THE **PENGUIN** GOOD AUSTRALIAN WINE GUIDE

Huon Hooke is a wine-marketing and production graduate of Roseworthy Agricultural College and has been a weekly columnist for the John Fairfax Group newspapers for 20 years. Currently he writes columns in the 'Good Living' section of the *Sydney Morning Herald* and the *Good Weekend* magazine of the *Herald* and Melbourne's *Age*. He's also contributing editor of *Australian Gourmet Traveller* WINE magazine and writes for various other publications, such as *Decanter* and *Slow Wine*. He's been judging in wine competitions for 16 years and judges eight to ten shows a year in Australia and abroad. He's judged in New Zealand, South Africa, Chile, Belgium, Slovenia, Canada and the USA. He currently chairs several Australian competitions and is a senior judge at Adelaide and Sydney.

Huon has many favourite wines, but asked to name one he cites red Burgundy, because it's complex, long-living, can be enjoyed at any age, is great with duck, and provides endless fascination. Which is what wine is all about, really.

Ralph Kyte-Powell has nearly 30 years' experience in the wine business and hospitality industry. His first wine job was with Seppelt during university vacation. Since then he has worked in marketing and sales for some of Australia's leading wine merchants, managed wine stores, been sommelier at some of Melbourne's best restaurants, worked in vineyards and wineries in Australia and France, and lectured on wine for a TAFE college. He's also owned a successful small hotel, and managed a restaurant. He started writing about wine 10 years ago and now has regular columns with Melbourne's *Age* and Sydney's *Sun-Herald*, and has contributed to other newspapers and magazines, including *Australian Gourmet Traveller* WINE magazine and Tourism Victoria's *Wine Regions of Victoria* guide. He has a regular radio spot talking about wine, and judges at regional wine shows each year.

A list of Ralph's favourite wines would be encyclopaedic and variable from time to time, but would always include champagne, great pinot noir and liqueur muscat.

the penguin good australian
WINE GUIDE
2003/2004

HUON HOOKE AND RALPH KYTE-POWELL

PENGUIN BOOKS

Penguin Books

Published by the Penguin Group
Penguin Books Australia Ltd
250 Camberwell Road, Camberwell, Victoria 3124, Australia
Penguin Books Ltd
80 Strand, London WC2R 0RL, England
Penguin Putnam Inc.
375 Hudson Street, New York, New York 10014, USA
Penguin Books, a division of Pearson Canada
10 Alcorn Avenue, Toronto, Ontario, Canada M4V 3B2
Penguin Books (NZ) Ltd
Cnr Rosedale and Airborne Roads, Albany, Auckland, New Zealand
Penguin Books (South Africa) (Pty) Ltd
24 Sturdee Avenue, Rosebank, Johannesburg 2196, South Africa
Penguin Books India (P) Ltd
11, Community Centre, Panchsheel Park, New Delhi 110 017, India

First published by Penguin Books Australia Ltd 2003

10 9 8 7 6 5 4 3 2 1

Copyright © Penguin Books Australia Ltd 2003

The moral right of the authors has been asserted

Cover design by Melissa Fraser, Penguin Design Studio
Cover photography by Adrian Lander
Author photograph by Peter Mack
Map illustration by Pat Kermode
Typeset in Stone Sans by Post Pre-press Group, Brisbane, Queensland
Printed and bound in Australia by McPherson's Printing Group, Maryborough, Victoria

National Library of Australia
Cataloguing-in-Publication data:

Hooke, Huon, 1954– .
   The Penguin good Australian wine guide: 2003/2004.

   Includes index.
   ISBN 0 14 300205 8.

   1. Wine and wine making – Australia. 2. Wine and wine
   making – New Zealand. I. Kyte-Powell, Ralph. II. Title.

641.220994

www.penguin.com.au

Contents

Penguin Wine Awards 2003

Choosing the best wines for this *Guide* is always a difficult job, and it just keeps on getting harder. We have to weigh up the relative merits of so many great drops and, despite the constant growth in Australian wine production, many of the best wines are always in short supply, mainly due to the tiny vintages experienced in so many regions in the last few years. Happily this year's Penguin Wine of the Year shouldn't be too hard to find. It's an example of the great 2002 Clare Valley riesling vintage that's been wowing us for some time. It's great value, it drinks beautifully now, and it should develop well with age. What more could you want?

Riesling won the big one, but we were mightily impressed by many other great Australian whites. Chardonnay continues to be everybody's darling and it featured twice in the awards this year, with wines from both ends of the scale. Our Best Chardonnay Award went to the latest edition of a modern Australian classic, and Best Bargain White was won by an astonishingly good chardonnay that will give change out of $15. And just to show what variety there is on the Australian wine scene these days, our Best White Blend/Other Variety went to an exotic Victorian viognier.

The 2001 vintage was a great one for reds right across southern Australia, so we had plenty of truly exciting wines to choose from. The Best Red Wine Award went to the latest vintage of a red from Coonawarra. Our Best Bargain Red also comes from that prolific strip of vineyards in South Australia's southern corner. It's a wine with a long pedigree, yet it remains very affordable. By contrast our Best Shiraz is a relative newcomer, the second vintage of shiraz from a winery widely experienced with other varieties.

We'd love to be able to announce that fortified wines are back in favour with wine drinkers all over Australia, but sadly it's not true – they still occupy a twilight zone bypassed by so many modern Aussie wine sippers that it's a tragedy. But their quality and value has never been greater, so please, do yourself a favour and try our Best Fortified Wine and our Best Bargain Fortified. You'll be amazed at how such wonderful wines can be on the market at such extraordinarily low prices.

So enough of the preamble, the awards await. And the winners are . . .

PENGUIN WINE OF THE YEAR
BEST WHITE WINE
BEST RIESLING

Mitchell Watervale Riesling 2002

The 2002 Clare-Watervale rieslings are superb and this great wine is one of the best. It's a riesling with everything: finesse, power, freshness and depth, and a reasonable price tag. Hurry to make sure you get some while it lasts. (See page 291.)

BEST RED WINE
BEST CABERNET SAUVIGNON/CABERNET BLEND

Petaluma Coonawarra 2000

A majestic example of modern Coonawarra red wine, Petaluma's 2000 vintage red flagship is a 50–50 cabernet–merlot blend of unusual concentration that promises to build superbly with long bottle-age. (See page 146.)

BEST SPARKLING WINE

Chandon Rosé Vintage Brut 1998

The days when pink fizz was considered a bit gauche are long gone, and Chandon's version confirms it. A rich mouthful of lovely subtle complexity, this blushing sparkler is equally at home as a classy party starter and as a great accompaniment to fine cuisine. (See page 358.)

BEST FORTIFIED WINE

Seppelt Show Oloroso DP38

If you think that sherry is a sort of prehistoric granny's drink, you're missing out badly. This gorgeously complex, amber-coloured wine treads a fascinating line between sweet and dry. And Seppelt's generous recent policy of doubling the size of the bottle, while actually reducing the already very reasonable price, makes it an all-time bargain. (See page 395.)

PICKS OF THE BUNCH

BEST PINOT NOIR

Freycinet Pinot Noir 2001

Few Tasmanian pinot noir makers have anything like the record for quality and consistency of Freycinet. Their 2001 wine eloquently sums up the best Tassie pinot style – perfumed, velvety and fine. (See page 93.)

BEST SHIRAZ

Voyager Estate Shiraz 2001

Voyager is kicking lots of goals lately with whites and reds, and this is a ripper of a shiraz, full of spicy, cherry, plum and meaty complexities. It's almost lusciously fruity in the mouth. A classy Margaret River style. (See page 190.)

⚘ BEST RED BLEND/OTHER VARIETY
Henschke Johann's Garden Grenache 2001

Stephen and Prue Henschke are among Australia's best winemakers and viticulturists, making justifiably famous shiraz and great riesling. Now they've added succulent grenache to their range and, not surprisingly, it's one of the best around. (See page 105.)

⚘ BEST CHARDONNAY
Bannockburn Chardonnay 2001

Gary Farr's intuitive expertise has given us some great 'new wave' Australian wines over the years, and his chardonnay is always one of the best. The excellent 2001 is no exception. (See page 214.)

⚘ BEST SAUVIGNON BLANC
Shaw and Smith Sauvignon Blanc 2002

Is this Australia's best sauvignon blanc? We reckon it might be and it's never been better than this 2002 release. Simply delicious! (See page 327.)

⚘ BEST SEMILLON
Tyrells Stevens Reserve Semillon 1998

We always say that Hunter semillon needs slow ageing to be at its best, and this one's already on the way to becoming a classic. Still youthful at five years of age and selling at the same price as a lot of youngsters, it's fantastic value. (See page 342.)

⚘ BEST SWEET WINE
McWilliams Riverina Botrytis Semillon 2000

The Riverina winemakers excel with botrytised sweet whites. McWilliams is as lush and hedonistic as any, but this also has surprising freshness, finesse and a real touch of class. (See page 286.)

⚘ BEST WHITE BLEND/OTHER VARIETY
Elgee Park Family Reserve Viognier 2001
No Australian winery has worked harder or longer with viognier than Elgee Park on the Mornington Peninsula and this is their best yet. Exotic, sexy, fascinating. (See page 245.)

⚘ BEST BARGAIN RED
Wynns Shiraz 2001
It's so gratifying to see a time-honoured label like this still coming up with the goods after 50 vintages. A great wine at a great price. (See page 202.)

⚘ BEST BARGAIN WHITE
Miranda High Country Chardonnay 2002
We really thought Miranda had made a mistake with this one. It's as though an expensive cool-climate chardonnay has been mis-labelled as an under-$15 wine – it's that good. You simply won't find better value. (See page 290.)

⚘ BEST BARGAIN BUBBLY
Brown Brothers King Valley Pinot Chardonnay NV
Lots of work has gone into sparkling wine at Brown Brothers and it's paid off with some very smart fizz. This non-vintage bubbly is available just about everywhere and it's perfect for lip-smacking refreshment any time. (See page 358.)

⚘ BEST BARGAIN FORTIFIED
DeBortoli Show Liqueur Muscat
Amazing. How do DeBortoli blend a wine this good at the price? We think Australian fortified wines are bargains anyway, but this is ridiculously cheap for such a superb wine. Grab a bottle and see what we mean. (See page 385.)

🐧 BEST NEW PRODUCER

Two Hands

Rarely are we as impressed with a new wine producer as we've been with this eccentric Barossa Valley–based outfit. Michael Twelftree and Richard Mintz have hit the ground sprinting! They've turned our heads with a stunning array of red wines, mainly shiraz, from the Barossa and McLaren Vale regions, made in the opulent, extravagantly rich-fruit style that is making waves overseas as well as at home. They've packaged them with quirky labels and distinctive names, and the marketing effort does full justice to the quality in the bottle. These are wines that cannot be ignored, jam-packed with flavour and character. In early 2003 they completed a cellar door in the Greenock area of the Barossa. We predict they'll go far.

Introduction

THE GLOBALISATION, AND COCA-COLA-ISATION, OF WINE

As the old Chinese proverb says: 'May you live in interesting times'.

We do!

In the past year, Australia's biggest wine company Southcorp has performed a spectacular belly-flop, returning an appalling financial performance and seeing its stock-market value decimated as a result. And Australia's second-biggest wine company (biggest, if you look at tonnes crushed), BRL Hardy, has been sold to a huge Yankee grog company, Constellation Brands. It's a bit of a mystery who owns Beringer Blass now, since it merged with the American Beringer organisation under the Fosters umbrella. McWilliams is deeply imbedded with America's number one winemaker, E & J Gallo, and there are rumours of a takeover (we don't take them seriously); Southcorp is ripe for one (it's likely to be foreign if it comes), and Orlando is already French-owned.

What is going on?

It seems to us the Aussie wine world is increasingly polarised. It has split neatly into two areas: the big and the small. The big are characterised thus: they're heavily into exporting because that's the only way they can grow. They're crowned by the publicly listed companies, which have the best access to the chain of distribution both domestically and overseas. They benefit most from government policy, especially taxation policy, which favours the producers of casks and other cheaper wines.

The small are typically thus: they're independent and owner-operated; they have difficulty getting their wines into the usual chain of distribution – especially wholesalers and retail liquor stores; they're run by people who are devoted to the ideal of producing special wine and who value lifestyle more than money. They tend not to pay much heed to what others think, but follow their own star. They feel alienated from wine-industry organisations and politics, and victimised by tax policies. Their wines are expensive because they have poor economies of scale. They tend to sell from the cellar door, by mail order and in restaurants. The bosses of the publicly listed groups probably wake up every morning to scan the financial pages over brekkie, anxious about their share price, and sometimes appear to be distracted from the goal of making great wine.

Understandably, wine enthusiasts feel closer to the smaller, human-scale wineries, than they do to the big, and regard them as being the soul of the wine industry. Often, they mistakenly equate the small with high-quality wine, and dismiss the big companies as producers of industrial swill. A gross over-generalisation!

Pipers Brook was taken over by Belgian raider Kreglinger, and founder/chief winemaker/CEO/spiritual guide for 30 years, Andrew Pirie, was unceremoniously shown the door. Pirie is writing a book (not his memoirs – yet!) and working part-time for Parker Coonawarra Estate (at last: a decent cabernet, some wit was heard to remark).

Brian Croser is going through the motions of working for Petaluma, which he founded and built into a great wine company over 25 years, and we don't know what the future holds for him. Petaluma is part of Banksia is now part of Lion Nathan is a public grog company that wants to get even bigger. So Croser is swinging in winemaker limbo.

Rosemount took over Southcorp (actually it was the reverse, but you'd never have known) and kicked out around 150 staff, including senior winemakers who took a great deal of corporate memory with them. They included Penfolds chief winemaker John Duval (we think he jumped, as distinct from being pushed) – only the third man to wear the mantle of Grange custodian, and although he's been replaced by a more than capable successor in Peter Gago, the whole episode was a bit sad. Rosemount's Keith Lambert became Southcorp CEO and presided over the conversion of a once-great company into one of total disarray. In mid-May, Southcorp warned it was expecting to announce precisely half the EBITA (earnings before interest, tax and amortisation) for the 2002–3 financial year that it made the year before. And in the second half of 2002–3, it earned only a third of what it made in the same period the previous year. HOW CAN THEY BE DOING SO BADLY??, everyone is asking. The Australian wine industry wants and needs a strong and healthy Southcorp. Our big companies seem besotted with the idea of selling ever more wine to a world that already has quite enough wine in it, thank you. BRL Hardy boss-man Stephen Millar reckons he'd like to make BRL the Coca-Cola of wine. Get a life, Stephen!

And Southcorp, before booting Keith Lambert out (with a $4.4-million golden handshake), announced it was going to increase sales of Penfolds-branded wines by close to treble – from 1.8 million to 5 million cases. The sceptics knitted their brows: it looked like the new Southcorp regime planned to plunder the good name of Penfolds for all it was worth. Are we alone in asking the questions: 'Why?' and 'At what cost to the good name of Penfolds?'

What gives the authors heart is that there are passionate new people constantly coming into the wine industry in this country who are driven to do great things. And they – and the dedicated ones who are still practising their craft in a friendly environment – continue to make the world of wine a vibrant, diverse and fascinating place.

Our Best New Producer for 2003–4 is Barossa-based excitement package, Two Hands. New winemakers such as Two Hands, Mitolo, Ferngrove, Kooyong, Casa Freschi, Torbreck, Thomas, Meerea Park and Castagna continue to leap from the shadows and thrill us with mesmerising booze! That's what keeps us going: the idea that somewhere, someone is hatching a plot at this very moment to pounce into the spotlight and create The Next Great Australian Wine.

Save us from the tedium of annual reports, stock-exchange statements and takeover terror. We don't need it.

(It is ironic that in March 2003, a woman who for many of us epito-mised the heart and soul of the small, high-quality winemaker, Di Cullen, passed away at the age of 80. She was a woman who pursued quality at any cost; whose integrity was a model for us all; who knew that wine and the stock exchange don't mix, and that winemakers as much as anyone need to respect the environment. Happily, her daugh-ter Vanya continues the tradition and Cullen's continues to go onwards and upwards. We wish there were more among us like Di.)

THE RETAIL REVOLVING DOOR

If there are weird things happening in the production end of the wine industry, with 92 per cent of Australia's wine now produced by the 22 biggest companies, and the other 1600 battling it out for the other 8 per cent of the market, even weirder stuff is happening in retail.

The big news is Woolworths making a major assault on the liquor retailing market, launching a new chain, First Estate, and taking its famous Melbourne brand Dan Murphy's into New South Wales and the ACT. Having bought up a lot of independent liquor stores across the nation in recent years, Woolies is aiming to beat Coles Myer – owner of Liquorland and Vintage Cellars – at its own game. Its weapons are discounting and massive advertising campaigns. The discount surge has been fuelled by the big winemaking companies' burning need to sell more wine in a flat market: led by Southcorp, the big com-panies have been offering retailers terrific deals. Deals that Southcorp couldn't really afford to offer, as it turns out. This dealing has infected much of the wine market, so that other medium and even some small producers are forced to also cut prices. It is rather unhealthy for all wine producers, although it's a field day for drinkers.

Amazingly, less than two years after First Estate was launched, with expensive fit-outs and all, it seems it's already a failure, and the Woolies brains trust is heading back to the drawing board.

At Coles Myer/Liquorland, they're not sitting on their hands either.

In May 2003, the ACCC finally approved Coles' takeover of the Theo's Liquor Markets chain, further increasing Coles' power. This gave Coles an extra 48 stores and four hotels, taking its total to 610 liquor outlets across Australia.

Because wine retailers' shelves are increasingly unable to represent all the wineries of Australia at retail level, there is more direct selling of wine than ever before. Internet web-sites are catching on quickly; sales by email and Internet are augmenting traditional snail-mail direct sales. And a lot of small wineries exist with little or no presence in the retail bottle-shop network. Extra effort and money has gone into developing cellar-door sales and other attractions at wineries, and winery tourism is growing strongly.

There is a polarisation happening in retail, with the big chains selling more and more of the big companies' wines, and increasing numbers of small retailers not keeping big-company wines at all. The small are forced to focus increasingly on rare, cultish, small-output, often dearer wines that big chains don't trifle with. Many small independent retailers haven't bought a bottle from Southcorp for years. And these are Southcorp's own figures: in the year 2002, Southcorp increased its business with the super-markets from 29 per cent to 42 per cent of its total sales.

Meanwhile, there is much wringing of hands in the cities, espe-cially Sydney where the biggest rationalisation of liquor stores has occurred and the big chains have been most aggressive. Independent retailers feel they are under siege, because they cannot compete on price against chains that sometimes have wine specials at prices lower than those at which small retailers can buy them from suppliers. The smart ones realise they will survive if they offer good service and other benefits the chains cannot.

We've checked out the Dan Murphy's shops in New South Wales and the ACT and they are well designed, well stocked, and have some excel-lent exclusive lines, including imports. But they are sterile places. They are the place to go if you're only interested in the cheapest price. They're the last place if you're a young wine enthusiast seeking nourishment for your new-found passion. In Melbourne's Dan Murphy's outlets there are some excellent staff, but in other places Woolies seems to have run into the usual staffing problems, and you'll be lucky to find a shelf-stocker drone who'll say hello, let alone give you sensible wine advice.

And be warned: huge newspaper advertisements offering apparently huge discounts are designed to get you into the shop. They do not guarantee the price won't have returned to the full retail price by the time your Daewoo rattles into the carpark.

THE WINE INDUSTRY'S HIDDEN CRISIS

It's often said the boutique wineries are the heart and soul of the wine industry. They provide the colour, the character, and many of the personalities behind wine that attract the public to the product. But many of them are in dire straits, and are trying to sell up, or find backers, or amalgamate with other wineries.

The combined effect of shaved profit margins, a flat domestic market, and the continuing growth in wine-producer numbers (about 100 a year), means that many small winemakers are poised on the edge of the abyss. Some say it's just a matter of time till many of them go broke. When they do, there will be shock waves throughout the rural economy, which has benefited in so many ways, in so many regional areas, from the winemaking boom of recent years.

Meanwhile, the Federal Government in early 2003 insulted the wine industry by handing out a $500 000 grant to help small wine producers with marketing workshops around the rural areas, then followed that with a Federal Budget that contained absolutely zilch for the beleaguered small producers. The same government is robbing $340 million extra each year from the wine sector, since it introduced the iniquitous WET (Wine Equalisation Tax) alongside its GST in July 2000. The WET was supposed to make up the shortfall in tax revenue when the 10 per cent GST replaced the 41 per cent wholesale sales tax on wine. Instead, the Government imposed the WET at a higher level than it needed, filching an extra $340 million a year by stealth. This is paid by all of us, the wine buyers.

To read about the tearaway success of Australia's wine exporting (still roaring along with volume up 27 per cent to 493 million litres and value up 31 per cent to $2.4 billion for the year ended March 2003), you might not realise that our wine industry is actually in crisis. Only 50 per cent of our winemakers export at all. In fact, Southcorp and BRL Hardy account for about half of all exports by volume (and they seem to be literally giving the stuff away), while the top 22 account for about 98 per cent. If only 50 per cent of all producers export, these 793 exporters are chasing the remaining 2 per cent of the market. There is barely any growth in the domestic wine market.

The other cheery feature that vignerons contemplate as they bounce along their vine rows on their tractors is the ongoing drought. It's been drought for five years in some regions. Irrigation water restrictions were in force last summer, and this coupled with an already dire situation meant some seriously water-stressed vineyards produced very little fruit. In some cases stressed vines failed to ripen their crops, and in others the quality was compromised. The drought has brought to a head the debates about water-use and the sustainability of viticulture in the driest continent on earth. The logic of irrigating vineyards is being questioned, and some new vineyards are already being established the old-fashioned way – without water. Theoretically, this encourages vines to put their roots down deep and make themselves more drought-resistant – if they survive the first two seasons.

Greedy modern techniques of establishing vineyards – where water and fertilisers are piled on to force profitable yields earlier than once deemed possible – are rightly being questioned. Especially as the grapes off these vineyards are seldom much good. And salination of the land continues to spread. Over the decades, excessive irrigation has caused the watertable to rise, bringing salt to the surface from deep underground. This kills vegetation and stops new growth. Dead soil then becomes eroded by wind. Not a pretty picture.

Most of our continent has dry summers, with little rain falling in the growing season of the grapevine. But, before irrigation technology changed the face of viticulture, perfectly good grapes were grown without it. Why shouldn't it happen again? There would be lower yields, which wouldn't be a bad thing, fewer get-rich-quick schemes, and viticulture would be more sustainable.

Which Wines to Cellar?

One of the great joys of wine is to take a bottle out of your own collection, that you've been storing for some years, draw the cork and enjoy it with friends. You can marvel at the changes brought on by maturity; and as a bonus you can gloat over the price you paid – time invariably makes wine prices seem paltry. You can congratulate yourself for picking up such a bargain!

But not all wines improve with age. Indeed, not all wines even *survive* with age. There is a great myth among those who are less-experienced in such matters: that all wines improve over time.

The truth is that only a relatively small proportion of all the wine made in the world every year is worth keeping. Most of it is cheap, light, innocuous quaffing stuff that's designed to be consumed as soon as it's purchased. In this country, that includes all cask wine, for starters, and that means about 50 per cent of all the Australian wine sold within Australia. It includes all the really cheap bottled wine, too. It includes most pink or rosé wine. It includes most sparkling wine – with the exception of really good-quality Champagne and the very best bubblies from other places such as Australia, New Zealand and the US. The greatest deluxe cuvée Champagnes will last for many years, and the cork – which is made of glued fragments and isn't designed for long ageing – becomes the main limiting factor.

While most reds, even fairly inexpensive drops, will hang on for several years if kept under good conditions, most white wines don't improve with age. Only the very best of them do: that means the right grape varieties, grown under the right conditions in the right places and packaged suitably, with good corks or screw-caps, but probably not plastic seals.

Generally, the wines that age the best are fuller-bodied reds, vintage ports and other fortified wines (but not dry sherry); rich sweet whites that are intended for keeping (such as French Sauternes and Alsace and German late-harvest wines); and a few dry whites. The latter include the best French Chablis and white Burgundy (which are made from chardonnay), but relatively few New World chardonnays (the top Margaret River chardonnays are an exception). In Australia the best-cellaring dry whites are the traditional-style dry, unoaked semillons of the Hunter Valley and rieslings from the Clare Valley, Eden Valley, Western Australia's Great Southern region, and other isolated pockets in Victoria and Tasmania. Alsatian, German and Austrian rieslings also age very well. Other famous French whites such as Loire Valley chenin blanc (especially Vouvray), dry Graves and other white Bordeaux (made from semillon and sauvignon blanc) can age well, as can the other great Alsace varieties like gewürztraminer, pinot gris and even pinot blanc.

The longest-ageing wines in the world are sweet wines, and ancient bottles of Hungarian tokaji, German trockenbeerenauslese, French Sauternes and Portuguese vintage port have been drunk in excellent condition at well over 100 years of age. In red wines, generally the fuller-bodied, richer wines with good alcoholic strength, tannin structure and flavour intensity will age the longest. In Australia, cabernet and shiraz from Coonawarra, shiraz from the Hunter Valley, shiraz from Great Western and central and southern Victoria (Sunbury, the Goulburn Valley and the Yarra Valley) have proved they can age very long-term. Reds from other South Australian regions have also shown good long-term ageing, and here we are thinking of the Barossa, Clare, Langhorne Creek and McLaren Vale, but especially Coonawarra. Again, shiraz has more runs on the board than the other varieties, but cabernet can be just as good. Only exceptional examples of Australian pinot noir and grenache are recommended for extended cellaring, although French Burgundy is one of the world's great cellaring reds. As always, the maker's reputation is the best guide.

Most wood-aged fortified wines, such as Australian muscats, tokays and tawny ports, will keep for many years, but they don't improve and their makers don't suggest you keep them. Vintage port, whether Australian or Portuguese, and Madeira are the greatest fortified wines for long cellaring.

Always, the potential longevity of any wine depends as much on the conditions of cellaring as on the wine itself. Cork variation is the other wild-card, but there's little you can do about that. What you can control is the cellar environment (temperature, humidity, etc.) and care of bottles (lay them down to keep corks moist; monitor corks for leakage; treat your bottles gently).

With each review in this *Guide* we make some very general cellaring recommendations. Check the Penguin Rating System chapter for a full explanation of our cellaring guidelines (see page 41). And remember: the best way to learn is by experience. There's no time like the present to start a cellar!

Fad and Fashion

What's the new chardonnay going to be? We've heard this question, or similar ones, a lot lately. It's a sign of the times and we don't think it's a good one. Wine fashions change of course, new styles emerge, new grape varieties are planted, but in the past it's been up to the winemakers and growers to generate new directions, and consumers to embrace or reject them. Nowadays there's a growing army of stylemeisters who promote the idea that just about everything is a fashion statement, and wine is very much in their sights. Wine is fashion and it's become very groovy.

Thus New Zealand sauvignon blanc was de rigueur on the right tables, that is until the next trend came along. At 'society' parties everybody absurdly sucks French Champagne from little bottles through a straw, at smart bars designer-scruffy fashion slaves nibble tapas and sip chilled sherry. Magazines and papers print lists that tell us that chardonnay is out, pinot gris is in. It's all about fashion.

What does it matter? Not much, we suppose at the moment, but there are possible future dangers in a growing reliance on fashion, marketing spin and fadism to determine where the wine industry heads. For a start, it's disrespectful to all those honest grapegrowers and winemarkers out there who work so hard to bring us the best fruits of their labours. What is it all worth if some style guru determines that your stuff is on the outer? Do you rip all your uncool grape vines out and start again with something that's more with it?

Trendiness also threatens to obscure the idea of fair value when it comes to parting with your hard-earned cash for a good bottle. We've tasted an increasing number of designer wines lately that are contrived from the ground up to fit a marketing strategy; the wine inside is incidental. Prices are forced up, value is compromised.

And what about the attack on the constants of wine that all this entails? If something is old hat, should it disappear? What a pity if Australian 'sherry' disappeared completely, while groovy barflies still sipped the fashionable Spanish original. Or gewürztraminer, or Rutherglen shiraz. There are so many wine types in Australia that mean something to our vinous history, what a pity it would be if they were to die due to vacuous trendiness.

Happily there's still an army of wine drinkers out there who are oblivious to the idea of wine as a fashion statement. They're happy to try something new, but they are their own people. They constantly hear that chardonnay is out, and respond by drinking it in record quantities; they hear that sparkling shiraz is in, but still can't work out why they should bother with it. They love sweet wines, or they hate them. They understand what wine really is: a favourite drink, a sensory delight, conviviality, relaxation, a food, a part of life.

Vintage Round-up 1999–2003

Most good-quality table wines are the product of a single annual harvest. The year is usually displayed prominently on the label. At the most basic level, the vintage year is like the use-by dates on groceries and the 'best-before' labels on bottles of beer – a simple indication of freshness or maturity. But unlike most food products, the year of production can also say a great deal about the wine inside. If that vintage was stifling hot, chances are you'll have big, over-the-top wines that lack refinement; a miserable, wet year with little sunshine and the wines might be thin, mean and harsh. If the conditions were perfect, the wines of that vintage will be highly prized and well worth seeking out.

The differences in quality can be dramatic, and for the savvy consumer a knowledge of vintage conditions is a great aid when purchasing and enjoying wine. The top vintages also provide a windfall for the wine trade. A great year of Penfolds Grange, like the 1998, has retailers popping the champagne corks at the prospect of some seriously opportunitistic profit margins to be had.

Until fairly recently, vintage variations in Australian wine weren't considered anywhere near as important as they were in Europe, particularly by the international wine trade. But there were great years and lesser ones, even in our long-established warmer vineyards, such as the Barossa and Rutherglen. Developments in regional variations and vintages have become much more apparent in recent years. Cooler vineyard sites have been explored, delicate new wine styles have started appearing, made from new grape varieties using new methods. The old traditional styles have continued in strength, but they have been joined by an exciting new crop of previously unheard of wines. Geelong pinot noir, Tasmanian riesling and Pemberton shiraz have become as much a part of the knowledgeable wine buff's palette as Coonawarra cabernet and Hunter semillon. With this came more vintage variation, as many new regions experienced the sort of marginal weather that brought climatic fluctuations more akin to the European experience.

All this means that vintage is now an important factor in choosing modern Australian wine. To that end, this *Guide* includes an independent, five-year, region-by-region vintage overview. This year we visit the vintages 1999–2003, the years most likely to be seen on the shelves of a wine shop. We base our vintage appraisals on our own tasting experience and conversations with winemakers, rather than hearsay. Remember though that no vintage guide is 100 per cent accurate; just as in Europe, good winemakers can produce fine wine in bad years, others can make a hash of the perfect vintage, and the name of a reliable producer can be just as important as a particular vintage date.

2003 VINTAGE

It's early days and it's always hard to evaluate the latest crop of wines when so many are yet to be released, but here is our initial assessment of the 2003 crop. The main feature of 2003 was drought across a large part of the continent. This meant reduced yields, as much as 20 per cent down on forecasts by some estimates. In addition, rain close to harvest in some places damaged fruit and further reduced yields. Despite these problems, the quality across Australia looks good. Shiraz and chardonnay look to be the most favoured by the conditions, and generally reds are powerful, ripe wines, while some whites lack vibrancy. Specific high-points in our opinion will be Yarra Valley pinot noir, Coonawarra cabernet sauvignon, Eden Valley riesling and Adelaide Hills sauvignon blanc.

2002 VINTAGE

NEW SOUTH WALES

Hunter Valley: late-vintage rain made this a vintage of two parts. Early-picked semillons and chardonnays are very good. Reds are more problematic.

Riverina: relatively cool conditions gave the Riverina a superb vintage. Expect to taste some surprisingly fine wines from this large region.

Orange/Hilltops: a cool year with some ripeness problems. Whites were better than the reds, the best are very good indeed.

Mudgee: after a series of awful vintages, Mudgee finally enjoyed an excellent season. Reds are the stars, perhaps in a more elegant style than usual.

Cowra: a cool year saw the normally warm vineyards of Cowra produce wines of unusual elegance. A very good vintage.

Canberra: cool conditions presented difficulties. Choose carefully.

VICTORIA

Rutherglen: moderate summer temperatures made for somewhat more elegant Rutherglen reds than the norm. Fortifieds benefited greatly from a warm, dry autumn. An excellent year.

Murray Valley: an excellent year.

Pyrenees/Great Western: a tiny crop, and cool conditions, but some good whites were made. Reds are elegant rather than robust. A mixed vintage.

Bendigo/Heathcote: a small vintage but a good one with some tasty, aromatic reds the highlight.

Yarra Valley: a cool year followed by a mild, dry autumn resulted in a good year for chardonnay and pinot noir, less so for the other red varieties. A very small crop.

Mornington Peninsula: a small crop and variable weather conditions meant difficulties for many vignerons. As usual, the well-established, most experienced producers made the best wines with some good pinot noirs.

Geelong: a tiny crop and a testing vintage. Look for the best makers.

SOUTH AUSTRALIA

Barossa/Eden Valley: a cooler year with more elegant reds than usual. Good but not special is the general verdict, with the exception of the rieslings from the high country. They are simply superb.

McLaren Vale: a cool summer and warm autumn resulted in an excellent vintage. The best reds combine power with unusual refinement and elegance.

Clare Valley: an absolutely outstanding year for riesling, the authors can't remember better. Reds can be very good.

Adelaide Hills: a cool year gave some problems and early ripeners succeeded. Whites were good with superb sauvignon blanc, pinot noir was successful too, but other reds less so.

Coonawarra/Limestone Coast: Whites outperformed reds in this cool year down south. The wines are generally fresher and more elegant than usual.

Riverland: cool conditions meant possibly the best Riverland vintage ever. Both reds and whites were made with outstanding balance and intensity. A vintage that might earn these vast 'industrial' vineyards new respect.

WESTERN AUSTRALIA

Margaret River: in common with the eastern states, this was a cooler than normal year. The wines are refined and stylish, rather than powerful. A good year for chardonnay and reds from the best producers.

Great Southern: a cooler year meant a mixed vintage, but some excellent wines. Whites are very good, and don't dismiss the reds, particularly varieties like pinot noir.

TASMANIA
An unusual Indian summer resulted in some very good wines.

2001 VINTAGE

NEW SOUTH WALES
Hunter Valley: a deluge caused problems in the Lower Hunter. A heatwave in January saved the day, and good, unusually intense semillons resulted. Other whites were good, reds more of a mixed bag. The Upper Hunter enjoyed a better deal with good wines across the board.

Riverina: another very good vintage on these sunburnt plains.

Orange/Hilltops: good whites, reds less so with merlot the best of them. Nevertheless a reasonable year overall.

Mudgee: a difficult year due to rain, hail and tropical heat. Despite this some makers produced good wines with whites being more successful than reds. Buy carefully.

Cowra: rain was a problem. Good whites, ordinary reds.

Canberra: a variable year with some stand-outs, including some superlative shiraz.

VICTORIA
Rutherglen: a very good year. Good fortified material.

Murray Valley: a very good year.

Pyrenees/Grampians: like most Victorian regions, this was an excellent vintage. Shiraz was a true highlight.

Bendigo/Heathcote: an outstanding vintage.

Yarra Valley: an outstanding vintage, but choose carefully.

Mornington Peninsula: generally an excellent year, but as always in this area choose carefully.

Geelong: an excellent vintage.

SOUTH AUSTRALIA

Barossa Valley/Eden Valley: an excellent vintage for reds, less so for whites with the exception of steely, fine Eden Valley rieslings.

McLaren Vale: a great vintage for reds made for the long haul. Whites so-so.

Clare Valley: a hot year resulting in reds of great extract and power. Whites were excellent too with great riesling. South Australia's best 2001 wines.

Adelaide Hills: an excellent vintage for just about everything.

Coonawarra/Limestone Coast: a good vintage, particularly from the established makers who made some great reds.

Riverland: an average year. Torrid conditions resulted in some pretty stewed wines.

WESTERN AUSTRALIA

Margaret River: a wonderful vintage with superbly concentrated reds and beautifully balanced whites. Real classics that should cellar well.

Great Southern/Pemberton: an excellent vintage.

TASMANIA

A variable vintage which was better in the north of the island. In fact the more mature of the northern vineyards produced some of the best Tassie wines to date. Other districts had problems due to rain and frost. Choose carefully.

2000 VINTAGE

NEW SOUTH WALES

Hunter Valley: a generally hot vintage made classical semillons for long keeping. Good chardonnays and reds too.

Riverina: generally good with botrytised wines a high-point as usual.

Orange/Hilltops: wet conditions meant a pretty poor year.

Mudgee: an awful year of heavy rain. Some whites are okay, avoid the reds.

Cowra: a variable year with whites the safest bet.

Canberra: a mixed vintage, but the best makers still provided good wines.

VICTORIA

Rutherglen: an excellent year.

Murray Valley: a very good year.

Pyrenees/Grampians: a mixed vintage due to rains at harvest. Generally good though, especially for reds.

Bendigo/Heathcote: a very good vintage, though very small due to drought. Reds particularly have great concentration.

Yarra Valley: an excellent vintage, especially for chardonnay and pinot noir.

Mornington Peninsula: drought conditions and a very warm summer meant a superb vintage with some of the best wines ever from this region.

Geelong: a very good vintage, but stick with the best producers to be sure of quality. Shiraz, pinot noir and chardonnay all fared very well.

SOUTH AUSTRALIA

Barossa/Eden Valley: a patchy vintage with average-quality reds, lacklustre whites. Shop with care.

McLaren Vale: a dry winter and variable weather prior to vintage led to ripeness problems with some reds showing both overripe and underripe qualitites at the same time – weird. At best an adequate vintage with a few exceptions.

Clare Valley: a generally good vintage with austere, classically proportioned rieslings, and a some good reds.

Adelaide Hills: rain caused problems and whites were generally a lot better than the reds. A year of generally ordinary quality.

Coonawarra/Limestone Coast: the third great year in a row.
Riverland: a good year.

WESTERN AUSTRALIA

Margaret River: a wet year where the name of the maker is important. The best made some good wines, and whites were often more successful than the reds.
Great Southern/Pemberton: a dry winter followed by a wet summer meant an ordinary year of wines that were mostly uninspiring.

TASMANIA

A very good vintage in most vineyards with some excellent pinot noirs and chardonnays from more mature vineyards and experienced makers.

1999 VINTAGE

NEW SOUTH WALES

Hunter Valley: a generally good year for semillons and shiraz.
Riverina: a good year despite problems with rain.
Orange/Hilltops: a middling year – some stylish wines, some less impressive.
Mudgee: a mixed year. Problems with rain. Makers who made a rigorous fruit selection were successful.
Cowra: so-so.
Canberra: rain at vintage gave some problems. An average year, yet still with some good wines.

VICTORIA

Rutherglen: a good year.
Murray Valley: a good year.
Pyrenees/Grampians: a very good year. The best reds were excellent.
Bendigo/Heathcote: a very good year.

Yarra Valley: bizarre weather at various times during the year made for a variable vintage. Wine quality was generally quite good.

Mornington Peninsula: a small and generally good vintage for chardonnay and pinot noir. One or two shirazes surprised us with their quality.

Geelong: an excellent year. Superb chardonnays and pinot noirs from the best producers.

SOUTH AUSTRALIA

Barossa/Eden Valley: a very good vintage that will probably always be in the shadow of the great 1998 harvest. Nevertheless some excellent reds.

McLaren Vale: unlike other South Australian regions, this was a fairly ordinary vintage due to rain. As ever there are exceptions, and a few very good reds resulted. Shop carefully.

Clare Valley: an excellent vintage producing fine regional styles.

Adelaide Hills: a cool but not wet vintage resulted in white wines of good quality, reds inconsistent.

Coonawarra/Limestone Coast: a superb vintage.

Riverland: an average vintage.

WESTERN AUSTRALIA

Margaret River: a very good vintage despite a scare as a result of cyclonic activity to the north. Reds are generally better than the whites.

Great Southern/Pemberton: a cool year where the early-ripening varieties succeeded but the later ones had problems. Pinot noir can be good.

TASMANIA

Good chardonnay and pinot noir from vineyards with expert viticulture. Less so from others.

The Top-quality Wines (🍷🍷🍷🍷🍷)

Each year, among the 1000-plus wines we review in this *Guide*, there are some that make a special impression. These wines represent, to us, the pinnacle of wine quality in Australia. Not surprisingly some are expensive, but many are not, and in fact some of them are amazing bargains.

This list includes only our five-glass rated wines, so you can see at a glance which wines really wowed us. Each one is accompanied by its price and value-for-money star-rating. All the five-glass wines are included, right down to the lowest value-for-money rating – because if you want the very best and can afford it, you'll still want to know that we loved it, despite its price tag!

This year white wines were revealed as the biggest strengths of Aussie wine, although there are plenty of reds and fortifieds there, too. You could mount a strong argument that Australia is running third only to France and Italy for the sheer numbers of high-quality red wines it produces.

A word of warning: the best of anything is usually in short supply, so grab 'em while you can!

Wine	Price	Value
RED WINES		
Plantagenet Hazard Hill Shiraz Grenache 2001	$11.00	*****
Penley Estate Hyland Shiraz 2001	$20.70	*****
Coal Valley Vineyard Pinot Noir 2001	$22.00	*****
Fox Creek JSM Shiraz Cabernet Franc 2001	$23.00	*****
Punt Road Shiraz 2001	$23.00	*****
M Chapoutier Shiraz 2001	$24.50	*****
Fox Creek Short Row Shiraz 2001	$27.00	*****

Voyager Estate Shiraz 2001	$28.00	★★★★★
Chatto Pinot Noir 2000	$35.00	★★★★★
Milford Pinot Noir 2001	$22.00	★★★★⁴
Hewitson Ned & Henry's Shiraz 2001	$25.00	★★★★⁴
Willow Creek Cabernet Sauvignon 2001	$25.00	★★★★⁴
Willow Bridge Estate Winemaker Reserve		
Shiraz 2000	$30.00	★★★★⁴
Peter Lehmann Mentor 1998	$36.50	★★★★⁴
Voyager Estate Cabernet Sauvignon Merlot 1999	$39.50	★★★★⁴
Wendouree Cabernet Sauvignon 2000	$40.00	★★★★⁴
Parket Estate Terra Rossa Merlot 2000	$45.00	★★★★⁴
Freycinet Pinot Noir 2001	$50.00	★★★★⁴
Petaluma Coonawarra 2000	$58.00	★★★★⁴
Tamar Ridge Cabernet Sauvignon 2000	$26.00	★★★★
Mount Broke River Bank Shiraz 2000	$30.00	★★★★
Yalumba The Signature Cabernet Sauvignon		
Shiraz 1998	$35.00	★★★★
Dal Zotto Shiraz 2000	$36.00	★★★★
McWilliams Mount Pleasant Old Paddock and		
Old Hill Shiraz 1999	$40.00	★★★★
Seppelt St Peters Shiraz 1999	$40.00	★★★★
Tower Estate Barossa Shiraz 2001	$40.00	★★★★
Tatachilla 1901 Cabernet Sauvignon 2000	$42.00	★★★★
Two Hands Bad Impersonator 2001	$45.00	★★★★
Bannockburn Shiraz 2001	$47.50	★★★★
Lindemans St George Cabernet Sauvignon 1999	$49.00	★★★★
Torbreck The Struie 2001	$50.00	★★★★
Paringa Estate Pinot Noir 2001	$52.00	★★★★
By Farr Pinot Noir 2001	$53.00	★★★★
Summerfield Reserve Cabernet 2001	$55.00	★★★★

Diamond Valley Estate Pinot Noir 2001	$59.60	★★★★
Diamond Valley Close Planted Pinot Noir 2000	$65.00	★★★★
McWilliams 1877 Cabernet Sauvignon Shiraz 1999	$90.00	★★★★
Knappstein Enterprise Shiraz 2000	$40.00	★★★⧎
Majella Cabernet 2001	$40.00	★★★⧎
Coldstream Hills Reserve Merlot 2000	$47.50	★★★⧎
Castagna Genesis Syrah 2001	$48.00	★★★⧎
Annie's Lane Copper Trail Shiraz 1999	$48.00	★★★⧎
Peter Lehmann Eight Songs Shiraz 1999	$49.70	★★★⧎
Bindi Original Vineyard Pinot Noir 2001	$50.00	★★★⧎
Dromana Estate Reserve Pinot Noir 2001	$53.00	★★★⧎
Yering Station Reserve Shiraz Viognier 2001	$58.00	★★★⧎
Cape Mentelle Cabernet Sauvignon 1999	$59.00	★★★⧎
Houghton Gladstones Shiraz 1999	$60.00	★★★⧎
Brand's Paton's Reserve 1999	$66.00	★★★⧎
Cullen Cabernet Sauvignon Merlot 2001	$80.00	★★★⧎
Mount Mary Quintet 2000	$82.50	★★★⧎
Houghton Jack Mann Cabernet Sauvignon Malbec 1999	$90.00	★★★⧎
Giaconda Warner Vineyard Shiraz 2001	$75.00	★★★
Giaconda Pinot Noir 2001	$80.00	★★★
Parker Estate Terra Rossa First Growth 2000	$82.00	★★★
Warrenmang Red Gold Reserve Shiraz 1997, 1998, 2000	$120.00	★★★
Wolf Blass Platinum Label Shiraz 2000	$170.00	★★
Penfolds Grange 1998	$400+	★★

WHITE WINES

Woodstock Semillon Sauvignon Blanc 2002	$14.00	★★★★★
Rosily Vineyard Sauvignon Blanc 2002	$16.00	★★★★★
Tyrrells Lost Block Semillon 2002	$17.00	★★★★★
Capercaillie Hunter Gewürztraminer 2002	$17.00	★★★★★
Richmond Grove Watervale Riesling 2002	$17.20	★★★★★
Mitchell Watervale Riesling 2002	$18.00	★★★★★
Orlando St Helga Riesling 2002	$18.00	★★★★★
Nepenthe Sauvignon Blanc 2002	$18.00	★★★★★
McWilliams Mount Pleasant Elizabeth 1999	$18.50	★★★★★
Chatto Riesling 2000	$19.50	★★★★★
Skillogalee Riesling 2002	$19.50	★★★★★
Burge Family Winemakers Olive Hill Semillon 2002	$19.80	★★★★★
Rosemount Estate Giants Creek Chardonnay 2001	$20.00	★★★★★
Rosemount Estate Hill of Gold Chardonnay 2002	$20.00	★★★★★
Knappstein Riesling 2002	$21.00	★★★★★
O'Leary Walker Watervale Riesling 2002	$21.00	★★★★★
Pikes Reserve Riesling 2002	$21.00	★★★★★
Lenswood Vineyards Sauvignon Blanc 2002	$21.50	★★★★★
Shaw and Smith Sauvignon Blanc 2002	$22.00	★★★★★
Tyrrells Stevens Reserve Semillon 1998	$23.00	★★★★★
Petaluma Hanlin Hill Riesling 2002	$24.00	★★★★★
Peter Lehmann Reserve Riesling 1997	$24.85	★★★★★
Howard Park Chardonnay 2001	$35.00	★★★★★

O'Leary Walker Polish Hill River Riesling 2002	$19.80	★★★★½
Thomas Semillon 2002	$20.00	★★★★½
Houghton Pemberton Sauvignon Blanc 2002	$23.00	★★★★½
Frankland Estate Isolation Ridge Vineyard Riesling 2002	$23.50	★★★★½
Rothbury Estate Brokenback Semillon 2002	$24.00	★★★★½
Howard Park Riesling 2002	$25.00	★★★★½

Provenance Pinot Gris 2002	$25.00	★★★★+
Reynolds Moon Shadow Chardonnay 2000	$25.00	★★★★+
Keith Tulloch Hunter Semillon 2002	$26.00	★★★★+
Seppelt Jaluka Chardonnay 2002	$29.00	★★★★+
Grosset Watervale Riesling 2002	$32.00	★★★★+
The Green Vineyards Chardonnay 2001	$36.00	★★★★+
Grosset Polish Hill 2002	$38.00	★★★★+
Wellington Iced Riesling 2002	$24.85 (375 ml)	★★★★
McWilliams Riverina Botrytis Semillon 2000	$25.00	★★★★
Pikes Reserve Riesling 2002	$27.00	★★★★
Mesh Eden Valley Riesling 2002	$27.00	★★★★
Mount Horrocks Riesling 2002	$27.80	★★★★
Annie's Lane Copper Trail Riesling 2002	$37.00	★★★★
Hardys Eileen Hardy Chardonnay 2000	$40.00	★★★★
Stonier Reserve Chardonnay 2001	$41.50	★★★★
Dalwhinnie Moonambel Chardonnay 2001	$42.00	★★★★
McWilliams Mount Pleasant Lovedale Semillon 1998	$42.00	★★★★
Bindi Quartz Chardonnay 2001	$45.00	★★★★
Bannockburn Chardonnay 2001	$47.50	★★★★
Penfolds Reserve Bin 00A Chardonnay 2000	$60.00	★★★★
By Farr Viognier 2001	$53.00	★★★+
Cullen Chardonnay 2001	$53.00	★★★+
Yering Station Reserve Chardonnay 2001	$58.00	★★★+
Giaconda Aeolia 2002	$85.00	★★★
Giaconda Chardonnay 2001	$120.00	★★★
Petaluma Tiers Chardonnay 2000	$130.00	★★★

SPARKLING WINES

Hardys Sir James Pinot Noir Chardonnay 1998	$25.00	★★★★★
Radenti Chardonnay Pinot Noir 1997	$34.00	★★★★⌐
Touchwood Coal River Cuvée 1998	$28.00	★★★★
Chandon Rosé Vintage Brut 1998	$33.00	★★★★
Tamar Ridge Josef Chromy Selection		
Blanc de Noirs 1996	$38.00	★★★★
Seppelt Show Sparkling Shiraz 1991	$65.00	★★★⌐

FORTIFIED WINES

Noon Winery V.P. 2001	$18.00 (500 ml)	★★★★★
Seppelt Show Amontillado DP116	$20.00	★★★★★
Seppelt Show Oloroso DP38	$20.00	★★★★★
Chambers Oloroso	$23.00	★★★★★
Stanton and Killeen Vintage Port 1997	$27.00	★★★★★
Morris Old Premium Liqueur Muscat	$45.70 (500 ml)	★★★★★
Morris Old Premium Liqueur Tokay	$45.70 (500 ml)	★★★★★
Seppelt Rutherglen Rare Muscat GR113	$65.00 (500 ml)	★★★★★
Seppelt Rutherglen Rare Tokay DP59	$65.00 (500 ml)	★★★★★
Chambers Old Vine Muscadelle	$46.00 (375 ml)	★★★★⌐
Chambers Grand Rutherglen Muscat	$56.00 (375 ml)	★★★★⌐
Seppelt Barossa Valley Rare Tawny DP90	$65.00 (500 ml)	★★★★⌐
McWilliams Show Reserve Liqueur Muscat	$69.50	★★★⌐
Penfolds Grandfather Port	$89.50	★★★
All Saints Museum Release Rare Muscat	$395.00 (500 ml)	★★★
All Saints Museum Release Rare Tokay	$395.00 (500 ml)	★★★

Best-value Wines under $15

Each year when we release this *Guide*, the most-often asked question is: 'What's the best value?' or 'Which are the best wines under $15?' So, to make it easier for you to find the best-value wines, we list them using $15 as the cut-off point. The wines are sequenced in descending order of value-for-money, using our star ratings (from five down to four), and in ascending order of price, so that you can easily spot the best buys. To save space, we've left out the quality ratings (out of five glasses) but you can easily check these by turning to the review pages.

The prices quoted here are full retail prices, but don't forget that most of these wines can often be found discounted. You will very likely find them substantially cheaper if you shop around, especially if you buy by the dozen. Retailers commonly charge around 10 per cent less for a case purchase, as an incentive to buy more. That discount is usually for both unbroken and mixed dozens. Theoretically, you should be able to buy 11 bottles of Jacob's Creek for Grandma and one bottle of deluxe Champagne for yourself, at the case price! So take advantage!

Wine	Price	Value
RED WINES		
Zilzie Buloke Reserve Sangiovese 2002	$10.00	★★★★★
Plantagenet Hazard Hill Shiraz Grenache 2001	$11.00	★★★★★
Lindemans Reserve Shiraz 2001	$14.00	★★★★★
Stonehaven Stepping Stone Cabernet Sauvignon 2001	$14.00	★★★★★
Leasingham Bastion Shiraz Cabernet Sauvignon 2001	$14.50	★★★★★

36 **RED WINES UNDER $15**

DeBortoli Sacred Hill Cabernet Merlot 2002	$7.00	★★★★
Grant Burge Barossa Vines Shiraz 2001	$13.50	★★★★
Queen Adelaide Cabernet Sauvignon 2002	$8.25	★★★★
Queen Adelaide Pinot Noir 2001	$8.25	★★★★
Eaglehawk Cabernet Sauvignon 2001	$10.00	★★★★
Zilzie Buloke Reserve Petit Verdot 2002	$10.00	★★★★
Orlando Jacob's Creek Shiraz Cabernet 2001	$11.00	★★★★
McWilliams Hanwood Shiraz 2001	$11.50	★★★★
Poet's Corner Shiraz Cabernet Sauvignon		
Cabernet Franc 2001	$11.70	★★★★
Rosemount Cabernet Merlot 2002	$11.70	★★★★
Rosemount Shiraz Cabernet 2002	$11.70	★★★★
Palandri Baldivis Estate Cabernet Merlot 2001	$12.00	★★★★
Penfolds Rawson's Retreat		
Cabernet Sauvignon 2002	$12.40	★★★★
Ashwood Grove Merlot 2002	$12.75	★★★★
Grant Burge Barossa Vines Cabernet Sauvignon		
Merlot 2001	$13.50	★★★★
Bloodwood Big Men in Tights 2002	$14.00	★★★★
Kingston Shiraz 2001	$14.00	★★★★
Lindemans Reserve Cabernet Sauvignon 2001	$14.00	★★★★
Stonehaven Stepping Stone Shiraz 2001	$14.00	★★★★
DeBortoli Windy Peak Cabernet Rosé 2002	$14.40	★★★★
Xanadu Secession Merlot 2002	$14.90	★★★★
Garry Crittenden I Rosato 2002	$15.00	★★★★

WHITE WINES

Lindemans Bin 75 Riesling 2002	$9.00	★★★★★
Orlando Jacob's Creek Riesling 2002	$10.00	★★★★★
McWilliams Hanwood Chardonnay 2002	$11.50	★★★★★
Peter Lehmann Semillon 2002	$12.00	★★★★★

Grant Burge Barossa Vines Semillon 2002	$13.50	★★★★★
Miranda High Country 2002	$13.50	★★★★★
Chrismont Riesling 2002	$14.00	★★★★★
Woodstock Semillon Sauvignon Blanc 2002	$14.00	★★★★★
Leasingham Bastion Riesling 2002	$14.50	★★★★★
Meeting Place Chardonnay 2001	$14.95	★★★★★
Boggy Creek Vineyards Riesling 1999	$15.00	★★★★★
Shane Warne Collection Chardonnay 2002	$15.00	★★★★★
Queen Adelaide Chardonnay 2002	$8.25	★★★★┥
Deen DeBortoli Vat 2 Sauvignon Blanc 2002	$10.00	★★★★┥
Palandri Baldivis Estate Chardonnay 2002	$12.00	★★★★┥
Wolf Blass Chardonnay 2002	$12.00	★★★★┥
Huntington Estate Semillon Bin W1 2002	$13.50	★★★★┥
Stonehaven Stepping Stone Chardonnay 2002	$13.80	★★★★┥
Zilzie Viognier 2002	$14.00	★★★★┥
Galli Estate Chardonnay 2001	$15.00	★★★★┥
Ingoldby Chardonnay 2002	$15.00	★★★★┥
Mount Trio Sauvignon Blanc 2002	$15.00	★★★★┥
Yangarra Park Chardonnay 2001	$15.00	★★★★┥
Orlando Jacob's Creek Chardonnay 2002	$10.00	★★★★
Zilzie Buloke Reserve Sauvignon Blanc 2002	$10.00	★★★★
Saltram Semillon 2002	$10.25	★★★★
R.L. Buller & Son Magee Semillon		
Chardonnay 2002	$11.00	★★★★
Jane Brook Plain Jane 2002	$12.00	★★★★
Miramar Semillon 2002	$12.00	★★★★
Ashwood Grove Sauvignon Blanc 2002	$12.75	★★★★
Element Chardonnay 2002	$13.25	★★★★
Grant Burge Barossa Vines Chardonnay 2002	$13.50	★★★★
Houghton Semillon Sauvignon Blanc 2002	$14.00	★★★★

Dalfarras Sauvignon Blanc 2002	$14.00	★★★★
Xanadu Secession Chardonnay 2002	$14.90	★★★★
Xanadu Secession Semillon Sauvignon Blanc 2002	$14.90	★★★★
D'Arenberg The Hermit Crab Marsanne		
Viognier 2002	$15.00	★★★★
Sticks Chardonnay 2002	$15.00	★★★★
Wyndham Estate Bin 777 Semillon 2002	$15.00	★★★★

SPARKLING WINES

Seppelt Fleur de Lys Pinot Noir Chardonnay	$12.60	★★★★★
Seaview Brut Vintage 2001	$9.60	★★★★⁺
McWilliams Hanwood Pinot Noir Chardonnay Brut	$11.50	★★★★⁺
McWilliams Hanwood Sparkling Shiraz	$11.50	★★★★⁺
Wolf Blass Chardonnay Pinot Noir	$13.00	★★★★⁺
Meeting Place Chardonnay Pinot Noir		
Meunier 2000	$14.95	★★★★⁺
Seppelt Great Western Brut Reserve	$8.25	★★★★
Orlando Trilogy	$14.90	★★★★

FORTIFIED WINES

Wynns Samuel Port	$12.50	★★★★★
Chambers Dry Flor Sherry	$15.00	★★★★★
Queen Adelaide Tawny	$7.00	★★★★⁺
McWilliams Family Reserve Old Tawny Port	$13.25	★★★★⁺
All Saints The Keep Tawny Port	$15.00	★★★★⁺

The Penguin Rating System

The rating system used in this *Guide* is designed to give you an immediate assessment of a wine's attributes, as they will affect your purchasing decision. The symbols provide at-a-glance information, and the written descriptions go into greater depth. Other wine guides are full of numbers, but this one places importance on the written word.

The authors assess quality and value; provide an estimate of cellaring potential and optimum drinking age; and give notes on source, grape variety, organic cultivation where applicable, decanting, and alcohol content. We list previous outstanding vintages where we think they're relevant.

We assess quality using a cut-down show-judging system, marking out of a possible 10. Wine show judges score out of 20 points – three for nose, seven for colour, 10 for palate – but any wine scoring less than 10 is obviously faulty, so our five-glass range (with half-glass increments) indicates only the top 10 points. When equated to the show system, three glasses is roughly equivalent to a bronze medal, and five glasses, our highest award, equals a high gold medal or trophy-standard wine.

Value is arrived at primarily by balancing absolute quality against price. But we do take some account of those intangible attributes that make a wine more desirable, such as rarity, great reputation, glamour, outstanding cellarability, and so on. We take such things into account because they are part of the value equation for most consumers.

If a wine scores more for quality than for value, it does not mean the wine is overpriced. As explained below, any wine scoring three stars for value is fairly priced. Hence, a wine scoring five glasses and five stars is extraordinary value for money. Very few wines manage this feat. And, of course, good and bad value for money can be found at $50 just as it can at $5.

If there are more stars than glasses, you are looking at unusually good value. We urge readers not to become star-struck: a three-glass three-star wine is still a good drink.

Where we had any doubt about the soundness of a wine, a second bottle was always sampled.

Quality

🍷🍷🍷🍷🍷	The acme of style, a fabulous, faultless wine that Australia should be proud of.
🍷🍷🍷🍷⸦	A marvellous wine that is so close to the top it almost doesn't matter.
🍷🍷🍷🍷	An exciting wine that has plenty of style and dash. You should be proud to serve this.
🍷🍷🍷⸦	Solid quality with a modicum of style; good drinking.
🍷🍷🍷	Decent, drinkable wine good for everyday quaffing. You can happily serve this to family and friends.
🍷🍷⸦	Sound, respectable wines, but the earth won't move.
🍷🍷	Just okay but, in quality terms, starting to look a little wobbly.

(Lower scores are not usually included.)

Value

★★★★★	You should feel guilty for paying so little: this is great value for money.
★★★★⸦	Don't tell too many people because the wine will start selling and the maker will put the price up.
★★★★	If you complain about paying this much for a wine, you've got a death adder in your pocket.
★★★⸦	Still excellent wine, but the maker is also making money.
★★★	Fair is fair, this is a win–win exchange for buyer and maker.

★★┧	They are starting to see you coming, but it's not a total rip-off.
★★	This wine will appeal to label drinkers and those who want to impress their bank manager.
★┧	You know what they say about fools and their money . . .
★	Makes the used-car industry look saintly.

Grapes

Grape varieties are listed in order of dominance; percentages are cited when available.

Region

Where the source of the grapes is known, the region is stated. If there is more than one region, they are listed in order of dominance. Many large commercial blends have so many source regions that they are not stated.

Cellar

Any wine can of course be drunk immediately, but for maximum pleasure we recommend an optimum drinking time, assuming correct cellaring conditions. We have been deliberately conservative, believing it's better to drink a wine when it's a little too young than to risk waiting until it's too old.

An upright bottle ▮ indicates that the wine is ready for drinking now. It may also be possible to cellar it for the period shown. Where the bottle is lying on its side ➥ the wine is not ready for drinking now and should be cellared for the period shown.

▮ Drink now: there will be no improvement achieved by cellaring.

▮ 3 Drink now or during the next three years.

➥ 3–7 Cellar for three years at least before drinking; can be cellared for up to seven years.

➥ 10+ Cellar for 10 years or more; it will be at its best in 10 years.

Alcohol by Volume

Australian labelling laws require that alcohol content be shown on all wine labels. It's expressed as a percentage of alcohol by volume, e.g. 12.0% A/V means that 12 per cent of the wine is pure alcohol.

Recommended Retail Price

Prices were arrived at either by calculating from the trade wholesale using a standard full bottle-shop mark-up, or by using a maker-nominated recommended retail price. In essence, however, there is no such thing as RRP because retailers use different margins. The prices in this book are indicative of those in Sydney and Melbourne, but they will still vary from shop to shop and city to city. They should only be used as a guide. Cellar-door prices have been quoted when the wines are not available in the retail trade.

ⓢ Special

The wine is likely to be 'on special', so it will be possible to pay less than the recommended retail price. Shop around.

⊘ Organic

The wine has passed the tests required to label it as 'organically grown and made'.

▌ Decant

The wine will be improved by decanting.

⬦ Screw-cap

This wine is available with a screw-cap seal. Some of these wines are also available with a cork finish, but at least part of the production has a screw-cap. We recommend them, as a guarantee against cork-taint and random oxidation.

Red Wines

The Advocate Langhorne Creek Red

This wine is dedicated to David Owen, a director of Bleasdale wines from 1989 to '97, who was a tireless advocate for the Langhorne Creek region. (N.B. It's exclusive to Cellarmasters.)
CURRENT RELEASE 2000   There's a hint of Ribena on the nose here, with some minty and earthy notes, and balanced sweet oak. The palate is medium in body with minty dark fruit flavour, a briary texture and good length. It finishes savoury and satisfying with dry tannins. Serve it with roast vegetable pasta.

Quality	🍷🍷🍷🍷
Value	✷✷✷
Grapes	shiraz; cabernet sauvignon; petit verdot; merlot
Region	Langhorne Creek, SA
Cellar	🍾 6
Alc./Vol.	13.0%
RRP	$25.00

Ainsworth Estate Reserve Cabernet Sauvignon

Ainsworth's red wines first arrived with us only a couple of years ago and they impressed us from the word go. We're pleased to report that they weren't a flash in the pan; consistency has been good.
CURRENT RELEASE 2002   Tasted in the first flush of youth, this has good cool-grown varietal character with aromas of blackcurrant and spicy herbs, a leafy touch and some skilfully applied sweet oak. There's a medium intensity, tight palate with blackcurranty, foresty fruit of good intensity and balanced dry tannins. An elegant style that needs time to flower. Serve it with lamb cutlets and mint salsa.

Quality	🍷🍷🍷🍷
Value	✷✷✷
Grapes	cabernet sauvignon
Region	Yarra Valley, Vic.
Cellar	�‑ 2–6
Alc./Vol.	13.5%
RRP	$35.00

Ainsworth Estate Shiraz

Quality	♀♀♀♀
Value	★★★⁺
Grapes	shiraz
Region	Yarra Valley, Vic.
Cellar	⌐ 1–4
Alc./Vol.	13.0%
RRP	$18.00 ⅏

Ainsworth Estate occupies a lovely hilly part of the Yarra Valley, just off the beaten track. The restaurant is a great place to try one of the region's better shirazes, now sensibly screw-capped.
CURRENT RELEASE 2002   A bright young wine with plenty of good cool-climate shiraz cues to it, and none of the unpleasant ones. The nose has spicy, slightly peppery black cherry fruit and underplayed oak. The pepper continues on the palate, which is soft and light in substance, with a moderate tannic grip underneath. It needs a year or so, then it should work well with Chinese black pepper lamb.

Aldgate Ridge Pinot Noir

Quality	♀♀♀♀
Value	★★★
Grapes	pinot noir
Region	Adelaide Hills, SA
Cellar	▮ 2
Alc./Vol.	13.5%
RRP	$30.00

This Adelaide Hills wine was made using new Burgundian clones of pinot noir. Oddly enough its personality is more ocker than French – a pinot that should suit shiraz drinkers perfectly. Maker: David Powell of Torbreck.
CURRENT RELEASE 1999   More in the style of a traditional Aussie dry red than an elegant Adelaide Hills pinot noir. The nose is warm and generous with leathery smells and dark plum/prune fruit. In the mouth it has straightforward berry and plum flavours that are unfussed, soft and dry-reddish. It has good body and length of flavour with soft ripe tannins behind. A match for braised duck.

Alexandra Bridge Cabernet Merlot

Quality	♀♀♀♀
Value	★★★
Grapes	cabernet sauvignon; merlot
Region	Margaret River, WA
Cellar	⌐ 1–6
Alc./Vol.	14.0%
RRP	$26.50 ▮

The Alexandra Bridge vineyard is in the southern part of Margaret River, a region that in our opinion sometimes has problems getting true ripeness in cabernet. Any difficulties aren't apparent in this wine.
CURRENT RELEASE 2001   A youthful ruby colour introduces an attractive middleweight cabernet merlot. On the nose there's soft plummy fruit with some warm spices and bitter chocolate. Cedary oak underpins it well. In the mouth it's smooth and medium-bodied with ripe, slightly leafy fruit flavour of good length and intensity. Tannins are firm. Serve it with barbecued lamb steaks.

Alkoomi Jarrah Shiraz

The second release of a new super-red from this well-run Frankland River winery, Jarrah is made from the best parcels of shiraz in what is a pretty marginal shiraz area.
CURRENT RELEASE 1999   Very closed-up on the nose, this wine is hiding its charms from us very effectively. There's a plummy whiff to it, some understated spice and smoky oak. A hint of volatility enters the equation but doesn't upset us much. In the mouth it has peppery berry fruit of light flavour intensity but forceful structure and body, finishing in dry firm tannins. A shiraz that doesn't quite deliver as expected. Try it with four cheese risotto.

Quality	♟♟♟♟
Value	★★♦
Grapes	shiraz
Region	Great Southern, WA
Cellar	▮ 6
Alc./Vol.	13.5%
RRP	$41.00

All Saints Cabernet Sauvignon

These standard varietal reds slot in below the prestigious, heavy-bottle Carlyle range in the All Saints scheme of things. We reckon that they're usually a better drink, being less heavily extracted and mercifully far less oaky than some of those top drops.
CURRENT RELEASE 2000   A well-made young cabernet that avoids the portiness of some Rutherglen reds. It has an attractive nose with blackberry and blackcurrant aromas dressed in notable dusty, cedary oak. The palate is medium intensity with nice carry and a slightly oaky berry flavour in the middle. Tannins are dry and unobtrusive. Good with roast lamb.

Quality	♟♟♟♟
Value	★★★♦
Grapes	cabernet sauvignon
Region	Rutherglen, Vic.
Cellar	▮ 3
Alc./Vol.	13.5%
RRP	$19.70

All Saints Carlyle Durif

A speciality of north-east Victoria, durif is made into a typically formidable red at All Saints.
CURRENT RELEASE 2000   This is a powerful-smelling drop, with subtlety and refinement definitely on hold. The nose has road tar, black fruit and spice aromas power-dressed in a big dose of vanillin, camphory oak. The palate is big and alcoholic, and happily the fruit flavour is nicely ripe, not too jammy or sweet. Oak is there in big measure too, and tannins are firm and grippy. Still totally immature, has it the balance for the long haul? Right now, serve with the biggest, charriest T-bone.

Quality	♟♟♟♟
Value	★★★
Grapes	durif
Region	Rutherglen, Vic.
Cellar	▬ 1–10+
Alc./Vol.	14.1%
RRP	$38.00

All Saints Shiraz

Quality 🍷🍷🍷🍷
Value ★★★
Grapes shiraz
Region Rutherglen, Vic.
Cellar 4
Alc./Vol. 13.5%
RRP $19.70

Like most Rutherglen district wineries, All Saints makes a comprehensive range of table wines, even though the main game is fantastic fortifieds. Shiraz has always been the main red table wine variety.

CURRENT RELEASE 2000 This is a well-made north-east Victorian shiraz that's miles away from the tired, jammy reds that were typical of the region not all that long ago. It has cherry-berry aromas with a controlled touch of vanillin oak. The palate is smooth and appealing with sweet fruit at the core, well-regulated tannins and a soft finish. Try it with a meal of baked root vegetables and crusty bread.

Amberley Margaret River Shiraz

Quality 🍷🍷🍷🍷
Value ★★★★★
Grapes shiraz
Region Margaret River, WA
Cellar 3
Alc./Vol. 13.5%
RRP $16.50

Amberley Estate has a lower profile than some of its neighbours. Its red wines deserve much wider acceptance for their balance and style.

CURRENT RELEASE 2001 A modern shiraz of good character and ready drinkability, this smells clean and appealing with aromas of aniseed, plums and peppery spice, enhanced by a touch of dusty oak. In the mouth it's ripe with plummy fruit of good intensity and balanced flavour and finely integrated soft tannins. Try it with boned and grilled chicken with black pepper and lemon.

Amberton Shiraz

Quality 🍷🍷🍷🍷
Value ★★★★½
Grapes shiraz
Region Barossa Valley, SA
Cellar 3
Alc./Vol. 14.0%
RRP $16.50

Amberton vineyard was a labour of love for a group of wine-loving doctors from Sydney who planted it in 1975. This vintage is exclusive to the Cellarmasters wine club. Maker: John Schwartzkopff.

CURRENT RELEASE 2001 Hooray for a moderately priced shiraz with a bit of refinement. This is a medium intensity red with spicy, slightly jammy fruit character that's pleasantly earthy and well balanced. In the mouth it has generous, lasting flavour in a medium-bodied package that winds up with unobtrusive, ripe, dry tannins. Great value. Try it with grilled lamb chops.

Andrew Garrett Bold Shiraz

Bold? Oh well, you have to call your wine something, and bold suits shiraz better than bashful; Australia's signature red grape rarely makes wine of shy, retiring personality.

CURRENT RELEASE 2001   Jammy berries and plums lead on the nose, and there are hints of mint, clove, spice and graphite. The palate isn't quite as bold as we thought it would be, with a little hollowness in the middle and flavours somewhat driven by wood rather than fruit. It finishes with sinewy drying tannins. Try it with spaghetti and veal sauce.

Quality	🍷 🍷 🍷
Value	★ ★ ★
Grapes	shiraz
Region	Limestone Coast, SA
Cellar	🍷 2
Alc./Vol.	13.0%
RRP	$15.25 Ⓢ

Andrew Harris Merlot

Mudgee has a long history with wine, but the large Andrew Harris vineyard is one of the newer players on the scene. It was first planted in 1991.

CURRENT RELEASE 2001   There's some good merlot character at the heart of this generous red, as well as oak-derived and regional elements. The nose reminds us of vanilla, squeaky leather, and boot polish over very plummy ripe fruit. The palate is medium in body with sweet berry flavour in the middle, seasoned with a dose of toasty oak. Dry fine-grained tannins underpin it well. Good with roast beef.

Quality	🍷 🍷 🍷 🍷
Value	★ ★ ★ ★
Grapes	merlot
Region	Mudgee, NSW
Cellar	🍷 4
Alc./Vol.	14.0%
RRP	$16.00

Angoves Bear Crossing Cabernet Merlot

The 'Warning: Koalas Crossing' style of label might not be everybody's cuppa but this wine does the right thing, with some of the proceeds going to help our little marsupial friends.

CURRENT RELEASE 2002   A pleasant soft nose of red and blackcurrant, some licorice and a light dusting of oak. It tastes clean and fresh and it's on the light side of medium-bodied, but with almost enough presence and flavour intensity to satisfy the financially challenged red drinker. The finish is soft. Try it with pizza.

Quality	🍷 🍷 🍷
Value	★ ★ ★
Grapes	cabernet sauvignon; merlot
Region	Murray Valley, SA
Cellar	🍷 2
Alc./Vol.	14.0%
RRP	$10.75 Ⓢ

Annie's Lane Cabernet Merlot

Quality	🍷🍷🍷🍷
Value	★★★★
Grapes	cabernet sauvignon; merlot
Region	Clare Valley, SA
Cellar	🍷 7
Alc./Vol.	13.0%
RRP	$18.00

The big wine companies are engaged in a constant battle to capture market share in the low and medium price ranges. This makes the consumer the winner, with great value available in brands like Annie's Lane.
CURRENT RELEASE 2001   Not quite the wine that the 2000 was, this is still a welcoming drop that's very good value. The nose has leafy dark-berry aromas that are intense and appetising, and oak is used with admirable restraint. The palate is full of ripe fruit and it's well supported by grainy-textured tannins. A good thing to enjoy with T-bone steak.

Annie's Lane Copper Trail Shiraz

Quality	🍷🍷🍷🍷🍷
Value	★★★
Grapes	shiraz
Region	Clare Valley, SA
Cellar	➡ 2–12+
Alc./Vol.	14.0%
RRP	$48.00

The Clare Valley's vineyards sit astride the Copper Trail, the track prospectors followed to reach the copper mines of the Burra district 150 years ago. Maker: Caroline Dunn.
CURRENT RELEASE 1999   A fine type of Clare shiraz: modern but with a welcome traditional thread. The colour is deep and the nose is concentrated with berry, spice, ironstone and mocha oak aromas of richness and power. The mouth-filling palate has deep flavours, full body and a firm foundation of ripe tannins. The aftertaste is long and powerful. Immature, but give it cellar time and you should have a classic. Roast beef will work well.

Annie's Lane Shiraz

Quality	🍷🍷🍷🍷
Value	★★★
Grapes	shiraz
Region	Clare Valley, SA
Cellar	🍷 3
Alc./Vol.	13.0%
RRP	$18.00 $

These Annie's Lane reds have often been favourites of ours due to the honest flavour and good value they represent.
CURRENT RELEASE 2001   This latest edition is a bit light-on compared to some previous vintages. Still good drinking but with less concentration. On the nose there's a good measure of slightly jammy, sweet blackberry aroma which has a hint of spice to it. The palate has simple fruit character that's a little lighter than usual and without the normal persistence. That said, it's still a pleasantly drinkable soft red wine. Try it with a homemade Cornish pastie.

Arakoon Doyen Shiraz

The label tells us that this Schwarzeneggeresque red is made from 'super-ripe' grapes. It's formidably constructed, with muscles on its muscles. Maker: Patrick Jones.

CURRENT RELEASE 2001   Very deep, blackish colour tells the tale here: it's a huge red designed for cigar smokers and Americans. The potent nose has liqueur cherry, raisin and menthol aromas, and it tastes dense and warm with some of the character of vintage port. A solid wall of tannins backs it up, but it's well tuned to the massive fruit weight. Try this highly alcoholic red with a steak from a rampaging bull elephant.

Quality	🍷🍷🍷🍷🍷
Value	★★★
Grapes	shiraz
Region	McLaren Vale, SA
Cellar	10
Alc./Vol.	16.5%
RRP	$44.00

Arakoon Sellicks Beach Shiraz Grenache

Arakoon wines have labels of very snappy, minimalist design that would fit perfectly on the tables of those who make wine a fashion statement.

CURRENT RELEASE 2001   This looks a friendlier proposition than the bullyboy Doyen. The nose has prune, mixed berry and earth aromas of ripe regional/varietal identity. There's also a dimension of chocolatey richness. The palate is dark-berry flavoured, concentrated and warm with soft tannins and a long finish. Serve it with lamb's fry and bacon.

Quality	🍷🍷🍷🍷
Value	★★★⁴
Grapes	shiraz; grenache
Region	McLaren Vale, SA
Cellar	3
Alc./Vol.	14.5%
RRP	$22.00

Ashwood Grove Merlot

Like a number of Murray Valley and Riverina wine producers, Ashwood Grove has taken a step into the prestige end of the market with involvement in a cooler climate vineyard, in this case in Victoria's Yarra Valley.

CURRENT RELEASE 2002   Lots of sweet fruit and sweet spice fills the nose here. It has good varietal identity with plummy fruit of attractive intensity. It tastes mouth-filling and smooth, rich and warm, and the tannins are supple. Drink it reasonably young with roast veal.

Quality	🍷🍷🍷
Value	★★★★
Grapes	merlot
Region	Murray Valley, Vic.
Cellar	2
Alc./Vol.	14.5%
RRP	$12.75 Ⓢ

Austin's Barrabool Cabernet Sauvignon

Quality	♥♥♥♥
Value	★★★
Grapes	cabernet sauvignon
Region	Geelong, Vic.
Cellar	▯ 3
Alc./Vol.	12.0%
RRP	$25.00

Austin's at Barrabool persevere with cabernet sauvignon when some of the best growers in the Geelong region have lost interest. And maybe they have a point: the cab from their vineyard is good.
CURRENT RELEASE 2001   The colour is a bright ruby and the nose has berry, earth and savoury tobaccoey aromas of moderate intensity. The palate has middling concentration, subtle flavour and a soft finish. There's a quiet succulence to this understated red. It hasn't great power or individuality, but it's very drinkable, fragrant in the mouth and easy on the gums. Try it with pork fillets.

Bannockburn Shiraz

Quality	♥♥♥♥♥
Value	★★★★
Grapes	shiraz
Region	Geelong, Vic.
Cellar	▯ 10
Alc./Vol.	13.5%
RRP	$47.50

Around 15 years ago, Bannockburn Shiraz veered away from the Aussie shiraz tradition, taking in technical and stylistic hints derived from winemaker Gary Farr's extensive experience in France. The result is a most interesting and complex wine.
CURRENT RELEASE 2001   Deep, dense colour looks the goods here, and the nose is wonderful. It harmoniously brings together spices, black pepper, ripe black cherry, a very light floral note, and subtle spicy oak. The palate has concentration, yet it's fine and savoury and won't weigh you down. There's real length and it finishes fine textured with ripe, balanced tannins. Serve it with spiced venison.

Banrock Station The Reserve Merlot

Quality	♥♥♥
Value	★★★
Grapes	merlot
Region	Murray Valley, SA
Cellar	▯ 3
Alc./Vol.	13.0%
RRP	$13.00 Ⓢ

Wine marketers are forever nailing new products onto other products. Last year, Banrock Reserve appeared. A $13 reserve wine seems a little like gilding the lily to us. But the wines are okay.
CURRENT RELEASE 2001   The only problem with this merlot is that it's dominated by charred American oak, which gives it a pervasive aroma and taste of burnt coconut. Cynics would say the difference between reserve wines and standard wines is always more oak! Those who like this sort of thing will be made happy by it, but not us. It demands a burnt barbecued chop.

Banrock Station The Reserve Shiraz

The BRL Hardy empire contributes a few cents from the sale of each bottle to a wetlands fund, which probably makes them feel better about the salinity problems of the Murray Valley.
CURRENT RELEASE 2001   The colour is fairly developed for its age, and the bouquet is dominated by charry oak aromas, which overpower the fruit. It is a little dried out. The palate is likewise savoury and drying, and the oak results in an astringent, oak-pumped taste. It lacks the fruit and softness expected in a red of this price level. Try it with shish kebabs.

Quality	🍷 🍷 ﹖
Value	★ ★ ★
Grapes	shiraz
Region	Murray Valley, SA
Cellar	🍷 3
Alc./Vol.	13.0%
RRP	$13.00 Ⓢ

Baptista The Graytown Heathcote Shiraz

When David Traeger bought this 112-year-old vineyard, it was in rundown condition. He's revived the 22 acres, but it's erratic and low-yielding, with high running costs, so the wine isn't cheap. There's also history and nostalgia factored into the price.
CURRENT RELEASE 1997   A minty, eucalyptus-scented red which has an angular, lean palate with slightly elevated acidity. It's medium-bodied, not rich, fleshy or tannic, and although it looks certain to live for ages, it hasn't acquired much complexity in its first six years. It's a conversation piece but not really worth $115. It would suit minted roast lamb.

Quality	🍷 🍷 🍷 🍷
Value	★ ★ ﹢
Grapes	shiraz
Region	Heathcote, Vic.
Cellar	🍷 8+
Alc./Vol.	14.5%
RRP	$115.00

Barossa Valley Estate Spires Shiraz Cabernet

Barossa Valley Estate is part of the BRL Hardy Group these days. Spires usually stands for good value inexpensive quaffers, but we've seen much better examples than the 2001.
CURRENT RELEASE 2001   The greenish, herbal aromas and flavours hint at some underripe grapes in the blend. It takes herbal/spicy characters to an extreme. It has plenty of flavour and a firm spine, but finishes with a little bitterness from green tannins. Serve it with lamb's fry, bacon and onions.

Quality	🍷 🍷 🍷
Value	★ ★ ★ ﹢
Grapes	shiraz; cabernet sauvignon
Region	Barossa Valley, SA
Cellar	🍷 3
Alc./Vol.	13.5%
RRP	$11.00 Ⓢ

Bazzani Cabernet Shiraz Dolcetto

Quality	♟ ♟ ♟ ♟
Value	★ ★ ★ ★
Grapes	cabernet sauvignon; shiraz; dolcetto
Region	Pyrenees, Vic.
Cellar	◊ 5+
Alc./Vol.	14.0%
RRP	$19.80

Luigi and Athalie Bazzani are the folks behind the Warrenmang vineyard, winery, restaurant and resort in the Pyrenees. It's a great place to dine on a cold winter's night.

CURRENT RELEASE 2000   The central Victorian provenance shows in the minty, eucalyptus character of this unusual blend. It is redolent of clean ripe fruit and well-handled background oak, and is big and lively in the mouth, with trademark Pyrenees tannins. It needs food to soften the astringency. Decanting also helps. Try it with aged hard cheeses.

Best's Bin 0 Great Western Shiraz

Quality	♟ ♟ ♟ ♟ ♟
Value	★ ★ ★ ★
Grapes	shiraz
Region	Grampians, Vic.
Cellar	⬤ 2–20
Alc./Vol.	14.0%
RRP	$36.40

We like the way Best's don't overwork, over-oak or otherwise tinker too much with their shirazes. You know you're tasting the fruit and that the fruit faithfully reflects the vineyard and season. Makers: the Thomson family and Hamish Seabrook.

CURRENT RELEASE 2000   The aroma is vibrant and youthful, sweetly aromatic from a deft combination of raspberry, blackberry fruit and scented oak, with a sprig of peppermint thrown in. In the mouth, it's lean and elegant, not fleshy or dense but tautly structured, with plenty of flavour, tannin and spine. It will age superbly. Drink with hard cheese, like Heidi gruyère.

Bidgeebong Gundagai Shiraz

Quality	♟ ♟ ♟ ♟
Value	★ ★ ★ ★
Grapes	shiraz
Region	Gundagai, NSW
Cellar	◊ 8
Alc./Vol.	13.5%
RRP	$22.00 ⑤

Cute name! It couldn't come from anywhere else but Australia, could it? Andrew Birks, wine science lecturer at Charles Sturt University in Wagga, is the brains behind it.

CURRENT RELEASE 2001   This is a clean, intense red wine with attractive plum, chocolate, aniseed and earth aromas. There's a good balance between oak and fruit. The fairly firm tannin on palate makes it taste leaner than it would with food. There's a bitter chocolate aftertaste and it lingers well. Would suit braised venison.

Bidgeebong Tumbarumba Merlot

Andrew Birks, the man behind Bidgeebong, talks about the Bermuda triangle bounded by Tumbarumba, Gundagai and Hilltops, from where he buys grapes. Bermuda because the wines tend to disappear! CURRENT RELEASE 2001   This is a bold and slightly aggressive red. The accent is firmly on the fruit, rather than oak or other secondary characteristics. The aromas are of raspberry and mulberry, and it seems slightly sweet on entry. The tannins are somewhat fierce, giving a disjointed 'arms and legs' perception. This could be remedied by time. It would suit mature cheeses.

Quality	♟♟♟♟
Value	★★★↗
Grapes	merlot
Region	Tumbarumba, NSW
Cellar	⬤ 2–7+
Alc./Vol.	13.0%
RRP	$22.00

Big Hill Vineyard Reserve Shiraz

The Big Hill in question is near Bendigo, a region that is providing some excellent shiraz. This reserve wine received 100 per cent new American oak but it doesn't dominate.
CURRENT RELEASE 2001   This young Bendigo shiraz introduces itself with plenty of minty scents that are fresh and savoury. Blackcurrant and blackberry pastille aromas combine with well-modulated vanillin oak to give a sweet-and-sour savoury feel to things. The palate has intense minted black-fruit flavours that are long and intense, and 100 per cent charry new American oak reveals itself as a seasoning rather than a dominant factor. A wine that should develop well medium term. Try it with Greek herbed lamb.

Quality	♟♟♟♟♟
Value	★★★★
Grapes	shiraz
Region	Bendigo, Vic.
Cellar	⬤ 1–6
Alc./Vol.	14.0%
RRP	$30.00

Big Hill Vineyard Shiraz

Quality	♟ ♟ ♟ ♟
Value	★ ★ ★ ⸼
Grapes	shiraz
Region	Bendigo, Vic.
Cellar	▮ 5
Alc./Vol.	13.0%
RRP	$25.00

At the Big Hill Vineyard café they serve 'Granite Burgers'. Make sure you consult your dentist before ordering. The wines are typically solid Bendigo types. Maker: John Ellis.

CURRENT RELEASE 2000   Robust Bendigo shiraz, this has dense colour and a juicy, concentrated nose of blackberries and spice. The mintiness that sometimes overwhelms Bendigo shiraz is nowhere to be seen. The palate is well-constructed with ripe flavour that isn't at all jammy or overripe. It has fine texture and good length with ripe tannins and civilised balance. Good to sip with roast beef.

Quality	♟ ♟ ♟ ♟
Value	★ ★ ★ ⸼
Grapes	shiraz
Region	Bendigo, Vic.
Cellar	▮ 5
Alc./Vol.	14.0%
RRP	$25.00

CURRENT RELEASE 2001   There's a touch of eucalypt here and the nose also has some savoury meaty notes to dark plum fruit. Oak backs it up well. The medium-bodied palate has silky texture and good length with mint, berry and mocha flavours that fold into balanced furry tannins. Try it with a good steak pie.

Bindi Original Vineyard Pinot Noir

Quality	♟ ♟ ♟ ♟ ♟
Value	★ ★ ★ ⸼
Grapes	pinot noir
Region	Macedon Ranges, Vic.
Cellar	▮ 5+
Alc./Vol.	14.0%
RRP	$50.00 (mailing list)

The average annual output of this tiny property is just 1000 dozen, but they have planted more recently. The total area stands at 6 hectares: two-thirds pinot noir, one-third chardonnay.

Previous outstanding vintages: '94, '97, '98, '99, '00
CURRENT RELEASE 2001   Another winner from Bindi: it's right up among the best pinots in the country. The colour is medium–full purple–red and it has a superb black cherry fragrance. Oak is present but not overt, while in the mouth it's fine and tautly structured, very intense and lingering, with a light tannin grip on a velvet-textured palate. It cries out for roast squab.

Bird in Hand 'Two In The Bush' Merlot Cabernet

Phew, what a mouthful. This wine is from the 26-hectare vineyard of Andrew and Justin Nugent, at Woodside. It's all very new: the business was established in 2001.

CURRENT RELEASE 2001   This is a light, fruity, simple red – probably reflecting young vines. It has a good colour and some attractive sweet berry, minty, raspberry aromas. The palate is lean and tightly wound, but the tannins are measured. It would go well with Italian veal escalopes.

Quality	🍷🍷🍷❵
Value	★★★
Grapes	merlot; cabernet sauvignon
Region	Adelaide Hills, SA
Cellar	🍷 5
Alc./Vol.	13.8%
RRP	$25.00

Bloodwood Big Men In Tights

The zany Stephen Doyle dreams up some curious names for his wines. Well, given the negativity surrounding the word 'rosé', this just has to be better.

CURRENT RELEASE 2002   Nice body! Did we say that? Ahem: this is a fuller bodied style of rosé as you might deduce from the title. The colour is medium–full pink with purple tinges. This fresh, clean appearance is reflected in the strawberry tutti-frutti aromas and taste, which is enhanced by a trace of sweetness. Nicely balanced and would go with heartier rosé foods, such as quail.

Quality	🍷🍷🍷🍷
Value	★★★★
Grapes	not stated
Region	Orange, NSW
Cellar	🍷 1
Alc./Vol.	12.5%
RRP	$14.00 (cellar door)

Bloodwood Pinot Noir

Pinot is micro-winemaking territory: this one ran out at just 100 cases, and is likely to all be sold at the cellar door. Winemaker: Stephen Doyle.

CURRENT RELEASE 2002   A fragrant 'pretty' pinot that really grows on you as you sip. It's a lighter style but no less a wine for that: just make sure you suit it to appropriate food, and we recommend whole baked salmon. The aromas remind us of strawberry and mint, while the taste is lively and fresh. The palate has surprising intensity and length. A promising debut.

Quality	🍷🍷🍷🍷
Value	★★★❥
Grapes	pinot noir
Region	Orange, NSW
Cellar	🍷 4
Alc./Vol.	14.0%
RRP	$35.00 (cellar door)

Blue Pyrenees Cabernet Sauvignon

Quality	♥♥♥♥♪
Value	★★★★★
Grapes	cabernet sauvignon
Region	Pyrenees, Vic.
Cellar	▮ 8+
Alc./Vol.	14.0%
RRP	$18.50

There's a subtle difference in label now between the flagship Blue Pyrenees Estate red, and a host of other me-too wines whose Pyrenees provenance is less clearly stated. Maker: Greg Dedman.

CURRENT RELEASE 2001   Terrific value for a sub-$20 red! It's a lovely big mouthful of flavour, well concentrated, smooth and easy to enjoy young. The aromas are mainly of dark chocolate, vanilla and various red fruits, including blackberry and blackcurrant. The palate is lean and lively with a touch of typical cabernet austerity, with balanced tannin astringency which will see it age for many years. You could drink now, with a hearty steak.

Blue Pyrenees Estate Reserve

Quality	♥♥♥♥♪
Value	★★★♪
Grapes	cabernet sauvignon; shiraz; merlot
Region	Pyrenees, Vic.
Cellar	➥ 2–10+
Alc./Vol.	14.0%
RRP	$36.50 ▮

This is the big cheese at Blue Pyrenees. It's been made for over twenty years from the best of the estate-grown fruit, and is always a multi-varietal blend. Maker: Greg Dedman.

CURRENT RELEASE 2000   This big bruiser has a gumleafy nose and is unequivocally full-bodied with a firm, astringent finish. It's solidly structured and gutsy, with lively acidity accentuating the tannins. Except for the use of oak, subtlety is not in the game plan. It's a good food wine and will age long term. Try it with venison pot-roast.

Blue Pyrenees Pinot Noir

Quality	♥♥♥♪
Value	★★★★
Grapes	pinot noir
Region	Pyrenees, Vic.
Cellar	▮ 3
Alc./Vol.	13.5%
RRP	$18.00 Ⓢ

This company, a stalwart of the Pyrenees region, was sold during 2002 by the Remy Cointreau group, which founded it way back in 1963. We hope to see it returned to a high position in the wine market.

CURRENT RELEASE 2001   A good red wine, but not a great pinot. There is a difference. It has a deep colour and an oak-led bouquet reminding us of vanilla and chocolate – with possibly a hint of American barrels. It's a stolid sort of wine which has plenty of muscle and intensity. A satisfying drink, to go with roast saddle of hare.

Brand's Patron's Reserve

This wine, made from 30-year-old vines, and produced in honour of founder Eric Brand, was named best red wine at the 2003 Sydney International Wine Competition.
CURRENT RELEASE 1999   This is Coonawarra played loud! It's a very deeply and youthfully coloured wine; the fruit aromas are ultra-ripe and border on jammy, and it has a plushly opulent, full-bodied flavour and texture that fills the senses. There are oak vanillin and regional mint aromas, too. This is about as forceful as Coonawarra gets, and it needs big flavours like barbecued kangaroo with pepper-berry sauce.

Quality	♥♥♥♥♥
Value	★★★✦
Grapes	cabernet sauvignon 50%; shiraz 22%; merlot 22%; cabernet franc 6%
Region	Coonawarra, SA
Cellar	10+
Alc./Vol.	14.5%
RRP	$66.00

Brindabella Hills Shiraz

Roger and Fay Harris's Brindabella Hills is making better and better wines; both vineyard and winemaker (Roger) are maturing. They're at 540 m altitude and take fruit from three vineyards as well as their own in the warmer sites of the Canberra region.
CURRENT RELEASE 2001   This is a lovely elegant, natural tasting shiraz. It ain't huge, but neither has the lovely spicy fruit been bolstered with oak or extra tannin, and it doesn't taste artificially concentrated. The aromas are of raspberry, white pepper and other spices, with fruit leading the charge, and the light-bodied palate is finely balanced. It would suit veal.

Quality	♥♥♥♥♥
Value	★★★★
Grapes	shiraz
Region	Canberra, ACT
Cellar	8+
Alc./Vol.	13.5%
RRP	$25.00

Brokenwood Cabernet Sauvignon Merlot

The fruit for this popular red blend was sourced from the King Valley, mainly from Guy Darling's famous Koombahla, which is now a mature vineyard. Makers: Iain Riggs and P J Charteris.
CURRENT RELEASE 2000   This red is designed as an each-way style; that is, you can drink it young or cellar it in the medium term. It has attractive raspberry and peppermint aromas, and tastes elegant and medium-bodied with good fruit intensity, focus and structure. A lick of tannin firms up the finish. It goes well with pink-roasted rack of lamb.

Quality	♥♥♥♥
Value	★★★✦
Grapes	cabernet sauvignon; merlot
Region	King Valley, Vic.
Cellar	6
Alc./Vol.	13.5%
RRP	$26.50

Brookland Valley Verse One Cabernet Merlot

Quality 4 glasses
Value ★★★½
Grapes cabernet sauvignon; merlot
Region Margaret River, WA
Cellar 1–6+
Alc./Vol. 14.5%
RRP $22.00

Verse One is Brookland Valleys' second rung of wines. The eccentric name refers to the sheets of music on the label and the statue of a piping Pan that's a centrepiece of the property.

CURRENT RELEASE 2001 This has some oddball sweaty, funky aromas which don't have a lot to do with cabernet or merlot, but it is a decent drink and fair value. It's very young and a tad raw, and would benefit from another year or two's ageing. There are cassisy cabernet flavours in the mouth, and the flavour is bold and generous. Try roast beef.

Bundaleera Pinot Noir

Quality 4 glasses
Value ★★★
Grapes pinot noir
Region Tamar Valley, Tas.
Cellar 4+
Alc./Vol. 12.4%
RRP $27.50 (mailing list)

This tiny 2.2 hectare vineyard is at Relbia, just outside Launceston. Owner David Jenkinson's day job is as a mining industry metallurgist; the wines are made at Rosevears Estate.

CURRENT RELEASE 2001 As pinots come, this is a whopper! It has a leathery bouquet reflecting lots of new oak, plus ripe plum fruit aromas. It has a lot of stuffing, and the finish carries for a long duration. The controversial issue is tannin: is there too much? Whatever your verdict, you'll want to drink it with a meal, so try roast duck.

Burge Family Garnacha Old Vine Grenache

Quality 3½ glasses
Value ★★★
Grapes grenache
Region Barossa Valley, SA
Cellar 4
Alc./Vol. 15.5%
RRP $27.00 (cellar door)

Somebody once said, 'Those who like this sort of thing will find this is the sort of thing that they like.' It neatly, if evasively, encapsulates the way we feel about this wine. Maker: Rick Burge.

CURRENT RELEASE 2001 The first thing you notice is the odour of alcohol. It smells spirity and porty and tastes very hot, like a dose of brandy has been added. The other aromas are of preserved fruits – berry and plum jams – and the mouth-feel is sweet and syrupy, clumsy and lacking shape or structure. Some people love this kind of wine . . . Food matches are too difficult.

Burge Family Olive Hill Shiraz Grenache Mourvèdre

Olive Hill is the name of Rick Burge's main vineyard, and is seen on the labels of several of his superb Barossa wines. He has 10 hectares of vines at Lyndoch. CURRENT RELEASE 2001   Strictly for lovers of humungous, jammy, sweet/syrupy Rhône-style reds, and that obviously includes American wine critic Robert Parker. The combination of vegetal and raisiny, porty aromas is extraordinary, as is the dimension of the broad, almost unctuous palate. There is no shortage of texture and flavour, but this is at the expense of structure. An unsubtle hot-area style, but a massive mouthful of flavour. Steak and kidney pie here.

Quality	♥♥♥♥♥
Value	★★★★
Grapes	shiraz; grenache; mourvèdre
Region	Barossa Valley, SA
Cellar	▮ 4
Alc./Vol.	14.5%
RRP	$29.00 (cellar door)

Burge Family Winemakers The Renoux

This brand is a simple solution to the complex problem of how to list several grape varieties on a label and not turn people off.
CURRENT RELEASE 2001   Rick Burge's style these days is very big and overripe; some would term it Parkerised. The bouquet suggests oak plus jammy overripe berries, treading into porty territory. The palate is extractive, meaning the porty flavours and sharp tannins result in astringency, which makes it hard to drink young. Cellar it and then serve with kassler.

Quality	♥♥♥♥
Value	★★★♦
Grapes	shiraz 45%; merlot 38%; cabernet sauvignon 17%
Region	Barossa Valley, SA
Cellar	➤ 2–8+
Alc./Vol.	14.5%
RRP	$27.00 ▮ (cellar door)

Burton Coonawarra Cabernet Sauvignon

Nigel Burton started his own wine venture quite recently and sources grapes from South Australian regions, including Coonawarra and McLaren Vale. Winemaker is veteran Pat Tocaciu. This won a gold medal at Perth in 2002.
CURRENT RELEASE 2000   Oak plays a big part in this big red. It's solid, concentrated, tannic and doesn't really speak to us of Coonawarra. The colour is very deep and youthful, and the finish is a bit heavy on the oak and acid combination. It needs food to soak up the acid: try it with a rare steak.

Quality	♥♥♥♥
Value	★★★
Grapes	cabernet sauvignon
Region	Coonawarra, SA
Cellar	➤ 1–5
Alc./Vol.	13.0%
RRP	$33.00 ▮

By Farr Pinot Noir

Quality	🍷🍷🍷🍷🍷
Value	★★★★
Grapes	pinot noir
Region	Geelong, Vic.
Cellar	🍾 5
Alc./Vol.	13.5%
RRP	$53.00

Gary and Robyn Farr don't have a marketing department; indeed, Gary's philosophy could be construed as anti-marketing. 'I make wines I like to drink,' he says gruffly.

CURRENT RELEASE 2001   Further evidence of Gary Farr's deft hand with pinot noir: this is a beautiful pinot with fine strawberry and cherry aromas, traces of leaf and mint – but no greenness. There's a whiff of the barnyard, a touch of straw and funk, while the palate has excellent depth and richness with nicely measured firm, fine tannins to close. A top drink with duck risotto.

Campbells Bobbie Burns Shiraz

Quality	🍷🍷🍷🍷🍷
Value	★★★★★
Grapes	shiraz
Region	Rutherglen, Vic.
Cellar	🍾 6
Alc./Vol.	14.5%
RRP	$19.00

Bobbie Burns is a benchmark Rutherglen red with a consistent record over many years. It has plenty of warm regional personality, but it has rarely strayed into the porty, stewed style of red wine that was once the Rutherglen norm.

CURRENT RELEASE 2000   This is a hearty regional style with plenty to recommend it. The nose is full of impact with dark plum, prune, spice, licorice and cedar aromas. A velvety big mouthful follows, warm with berry, prune and alcohol, backed up by firm tannins. It's well-made and generously constructed. Worth cellaring mid-term. Try it with a lamb casserole.

Cannibal Creek Merlot

Quality	🍷🍷🍷🍷
Value	★★★
Grapes	merlot
Region	Gippsland, Vic.
Cellar	🍾 3
Alc./Vol.	13.2%
RRP	$28.00

At Cannibal Creek there's an air of relaxed timelessness, heightened by tin-roofed buildings and a very country feel. By contrast the wines are very today.

CURRENT RELEASE 2001   The term 'cool climate' can mean a multitude of things, not all of them desirable, but this cool-grown merlot is ripe enough, with briary red and dark berry aromas and a lightly earthy touch. The palate combines sweet fruit and more savoury elements in good balance. The gentle, ripe berry flavour makes it easy to drink and so does the soft finish. Serve it with a veal casserole.

Cannibal Creek Pinot Noir

This back-blocks vineyard, a few kilometres off the main Melbourne–Gippsland road, is a little oasis of pinot noir, skillfully made into a delicate drop by winemaker Pat Hardiker.

CURRENT RELEASE 2001   This vintage captures the essence of pinot noir well, without the weird characters that blight a number of cool-climate pinots from young vineyards. The nose is juicy and fruity smelling, reminiscent of raspberries and strawberries; it's light, fresh and appealing with little apparent oak. In the mouth it's intense, ripe and soft with a delicious succulent quality helped by sweet fruit and mouth-watering acidity. Great alongside roasted quail with grapes.

Quality	♟♟♟♟
Value	★★★⊰
Grapes	pinot noir
Region	Gippsland, Vic.
Cellar	🍾 3
Alc./Vol.	13.4%
RRP	$28.00

Cape Mentelle Cabernet Sauvignon

Cape Mentelle has sometimes flirted with slightly green, herbal notes that aren't to everyone's taste, but the last couple of vintages have been in top form.
Previous outstanding vintages: '82, '83, '86, '88, '90, '91, '93, '94, '95, '98
CURRENT RELEASE 1999   There's a slight suggestion of red Bordeaux to it – the nose is complex with unevolved black fruit aromas, along with briar, earth, herbal and cedary notes. The long-flavoured palate is based on dense-packed fruit and classy oak flavours, on a firm structure of supporting tannins. Still immature, it should be an ideal partner to roast lamb one day in the future.

Quality	♟♟♟♟♟
Value	★★★⊰
Grapes	cabernet sauvignon
Region	Margaret River, WA
Cellar	➖ 2–10
Alc./Vol.	14.6%
RRP	$59.00

Cape Mentelle Shiraz

Cape Mentelle has done a lot for Margaret River, not least helping to popularise the region's shiraz. Recent years have seen some very good wines.
CURRENT RELEASE 2001   This red has a lot of savoury interest instead of just plain shiraz fruit. The colour is dense and it smells of dirt, spice and blackberries with a wild salt and pepper touch. The complex flavour is spicy and long with good concentration and a balanced foundation of tannins. A savoury accompaniment to raan (Indian marinated leg of lamb).

Quality	♟♟♟♟♟
Value	★★★
Grapes	shiraz
Region	Margaret River, WA
Cellar	🍾 6
Alc./Vol.	14.8%
RRP	$32.40

Cape Mentelle Trinders Cabernet Merlot

Quality	♥♥♥♥
Value	★★★
Grapes	cabernet sauvignon; merlot
Region	Margaret River, WA
Cellar	🍷 6
Alc./Vol.	14.5%
RRP	$29.00

Trinders is Cape Mentelle's lesser red, but that's only relative to the top-of-the-tree cabernet sauvignon and zinfandel. It more than holds its own with much of the Margaret River competition.

CURRENT RELEASE 2000   Many young cabernet blends are driven by ripe fruit-sweet character, but this Trinders is a more savoury expression of the grape. It has leafy, briary aromas that are very appetising with blackcurranty fruit underneath. In the mouth it's medium-bodied with savoury flavours on a smooth background of berry flavour. Oak is moderately applied and tannins are fine. Serve it alongside racks of lamb.

Quality	♥♥♥♥
Value	★★★
Grapes	cabernet sauvignon 55%; merlot 38%; cabernet franc 6%; petit verdot 1%
Region	Margaret River, WA
Cellar	⊶ 2–7
Alc./Vol.	14.5%
RRP	$29.00

CURRENT RELEASE 2001   The herbal aromas of south Margaret River combine with blackcurrant fruit, cedary oak and a slightly medicinal edge in a complex nose. The palate follows the same savoury theme with intense herb and blackcurrant flavours of good intensity and length. Chewy tannins back things up well. Try it with mint-crusted racks of lamb.

Cape Mentelle Zinfandel

Quality	♥♥♥♥♥
Value	★★★♦
Grapes	zinfandel (primitivo)
Region	Margaret River, WA
Cellar	🍷 10
Alc./Vol.	15.0%
RRP	$39.00

Cape Mentelle 'zin' is a wild and woolly wine with tons of personality. Until recently most thought of zinfandel as uniquely and mysteriously Californian; in fact it is the primitivo of southern Italy.

CURRENT RELEASE 2001   As ever, this is a potently built wine, souped-up with loads of go. The nose has panforte-like aromas of dried fruits, chocolate, spices and coffee. The palate is full of warmly decadent berry, prune and chocolatey flavours, with a wild chewy texture and there's a firm grip in the background. Try it with Chinese braised gravy beef.

Capercaillie The Ceilidh Shiraz

A ceilidh (pronounced *kay-lee*) is a gathering of the clans, and what better brew to serve when your clan is gathered than this one. The maker is Alasdair Sutherland. CURRENT RELEASE 2001   This wine is not terribly distinctive but it's a damn good drink. Pommy wine writers would probably say it lacks *terroir*. The aromas remind of toasted nuts, earth, plum and spices. It's soft and lean on the tongue, with lighter body and good harmony. It's very approachable already, and would suit braised meats.

Quality	♀ ♀ ♀ ♀ ♀
Value	★ ★ ★ ★
Grapes	shiraz
Region	McLaren Vale, SA & Hunter Valley, NSW
Cellar	♦ 5
Alc./Vol.	13.8%
RRP	$28.00

Capercaillie The Clan

The Sutherlands of Capercaillie are Scottish down to their bootstraps. Al Sutherland is a big bear of a man who has a long history of winemaking in the Hunter. He's not scared to source grapes from further afield if they improve his wines.
CURRENT RELEASE 2001   This is a bright, nervy red which smells of mint and crushed blackcurrants with some of the gunsmoke/herbal characters of very cool-grown cabernet. The palate is lively and lean with plenty of acid, and finishes a touch sharpish. It needs food, and would suit veal.

Quality	♀ ♀ ♀ ♀
Value	★ ★ ★
Grapes	cabernet sauvignon 80%; merlot 10%; petit verdot 10%
Region	Coonawarra & Barossa, SA 60%; Orange, NSW 40%
Cellar	➛ 1–5+
Alc./Vol.	13.5%
RRP	$28.00

Cascabel Monastrell

Monastrell originated in Spain but it successfully emigrated to France as mourvèdre, and later to Australia as mataro. Maker: Susana Fernandez.
CURRENT RELEASE 2001   With only 130 dozen of this wine produced, it's not easy to find. It has a savoury, strongly earthy European-style nose and there's a touch of licorice to black plum and cedar aromas. The palate is medium-bodied with dry savoury flavour, great briary, chewy texture, and a tight, firm grip of tannins. An unorthodox savoury style, far from the squeaky-clean Australian norm, that would work well with charry barbecued lamb.

Quality	♀ ♀ ♀ ♀
Value	★ ★ ★
Grapes	mourvèdre 92%; grenache 8%
Region	McLaren Vale, SA
Cellar	♦ 3
Alc./Vol.	13.5%
RRP	$40.00

Cascabel Shiraz

Quality	❦❦❦❦
Value	★★★
Grapes	shiraz
Region	Fleurieu Peninsula, SA
Cellar	➛ 1–5+
Alc./Vol.	14.0%
RRP	$30.00

The Cascabel Shiraz has a savoury European feel to it that's worlds away from the South Australian mainstream. This comes from a vineyard close to picturesque Victor Harbour.

CURRENT RELEASE 2001   There's a complex, rustic bouquet and palate to this wine that doesn't have much to do with conventional ideas of Aussie shiraz. It's all about earth, dry undergrowth, feral notes, walnuts and cedar rather than bright, ripe fruit characters. A hit of raspberry emerges and it flows smoothly across the palate into textured, ripe tannins. Ve-e-e-ery interesting. Serve it with a dish of braised lamb and vegetables.

Cascabel Tempranillo Graciano

Quality	❦❦❦❦
Value	★★★
Grapes	tempranillo; graciano
Region	McLaren Vale, SA
Cellar	▮ 4
Alc./Vol.	13.5%
RRP	$40.00

Winemaker Susana Fernandez's heritage is readily apparent in the Spanish-inspired wines she makes at McLaren Vale. Tempranillo and graciano are red grapes grown in the Rioja region of north-central Spain.

CURRENT RELEASE 2001   There really is a piece of Spain in this limited production red wine. It's rustic, wild and unrefined – more Andalucian gypsy than gentleman of Castille – with dark berry fruit and a gamy touch that's very savoury rather than sweet in fruit. It's medium in body with good texture and a foundation of firm, dry tannins. Try it beside paella with game and chorizo and it all makes sense.

Castagna Genesis Syrah

Quality	❦❦❦❦❦
Value	★★★❦
Grapes	shiraz; viognier
Region	Beechworth, Vic.
Cellar	➛ 1–5
Alc./Vol.	13.8%
RRP	$48.00

Set in Alpine foothills in Victoria's north-east, Beechworth is proving a superb place to produce wine. Castagna is a stunning new operator.

CURRENT RELEASE 2001   This hard-to-find drop is made in the modern Rhône-inspired style that's putting a different perspective on Australian shiraz, even down to the addition of a little viognier à la Côte-Rôtie. It's exotic and richly aromatic with a complex nose and palate of dark cherries and berries, flowers, pepper and gamy/meaty touches. Middling in body, it tastes perfumed and spicy with silky texture, lovely intensity and fine tannins. A good companion to Peking duck.

Castagna La Chiave

Ex-filmmaker Julian Castagna's wines have added lustre to the quietly famous Beechworth region in recent years. This is made from sangiovese, the red grape of Tuscany. CURRENT RELEASE 2001   An unusual expression of sangiovese that had the authors scratching their heads. The nose has herbal, briary and spicy aromas that initially dominate cherry-like sangiovese fruit. That fruit comes through with air and the palate is rather stewed, with medium body and fine-grained tannins. It's a sound wine but it lacks the savoury cut of the best sangioveses. Try it with mixed salamis and prosciutto.

Quality	♀ ♀ ♀ ♀
Value	★ ★ ┤
Grapes	sangiovese
Region	Beechworth, Vic.
Cellar	▮ 2
Alc./Vol.	13.6%
RRP	$38.00 (cellar door)

Castle Rock Estate Pinot Noir

Each state has its number one pinot noir district, except perhaps Queensland. In Western Australia it's the Great Southern, although like most specialty pinot regions, standards are far from consistent. Castle Rock is one of the reliable ones.
CURRENT RELEASE 2001   This is a fresh, juicy pinot with the sort of light raspberry and cherry aromas that suggest some whole bunches in the ferment. There's a hint of tea-leaf on the nose too, and the palate is soft and light to medium in body. The finish is soft and clean. Best served cool, with a prosciutto and charcuterie selection.

Quality	♀ ♀ ♀ ♀
Value	★ ★ ★ ┤
Grapes	pinot noir
Region	Great Southern, WA
Cellar	▮ 2
Alc./Vol.	14.0%
RRP	$23.00

Cathedral Lane Pinot Noir

The central Victorian High Country is a lovely region with a variety of vineyards, some of which can even get snow on them in winter. As you can imagine this is cool-climate viticulture, the sort of place where vignerons harbour great hopes for pinot noir.
CURRENT RELEASE 2000   This vintage of Cathedral Lane Pinot has been around for a while now. The nose is very pinot with plum, earth and light oak aromas, and the palate has medium intensity briary plum fruit. The finish has marked bitterness that may not be to everybody's taste, but the fruit quality is good. Try it with pork spare ribs.

Quality	♀ ♀ ♀ ♀
Value	★ ★ ★
Grapes	pinot noir
Region	Central High Country, Vic.
Cellar	▮ 2
Alc./Vol.	13.2%
RRP	$25.00

Celtic Farm Firkin Hall Shiraz

Quality	♟ ♟ ♟ �
Value	★ ★ ★
Grapes	shiraz
Region	Yarra Valley, Vic.
Cellar	🍷 2
Alc./Vol.	13.4%
RRP	$28.00

Those Celtic Farm boys Gerry Taggert and Mark McKenzie don't reckon the wine world should take itself as seriously as it sometimes does. (Nor do we.) Wines labelled Far Canal and Firkin Hall cause a few sniggers, but we don't get the joke. Do you? Maybe bar stewards like us should wait in the far queue . . .

CURRENT RELEASE 2001   This is a slightly underdone Yarra shiraz with red berry aromas in the jujube/pastille vein, plus a slightly gamy, mulchy edge. The palate is pleasant with fresh red berry flavours of middling depth and body, finished off with balanced tannins. Drink it with veal chops.

Chain of Ponds Cabochon

Quality	♟ ♟ ♟ ♟
Value	★ ★ ★
Grapes	merlot 59%; cabernet sauvignon 34%; cabernet franc 7%
Region	Adelaide Hills, SA
Cellar	🍷 2
Alc./Vol.	14.0%
RRP	$16.00 🍷

A 'cabochon' is a French word meaning 'polished gem'. The link between a cabochon and this wine is a bit tenuous, something about attention to detail and so forth. Maker: Neville Falkenberg

CURRENT RELEASE 2001   This is a slightly European style with a balance of ripe and savoury qualities. The nose has dried leaves, red berry, spice and earth aromas, and it tastes succulent yet dry, with medium body and good persistence. Tannins are finely textured and dry but not intrusive. A good early-drinking style to enjoy with some pasta.

Chalk Hill Shiraz

Quality	♟ ♟ ♟ ♟
Value	★ ★ ★
Grapes	shiraz
Region	McLaren Vale, SA
Cellar	🍷 5
Alc./Vol.	14.5%
RRP	$26.00

There are labels and there are labels, but for our money the current Chalk Hill label is one of the catchiest. It features a fragment of blackboard with chalk drawings of grapes, a glass and the sunny coastline of the Southern Vales wine region on it.

CURRENT RELEASE 1999   This has a sweet nose of blackberry that's well-proportioned with vanillin oak in support. In the mouth it's fullish medium-bodied with more of that juicy blackberry fruit that's spicy and intense. The background of oak is noticeable but not overwhelming, and it's pleasantly dry and fresh on the finish. Good with Turkish-inspired lamb.

Chapel Hill Cabernet Sauvignon

Pam Dunsford blends wines from different regions in the belief that the sum of the parts is greater than the parts themselves. It's a philosophy that always works well in Australia, to the bemusement of Europeans.
CURRENT RELEASE 2000   Chapel Hill cabernets have evolved over the years into less oaky, more fruit-dominant styles. The 2000 seems a bit leaner than usual, but remains good drinking. The nose has blackcurrant, briary and bitter chocolate notes in a savoury mix with some toasty oak. In the mouth it's medium-bodied with middling ripeness of flavour and dry tannins underneath. Serve it with roast lamb.

Quality	♈♈♈♈
Value	★★★)
Grapes	cabernet sauvignon
Region	McLaren Vale 79% & Coonawarra 21%, SA
Cellar	➥ 1–5
Alc./Vol.	13.0%
RRP	$24.00

Charles Melton Rose of Virginia

Despite toying with a little sweetness, Rose of Virginia is further down the track to real, substantial red wine than the pink frivolities of many wineries and is consistently one of our best grenache-based rosés.
CURRENT RELEASE 2002   Charlie Melton's rosé is deeper in colour than most – the word magenta comes to mind. On the nose there are suggestions of red cherries, flowers, berries and earthy spice. The red fruit flavour flirts with sweetness on the palate and it has some depth and weight, ahead of a fresh, clean finish. Great with special fried rice and char siew (barbecued pork).

Quality	♈♈♈♈(
Value	★★★★
Grapes	grenache; cabernet sauvignon; shiraz; pinot meunier
Region	Barossa valley, SA
Cellar	▮ 2
Alc./Vol.	12.0%
RRP	$17.90

Chateau Leamon Cabernet Sauvignon Cabernet Franc Merlot

Chateau Leamon, once known tongue-teasingly as Chateau Le Amon, is one of the oldest of the modern Bendigo vineyards. This year it celebrated 30 years of providing good regional wines. Maker: Ian Leamon.
CURRENT RELEASE 2001   The current batch of Leamon reds are formidably alcoholic. It doesn't show unduly until your palate encounters the heat on the finish. This medium-bodied cabernet blend is a case in point: a distinctly regional wine with fresh, minty, leafy, herbal notes, interwoven with mixed berry fruit and a hint of spicy oak, leading to a very warm astringent finish. Try it with spring lamb cutlets.

Quality	♈♈♈(
Value	★★★
Grapes	cabernet sauvignon; cabernet franc; merlot
Region	Bendigo, Vic.
Cellar	▮ 4
Alc./Vol.	15.0%
RRP	$22.00

Chateau Leamon Reserve Cabernet Sauvignon

Quality	🍷🍷🍷🍷
Value	★★★
Grapes	cabernet sauvignon
Region	Bendigo, Vic.
Cellar	2–8+
Alc./Vol.	15.0%
RRP	$38.00

Ian Leamon's Reserve reds are a step up from the standard wines in ripeness and power. They still maintain a distinct minty regionality.
CURRENT RELEASE 2001   The nose is ripe and fairly complex with plum and dark berry aromas meeting briary touches, a hint of menthol and well-integrated spicy oak in good combination. In the mouth it's full-bodied with real depth, finishing in a solid wall of dry, grippy tannins. A well-made Bendigo cabernet that needs time to mellow. Serve it with roast lamb.

Chateau Leamon Reserve Shiraz

Quality	🍷🍷🍷🍷
Value	★★★
Grapes	shiraz
Region	Bendigo, Vic.
Cellar	1–10
Alc./Vol.	15.0%
RRP	$38.00

The historic Bendigo region was one of Victoria's great vineyard regions in the 1800s. Now it's well and truly re-emerged, and in most people's minds shiraz is its best wine.
CURRENT RELEASE 2001   Let this young Bendigo shiraz breathe in a decanter for a while and it builds personality, albeit of the robust kind. The nose has blackberry, mint, chocolate and smoky oak in true harmony, and the palate is surprisingly supple, ripe and smooth. There's power there though, and the flavour's deep and smooth, full-bodied and persistent . Firm tannins promise long life. Try it with Chinese braised beef ribs.

Chatto Pinot Noir

A winemaker at Rosevears Estate before moving to contract winemaking firm Monarch in the Hunter, Jim Chatto still consults in Tassie and makes a bit of Tassie pinot and riesling on the side.

CURRENT RELEASE 2000   An impressive pinot from a top Tassie harvest. This is jam-packed with complex earthy, fungal, undergrowth, dried red fruit and Bonox-like characters. The palate is savoury and quite firm with tannin to burn. It's unusual to see Aussie pinot with this much tannin. Drink it with grilled lamb chops and you'll find it has a power of lovely luscious black-cherry fruit: deep, structured and very long. It responds to breathing, too.

Quality	♀♀♀♀♀
Value	★★★★★
Grapes	pinot noir
Region	Tamar Valley, Tas.
Cellar	▮ 5+
Alc./Vol.	13.5%
RRP	$35.00

CURRENT RELEASE 2001   The unlabelled pre-release sample was looking disjointed and somewhat unready when we tried it. Spicy herb and peppermint aromas were dominated by an unusual ginger character, probably oak-derived, and the palate seemed a little dominated by oaky tannins. The palate is big and concentrated and opens with high drama. Flavour and tannin coat the mouth and there's a kick of acid to finish. We'd like to see this again when it's released in late 2003.

Quality	♀♀♀♀
Value	★★★↓
Grapes	pinot noir
Region	Tamar Valley, Tas.
Cellar	➥ 1–5+
Alc./Vol.	13.5%
RRP	$35.00

Chestnut Grove Merlot

The Kordics of Chestnut Grove aim to make their merlot a benchmark wine for the Pemberton/Manjimup end of Western Australia's wine regions.

CURRENT RELEASE 2001   At the moment there's a heap of raw oak in this wine that tends to obscure any other virtues it might have. It has spicy, earthy, blackberry fruit but the wood is laid on in spades. The palate has great concentration but clove and vanillin oak dominates. As it ages that woodiness may recede a little but we aren't overly optimistic. Try it with chargrilled rump steak.

Quality	♀♀♀♀
Value	★★↓
Grapes	merlot
Region	Pemberton/Manjimup, WA
Cellar	▮ 5
Alc./Vol.	14.5%
RRP	$50.00

Cheviot Bridge Pinot Noir

Quality	♥♥♥♥♥
Value	★★★★
Grapes	pinot noir
Region	Yea Valley, Vic.
Cellar	3
Alc./Vol.	13.5%
RRP	$25.00

Hugh Cuthbertson claims to 'make wine you can sit down and drink a bottle of', meaning his Cheviot Bridge wines are gentle gluggable things, unlike the aggressive young fightin' wines that make drinking a real task.
CURRENT RELEASE 2001   Like the other Cheviot Bridge reds, this hits the spot perfectly for varietal correctness, customer appeal and value. It has plummy pinot smells, along with light hints of almond, spice and well-integrated subtle oak. On the palate it's intense, long and ripe, with attractive fruit and oak flavours gently supported by soft tannins. A poised pinot that's perfect with grilled quail.

Chris Hackett Coonawarra Shiraz

Quality	♥♥♥♥
Value	★★★
Grapes	shiraz
Region	Coonawarra, SA
Cellar	2
Alc./Vol.	13.6%
RRP	$30.00

Chris Hackett has wide experience as a winemaker. Until recently his own merchant label was reserved for export, but now he's having a go at the local market.
CURRENT RELEASE 2000   Simple, ripe shiraz fruit is at the core of this Coonawarra shiraz. The complications of oak and all other paraphernalia are hidden. The result is a friendly soft red with a nose of blackberry and sweet spice aromas, smooth ripe flavour and a soft, giving palate. The whole package suggests slightly elevated pH values, but what the heck if it's easy drinking. Try it with a steak and mushroom pie.

Clarence Hill Cabernet Sauvignon

Quality	♥♥♥♥
Value	★★★★
Grapes	cabernet sauvignon
Region	McLaren Vale, SA
Cellar	5
Alc./Vol.	13.5%
RRP	$21.00

Wait for it . . . The Curtis family, who own the Clarence Hill vineyard, have been in the wine business for 532 years. That makes fifth-generation South Australian winemaking aristocracy a really nouveau crowd!
A Curtis ancestor started the ball rolling, purchasing Papal vineyards in Italy, still in the family's hands today.
CURRENT RELEASE 2000   A crowd-pleaser from McLaren Vale. The nose is clean and tangy with plum, blackberry and light leafy aromas, clothed in a veneer of vanillin oak. In the mouth it's medium in body with good black-fruit flavour of length and intensity. Try it with herbed roast veal.

Coal Valley Vineyard Pinot Noir

This new brand is the former Treehouse vineyard at Cambridge, north of Hobart, which was bought by new owners and renamed. Contract winemaker is Andrew Hood.

CURRENT RELEASE 2001   This topped a very strong 2001 pinot noir class at the 2003 Tasmanian Regional Wine Show. It is a gorgeous pinot that's deep, rich, multi-layered and succulent. Black cherry, cedar and leather figure in the bouquet, and the palate is dense and fruit-sweet. It would set off a confit of duck beautifully.

Quality	♟ ♟ ♟ ♟ ♟
Value	★ ★ ★ ★ ★
Grapes	pinot noir
Region	Coal Valley, Tas.
Cellar	▮ 4+
Alc./Vol.	13.0%
RRP	$22.00

Cofield Quartz Vein Durif

The Quartz Vein range are Cofield's top reds: wines of true regional substance and intensity, but a shade more civilised than some north-east Victorian drops.

CURRENT RELEASE 2001   This is a powerful, tightly closed-up young durif with deep colour and a nose of blackcurrants, prunes and tea leaves. It seems marginally less brutish than its 15 per cent alcohol might lead you to expect, but it's still all youthful power and macho attitude. Firm tannins support it well and we reckon it will develop well over many years. Serve it with braised oxtail.

Quality	♟ ♟ ♟ ♟
Value	★ ★ ★
Grapes	durif
Region	Rutherglen, Vic.
Cellar	➥ 2–10
Alc./Vol.	15.1%
RRP	$32.00

Cofield Quartz Vein Malbec

Malbec is one of those red grapes that crops up here and there as a straight varietal, but its role in Australia has mostly been as a blender with cabernet.

CURRENT RELEASE 2001   Less dense in colour than most other 2001 Rutherglen reds, this has a ripe, potent aroma of blackberries and tar, maybe with a hint of aniseed. It's well-concentrated and a bit porty, especially on the palate, which has a slightly spirity touch. In the mouth it has medium depth and a fair belt of tannin. Try it with mild cheddar.

Quality	♟ ♟ ♟ ♟
Value	★ ★ ✦
Grapes	malbec
Region	Rutherglen, Vic.
Cellar	▮ 4
Alc./Vol.	12.9%
RRP	$32.00

Cofield Quartz Vein Shiraz

Quality	♟♟♟♟♟
Value	★★★★
Grapes	shiraz
Region	Rutherglen, Vic.
Cellar	🍷 5
Alc./Vol.	14.7%
RRP	$32.00

The Cofields have given away their plain-Jane pale blue labels on these wines for something smart and contemporary. They remain among the best Rutherglen table wines.

CURRENT RELEASE 2001   A slightly paler colour than we expected here, but the wine still has plenty of oomph. The nose has ripe plum, warm spice and a touch of vanillin oak. In the mouth it's a generously proportioned wine of seductive softness and silky texture. The flavour is clean and ripe with good length and fine soft tannins underneath. An easy-drinking red now, but one that should repay cellaring for some years.

Coldstream Hills Briarston

Quality	♟♟♟♟
Value	★★★
Grapes	cabernet sauvignon; merlot
Region	Yarra Valley, Vic.
Cellar	🍷 3
Alc./Vol.	13.5%
RRP	$26.50

This was once known as Cabernet Merlot, but was renamed Briarston after a large Coldstream Hills vineyard development some distance from the estate's original Coldstream plantings.

CURRENT RELEASE 2001   Briarston by name, briary by nature. There's a distinct touch of briary character to this wine, as well as plum and berry fruits, giving it a slightly herbal edge. This savoury quality doesn't detract from a core of ripe fruit and the oak input is moderate. There's almost a suggestion of Bordeaux to it, such is its savoury personality. Try it with grilled pink lamb cutlets.

Coldstream Hills Merlot

Quality	♟♟♟♟♟
Value	★★★⭒
Grapes	merlot
Region	Yarra Valley, Vic.
Cellar	🍷 5
Alc./Vol.	14.0%
RRP	$26.50

Merlot does well at Coldstream Hills and this basic edition is often joined by a Reserve wine when vintage conditions are just right.

CURRENT RELEASE 2001   This deep-coloured merlot has a smooth nose of plum pud, earth and dark chocolate. It's clean and ripe without the leafiness that's sometimes present. A thread of cedary oak runs through it, and the palate has plump fruit flavour of good depth and persistence. It's a very friendly red to drink right now, but it won't disappoint with a few years in bottle. Serve it with venison.

Coldstream Hills Pinot Noir

For many years now the team at Coldstream Hills has put a lot of work into pinot, employing a Burgundy-inspired regime to build character.

CURRENT RELEASE 2002   There's a good measure of mystery here: plummy fruit aromas with some of the thorny undergrowth and meaty notes that get pinot-philes all a-twitter. In the mouth it has plum and spice flavours sitting on lightly astringent, unobtrusive tannins. It will be better in a year or two, when it will start to build typical Coldstream Hills complexity. Try it with rillettes and toasted sourdough.

Quality	♥♥♥♥
Value	★★★
Grapes	pinot noir
Region	Yarra Valley, Vic.
Cellar	☛ 1–4
Alc./Vol.	13.5%
RRP	$28.50

Coldstream Hills Reserve Merlot

This very fine merlot is the companion wine to the Reserve Cabernet Sauvignon that captivated us in the last *Guide*. It hasn't disappeared totally from the shelves and is worth searching out.

CURRENT RELEASE 2000   A sweetly fragrant, ripe merlot of real substance. The nose is subtly complex and richly endowed with spiced plum, mocha and loganberry-like smells. Beautifully integrated Bordeaux-style oak adds to the wine's aromatic appeal. In the mouth it's smooth and velvety, rich and long, with ripe, fine-textured tannins woven through it. Serve it with roast beef.

Quality	♥♥♥♥♥
Value	★★★♪
Grapes	merlot
Region	Yarra Valley, Vic.
Cellar	▯ 5
Alc./Vol.	14.0%
RRP	$47.50

Connor Park Cabernet

Cabernet sauvignon plays second fiddle to shiraz these days in many regions of Australia. Bendigo is no exception, although it was different when the vineyards were planted – then, cabernet was king.

CURRENT RELEASE 2001   The regionality of some central Victorian vineyards makes fruit-sweet reds uncommon. Instead savoury elements rule the day with herbal, eucalypt and spicy touches dominating. This is an example with initial green peppercorn and cedar touches to a core of blackberry fruit character. As it airs in the glass, dark fruit of good depth emerges. It's a medium-bodied, dry and interesting wine that goes well with slow-roasted lamb.

Quality	♥♥♥♥
Value	★★★★♪
Grapes	cabernet sauvignon
Region	Bendigo, Vic.
Cellar	▯ 3
Alc./Vol.	13.5%
RRP	$18.00

Connor Park Shiraz

Quality	🍷🍷🍷🍷
Value	★★★★
Grapes	shiraz
Region	Bendigo, Vic.
Cellar	⌐ 2–8
Alc./Vol.	15.0%
RRP	$20.00

The recent succession of drought years has made the area around Connor Park pretty desolate. The vineyard is like an oasis on a dry plain.

CURRENT RELEASE 2001   Earthy regional smells head the bill in this black–purple wine. There's blackberry fruit dominating the nose, as well as hints of pepper and spice. The dense fruit character hasn't been compromised by twelve months in oak, but there is a whisper of volatile lift there. The palate is solid with firm, ripe flavour and a fair whack of tannin. Good value but it needs time. Serve with roasted racks of lamb.

Cookoothama Limited Release Pigeage Merlot

Quality	🍷🍷🍷🍷
Value	★★★
Grapes	merlot
Region	Riverina, NSW
Cellar	🍷 4
Alc./Vol.	13.0%
RRP	$30.00

During fermentation the mass of grape skins, pips and stalks floats to the top of the fermenting wine. 'Pigeage' is the French term for breaking this cap up and pushing it down into the wine to extract colour, flavour and tannins.

CURRENT RELEASE 2001   Not much that says merlot here, but there's no questioning its quality aspirations. The nose is intense and promising, with mellow blackberry, plum and dark chocolate aromas dressed up in toasty-sweet oak. In the mouth, succulent fruit is mixed up with charry oak into a flavoursome, concentrated mouthful that finishes with ripe, dry tannins. An up-market wine, serve with roast beef.

Craiglee Pinot Noir

Quality	🍷🍷🍷🍷
Value	★★★
Grapes	pinot noir
Region	Sunbury, Vic.
Cellar	🍷 3
Alc./Vol.	14.0%
RRP	$28.00

Craiglee's Pat Carmody reckons shiraz and cabernet suit his vineyard well, but he's still undecided about pinot noir. That said he can still make a pretty good fist of it.

CURRENT RELEASE 2001   An attractive medium-bodied red with some floral fragrance and light red berry aromas. It lacks some true pinot noir richness and complexity, but it's not a bad drink at all. In the mouth sappy red fruit flavour is clean-tasting and persistent, and soft tannins finish it off in easy-drinking style. Try it with cheesy pasta.

Crawford River Cabernet Sauvignon

Crawford River is in Victoria's cool south-west, the sort of place conventional wisdom would dictate was a bit extreme for cabernet sauvignon. But the Thomsons often succeed admirably with it.

CURRENT RELEASE 2000 There is more savoury than direct fruity appeal in this cabernet. There's a foresty touch on the nose and some herbal notes, but it's not green. The palate is clean with firm herby blackcurrant fruit and a succulent balance of acid. Dry, slightly sinewy tannins don't intrude too much and make it a good wine to drink with the right food, say, herbed roast veal.

Quality	🍷🍷🍷🍷
Value	★★★
Grapes	cabernet sauvignon; cabernet franc; merlot
Region	Portland, Vic.
Cellar	4
Alc./Vol.	13.0%
RRP	$39.00

Cullen Cabernet Sauvignon Merlot

With the passing this year of Di Cullen, matriarch of the Cullen family, we lost one of Australian wine's great personalities. Her memory lives on in these wines, superbly made by her daughter, Vanya.

CURRENT RELEASE 2001 One of Australia's best reds continues in fine form. Intense dark fruit and cassis aromas, with touches of black olive and cigar box oak in seamless harmony, and an elegant palate, intense and long, with understated richness backed by a finely tuned foundation of ripe tannins. It's ripe yet savoury at the same time, a wine of real presence which will greatly reward cellaring. Serve it with boned, marinated leg of lamb.

Quality	🍷🍷🍷🍷🍷
Value	★★★½
Grapes	cabernet sauvignon; merlot; malbec; petit verdot; cabernet franc
Region	Margaret River, WA
Cellar	2–10
Alc./Vol.	14.0%
RRP	$80.00

Cullen Mangan

An unorthodox blend of Margaret River malbec, petit verdot and merlot, this recent addition to the Cullen range is named after Vanya Cullen's sister-in-law Bettina Mangan, whose vineyard provided the grapes.

CURRENT RELEASE 2002 Wow! A real glass-stainer, with a dense appearance and a rawness that will need time to sort itself out, though it's already friendly in a bolshy way. It smells of dark plums, violets, fountain pen ink and gravel. The palate is less rugged than the 2000 edition, but still with intense black fruit flavours and a firm backbone of tannins. Try it with braised oxtail and gnocchi.

Quality	🍷🍷🍷🍷
Value	★★★
Grapes	malbec 43%; petit verdot 32%; merlot 25%
Region	Margaret River, WA
Cellar	1–5+
Alc./Vol.	14.0%
RRP	$45.00

Dal Zotto Shiraz

Quality	🍷🍷🍷🍷🍷
Value	★★★★
Grapes	shiraz
Region	King Valley, Vic.
Cellar	🍷 8+
Alc./Vol.	14.0%
RRP	$36.00

This won the trophy for the best shiraz in the 2002 Australian Boutique Winemakers' Awards, quite an achievement for a relatively new player; it's always a strong class of wines with several gold medallists. CURRENT RELEASE 2000 This is a lovely big, rich, smooth mouthful of shiraz, smelling of blackberries and nicely balanced oak. It's full-bodied and generously flavoured, with firm, balanced tannins together with perfectly ripe fruit flavours. A real crowd pleaser that would go nicely with rare roast beef.

Dalrymple Pinot Noir

Quality	🍷🍷🍷🍷
Value	★★★★
Grapes	pinot noir
Region	Pipers River, Tas.
Cellar	🍷 3+
Alc./Vol.	13.4%
RRP	$25.00

This 12-hectare vineyard was established in 1987 by a former oncologist, Dr Bertel Sundstrup, and his wife Anne. Bert makes his own wines, usually with the help of itinerant young French winemakers gathering New World experience. CURRENT RELEASE 2001 A succulent, cherry-ripe and vanilla scented young pinot, this has lovely smooth flavours reflecting very ripe – but not overripe – grapes. It's a silky, rounded, cuddly drink. The colour is on the lighter side of full, but in pinot this doesn't always reflect the depth of flavour. It would do justice to marinated barbecued quail.

D'Arenberg The Coppermine Road Cabernet Sauvignon

Quality	🍷🍷🍷🍷
Value	★★★⯪
Grapes	cabernet sauvignon
Region	McLaren Vale, SA
Cellar	⬤ 3–12+
Alc./Vol.	13.5%
RRP	$60.00

Chester Osborn is making some wonderful wines, thanks at least in part to the heritage of great mature vineyards at D'Arenberg. He was a finalist in the 2002 Qantas/*Gourmet Traveller Wine Magazine* Winemaker of the Year competition. CURRENT RELEASE 2000 This International Wine Challenge trophy winner has real weight and grip, smelling meaty, smoky and toasty-oaky, with lots of appeal and complexity. There are some green-leafy varietal aspects, and quite a lot of oak. It's firmly structured – almost grippy – with ample tannin, and it demands patient cellaring. Best served with aged cheddar.

D'Arenberg The Dead Arm Shiraz

Why the name? If you read the black label, the story is that dying-arm, or 'phomopsis', is a fungal disease that attacks very old vines, drastically reducing the amount of fruit on each plant. This has the perverse effect of giving more concentrated flavour.
CURRENT RELEASE 2000   This is a very dense, oaky style of shiraz. The nose is pungently spicy, gamy, vegetal and toasty from oak, while the palate is very savoury and drying because of extended oak maturation and sandy tannins. The finish carries a lot of oak flavour. It will have plenty of fans. Would go best with aged cheeses.

Quality	♟♟♟♟
Value	★★♦
Grapes	shiraz
Region	McLaren Vale, SA
Cellar	▮ 12+
Alc./Vol.	14.5%
RRP	$60.00 ▮

D'Arenberg The Feral Fox Pinot Noir

D'Arenberg's quirky wine names are explained in their back labels, making entertaining reading for the lone diners among us. This new wine's front label seems heavily inspired by traditional Burgundy packaging.
CURRENT RELEASE 2001   As you might expect, this is a pinot with structure! Its colour is fairly light, but don't be deceived. There are lots of meaty, toasty and forest-floor aromas and again it reminds us of Burgundy, with its 'feral' or somewhat wild flavours. Fresh acid and fine tannins complete the picture. An intense wine, crammed with interest, and a really promising start. Try it with veal sweetbreads.

Quality	♟♟♟♟
Value	★★★★
Grapes	pinot noir
Region	Adelaide Hills, SA
Cellar	▮ 3
Alc./Vol.	14.5%
RRP	$25.00

D'Arenberg The Ironstone Pressings

Ironstone Pressings is a succinct way of describing this 'GSM', but we're not sure how much of the wine is technically pressings. Maker: Chester Osborn.
CURRENT RELEASE 2000   The colour is a little light thanks to grenache being the main component of the blend. The nose reminds of tinned peas or asparagus, as well as raspberry jam and blackcurrant juice. It has very sweet jammy flavour, ultra-ripe but not all that big in structure. It's thickly textured, almost oily, with a tannic finish. This fruit would have made great port! Those who love this sort of wine will rate it higher. Nice with pork ribs and plum sauce.

Quality	♟♟♟♟
Value	★★★
Grapes	grenache; shiraz; mourvèdre
Region	McLaren Vale, SA
Cellar	▮ 7
Alc./Vol.	14.5%
RRP	$60.00 ▮

D'Arenberg The Stump Jump

Quality	♥♥♦
Value	★★★
Grapes	grenache; shiraz; mourvèdre
Region	McLaren Vale, SA
Cellar	♦ 3
Alc./Vol.	14.0%
RRP	$11.00 ⑤

The stump jump plough is a part of Australian agricultural history. It was developed to bounce over stumps left in the ground after the land was cleared by the early settlers.
CURRENT RELEASE 2001   This is a light, lean, narrow structured red which smells of berries, gamy meat, mint and mulch. The minty theme develops further in the mouth, where it has leafy berry flavours and a smidgin of green tannin, which adds astringency to the finish. It's a fair drink at the price. It would go with a Four 'n' Twenty meat pie.

De Iuliis Show Reserve Shiraz

Quality	♥♥♥♥
Value	★★★♦
Grapes	shiraz
Region	Hunter Valley, NSW
Cellar	♦ 5+
Alc./Vol.	14.0%
RRP	$20.00 (cellar door)

The De Iuliis family are located on Broke Road, Pokolbin. Their label bears a stylised waratah, the state floral emblem of New South Wales.
CURRENT RELEASE 2000   This is an unusual shiraz, combining the anticipated leathery, earthy and peppery savoury aromas typical of the region with fragrant mint and leafy cassis sidelights. It has character and complexity in abundance. It's smoothly textured and soft enough to enjoy now but will last for many years. Try it with lamb kebabs.

Deakin Estate Shiraz

Quality	♥♥♥♦
Value	★★★♦
Grapes	shiraz
Region	Murray Valley, Vic.
Cellar	♦ 2
Alc./Vol.	13.5%
RRP	$10.00 ⑤

Deakin Estate is based at Red Cliffs, near Mildura in the Riverland. Winemaker is Linda Jakubans.
CURRENT RELEASE 2001   The colour is mid-purple–red and it's an all-round light-bodied wine, with a dusty plum aroma that doesn't show much – if any – oak. There are some slightly bitter extractives on the palate and it's suited to quaffing fairly soon, with lighter meat dishes such as bangers and mash.

DeBortoli Sacred Hill Cabernet Merlot

Sacred Hill really exists, just outside Griffith in the DeBortoli stamping-ground. This is the basic DeBortoli range, which often surprises with great value for money. CURRENT RELEASE 2002   It's very young for a red wine but it's designed to drink young. The nose shows plum-skin and cherry-stone aromas, with little or no sign of wood. It's clean and well-made but not especially cabernet-like, except for a little leafiness. A touch of firm tannin completes the finish. It's very good value for the price, and goes with Lebanese kofta.

Quality	♥♥♥♥
Value	★★★★↓
Grapes	cabernet sauvignon; merlot
Region	Riverina, NSW
Cellar	▮ 2
Alc./Vol.	14.0%
RRP	$7.00 ⑤

DeBortoli Windy Peak Cabernet Rosé

Cabernet rosés are loosely based on the Anjou rosé style from France's cool-climate Loire Valley. The other classic French style is the grenache rosé from the warmer southern Rhône Valley.
CURRENT RELEASE 2002   This is barely rosé, but more like a cross between Beaujolais and rosé. The colour is medium–deep purple–red, the body more a light-bodied red. It has loads of fruit and a fair dollop of sweetness: plenty of weight and presence. It smells of blackberry jam, cherry jelly and chocolate. Clean and well-made, it would suit beef carpaccio.

Quality	♥♥♥♥
Value	★★★★
Grapes	cabernet sauvignon
Region	Yarra Valley, Vic.
Cellar	▮ 2
Alc./Vol.	13.0%
RRP	$14.40 ⑤

DeBortoli Yarra Valley Cabernet Sauvignon

The Griffith-based DeBortoli family celebrated its 75th anniversary during 2003. It's been involved in the Yarra since the late '80s. Makers: Steve Webber and David Slingsby-Smith.
CURRENT RELEASE 2000   Ripe meaty, blackberry and blueberry aromas are sweet and attractive, while the sweetly ripe flavours translate perfectly onto the palate, which still has some youthful astringency that time (or food) will soften. It's a very promising youngster, with the ability to age long term. Cellar, then serve it with rare steak and a reduction sauce.

Quality	♥♥♥♥
Value	★★★↓
Grapes	cabernet sauvignon
Region	Yarra Valley, Vic.
Cellar	➤ 2–10+
Alc./Vol.	13.0%
RRP	$33.80 ▮

Deen DeBortoli Vat 9 Cabernet Sauvignon

Quality	♥♥♦
Value	★★★
Grapes	cabernet sauvignon
Region	Riverina, NSW
Cellar	▮ 2
Alc./Vol.	13.5%
RRP	$10.80 ⓢ

DeBortoli is the seventh-biggest Australian wine company in terms of tonnes of grapes crushed. It admits to taking in 46 000 tonnes at vintage time. CURRENT RELEASE 2001   This is a fair to middling cheap cabernet with minty, crushed-leaf aromas and some rather astringent greenness on the palate. It is no different to many Aussie reds in its price bracket in this regard. It rates as a reasonable red at its price, but won't raise too many eyebrows. It would go with burnt chops at a barbie.

Deen DeBortoli Vat 1 Durif

Quality	♥♥♥
Value	★★★
Grapes	durif
Region	Riverina, NSW
Cellar	▮ 3
Alc./Vol.	13.0%
RRP	$10.00 ⓢ

When grown in Rutherglen, its Australian home, durif is a big, ballsy style of red wine. But this is altogether different: a lighter, cheaper red with more modest aspirations. CURRENT RELEASE 2001   The colour is youthful medium purple–red and it has the scent of cherry pips, which together with the palate style suggests slightly underripe fruit. It's a lighter-bodied, simple style of durif, not over endowed with fruit, and showing some tannin firmness to close. It's a good current drinking red, to team with grilled pork chops and mustard.

Delatite Dungeon Gully

Quality	♥♥♦
Value	★★★
Grapes	malbec; merlot; cabernet; shiraz
Region	Mansfield, Vic.
Cellar	▮ 2
Alc./Vol.	12.5%
RRP	$19.40

Delatite's general purpose bistro red is blended from 45 per cent local Mansfield growers and 55 per cent Delatite vineyards. Maker: Rosie Ritchie. CURRENT RELEASE 2001   The colour is light but youthfully purple, and it smells young and fresh – minty, coconutty and raspberry grapey. The mint thing almost verges into Dencorub territory. It's light-bodied in the mouth, lean and not especially ripe or generous, but it's a simple early-drinking red to quaff without too much introspection. Try it with a meat pie and chips.

Devil Bend Creek Pinot Noir

Moorooduc Estate has several pinot bottlings and this is the 'entry-level' or cheapest of them. Maker is surgeon-come-vigneron Richard McIntyre, yet another winemaker who can be seen blatting around in a Subaru WRX! CURRENT RELEASE 2001   This is a light, fruit-driven, less-complex but no less valid style of pinot. The aromas are full of charm and remind us of strawberry conserve and red cherry, and there is no doubting the grape variety. It's soft and fruit-sweet in the mouth, with mild tannins and fine, gentle structure. A remarkable wine at the price. It would go with lightly seared tuna steaks.

Quality	♙ ♙ ♙ ♙
Value	★ ★ ★ ★ ⃕
Grapes	pinot noir
Region	Mornington Peninsula, Vic.
Cellar	▯ 3
Alc./Vol.	13.5%
RRP	$20.00

Devil's Lair Fifth Leg

Many years ago paleontologists found an ancient dog skeleton in a cave in the Margaret River region. Funny thing, they found an extra leg with it, and the mystery was never solved.
CURRENT RELEASE 2001   The wine breathes to show some of the mulberry and cassis aromas of good cabernet-based red, although the wine is fairly closed and has a lot of dusty, earthy and gamy aromas in its bouquet. It has some of the acid and austerity we expect in cabernet-based reds from this region, and it will improve with a little cellaring. Try it with lamb's fry and onions.

Quality	♙ ♙ ♙ ♙
Value	★ ★ ★
Grapes	cabernet sauvignon; shiraz
Region	Margaret River, WA
Cellar	▭ 1–5
Alc./Vol.	14.0%
RRP	$21.40 Ⓢ

Diamond Valley Close Planted Pinot Noir

This block is beside the original vineyard on the Lances' property at St Andrews. The vines were planted close together, more in the way of Burgundy than Australian vineyards. It's possible to decrease the yield per vine but maintain the yield per hectare.
CURRENT RELEASE 2000   The colour is deepish red–purple and the bouquet has a complex array of undergrowth or foresty aromas, with some meatiness and black cherry, plus a hint of cooked vegetables. The taste is very deep and finely nuanced: soft in tannins, medium-bodied and gentle, with a long finish that is beautifully balanced. Try it with Peking duck.

Quality	♙ ♙ ♙ ♙ ♙
Value	★ ★ ★ ★
Grapes	pinot noir
Region	Yarra Valley, Vic.
Cellar	▯ 6
Alc./Vol.	13.0%
RRP	$65.00

Diamond Valley Estate Pinot Noir

Quality	♟♟♟♟♟
Value	★★★★
Grapes	pinot noir
Region	Yarra Valley, Vic.
Cellar	🍷 6
Alc./Vol.	13.0%
RRP	$59.60

The Lance family of Diamond Valley Vineyards have been leading pinot producers for at least fifteen years. This is their middle-rank wine, with the blue label Yarra Valley wine below it and the single-vineyard Close Planted above.

CURRENT RELEASE 2001   The colour is quite deep and the nose offers delicious plum, cherry and hints of vanilla and toast, together with that trace of forest-floor that is a mark of their house style. It's firm, fine and concentrated in the mouth, with superb complexity and structure. The finish lingers on and on. This wine really benefits from breathing. Serve it with barbecued marinated quails.

DiGiorgio Family Merlot

Quality	♟♟♟♟
Value	★★★
Grapes	merlot
Region	Limestone Coast, SA
Cellar	🍷 3
Alc./Vol.	13.0%
RRP	$25.50

What's this? Another new brand? It's baffling for us to keep up; we can't imagine what it must be like for the average wine drinker on the street, so to speak. This apparently won gold medals at Cowra and Hobart in 2001, presumably as an unfinished, unbottled wine.

CURRENT RELEASE 2000   It's a fairly light-bodied merlot, with a developed medium red colour and a savoury developed bouquet of dried herbs, toasted nuts and earth. It's soft and sweetly fruity in the mouth, with mild, gentle tannins, and it fades a little towards the finish. Drink soon, with pasta and mushrooms.

Domaine A Cabernet Sauvignon

Quality	♟♟♟♟
Value	★★★
Grapes	cabernet sauvignon
Region	Coal Valley, Tas.
Cellar	🍷 15+
Alc./Vol.	13.5%
RRP	$55.00 🍷 (cellar door)

The back label tells us it was unfiltered, an indication that maker Peter Althaus wanted to leave as much flavour, colour and extract as possible in the wine.

CURRENT RELEASE 1999   The Domaine A cabernets are lean and elegant, as befits their cool-climate origin. This is riper than some vintages: it has an intense aroma of lifted, fragrant raspberry and mint, with dusty and Ribena cordial overtones. The structure is taut and firm. You would never describe it as rich, but it finishes with elegance and balance. It would suit roast leg of lamb.

Domaine A Pinot Noir

It's expensive, but Stoney Vineyard owner Peter Althaus kept this top label nearly three years before release. Unfiltered; 4850 bottles made.

CURRENT RELEASE 2000   The colour is amazingly youthful for a 2000. The nose has ripe plummy pinot fruit backed by plenty of vanillin oak, well integrated. There are herb, stalk and mint/anise aromas, too. In the mouth there's no shortage of body and flavour: concentrated fruit and rich tannins coat the tongue. Black cherry and herb flavours linger. Slightly raw and unevolved and needs time, promising a long cellaring future. One of the better Domaine A pinots. Try it with Peking duck.

Quality	🍷🍷🍷🍷🍷
Value	★★⯪
Grapes	pinot noir
Region	Coal Valley, Tas.
Cellar	🍾 8+
Alc./Vol.	13.5%
RRP	$60.00 (cellar door)

Domaine Epis Pinot Noir

Alec Epis has quickly emerged as one of the best pinot noir producers in the Macedon region. His viticulture is excellent and the winemaking help he receives from Stuart Anderson is first class.

CURRENT RELEASE 2001   This has a middling colour for pinot, and the nose shows none of the green characters that bedevil other Macedon pinots. There are smooth strawberry caramel aromas with a hint of undergrowth to them. In the mouth it's light, ripe and easy with uncomplicated clean pinot flavour that's soft and long. A very easy-drinking pinot noir of good quality and style. Serve it with squab.

Quality	🍷🍷🍷🍷
Value	★★★
Grapes	pinot noir
Region	Macedon Ranges, Vic.
Cellar	🍾 4
Alc./Vol.	13.0%
RRP	$40.00

Dominique Portet Cabernet Sauvignon

Dominique Portet's new Yarra Valley operation is ideally sited and the smart cellar door and winery bring a breath of Provence to the region. The red wines he makes are more elegant in style than the brawny drops he created during his years at Taltarni.

CURRENT RELEASE 2001   Like the 2000, this young cab has a hint of Bordeaux to it. The nose has briary blackcurrant and plum aromas with a thread of cedar through it. In the mouth it has a fine, elegant feel with lightish–medium body and a long savoury aftertaste. Try it with lamb.

Quality	🍷🍷🍷🍷
Value	★★★
Grapes	cabernet sauvignon
Region	Yarra Valley, Vic.
Cellar	🍾 5
Alc./Vol.	13.5%
RRP	$42.00

Dromana Estate Pinot Noir

Quality 🍷🍷🍷🍷
Value ★★★
Grapes pinot noir
Region Mornington Peninsula, Vic.
Cellar 🍾 3
Alc./Vol. 13.0%
RRP $30.00

Dromana's reserve is made only from grapes grown on Dromana Estate; this one is partly from Dromana and partly from local growers. Makers: Judy Gifford and Garry Crittenden.

CURRENT RELEASE 2001 This is certainly a step or two behind the Reserve: it has a sweaty, vegetal and slightly raspberryish bouquet and there are mint and cherry/raspberry flavours on the palate, too. It starts off well, but falls away a little at the finish. Nice wine; could improve with another six to twelve months in bottle, and deserves food. Try it with barbecued quail.

Dromana Estate Reserve Pinot Noir

Quality 🍷🍷🍷🍷🍷
Value ★★★½
Grapes pinot noir
Region Mornington Peninsula, Vic.
Cellar 🍾 5
Alc./Vol. 14.0%
RRP $53.00

Reserve wines are a dangerous sport: sometimes the standard wine seems emasculated by the loss of the maker's best fruit. That's less of an issue with Dromana Estate, as they have a lot of vineyard to choose from.

CURRENT RELEASE 2001 An encouraging medium–full red–purple, the first sniff reveals some volatile acidity, which may be due to wild ferments. Whatever, this is a deep, complex and highly attractive wine. The palate has marvellous texture, mouth-filling richness, and persistence. There are dark-chocolate flavours together with black cherry and plum, heaps of sweet fruit dried off by nicely balanced tannins that lend structure. Serious stuff! Try it with roast pigeon.

Dunsborough Hills Merlot Cabernet Sauvignon

Quality 🍷🍷🍷🍷
Value ★★★★
Grapes merlot; cabernet sauvignon
Region Margaret River, WA
Cellar 🍾 1–7
Alc./Vol. 13.5%
RRP $18.20

This is a sister wine to Flinders Bay, priced a little below that wine. Dunsborough is a small town in the north of the Margaret River Region.

CURRENT RELEASE 2001 The deep purple colour looks very youthful, which reflects the brash rawness of the wine. The dominant aroma is of seaweed or iodine, which is unusual. There are some stalky/leafy and oak characters too, and the wine has good concentration. It tastes as though the grapes were properly ripe. Sweet berries aplenty and a shock of tannin to finish. It needs more time, then serve with rack of lamb.

Eaglehawk Cabernet Sauvignon

The old Quelltaler enterprise in the Clare Valley has had many incarnations in Beringer Blass ownership. One of them was Eaglehawk. These days the Eaglehawk wines make no claims to regionality.

CURRENT RELEASE 2001   This is a passable young red, given its modest price. The nose is simple with fruity aromas, and flavours of red and black berries are light and fresh. In the mouth it's fruity and soft with little apparent tannin. A good match for pasta dishes.

Quality	♥♥♥♥
Value	★★★★
Grapes	cabernet sauvignon
Region	not stated
Cellar	▮ 1
Alc./Vol.	13.0%
RRP	$10.00 Ⓢ

Eaglehawk Merlot

Yet another of the flood of lower-priced merlots pouring into the shops. This creation of the Beringer Blass crowd is typically easy drinking.

CURRENT RELEASE 2001   The nose has spice, berries, and a hint of chocolate to it. The palate is soft and supple, made in an easy, quaffable style to drink young. Soft tannins suit it to people who aren't really red wine fans, and it should go nicely with cold cuts.

Quality	♥♥♥
Value	★★★
Grapes	merlot
Region	not stated
Cellar	▮ 1
Alc./Vol.	13.0%
RRP	$10.00 Ⓢ

Elderton Ashmead Cabernet Sauvignon

This is Elderton's top cabernet, equivalent to Command Shiraz in the scheme of things. Of the two, we prefer this wine – it's a tour de force, but with more refinement.

CURRENT RELEASE 1999   A powerful big red, deep and dark with a nose of exotic spices, camphorwood chests and essency blackcurrant fruit. It smells clean and concentrated. In the mouth it's big and solid with concentrated flavours of black fruits, an oaky edge and a foundation of firm ripe tannins. An epic wine, not easy to drink in quantity due to its monumental construction, but of high quality. Serve with a roast rib of beef.

Quality	♥♥♥♥♥
Value	★★⊀
Grapes	cabernet sauvignon
Region	Barossa Valley, SA
Cellar	▮ 8
Alc./Vol.	14.5%
RRP	$83.00

Elderton Command Shiraz

Quality	🍷🍷🍷🍷
Value	★★
Grapes	shiraz
Region	Barossa Valley, SA
Cellar	🍷 8
Alc./Vol.	14.5%
RRP	$83.00

Here's a wine that receives grand accolades from the USA, and like most Yankee favourites, subtlety is not what it's all about

CURRENT RELEASE 1998   A big, solid wine that's not as ugly as some of its hairy-chested brethren. It's a good example of the bigger-is-better Barossa shiraz style. The nose has potent blackberry, chocolate and vanilla scents, power-dressed in loads of toasty sweet oak. In the mouth it's very full-bodied and thick-textured with a Cherry Ripe sort of flavour at the core, and strong charry oak around it. It finishes with plentiful fine-grained tannins. Roast some beef to go with this big red.

Quality	🍷🍷🍷🍷
Value	★★
Grapes	shiraz
Region	Barossa Valley, SA
Cellar	➡ 2–10+
Alc./Vol.	14.5%
RRP	$83.00

CURRENT RELEASE 1999   Command always commands attention and this is no exception. It's a deep, dark wine with a nose of densely packed black fruit – tight, powerful and juicy – combined with lots of sophisticated and prolonged (three years!) oak treatment, which adds mocha and charry/smoky elements to the mix. In the mouth it's power-packed, full-bodied, thick-textured and oaky with a solid backbone of grippy tannins. Try it with a brontosaurus burger.

Eldredge Blue Chip Shiraz

Quality	🍷🍷🍷🍷
Value	★★★
Grapes	shiraz
Region	Clare Valley, SA
Cellar	🍷 5
Alc./Vol.	14.0%
RRP	$29.00

This relatively recent Clare Valley enterprise grew out of Leigh and Karen Eldredge's deep interest in the wine industry, and their despair at the state of the high interest rate, low commodity price regime of Australian agriculture.

CURRENT RELEASE 2000   This is a modern Clare Valley red rather than a very traditional style, but it's still attractive. The nose has mocha, spice and blackberry aromas, dressed up in toasty, coconutty oak. In the mouth there's good intensity and length, and medium body. It's a tasty wine, and not overpowering, finishing with soft dry tannins.

Eldridge Estate Gamay

Eldridge Estate has made Australia's best gamay for a few years now, somehow perfectly capturing the spirit of its French prototype, the fresh red wine of Beaujolais. CURRENT RELEASE 2002   This bright purple wine has a typically vibrant nose with a surge of red berries and plums that's mouth-wateringly attractive. There's a light touch of spice and it tastes juicy, light and deliciously fruity, with a soft finish that will make plenty of friends. An eminently gulpable young red that could be served with a gentle chill in hot weather. Serve it outdoors with antipasto.

Quality	♟ ♟ ♟ ♟ ♟
Value	★ ★ ★ ★
Grapes	gamay
Region	Mornington Peninsula, Vic.
Cellar	♦ 1
Alc./Vol.	13.0%
RRP	$20.00

Eldridge Estate Pinot Noir

David Lloyd is a great champion of pinot noir. To that end he successfully organised the 2003 Pinot Noir Celebration on the Mornington Peninsula, bringing together pinot makers from all over the world. CURRENT RELEASE 2001   Typically pale in colour, this has authentic varietal aromas that hint at sap, forest glades, cherries and game. In the mouth it's not a 'pretty' little frippery of a pinot: nor is it a big wine but it has presence. There's good textural interest with light, soft fruit character in the middle, a little firmness and fine tannins on the finish. Try it with grilled quail.

Quality	♟ ♟ ♟ ♟
Value	★ ★ ★
Grapes	pinot noir
Region	Mornington Peninsula, Vic.
Cellar	♦ 3
Alc./Vol.	13.5%
RRP	$34.00

Elmswood The Grand Elm Cabernet Sauvignon

This Yarra Valley winery must have one of the most scenic outlooks of any Australian vineyard, with a beautiful view of rolling hills, pasture and forest. Recently, they've shown ambition and decided to step up a notch in the marketplace. CURRENT RELEASE 2001   A young Yarra Valley cabernet of dense appearance with a Bordeaux-style nose of cedar and blackcurrant fruit. In the mouth it is middling in intensity with savoury, persistent cabernet flavour, good depth and attractive texture. French oak leads the way at the moment; it needs a couple of years to mellow and settle down. Try it with yearling beef.

Quality	♟ ♟ ♟ ♟ ♟
Value	★ ★ ★
Grapes	cabernet sauvignon
Region	Yarra Valley, Vic.
Cellar	➝ 1–6
Alc./Vol.	13.5%
RRP	$50.00

Epis and Williams Cabernet Sauvignon

Quality	🍷🍷🍷🍷
Value	★★★
Grapes	cabernet sauvignon
Region	Macedon Ranges, Vic.
Cellar	🍷 5
Alc./Vol.	12.9%
RRP	$35.00

This cabernet comes from the pioneering Macedon Ranges vineyard planted by Laurie Williams in 1976. Alec Epis purchased it in 1999 and he pays his respects to the late Williams by retaining his name on the label.
CURRENT RELEASE 2001   A more successful, riper wine than the 2000. It has a deep colour, and a very fragrant, aromatic nose, with blackcurrant, floral and minty/leafy notes, along with lightly cedary oak. The palate is savoury with succulent blackcurrant and minty flavours of good intensity, fine tannins, and a long fresh finish. Serve it with pink rack of lamb.

Eppalock Ridge Shiraz

Quality	🍷🍷🍷
Value	★★★
Grapes	shiraz
Region	Heathcote, Vic.
Cellar	2–6
Alc./Vol.	13.5%
RRP	$34.00

Victoria has hundreds of small, recently established vineyards. Eppalock Ridge, near Heathcote, is one of the older ones, dating back to the late '70s. Maker: Rod Hourigan.
CURRENT RELEASE 2000   The shiraz of Heathcote and Bendigo often has a particular Central Victorian tang, a bit minty, a bit like eucalypt. Eppalock Ridge misses out on most of this, which makes it a finer, more fragrant wine. The nose has spice and floral touches to plummy fruit of medium intensity. The middleweight palate has persistent ripe flavour of good length, finishing in astringent tannins that need time to settle down. Try it with grilled cevapcici.

Evans and Tate Margaret River Merlot

Quality	🍷🍷🍷
Value	★★★
Grapes	merlot
Region	Margaret River, WA
Cellar	🍷 3
Alc./Vol.	13.4%
RRP	$40.00

In recent years Evans and Tate has become one of the biggest Margaret River winemakers, largely centred on new plantings at Jindong, inland from the established strip. This merlot still comes from Evans and Tate's long established Redbrook vineyard.
CURRENT RELEASE 1999   This starts off with peaky oak, then a core of boiled-down loganberry fruit and dark chocolate aromas emerges. The palate has intense berry fruit, slightly dried out by the wood influence and some grippy tannins. It comes through in the mouth as firm and unyielding, not the sweetly soft image of merlot many people have. Serve it with baby lamb cutlets.

Evelyn County Estate Black Paddock Cabernet Sauvignon

Worth a visit, Evelyn County Estate is a friendly new Yarra Valley vineyard with a swish café/restaurant attached. Oh, and the wine is made by the Lances of Diamond Valley Estate, a good sign.

CURRENT RELEASE 2001 This deep-coloured young cab smells like it came out of French oak yesterday. It's immature and unyielding with a high-toned nose that smells of fountain pen ink and graphite, with spicy blackcurrant aromas hiding within. The palate is similarly tight and unyielding but we have a hunch that it will open up in bottle. When it does, try it with spiced Middle Eastern leg of lamb.

Quality 🍷🍷🍷🍷
Value ★★★
Grapes cabernet sauvignon
Region Yarra Valley, Vic.
Cellar 3–7
Alc./Vol. 13.5%
RRP $26.00

Farr Rising Merlot

Minted in 2002, this brand is the first foray into the wilds of wine marketing by Nick Farr, young son of Bannockburn winemaker Gary Farr. Nick takes grapes from, and makes the wines at, Innisfail vineyard at Batesford, not far from Bannockburn.

CURRENT RELEASE 2001 A delicious young merlot, with exactly the softness and charm that merlot often claims, but so rarely produces. It has a very good colour and smells plummy and slightly herbal, with mixed spices as well. The palate is light- to medium-bodied, with a touch of leanness, but good balance and drinkability. It goes well with roast Illabo lamb.

Quality 🍷🍷🍷🍷
Value ★★★★
Grapes merlot
Region Geelong, Vic.
Cellar 6
Alc./Vol. 14.0%
RRP $35.00

Ferngrove Merlot

A feature of the modern Australian wine industry is that brand-new companies are continually springing up with new vineyards, and serving up excellent wine. Three cheers to that! Ferngrove is one of them.

CURRENT RELEASE 2001 The colour is vivid youthful purple–red; the aromas are of vibrant red berries and supportive oak. In the mouth, it has concentration and weight, with ripe flavour and abundant tannin giving a big, firm finish. And it has good persistence. It would suit steak diane.

Quality 🍷🍷🍷🍷½
Value ★★★★★
Grapes merlot
Region Frankland River, WA
Cella 2–8+
Alc./Vol. 13.5%
RRP $18.00

Fire Gully Cabernet Sauvignon

Quality	♟♟♟♟
Value	★★⟩
Grapes	cabernet sauvignon
Region	Margaret River, WA
Cellar	🍷 5
Alc./Vol.	14.0%
RRP	$43.70

Pierro's Mike Peterkin bought the Fire Gully vineyard when it was 10 years old in 1998. He'd been making wine from it for a number of years before that, though. CURRENT RELEASE 2000   It shows the typical style of the maker: soft, savoury and fairly forward in maturity. The bouquet has some stalky and earthy aromas plus crushed-leaf and rose-petal complexities that reminds us of some Bordeaux reds. It's soft, developed and easy to drink. Try it with aged parmesan cheese.

Fire Gully Merlot

Quality	♟♟♟♟
Value	★★★
Grapes	merlot
Region	Margaret River, WA
Cellar	🍷 3
Alc./Vol.	14.0%
RRP	$43.70 🍷

This range of wines, effectively a second label of Pierro, has been expanding lately, and now encompasses a shiraz, pinot noir, merlot, cabernet merlot and cabernet sauvignon as well as a semillon and a semillon sauvignon. Maker: Mike Peterkin.
CURRENT RELEASE 2000   The nose is most unusual – a grassy, green-leaf scent and something else resembling lemonade – but it tastes good in the mouth, which is where it counts. It's light- to medium-bodied and there's a nice fleshy texture, with pleasant depth of flavour. Easy drinking with roast leg of lamb.

Fire Gully Pinot Noir

Quality	♟♟♟♟
Value	★★★
Grapes	pinot noir
Region	Margaret River, WA
Cellar	🍷 3
Alc./Vol.	14.0%
RRP	$22.50

When proprietor Mike Peterkin isn't making some pretty smart vino, he is also a medical doctor in the Margaret River Region.
CURRENT RELEASE 2001   The colour is medium–light red–purple and it's a fairly firmly structured pinot, showing some alcohol warmth on the finish. There are sweet cherry/confectionery aromas beneath earthy, foresty characters. It would go better with food than without: try stuffed chicken wings with satay sauce.

First Creek Merlot

Every year more than 100 new wine producers flood onto the market. First Creek is one of them. It's produced by the men behind Hunter Valley contract winemaker, Monarch.

CURRENT RELEASE 2000 This is a smooth, fleshy, enjoyable red, although it's a little left of centre. The aromas are toasty-nutty with a hint of seaweed. In the mouth it has plenty of extract and tannin, depth and dimension. The acid is a tad high on the finish. It could cellar well, but drinks well now with seared kangaroo fillets.

Quality	🍷🍷🍷🍷
Value	★★★★
Grapes	merlot
Region	Hunter Valley, NSW
Cellar	7
Alc./Vol.	13.5%
RRP	$25.00 (cellar door)

Flinders Bay Margaret River Shiraz

Bill Ireland's wines from both Margaret River and Clare (Old Station) have been steadily improving and some of the credit must go to contract winemakers David O'Leary and Nick Walker.

CURRENT RELEASE 2001 The colour is promisingly dark and dense and it smells of chocolate, vanilla and fruitcake. Lashings of dark berry flavour and ripe fruit sweetness fill the mouth. It's big and generous, fruit-driven and remarkably smooth, considering its youth and ample proportions. A yummy big red to cellar, or drink young with Shanghai duck.

Quality	🍷🍷🍷🍷½
Value	★★★★½
Grapes	shiraz
Region	Margaret River, WA
Cellar	10+
Alc./Vol.	13.5%
RRP	$24.85

Flinders Bay Merlot

Margaret River has truly distinguished itself with cabernet sauvignon and, to a lesser degree, shiraz; but as every year goes by it also has more runs on the board with merlot.

CURRENT RELEASE 2001 The vivid colour of this baby is almost blue–black! It's an excellent wine but too young, and needs to be cellared. There are discreet but ripe blackberry aromas, a touch of mocha and some well-handled oak. A stylish and seriously structured merlot, with impressive grip and concentration. We'd like to see it again in a few years. Age it, then drink with roast beef and yorkshire pudding.

Quality	🍷🍷🍷🍷½
Value	★★★★½
Grapes	merlot
Region	Margaret River, WA
Cellar	2–10+
Alc./Vol.	13.5%
RRP	$21.50

Flybrook Pemberton Shiraz

Quality	▼▼▼▼
Value	★★★
Grapes	shiraz
Region	Pemberton, WA
Cellar	� 1–6+
Alc./Vol.	13.9%
RRP	$20.00 (mail order)

Flybrook is the label of newish Pemberton vineyard Channybearup Wines. It's the latest in a rash of wines with names linked to fly fishing – a popular cool-climate sport with many synergies with wine.

CURRENT RELEASE 2001   A very promising start for a new brand. The colour is fresh and youthful looking; and the bouquet features black pepper, ironstone, dusty notes and a charry oak aspect. A taste reveals the wine is quite big and a little unresolved at this stage, with acid, oak and tannin all vying for our attention. Leave it a year, then try with a hearty meat dish like osso buco.

Fox Creek Duet Cabernet Merlot

Quality	▼▼▼▼
Value	★★★★
Grapes	cabernet sauvignon; merlot
Region	McLaren Vale, SA
Cellar	▮ 5
Alc./Vol.	14.5%
RRP	$21.00 ▮

What a nice, simple, succinct title for a two-way blend. Surprising it hasn't been used before, really. Makers: Daniel Hills and Tony Walker.

CURRENT RELEASE 2001   This is a big, bumptious but not overdone kind of red, showing the old one-two of rich, sweet fruit-and-oak for which the Vale has become famous. The bouquet features considerable vanillin oak, and there are some raisiny, super-ripe fruit flavours. It's powerful, solid and quite oaky, and could be served with civet of hare.

Fox Creek JSM Shiraz Cabernet Franc

Quality	▼▼▼▼▼
Value	★★★★★
Grapes	shiraz; cabernet franc; cabernet sauvignon
Region	McLaren Vale, SA
Cellar	▮ 8
Alc./Vol.	14.5%
RRP	$23.00

The bottle proudly bears two award stickers, boasting gold and a trophy at the 2000 Royal Adelaide Wine Show. Not only were the judges good at their job, they were apparently supernaturally able to judge into the future!

CURRENT RELEASE 2001   Another ripsnorter from Fox Creek, we'd award it gold any day! The hallmarks are terrific depth of colour and a marvellously rich nose of ripe plum and blackberry fruit with some pepper/spice. It's very ripe and concentrated on the palate, chock-a-block with flavour and fleshy extract. It's dense and smooth with lots of alcohol but doesn't taste overdone. Serve it with rare steak and bearnaise sauce.

Fox Creek Shadow's Run

The Watts family of Fox Creek created this wine to raise money for the Farmhand appeal, set up to provide relief to drought-stricken farmers. Six bucks from every case is donated. The handsome mutt on the label is for real, and his name is Shadow. CURRENT RELEASE 2001   This peppery, meaty, earthy wine is starting to show some early development, and has a lean palate without a huge amount of fruit – but the price is very reasonable. It's light-bodied and savoury with some tannin at the finish. Very drinkable if undistinguished. Try it with Irish stew.

Quality	♟ ♟ ♟
Value	★ ★ ★ ♦
Grapes	shiraz; cabernet sauvignon
Region	McLaren Vale, SA
Cellar	♠ 3
Alc./Vol.	13.5%
RRP	$12.00 ⑤ 🍾

Fox Creek Short Row Shiraz

This is the little brother to the famous Reserve Shiraz, but we actually have a secret preference for this because it is less massive, less woody and more approachable. CURRENT RELEASE 2001   A delicious shiraz in the full-blooded style that McLaren Vale, and Fox Creek specifically, have made their signature. Ripe plum, dark chocolate, vanilla, jam and dusty oak all figure in the complex bouquet, and the palate is very deep and lush with stacks of flavour, superb length and balance. The texture is almost chewy, with perfectly ripe fruit. It goes well with aged parmesan cheese.

Quality	♟ ♟ ♟ ♟ ♟
Value	★ ★ ★ ★ ★
Grapes	shiraz
Region	McLaren Vale, SA
Cellar	♠ 8+
Alc./Vol.	14.5%
RRP	$27.00

Freycinet Pinot Noir

Winemaker Claudio Radenti does very little in the winery and gives credit for this wine's consistent high quality to the vineyard and the fruit: there's no cold-soak and it's all rotary fermented.
Previous outstanding vintages: '94, '95, '96, '97, '98, '99, '00
CURRENT RELEASE 2001   Another lovely fine, scented pinot from this top producer. The colour is medium–full purple–red and it smells of sweet, ripe plums and vanilla, with some floral high notes. The perfume is a highlight. In the mouth it is sweetly ripe, rich as plush, medium-bodied and fleshy. It has the kind of velvety texture we love in pinot. Try serving it with salmon coulibiac.

Quality	♟ ♟ ♟ ♟ ♟
Value	★ ★ ★ ★ ♦
Grapes	pinot noir
Region	East Coast, Tas.
Cellar	♠ 8
Alc./Vol.	13.5%
RRP	$50.00

PENGUIN BEST PINOT NOIR

Gallagher Wines Shiraz

Quality	🍷🍷🍷🍷
Value	★★★
Grapes	shiraz
Region	Murrumbateman, NSW (Canberra)
Cellar	🍷 3
Alc./Vol.	12.5%
RRP	$24.00

Gallagher Wines is the business of ex-Taltarni winemaker Greg Gallagher, who has successfully set up shop in the Canberra district.

CURRENT RELEASE 2001   A bright young thing from the land of politicians, this shiraz smells of cooked plums and beef stock with a hint of white pepper, and smooth oak is folded in harmoniously. The palate is easy in texture with good length of silky fruit, kept succulent by tangy acidity and ripe tannins. It just lacks the bit of rich complexity that distinguishes top Canberra shiraz. A good drink though, and great with pasta and braised duck.

Galli Estate Cabernet Sauvignon Cabernet Franc Merlot

Quality	🍷🍷🍷🍷
Value	★★★⯪
Grapes	cabernet sauvignon; cabernet franc; merlot
Region	Sunbury, Vic.
Cellar	� 2–6
Alc./Vol.	13.0%
RRP	$22.00

The ambitious Galli Estate, on the Melbourne edge of the Sunbury region, has entered the fray with some impressive first efforts. The wines are well priced and quality is good under ex-Coldstream Hills winemaker Stephen Phillips.

CURRENT RELEASE 2001   An immediately attractive young cabernet blend with a deep ruby colour and a fresh, harmonious nose. There are aromas of leafy blackcurrant lightly dressed in a cedary touch of oak. The palate is elegant and medium-bodied with subtle savoury flavours rather than overt fruit, and the slightly astringent tannins of youth are in fair balance. This will improve. A good match for wet-roasted lamb.

Galli Estate Shiraz

Quality	🍷🍷🍷🍷
Value	★★★⯪
Grapes	shiraz
Region	Sunbury, Vic.
Cellar	🍷 5
Alc./Vol.	14.0%
RRP	$22.00

At Rockbank, near Melbourne, there's the impressive edifice of Galli Estate's winery, and a giant windmill down the road had us wondering whether we'd had too much shiraz when we visited!

CURRENT RELEASE 2001   A tasty red of medium depth and intensity. The nose has raspberry and plum fruit, some spices, attractive creamy notes and a light dressing of chocolatey oak. In the mouth there's a slightly Côtes-du-Rhônish feel to earthy fruit flavours. It has good intensity and length, with ripe dry tannins running all the way down the palate. A well put-together shiraz to sip with cotechino sausage.

Gapsted Ballerina Canopy Cabernet Sauvignon

Once known as Victorian Alps Winery, Gapsted originally sold bulk wine to the large companies. Now, part of the 6000 tonne-plus annual crush goes into their own range of table wines.

CURRENT RELEASE 2000   An extrovert type of cabernet with berries, briar and a fair dose of slightly raw, charred oak on the nose. The palate tracks the nose well with berry fruit and strong oak flavours that dry out the palate a bit. It's medium-bodied and firm on the finish – not bad, but not as friendly as it might be with less wood. Serve it with barbecued chops.

Quality	♥♥♥◊
Value	★★★
Grapes	cabernet sauvignon
Region	King Valley & Strathbogie Ranges, Vic.
Cellar	▮ 4
Alc./Vol.	14.0%
RRP	$20.00

Gapsted Ballerina Canopy Merlot

They're an adventurous lot at Gapsted – they have the Aussie 'standards' planted, fashion varieties like merlot, and household names like tempranillo, saperavi and petit manseng!

CURRENT RELEASE 2000   We thought the '99 was a pretty oaky drop and surprise, surprise . . . so is the 2000. There's a ripe sweet-fruited core there with some juicy plum and earth, but 'new-sawn' oak makes its presence felt with a powerful, savoury, charry overlay. It's medium-bodied with good depth and a firm drying end. Good with some charry T-bones.

Quality	♥♥♥◊
Value	★★★
Grapes	merlot
Region	King & Alpine Valleys, Vic.
Cellar	▮ 3
Alc./Vol.	14.0%
RRP	$20.00

Gapsted Limited Release Saperavi

After a hard day at the office there's nothing like a nice glass of saperavi, don't you think? For lovers of obscure grape varieties this takes the cake; saperavi originally comes from the Crimea in southern Russia.

CURRENT RELEASE 2001   An interesting, unusual varietal wine, just the thing for people bored with a diet of conventional Australian red wine. This has oriental spices on the nose with some cherry, licorice and vanillin oak. In the mouth it's ripe and structured by acidity rather than tannin, although there's a dry tannic undercurrent there. It finishes clean and mouth-watering. Suits sausage and lentil salad.

Quality	♥♥♥♥
Value	★★★
Grapes	saperavi
Region	King & Alpine Valleys, Vic.
Cellar	▮ 2
Alc./Vol.	14.0%
RRP	$25.00

Garry Crittenden I Barbera

Quality	♟♟♟♟♟
Value	★★★★
Grapes	barbera
Region	King Valley, Vic.
Cellar	▮ 4
Alc./Vol.	13.0%
RRP	$25.00

Garry Crittenden has now officially handed over the making of his ever-improving range of Italian varietals to son Rollo, the de facto winemaker for some years already. The wines continue to excite us.

CURRENT RELEASE 2001   This is a beaut drink. The nose has plum, Siena cake and earthy notes with a savoury touch. In the mouth there's richness, yet tangy acidity keeps it light and palatable. A little Italianate semi-bitterness on the finish should smooth out with time in bottle, and with the right food. It should also suit medium-term cellaring – a '97 tasted alongside the 2001 was very good. Serve with vitello tonnato.

Garry Crittenden I Dolcetto

Quality	♟♟♟♟
Value	★★★⁺
Grapes	dolcetto
Region	Great Western & King Valley, Vic.
Cellar	▮ 1
Alc./Vol.	12.0%
RRP	$25.00

Dolcetto is the wine the Piedmontese drink while they're waiting for their nebbiolos to mature; those Italians are right, dolcetto is delicious to glug down in the first flush of youth.

CURRENT RELEASE 2002   A delicious young wine that's almost too easy to drink. It has a brilliant purplish colour and a fresh appetising nose reminiscent of juicy cherries, unfermented black grape juice, spices and Italian herbs. It's clean in the mouth with a light fruity flavour and mouth-watering acidity. A succulent outdoorsy red wine to drink with enthusiasm over the next year or so. Good with meat and vegetable antipasto.

Garry Crittenden I Nebbiolo

Quality	♟♟♟♟
Value	★★★⁺
Grapes	nebbiolo
Region	King Valley, Vic.
Cellar	➤ 2–6+
Alc./Vol.	14.0%
RRP	$25.00

In Italy's north, nebbiolo makes the most powerfully tannic, age-worthy red wines. They live for decades and, when mature, coax superlatives from even the most jaded palates.

CURRENT RELEASE 2000   This opens up reserved but builds in the glass, developing floral and dark fruit aromas, fruitcakey spiced notes, and maybe a hint of road tar (a characteristic of the best): a solid, un-giving, yet mysteriously addictive smell. The palate is dry and dense in texture with a core of black fruit threaded through a solid fortress of tannin. Fascinating now, but age will ideally mellow that strong personality. Drink it with firm cheeses.

Garry Crittenden I Rosato

Garry Crittenden's pink wine is made into a dry type that has some affinity with the wines that grace alfresco summer tables in Europe.
CURRENT RELEASE 2002   Don't dismiss pink wines: some of the recent crop can be pretty good. This example is made from Italian grape varieties, which gives it a much more savoury personality than the sometimes cloying grenache-based wine, standard in the past. This has rose-pink colour and a light, fresh nose combining raspberry-like sangiovese with the florals and earth of nebbiolo. The palate is simple, dry and savoury, with a pleasantly earthy grip to it and succulent acidity.

Quality	♀♀♀♀
Value	★★★★
Grapes	sangiovese; nebbiolo
Region	King Valley & Pyrenees, Vic.
Cellar	▮ 1
Alc./Vol.	14.0%
RRP	$15.00

Garry Crittenden I Sangiovese

Italian grape varieties take a bit of getting used to, especially if you were weaned on a diet of ripe Aussie reds, but persevere. The rewards are well worth it.
CURRENT RELEASE 2001   This encapsulates the mysteries of good sangiovese. Restrained fruit gives way on the nose to appetising complex aromas of spices, earth and dessert nougat. In the mouth, it's dry and savoury with a slightly chewy texture and intense flavour. It finishes with a light grip, but enough give to make it a great drink in its youth and even better in a couple of years. Try it with saltimbocca alla romana.

Quality	♀♀♀♀♀
Value	★★★★
Grapes	sangiovese
Region	King Valley & Pyrenees, Vic.
Cellar	▮ 4
Alc./Vol.	14.0%
RRP	$25.00

Gartelmann Merlot

The Gartelmanns have a 16-hectare vineyard in the Lovedale Road area. It used to be Sydney restaurateur Oliver Shaul's George Hunter Estate. The wines are contract-made at Monarch.
CURRENT RELEASE 2001   The notes say it was hand-picked and basket-pressed, for what it's worth. The wine has an appealingly complex plummy nose, with some meaty, earthy regional inflexions. It has good flavour in the mouth although the acidity is slightly prominent. It's ready to drink young. Pair it with gourmet sausages.

Quality	♀♀♀♀
Value	★★★
Grapes	merlot
Region	Hunter Valley, NSW
Cellar	▮ 5
Alc./Vol.	13.0%
RRP	$23.50 (cellar door)

Gehrig Durif

Quality	♥♥♥
Value	★★★
Grapes	durif
Region	Rutherglen, Vic.
Cellar	3+
Alc./Vol.	13.5%
RRP	$23.50

Gehrig's winery at Barnawartha, near Rutherglen, is an imposing series of Victorian-era buildings with a three-storey tower that dominates the surrounding vineyards. It's an historic place to visit in one of Australia's most historic wine regions.

CURRENT RELEASE 2001   This is a typically rustic red with a dense, powerful nose of tobacco, plum pudding, walnuts and spice. The palate is intense and rather wild with ripe fruit, good body and a dry, sharp edge that flirts with volatility. A durif for Gehrig aficionados. Serve it with a braised lamb dish.

Gemtree Tatty Road

Quality	♥♥♥♥
Value	★★★
Grapes	cabernet sauvignon; merlot; petit verdot
Region	McLaren Vale, SA
Cellar	3
Alc./Vol.	14.0%
RRP	$19.00

Tatty Road is Tatachilla Road vineyard, one of the sources of grapes for this cabernet blend. Fruit also comes from the main Gemtree vineyard, which is in slightly cooler foothills country.

CURRENT RELEASE 2001   There's a leafy thread and some florals through the nose here and the fruit character is more piercing than many Southern Vales reds: more redcurrant than blackberry, if you know what we mean. The palate is medium in body with intense blackcurranty cabernet flavour, ahead of drying tannins. Good with pasta and chicken livers.

Giaconda Pinot Noir

Quality	♥♥♥♥♥
Value	★★★
Grapes	pinot noir
Region	Beechworth, Vic.
Cellar	6+
Alc./Vol.	13.5%
RRP	$80.00

Giaconda's pinot noirs attract less attention than the chardonnays, but they are worth seeking out for their powerful personalities. They age well too.

CURRENT RELEASE 2001   A medium-depth colour introduces a pinot noir of good weight and intensity. It has a fascinating complex nose that hints at maraschino cherries, chopped tomato, briar, spicy fruitcake and cedar. The palate is medium- to full-bodied for a pinot with rich gamey flavours of cherry and plum. The texture is quite dense and there's some tannic firmness in the background. A powerful pinot that will improve with age. Try it with roast fillet of beef.

Giaconda Warner Vineyard Shiraz

Rick Kinzbrunner only started messing around with
Beechworth shiraz in 1999, but he's already a master.
These wines have all the makings of Australian classics.
CURRENT RELEASE 2001   There's a touch of the Rhône
here; it's spicy, meaty, earthy, and exotically rich and
seductive. Oak is folded in seamlessly. Plummy fruit of
eau-de-vie-like fragrance and smooth intensity rests
easily with rustic touches, in effortless harmony. It's
smooth and long, and fine-grained tannins dovetail
in perfectly. Great with veal kidneys in brioche.

Quality	♟♟♟♟♟
Value	★★★
Grapes	shiraz
Region	Beechworth, Vic.
Cellar	🍷 6
Alc./Vol.	13.5%
RRP	$75.00

Glaetzer Shiraz

The Glaetzer family feature large in Barossa Valley
winemaking. John is Wolf Blass winemaker, and twin
brother Colin and son Ben make hearty Barossa reds
under this label.
CURRENT RELEASE 1999   Generous Barossa reds like
this have a great following. The colour is an attractive
ruby and the nose has sweet cherry and berry fruit
character that's juicy and fresh. A charry seasoning of
oak doesn't take over. In the mouth it has fullish
medium body, mellow flavours, supple feel, and ripe
tannins. A well-made red, with a welcome touch of
maturity. Try it with steak and mushroom pie.

Quality	♟♟♟♟♟
Value	★★★
Grapes	shiraz
Region	Barossa Valley, SA
Cellar	🍷 4
Alc./Vol.	14.0%
RRP	$53.75

Glaetzer The Bishop Shiraz

The Glaetzer reds are based on old, low-yielding, dry-
grown vineyards in the Barossa Valley. The last 15 years
have seen such vines rise from irrelevance to rightly
become a Barossa (and national) treasure.
CURRENT RELEASE 1999   A medium-depth Barossa
shiraz with blackberry, plum, spice and earth aromas
that are ripe and full. The medium-intensity palate has
chocolatey-ripe fruit of good texture with oak folded
in seamlessly. It's very Barossa in its generosity, and
thankfully it lets the fruit speak clear and long. Soft
tannins finish things off in a smooth red that would
suit veal sautée.

Quality	♟♟♟♟
Value	★★★
Grapes	shiraz
Region	Barossa Valley, SA
Cellar	🍷 2
Alc./Vol.	14.0%
RRP	$31.50

The Gorge Shiraz

Quality	🍷🍷🍷🍷
Value	★★★★﹚
Grapes	shiraz
Region	McLaren Vale, SA; Mudgee & Hunter Valley, NSW
Cellar	🍷 6
Alc./Vol.	13.0%
RRP	$16.00

Hunter winemaker David Hook has blended grapes from three regions in 2001 to achieve the desired result. It wasn't such a great red year in the Hunter, whereas the 2000 vintage was all Hunter.

CURRENT RELEASE 2001   The colour is good: medium–full purple–red, and it smells invitingly of sweet mint and pepper/nutmeg spice. There's a dried banana savouriness to it as well. The taste is focussed and tight with mild tannins and plenty of depth and spine. Far from a mono-dimensional wine, it has character. It would suit lamb kebabs.

Grant Burge Barossa Vines Cabernet Sauvignon Merlot

Quality	🍷🍷🍷
Value	★★★★
Grapes	cabernet sauvignon; merlot
Region	Barossa Valley, SA
Cellar	🍷 2
Alc./Vol.	13.5%
RRP	$13.50 ⑤

The Barossa Vines wines offer honest, generous Barossa character on a budget, a formula for success.

CURRENT RELEASE 2001   There's no great refinement or sophistication in this wine, but it does get better as you drink it. Initially the nose is simple. Just plum and berry fruit aromas, and a layer of lead pencilly oak. The palate is light–medium in body with pleasant fruity flavour, a nice dab of oak and ripe, fine tannins. It has an unusually long finish for a wine in this price category and this takes it into above average territory. Try it with lamb cutlets.

Grant Burge Barossa Vines Shiraz

Quality	🍷🍷🍷﹚
Value	★★★★﹚
Grapes	shiraz
Region	Barossa Valley, SA
Cellar	🍷 3
Alc./Vol.	13.5%
RRP	$13.50 ⑤

An old Barossa boy like Grant Burge ought to know a thing or two about shiraz. He also knows how to provide it in a keenly priced format. These Barossa Vines wines are great value.

CURRENT RELEASE 2001   Straightforward shiraz all the way here. The nose has syrupy blackberry fruit, some spiciness and a measure of aromatic sweet oak. In the mouth it's medium-bodied with good depth of ripe flavour, a lick of vanillin oak and kindly tannins. Easy Barossa on a budget, this tastes good with a steak.

Grant Burge Cameron Vale Cabernet Sauvignon

The Grant Burge range of wines gets bigger all the time, but with the reds the house style remains pretty much the same: ripe fruit, sweet oak, easy drinkability. CURRENT RELEASE 2001   This is a smooth customer, designed to drink well in youth, but also capable of a few years in the cellar. It smells of blackcurrant with a light earthiness and a dab of smoky oak. The palate is easy to like with good depth of fruit and a pleasant grip at the end. It's not especially complex or powerful, but it's still a very satisfying drop. Try it with braised beef and winter vegetables.

Quality	♥ ♥ ♥ ♥
Value	★ ★ ★ ❜
Grapes	cabernet sauvignon
Region	Barossa River, SA
Cellar	▮ 5
Alc./Vol.	13.5%
RRP	$24.00

Grant Burge Filsell Shiraz

Filsell used to be one of the more standard Grant Burge labels, but now it's been eased upwards with a new label and higher pricing. It remains good drinking. CURRENT RELEASE 2001   This opens with a very dense, dark colour and the nose is full with slightly stewed dark plum fruit and spices. Coconut/caramel oak is in good balance and it tastes smooth and forward with good depth and length. Charry oak sits nicely in the background and soft ripe tannins provide satisfying balance. Easy drinking with roast veal.

Quality	♥ ♥ ♥ ♥
Value	★ ★ ★
Grapes	shiraz
Region	Barossa Valley, SA
Cellar	▮ 6
Alc./Vol.	14.0%
RRP	$30.00

Grant Burge Hillcot Merlot

Grant Burge's first small plot of merlot vines were planted in the Hillcot vineyard in 1982. Things have grown and he now owns about 50 per cent of the entire commercial Barossa Merlot crop. CURRENT RELEASE 2001   Mouth-wateringly drinkable, this merlot is very attractive as a young wine. The nose is a sort of summer pudding of raspberry and tangy blackcurrant aromas that are clean and pure, with a light touch of spicy oak playing only a bit part. The palate is medium in body with plump juicy flavour in the middle and moderate tannins underneath. Try it with veal cutlets.

Quality	♥ ♥ ♥ ♥
Value	★ ★ ★ ❜
Grapes	merlot 90%; cabernet sauvignon 10%
Region	Barossa Valley, SA
Cellar	▮ 4
Alc./Vol.	14.0%
RRP	$18.00

Grant Burge Miamba Shiraz

Quality	♀♀♀♀
Value	★★★↓
Grapes	merlot
Region	Barossa Valley, SA
Cellar	🍷 4
Alc./Vol.	14.0%
RRP	$19.90

Miamba was a nineteenth-century property that was once the source of Orlando's low-priced 'Miamba Claret'. Incredibly the vines were pulled out as recently as 1980. Grant Burge put things right by replanting the vineyard in 1987.
CURRENT RELEASE 2000   A ripe nose of blackberry and sweet plum sets this deep coloured wine on its way, along with a dash of spice and a little graphite-like oak. The palate is smooth, ripe and complete in time-honoured Grant Burge fashion. It has medium depth and a dry lip-smacking finish. Serve it with mixed grilled and roasted vegetables.

Quality	♀♀♀♀
Value	★★★↓
Grapes	merlot
Region	Barossa Valley, SA
Cellar	🍷 4
Alc./Vol.	13.5%
RRP	$19.90

CURRENT RELEASE 2001   This has a good, dense, purplish colour and a slightly syrupy dark plum nose. It's ripe and mellow in the mouth, with less power than the nose would suggest. The flavours remind us of raspberry and plum, and it has a smooth, likeable texture. Oak treatment is subtle throughout and tannins are kept moderate. Try it with north Chinese braised lamb.

Grant Burge RSZ1 Eden Valley Shiraz

Quality	♀♀♀♀↓
Value	★★★
Grapes	shiraz
Region	Eden Valley, SA
Cellar	🍷 8+
Alc./Vol.	14.0%
RRP	$45.00

Grant Burge has adopted a system of numbering for his special binnings that makes them sound like secret rocket fuels. There's RBM1, MSJ2, RBS2, RSZ1, and so on. Very mysterious.
CURRENT RELEASE 1999   This smells a bit like a good old-fashioned roast dinner: meat, stuffing, baked pumpkin, salt and pepper . . . the lot. It's a savoury, ripe combo that endeared us immediately, and the whole thing is wrapped up in smart oak. It's full and round, long and satisfying, with a fine backbone of ripe tannins. Serve it with a good old-fashioned roast dinner.

Grant Burge The Holy Trinity

Grant Burge has all sorts of convoluted reasons for calling this wine The Holy Trinity, and some of them are on the back label.

CURRENT RELEASE 1999   While this wine bows in the direction of France's Rhône Valley, even down to an embossed bottle à la Chateauneuf du Pape, it's really very Barossa Australian due to the sweet fruit and the oak input. The oak has been toned down a bit, and that old vine Barossa fruit expresses itself very well. It's gently spicy with sweet berry and meaty aromas, and smoothly persistent flavour. It finishes pleasantly firm. Try it with roast veal.

Quality	🍷🍷🍷🍷
Value	★★★⌐
Grapes	grenache; shiraz; mourvèdre
Region	Barossa Valley, SA
Cellar	🍷 4
Alc./Vol.	14.5%
RRP	$33.00

Hamilton's Ewell Limestone Quarry Shiraz

In the south-east of South Australia around Coonawarra and Wrattonbully there's a lot of limestone under the ground. Hence the name of this wine.

CURRENT RELEASE 2001   Aromas of coffee, plum and some meaty feral sidenotes pour from the glass, and the texture is rich and very smooth indeed. It's medium-bodied but has a lot of flesh and texture from phenolics and glycerol. A very easy wine to drink, despite the high level of alcohol. Try it with barbecued pork spare ribs and plum sauce.

Quality	🍷🍷🍷🍷
Value	★★★★
Grapes	shiraz
Region	Wrattonbully, SA
Cellar	🍷 5
Alc./Vol.	14.2%
RRP	$19.00

Hardys Eileen Hardy Shiraz

Named in honour of the late Eileen Hardy, mother of Sir James, this flagship red is usually pure McLaren Vale, but this year three other regions are involved. Maker: Steve Pannell.

CURRENT RELEASE 1999   The style is big, statuesque, fairly oaky and tannic – a wine to cellar for maximum effect. Ripe, dark berry and plum aromas, coupled with a touch of gumleaf, mint/anise and mixed spices. There's plenty of oak character but it's not overdone. It's the subtlety of French oak rather than the brashness of American. It's full-bodied, dense and full of mouth-coating tannin. Never likely to be an elegant wine, this needs more time to mellow and build complexity. A good but not great Eileen. It goes with aged hard cheeses.

Quality	🍷🍷🍷🍷
Value	★★⌐
Grapes	shiraz
Region	McLaren Vale, Clare & Padthaway, SA; Frankland, WA
Cellar	➣ 2–8+
Alc./Vol.	13.5%
RRP	$90.00

Heartland Wirrega Cabernet Merlot

Quality	♟♟♟↓
Value	★★★
Grapes	cabernet sauvignon; merlot
Region	Limestone Coast, SA
Cellar	🍶 5
Alc./Vol.	13.8%
RRP	$19.00

Heartland is a new brand produced by a group of South Australian wine men including Scott Collett of Woodstock.

CURRENT RELEASE 2001   This is a decent wine despite a thread of greenness running through it. It smells of menthol and garden mint, while the palate is all about crushed leaves, raspberry and eucalyptus. It has decent flavour on the middle palate, although the tannins turn a bit green towards the finish. It would suit mint-sauced lamb.

Heggies Merlot

Quality	♟♟♟↓
Value	★★★
Grapes	merlot
Region	Eden Valley, SA
Cellar	🍶 5
Alc./Vol.	14.0%
RRP	$25.00 🍶

Heggies is one of Yalumba's several noted Eden Valley vineyards. It was bought and planted by Yalumba in 1971 and is named after the previous owner.

CURRENT RELEASE 2000   This is a somewhat unwieldy merlot, which starts off promisingly with aromas of herbs, spices, fennel and anise, with raspberry jam undercurrents. But it's tannic and acidic in the mouth, giving the wine a hard astringency. It is better with food, such as osso buco.

Henschke Henry's Seven

Quality	♟♟♟♟
Value	★★★↓
Grapes	shiraz 70%; grenache 25%; viognier 5%
Region	Eden Valley, SA
Cellar	🍶 3+
Alc./Vol.	14.2%
RRP	$28.00 🥂

Henry Evans was a pioneer vigneron of Keyneton. He planted seven acres of vines in 1853. When he died his wife, who was a temperance wowser, pulled out his vines.

CURRENT RELEASE 2001   The sweet raspberry grenache aromas mingle with mint and coconut in a simple, basic fruity red wine that is Rhône-ish in character. It's youthful, purple and fresh, and just lacks a little weight and complexity. It would suit steak and kidney pie.

Henschke Johann's Garden Grenache

For a long-established, outwardly conservative family company, Henschke come up with exciting new wines on a pretty regular basis. This is one such, and it's lobbed fair and square into the upper echelon of Rhône blends the way we see it.

CURRENT RELEASE 2001   This is very smart stuff. It is the essence of the grenache grape, picked ultra-ripe as it should be. Confectionery, ripe raspberries, boiled lollies, sweet spices and a slight vegetable undertone. It's sweetly ripe-to-overripe but not porty. There are tight tannins holding the palate together. A real charmer. It would suit aged manchego cheese.

Quality	🍷🍷🍷🍷🍷
Value	★★★★
Grapes	grenache
Region	Eden Valley, SA
Cellar	🍾 5
Alc./Vol.	15.0%
RRP	$30.80

PENGUIN BEST RED BLEND/ OTHER VARIETY

Hewitson Ned & Henry's Shiraz

Dean Hewitson won our 'Best New Producer' award three editions ago. He's managed to gather grapes from some seriously good old vineyards and turn them into mouth-watering booze. Dean's careful use of oak is a feature. CURRENT RELEASE 2001   A deep, rich, chunky red wine, this has Barossa generosity of flavour but doesn't sacrifice elegance or harmony. The nose reminds of dried banana and sundry dry spices, with flecks of aniseed or licorice. It turns more to plum and blackberry in the mouth. Flavour is delicious and the tannins are positive and in good balance. A clean, dry finish. Great with roast lamb.

Quality	🍷🍷🍷🍷🍷
Value	★★★★⸼
Grapes	shiraz
Region	Barossa Valley, SA
Cellar	🍾 8
Alc./Vol.	14.0%
RRP	$25.00

Highbank Coonawarra Basket Pressed

Dennis and Bonnie Vice try to run an organic vineyard in Coonawarra, where chemical viticulture has held sway for many years. They have quite a challenge. CURRENT RELEASE 2000   This is a typical Highbank red, in that it is smooth, forward in development and easy to drink, with savoury flavours predominating. The colour is already showing some brick-red and it smells of fresh earth, dried bay leaf and brazil-nut, with a whiff of Vegemite too. The taste is mellow and developed, with wood-matured characters uppermost and a hint of rhubarb beneath. It would suit slow-roasted Greek lamb.

Quality	🍷🍷🍷🍷
Value	★★★
Grapes	cabernet sauvignon 75%; merlot 20%; cabernet franc 5%
Region	Coonawarra, SA
Cellar	🍾 5
Alc./Vol.	13.5%
RRP	$45.70 🍾 ⊛

Higher Plane Cabernet Merlot

Quality	♟♟♟♟
Value	★★★
Grapes	cabernet sauvignon; merlot
Region	Margaret River, WA
Cellar	➾ 1–5+
Alc./Vol.	14.0%
RRP	$31.00

What have these people been smoking? Higher Plane indeed! Perhaps if you drink enough of their wine you'll elevate your consciousness. Hmmm.

CURRENT RELEASE 2001   The colour is excellent: a deep purple–red. It smells invitingly of ripe plums and blackberries, almost into the jammy spectrum, while the taste is deep, rich and concentrated, finishing with solid structure and gripping tannins. It needs food, or short-term cellaring. It would suit braised venison.

Higher Plane Pinot Noir

Quality	♟♟♟♟
Value	★★★
Grapes	pinot noir
Region	Margaret River, WA
Cellar	♦ 2
Alc./Vol.	12.5%
RRP	$22.50

This is the first vintage from a new individual vineyard at Margaret River. The brand-name at least gives them something to aim for.

CURRENT RELEASE 2001   The colour is light red–purple, almost as light as a rosé. The aromas are of cherry pips and sap, with plenty in the greener spectrum. It is clean and aromatic. In the mouth, it's light-bodied, simple and a trifle short, with a clean, dry finish. It is a well-made first effort. It would suit barbecued octopus.

Home Hill Pinot Noir

Quality	♟♟♟♟♟
Value	★★★♦
Grapes	pinot noir
Region	Huon Valley, Tas.
Cellar	♦ 3+
Alc./Vol.	13.5%
RRP	$30.00

Home Hill is owned by Terry and Rosemary Bennett. It has an acclaimed restaurant attached to the winery, and cellar door sales.

CURRENT RELEASE 2001   This is a 'pretty' style of pinot, which is not to say that it isn't a good or serious wine. It has high-toned strawberry, leafy, minty aromas which are telltale cool-climate scents. Lively acid and tannin gives a taut firmness to the palate. There is a subtle oak background and the wine just lacks the body to be higher rated. Delicious with beef carpaccio and all the trimmings.

Houghton Gladstones Shiraz

This new wine commemorates a leading figure in the Western Australian wine world: Dr John Gladstones is a renowned viticultural scientist and author of the excellent *Viticulture and Environment*.

CURRENT RELEASE 1999 Its two gold medals are thoroughly deserved. A dense, profound, multi-layered shiraz which is just starting to open up and has a very long life ahead of it. The aromas remind us of dark chocolate and mocha, nuttiness from toasted barrels and concentrated dark plum fruit. It is dense, essency and almost thick in its chewy texture. The abundant tannins are grainy and ripe. It needs time, and would suit rare rump steak.

Quality	🍷🍷🍷🍷🍷
Value	★★★½
Grapes	shiraz
Region	Frankland River, WA
Cellar	2–15+
Alc./Vol.	14.0%
RRP	$60.00

Houghton Jack Mann Cabernet Sauvignon Malbec

Jack Mann would probably not recognise this style of wine: it's a far cry from the vogue during his prime as Houghton's chief winemaker in the '50s. Maker: Larry Cherubino.

CURRENT RELEASE 1999 The incredible inky black purple–red colour accurately sets the scene. An extraordinary wine. Concentration is the key. It smells of plum and blackberry, very deep, ripe and rich. The not quite overripe fruit theme continues on palate, where it has masses of sweet fruit firmed up by cedary oak and smooth tannins that aren't aggressive. Just a pup, it's ageing very slowly, and should have a huge future. A great wine in the making.

Quality	🍷🍷🍷🍷🍷
Value	★★★½
Grapes	cabernet sauvignon; malbec
Region	Frankland River, WA
Cellar	3–20+
Alc./Vol.	14.5%
RRP	$90.00

House of Certain Views Mt Kaputar Merlot

Hunter winemaker Andrew Margan sources the grapes for this wine from a new and somewhat isolated vineyard on the slopes of Mt Kaputar, in central-northern New South Wales.

CURRENT RELEASE 2001 This is a lighter model than the show-stopping first vintage, 2000. It has fresh purple tints and is scented by coconutty oak and minty fruit. It's lean and linear in the mouth, light- to medium-bodied, and although it isn't very powerful, it does have length and attractive balance. It would suit pan-fried veal escalopes.

Quality	🍷🍷🍷🍷
Value	★★★
Grapes	merlot
Region	Mt Kaputar, NSW
Cellar	3
Alc./Vol.	13.5%
RRP	$38.00

Howard Park Cabernet Sauvignon

Quality	♟♟♟♟
Value	★★┥
Grapes	cabernet sauvignon
Region	Margaret River 76% & Great Southern 24%, WA
Cellar	⬛ 2–5+
Alc./Vol.	14.5%
RRP	$76.00 ⬛

This wine was originally created by accomplished winemaker John Wade and given a beautiful label depicting the karri trees of south-west Western Australia. Both Wade and the label are now long gone. CURRENT RELEASE 2000   In making this wine more concentrated and more 'impressive', the Howard Park team are in danger of losing its essence. It is loaded with heavy char oak, and is very packed, dense and concentrated, but lacks the elegance and clear cabernet identity it used to have. It's very spicy, we suspect from the new barrels, and slightly disjointed. It needs time, then try with aged reggiano cheese.

Hungerford Hill Shiraz

Quality	♟♟♟
Value	★★★
Grapes	shiraz
Region	Central Ranges, NSW
Cellar	⬛ 3
Alc./Vol.	13.5%
RRP	$16.50 ⓢ

Under the new ownership and management, Hungerford Hill has two tiers of wines: a very fine range of more expensive, regionally specific wines and a cheaper, less exciting range, of which this shiraz is part. CURRENT RELEASE 2001   It's a lighter coloured and weighted shiraz which is fairly basic, but fair value. It has minty, coconutty and raspberry aromas and a definite whiff of American oak, plus a suspicion of green fruit on the slightly pinched finish. Decent quaffing with a hamburger.

Jamiesons Run Cabernet Sauvignon

Quality	♟♟♟┋
Value	★★★┥
Grapes	cabernet sauvignon
Region	Coonawarra, SA
Cellar	⬛ 4
Alc./Vol.	13.5%
RRP	$16.00 ⓢ

This is a controversial wine, with considerable batch variation. In reviewing this, the merlot and the shiraz, we based our tasting notes and ratings on the poorest of the wines we sampled. CURRENT RELEASE 2001   We rated the first bottle five glasses, which accords with the gold medal it won at the Sydney Show, but the last bottle sampled was not nearly as good. It's a nice wine and fair value, though: medium–deep red–purple with strongly varietal aromas of blackcurrant, blackberry, cedar and crushed leaves. The palate is rather firm and has some green tannins, giving a trace of bitterness towards the finish. It's a nice enough wine but a bit angular and needs food. Try Italian-style braised beef.

Jamiesons Run Merlot

It's interesting that the merlot is the least of the three
Jamiesons Run single variety reds: we find this is usually
the case, whichever winery you talk about. Merlot is an
overrated, under-performing grape in Australia.
CURRENT RELEASE 2001   Again, the last bottle we
sampled is a lesser wine than the first. It's medium–light
red with a faint purple tint. The bouquet is soft, nutty,
lightly vanillin and fairly basic. It's a clean, pleasant red,
although the palate is fairly light, weak and innocuous,
with a somewhat hollow middle and short finish. It
goes with shawarma or yeeros.

Quality	🍷 🍷 🍷
Value	★ ★ ★
Grapes	merlot
Region	Coonawarra, SA
Cellar	🍾 2
Alc./Vol.	13.0%
RRP	$20.00 Ⓢ

Jamiesons Run O'Dea's Block Cabernet Sauvignon

One good turn deserves another, so Beringer Blass keep
turning out more and more wines under the Jamiesons
Run banner. This is one of their super-premium,
individual vineyard numbers. Maker: Andrew Hales.
CURRENT RELEASE 2000   Very appealing stuff that
shows this company hasn't lost the plot in Coonawarra,
as far as top-shelf reds go. The colour is excellent –
deep and purplish – and aromas of sweet mulberries
and blackberries burst from the glass. It's an elegantly
weighted wine, with good fruit sweetness and fine-
grained tannins. A real charmer. Try it with kangaroo
backstraps, barbecued.

Quality	🍷 🍷 🍷 🍷 🍷
Value	★ ★ ★ ★
Grapes	cabernet sauvignon
Region	Coonawarra, SA
Cellar	🍾 15
Alc./Vol.	13.0%
RRP	$35.00

Jamiesons Run Shiraz

First there was just a blended Coonawarra red under
this hugely successful label. Now a straight shiraz,
cabernet and merlot have appeared as companion
wines. Maker: Andrew Hales.
CURRENT RELEASE 2001   The colour is medium
red–purple and it has a nice Rhône-like spicy nose that's
slightly vegetal and plummy, revealing good varietal
character. It has a hint of charry oak but isn't too woody.
The palate is light- to medium-bodied: soft, plain and
fairly average. It's an elegant Coonawarra style with
good balance, but lacks weight and intensity – especially
when compared with the sample we tried some months
earlier. Like the cab and the merlot, it's variable.

Quality	🍷 🍷 🍷 🍷
Value	★ ★ ★ ⁴
Grapes	shiraz
Region	Coonawarra, SA
Cellar	🍾 3
Alc./Vol.	13.5%
RRP	$18.00 Ⓢ

Juniper Crossing Cabernet Sauvignon Merlot

Quality	🍷🍷🍷🍷
Value	★★★★⟩
Grapes	cabernet sauvignon; merlot
Region	Margaret River, WA
Cellar	🍾 6+
Alc./Vol.	14.5%
RRP	$19.00

Lower priced than Juniper Estate and made partly from purchased fruit, the Juniper Crossing wines are consistently impressive and excellent value. We wish there were more like them around.

CURRENT RELEASE 2001   The nose is all about pristine cabernet: sweet ripe cassis-like fruit, embellished with toasty, cedary oak. There's a hint of feral character but not enough to worry us. It's soft and starting to mellow nicely. The oak is well handled and it has a pleasing claret-style structure, with a little tannin firmness to close. It would suit braised beef cheeks and reduction sauce.

Juniper Crossing Shiraz

Quality	🍷🍷🍷🍷
Value	★★★★
Grapes	shiraz
Region	Margaret River, WA
Cellar	🍾 5
Alc./Vol.	14.5%
RRP	$19.00

The Juniper family is well known in the Margaret River region. Robert Juniper, whose artworks appear on the labels, is a highly regarded and well-established local artist. This won a gold medal at the 2002 Adelaide Show.

CURRENT RELEASE 2001   This wine is a bit of a bruiser. The alcohol heat adds to the astringency of the palate, and the oak sits slightly apart from the fruit. It's a big, rather unsubtle red which smells of plum skins and toasty oak, and tastes full-bodied, tannic and a bit heavy-handed. You could try it with lamb's fry and bacon.

Juniper Estate Shiraz

Quality	🍷🍷🍷🍷🍷
Value	★★★⟩
Grapes	shiraz
Region	Margaret River, WA
Cellar	🍾 8+
Alc./Vol.	14.5%
RRP	$29.00 🍾

Juniper Estate is the former Wright's vineyard in Willyabrup, opposite Vasse Felix; it is a mature vineyard of some distinction. Juniper Crossing is the cheaper label for bought-in grapes.

CURRENT RELEASE 2000   This is a serious red: it has an appealing aroma of dry spices, ripe plums and toasty, spicy oak with a meaty undertone. The taste is rich and full-bodied, chunky in structure and dense almost to the point of being thick on the palate. There's a lot of oaky tannin and it has a density that reminds us of heavily reduced stock. You could serve it with seared kangaroo fillets.

Kangarilla Road Shiraz

Kangarilla Road was once Graham Stevens' Cambrai. And surprise, surprise, it's on Kangarilla Road! CURRENT RELEASE 2001   True to region and variety, this is a straightforward young shiraz with bitter chocolate and raspberry aromas that would make a confectioner proud. There are also some attractive hints of spice and earth. The palate is medium-bodied with soft berry flavours that are juicy and ripe. Oak is very restrained and it finishes with a light grip of tannin. Try it with braised gravy beef and dumplings.

Quality	🍷🍷🍷🍷
Value	★★★★★
Grapes	shiraz
Region	McLaren Vale, SA
Cellar	4
Alc./Vol.	14.0%
RRP	$20.00

Kara Kara Shiraz

Kara Kara is an Aboriginal term meaning 'gold quartz'. Much of the vineyard country of central Victoria was goldfields in the rip-roarin' days of the gold rush. CURRENT RELEASE 2001   Strong regionality is a feature of most red wines from the Pyrenees and Kara Kara usually has it, but it's less pronounced in this 2001. It has spice and a touch of vegetal leafiness on the nose, but ripe fruit leads the way with berry and plum-like aromas and flavours. The palate is strongly flavoured, but it has balance, with dry tannins chiming in nicely at the end. Try it with barley risotto with lamb.

Quality	🍷🍷🍷
Value	★★★
Grapes	shiraz
Region	Pyrenees, Vic.
Cellar	5
Alc./Vol.	14.5%
RRP	$30.00

Katnook Estate Cabernet Sauvignon

Over 22 vintages, Katnook Cabernet has come to epitomise the modern Coonawarra style: a classy wine of great intensity and balance. Maker: Wayne Stehbens. *Previous outstanding vintages: '91, '92, '96, '97, '98, '99* CURRENT RELEASE 2000   There's a slightly mulch/leafy touch to this cabernet that keeps it short of the superb '99, but it's still an excellent regional style. The nose has tart leafy blackcurrant folded into measured cedary oak and the palate is concentrated but not too potent. There's ripe, leafy cassis-like fruit and measured oak in the mouth, and tangy acidity coupled to ripe, dry tannins provides good structure. Roast a leg of lamb.

Quality	🍷🍷🍷🍷
Value	★★★⅃
Grapes	cabernet sauvignon
Region	Coonawarra, SA
Cellar	1–5+
Alc./Vol.	14.0%
RRP	$40.00

Katnook Estate Merlot

Quality	♟ ♟ ♟ ♟
Value	★ ★ ★
Grapes	merlot
Region	Coonawarra, SA
Cellar	🍷 4
Alc./Vol.	13.0%
RRP	$40.00

The Katnook Merlot style has changed. It started off as a lighter, more fruit-dominant style, but recent vintages have often had more substance. Maker: Wayne Stehbens.

CURRENT RELEASE 2000   This has good varietal character in its plum and warm spice aromas. Dusty oak is there too, and the impression is smooth, but for a slightly vegetal hint of stems and herbs. The smooth fruit continues across the palate, ripe and complete, but that vegetal thing appears again, giving a slightly mulchy touch. Ripe, easy tannins finish things off in good balance. Try it with veal scaloppine.

Katnook Estate Prodigy

Quality	♟ ♟ ♟ ♟ ♟
Value	★ ★ ★
Grapes	shiraz
Region	Coonawarra, SA
Cellar	➤ 2–10
Alc./Vol.	15.0%
RRP	$83.00

Prodigy is the shiraz made to partner Odyssey, which is Katnook's super-dooper cabernet. They are both wines of some potency.

CURRENT RELEASE 1999   This is a power-packed shiraz with a deep purplish-red appearance of great concentration. On the nose smoky bacon bone and vanillin oak aromas are strong, with essency black plum fruit buried within. It has forceful long flavours, slightly fumy alcohol, great depth, and a solid backbone of tannins. Toasty oak is a strong feature and less might have been better. Fans of potent shiraz won't be disappointed here. Try it with thick florentine beefsteak.

Killerby Shiraz

Quality	♟ ♟ ♟ ♟
Value	★ ★ ★ ⁾
Grapes	shiraz
Region	Geographe, WA
Cellar	🍷 5
Alc./Vol.	14.5%
RRP	$24.00

The Killerby family have a century-long association with Western Australia's south-west. Their first vineyards were planted in 1973 near Bunbury and they have progressively expanded since then to take in a property at Margaret River.

CURRENT RELEASE 2000   There's real concentration here – deep colour, and an intense nose of ripe berries, earth, spice and vanillin oak. In the mouth it has a dense feel, solid berry and wood flavours, and grippy tannins that creep up on you from behind. It's not especially fine, but satisfying and well put together. Just right with Chinese braised beef and ribbon noodles.

Kingston Shiraz

A new label with a stylised head of Dionysus, the ancient Greek god of wine, gives a new feel to Kingston Estate's range. The wine is probably better than anything in those far-off days. Ancient Greek wine was often adulterated with things like powdered marble, salt water, resin and perfumes.
CURRENT RELEASE 2001   This is an appealing everyday red with a surge of blackberry fruit, earthy and spicy and fresh. In the mouth there's smooth fruit flavour that's uncomplicated and easy to slurp down. Oak is kept to a restrained seasoning and it finishes ripe and tasty. Try it with moussaka.

Quality	♥♥♥
Value	★★★★
Grapes	shiraz
Region	Murray Valley, SA
Cellar	3
Alc./Vol.	14.0%
RRP	$14.00 ⑤

Knappstein Enterprise Cabernet Sauvignon

The Enterprise label is kept for the biggest, brawniest products of the Knappstein Clare Valley vineyard. It's sort of a reserve label with more of everything.
CURRENT RELEASE 2000   As usual impenetrable in colour, this has real power on the nose with lush blackberry and blackcurrant fruit, and a touch of new leather. Oak is there in good measure but the concentrated fruit is the thing. The palate has great power and richness with truly profound flavour, and smooth velvet texture in the middle. Tannins are ripe and surprisingly softish, given the fruit weight in the wine. Serve it with lamb shanks braised in red wine.

Quality	♥♥♥♥
Value	★★★
Grapes	cabernet sauvignon
Region	Clare Valley, SA
Cellar	2–12
Alc./Vol.	14.5%
RRP	$40.00

Knappstein Enterprise Shiraz

Quality	▉ ▉ ▉ ▉
Value	✹ ✹ ✹
Grapes	shiraz
Region	Clare Valley, SA
Cellar	➥ 1–10
Alc./Vol.	14.5%
RRP	$40.00

This competes with the Enterprise Cabernet Sauvignon in the bigger is better stakes. No shy, retiring type, it jumps out and wrestles you into submission.
CURRENT RELEASE 1999   Formidable is the word. The nose is super-concentrated with black plum, blackberry and spicy oak, big but all in nice equilibrium. In the mouth the big flavour continues across the full-bodied palate. The texture is dense and chewy, but the tannins are in good balance for such a forceful wine. It actually drinks well now, however it should live on for many years. Serve it with something similarly robust, perhaps oxtail braised in big red.

Quality	▉ ▉ ▉ ▉ ▉
Value	✹ ✹ ✹ ⟊
Grapes	shiraz
Region	Clare Valley, SA
Cellar	➥ 1–12
Alc./Vol.	14.5%
RRP	$40.00

CURRENT RELEASE 2000   A super-ripe, super-concentrated shiraz, with fruit admirably dominating oak. It smells powerfully of dark berries, plums, chocolate and earth, with a vanillin touch in the background. In the mouth it's big and round with profound dark-fruit flavour that isn't jammy or overdone. Despite its potency, there's a purity about it, and a refinement that lifts it above the ruck. It should develop well in bottle. Serve with a steak.

Knots Capstan Cabernet Sauvignon

Quality	▉ ▉ ▉ ▉
Value	✹ ✹ ✹
Grapes	cabernet sauvignon
Region	central Victoria
Cellar	▮ 4
Alc./Vol.	13.5%
RRP	$27.00

Ex-boy scouts and girl guides everywhere will find these labels of great interest. They refresh your memory about all those knots you used to tie. The capstan knot is a useful mooring knot for a small boat. Fascinating.
CURRENT RELEASE 2001   There's juicy blackcurrant on the nose, with hints of mint and gamy complexity. Oak is subtle. In the mouth it has easy medium body with a supple texture that invites another glass. The finish is savoury with an agreeable bit of firmness to it. An easy-drinking central Victorian red that's really quite gentle-hearted. Try it with pasta with braised veal sauce.

Kooyong Pinot Noir

Kooyong winery was conceived as a top of the range Mornington Peninsula estate, dedicated to quality, through attention to detail in every aspect of wine production. Maker: Sandro Mosele.

CURRENT RELEASE 2001   An attractive young pinot in a fresh, light vein. The nose is appetising with sappy red fruit aromas that are succulent and nicely savoury. It tastes clean and fresh with light red berry flavour of reasonable persistence. There's a slightly bitter end to the palate and age may soften it, but the fruit weight suggests it be consumed young. Try it with quail.

Quality	♟♟♟♟
Value	✷✷✷
Grapes	pinot noir
Region	Mornington Peninsula, Vic.
Cellar	🍶 3
Alc./Vol.	13.0%
RRP	$39.00

The Lane Reunion Shiraz

The Lane is the new name for Ravenswood Lane, the Adelaide Hills vineyard of John Edwards. He shortened it because of conflicts with other wines.

CURRENT RELEASE 2000   The colour is nicely deep and rich, while the wine is complex but also full of meaty, gamy, feral characters, which purists might find confronting. It's chunky and rich in the mouth, with lots of fleshy extract and smooth tannins, and again a sweaty, less than pristine character. We liked it much more than the even more feral cabernet. Flawed brilliance! It will have plenty of fans. Try it with steak and kidney pie.

Quality	♟♟♟♟
Value	✷✷✷
Grapes	shiraz
Region	Adelaide Hills, SA
Cellar	🍶 4
Alc./Vol.	12.5%
RRP	$50.00

Langhorne Creek Area Red Blend

Cellarmasters, the direct wine marketers, decided to cobble together small parcels of the best grapes from its growers in Langhorne Creek, and get Michael Potts to vinify the wine at Bleasdale. An unusual concept, highly successful over the seven vintages it's been made.

CURRENT RELEASE 1999   The smooth, fleshy texture, high extract and supple tannins are a feature of this eminently drinkable, cuddly, warm-climate red. It smacks of vanilla and toasty oak, plus plum and blackberry, and it's rich and dense without being overpowering or astringent. On the contrary, it's dangerously easy to drink. It goes well with grilled bangers and mash.

Quality	♟♟♟♟♟
Value	✷✷✷✷
Grapes	shiraz; cabernet sauvignon; etc.
Region	Langhorne Creek, SA
Cellar	🍶 6+
Alc./Vol.	14.0%
RRP	$31.50 🍶 (from Cellarmasters)

Lark Hill Shiraz

Quality	🍷🍷🍷
Value	★★★
Grapes	shiraz
Region	Canberra region, NSW
Cellar	➥ 1–5
Alc./Vol.	13.0%
RRP	$28.00

The Carpenters of Lark Hill have been Canberra vignerons for 25 years now, and their wines are always among the region's best.

CURRENT RELEASE 2000   Dense, deep colour gives an impression of intensity here and the nose confirms it. There's that lovely balance that the best Canberra shiraz has – plummy fruit, a dash of pepper, and sweet spices are all in easy accord. Oak is folded in with a light hand, and it tastes complete, but there's a slight stemmy astringency that needs time to integrate properly. Keep it a couple of years then sip it with veal ribs.

Leasingham Bastion Shiraz Cabernet Sauvignon

Quality	🍷🍷🍷🍷
Value	★★★★★
Grapes	shiraz; cabernet sauvignon
Region	Clare Valley, SA
Cellar	🍾 5
Alc./Vol.	13.5%
RRP	$14.50 $

Like its predecessors, this edition is an extraordinary bargain. Usually new brands start off 'over-delivering' and fall away with subsequent vintages. Not this one. Maker: Kerri Thompson.

CURRENT RELEASE 2001   Like the 2000, this has dinky-di Clare style at a bargain price. How can they do it? Dusty, earthy, subdued plum aromas; good intensity in the mouth, with fleshy richness and superior extract. It has a slight dip in the middle but is soft and very agreeable. The finish is quite big, with serious persistence. It's a satisfying, grown-up red. Try it with your favourite sausages and mash.

Leasingham Bin 56 Cabernet Malbec

Quality	🍷🍷🍷🍷
Value	★★★
Grapes	cabernet sauvignon; malbec
Region	Clare Valley, SA
Cellar	🍾 5
Alc./Vol.	13.5%
RRP	$22.00 $

What is BRL Hardy doing to its red wines, especially the Leasinghams? Many of them have a vegetal, compost, mulchy earthiness about them. We're not sure it's a great new direction.

CURRENT RELEASE 2000   The colour is medium–deep and the nose has the corporate uniform of a meaty, vegetal, mulchy, gamy character, and it doesn't have much varietal definition. If anything, it tastes like a shiraz! The palate is smooth and mild, with a little sweetness balancing a dash of tannin astringency. Unusual but fair value, especially when discounted. Try meat pie and tomato sauce here.

Leasingham Classic Clare Cabernet Sauvignon

Even though chief winemaker Kerri Thompson, who took over in '99, professes to have throttled back the oak, these wines are still anything but classic Clare in our view. They're just too oaky and astringent.

CURRENT RELEASE 1999   It may be less oaky than earlier releases but it's still a show pony. The colour is very dark and rich. The bouquet is loaded with chocolate/mocha and toasty oak, but also good cabernet character with crushed-leaf, mulberry and blueberry aromas. It's concentrated and tannic, with a spirity alcohol finish and grippy astringency. Chargrilled kangaroo, here.

Quality	▼▼▼▼
Value	★★★
Grapes	cabernet sauvignon
Region	Clare Valley, SA
Cellar	● 2–8+
Alc./Vol.	14.0%
RRP	$46.00

Leasingham Classic Clare Shiraz

The winds of change need to blow a bit harder. These wines still taste like they're designed to win trophies rather than drink.

CURRENT RELEASE 1999   It's won three gold medals so far, and there's no denying its power or concentration. The colour is almost black–purple and it smells of smoked meats, fruitcake and coconuts, and the whiff of American oak barrel staves is bell-clear. The palate is dense and very tannic, and leaves you with a lingering aftertaste of oak. Try before you buy!

Quality	▼▼▼▼
Value	★★⁺
Grapes	shiraz
Region	Clare Valley, SA
Cellar	● 2–9+
Alc./Vol.	14.0%
RRP	$46.00

Lenswood Vineyards Pinot Noir

Tim Knappstein makes one of the bigger styles of pinot in the Adelaide Hills, partly a function of the site and partly the way he makes it, with plenty of oak and extraction. For this vintage, 970 dozen were made.

CURRENT RELEASE 2000   This is quite a big, solid and somewhat chunky pinot, certainly not the delicate, prettily perfumed, ethereal style. There are meaty, oaky, funky aromas over dried cherry, and the dominant secondary flavours continue on the palate. There are stewed plum flavours and the finish is quite drying. It would suit roast pork belly.

Quality	▼▼▼▼⁺
Value	★★★
Grapes	pinot noir
Region	Adelaide Hills, SA
Cellar	▮ 3
Alc./Vol.	13.5%
RRP	$50.00

Lillydale Cabernet Merlot

Quality	🍷🍷🍷🍷
Value	✱✱✱
Grapes	cabernet sauvignon; merlot
Region	Yarra Valley, Vic.
Cellar	🍷 5
Alc./Vol.	13.0%
RRP	$23.00

Lillydale Vineyards is owned by McWilliams and has produced some pleasant, elegantly weighted cabernet merlots over the years, although they seem to lack the intensity and structure of the best Yarra cabernets. CURRENT RELEASE 2000 The colour is medium red–purple and the bouquet is dominated by oaky and stalky/leafy aromas. It's a light- to medium-bodied red with a lightness on the mid-palate which is not unusual in cabernet on its lonesome. (Merlot is supposed to plug the gap.) The oak is seductive but we wonder if there's enough fruit depth to carry the wine in time. Try it with chargrilled veal cutlets.

Lindemans Cawarra Cabernet Merlot

Quality	🍷🍷🍷
Value	✱✱✱⸍
Grapes	cabernet sauvignon; merlot
Region	not stated
Cellar	🍷 2
Alc./Vol.	13.5%
RRP	$8.10 Ⓢ

Cawarra was the name of Dr Henry John Lindeman's first vineyard, at East Gresford, a part of the Hunter Valley that's been overlooked for grapegrowing almost ever since. CURRENT RELEASE 2001 This is little better than cask quality, but it doesn't offend, either. At the price, it's pitched right on middle stump. The colour is medium–light but of good hue, and it smells grapey – cherry scented – without obvious oak or other complexities. It's light and simple in the mouth, a tad weak and mono-dimensional, with barely any tannin. A quaffing red to take to a smoky barbecue.

Lindemans Limestone Ridge

Quality	🍷🍷🍷🍷
Value	✱✱✱
Grapes	shiraz; cabernet sauvignon
Region	Coonawarra, SA
Cellar	⬤ 1–7+
Alc./Vol.	13.5%
RRP	$49.00 🍷 Ⓢ

The Limestone Ridge is usually a bit too oaky for our tastes. The other Lindemans Coonawarras also push oak to the limit, but in the '99 vintage their balance is better. CURRENT RELEASE 1999 The Lindemans Coonawarra red wine style is nothing if not consistent. It's still very oaky! This vintage has a savoury, somewhat dried-out bouquet of toasty oak and earthy developing fruit. In the mouth it is oaky/tannic and a trifle austere. Oak and acid dominate the finish. It may benefit from cellaring. Try it with chargrilled venison sausages.

Lindemans Pyrus

This is usually the softest of the Lindemans Coonawarra trio, and the most 'fruit forward'. Maker: Greg Clayfield and team.

CURRENT RELEASE 1999   At four years this is still very young, smelling of rose petals, mint and raspberry. There are Ribena and cassis touches, too. It's an elegant-weight wine, medium-bodied, with a nice balance of fruit and tannin, the oak not at all assertive. It's starting to mellow and build cigar-box, smoky and black-olive characters. It has the sinewy rather than fleshy palate that's typical of all three members of the Trio. Try it with aged cheese.

Quality	🍷🍷🍷🍷
Value	★★★↓
Grapes	cabernet sauvignon; merlot; cabernet franc
Region	Coonawarra, SA
Cellar	🍷 7+
Alc./Vol.	14.0%
RRP	$49.00 Ⓢ

Lindemans Reserve Cabernet Sauvignon

These days the Lindemans Reserve selection reds are the best buys in the Lindeman stable. They are very good and usually surpass expectations.

CURRENT RELEASE 2001   It's a pleasant medium-bodied red wine without real distinction, but offers very enjoyable current drinking at a more than reasonable price. There's a hint of raspberry but it generally doesn't show a lot of cabernet definition. The texture is smooth and supple, with balance and quality. It would suit a mild washed-rind cheese such as Pont Leveque.

Quality	🍷🍷🍷
Value	★★★★
Grapes	cabernet sauvignon
Region	various, SA
Cellar	🍷 3
Alc./Vol.	13.0%
RRP	$14.00 Ⓢ

Lindemans Reserve Padthaway Merlot

Padthaway was first planted to grapevines in the late 1960s and has steadily risen in the quality stakes. These days, some of Southcorp's and Hardys' finest reds have a Padthaway component.

CURRENT RELEASE 2000   This is another decent, easy drinking, well-priced red from Lindemans. It has somewhat indistinct varietal provenance, and is starting to show some age development. It's smooth and medium-weight in the mouth. It may lack some freshness and fruit definition but it does have drinkability. Try it with Lebanese lamb shawarma.

Quality	🍷🍷🍷
Value	★★★↓
Grapes	merlot
Region	Padthaway, SA
Cellar	🍷 2
Alc./Vol.	13.5%
RRP	$14.00 Ⓢ

Lindemans Reserve Shiraz

Quality	★★★★
Value	★★★★★
Grapes	shiraz
Region	various, SA
Cellar	🍶 5+
Alc./Vol.	14.0%
RRP	$14.00 Ⓢ

The new label for what used to be Lindemans' Padthaway series scrapes the bottom of the barrel: dark, dull, bland = instantly forgettable. At least what's inside is good!

CURRENT RELEASE 2001   This is simply one of the best value reds we've seen for ages. A lovely spicy, elegant, very drinkable wine, it has black cherry and plum aromas, a hint of herbal character, and oak is tucked neatly in the background. The palate is concentrated with a taut, firm, linear profile, and good fleshy extract. Mixed spices and peppercorns to close. It's lively but smooth: a delicious drink right now, with aged parmesan cheese.

Lindemans St George Cabernet Sauvignon

Quality	★★★★★
Value	★★★★
Grapes	cabernet sauvignon
Region	Coonawarra, SA
Cellar	🍶 10+
Alc./Vol.	13.5%
RRP	$49.00 Ⓢ 🍾

The St George vineyard was named after Major-General Hinton St George, who bought the land from John Riddoch in the 1890s. Lindemans was first to plant vines there. It is always a single-vineyard wine.

CURRENT RELEASE 1999   Attractive bottle-age is starting to be evident in this elegant Coonawarra cabernet. It has a bouquet of dusty, earthy, cedar-cigar-box developing cabernet, with flecks of mint and toasty oak. The structure is fine and firm, elegant and very much alive in the mouth, with serious backbone and amazing persistence. A finely textured red of very good balance. Try it with venison stewed with cherries.

M Chapoutier Cabernet Sauvignon

Quality	★★★★
Value	★★★★⟩
Grapes	cabernet sauvignon
Region	Limestone Coast, SA
Cellar	🍶 5
Alc./Vol.	13.2%
RRP	$24.50 ⓥ

Michel Chapoutier has entered into cooperative arrangements with some established producers in Victoria, in addition to his own vineyard development at Mount Benson in South Australia.

CURRENT RELEASE 2001   This is really an un-cabernet cabernet, and that's not necessarily a criticism. It's a rustic wine with an earthy note through it; black fruit characters are well concentrated; oak adds subtle complexity. The palate has medium weight with good texture and ripe integrated tannins. Serve it with daube of beef.

M Chapoutier Shiraz

The irrepressible Michel Chapoutier of Rhône Valley
fame embarked on his Australian odyssey about five
years ago now. His biodynamic Limestone Coast
property in South Australia already produces wines
that demand attention.

CURRENT RELEASE 2001   A brilliantly coloured wine
with real density of hue. The nose is superb: very pure,
deep, cherry-like shiraz fruit aromas meet some lightly
earthy and cedary notes in subtle, smooth harmony.
The palate is silky in texture and beautifully restrained
in flavour with an almost gentle background of ripe
tannins. An understated red of real style. Try it with
coq au vin rouge.

Quality	▟ ▟ ▟ ▟ ▟
Value	★ ★ ★ ★ ★
Grapes	shiraz
Region	Limestone Coast, SA
Cellar	▐ 6
Alc./Vol.	14.0%
RRP	$24.50 ✿

Mad Fish Shiraz

This is a second-string wine from the esteemed Howard
Park winery. The label features an impressive piece of
Aboriginal art.

CURRENT RELEASE 2001   This really is very good for
a second-fiddle shiraz. The nose has black cherry, spice
and classy oak with a savoury gamy touch. The palate
has good flesh with a grainy textured feel that's very
satisfying. It works well alongside roast beef.

Quality	▟ ▟ ▟ ▟
Value	★ ★ ★ ⧪
Grapes	shiraz
Region	south western WA
Cellar	▐ 4
Alc./Vol.	14.5%
RRP	$22.00

Main Ridge Half Acre Pinot Noir

All wine buffs should make a point of visiting the
Mornington Peninsula. It has great beaches, lovely
countryside and historic townships, and the wineries are a
real journey of discovery. Main Ridge was one of the first.

CURRENT RELEASE 2001   Winemaker Nat White's
thing is subtlety and complexity. This description fits
the 2001 Half Acre well. It has strawberry and
raspberry eau-de-vie aromas, with some foresty/earthy
notes. The palate has medium intensity flavours that
are fragrant and lasting with some slightly stemmy
tannins beneath. This really needs a little bottle-age to
hit its stride. Serve it with grilled quail.

Quality	▟ ▟ ▟ ▟
Value	★ ★ ★
Grapes	pinot noir
Region	Mornington Peninsula, Vic.
Cellar	➥ 1–5
Alc./Vol.	14.0%
RRP	$48.00

Majella Cabernet

Quality	♟♟♟♟♟
Value	★★★➵
Grapes	cabernet sauvignon
Region	Coonawarra, SA
Cellar	➥ 2–10
Alc./Vol.	14.0%
RRP	$40.00

Majella successfully made the transition from grapegrower to wine producer around 10 years ago and hasn't looked back.

CURRENT RELEASE 2001   A densely coloured, blackish young cabernet, it's still very youthful and yet to come together properly, making the oak component seem beefed up over other recent vintages. That said, there's real fruit concentration hidden in there. The nose has super-intense, juicy, leafy blackcurrant aromas, lots of spicy oak and charry scents. It opens up on the palate with great purity, concentration and length of fine flavour. Needs time, then serve it with racks of lamb char siew style.

Majella Shiraz

Quality	♟♟♟♟
Value	★★★
Grapes	shiraz
Region	Coonawarra, SA
Cellar	➥ 2–8
Alc./Vol.	13.5%
RRP	$40.00

The Majella vineyard is one of Coonawarra's most highly regarded and has been the source of some prestigious wines over the years.

CURRENT RELEASE 2001   There's a good dose of oak here and it gives vanilla, sawmill and slightly coconutty aromas. Redcurrant and berry fruit hides in the midst of it, giving it clean flavour, seemingly without great fruit weight or power, but it's still a pup and consequently difficult to assess. Tannins are soft and fine, giving a rather gentle and elegant finish. Try it with pink lamb cutlets.

Majella The Malleea

Quality	♟♟♟♟♟
Value	★★★
Grapes	cabernet sauvignon; shiraz
Region	Coonawarra, SA
Cellar	➥ 1–10+
Alc./Vol.	14.0%
RRP	$70.00

For their flagship wine, Majella choose the traditional Coonawarra blend of cabernet sauvignon and shiraz.

CURRENT RELEASE 2000   The Malleea always has an essency quality to it: clean, pure blackcurranty fruit, light touches of spice, earthiness, and an emphatic measure of cedary oak. The palate is medium-bodied with an intensity that exactly follows the nose. Texture is fine and ripe; dry tannins support things in good balance. Try it with braised beef cheeks with blackcurrants.

Mandurang Valley Cabernet Sauvignon

Bendigo meant gold in wild and woolly frontier Victoria
140 years ago. It also meant wine, with large vineyards
here, there and everywhere. Now they're back making
wine, but for more genteel patrons than a crowd of
knuckleheaded gold diggers.

CURRENT RELEASE 2001   Heavily extracted and very
potent, this is a macho Bendigo cabernet with a
difference. It has impenetrable colour and a meaty nose
of prune, dark plum, licorice and sweet oak. In the
mouth it's a very full, drought-affected wine – a touch
porty with big, firm structure, tooth-gripping tannins
and butch personality. Fightin' wine. Serve it with
braised oxtail.

Quality	♟♟♟♟
Value	★★★
Grapes	cabernet sauvignon
Region	Bendigo, Vic.
Cellar	➡ 2–8
Alc./Vol.	14.5%
RRP	$22.00

Mandurang Valley Shiraz

Mandurang Valley's owners' surname is Vine. What else
could you do with a moniker like that but grow grapes?
CURRENT RELEASE 2001   The attractive savoury
aspects of tasty Bendigo shiraz are all here in good
balance. It smells really appetising and fresh with some
savoury minty notes to ripe blackcurrant and berry
fruit. Cedary oak dresses it up tastefully. The palate has
mouth-watering fruit–acid balance, good intensity and
medium body. Tannins are soft and it should profit
from a few years in bottle.

Quality	♟♟♟♟
Value	★★★
Grapes	shiraz
Region	Bendigo, Vic.
Cellar	🍷 4
Alc./Vol.	14.2%
RRP	$22.00

Maxwell Ellen Street Shiraz

There are a number of small to medium-sized wineries
like Maxwells in McLaren Vale. They can make a visit to
the region a real voyage of discovery.
CURRENT RELEASE 2000   This is a delicious McLaren
Vale red with great purity of regional and varietal
qualities. On the nose there's blackberry and sweet
spice, only a smidgen of McLaren Vale earthiness, and
underplayed oak. In the mouth it's smooth, round and
juicy with good length and soft tannins. A generous
shiraz to drink with beef ribs.

Quality	♟♟♟♟♟
Value	★★★★
Grapes	shiraz
Region	McLaren Vale, SA
Cellar	🍷 5
Alc./Vol.	14.0%
RRP	$29.00

Maxwell Four Roads Shiraz

Quality	♥♥♥♥
Value	★★★⸣
Grapes	shiraz
Region	McLaren Vale, SA
Cellar	▮ 3
Alc./Vol.	14.0%
RRP	$19.50

Maxwells is one of the new old wave McLaren Vale wineries, or is that the old new wave? Whatever, the vineyard was planted with a number of others in the 1970s. Shiraz makes very good wine here.
CURRENT RELEASE 2000   This is very much in the honest, hearty McLaren Vale mainstream with earthy, raspberry and blackberry aromas along with a light touch of oak. The palate is full of ripe flavour with some dark-chocolatey richness in the middle and ripe tannins at the end. A good match for braised steak and onions.

Maxwell Lime Cave Cabernet

Quality	♥♥♥♥
Value	★★★
Grapes	cabernet sauvignon
Region	McLaren Vale, SA
Cellar	➥ 1–7
Alc./Vol.	14.0%
RRP	$29.00

The Maxwell winery has come a long way and today occupies a swish new winery on a lime cave hill, just north of McLaren Vale.
CURRENT RELEASE 2000   There's something friendly and familiar about this traditional style of McLaren Vale red wine. The nose is attractive with ripe black fruit aromas of moderate intensity, along with an interesting bit of regional earthiness. In the mouth, pleasant ripe fruit flavour is juicy and mellow, but it's backed up by some sinewy tannins that give it a slightly unyielding feel. Time in bottle should iron things out nicely. It suits a good, old-fashioned beef and vegetable stew.

McWilliams 1877 Cabernet Sauvignon Shiraz

Quality	♥♥♥♥♥
Value	★★★★
Grapes	cabernet sauvignon 73%; shiraz 20%; merlot 7%
Region	Hilltops, NSW 64% & Coonawarra, SA 36%
Cellar	▮ 10
Alc./Vol.	14.0%
RRP	$90.00

Introduced last year to celebrate McWilliams' 125th anniversary, this new super-premium red wine hit the mark straight away. A worthy flagship for a company that's become surprisingly dynamic of late.
CURRENT RELEASE 1999   An immensely satisfying wine – concentrated, ripe and fleshy. The nose has character and smooth complexity, with deep dark fruit, demiglace-like savoury richness, and harmonious oak. The long-flavoured palate is complete, velvety and mellow, with fine-tuned ripe tannins. A great match for venison pie.

McWilliams Hanwood Shiraz

An everyday sort of wine, but fault-free and very pleasant drinking. It's often discounted below its already reasonable price, another reason to make it your 'house red'.

CURRENT RELEASE 2001   Simple, clean cherry and kernelly aromas have a hint of earthiness to them, and a light whisper of oak is a subtle condiment. In the mouth there's light berry flavour that's soft and undemanding, along with very easy tannins. Easy drinking within a year or two of vintage. This would work well with a vegetarian pizza.

Quality	▼▼▼
Value	★★★★
Grapes	shiraz
Region	Riverina, NSW
Cellar	🍶 1
Alc./Vol.	13.5%
RRP	$11.50 Ⓢ

McWilliams Mount Pleasant Old Paddock and Old Hill Shiraz

A blend of two plots of shiraz planted in the 1880s and 1920s at Mount Pleasant, this wine gets 18 months in new oak, but the character of the vineyard and region shines through: testament to old vines and low yields.

CURRENT RELEASE 1999   This classic Hunter shiraz can polarise tasters between the traditionalists and the others. The nose reveals itself slowly and is very complex. At the core are intense earthy, plum, berry and liqueur cherry aromas, along with some faded leathery tones and just a hint of chocolatey oak coming through. The palate is savoury and deeply flavoured with earthy Hunter shiraz. It's medium in body and fine in tannins. Drink it with roast lamb.

Quality	▼▼▼▼▼
Value	★★★★
Grapes	shiraz
Region	Hunter Valley, NSW
Cellar	�‒ 1–8+
Alc./Vol.	14.0%
RRP	$40.00

McWilliams Mount Pleasant Rosehill Shiraz

Brought into the fold by the legendary Maurice O'Shea in 1945, Rosehill is one of the occasional individual vineyard bottlings that have been a feature of the Mount Pleasant range for decades.

CURRENT RELEASE 1999   When the vintage is kind, the understated personality of good Hunter shiraz makes it one of Australia's most charming wines. Rosehill sums it all up – a complex bouquet of earth, plum, smoke and leather-furnished drawing rooms, rather like a gentleman's club in a bottle. It has a savoury regional palate of medium body that's pleasantly intense with soft integrated tannins and a very long aftertaste. Try it with yearling beef.

Quality	▼▼▼▼▸
Value	★★★▸
Grapes	shiraz
Region	Hunter Valley, NSW
Cellar	🍶 5
Alc./Vol.	14.0%
RRP	$32.00

McWilliams Regional Collection Coonawarra Cabernet Sauvignon

Quality	🍷🍷🍷
Value	★★★
Grapes	cabernet sauvignon
Region	Coonawarra, SA
Cellar	🍾 3
Alc./Vol.	13.5%
RRP	$17.50

Recent years have seen wines from well outside the company's traditional New South Wales base incorporated smoothly into the portfolio. The Regional Collection showcases some of these.
CURRENT RELEASE 2000   An unusual style for a Coonawarra cabernet, it's made with a light hand into a fresh, almost foreign wine. It smells herbal and slightly mulchy with redcurrant fruit and a touch of capsicum. The palate has medium intensity with a herbal edge to light currancy flavour. Fine tannins and clean acidity provide a framework for the light fruit; it's quite lean in structure but still satisfying. Serve it alongside lamb cutlets, oregano and lemon.

Meadowbank Pinot Noir

Quality	🍷🍷🍷🍷
Value	★★★★
Grapes	pinot noir
Region	Derwent Valley, Tas.
Cellar	🍾 4
Alc./Vol.	13.5%
RRP	$28.00

In Tasmania, growers make a speciality of pinot noir. Standards aren't uniformly high but Meadowbank is one of the consistent success stories. Maker: Andrew Hood.
CURRENT RELEASE 2002   This is from a great vintage. The colour here is a deep purplish red and the nose shows good concentration. It's fragrant with black cherry, vanilla and lightly foresty hints. The succulence of the nose leads to a similarly juicy palate – rich and long, yet fresh, it dances on the tongue. The finish is soft and it has a light structure that makes it very silky and easy to slurp down. Serve with grilled chicken.

Meerea Park The Aunts Shiraz

Quality	🍷🍷🍷🍷
Value	★★★
Grapes	shiraz
Region	Hunter Valley, NSW
Cellar	➡ 2–6
Alc./Vol.	14.0%
RRP	$26.00

The Aunts in question were three pioneering sisters who lived on the Meerea estate in the 1830s. We're not sure if they were wine drinkers.
CURRENT RELEASE 2001   This is a slightly rustic red, made in the earthy 'Hunter Burgundy' tradition. On the nose there's the smell of the soil, as well as plum and berry fruit and a light dab of vanillin oak. In the mouth it's a round, generous red of surprisingly full body. Some lightly astringent edges should soften in bottle. Try it with a mild cheese.

Meeting Place Cabernet Sauvignon

Thankfully, the vineyards in the Canberra region largely
survived the bushfires that ravaged the area recently.
CURRENT RELEASE 2000   A good style of red of the
sort only the big makers can manage. While it's not
strongly cabernet varietal, it's still very agreeable.
The nose has blackberries, spice, a leafy minty touch
and some well-measured vanillin oak. The palate is
designed for easy drinking young, with smooth fruit
flavour and soft tannins. A tad short in flavour, but the
price is sharp, even better when discounted. Try it with
a barbecue.

Quality	🍷🍷🍷🍷
Value	★★★
Grapes	cabernet sauvignon
Region	Canberra, ACT;
	Hilltops, NSW
Cellar	🍾 2
Alc./Vol.	12.5%
RRP	$14.95 🍾

Melaleuca Grove Cabernet Sauvignon

Jeff and Anne Wright's 2000 vintage Melaleuca
Grove wines come from Yea, which is beyond the
Yarra Valley. Some of the initial wines were a bit
problematic, but things are improving.
CURRENT RELEASE 2000   This middle-of-the-road
cabernet has already been around for a while, which
probably shows just how hard it is to flog new wines
in a market saturated with boutique labels. The nose
has briary blackcurrant aromas of middling intensity
and pure varietal personality, and the palate is clean
and tasty with a touch of toasty oak at the end and
balanced tannins. Try it with a North Chinese
lamb dish.

Quality	🍷🍷🍷🍷
Value	★★★★★
Grapes	cabernet sauvignon
Region	Yea Valley, Vic.
Cellar	🍾 3
Alc./Vol.	13.0%
RRP	$19.00

Metala Original Plantings Shiraz

This black label Metala is based on the 1891 plantings of
shiraz in the Metala vineyard at Langhorne Creek. There's
history in the label too: its typeface and design were
originally used on early bottlings of Metala, in the 1950s.
CURRENT RELEASE 2000   A wine of typical Langhorne
Creek concentration with a very ripe nose of raisiny fruit,
blackberries, wood smoke, mocha and sweet oak. It
tastes powerful with lots of dense fruit, a rich chewy
texture, and plenty of charry oak flavours. It has good
length and a ripe backbone of tannins. Serve it with a
charred rib of beef.

Quality	🍷🍷🍷🍷
Value	★★★
Grapes	shiraz
Region	Langhorne Creek,
	SA
Cellar	➻ 1–10
Alc./Vol.	14.5%
RRP	$49.50

Milford Pinot Noir

Quality 🍷🍷🍷🍷🍷
Value ★★★★½
Grapes pinot noir
Region Coal Valley, Tas.
Cellar 4+
Alc./Vol. 13.0%
RRP $22.00

How small can a commercial vineyard be? Well, this one has been just 1 hectare (3000 vines) since Charlie Lewis planted it in 1985. Maker: Andrew Hood.

CURRENT RELEASE 2001 A gold medal winner at the 2003 Tasmanian Regional Wine Show, this has a deep red–purple hue and is a pretty big wine for a Tassie pinot. The aromas display marked oak, with a touch of mint gracing dark cherry and plum aromas. It's very full on the palate, with a high impact attack, and needs food to come into its own. An excellent pinot of structure and power. It would suit roast duck.

Miramar Eljamar Shiraz

Quality 🍷🍷🍷🍷
Value ★★★★½
Grapes shiraz
Region Mudgee, NSW
Cellar 8
Alc./Vol. 13.5%
RRP $19.00 (cellar door)

Ian McRae has made a very handy wine off three-year-old vines in a new vineyard at Mudgee. It has less oak influence than his regular Mudgee shiraz.

CURRENT RELEASE 2001 This little baby, screw-capped for freshness, is very youthful and boisterous. It has a vibrant purple–red colour and smells of sweet, plummy, ripe shiraz fruit. There are hints of clove and cinnamon. The oak is low-key and the tannins are fine-grained but drying on the finish, typical of Mudgee shiraz. It has intensity and elegance. A very promising start. Try it with barbecued steak.

Miramar Mudgee Shiraz

Quality 🍷🍷🍷🍷½
Value ★★★★★
Grapes shiraz
Region Mudgee, NSW
Cellar 3–20+
Alc./Vol. 13.0%
RRP $19.00 (cellar door)

The shiraz vines that made this wine are 25-year-olds. In a bold, brave move, Ian McRae has bottled all his latest release of wines under screw-caps.

CURRENT RELEASE 2001 This is a very immature, raw and somewhat aggro youngster, but with time (especially under the screw-cap) it should bring rich rewards. It has a very expressive aroma of plum and spices, bayleaf and nutmeg to the fore, with a hint of dried banana. There is noticeable oak and also some lively acidity. Tannins are well-managed and in balance. As a cellaring proposition, this is an absolute steal! Cellar, then drink with beef casserole.

Mitchell Peppertree Vineyard Shiraz

Andrew and Jane Mitchell are keen advocates of the Stelvin-type screw-cap as a safe alternative to cork. With many other Clare Valley vignerons, they started sealing riesling this way; the shiraz followed.
CURRENT RELEASE 2001   Very much the deep colour of new wine, this needs breathing to bring out its latent quality. The nose has red berry shiraz fruit and a slightly reductive, earthy pong which gives it a touch of the Rhône. In the mouth it's a middling weight earthy shiraz with raspberryish fruit, little perceptible oak and soft tannins. Try it with Chinese braised duck and shitake mushrooms.

Quality	♟ ♟ ♟ ♟
Value	★ ★ ★ ⁜
Grapes	shiraz
Region	Clare Valley, SA
Cellar	▮ 6+
Alc./Vol.	14.0%
RRP	$25.00 ▮ ⧖

Mitchelton Blackwood Park Cabernet Sauvignon

The Blackwood Park name, originally reserved for Mitchelton's rieslings, has now been expanded to include red wines like this one.
CURRENT RELEASE 1999   This middle of the road red has a clean and attractive nose of mixed berries, chocolate and mint with a notable touch of sweet oak. The palate is medium in body with attractive ripe fruit and oak flavours, a savoury touch and a firm dry finish. Serve with lamb cutlets with lemon and thyme.

Quality	♟ ♟ ♟ ♟
Value	★ ★ ★
Grapes	cabernet sauvignon
Region	not stated
Cellar	▮ 3
Alc./Vol.	13.5%
RRP	$17.00

Mitchelton Crescent Shiraz Mourvèdre Grenache

The Rhône blend of shiraz, grenache and mourvèdre could just as readily be called the Australian blend – it has a very long history in this country. Mitchelton's version is a modern interpretation.
CURRENT RELEASE 2001   Bright colour is a good introduction here and it smells spicy and fresh with earth, berry and mint aromas. The palate has good texture and medium intensity. It's a savoury, easy-drinking red with relatively light tannins. Not really a Côtes-du-Rhône style but it fulfils the same purpose of honest, tasty drinking without fuss. Try it with wild mushroom tarts.

Quality	♟ ♟ ♟ ♟
Value	★ ★ ★
Grapes	shiraz; mourvèdre; grenache
Region	Goulburn Valley, Vic.
Cellar	▮ 3
Alc./Vol.	13.5%
RRP	$24.00

Mitchelton Print Shiraz

Quality	🍷🍷🍷🍷◗
Value	★★★
Grapes	shiraz
Region	Goulburn Valley, Vic.
Cellar	🍷 6
Alc./Vol.	14.0%
RRP	$50.00

We used to look forward to each new Print to see what etching or lithograph was on the label, via the Mitchelton Print Award. Now the labels seem standardised with Tim Jones's 'In Woo's Wood', originally printed on the 1992 vintage.
CURRENT RELEASE 1999   Mitchelton's top shiraz is a satisfying, powerful red with a ripe nose of syrupy blackberry and plum. There's notable sweet oak there as well, giving a rich chocolatey dimension. The palate is ripe and tasty with a smooth, full-bodied feel, full of dark fruit and toasty oak. It finishes long with fine tannins. Serve it with veal shanks.

Moorooduc Estate The Moorooduc Wild Yeast Pinot Noir

Quality	🍷🍷🍷🍷◗
Value	★★★
Grapes	pinot noir
Region	Mornington Peninsula, Vic.
Cellar	🍷 4
Alc./Vol.	13.5%
RRP	$60.00

Wild yeast starts fermentation spontaneously in many European vineyards, but it's still a pretty radical concept in Australia. Practitioner numbers are growing, however, and it's now standard procedure at Moorooduc Estate.
CURRENT RELEASE 2001   This opens up shy and reserved but grows in stature as it rests in the glass. Its nose captures some of the mystery of pinot noir with aromatic woodsy smells, and suggestions of plum and game. In the mouth it has a silky, long palate of medium concentration and complex flavour. Good acidity keeps it fresh and it finishes long and slightly firm. Try it with mushroom risotto.

Moorooduc Estate Wild Yeast Pinot Noir

Quality	🍷🍷🍷🍷
Value	★★★
Grapes	pinot noir
Region	Mornington Peninsula, Vic.
Cellar	🍷 3
Alc./Vol.	13.5%
RRP	$36.00

There's a great deal of winemaking expertise and experience on the Mornington Peninsula these days. What was once a hobbyist's wine region has got serious and wines like Moorooduc Estate show how it's done.
CURRENT RELEASE 2001   A typically pale Moorooduc pinot with a foresty, complex nose. There's some strawberryish fruit in the middle and a briary touch. The palate tracks the nose well with harmonious flavours of well-integrated fruit and lightly cedary oak that are soft and friendly. The finish is long and gentle. A more-ish understated pinot to sip with a platter of smallgoods and charcuterie.

Mount Broke River Bank Shiraz

Here's yet another new brand from the Hunter. The labels are a striking orange sash and the quality inside is very encouraging. The McNamaras began planting their 9.5-hectare vineyard in 1997 and already the rewards are rolling in. The wines are contract-made.

CURRENT RELEASE 2000 A big, ripe red that has loads of everything we like in Hunter shiraz. The earthy, savoury nose shows some development and there are plum and cherry aromas too, joined by mushroom, aniseed and spice characters. Mercifully, it's not oaky and the palate is chunky with ample smooth tannins. Plenty of yum factor here! Try roast lamb.

Quality	🍷🍷🍷🍷🍷
Value	★★★★
Grapes	shiraz
Region	Hunter Valley, NSW
Cellar	8+
Alc./Vol.	14.0%
RRP	$30.00 (cellar door)

Mount Horrocks Cabernet Merlot

Stephanie Toole has bitten the bullet and put her reds in screw-capped bottles. Mount Horrocks wines will henceforth always be of uniformly high quality. We applaud her.

CURRENT RELEASE 2001 Even though it's an absolute infant, this shares the refinement that's such a mark of the Mount Horrocks red wines. The nose has plum and blackcurrant aromas of succulent purity, clothed in restrained French oak. In the mouth it's silky smooth and long, with real elegance of flavour and structure. Try it with a Korean barbecue.

Quality	🍷🍷🍷🍷½
Value	★★★½
Grapes	cabernet sauvignon 90%; merlot 10%
Region	Clare Valley, SA
Cellar	2–6
Alc./Vol.	14.0%
RRP	$38.50

Mount Horrocks Shiraz

Quality	🍷🍷🍷🍷
Value	★★★
Grapes	shiraz
Region	Clare Valley, SA
Cellar	🍾 3
Alc./Vol.	13.5%
RRP	$38.00

Red wines from Mount Horrocks are among the Clare Valley's most stylish, made with elegance rather than sheer power in mind. Maker: Stephanie Toole.

CURRENT RELEASE 2000   Inky-purple colour indicates some depth and intensity here, but the nose, though attractive, hasn't the substance of some previous vintages. It has black cherry, blackberry and spice aromas with a restrained robe of oak behind. In the mouth it's easy in texture, but less plump than usual, with medium body and rather astringent sinewy tannins. This should develop more satisfying softness with a couple of years' bottle age. Try it with a minute steak.

Quality	🍷🍷🍷🍷🍷
Value	★★★⯪
Grapes	shiraz
Region	Clare Valley, SA
Cellar	➲ 1–5+
Alc./Vol.	14.0%
RRP	$38.00 🥂

CURRENT RELEASE 2001   Deep, glass-staining colour looks just right, and the nose has sumptuous black-cherry fruit, a dab of mint and subtle oak. It has impact, but it comes from a different school to the big tough shiraz that is often seen as archetypically Clare. This has a smooth velvety palate that is supple and long-flavoured with soft, layered tannins underneath. An understated Clare shiraz of real style. A screw-cap too. Try it with fillet of beef.

Mount Mary Quintet

Quality	🍷🍷🍷🍷🍷
Value	★★★⯪
Grapes	cabernet sauvignon; merlot; cabernet franc; malbec; petit verdot
Region	Yarra Valley, Vic.
Cellar	➲ 2–15+
Alc./Vol.	12.2%
RRP	$82.50 (cellar door)

John Middleton makes reds for drinking, not for wine shows. In blind tastings they don't always rise to the very top, but drink a glass or two with appropriate food, and they really shine.
Previous outstanding vintages: '78, '79, '80, '84, '88, '90, '91, '94, '95, '96, '97, '98, '99
CURRENT RELEASE 2000   What a delicious, refined, elegant red wine! It is the product of a vineyard where the vines are in balance, and the grapes are properly ripe without excessive levels of alcohol. It has a fine purplish hue and smells of leafy blackcurrants and meaty, cedary touches. It's light- to medium-bodied, subtle, tautly structured and intense. It has superb balance and lingers well after you swallow. It goes well with aged parmesan cheese.

Mount Trio Pinot Noir

The Mount Trio vineyard of Gavin Berry and Gill Graham occupies a hillside with the rugged Porongorups behind and a panoramic view over the distant Stirling ranges in front. Lovely vineyard country. CURRENT RELEASE 2001   This pinot sits on the edge of ripeness, not exactly green but close. The nose has cherry and plum fruit aromas, along with touches of stewed tomato, leaves, stems and foresty notes. It's better in the mouth, with medium intensity and wild flavours that are clean and slightly tart with acidity. It finishes long and earthy with an edge of bitterness. Try it with sautéed chicken livers.

Quality	🍷🍷🍷
Value	★★★
Grapes	pinot noir
Region	Great Southern, WA
Cellar	🍾 3
Alc./Vol.	13.0%
RRP	$17.90

Mr Riggs Shiraz

Mr Riggs is ex-Wirra Wirra winemaker Mr Ben Riggs. We're pleased to see wine from someone who respects formalities that are sadly lacking in this first-names-only world. We hear that there is a Señor Riggs Tempranillo and a Monsieur Riggs Viognier in the wings. CURRENT RELEASE 2001   A wine of scandalously informal personality. The nose has sweet ripe red and blackberry aromas that are improperly succulent, some McLaren Vale 'earth' and a whiff of licorice. The palate is open with jammy, dense berry flavour and fine tannins. Oak keeps a respectful measure of quiet throughout. Try roast beef.

Quality	🍷🍷🍷🍷
Value	★★★
Grapes	shiraz
Region	McLaren Vale, SA
Cellar	🍾 8
Alc./Vol.	14.5%
RRP	$38.00

Munari Cabernet

The Munari winery is homey and uncomplicated, and the wines are tasty regional styles of good balance. Makers: Adrian and Deborah Munari. CURRENT RELEASE 2001   There's a lot of interest in this typically central Victorian cabernet. The nose has a blackcurrant fruit aroma that's fresh and bracing. Minty/herbal and foresty notes add dimension, as does nicely integrated cedary oak. In the mouth it's not as powerful as some Heathcote reds – not necessarily a bad thing. It has good intensity and balance, middling weight, and an attractive mouth-feel, finishing with ripe tannins. Good with roast lamb.

Quality	🍷🍷🍷🍷
Value	★★★⸱
Grapes	cabernet sauvignon; cabernet franc
Region	Heathcote, Vic.
Cellar	➶ 2–6
Alc./Vol.	13.9%
RRP	$34.00

Munari Schoolhouse Red

Quality	♀♀♀♀
Value	★★★
Grapes	shiraz; cabernet sauvignon
Region	Bendigo & Heathcote, Vic.
Cellar	➥ 1–5
Alc./Vol.	15.0%
RRP	$38.00

The Munari vineyard is on the corner of the Northern Highway and Schoolhouse Lane, hence the name. CURRENT RELEASE 2001   Regional characters come to the fore in Munari reds, making them savoury and full of interest. This blend smells ripely of dark berries and plums with plenty of minty, gum-tree-like touches folded in. The dense palate has good concentration with quite lush black fruit flavours that are long and tangy. Ripe, well-balanced tannins support it nicely. Serve it with a grill of mixed meats.

Ninth Island Pinot Noir

Quality	♀♀♀♀
Value	★★★★
Grapes	pinot noir
Region	Pipers River, Tas.
Cellar	▮ 3
Alc./Vol.	13.5%
RRP	$23.20

Ninth Island is the second label of Pipers Brook, and it's their lowest priced of several pinots, designed to drink young. Makers: Rene Bezemer and Misha Taylor. CURRENT RELEASE 2002   This looks to be the best Ninth Island pinot yet, and they've been getting better year by year. It has a deepish red–purple colour and is fruit-driven, with lovely plum and cherry aromas, delicious sweet fruit in the mouth, excellent style and balance. Drink young with boudin blanc.

Noon Winery Eclipse

Quality	♀♀♀♀
Value	★★★★⁺
Grapes	grenache; shiraz
Region	McLaren Vale, SA
Cellar	▮ 5
Alc./Vol.	15.8%
RRP	$20.00 (cellar door)

Some of the Noon wines have names that play on the family surname. There's a Solaire reserve grenache, as well as this Eclipse grenache shiraz blend. The prices are extraordinarily reasonable considering the acclaim and demand. That means the wines are exceedingly difficult to get. Maker: Drew Noon. CURRENT RELEASE 2001   The colour of this overripe, jammy wine is a dense dark purple–red. The bouquet reminds of dusty earth, straw and cured hay, together with oaky and sweet raspberry jam aromas. It's generously flavoured and opulent, a real in-your-face, gutsy wine. It could go with hearty sausages and mustard sauce.

Noon Winery One Night Rosé

One night what? Well, we suspect Drew Noon is leaving that up to your imaginations. Perhaps the next sales pitch for rosé should be 'the wine of passion'.
CURRENT RELEASE 2002   This is at the big end of town for rosé style. It has a hot-pink, light purple–red colour and smells sweetly cherry-jammy and very ripe. It's simple but clean and good. The alcohol warmth combines with the acid to give a slight burn across the tongue. A very unusual style. You could try it with a tomatoey frittata.

Quality	🍷🍷🍷
Value	★★★
Grapes	not stated
Region	McLaren Vale, SA
Cellar	🍷 1
Alc./Vol.	13.5%
RRP	$15.00 (cellar door)

Noon Winery Reserve Shiraz

Drew Noon was the state oenologist in Victoria before he headed to McLaren Vale to take over the family wine business. While in Victoria he helped the Summerfields get on track. You can see a similarity in style here.
CURRENT RELEASE 2001   At 15.8 per cent alcohol, the label helpfully informs us, the bottle contains 9.3 standard drinks! This is a dense, syrupy red wine that's strictly for lovers of unfortified port. With flavours of plum essence, licorice and aniseed, this huge, thick wine has eye-watering density and concentration, and we wonder if it will ever mellow. It's soaked up a lot of oak and you can taste the sunshine! It's not a food-friendly style, but you could try spicy sausages and tomato sauce.

Quality	🍷🍷🍷🍷
Value	★★★★
Grapes	shiraz
Region	McLaren Vale, SA
Cellar	➡ 2–6+
Alc./Vol.	15.8%
RRP	$20.00 (cellar door)

Noon Winery Solaire Reserve Grenache

This grenache bears a closer resemblance to Italian Amarone than most Australian reds. So does the alcohol which, we assume, is all natural. Only one barrel was made.
CURRENT RELEASE 2001   The colour is a developing red–brick red of moderate depth and it smells bizarre! It's herbal, sweetly jammy, floral and has some earthy development. There is some residual sugar and some tannin, while it's not as big and sweet as vintage port, nor as tannic. It tastes like a young, high alcohol (but unfortified) sweet red that's had time in older barrels. Probably best drunk with a creamy blue cheese.

Quality	🍷🍷🍷🍷
Value	★★★★
Grapes	grenache
Region	McLaren Vale, SA
Cellar	🍷 5+
Alc./Vol.	17.2%
RRP	$21.00 (500 ml)
	(cellar door)

Normans Chais Clarendon Shiraz

Quality	♟ ♟ ♟ ♟
Value	★ ★ ★ ♪
Grapes	shiraz
Region	Barossa Valley & McLaren Vale, SA
Cellar	▣ 8+
Alc./Vol.	14.5%
RRP	$35.00 ▣

Normans is now part of the public company Xanadu Wines. The Normans winery at Clarendon has been renamed Xanadu Clarendon Winery. Maker: Rebecca Kennedy.

CURRENT RELEASE 1999   Here's another entrant in the mine's-bigger-than-yours stakes. It has lots of guts, and plenty of flavour but is very much on the oaky side. The bouquet has mulchy, earthy and timber smells, burnt-toasty and cedary. In the mouth it's drying and savoury, from substantial barrel maturation. It will have plenty of fans. Best served with barbecued meats.

Nugan Estate Manuka Grove Vineyard Durif

Quality	♟ ♟ ♟ ♪
Value	★ ★ ★
Grapes	durif
Region	Riverina, NSW
Cellar	▣ 4
Alc./Vol.	13.5%
RRP	$25.00

No wonder there's a baffling array of new labels every year. Not only are there more than 100 new producers – many of them have more than one brand. The Nugans also have Cookoothama.

CURRENT RELEASE 2001   The colour is a tad light, but it's a pleasant light- to medium-bodied red, with some smoky, charry oak aromas, and simple cherry and vanilla flavours. It's a clean, bright fruit wine without much complexity, and is soft enough to drink well young, with a game and mushroom risotto.

Oakridge Yarra Valley Cabernet Merlot

Quality	♟ ♟ ♟ ♪
Value	★ ★ ★
Grapes	cabernet sauvignon; merlot
Region	Yarra Valley, Vic.
Cellar	▣ 3
Alc./Vol.	13.0%
RRP	$20.75

Oakridge is now owned by the energetic Evans & Tate wine company of Western Australia, giving them a handy foothold in the Yarra Valley.

CURRENT RELEASE 2000   A Yarra cabernet that veers more towards the herbal spectrum than the sweetly ripe end of the scale. The nose has aromas of mulberries, blackcurrants and definite mocha-vanillin oak. In the mouth it's clean and fresh-tasting, but marginally simple, finishing in quite astringent tannins. Try it with Lebanese lamb pastries.

Orlando Jacob's Creek Grenache Shiraz

Jacob's Creek is an actual stream in the Barossa Valley, and the site of the first commercial vineyard in the region, planted in 1847. Today's Jacob's Creek wines come from much further afield.

CURRENT RELEASE 2002   You have to love grenache to enjoy this. It has a sweet raspberry jam-like nose and some hints of licorice and savoury earthiness that are typically grenache-varietal. The palate has medium depth and ripe, juicy flavour that has notable fruit sweetness. A savoury touch stops it being too syrupy in the mouth and soft tannins keep it easy to glug down. Serve with a good meat pie.

Quality	♟♟♟
Value	★★★
Grapes	grenache; shiraz
Region	various, SA
Cellar	1
Alc./Vol.	13.5%
RRP	$11.00 Ⓢ

Orlando Jacob's Creek Shiraz Cabernet

In just over 25 years, Jacob's Creek has become one of the English-speaking world's favourite wine brands. Today it's sold in over 65 countries and demand just keeps growing.

CURRENT RELEASE 2001   This is the wine that launched the Jacob's Creek success story and it's not hard to see why. It's a tasty combination of ripe, dark berry aromas with a savoury touch of earthiness and a clever dab of sweet oak. In the mouth the 2001 seems a little more substantial than some recent editions, with ripe fruit, chewy texture and soft tannins. Just the thing for pasta.

Quality	♟♟♟♟
Value	★★★★
Grapes	shiraz; cabernet sauvignon
Region	various, SA
Cellar	2
Alc./Vol.	13.5%
RRP	$11.00 Ⓢ

Orlando Lawson's Shiraz

Surprisingly, Orlando's flagship shiraz isn't sourced from the vineyards of the company's Barossa heartland but from Padthaway in the south of South Australia. It's always a big, powerful wine.

CURRENT RELEASE 1997   At six years of age the colour is still youthful. The nose is very ripe and powerful with aromas of mint, blackberries and spices. Sweet vanillin oak makes a big contribution, and the palate follows suit in big flavoury manner with choc-minty black fruit, spicy oak and gripping tannins. Only just emerging from infancy, this has a long life ahead of it. Cellar, then serve it with fillet of beef.

Quality	♟♟♟♟
Value	★★★
Grapes	shiraz
Region	Padthaway, SA
Cellar	2–10
Alc./Vol.	13.5%
RRP	$55.00

Orlando St Hugo Cabernet Sauvignon

Quality	❦❦❦❦❦
Value	★★★★
Grapes	cabernet sauvignon
Region	Coonawarra, SA
Cellar	➛ 1–10
Alc./Vol.	13.5%
RRP	$36.00

Show St Hugo to the smartypants who thinks large wineries only make dull homogenised red wines. They just might be convinced otherwise.
Previous outstanding vintages: '88, '90, '91,'92, '94, '96, '98
CURRENT RELEASE 1999   There's real class to the '99 St Hugo. The bouquet is clean and intense with a tang of mint emphasising its fresh blackcurrant and savoury black olive aromas. High-toned cedary oak is worked in with skill to season rather than dominate. The middleweight palate is intensely flavoured, and it has the satiny texture of good ripe Coonawarra cabernet. Fine-grained tannins are in perfect balance. A tasty companion to pink-roasted racks of lamb.

Palandri Aurora WA Cabernet Sauvignon

Quality	❦❦❦❦
Value	★★★➍
Grapes	cabernet sauvignon
Region	Great Southern & Margaret River, WA
Cellar	▮ 4
Alc./Vol.	14.0%
RRP	$15.00 ⑤

Ironically, co-founder Robert Palandri, who gave his name to this bold and expansionary venture in Margaret River, is no longer involved – save as a shareholder.
CURRENT RELEASE 2001   The wine has very good colour; it's a rich medium–deep red–purple, and is dominated in its youth by somewhat chippy oak aromas. The palate is quite drying and there's some astringency from oak and tannin. It needs more fruit to be well balanced. A reasonable wine at the price. Serve with chargrilled hamburgers.

Palandri Baldivis Estate Cabernet Merlot

Quality	❦❦❦❦
Value	★★★★
Grapes	cabernet sauvignon; merlot
Region	not specified, WA
Cellar	▮ 4
Alc./Vol.	13.5%
RRP	$12.00 ⑤

The Palandri juggernaut bought the Kailis family's Baldivis Estate on Western Australia's south-west coastal plain, and rolled it into Palandri Wines. The prices seemed to tumble and it's not clear if all the fruit is from Baldivis or not.
CURRENT RELEASE 2001   At this price, probably no one bothers about where the grapes were grown. It's very good value for money. There's a lot of clean, bright, berry flavour and there's some sweetness to begin with, then an unexpectedly firm tannin finish. It has a little residual sugar. A bold flavoured, stroppy young red, which would suit barbecued chops and sausages.

Palandri Shiraz

Palandri is a bold, brash new venture in Western
Australia, and the recipient of much negativity from
established producers. It planted like crazy, with 350
hectares in the Great Southern, including WA's largest
single-vineyard development.
CURRENT RELEASE 2001   This is a pleasant surprise.
A youthful purple in hue, it smells of sweet ripe berry
jam – arguably a tad overripe. It has excellent weight
and intensity in the mouth, with clean ripe fruit, again
bordering on jammy, and finishing with firm tannins.
It's chewy and concentrated – a style many red drinkers
love. Time should improve it further. It goes with grilled
venison cutlets.

Quality	▯▯▯▯▮
Value	★★★★
Grapes	shiraz
Region	Margaret River, WA
Cellar	▬ 1–8+
Alc./Vol.	14.5%
RRP	$25.00

Palandri WA Merlot

It's hard to miss the deep-etched Palandri label, with its
bright colour coding and gecko lizard winding around
the bottle. Maker: Tony Carapetis.
CURRENT RELEASE 2001   This is very young and bold,
with a deep blood-red colour and an assertive gumleaf/
mint aroma that will divide tasters. There are mulberry
flavours too, and it has plenty of body and youthful aggro,
with a somewhat astringent aftergrip. It could mellow
given more time, but there is a slight streak of greenness
running through it. Cellar, then try serving it with veal.

Quality	▯▯▯▮
Value	★★★
Grapes	merlot
Region	various, WA
Cellar	▬ 1–5+
Alc./Vol.	14.0%
RRP	$27.00 Ⓢ

Panorama Pinot Noir

Michael Vishacki joined the wine industry just eight
years ago, when he and his wife Sharon bought this
established vineyard. But he's a quick learner, has
rapidly risen to the highest levels of Tasmania's wine
industry and is also valued as a contract winemaker
and viticulturist.
CURRENT RELEASE 2001   This has some of the
opulent, super-ripe fruit flavours of Panorama's
spectacular 2000 and '98 vintages, although there's
a serious acid kick in the finish. Plum, chocolate and
vanilla aromas are very appealing, and there's plenty
of fruit sweetness in the mouth. Try it with roast
saddle of hare.

Quality	▯▯▯▯
Value	★★★⬦
Grapes	pinot noir
Region	Huon Valley, Tas.
Cellar	▮ 3+
Alc./Vol.	13.8%
RRP	$39.00

Paringa Estate Pinot Noir

Quality	🍷🍷🍷🍷🍷
Value	★★★★
Grapes	pinot noir
Region	Mornington Peninsula, Vic.
Cellar	🍶 5
Alc./Vol.	14.5%
RRP	$52.00

The McCalls of Paringa have a superb vineyard site on a steep, north-facing hill. It acts as a suntrap and at the same time is sheltered from what can be damaging weather from Bass Strait.
Previous outstanding vintages: '97, '98, '00
CURRENT RELEASE 2001   This is yet another sensational wine from Paringa. Quite deeply coloured, it has an arresting bouquet of black cherry with some meaty and sousbois undertones, complex and not overtly oaky, rich and fruit-sweet on the tongue. A feature is its lovely balance and harmony in the mouth; a succulent pinot that has it all. It suits Peking duck.

Parker Estate Terra Rossa First Growth

Quality	🍷🍷🍷🍷🍷
Value	★★★
Grapes	cabernet sauvignon; merlot
Region	Coonawarra, SA
Cellar	🍶 15
Alc./Vol.	14.0%
RRP	$82.00 🍶 (cellar door)

John Parker, who started Hungerford Hill and later Parker Estate, died in late 2002 after a long illness. He was one of the lesser-known key players in the wine industry over the last 40 years. Maker: Peter Bissell.
CURRENT RELEASE 2000   The 2000 fully supports the lofty reputation of this grandly named red. It's a lovely ripe, concentrated, supremely elegant blend which speaks clearly of the region and the grape varieties used. The nose is vibrant blackberry with a hint of jam; the palate contains masses of sweet ripe cabernet fruit, with fine tannins and great persistence. Majestic stuff. Serve it with roast beef.

Parker Estate Terra Rossa Merlot

Quality	🍷🍷🍷🍷🍷
Value	★★★★⁹
Grapes	merlot
Region	Coonawarra, SA
Cellar	➡ 2–10+
Alc./Vol.	13.5%
RRP	$45.00 🍶

This 500-case wine was offered mainly to mailing list customers and through restaurants. Made by Peter Bissell at Balnaves.
CURRENT RELEASE 2000   This is a great merlot! It has lashings of sweet, ripe blackberry fruit, with an echo of cabernet not unusual in pure merlots, together with lots of dusty oak. The taste is full-bodied, intense and vibrant, with sumptuous fruit-sweetness and fleshy mouth-feel. It needs time, and would go best with rare steak.

Peerick Vineyard Merlot

This is Peerick's first merlot, made from vines planted in 1991. Its makers, Chris and Merryl Jessup, reckon it's made in a fuller, firmer style than most merlots.
CURRENT RELEASE 2000   The 14.5 per cent alcohol and high ripeness are reflected in the thick legs that run down the glass and the slightly oily viscosity of this wine. It's a dense, thick, slightly hefty warm-area style with a savoury, earthy, oak-infused bouquet and a drying, slightly oaky taste. There's plenty of tannin on the finish and it is a firmer style. It needs food: try kangaroo fillets.

Quality	♟♟♟♟
Value	★★★
Grapes	merlot
Region	Pyrenees, Vic.
Cellar	🍷 3
Alc./Vol.	14.5%
RRP	$28.00 ⓢ

Penfolds Bin 28 Kalimna Shiraz

This wine is something of an institution, being first made in 1962. The 2000 vintage was not an easy one, with extremes of heat and rain, and yields of the Penfolds premium reds were down.
CURRENT RELEASE 2000   The style is very Penfolds, with a particular oak character they get which, when combined with rich warm-area shiraz, develops an almost sump oily character. There are smoked-meat and reduced-stock flavours, too; with breathing the wine is not so oaky and drinks really well. It has fleshy, chewy depths and heaps of character. It goes well with game.

Quality	♟♟♟♟
Value	★★★⤙
Grapes	shiraz
Region	McLaren Vale, Barossa & Clare Valleys, Robe & Padthaway, SA
Cellar	🍷 8
Alc./Vol.	13.5%
RRP	$26.00 ⓢ

Penfolds Bin 128 Coonawarra Shiraz

This is all aged in French oak and, since the mid-1980s, more attention has been paid to picking the fruit properly ripe, resulting in a change to a fuller style, says winemaker Peter Gago.
CURRENT RELEASE 2000   The nose is quite reticent and failed to really bloom with breathing, but it's a pretty good wine all the same. There are stalky and peppery flavours and obvious oak, while the palate reveals real concentration, density and plenty of tannin. It's dry and mellow to finish, with good length and balance in that savoury, less fruity Penfolds style. Try it with braised beef.

Quality	♟♟♟♟
Value	★★★★
Grapes	shiraz
Region	Coonawarra, SA
Cellar	🍷 10+
Alc./Vol.	13.5%
RRP	$26.00 ⓢ

Penfolds Bin 138 Old Vine Shiraz Grenache Mourvèdre

Quality 🍷🍷🍷🍷
Value ★★★½
Grapes shiraz; grenache; mourvèdre
Region Barossa Valley, SA
Cellar 4+
Alc./Vol. 14.0%
RRP $26.00 (S)

The grape composition of this Rhône blend varies according to the season. This was aged for 17 months in used American and French oak, so it's not overtly oaky.
CURRENT RELEASE 2001 The colour is bright purplish and it has a savoury, wood-matured character with some herbal and spicy, earthy shiraz flavours leading the way. It opens up with breathing into a rich, fleshy, almost chunky red wine with some meat-stocky complexity as opposed to simple grapey fruit flavour. It would suit lamb's fry and bacon.

Penfolds Bin 407 Cabernet Sauvignon

Quality 🍷🍷🍷🍷½
Value ★★★★
Grapes cabernet sauvignon
Region Coonawarra, Bordertown & McLaren Vale, SA & Margaret River, WA
Cellar 10+
Alc./Vol. 13.5%
RRP $30.00 (S)

The company line is that this wine was inspired by Bin 707 Cabernet, and invented by former chief winemaker John Duval in response to a freer availability of cabernet grapes in 1990.
CURRENT RELEASE 2000 This is a very fine Aussie cabernet, showing raspberry and cassis fruit backed by leather, walnut and cedar overtones from oak maturation. The palate is lively and firm with plenty of tannin giving density, authority and grip. It will cellar well and cope with hearty food, such as beef wellington.

Penfolds Grange

Quality 🍷🍷🍷🍷🍷
Value ★★
Grapes shiraz 97%; cabernet sauvignon 3%
Region Barossa Valley, Padthaway & Magill, SA
Cellar 4–30+
Alc./Vol. 14.5%
RRP $400+

Proof that wine has transcended the realm of mere drink and become a collector's item, the hoo-haa surrounding the release of this stellar 1998 Grange eclipsed even that of the 1990. Chief winemaker for this vintage was John Duval. Peter Gago took over late 2002.
Previous outstanding vintages: '53, '55, '62, '63, '66, '71, '72, '76, '80, '83, '86, '88, '90, '91, '94, '96
CURRENT RELEASE 1998 Undoubtedly one of the greatest Granges, this magnificent, majestic red fully justifies the attention, if not the price. Aromas of mixed spices, plums, toasted nuts and vanilla vault from the glass. It has a sensational nose! Flavour is nigh on perfect too. The fruit ripeness is outstanding, and it has extraordinary depth and backbone, muscularity and concentration. Nothing seems out of place. In a word: balance. A fabulous wine with a great future. The best aged cheddar, here.

Penfolds Rawson's Retreat Cabernet Sauvignon

Rawson's is Southcorp's great white hope to boost sales of Penfolds branded products about three-fold. It's been launched in the US, where it is hoped the major growth will come.
CURRENT RELEASE 2002   The colour is excellent: medium–deep red–purple, and it has definite cabernet overtones, with mulberry, gamy, leafy and mulchy characters. In the mouth, there's no shortage of flavour and style. There is some extractive bitterness on the finish, but the wine has good weight and length. Good value. It goes with shish kebabs.

Quality	♥♥♥♥
Value	★★★★
Grapes	cabernet sauvignon
Region	various, SA
Cellar	🍷 4
Alc./Vol.	14.0%
RRP	$12.40 ⑤

Penfolds St Henri Shiraz

This wine was first produced at the now-defunct Auldana winery in the Adelaide foothills in the late nineteenth century, and the name and label were resurrected in the 1950s by senior Penfolds winemaker John Davoren. It's one of Penfolds' most famous wines.
CURRENT RELEASE 1998   This deep, plush, concentrated, ample red is lovely to drink now, but will mature into one of the great St Henris. The nose has developing plummy, earthy, foresty smells with minty vegetal/spicy nuances. The palate is big and full for a St Henri, with lashings of tannin that will help it age. It needs food now: try it with chargrilled T-bone steak.

Quality	♥♥♥♥♥
Value	★★★★
Grapes	shiraz
Region	various, SA
Cellar	🍷 15+
Alc./Vol.	14.0%
RRP	$50.00 (375 ml: $30.00) 🍾

Penfolds Thomas Hyland Cabernet Sauvignon

Thomas Hyland married Georgina Penfold, daughter of the founder, Christopher Rawson Penfold, and helped build the fledgling wine company into the empire it became. Maker: John Duval and team.
CURRENT RELEASE 2001   Minty, raspberry, American oak-lifted aromas are the main event here, with talc and green leaf aspects. There's a thread of greenness in the wine coupled with oak. The finish is slightly astringent. It needs food to soften it: you could try chorizo sausages.

Quality	♥♥♥♥
Value	★★★★
Grapes	cabernet sauvignon
Region	Robe, Coonawarra, Padthaway & Bordertown, SA
Cellar	🍷 4
Alc./Vol.	13.5%
RRP	$20.00 ⑤

Penfolds Thomas Hyland Shiraz

Quality	🍷🍷🍷🍷
Value	★★★★⟩
Grapes	shiraz
Region	McLaren Vale, Barossa Valley & Padthaway, SA
Cellar	🍷 7
Alc./Vol.	14.0%
RRP	$20.00 ⑤

Southcorp intends to double, even treble, the output of Penfolds branded wines. This new brand is positioned between Koonunga and the Bin range.
CURRENT RELEASE 2001   A very fine debut! This has good depth of colour and plenty of weight and flavour. It's a medium- to full-bodied, typically savoury Penfolds red with mild oak input, emphasising more the peppery, spicy, vegetal and cherry-plum fruit characters. Pleasingly concentrated, with excellent balance and drinkability. This hits the spot. Try hard cheeses.

Penley Estate Hyland Shiraz

Quality	🍷🍷🍷🍷🍷
Value	★★★★★
Grapes	shiraz
Region	Coonawarra, SA
Cellar	🍷 13+
Alc./Vol.	13.5%
RRP	$20.70

Kym Tolley probably has more right than Southcorp to the Hyland name, since he is a direct descendant of Thomas Hyland and the Penfold-Hyland brothers who built Penfolds into such a great company. Yet Southcorp is now marketing a Thomas Hyland brand . . .
CURRENT RELEASE 2001   A brilliant shiraz, showcasing the world-famous Coonawarra elegance and style. It has excellent deep purple–red colour, and a beautifully balanced, young sweet-berry aroma, in which cherry, plum and blackberry mingle with discreet oak giving subtle cedar, floral, fresh-turned earth and a multitude of other beguiling perfumes. The texture is smooth and fleshy with plenty of tannin that's ripe and supple. A marvellous drink with roast leg of lamb.

Penley Estate Phoenix Cabernet Sauvignon

Quality	🍷🍷🍷🍷🍷
Value	★★★★★
Grapes	cabernet sauvignon
Region	Coonawarra, SA
Cellar	🍷 7
Alc./Vol.	13.5%
RRP	$23.30

This won three major trophies at the 2003 Royal Sydney Wine Show, no surprise when you consider chairman Brian Croser likes to champion elegant reds.
Previous outstanding vintage: '00
CURRENT RELEASE 2001   A serious red wine – and seriously great value! The fruit tastes ripe and rich, with oak discernible but tucked neatly into the background, where it should stay. There are some nice toasty overtones. It's quite savoury in the mouth, elegant and medium-bodied, and there's enough acidity to keep the palate lively and refreshing. It's already quite complex, too. Drink with pink lamb loin.

Penley Estate Shiraz Cabernet

Kym Tolley's red wines have been moving steadily upwards in quality over the past decade or so. The sub-$30 reds are reliably good value and in our view offer some of the best, and most elegant, drinking reds in Coonawarra.

CURRENT RELEASE 2000   The colour is rich and purplish; the bouquet is likewise rich, complex and beef-stocky, with plenty of oak presence but this is well-handled. It's smooth and fleshy on the palate and well balanced despite plenty of oak. Cedar cigar-box flavours and ripe, grainy tannins are long and lovely. A delicious drink, especially with pink lamb chops.

Quality	♥♥♥♥♥
Value	★★★★→
Grapes	shiraz; cabernet sauvignon
Region	Coonawarra, SA
Cellar	🍷 10+
Alc./Vol.	14.0%
RRP	$29.00

Penmara Five Families Cabernet Franc

Penmara is a puzzling new brand: wines from the Orange district generally cost a lot more, mostly because the production costs are fairly high.

CURRENT RELEASE 2001   It's hard to know why anyone persists with trying to make good wine from cabernet franc, let alone a new outfit in a cool climate! It's not a high percentage punt! This has a good young colour but smells mulchy and vegetal and tastes fairly hard and acidic. There are some feral characters, too. It would be best served with food: try a beef and vegetable casserole.

Quality	♥♥♥
Value	★★→
Grapes	cabernet franc
Region	Orange, NSW
Cellar	🍷 1
Alc./Vol.	14.0%
RRP	$14.00

Penny's Hill Shiraz

The vineyard is 44 hectares and the wines are made under contract by Ben Riggs, while David Paxton looks after the viticulture: a very professional team.

CURRENT RELEASE 2000   This is a big, smooth dark-berry flavoured shiraz and thoroughly typical of the region. It has some vegetal and spicy overtones, too; the palate is fruit-sweet and the ripeness level verges on jammy. It's big and bold in the mouth with a generous tannin finish. It would suit chargrilled kangaroo.

Quality	♥♥♥♥♥
Value	★★★★
Grapes	shiraz
Region	McLaren Vale, SA
Cellar	🍷 7
Alc./Vol.	14.5%
RRP	$28.00

Penny's Hill Specialised

Quality	♥♥♥♪
Value	★★★
Grapes	shiraz 41%; cabernet sauvignon 32%; merlot 27%
Region	McLaren Vale, SA
Cellar	🍾 5
Alc./Vol.	14.0%
RRP	$26.00

Sure, it's an odd name for a wine, but at least it's original. Both this wine and the shiraz won blue–gold awards in the 2003 Sydney International Wine Competition, and the shiraz got into the Top 100. CURRENT RELEASE 2000   It's often hard to tell cabernet from shiraz in McLaren Vale, especially when they get the grapes so ripe. This has an interesting blend of spicy shiraz and vegetal/leafy cabernet-type aromas, together with raspberry. There's green-leafy cabernet character and it finishes much leaner than the shiraz. Good for roast lamb and mint sauce.

Pepperjack Barossa Cabernet Sauvignon

Quality	♥♥♥♪
Value	★★★
Grapes	cabernet sauvignon
Region	Barossa Valley, SA
Cellar	🍾 4
Alc./Vol.	13.5%
RRP	$22.00 Ⓢ

Another semi-new brand from the sprawling Beringer Blass empire. The wines are made by Saltram winemaker Nigel Dolan at the new Bilyara winery in the Barossa. CURRENT RELEASE 2000   The stalky, herbal, minty aromas remind us that 2000 wasn't a great Barossa vintage. Cabernet is a choosy critter in the Barossa, too, and is far less consistent than shiraz. The wine lacks intensity and is a bit hollow in the middle. It finishes with a twist of tannin. It could go with moussaka.

Petaluma Coonawarra

Quality	♥♥♥♥♥
Value	★★★★♪
Grapes	cabernet sauvignon 50%; merlot 50%
Region	Coonawarra, SA
Cellar	🍾 20+
Alc./Vol.	14.0%
RRP	$58.00 🍾

In 2002, founder Brian Croser conducted 20-year vertical tastings of this wine, proving how well it ages and how the style has evolved into a consistently richer, riper wine without sacrificing its essential elegance. *Previous outstanding vintages: '79, '82, '86, '88, '90, '91, '92, '95, '97, '98, '99*

CURRENT RELEASE 2000   This is the first vintage where the merlot component hasn't been substantially less than the cabernet. It's a wine of great concentration, a blackish purple hue with extraordinary intensity of complex blackberry, blackcurrant, dark-chocolate, vanilla and gunsmoke aromas. A little atypical, being so full-bodied and packed, but this is a very great wine with a huge future. Serve with aged reggiano cheese.

PENGUIN BEST RED WINE & BEST CABERNET SAUVIGNON/ CABERNET BLEND

Peter Lehmann Clancy's Classic Red

This has long been a decent value for money, easy-drinking red, although it's no longer pure Barossa Valley fruit.

CURRENT RELEASE 2001   Sweet, almost overripe raspberry fruit aromas get you in the mood, and it doesn't disappoint in the mouth. It's a tidy, well-balanced red with plenty of sweet fruit on palate and the weight is medium-bodied. It finishes with a lick of tannin but is soft enough to drink well young. Serve with roast pork.

Quality	♟♟♟♟
Value	★★★★
Grapes	shiraz; cabernet sauvignon; merlot; cabernet franc
Region	various, SA
Cellar	▮ 4
Alc./Vol.	13.5%
RRP	$15.70 Ⓢ

Peter Lehmann Eight Songs Shiraz

This is an alter ego to Stonewell, created out of a desire to do something completely different with the fruit that didn't quite measure up to Stonewell specifications, and finish it off with French rather than American oak.

CURRENT RELEASE 1999   The vivid purple–red colour is startling. This is a finer wine than Stonewell, but still big and powerful with lots of toasty, smoky vanilla and cedar oak-infused complexities. It has more backbone than Stonewell, a kind of linear structure with very good balance and length. It would suit Barossa mettwurst.

Quality	♟♟♟♟♟
Value	★★★⁂
Grapes	shiraz
Region	Barossa Valley, SA
Cellar	▮ 6+
Alc./Vol.	14.0%
RRP	$49.70 ▮

Peter Lehmann Mentor

Peter Lehmann has mentored so many people in the Barossa over his long life there, and chief winemaker Andrew Wigan figures high on the list.

CURRENT RELEASE 1998   This is an ace red wine, certainly the best Mentor we've ever tasted. 1998 was a good year for cabernet, and the wine retains its deep, dense colour even at five years old. Ideal fruit ripeness, a trace of varietal herbs and mint, plus rich sweet ripe berries and lashings of vanillin oak. Fruit, wood and development combine in a lovely dark chocolate character. It's smooth, fleshy and concentrated and has tremendous texture. A top wine. Serve it with steak and kidney pie.

Quality	♟♟♟♟♟
Value	★★★★⁂
Grapes	cabernet sauvignon 70%; malbec 15%; shiraz 15%
Region	Barossa Valley, SA
Cellar	▮ 5+
Alc./Vol.	13.5%
RRP	$36.50 ▮

Peter Lehmann Stonewell Shiraz

Quality	🍷🍷🍷🍷
Value	★★★
Grapes	shiraz
Region	Barossa Valley, SA
Cellar	🍾 7+
Alc./Vol.	14.0%
RRP	$69.50 🍾

Big reds like this tend to do well in wine shows. This one has harvested gold medals at Melbourne and Sydney, and a blue–gold and Top 100 rating in the Sydney International Wine Competition.
Previous outstanding vintages: '88, '89, '91, '94, '96
CURRENT RELEASE 1997   If you like huge, dense, thick red wines and aren't afraid of oak, tannin or alcohol, this is your bag! That said, the '97 isn't as extreme as some earlier vintages. It is concentrated, rich and fruitcakey, with vanilla, plum cake, charred oak and dark chocolate flavours, but the taste is softer with a seductive smoothness. There's fruit sweetness aplenty here. It could work well with aged cheddar.

Pike & Joyce Pinot Noir

Quality	🍷🍷🍷
Value	★★⁴
Grapes	pinot noir
Region	Adelaide Hills, SA
Cellar	🍾 2
Alc./Vol.	13.5%
RRP	$28.00

The Pike family of winemaker Neil and viticulturist Andrew have linked up with the Joyces to make a crop of Adelaide Hills wines.
CURRENT RELEASE 2001   This is pinot with training wheels: it'd be a bit much to expect them to produce a great wine first-up! The colour is fairly light and advanced; the aromas reflect green, underripe grapes with a weedy, capsicum-like smell. The palate certainly has depth and weight, but it lacks ripe-fruit charm and the tannins are a bit harsh on the finish. It needs food: try pork spare ribs and plum sauce.

Pipers Brook The Lyre Pinot Noir

Quality	🍷🍷🍷⁴
Value	★★⁴
Grapes	pinot noir
Region	Pipers River, Tas.
Cellar	🍾 4+
Alc./Vol.	12.8%
RRP	$70.00

This is one of Pipers Brook's two individual vineyard pinots, and reflects the heavily extracted style that results from Andrew Pirie's pre- and post-fermentation skin maceration techniques. Only 150 dozen were made.
CURRENT RELEASE 2000   This is quite a big, solid pinot whose bouquet is, at present, dominated by toasty oak and the palate by firm tannins. There's also a hint of funkiness, and we struggle to find the fruit and pinot charm in it all. Hopefully, time will bring it all together, but we are not totally convinced. It needs food, so serve it with duck confit.

Pipers Brook Reserve Pinot Noir

To add to his list of achievements, Andrew Pirie has emerged as a pinot noir specialist. The range starts with Ninth Island, moving up to the Estate pinot, then the Reserve, and finally the two Individual Vineyard bottlings. Prices rise accordingly!

CURRENT RELEASE 2000   This 430-case wine is a good pinot in the savoury, structured Pipers style. The nose shows chocolatey, earthy, undergrowth complexities with some barnyard funkiness that seems to be controlled at this stage. It has a drying, savoury palate that borders on the rustic, and the finish is tight and firm. Best served with food: try pork spare ribs.

Quality	♥♥♥♥
Value	★★★
Grapes	pinot noir
Region	Pipers River, Tas.
Cellar	3+
Alc./Vol.	13.3%
RRP	$50.00

Plantagenet Hazard Hill Shiraz Grenache

This wine's cleverly worded back label talks about the Hazard Hill vineyard, but we are left doubting whether this wine actually comes from there: many Australian wineries indulge in a kind of doubletalk.

CURRENT RELEASE 2001   If there's a better $11 red out there at present, we'd like to see it! This is an absolute ripper. The colour is a youthful deep red-purple and it has a clean and inviting aroma of blackberry, plum, chocolate and toasty barrels. It has remarkable concentration for its price: a big, ripe, fruit-sweet palate, plus nice balance and structure. Far from being a simplistic cheapie, it has plenty of character too. Enjoy with rare roast beef.

Quality	♥♥♥♥♥
Value	★★★★★
Grapes	shiraz; grenache
Region	various, WA
Cellar	7+
Alc./Vol.	14.5%
RRP	$11.00 Ⓢ

Plantagenet Omrah WA Shiraz

It's interesting how many wineries' second-tier reds are often more enjoyable to drink than their top-priced reds. That doesn't apply at Plantagenet, whose flagship reds are excellent – it's just that the Omrah label is surprisingly good, too.

CURRENT RELEASE 2001   This is a soft, plummy, easy-drinking red that won't break the bank. It has some pruney, jammy aromas in the mix, too, and the palate is soft, fruit-sweet and nicely balanced, with gentle tannin. It would go well with a steak sandwich.

Quality	♥♥♥
Value	★★★
Grapes	shiraz
Region	various, WA
Cellar	3
Alc./Vol.	14.5%
RRP	$17.90 Ⓢ

Plunkett Reserve Shiraz

Quality	🍷🍷🍷🍷
Value	★★★
Grapes	shiraz
Region	Strathbogie Ranges, Vic.
Cellar	2–8+
Alc./Vol.	13.5%
RRP	$35.00

The Plunkett family goes back a long way in the Strathbogies, having planted their first vines in 1968. They sold grapes to major wineries for years before lashing out on their own.

CURRENT RELEASE 2001 The colour is a promising deep purple–red and it smells richly of sweet oak, peppermint and dark berries. The dominant oak gives an aromatic lift. The palate reveals some stalky, spicy and peppery cool-climate characters, coupled with a firm, slightly astringent finish that just needs time. It has depth and richness too, and should reward the patient. Cellar and then serve with aged parmesan.

Poet's Corner Shiraz Cabernet Sauvignon Cabernet Franc

Quality	🍷🍷🍷½
Value	★★★★
Grapes	shiraz; cabernet sauvignon; cabernet franc
Region	not stated
Cellar	3
Alc./Vol.	13.5%
RRP	$11.70 ($)

This deservedly popular blend is also available in 187 ml airline-type screw-capped bottles. Maker: James Manners and crew.

CURRENT RELEASE 2001 This tidy medium-weight red is smooth and finely balanced, with nutty aromas hinting at the use of some fresh oak, while the profile is streamlined and quite fine for such an affordably priced wine. It's soft and smooth for immediate drinking. It would go well with veal scaloppine.

Politini Merlot

Quality	🍷🍷🍷🍷
Value	★★★★
Grapes	merlot
Region	King Valley, Vic.
Cellar	5
Alc./Vol.	13.5%
RRP	$19.50 (cellar door)

Here's another new producer from Victoria's King Valley with a mellifluous Italian name. Good value wine, too.

CURRENT RELEASE 2000 It's a well-balanced, quite stylish wine that has some of the softness and suaveness so often promised with merlot but so rarely produced. It has a medium red–purple colour and smells tobaccoey and green-leafy, but ripe, with some lifted aromatic American oak. It's medium-bodied, smooth and fleshy with balanced tannin, and the drinkability factor is high. It goes well with calves' liver, onions and mash.

Polleters Moonambel Merlot

This is a newer name from the Pyrenees and still pretty well unknown. The wines are made by the Summerfields, who know how to turn Pyrenees grapes into good wine. They deserve a wider audience.

CURRENT RELEASE 2001   This is a big, somewhat oaky wine at present, but we suspect it has the guts to turn into a ripper with a little time in the cellar. There are coconutty American oak aromas, a trace of licorice, and the colour is deep. A big, very ripe, concentrated blockbuster that needs time, and then a mooing steak.

Quality	♟♟♟♟
Value	★★★★
Grapes	merlot
Region	Pyrenees, Vic.
Cellar	➡ 2–8
Alc./Vol.	14.5%
RRP	$25.00

Polleters Moonambel Shiraz

This Pyrenees vineyard supplies grapes to Summerfield's. The wines are made at Summerfield, and they're certainly cast in the Summerfield mould.

CURRENT RELEASE 2001   The colour is impressively deep and purplish; the aromas of concentrated plum jam, mint/anise, liquorice and almost porty fruit don't fail to impress. It's big and syrupy and has a heap of alcohol but somehow avoids hotness. Some will love this, but we wonder how you'd drink it! Try it with barbecued pork spare ribs and plum sauce.

Quality	♟♟♟♟
Value	★★★★
Grapes	shiraz
Region	Pyrenees, Vic.
Cellar	➡ 2–10+
Alc./Vol.	15.0%
RRP	$25.00

Polleters Moonambel Shiraz Merlot Cabernet Franc

The Polleters style will appeal to lovers of big, very ripe reds. They're a bit on the Robert Parker side, but it's hard to dislike their opulence.

CURRENT RELEASE 2001   The colour is, in a word, colossal. Its density is paralleled by the thick texture and full body of this wine. It has flavours of jam and blackberry syrup, with gunpowder, aniseed and gumleaf/mint overtones. An essency wine that needs cellaring. Then serve with beef ribs and hoisin sauce.

Quality	♟♟♟♟
Value	★★★★
Grapes	shiraz; merlot; cabernet franc
Region	Pyrenees, Vic.
Cellar	▮ 10
Alc./Vol.	14.5%
RRP	$25.00

Pondalowie Vineyards Shiraz

Quality	♟♟♟♟
Value	★★★
Grapes	shiraz
Region	Bendigo, Vic.
Cellar	🍷 5
Alc./Vol.	14.0%
RRP	$25.00

Keeping abreast of new vineyards is a full-time job for both authors. New labels appear to the tune of several a week; some sink without trace, others, like Pondalowie, look to have a future.

CURRENT RELEASE 2001   Pondalowie Vineyards aim to showcase grape variety and region, rather than being styled in the universal Australian way. This shiraz comes up roses on both counts. The nose has pepper, mint and blackberry fruit that's clean-smelling and full of spicy interest. Charry barrel influence is subtle and the palate has ripe spicy flavour of good intensity and persistence. Not a big wine but it has impact. Try it with fillet steak.

Preece Cabernet Sauvignon

Quality	♟♟♟
Value	★★★
Grapes	cabernet sauvignon
Region	Goulburn Valley & King Valley, Vic.
Cellar	🍷 2
Alc./Vol.	14.0%
RRP	$15.75 (S)

Colin Preece's name lives on. He was the legendary winemaker at Seppelt's Great Western in the 1940s and '50s, and helped set Mitchelton up in the '60s.

CURRENT RELEASE 2001   It's a fairly ordinary red, but at least it isn't too exxy. The colour is medium-red and it has an odd, slightly oaky, slightly camphor-like bouquet. It's lean and somewhat lacking mid-palate fruit richness. The finish rides in with firm acid and tannin, leaving a tart aftertaste. It needs food: try well-herbed rissoles.

Preece Merlot

Quality	♟♟♟
Value	★★★
Grapes	merlot
Region	King Valley & others, Vic.
Cellar	🍷 3
Alc./Vol.	13.5%
RRP	$16.50 (S)

Preece, by virtue of being part of Mitchelton, which was part of Petaluma, is now part of the Lion Nathan wine group. Whew! Who owns what is a complicated business these days.

CURRENT RELEASE 2000   This has a nice fresh red–purple colour and smells interesting – as in full of character. There are some funky, barnyard-type scents as well as bright mint and berry fruit aromas, together with some charred oak smells. The chippy oak taste is also apparent in the mouth and it finishes with a little too much astringency to drink solo. Have it with food, such as moussaka.

Preston Peak Leaf Series Merlot

This winery is located at Wyberba, in Queensland's pre-eminent wine region, the Granite Belt.

CURRENT RELEASE 2001 This unusual red has a slightly muffled bouquet which features some stalky aromas and a lemony overtone. The palate is a little hollow and lacks a bit of richness from ripe, fruit-sweet grapes. It finishes with some tannin astringency and could benefit from short-term cellaring. It would suit a gourmet hamburger.

Quality	🍷🍷🍷
Value	★★★
Grapes	merlot
Region	Granite Belt, Qld.
Cellar	4
Alc./Vol.	13.0%
RRP	$19.00

Preston Peak Reserve Shiraz

Preston Peak has about 10 hectares of vineyards at Preston and Wyberba in the Granite Belt. Winemaker is Philippa Hambleton.

CURRENT RELEASE 2000 It's an unusual wine, smelling of mulch and vegetable scents, a little roasted capsicum, and some richer, meaty notes. The palate is lean and just a little hollow, although it's soft and approachable enough. Easy current drinking, perhaps with grilled meatballs.

Quality	🍷🍷🍷
Value	★★½
Grapes	shiraz
Region	Granite Belt, Qld.
Cellar	3
Alc./Vol.	13.5%
RRP	$28.00

Primo Estate Il Briccone Shiraz Sangiovese

This is a real bitzer: a multi-breed, like the proverbial junkyard dog. While mainly shiraz and sangiovese, it also contains small amounts of barbera, nebbiolo and cabernet.

CURRENT RELEASE 2001 A departure from conventional Aussie red style, the 2001 continues the rustic style of earlier vintages. The bouquet is subdued but non-specific varietally, with chocolate, vanilla and earth aromas. The structure is chunky, viscous and fairly broad with good texture but a slight lack of 'shape'. It has an awkward finish of alcohol, oak, tannin and again that syrupy texture. Maybe it needs more time. An unusual wine: try it with oxtail.

Quality	🍷🍷🍷½
Value	★★★
Grapes	mainly shiraz & sangiovese
Region	Adelaide Plains, SA
Cellar	4
Alc./Vol.	14.0%
RRP	$23.30 (S)

Provenance Geelong Pinot Noir

Quality	♥♥♥◗
Value	★★★
Grapes	pinot noir
Region	Geelong, Vic.
Cellar	▮ 2
Alc./Vol.	13.5%
RRP	$29.00

Geelong has plenty of runs on the board as a pinot-producing region, but this falls a little short of the mark. Pinot seems very responsive to vine age, and perhaps this, like so many of its kind, was made from young vines.

CURRENT RELEASE 2001   The colour is fairly light but quite acceptable and the aromas are dominated by mint. The palate is lean and angular and lacks good pinot fleshiness. There are some firm tannins to finish. It's a fair wine that might go with minted lamb.

Provenance Geelong Shiraz

Quality	♥♥♥◗
Value	★★★
Grapes	shiraz
Region	Geelong, Vic.
Cellar	▮ 5
Alc./Vol.	13.3%
RRP	$29.00

Provenance is everything in wine, as any collector or auction-goer knows. The name of this wine, though, probably refers to the provenance of the grapes, which is of primary concern to the winemaker. His name is Scott Ireland.

CURRENT RELEASE 2001   The colour is only medium–full and the bouquet suggests black peppercorns, together with mulchy forest-floor and other vegetal cool-climate shiraz characters. The palate is correspondingly lean and light- to medium-bodied, and it has plenty of appeal as an early-drinking style. We suggest teaming it with duck, perhaps a confit.

Punt Road Cabernet Sauvignon

Quality	♥♥♥♥
Value	★★★★
Grapes	cabernet sauvignon
Region	Yarra Valley, Vic.
Cellar	▮ 4
Alc./Vol.	13.0%
RRP	$23.00 ⑤

In the 1950s, traffic was carried across Melbourne's Yarra River by punt. There were vineyards along the road at the time, long gone now. Maker: Kate Goodman.

CURRENT RELEASE 2001   So 2001 wasn't much of a cabernet year in the Yarra? Think again: this is a pretty decent drink. Chocolate, vanilla and caramel oak influences somewhat dominate the varietal fruit aromas but the wine has flavour and drinkability. It has a lively acid palate, which has some of the native austerity of cabernet, but overall is soft and easy to drink young. Try it with charred steak.

Punt Road Shiraz

The Yarrahill winery, with Kate Goodman making the wines, has turned out a bevy of lovely, user-friendly reds and whites under the new Punt Road brand. Clever name, clever wines.

CURRENT RELEASE 2001   A superb shiraz and great value for money! This is a real trimmer: elegant, medium-bodied, spicy and somewhat Rhone-ish. It has a deep purple–red hue and smells of flowers – especially violets – pepper and other spices, a trace of anise, and a hint of vegetal character all adding to its complexity. The taste is smooth and refined yet concentrated, with subtle but effective use of French oak. An utterly lovely shiraz to drink with kangaroo fillets.

Quality	🍷🍷🍷🍷🍷
Value	★★★★★
Grapes	shiraz
Region	Yarra Valley, Vic.
Cellar	🍾 6
Alc./Vol.	13.0%
RRP	$23.00 Ⓢ

Queen Adelaide Cabernet Sauvignon

Queen Adelaide Claret was once a favourite of budding execs bunging on side while watching their pennies. That was 30 years ago; since then Queen Adelaide has been on a steady slide into the bargain basement.

CURRENT RELEASE 2002   This has promising crimson colour and a nose of dark berries and earth. In common with a lot of low-priced reds, it tastes fruit-sweet and juicy. There are soft tannins and no apparent oak influence. It falls away a bit on the finish, but its ripe fruity appeal (not to mention its price tag) will make it a lot of friends. Try it with a meat pie.

Quality	🍷🍷🍷
Value	★★★★
Grapes	cabernet sauvignon
Region	not stated
Cellar	🍾 1
Alc./Vol.	13.0%
RRP	$8.25 Ⓢ

Queen Adelaide Pinot Noir

Few low-priced pinots make the cut in the *Guide* – quite justifiably, because most of them are hogwash – but occasionally we find one that has a modicum of appeal.

CURRENT RELEASE 2001   This makes you wonder where in Australia you could get pinot noir grapes at such a low price. No matter, it actually has a light, almost pinot-ish aromas of red fruits, earth and some sappy notes. The palate is simple and fruity with attractive softness and a light thread of tannin to give it structure. Try it with stir-fried noodles and barbecue pork.

Quality	🍷🍷🍷
Value	★★★★
Grapes	pinot noir
Region	not stated
Cellar	🍾 1
Alc./Vol.	12.5%
RRP	$8.25 Ⓢ

Redman Cabernet Sauvignon Merlot

Quality	♥ ♥ ♥
Value	★ ★ ★
Grapes	cabernet sauvignon; merlot
Region	Coonawarra, SA
Cellar	➟ 1–8+
Alc./Vol.	14.0%
RRP	$28.00

The Redmans have a longer continuous history of winemaking in Coonawarra than any other family; Bill Redman worked for the 'father of Coonawarra', John Riddoch, way back in the early 1900s.

CURRENT RELEASE 1999   The nose is all chocolate and vanilla, with oak very evident. The fruit is a touch lacking in vibrancy. The wine is firm and steely on the palate, with plenty of grip and lively astringency. There is some good fruit buried at the core of the wine, and it needs time to emerge and for the structure to soften. Cellar, then drink with roast lamb and mint sauce.

Redman Shiraz

Quality	♥ ♥ ♥
Value	★ ★ ★
Grapes	shiraz
Region	Coonawarra, SA
Cellar	▮ 5+
Alc./Vol.	13.5%
RRP	$17.00 ⑤

This is a famous wine, although it doesn't enjoy the exalted status it had back in the 1970s. It's a higher alcohol wine than it was back then, but seemed to lose some of its elegance and finesse as the output increased.

CURRENT RELEASE 2001   The colour is an encouraging red–purple, while the aromas are minty, cedary and perfumed from slightly raw oak. It's only light- to medium-bodied but the palate is lean and slightly green, with some astringency and austerity. Some age could be beneficial. Try it with lamb chops.

Renard Pinot Noir

Quality	♥ ♥ ♥ ♥
Value	★ ★ ★ ★
Grapes	pinot noir
Region	Mornington Peninsula, Vic.
Cellar	▮ 4+
Alc./Vol.	13.0%
RRP	$35.60

Renard is a new label coming from another ambitious new pinot producer on the Peninsula. The wine is made by the highly competent Sandro Mosele at Kooyong, and you can see the resemblance to his own wines.

CURRENT RELEASE 2001   It's a biggie! The colour is deep and the palate carries a lot of tannin and a hint of bitterness towards the back. Because of this, it needs to be drunk with food, such as roast pork loin. The aromas bring lovely pinot scents of black cherry, sap and a discreet hint of mint. It has good concentration and oodles of character, but we wonder if those tannins will soften gracefully.

Reschke Empyrean Cabernet Sauvignon

The Reschke Coonawarra reds got people talking last year, mostly due to the $100 price tag. The 1998 wine was very good, but with the subsequent '99 and 2000 wines there is no question; they simply aren't worth anywhere near a hundred smackers.

CURRENT RELEASE 1999   A good mid-range Coonawarra cabernet nose of blackcurrant, earth, peppermint and cedar is a pleasant introduction. In the mouth it's attractively put together, with lightish medium body, good fruit intensity and freshness, and well-balanced drying tannins. Like most cabernets it's a good accompaniment to lamb.

Quality	♱ ♱ ♱ ♱
Value	✶ ⟩
Grapes	cabernet sauvignon
Region	Coonawarra, SA
Cellar	▋ 4
Alc./Vol.	13.8%
RRP	$100.00

CURRENT RELEASE 2000   This young cabernet smells appetising with cassis, mint and subtle cedary oak in nice balance. The palate disappoints a bit. It has lightish medium body, good length and direct cabernet flavour, but it gives a slightly desiccated impression – dried out and lacking depth and power. Tannins are relatively soft. Serve it with lamb leg steaks.

Quality	♱ ♱ ♱ ♱
Value	✶ ⟩
Grapes	cabernet sauvignon
Region	Coonawarra, SA
Cellar	▋ 4
Alc./Vol.	12.9%
RRP	$100.00

Reynolds of Orange Marble Man Merlot

Reynolds is a company that had a mid-life metamorphosis, moving from the Upper Hunter to Orange, where Jon Reynolds is chief winemaker at the spanking new Cabonne winery, now named Reynolds.
CURRENT RELEASE 2000   This wine opens with a touch of meaty pong, which clears to reveal appealing vanilla and chocolate aromas, which translate to a soft and fruit-sweet palate. It's fairly light and has a trace of vegetal character, with acid and tannin firming the finish. It's a decent effort from a difficult vintage. Try it with veal and mushrooms in a creamy sauce.

Quality	♱ ♱ ♱ ♰
Value	✶ ✶ ✶
Grapes	merlot
Region	Orange, NSW
Cellar	▋ 4
Alc./Vol.	13.5%
RRP	$29.00

Reynolds The Jezebel Orange Cabernet Sauvignon

Quality	♟ ♟ ♟
Value	★ ★ ⁴
Grapes	cabernet sauvignon
Region	Orange, NSW
Cellar	⬤ 3
Alc./Vol.	13.5%
RRP	$29.00

At the time of going to press, the Reynolds Wine Company was in all sorts of bother with the Australian Securities and Investments Commission, and its shares were suspended from trading. Watch this space . . .
CURRENT RELEASE 2000   From a difficult vintage in the Orange region, this is a light, acidic kind of cabernet that shows the lack of richness and ripe flavour often encountered in cool-climate, cool-year cabernet. The aromas are oaky and earthy and the finish is a little short. It could suit vegetarian lasagna.

Richmond Grove Barossa Vineyards Shiraz

Quality	♟ ♟ ♟ ♟
Value	★ ★ ★ ⁴
Grapes	shiraz
Region	Barossa Valley, SA
Cellar	⬤ 6
Alc./Vol.	14.0%
RRP	$21.00 ⑤

The home of Richmond Grove Barossa is the former Chateau Leonay at Tanunda, where Leo Buring plied his trade for so long in the first half of the twentieth century.
CURRENT RELEASE 2000   Oak plays a big part in this solid Barossa red. It has a big, toasty-barrel, chocolate and vanilla nose, with a sidenote of hay bales, and is soft, rich and round in the mouth, with plenty of persistence. A crowd-pleaser. Try it with barbecued hamburgers.

Richmond Grove Coonawarra Cabernet Sauvignon

Quality	♟ ♟ ♟ ♟
Value	★ ★ ★ ★
Grapes	cabernet sauvignon
Region	Coonawarra, SA
Cellar	⬤ 6
Alc./Vol.	13.0%
RRP	$21.00 ⑤

Richmond Grove is just a brand these days, and a brand that is best known for riesling. But that doesn't stop the Orlando group from turning out very good-value reds as well.
CURRENT RELEASE 2000   Dusty, straw, earthy and tobacco-like aromas are savoury as opposed to grapey, while the palate is lean of profile and medium-bodied. It's a red with balance and style, well tailored to early drinking. It would suit beef sausages baked in tomato.

Riddoch Cabernet Merlot

This is the second label of Katnook Estate, and not for the first time we fancy we see a once-reliable brand slipping because of the use of substandard grapes. CURRENT RELEASE 2000   The aromas are mulchy, vegetal and weird – a bit too much green bean for us. In keeping with the nose, the palate is hollow and weedy, lacking concentration and ripe fruit sweetness. It finishes with dominant acid. Best serve it with a greasy hamburger.

Quality	🍷🍷🥂
Value	★★
Grapes	cabernet sauvignon; merlot
Region	Coonawarra, SA
Cellar	🍷 2
Alc./Vol.	13.0%
RRP	$20.00 Ⓢ

Riverina Estate Kanga's Leap Shiraz

The Sergi family's Riverina Estate is one of the most active creators of new brands – every time we open the mail, there's a new label! No doubt they have a lot of wine to sell. Maker: Sam Trimboli. CURRENT RELEASE 2002   This is a very light, simple, apparently unwooded quaffer. The colour is light, it has a simple raspberry-cordial grapey aroma, and it's light, soft and easy to drink. It tastes a touch sweet and has little tannin. Ribena flavours dominate the palate. Serve at a smoky barbecue.

Quality	🍷🍷🍷
Value	★★★♪
Grapes	shiraz
Region	Riverina, NSW
Cellar	🍷 2
Alc./Vol.	13.5%
RRP	$9.00 Ⓢ

Robert Stein Reserve Shiraz

Robert Stein is descended from Johann Stein, who was brought out to Australia to tend the Macarthur family's Camden vineyards in 1838. Stein's wines are grown, made and bottled on the property. Maker: Michael Slater. CURRENT RELEASE 2001   This is remarkably approachable for a reserve-level Mudgee shiraz. It smells of roasted nuts, toasty barrels, chocolate and fruitcake, all of which are translated to the elegant, finely structured but intense palate. There are some ginger and spice flavours and the acid is noticeable at this stage. It goes well with aged parmesan cheese.

Quality	🍷🍷🍷🍷🥂
Value	★★★★
Grapes	shiraz
Region	Mudgee, NSW
Cellar	🍷 10+
Alc./Vol.	13.5%
RRP	$27.50 🍾
	(cellar door)

Rosabrook Estate Reserve Cabernets

Quality	♟♟♟♟
Value	★★★⅃
Grapes	cabernet sauvignon; cabernet franc; merlot
Region	Margaret River, WA
Cellar	➥ 2–15+
Alc./Vol.	15.0%
RRP	$39.75

Many of Western Australia's vineyards have the word 'brook' in their names. It's local parlance for a stream or small river.

CURRENT RELEASE 2001   This is just a babe, and has a very deep red–purple colour and a raw young aroma of grapey berries and cassis. It's very ripe and there's some slightly unintegrated oak plus subtle hints of mint and herb. The tannins are fine and powdery. It's a good wine but needs a year or two in a dark place. Then drink it with a meaty casserole.

Rosabrook Shiraz

Quality	♟♟♟♟
Value	★★★⅃
Grapes	shiraz
Region	Margaret River, WA
Cellar	➥ 2–8+
Alc./Vol.	13.5%
RRP	$24.40

Serious Margaret River reds need time, which is why it's a bit of a concern to us to see such wines as this coming onto the market at around 18–20 months old. They need to be cellared.

CURRENT RELEASE 2001   This is not a huge wine: it's medium-bodied, but it is quite firm and grippy and just a tad formidable. The nose offers sweet plummy, grapey, pepper/spicy scents, and in the mouth it has lots of spicy oaky tannins, peppery fruit and a little toughness. The structure is taut and linear. Cellar, then serve with aged cheddar.

Rosemount Cabernet Merlot

Quality	♟♟♟♟
Value	★★★★
Grapes	cabernet sauvignon; merlot
Region	not stated
Cellar	▮ 3
Alc./Vol.	14.0%
RRP	$11.70 Ⓢ

With cheap, early-release reds such as this, Rosemount has a reputation as a pioneer in the new trend of micro-oxygenation. This means bubbling small amounts of air through the wine to mature its tannins, and is very helpful for removing green or unripe flavours.

CURRENT RELEASE 2002   The colour is very sound and the aromas are young and grapey, mulberry and cherry, together with chocolate and vanilla hints of oak. It's clean and fruity to taste, with some firm tannins that give just a hint of bitterness. Young and simple at present, it's good value and would go with a veal chop.

Rosemount Estate Traditional

What's traditional about this wine? We suspect it's just a brand with a past: Nick (Shottesbrooke) Holmes started it when he worked at Ryecroft many moons past, and the name has lingered while just about everything around it has changed many times over.

CURRENT RELEASE 2000   A typical Rosemount wine – quite oaky, minty, almost palpably sweet in the mouth, and sort of contrived-tasting. It does have good depth and weight in its favour, and the sweet-oak/very ripe fruit style has plenty of fans. It's an easy wine to enjoy and has lots of gold medals to its credit. Try it with aged cheddar.

Quality	♟ ♟ ♟ ♟
Value	★ ★ ★ ★
Grapes	cabernet sauvignon; merlot; petit verdot
Region	McLaren Vale, SA
Cellar	▬ 5
Alc./Vol.	13.5%
RRP	$25.00 Ⓢ

Rosemount Hill of Gold Cabernet Sauvignon

Poor Mudgee has had a horror run of vintages lately. 2001 isn't too bad, but 2000 was a shocker and (at time of press) it looks like rain and flooding may have affected 2003.

CURRENT RELEASE 2001   Remarkably soft for a Mudgee red, which means you can drink it young. It has a youthful looking colour and a lean, cool-climate style of bouquet, with leafy edges and marked cabernet varietal character, despite its 14 per cent alcohol. The background oak is nicely handled and the profile is lean but not thin, elegant and suave. It has length, if not richness. Pair it with grilled veal cutlets.

Quality	♟ ♟ ♟ ♟
Value	★ ★ ★ ┥
Grapes	cabernet sauvignon
Region	Mudgee, NSW
Cellar	▬ 5+
Alc./Vol.	14.0%
RRP	$20.00

Rosemount Orange Vineyard Merlot

The Orange district should be well suited to merlot, as it's a cool-climate variety that tends to ripen properly when its mate, cabernet sauvignon, may have difficulty. Maker: Philip Shaw and team.

CURRENT RELEASE 2000   This is a lovely smooth, light- to medium-bodied red which drinks really well now and has no pretensions to greatness. It's fine value for money. The aromas are of soft, ripe, rich plum and sweet berries. Oak is in the background. It's elegantly structured, with mild, soft tannins and drinks well now with ripe brie-style cheeses.

Quality	♟ ♟ ♟ ♟
Value	★ ★ ★ ┥
Grapes	merlot
Region	Orange, NSW
Cellar	▬ 4+
Alc./Vol.	13.5%
RRP	$33.00 Ⓢ

Rosemount Orange Vineyard Shiraz

Quality	🍷🍷🍷🍷
Value	***
Grapes	shiraz
Region	Orange, NSW
Cellar	🍾 4
Alc./Vol.	14.0%
RRP	$33.00

This won two trophies, including one for best red wine, at the National Wine Show in Canberra, in late 2002. That's a victory for elegant reds over the blockbusters, but does it really have enough intensity for such a high accolade?

CURRENT RELEASE 2000 The wine opens with leafy, slightly green fruit aromas and breathes to reveal more peppery fruit. It is light- to medium-bodied, soft and easygoing, and is starting to show some developed secondary flavours. It is a trifle lean and lacks a bit in power and length, but it is a very attractive early drinker. You could serve it with veal saltimbocca.

Rosemount Shiraz Cabernet

Quality	🍷🍷🍷🍷½
Value	****
Grapes	shiraz; cabernet sauvignon
Region	not stated
Cellar	🍾 3
Alc./Vol.	14.5%
RRP	$11.70 (S)

This split-diamond label blend often carries off the trophy for best light-bodied red in the big wine shows. That's because it's always soft and fruity and drinks well young. Maker: Philip Shaw.

CURRENT RELEASE 2002 This won a trophy at the Perth Wine Show in 2002, so we hope it was actually finished and bottled at the time. It has a deepish red–purple hue and smells a dead ringer for a Beaujolais, due to a carbonic maceration character. The taste is soft and easy, with plenty of weight, but it doesn't lack drinkability. The softness is helped along by a big whack of residual sugar. It could go with sausages and sweet chilli sauce.

Rosevears Estate Rosé

Quality	🍷🍷🍷
Value	***
Grapes	pinot noir
Region	West Tamar, Tas.
Cellar	🍾 1
Alc./Vol.	14.0%
RRP	$21.00

Careful of that alcohol! This is not a gulping style of rosé. It's made from pinot noir, which is almost expected of a Tasmanian rosé, and the winemaker was Shane McKerrow.

CURRENT RELEASE 2001 The colour is a medium–light salmon pink, with orange tinges reflecting its age. The bouquet reveals some development, with dry grass/straw aromas prevailing. There is a trace of spirity alcohol also. It finishes dry, with a trace of hardness, possibly from the alcohol. It really needs food. Try it with tuna steaks.

Rothbury Estate Neil McGuigan Series Merlot

Neil McGuigan, an accomplished Hunter winemaker, moved to Rothbury as chief winemaker when Beringer Blass bought both Rothbury and Briar Ridge, where he was working at the time.
CURRENT RELEASE 2001   Garden mint, crushed vine leaves, and red berries figure in the aromas here. It tastes lean and lively on the tongue, as opposed to rich and fleshy, and there's a little tannin firmness on the finish. There's a thread of greenness in the wine. It's a pleasant drink, probably not with a big future, though. Try it with vitello tonnato.

Quality	♟♟♟♟
Value	★★★✦
Grapes	merlot
Region	Hunter Valley, NSW
Cellar	♦ 4
Alc./Vol.	12.5%
RRP	$20.00

Rouge Homme Shiraz Cabernet

Rouge Homme is still a Southcorp brand, although the winery of that name has been sold and winemaker Paul Gordon has moved on, to Leconfield.
CURRENT RELEASE 2000   This is very good red wine for the price. It's soft and easy to enjoy young, smelling of dark red berries and a subtle veneer of charry oak, while the palate is generously fruity with sweet, ripe blackberry flavour. It's finely balanced and more-ish, and would suit a grilled pork chop.

Quality	♟♟♟♟
Value	★★★★✦
Grapes	shiraz; cabernet sauvignon
Region	Coonawarra, SA
Cellar	♦ 5
Alc./Vol.	13.5%
RRP	$15.60 ⑤

Rymill Cabernet Sauvignon

Winemaker John Innes is not afraid of lining his reds up for the press, along with competing wines that he admires. He's done it with his cabernets and last year with his shirazes. Brave stuff!
CURRENT RELEASE 1999   They've done us a favour by holding the wine back for nearly four years, by which time it's developed its colour a little, and acquired a dusty, toasty, savoury bouquet and flavour. The palate is elegant and cedar/cigar-boxy, with a tight, dry, 'claret' structure and a long finish with persuasive, fine-grained tannin. It has the structure to age, and to go with hearty main courses like beef wellington.

Quality	♟♟♟♟♟
Value	★★★★
Grapes	cabernet sauvignon
Region	Coonawarra, SA
Cellar	♦ 6+
Alc./Vol.	14.5%
RRP	$28.50 ♟

Rymill MC2

Quality	🍷🍷🍷❘
Value	★★★
Grapes	cabernet sauvignon; merlot; cabernet franc
Region	Coonawarra, SA
Cellar	🍷 3
Alc./Vol.	13.5%
RRP	$19.00

It's almost e = mc², a sure-fire formula for success. If you're in the dark as to what it means, check the grape composition here. Maker: John Innes.

CURRENT RELEASE 2000   A highly aromatic red blend, which seems to be lifted by some American oak. It smells minty, leafy and vanillin with a hint of green bean. Its structure is lean, slightly hollow and a little strong on the green-leafy flavour spectrum. It would be best served with food, such as minted roast lamb.

Rymill Shiraz

Quality	🍷🍷🍷🍷
Value	★★★⟩
Grapes	shiraz
Region	Coonawarra, SA
Cellar	🍷 6+
Alc./Vol.	14.0%
RRP	$23.00

The Rymill label carries the winery's symbol, a pair of rampant racehorses, taken from a bronze sculpture that's proudly displayed in the cellar door area. Maker: John Innes.

CURRENT RELEASE 2000   The hallmarks of the Rymill style are evident here, in the wine's savoury mellowness and lack of obvious oak or bold simple fruit. There's a subtle hint of mint/anise, and the palate is dry and linear with abundant smooth tannin. It has the structure to go well with food, and suits osso buco.

Saddler's Creek Single Vineyard Hunter Shiraz

Quality	🍷🍷🍷🍷
Value	★★⟩
Grapes	shiraz
Region	Hunter Valley, NSW
Cellar	➤ 2–7+
Alc./Vol.	14.5%
RRP	$58.00 (cellar door)

The grapes were hand-picked off the Herlstone vineyard, which John Johnstone says is a non-irrigated low-yielding vineyard which produces very intensely flavoured grapes.

CURRENT RELEASE 2000   You need to like oak to enjoy these wines: they are very oaky, and this one is so despite the news that the barrels were all one year old. It has good colour and weight, but the pervading aroma and flavour is of toasty, charred oak and the tannins also taste woody. Perhaps age will bring it into balance but you'd need to be an optimist. It's a good wine of its style. Try it with charred barbecued sausages.

Saltram Cabernet Sauvignon

This is Saltram's 'no frills' label, reserved for everyday wines that are always sharply priced.

CURRENT RELEASE 2002   Bright colour is a good sign here, and the nose has pleasant aromas of raspberry and blackcurrant. A whisper of smoky oak is hiding in the background. In the mouth it has direct berry and currant flavour of medium intensity, finishing in soft tannins. Not a wine for contemplation, this is one to slurp down at a rowdy barbecue.

Quality	🍷🍷🍷
Value	★★★⯪
Grapes	cabernet sauvignon
Region	not stated
Cellar	🍷 2
Alc./Vol.	13.0%
RRP	$10.00 Ⓢ

Sandalford Cabernet Sauvignon

Sandalford Cabernet Sauvignon is made from 30-year-old vines at Willyabrup in the heart of the best Margaret River cabernet country.

CURRENT RELEASE 2001   This is a savoury young Margaret River cabernet, maybe not in the top league, but very attractive. On the nose there's a blackcurrant pastille aroma that's succulent and appetising, along with a light minty touch. Oak makes a casual entrance hereabouts but it knows it shouldn't intrude. The palate is middling in body with tangy fruit and a subtle thread of cedary oak. Everything is in equilibrium and dry tannins provide good flavour balance. Try this with roast lamb.

Quality	🍷🍷🍷🍷
Value	★★★⯪
Grapes	cabernet sauvignon
Region	Margaret River, WA
Cellar	🍷 5
Alc./Vol.	13.5%
RRP	$27.50

Sandalford Merlot

Winemakers in Western Australia's Great Southern region put great store in merlot. So far results have been mixed, but as vine age increases and regional expertise improves, the wines are starting to look very good indeed.

CURRENT RELEASE 2001   Unlike a lot of merlots, this actually *tastes* like a merlot. The nose combines the plum and berry fruit aromas, floral touches and earthy leafiness of merlot with hints of spicy oak. It tastes softly of plum with attractively smooth mouth-feel and a nicely poised background of powdery dry tannins. Works well with pasta and veal and tomato ragu sauce.

Quality	🍷🍷🍷🍷
Value	★★★⯪
Grapes	merlot
Region	Frankland River, WA
Cellar	⊂ 1–5
Alc./Vol.	13.5%
RRP	$22.50

Sandhurst Ridge Shiraz

Quality	▼▼▼▼
Value	★★★
Grapes	shiraz
Region	Bendigo, Vic.
Cellar	🍷 5
Alc./Vol.	14.0%
RRP	$36.00

Bendigo was a significant wine region 150 years ago, and now it has returned with a vengeance. The area's shiraz is one of the new Australian classics, and things can only get better.

CURRENT RELEASE 2000   Not as overtly regional as some of the very minty reds of Bendigo, this has a medium-intensity nose with some briary and cedary aromas that are nicely savoury. Some plummy fruit is there too, but it's restrained. The palate is clean and dry with middling intensity and a catchy thread of ripe yet savoury fruit through it. Tannins are well integrated and oak is subdued. Try it with some saltbush lamb.

Schild Estate Shiraz

Quality	▼▼▼▼
Value	★★★
Grapes	shiraz
Region	Barossa Valley, SA
Cellar	🍷 3
Alc./Vol.	14.0%
RRP	$24.00

The Schilds have followed a growing trend for long-established grape growers to start having part of their production contract-made and sold under their own label.

CURRENT RELEASE 2001   The colour suggests a little more maturity than most 2001 reds. On the nose it has a dry, old-fashioned feel with some chocolate and stewed raspberry aromas and notable oak influence. The palate is simple and pleasant, with the sort of desiccated fruit flavour that was once more common than it is now, finishing in dry tannins. It suits a mixed grill.

Scotchmans Hill Pinot Noir

Quality	▼▼▼▼
Value	★★★
Grapes	pinot noir
Region	Geelong, Vic.
Cellar	🍷 1
Alc./Vol.	13.5%
RRP	$29.80

One of Australia's best known pinot noirs, Scotchmans Hill is a favourite with the restaurant crowd for its soft, easy-drinking personality.

CURRENT RELEASE 2001   There's no doubting the softness and easy nature of this pinot with its raspberry and plum fruit, and it has hints of those gamy, earthy things that make pinot noir so intriguing. There's also a slight soapiness that may betray an elevated pH. It feels silky in the mouth and there's some gamy richness mid-palate, ahead of a soft finish. A wine to drink in the flush of youth, perhaps with some Chinese barbecued pork.

Seppelt Chalambar Shiraz

The Seppelt Chalambar name rings plenty of bells with the authors. Not only have we enjoyed some pretty good old bottles of it over the years, but the first bottle of wine RK-P ever 'cellared' was an old 1962 Chalambar he stashed in his bedroom cupboard as a teenager.
CURRENT RELEASE 2000   This is a step up from the '99 Chalambar. It's a generously proportioned red with deep colour and a lush, fruit-sweet nose of loganberry, sweet spices and dusty oak. It tastes smooth and complete with ripe spiced berry flavours and a dry undertone of fine-grained tannins. Try it with kofta kebabs.

Quality	♥♥♥♥♥
Value	★★★★★
Grapes	shiraz
Region	various, Vic.
Cellar	🍾 5
Alc./Vol.	13.0%
RRP	$23.00

Seppelt St Peters Shiraz

This was once Great Western Shiraz, one of Australia's great classics. Now 'Great Western' is in small print, marginalising one of Australia's great wine names . . . we think 'Great Western' should dominate the label in bold type.
CURRENT RELEASE 1999   This continues to be a very honest regional red of distinction and class. It has a restrained nose of spice, earth, raspberry and seasoned leather. In the mouth it's harmonious, long and smooth. Other reds demand more attention at first, this one grows on you gradually . . . then suddenly the bottle's empty and you're opening another! Try it with braised veal shanks.

Quality	♥♥♥♥♥
Value	★★★★
Grapes	shiraz
Region	Great Western, Vic.
Cellar	🍾 10
Alc./Vol.	14.0%
RRP	$40.00

Seppelt Victorian Premium Reserve Cabernet Sauvignon

Seppelt's Victorian Premium Reserve wines are blended from various vineyards across Victoria's wide range of regions. No state in the Commonwealth would have as diverse a range of vineyard climates.
CURRENT RELEASE 2000   A dense appearance introduces a well-built cabernet. The nose has real impact with ripely spicy black plum and blackcurrant aromas and a savoury veneer of sweet oak. In the mouth it has attractive concentration of fruit but it's quite fine in texture and flavour at the same time. It finishes with civilised dry tannins. A good wine to sip with roast lamb.

Quality	♥♥♥♥
Value	★★★★⧫
Grapes	cabernet sauvignon
Region	various, Vic.
Cellar	🍾 4
Alc./Vol.	13.0%
RRP	$17.00 ⑤

Seppelt Victorian Premium Reserve Shiraz

Quality	🍷🍷🍷🍷
Value	★★★★★
Grapes	shiraz
Region	various, Vic.
Cellar	🍾 5
Alc./Vol.	13.0%
RRP	$17.00 ⑤

The revamp of the Seppelt range under the Rosemount/ Southcorp regime was intended to streamline what was perceived as a confused Seppelt identity. We might be thick, but we reckon it's harder to work out where everything fits now than ever before.
CURRENT RELEASE 2000   For a junior version of Seppelt's great Victorian red range, this is really very good. The colour is dark and the nose has good concentration of berries, spice and licorice, even a floral touch. Oak is sympathetically used and the palate is densely packed, yet not heavy, with deep berry flavours of good persistence resting on fine-grained tannins. Serve it with a charry steak.

Settlers Rise Reserve Shiraz

Quality	🍷🍷🍷🍷
Value	★★★
Grapes	shiraz
Region	coastal Qld.
Cellar	🍾 2
Alc./Vol.	13.5%
RRP	$26.50

The label on this bottle has a little chart that takes all the work out of tasting it. It details its fullness of body, delicacy, oak, crispness, relative complexity and dryness, and so on.
CURRENT RELEASE 2000   A complex nose features aromas of black fruits, light spice, smoky tobacco and reasonably powerful dusty, toasty oak. The wood is strong on the palate too, stopping just short of overwhelming some juicy berry flavour in the middle. It's medium-bodied and dry in tannins with good persistence of flavour. Try it with little fillet steaks quickly seared on the barbecue.

Shane Warne Collection Cabernet Sauvignon Merlot Petit Verdot

Quality	🍷🍷🍷🍷
Value	★★★↓
Grapes	cabernet sauvignon; merlot; petit verdot
Region	Murray Valley, Vic.
Cellar	🍾 2
Alc./Vol.	14.0%
RRP	$14.95

The Warne family and the Forbes family who own Zilzie Wines have long been friends, and this wine has grown out of their relationship. A percentage of all sales will go towards the Shane Warne Foundation's charitable works.
CURRENT RELEASE 2002   Youthfully ruby in colour, this has raspberry, plum and a hint of licorice on the nose. The impression is of ripe sweetness with little or no oak input. In the mouth it's nothing cerebral or highbrow, just soft, juicy, easy-drinking red wine, soft in tannins, relaxed in demeanour. Drink it chilled when the heat's on at the 'Gabba, the 'Gee, or the WACA. Good with a gourmet burger.

Shelmerdine Heathcote Shiraz

The Shelmerdine family has been linked with Victoria's wine industry for many years as vineyard pioneers, wine producers, industry promoters, and good company over a glass or two of the product. This new range of wines looks promising.

CURRENT RELEASE 2001   There's a deceptive sort of intensity here – it's not a whopper, but it is quite concentrated in character. The nose has blackberry and spice, hints of licorice and prune, and commendably unobtrusive cedary oak. In the mouth it's smooth and fine-textured, well balanced and easy to like. Good with a cheese soufflé.

Quality	🍷🍷🍷🍷
Value	★★★⁴
Grapes	shiraz
Region	Heathcote, Vic.
Cellar	🍾 4
Alc./Vol.	13.0%
RRP	$24.00

Shottesbrooke Cabernet Sauvignon

Shottesbrooke proprietor Nick Holmes has a long history as a McLaren Vale winemaker. He once made wine at Ryecroft, one of the grand old names in McLaren Vale wine.

CURRENT RELEASE 2001   There's plenty of appeal here: it's a ripe regional red with a bit more refinement than some. The bouquet has dark berries, plum and balanced oak aromas of some impact, and the palate is true to the nose with tasty dark fruit flavours trimmed in vanilla and savoury touches. It's medium-bodied and dry-finishing with ripe tannins and a long aftertaste. Serve with sesame beef fillet and noodles.

Quality	🍷🍷🍷🍷
Value	★★★★⁴
Grapes	cabernet sauvignon
Region	McLaren Vale, SA
Cellar	🍾 5
Alc./Vol.	14.0%
RRP	$18.00

Skillogalee Shiraz

The Skillogalee reds have undergone a packaging revamp and this shiraz is now in a classy-looking heavy burgundy bottle. The wines retain their own distinctive style.

CURRENT RELEASE 2000   Minty/menthol aromas are pronounced in Skillogalee's reds and this is no exception. It's an attractive savoury feature, although it tends to shade raspberry and blackberry fruit in youth. Oak is well-integrated and subtle. The palate is where it comes into its own, with long, plush, black fruit flavour, touched by dark chocolate and mint, and built on ripe tannins. A good wine from a difficult vintage. Serve with Turkish lamb and pide.

Quality	🍷🍷🍷🍷🍷
Value	★★★⁴
Grapes	shiraz
Region	Clare Valley, SA
Cellar	🍾 6
Alc./Vol.	13.0%
RRP	$27.50

Skillogalee The Cabernets

Quality	🍷🍷🍷🍷
Value	★★★
Grapes	cabernet sauvignon; cabernet franc; malbec
Region	Clare Valley, SA
Cellar	🍾 5
Alc./Vol.	12.5%
RRP	$27.50

'Skillogalee' was a sort of thin gruel that sustained early Clare Valley explorer John Horrocks when provisions ran low. Modern Clare Valley vignerons tend to dine on much better fare.

CURRENT RELEASE 2000   That choc-minty freshness of the Skillogalee reds features on the nose of this cabernet, and blackberry aromas are there in the midst of it. Oak is restrained and it's medium-bodied with minty black fruit flavour of good intensity and savoury length. Serve roast lamb here.

Smith and Hooper Limited Edition Merlot

Quality	🍷🍷🍷🍷
Value	★★★★
Grapes	merlot
Region	Wrattonbully, SA
Cellar	🍾 3
Alc./Vol.	13.5%
RRP	$18.50

Packaging wine in flash, embossed bottles sometimes makes us suspicious as to the quality of the wine, but Smith and Hooper's special bottle does contain good stuff.

CURRENT RELEASE 2000   The first thing you notice on the nose of this wine is oak. The wood gives lead pencil and camphor-like aromas that tend to dominate the light fruit underneath, but with further acquaintance that fruit emerges. There's a hint of violets, plum and mulberry fruit notes, and a savoury meaty touch. The palate has medium intensity, easy texture and soft tannins, but it's slightly lacking in personality. Serve it with veal scallopine.

Smithbrook Cabernet Sauvignon

Quality	🍷🍷🍷🍷
Value	★★★⁴
Grapes	cabernet sauvignon
Region	Pemberton, WA
Cellar	➡ 1–6
Alc./Vol.	13.5%
RRP	$24.00

Smithbrook's wines are very fairly priced, given their quality and type. This cabernet sauvignon summarises the house-style well. Maker: Michael Symons.

CURRENT RELEASE 2000   This is quite unevolved at three years of age, and it doesn't leap out of the glass at you, but perseverance is rewarded. The nose opens up with fine floral cabernet fruit, some bitter chocolate and high-toned cedary notes, and the palate has good structure underpinning fine fruit. Tannins are sinewy and astringent, but give it time. Serve it with spiced lamb, couscous and Middle Eastern trimmings.

Smithbrook The Yilgarn

The Smithbrook team maintains that merlot has a great future among the beautiful forested hills of the Manjimup district, so it's little wonder that their flagship red is mainly merlot.

CURRENT RELEASE 2000   It's a ripe red with a nose and palate of medium intensity, nowhere near as concentrated or powerful as many 'flagship' reds. Plum, almond and berry aromas are dressed in a suggestion of smoky bacon from French oak; there's also a hint of cedar to it. The palate is succulent with fresh acidity, and it has good length and fine tannins. Yilgarn should improve medium term, and will suit Chinese barbecue pork well.

Quality	🍷🍷🍷🍷
Value	★★★↓
Grapes	merlot 85%; cabernet sauvignon 7.5%; petit verdot 7.5%
Region	Pemberton, WA
Cellar	━ 1–6
Alc./Vol.	14.0%
RRP	$36.50

Sorrenberg Gamay

Sorrenberg's Beechworth wines are not really mainstream, with French-influenced ideas contributing to an eclectic range. This red is typical of their individual approach.

CURRENT RELEASE 2001   An unusual wine, this has a rather feral touch with earthy scents, rhubarb and strawberry aromas, and a savoury foresty edge. In the mouth it has lightish–medium body and light intensity of red fruit flavour that's succulent enough, but leads to a slight bitterness at the end. Despite being made from gamay, it bears little resemblance to gulpable French Beaujolais, having more structure and firmness. Try it with lyonnaise sausage.

Quality	🍷🍷🍷
Value	★★★
Grapes	gamay 90%; pinot noir 10%
Region	Beechworth, Vic.
Cellar	🍷 2
Alc./Vol.	13.9%
RRP	$26.00

St Hallett Blackwell Shiraz

The Blackwell on the label is Stuart Blackwell, St Hallett's longtime winemaker who has 30 years experience with Barossa shiraz.

CURRENT RELEASE 1999   Very much in the house style, this is a substantial Barossa shiraz of good character. The nose combines plum and spice aromas with a good measure of vanillin, coconutty oak. There's also a slightly raisiny touch to it. In the mouth it has intense spicy fruit dressed in some slightly aggressive oak which adds astringency to the firm, dry finish. Serve it with steak and kidney pudding.

Quality	🍷🍷🍷🍷
Value	★★★
Grapes	shiraz
Region	Barossa Valley, SA
Cellar	🍷 6
Alc./Vol.	14.0%
RRP	$30.00

St Hallett Grenache Shiraz Touriga

Quality	♟♟♟♟
Value	★★★
Grapes	grenache 72%; shiraz 23%; touriga nacional 5%
Region	Barossa Valley, SA
Cellar	▯ 3
Alc./Vol.	15.5%
RRP	$19.00

This blend, incorporating a little of the Portuguese grape touriga, used to go into a lightish red called Gamekeeper's Reserve. This is a more robust version. CURRENT RELEASE 2002   A bright, purplish young wine with minty, herby touches adding savoury notes to berry fruit on the nose. It has a warmly spicy palate of straightforward flavour, and a mild sign-off of fine moderate tannins. Savoury drinking young, but beware of that 15.5 per cent alcohol! Try it with a spicy vegetarian pizza.

St Huberts Pinot Noir

Quality	♟♟♟♟
Value	★★★♪
Grapes	pinot noir
Region	Yarra Valley, Vic.
Cellar	▯ 3
Alc./Vol.	13.0%
RRP	$24.00

This vineyard was originally planted by Hubert de Castella, one of the Yarra Valley's pioneering vignerons in the nineteenth century. The modern label is based on the original, with a stag's head in honour of St Hubert, patron saint of hunters. CURRENT RELEASE 2001   This is a pleasant style of pinot with a nicely sappy nose, fresh with ripe cherry, dry leaves and light oak smells. It rests on the light side of medium-bodied yet it has reasonable intensity of juicy, tangy flavour mid-palate. It finishes soft without the green stemmy tannins that mark too many young pinot noirs. Try it with braised duck risotto.

St Leonards Wahgunyah Shiraz

Quality	♟♟♟♟
Value	★★♪
Grapes	shiraz
Region	Rutherglen, Vic.
Cellar	▯ 2
Alc./Vol.	14.5%
RRP	$45.00

The old St Leonards winery is very like a museum by a lagoon in the Murray River. There's a café and picnic area near the water and the winery captures the feel of bygone times perfectly. CURRENT RELEASE 1997   This recent aged release has been hanging around the St Leonards winery for some time. It remains a pretty oaky drop in the house style. Nose and palate have ripe blackberry, dark chocolate and powerful vanillin oak; it's quite full-bodied, mature and deep in flavour, but not jammy or porty like some older Rutherglen reds. Try it with roast beef.

Stanton and Killeen Cabernet Franc Merlot

A mix of cabernet franc and merlot is a highly
unconventional blend in the Rutherglen region,
but Stanton and Killeen have often made wines that
sit a little outside the regional mainstream. Maker:
Chris Killeen.

CURRENT RELEASE 2001   Those who think cabernet
franc and merlot are a bit wishy-washy should try this
blend. It has a very dense glass-staining colour and a
nose that's reminiscent of crushed blackberries, tar and
dried leaves. The palate is fullish medium-bodied with
velvety ripe flavour and satisfying fruitiness, ahead of
firm grippy tannins. Serve it with red wine-braised lamb.

Quality	🍷🍷🍷🍷🍷
Value	★★★★
Grapes	cabernet franc; merlot
Region	Rutherglen, Vic.
Cellar	🍷 7
Alc./Vol.	14.0%
RRP	$24.00

Stanton and Killeen Durif

Chris Killeen makes some of the best Rutherglen red
wines of all. They have plenty of honest regionality,
as well as a bit of civilisation.

CURRENT RELEASE 2000   Durif usually has deep
colour and this is no exception. The nose is ripe with
dark plum and spice, vanilla, mulchy earth and leather.
In the mouth it's intense and long-flavoured with good
body and ripe tannins. A satisfying durif that should
develop well. Serve it with a charry steak.

Quality	🍷🍷🍷🍷
Value	★★★
Grapes	durif
Region	Rutherglen, Vic.
Cellar	⬤ 1–8
Alc./Vol.	14.0%
RRP	$38.00

Stanton and Killeen Shiraz Durif

Made from almost equal parts of shiraz and durif, this
hearty wine highlights Rutherglen's two best red wine
grapes in a blend that works very well.

CURRENT RELEASE 2001   The colour is deep, so too is
the aroma and flavour. It has berries, prune and earth
on the nose. The palate follows with solid berry flavour
that's juicy and appealing at first, suggesting that it be
consumed young, but on further acquaintance a solid
foundation of grippy tannins shows that this is not a
wine to be trifled with. A robust, satisfying wine for
braised lamb shanks.

Quality	🍷🍷🍷🍷
Value	★★★★
Grapes	shiraz; durif
Region	Rutherglen, Vic.
Cellar	🍷 7
Alc./Vol.	14.0%
RRP	$22.00

Starvedog Lane Cabernet Sauvignon

Quality	▼ ▼ ▼ ▼
Value	★ ★ ★
Grapes	cabernet sauvignon
Region	Adelaide Hills, SA
Cellar	🍾 5
Alc./Vol.	13.5%
RRP	$29.00 🍾

The Starvedog Lane wines are the result of collaboration between John and Helen Edwards, who own some of the vineyards responsible, and BRL Hardy who make the wines.

CURRENT RELEASE 1999   A thoroughly modern Australian cabernet with a nose of mint, notable cedary oak, mocha and black plum. It tastes appetising with attractive savoury touches, although oak is a wee bit assertive. The palate is medium-bodied with good length and ripe tannins beneath. Serve it with roast veal.

Stella Bella Sangiovese Cabernet Sauvignon

Quality	▼ ▼ ▼ ▼
Value	★ ★ ★
Grapes	sangiovese; cabernet sauvignon
Region	Margaret River, WA
Cellar	🍾 3
Alc./Vol.	14.0%
RRP	$28.00

The Stella Bellas are an offshoot of the Suckfizzle Augusta wines from Margaret River. The Stella label is reserved for things that push the thresholds a bit.

CURRENT RELEASE 2001   We think sangiovese has a future in Australia, so we're pleased to taste each new one. This bright-coloured blend with cabernet has correct savoury notes on the nose reminiscent of Italian herbs, raspberry, earth and cedar. In the mouth it's lightish medium-bodied with dry, earthy, red berry flavours. There's a pleasantly grainy texture which is very Italianate and the finish is typically grippy. The cabernet component doesn't show much. Try it with braised kid.

Sticks Cabernet Sauvignon

Quality	▼ ▼ ▼ ▽
Value	★ ★ ★
Grapes	cabernet sauvignon
Region	Yarra Valley, Vic.
Cellar	🍾 2
Alc./Vol.	13.0%
RRP	$18.00

If you've ever met Rob Dolan, you'll know why he's called 'Sticks' – he sure is a long beanpole of a bloke. The wines that bear his nickname are made in an easy-going style that perfectly reflects his personality.

CURRENT RELEASE 2001   A simple young cabernet with adequate black plum fruit aromas and a lightly floral touch. Oak influence is moderate and the palate is middling in body and very tasty, although it falls away just a little. It finishes with a savoury touch and is well-made and fault-free. Try it with a schnitzel.

Stonehaven Stepping Stone Cabernet Sauvignon

It's usually worth grabbing new red wine labels from our big wine companies in the hotly competitive under-$15 category. To quickly capture a bit of turf on the supermarket shelf, the first few vintages of new wines often over-deliver on value for money. This BRL Hardy cabernet arrived last year with plenty of bang for your buck and this is a worthwhile follow-up.
CURRENT RELEASE 2001   A well-made, good-drinking cabernet with everything in the right place. The nose has aromas of blackcurrant, blackberry, herbs and background toasty oak. It tastes satisfyingly intense with medium weight, good balance and softer tannins than last edition. Try it with veal cutlets.

Quality	🍷🍷🍷🍷
Value	★★★★★
Grapes	cabernet sauvignon
Region	Coonawarra, SA
Cellar	🍷 4
Alc./Vol.	13.0%
RRP	$14.00 ⑤

Stonehaven Stepping Stone Shiraz

The Stepping Stone Cabernet Sauvignon was such a success when released last year that the range is expanding. Now there's this good value shiraz.
CURRENT RELEASE 2001   A pleasant-smelling young shiraz with aromas of blueberry and plum, aniseed and earth, and the regulation dose of oak is readily apparent. The palate is smoothly satisfying with spicy berry and oak flavours of medium intensity. There's a little 'hole' mid-palate and the finish is a smidge shorter than we'd ideally like, but it does inhabit the sharply priced everyday end of the market. The finish is dry with some grip. Try it with veal cutlets.

Quality	🍷🍷🍷🍷
Value	★★★★
Grapes	shiraz
Region	Padthaway, SA
Cellar	🍷 3
Alc./Vol.	14.0%
RRP	$14.00 ⑤

Stoney Vineyard Cabernet Sauvignon

Stoney is the regular label of Ruth and Peter Althaus; Domaine A is the vineyard's quite expensive and sought-after premium label.
CURRENT RELEASE 1999   This is a typically extreme, cool-climate cabernet: light bodied and leafy, with more of the capsicum, mint, crushed-leaf flavours than you'd expect from a big, warm-area red. There are some raspberry aromas, too, and the colour is fairly light. It's a bit lean and borders on unripe. It would suit grilled lamb chops and mint sauce.

Quality	🍷🍷🍷
Value	★★⸰
Grapes	cabernet sauvignon
Region	Coal Valley, Tas.
Cellar	🍷 6
Alc./Vol.	13.0%
RRP	$25.00 (cellar door)

Stonier Pinot Noir

Quality	♥ ♥ ♥ ♥
Value	★ ★ ★
Grapes	pinot noir
Region	Mornington Peninsula, Vic.
Cellar	🍷 2
Alc./Vol.	13.5%
RRP	$24.00

This is Stonier's junior pinot, a simpler, less substantial wine than the Reserve, but well-made and honest. Maker: Tod Dexter.

CURRENT RELEASE 2001   This is a rather pale young wine, but in common with most of Stonier's standard pinots it has reasonable varietal character in a light, fresh package. The nose has bright strawberry and raspberry aromas with a touch of mint. In the mouth it's light and simple, without much in the way of depth or complexity. It should build in bottle a bit, but it will never make the earth move. Try it with grilled salmon cutlets.

Quality	♥ ♥ ♥ ♥
Value	★ ★ ★ ⸙
Grapes	pinot noir
Region	Mornington Peninsula, Vic.
Cellar	🍷 3
Alc./Vol.	13.0%
RRP	$24.00

CURRENT RELEASE 2002   There's a bit more to this than the 2001. The nose has red berry aromas that are sweet and fresh, and pleasant foresty, lightly gamy touches come through to add interest. In the mouth it's light yet it has enough intensity of smoky pinot flavour. The finish is fruity and long. Serve it with roast quail.

Straws Lane Pinot Noir

Quality	♥ ♥ ♥ ♥
Value	★ ★ ⸙
Grapes	pinot noir
Region	Macedon Ranges, Vic.
Cellar	🍷 2
Alc./Vol.	12.9%
RRP	$31.00

The cool vineyards in the highlands to Melbourne's north are a marginal place to grow grapes. Pinot noir is a favourite of Macedon vignerons who make all sorts of claims for it. In truth the wines are very variable.

CURRENT RELEASE 2000   Like a lot of Macedon pinots there's a ripeness question here. A peppery overlay on the nose suggests it, but there are also delicately perfumed red fruit and foresty touches that save the day. The palate is light with spicy fruit flavours but it lacks a little length and substance. Well-made and clean-tasting, but it could have a bit more presence. Serve it with salmon.

Suckfizzle Augusta Cabernet Sauvignon

This smartly presented red comes from the southern end of Margaret River. We've often expressed our reservations about some green, weedy characters that creep into some cabernets down there, and Suckfizzle Augusta usually pushes the boundaries in that direction. CURRENT RELEASE 2000   Charry oak heads the bill here, and red and blackcurrant fruit are present too, but these influences aren't enough to cover the stemmy, green characters that lie beneath. The palate follows suit with mocha and cedary oak-derived flavours, black fruit of reasonable intensity and more of that greenness. Try it with roast lamb and mint sauce.

Quality	▼▼▼▼
Value	★★
Grapes	cabernet sauvignon
Region	Margaret River, WA
Cellar	➟ 1–5
Alc./Vol.	13.5%
RRP	$45.00

Summerfield Cabernet

Ian and Mark Summerfield have upped the ante in the last couple of vintages, making very powerful young reds that should develop over many years in bottle. Past vintages have aged well.
CURRENT RELEASE 2001   A densely coloured young cabernet. The nose is ripe with blackcurrant and blackberry fruit, with a touch of lead pencils to it. In the mouth it's medium in body and although it's quite solidly concentrated, it has style. Cassis flavours are smooth and fleshy and it has an attractively grainy texture ahead of slightly firm ripe tannins. It has length and balance with a long aftertaste. Try it with venison.

Quality	▼▼▼▼▼
Value	★★★⌐
Grapes	cabernet sauvignon
Region	Pyrenees, Vic.
Cellar	▮ 7+
Alc./Vol.	14.0%
RRP	$30.00

Summerfield Merlot

This is Summerfield's first straight varietal merlot – previously it all went into a blend with cabernet sauvignon. It's a promising beginning.
CURRENT RELEASE 2001   Another dense-looking, dark wine from Summerfield. The nose is richly complex with spiced plum, mocha and vanilla aromas, and the palate is smooth and generous with deep plum pud flavours and some charry oak for seasoning. There's some succulence in the middle and it finishes with fine-grained, dry tannins. A good match for kangaroo.

Quality	▼▼▼▼▼
Value	★★★
Grapes	merlot
Region	Pyrenees, Vic.
Cellar	▮ 5+
Alc./Vol.	14.5%
RRP	$40.00

Summerfield Reserve Cabernet

Quality	♟♟♟♟♟
Value	★★★★
Grapes	cabernet sauvignon
Region	Pyrenees, Vic.
Cellar	⬸ 2–12+
Alc./Vol.	15.0%
RRP	$55.00

Summerfield's Pyrenees reds are not as well known as some of the region's products, but they are right up there for quality, with far less of the love-it-or-hate-it eucalypt character prominent in neighbours' wines.
CURRENT RELEASE 2001   An impenetrable blackish purple wine with a powerful nose of syrupy blackcurrant and blackberry. There's a hint of mint and nicely understated oak in there and the palate has power-plus. It's full-bodied and densely packed with rich regional flavours. It's still immature but it has lovely velvety texture and tannins that are ripe and fine-grained. A big red with a touch of class. Drink it with roast beef.

Summerfield Shiraz

Quality	♟♟♟♟♟
Value	★★★★
Grapes	shiraz
Region	Pyrenees, Vic.
Cellar	⬸ 1–10
Alc./Vol.	15.0%
RRP	$30.00

This is Summerfield's 'standard' shiraz, but it's still a wine of some power.
CURRENT RELEASE 2001   This is big, black and beautiful, with a potent nose of dark plums, spices, meat, tar and graphite. It's round and full in the mouth with rich flavour and chewy texture. Tannins are dry and slightly astringent but not too much so. A long powerful finish underlines an excellent Pyrenees region shiraz. Excellent with fillet of beef.

Tahbilk Cabernet Sauvignon

Quality	♟♟♟♟
Value	★★★
Grapes	cabernet sauvignon
Region	Goulburn Valley, Vic.
Cellar	▮ 3
Alc./Vol.	13.0%
RRP	$20.00 Ⓢ

The regular Tahbilk bottlings have certainly lightened off in recent years. It may have something to do with the reserve wines bottled separately in recent years, and it may be a deliberate effort to make the wines more approachable young.
CURRENT RELEASE 2000   This is a touch light and ordinary. It lacks distinctive cabernet character and strength on palate. There are mulch and plum aromas while the palate flavours are savoury and a little hollow. It's mellow, as opposed to a simple, primary fruit wine. It could do with more freshness and mid-palate fruit, though. It would suit Wiener schnitzel.

Tahbilk Reserve Cabernet Sauvignon

Tahbilk wines actually hail from the southern Nagambie Lakes sub-region of the Goulburn Valley, around Nagambie, Tabilk and Seymour. It's where most of the wineries are and it's significantly cooler than the northern part, which stretches as far as the Murray River.
CURRENT RELEASE 1997   At six years old, this is a lovely, complex, aged cabernet, redolent of cigar boxes and cedar and a hint of sump oil (but nice!). It's very mellow and layered, with a developed colour and smoky, oak-infused nuances, and a lean, elegant palate profile. The finish still carries plenty of drying tannin. It would go well with aged hard cheeses.

Quality	🍷🍷🍷🍷
Value	★★★
Grapes	cabernet sauvignon
Region	Goulburn Valley, Vic.
Cellar	🍾 4+
Alc./Vol.	13.0%
RRP	$70.00

Tahbilk Reserve Shiraz

We were surprised to see this lovely aged red is only six years old. It tastes like 12 to 15! Maker: Alister Purbrick and team.
CURRENT RELEASE 1997   The colour is light, developed ruby to brick red, and the bouquet is mellow and nicely aged, evoking old leather armchairs, smoke and fresh earth, a hint of volatility, and other aged, secondary characters. It tastes dry and elegantly savoury in the mouth: a lovely soft, mellow oldie that's drinking at its best right now. It would suit mild cheese, such as aged French brie on savoury biscuits.

Quality	🍷🍷🍷🍷
Value	★★★
Grapes	shiraz
Region	Goulburn Valley, Vic.
Cellar	🍾 3
Alc./Vol.	13.5%
RRP	$70.00

Taltarni Cephas

This is Taltarni's signal that it has finally decided to get with the changing times and produce a modern style red wine. Hear! Hear! Maker: Peter Steer and team.
CURRENT RELEASE 2000   What a change from the dried-out, tannic and sometimes fruitless Taltarni reds of yore! This is an elegant, deliciously drinkable, smooth red of medium body which can be enjoyed young or cellared. It has a bright purple–red colour, a perfume of rose petals, raspberries and violets, lifted by high-toned American oak, and a finely structured palate with plenty of fruit and gentle, low-key tannins. It would go well with pink roast lamb.

Quality	🍷🍷🍷🍷
Value	★★★
Grapes	shiraz 60%; cabernet sauvignon 40%
Region	Pyrenees, Vic.
Cellar	🍾 6+
Alc./Vol.	13.8%
RRP	$45.00

Taltarni Fiddleback Red

Quality	♟ ♟ ⬩
Value	★ ★ ★
Grapes	shiraz; cabernet sauvignon; merlot
Region	Pyrenees 49% & Murray Valley 51%, Vic.
Cellar	◑ 2
Alc./Vol.	13.5%
RRP	$13.00 ⑤

Fiddleback is a type of native eucalypt found in the heavily forested Pyrenees region. Maker: Shane Clohesy.
CURRENT RELEASE 2001   The colour is good and sound, although the nose and palate reveal a certain green minty, mulchy character. This is attended by some astringency on the tongue. It's a fair drink at the price, and is often discounted, but we'd love to see some riper fruit flavours and softness. Try it with beef casseroled with olives.

Taltarni Rosé

Quality	♟ ♟ ♟ ⬩
Value	★ ★ ★ ⬩
Grapes	malbec; shiraz
Region	Pyrenees, Vic.
Cellar	◑ 1
Alc./Vol.	13.0%
RRP	$15.75

Taltarni has been producing rosé for as long as we can remember. It was always a malbec, now there's some shiraz in it as well, which may explain the softer, more easygoing style.
CURRENT RELEASE 2002   The colour is a vibrant, almost neon, medium-depth purple; it's a mid- to full-bodied rosé with a sweet confectionery-like aroma, with some chocolate, vanilla and jam nuances. It's not sweet, but has a fruity palate and a clean, dry finish of modest length. It would suit steak tartare.

Tamar Ridge Cabernet Sauvignon

Quality	♟ ♟ ♟ ♟ ♟
Value	★ ★ ★ ★
Grapes	cabernet sauvignon
Region	Tamar Valley, Tas.
Cellar	◑ 10+
Alc./Vol.	13.5%
RRP	$26.00 ▯

Tassie cabernet has been making great strides in recent years, thanks to site selection and improved viticulture – and some very good vintages. This won a trophy at the 2003 Tasmanian Regional Wine Show.
CURRENT RELEASE 2000   The product of a top vintage, this is a brilliant cabernet, smelling of sweet ripe berries, crème de cassis, and a background of smart new oak. It has freshness and balance, great intensity of flavour and real fruit sweetness in the middle. A perfect partner for a plate of Tasmanian cheeses.

Tatachilla Adelaide Hills Merlot

Tatachilla also makes an acclaimed Clarendon merlot, which is technically in McLaren Vale – and is also more expensive. Makers: Michael Fragos and Justin McNamee. CURRENT RELEASE 2000   The high-altitude aromas of crushed leaves and mint, coupled with sweet cassis/blackberry fruit, mark this as a cool-climate wine. The palate is medium-bodied and has the leanness and angularity of an elegant 'cool' style of merlot. It's clean and well-made and could benefit from keeping. Try it with veal cutlets.

Quality	♥♥♥♥
Value	★★★★
Grapes	merlot
Region	Adelaide Hills, SA
Cellar	5+
Alc./Vol.	13.0%
RRP	$25.00

Tatachilla 1901 Cabernet Sauvignon

This wine pulled a hat-trick at the 2003 Royal Sydney Wine Show. It won three trophies, topped off by the Gilbert Phillips for best red wine of show; not a bad achievement, and we agree with the judges. Only 515 dozen were produced.
CURRENT RELEASE 2000   The colour is still youthful: medium–deep red–purple, and the bouquet shows dusty cabernet and oak integration; it's toasty, cedary and slightly meat-stocky. The palate is superb: rich and smooth but not oversized. It has terrific fruit intensity but is savoury, mellow and complex, with richness and fruit-sweetness. There's persuasive tannin on the finish. It would be good with casseroled meats.

Quality	♥♥♥♥♥
Value	★★★★
Grapes	cabernet sauvignon
Region	McLaren Vale & Padthaway, SA
Cellar	10+
Alc./Vol.	13.5%
RRP	$42.00

Tatachilla Clarendon Vineyard Merlot

Tatachilla's Clarendon vineyard is on the border between the McLaren Vale and Adelaide Hills regions, and enjoys some of the best of both worlds. It's cooler than the Vale and drier than the Hills. Makers: Michael Fragos and Justin McNamee.
CURRENT RELEASE 2000   The 2000 vintage has produced a finer, leaner style with fairly high acid and a firm finish. It's medium-bodied at best, and as it airs it builds meat stock and leather complexities, and the palate fills out and becomes somewhat softer and more rounded. A quite delicious red, less gutsy than some earlier vintages, and goes well with pink roast lamb.

Quality	♥♥♥♥
Value	★★★
Grapes	merlot
Region	McLaren Vale, SA
Cellar	5
Alc./Vol.	13.5%
RRP	$42.00

Tatachilla McLaren Vale Shiraz

Quality	🍷🍷🍷
Value	★★★
Grapes	shiraz
Region	McLaren Vale, SA
Cellar	➡ 1–5+
Alc./Vol.	14.5%
RRP	$22.00 (cellar door)

Tatachilla these days is part of the Lion Nathan wine division, along with Petaluma, Mitchelton, Hillstowe, St Hallett, etc.

CURRENT RELEASE 2000   The nose of this rustic red offers green peppercorn and oak and a hint of volatility, while the palate is more astringent and fiery than we would have expected. It has a savoury flavour, and liberal toasty oak contributes to the grippy finish. It has plenty of guts, but not a lot of style! Try steak and kidney pie.

Taylors Cabernet Sauvignon

Quality	🍷🍷🍷
Value	★★★⁺
Grapes	cabernet sauvignon
Region	Clare Valley, SA
Cellar	🍾 5
Alc./Vol.	14.0%
RRP	$19.00 ⑤

Taylors reckons this is Australia's number one selling cabernet over $15 – a fact we wouldn't dispute. The family company has made a statement with this vintage and released a screw-capped version through Vintage Cellars.

CURRENT RELEASE 2001   It's a big, bold, typical Clare cabernet which features lashings of raspberry and blackberry jam flavour unencumbered by too much oak. It's a trifle undeveloped and 'fruit bomb-like' but it's excellent value and will improve over several years. It goes with steak diane.

Terrace Vale Collector Series Cabernet Sauvignon

Quality	🍷🍷🍷🍷
Value	★★★⁺
Grapes	cabernet sauvignon
Region	Hunter Valley, NSW
Cellar	🍾 7
Alc./Vol.	13.5%
RRP	$45.00 ⑤ 🍾

Cabernet isn't nearly as successful as shiraz in the Hunter, but if it ever succeeds it'll be in a year like 2000. This special bottling won a gold medal and trophy at the Hunter Boutique Wine Show.

CURRENT RELEASE 2000   This is a very complex, interest-packed red, and speaks more of the Hunter than of the grape variety. The bouquet is very regional, with funky/gamy, savoury, meaty characters that are somewhat wild. The palate continues in this vein, with complex, savoury flavour and plenty of oak and wood-maturation character. It's best with food: try savoury meatballs.

Tim Adams Clare Valley Shiraz

Tim Adams is one of the quiet achievers of the wine business. He beavers away in the Clare Valley without making any fuss, and his wines speak for themselves. CURRENT RELEASE 2001   This is a delicious red! It's big and concentrated, but not over the top. It's rich and layered with flavours of plums and blackberries and aniseed, with oak in balance and just a touch of meaty funk. The flavour is dense and fleshy and fills every corner of the mouth. A sumptuous, gutsy red. Try it with rare rump steak.

Quality	♥ ♥ ♥ ♥ ◗
Value	★ ★ ★ ★ ⁺
Grapes	shiraz
Region	Clare Valley, SA
Cellar	➥ 1–10+
Alc./Vol.	14.0%
RRP	$19.00

Tinderbox Pinot Noir

Liz McGown's maiden name was Vine, so it was probably predestined that she would plant this 3-hectare vineyard beside the water of d'Entrecasteaux Channel, just south of Hobart. Andrew Hood makes the wines. CURRENT RELEASE 2001   A deliciously fruit-driven pinot, this floods the glass with sweet strawberry and red-cherry aromas. In the mouth, it has lush sweet fruit with no hint of greenness, and the balance is impeccable. The texture is nice and soft, without obvious tannin grip. It would go with roast guinea fowl.

Quality	♥ ♥ ♥ ♥ ◗
Value	★ ★ ★ ★
Grapes	pinot noir
Region	Channel & Huon, Tas.
Cellar	▮ 3
Alc./Vol.	13.0%
RRP	$28.00 (cellar door)

Torbreck Descendant

A 'descendant' of Runrig, the big gun at Torbreck, and similarly fashioned from shiraz and viognier. If this is $150, you can imagine what Runrig costs – try $200 plus! CURRENT RELEASE 2001   The Torbreck reds seem cleaner and more composed this year: less feral and less porty too. The colour is, as usual, superb – deep purple–red – and the youthful plummy, meaty, minty and toasty aromas are neither overripe nor over-oaked. Indeed, it's a fruit-driven style, with berry jam, prune juice flavours edged in licorice/anise. A lovely big, soft, rich mouthful of wine, but we wouldn't pay $150 for it. Would suit steak and kidney pie.

Quality	♥ ♥ ♥ ♥ ◗
Value	★ ★ ⁺
Grapes	shiraz; viognier
Region	Barossa Valley, SA
Cellar	▮ 5
Alc./Vol.	14.5%
RRP	$150.00

Torbreck Juveniles

Quality	▽▽▽▽
Value	★★★★
Grapes	grenache; mourvèdre; shiraz
Region	Barossa Valley, SA
Cellar	🍾 4
Alc./Vol.	14.5%
RRP	$33.00

Created especially for Tim Johnston, proprietor of Juveniles winebar in Paris, this wine is an unwooded blend of grenache, mourvèdre and shiraz. Maker: Dave Powell.

CURRENT RELEASE 2002   This is the best Juveniles yet, we think. It is very young and fresh but not as raw as previous versions have been at the same age. There's a fascinating array of aromas and flavours, from grapey, greenish/herbal young grenache fruit, to raspberry jam, to subtle peppermint and even a hint of lemon/citrus. It's clean and vibrant, with a big, obvious, syrupy palate reflecting overripe, concentrated grapes. It could go with seared roo and chilli jam.

Torbreck The Steading

Quality	▽▽▽
Value	★★★
Grapes	grenache; mourvèdre; shiraz
Region	Barossa Valley, SA
Cellar	🍾 4
Alc./Vol.	14.5%
RRP	$40.00

Torbreck went through a shaky period in late 2002, with some financial stresses for founder David Powell. After a period in receivership, he refinanced the business and seems to have pulled it out of the fire.

CURRENT RELEASE 2001   There was a little dissolved gas in the wine, which can be a sign of a problem, but didn't seem to have damaged our sample. The aromas are bizarre, with a range of vegetal and ripe aromas from lime/citrus, herbs and even lemon through to sweet jammy/berry scents. It's a big, broad, unsubtle blend with generous flavour, but at least some of the grapes would have made good port! Try it with pungent cheese, like aged cheddar.

Torbreck The Struie

Torbreck's boss Dave Powell should get together with Capercaillie's Al Sutherland – they could trot out all their favourite Scottish words and have a ball! In this case, a 'struie' is a shiraz blended from the Barossa and Eden Valleys.

CURRENT RELEASE 2001   A new wine, but the style is recognisably Torbreck: concentrated, rich, fleshy and hedonistic. It's spicier and more Rhône-ish, no doubt thanks to the higher altitude components. The nose is very intense – spices and pepper, clean and vibrant. It's likewise intense in the mouth, taut and unusually elegant, again with Rhône-ish pepper/spice and vegetal nuances. The oak is subtle and nicely savoury/spicy. A beaut drink! Try it with osso buco.

Quality	♥♥♥♥♥
Value	★★★★
Grapes	shiraz
Region	Barossa & Eden Valleys, SA
Cellar	8+
Alc./Vol.	14.5%
RRP	$50.00

Tower Estate Barossa Shiraz

Winemaker Dan Dineen reckons this is the best Barossa shiraz he's made to date. The grapes came from Peter Lehmann, and only 1000 cases were produced.

CURRENT RELEASE 2001   A marvellous shiraz that avoids excessive use of obvious oak, a common sin among Barossa winemakers. It has a youthful deep purple–red hue and smells of rich, ripe, concentrated plummy shiraz fruit, with a little alcohol fuminess and beautifully judged background oak. Supple, ripe tannins run the length of the palate. It has serious depth of damson plum flavour which perfectly treads the line, avoiding both jammy overripe and greener underripe flavours. Serve with aged hard cheeses.

Quality	♥♥♥♥♥
Value	★★★★
Grapes	shiraz
Region	Barossa Valley, SA
Cellar	2–15+
Alc./Vol.	14.5%
RRP	$40.00 (cellar door)

Tower Estate Coonawarra Cabernet Sauvignon

Quality 🍷🍷🍷🍷½
Value ★★★★
Grapes cabernet sauvignon
Region Coonawarra, SA
Cellar 10+
Alc./Vol. 14.0%
RRP $35.00 (cellar door)

The grapes for the Tower Coonawarra cabernet come from Yalumba's vineyards. The latest attraction at the associated luxury hotel, Tower Lodge, is a mini-golf course, designed by the pro himself, Len Evans. Maker: Dan Dineen.

CURRENT RELEASE 2000 Delicious cabernet, and all the more remarkable by being made outside Coonawarra! Concentrated blackcurrant fruit is what it's all about, plus well-judged toasty oak. The flavours are rich and varied in the mouth, smooth and full, with adequate but not strongly assertive tannins. It will age well but drinks nicely now, with barbecued rump steak.

Trentham Estate Cellar Reserve Shiraz

Quality 🍷🍷🍷🍷
Value ★★★★
Grapes shiraz
Region Murray Valley, NSW
Cellar 5
Alc./Vol. 14.0%
RRP $20.00

The Cellar Reserve is a new premium label for Trentham, and signals a higher level of quality, but still at very reasonable prices. They're off superior 50-year-old vines in the Murphy family's estate-owned vineyards.

CURRENT RELEASE 1999 A little extra age is a bonus, too. This has a complex bouquet of mocha, coffee, earth and toasty oak, which hints at lengthy barrel ageing. It's very smooth and chunky in the mouth, with slightly grainy tannins, and cleverly infused oak character. Its warm climate origins show in its richness, softness and chocolatey flavour spectrum. It goes with beef casserole.

Trentham Estate Merlot

Quality 🍷🍷🍷½
Value ★★★½
Grapes merlot
Region Murray Valley, NSW
Cellar 3
Alc./Vol. 13.5%
RRP $16.50 (S)

Merlot is the big thing – everybody's doing it. From the baking plains of the Riverina to the coolest parts of Tassie to the lofty altitudes of Tumbarumba, there's merlot for all.

CURRENT RELEASE 2000 Even in the Riverland merlot can be a pretty good drop. This is a soft, savoury style, with nice ripe fruit and none of the herbaceousness you sometimes taste in cool-area wines. The colour is medium red; developed aromas and flavours prevail, with a lean, savoury style and grainy tannins. It shows some development and the finish is pleasantly dry. It would suit slow-braised meats.

Trentham Estate Petit Verdot

Riverland wineries have had remarkably good results with this Bordeaux variety recently. It is said to need more sun and warmth than Bordeaux can usually provide, and hence is well suited to our hotter regions. Maker: Tony Murphy.

CURRENT RELEASE 2001   Good concentration is a feature of this red – in colour, aroma and flavour. It has a nice ripe flavour of blackberries and blackcurrants, with a subtle backing of vanillin from oak, and in the mouth there's an abundance of sweet ripe flavours. The finish is tightened up by some fine-grained tannins. It should drink well for several years. Try veal cutlets as a match.

Quality	▮▮▮▮
Value	★★★★
Grapes	petit verdot
Region	Murray Valley, NSW
Cellar	4
Alc./Vol.	13.5%
RRP	$19.00 Ⓢ

Turkey Flat Rosé

Turkey Flat is the Schulz family venture at Bethany Road, Tanunda. It is consistently one of the better rosé producers in the land. Maker: Peter Schulz.

CURRENT RELEASE 2002   A vibrantly grapey, clean, fruity style of rosé which concludes with just a flick of sweetness. The aromas are banana-estery and floral, and the finish is soft and nicely balanced. It's the sort of wine you could drink with antipasto, or sip well chilled, as an aperitif.

Quality	▮▮▮▮
Value	★★★
Grapes	grenache; cabernet sauvignon; shiraz; dolcetto
Region	Barossa Valley, SA
Cellar	1
Alc./Vol.	12.0%
RRP	$18.00

Turramurra Estate Shiraz

David and Paula Leslie are the affable proprietors of one of Mornington Peninsula's quiet achievers: Turramurra Estate always provides wine of interest and quality.

CURRENT RELEASE 1999   This has been on the shelves for a while now and a little additional bottle-age hasn't done it any harm. Stylistically it's in the aromatic, spicy cool-climate mould. The nose has pepper and dark cherry fruit. In the mouth there's very spicy flavour to match the nose. It's dry and has a slight minerally austerity to it. The finish is dry and firm. Serve it with rice ribbon noodles and Chinese braised beef.

Quality	▮▮▮▮
Value	★★★
Grapes	shiraz
Region	Mornington Peninsula, Vic.
Cellar	2
Alc./Vol.	13.5%
RRP	$30.00

Two Hands Bad Impersonator

Quality	🍷🍷🍷🍷🍷
Value	★★★★
Grapes	shiraz
Region	Barossa Valley, SA
Cellar	🍷 6
Alc./Vol.	14.5%
RRP	$45.00

This nascent Adelaide-based company has created an extraordinary range of rich, warm-area 'concept reds' with such superb packaging and catchy names they ensure you always read the label.

CURRENT RELEASE 2001   It tastes like a shiraz from a slightly cooler region, because of its peppery aromas. It has dusty, earthy, plum and herbal aromas too. It really comes into its own in the mouth, though, where it has sumptuously rich, sweet, very ripe fruit galore. It's very deep and fleshy with smart style and elegance, and the finish carries on and on. Try it with a hearty beef casserole.

Two Hands Bella's Garden Shiraz

Quality	🍷🍷🍷🍷🍷
Value	★★★⭐
Grapes	shiraz
Region	Barossa Valley, SA
Cellar	🍷 6
Alc./Vol.	14.5%
RRP	$55.00

Several of the Two Hands wines are named after children or other females in the circle of the owners of the brand, Michael Twelftree and his silent partner (ssshhhh!).

CURRENT RELEASE 2001   We prefer Two Hands' Barossa shirazes to their McLaren Vales, which are thicker and soupier and less well structured. This has a dense colour and smells of chocolate, vanilla and toasty barrels. It's been thoroughly infused with oak, but not really overdone. There's a trace of mint and the palate is thick and chewy in its density. The texture is smooth and fleshy. A wine to sip with aged cheddar.

Two Hands Lily's Garden Shiraz

Quality	🍷🍷🍷🍷
Value	★★★
Grapes	shiraz
Region	McLaren Vale, SA
Cellar	🍷 5
Alc./Vol.	14.5%
RRP	$55.00

Michael Twelftree ran a building company before deciding to chuck it in and follow his heart into the wine industry. Lovers of big, rich reds are very glad he did.

CURRENT RELEASE 2001   How porty do you like your red wine? The colour is nicely deep, the aromas suggest licorice, port and earth, and it has a thick, sweet, oily texture that is so overripe it strays into port territory. A lot of people love this sort of thing, but we reckon it has little to do with stylish red wine, and is difficult to drink more than a sip or two. Food: not really!

Two Hands Sophie's Garden Shiraz

Two Hands recently built a winery in the Greenock sub-region of the Barossa Valley. They'll have a cellar-door sales outlet there, and various other attractions. CURRENT RELEASE 2001   This is another different expression of shiraz from the hard-working Two Hands mob. This time, a raisiny fruit character which borders on 'dead fruit' and lacks vibrancy, suggesting the grapes were left hanging a bit long. It's also chocolatey and has a hint of creosote. The maker's trademark opulence is still there, with stacks of concentrated, rich flavour, sweet and plum-jammy and all held together by a firm tannin finish. Serve with osso buco.

Quality	🍷🍷🍷🍷
Value	★★★
Grapes	shiraz
Region	Padthaway, SA
Cellar	🍷 4
Alc./Vol.	14.5%
RRP	$55.00

Two Hands The Bull & The Bear

We decided to review more Two Hands wines than we normally would for one very small producer, because they're such interesting, flavour-packed, exciting wines. CURRENT RELEASE 2001   Like most Two Hands offerings, this gives little clue to its varietal mix. Tasted blind, we thought it was a grenache blend! It has plenty of colour and a bouquet of straw/hay, toasty barrels, earth, dried herbs and raisins. There's a hint of the horse-stable, too. Pruney, black fruit flavours flood the palate and the tannins are coarse-grained. It's a bit funky and lacks shape, but has a tonne of flavour and character! Try it with game pie.

Quality	🍷🍷🍷🍷🍷
Value	★★★★
Grapes	shiraz; cabernet sauvignon
Region	Barossa Valley, SA
Cellar	🍷 6+
Alc./Vol.	14.5%
RRP	$45.00

Vintage Plane Wild Rosé

We are big fans of rosé. It is an underrated wine in this country, especially in the stinking hot mid-summer weather prevailing while this tasting note was penned! CURRENT RELEASE 2002   The vintage plane covers a fair bit of SA airspace, from Adelaide Hills to Clare at least. This has a vibrant purple–pink hue and smells of cherries, strawberries and crushed leaf. The entry is fairly tart due to acid, but there is good fruit flavour as well and it certainly avoids excessive sweetness, which is a trap unwary rosé hunters can fall into. It would go well with antipasto.

Quality	🍷🍷🍷🍷
Value	★★★
Grapes	grenache
Region	Clare Valley, SA
Cellar	🍷 1
Alc./Vol.	12.6%
RRP	$23.00

Voyager Estate Cabernet Sauvignon Merlot

Quality	▼ ▼ ▼ ▼
Value	★ ★ ★ ★ ⟩
Grapes	cabernet sauvignon; merlot
Region	Margaret River, WA
Cellar	🍾 15+
Alc./Vol.	14.2%
RRP	$39.50 🍷

The Voyager reds have been coming along in leaps and bounds. They used to be a touch on the herbaceous side, but it tastes like the vineyard is being pulled into gear. Maker: Cliff Royle.

CURRENT RELEASE 1999   This is a seriously good cabernet blend, a Margaret River classic. It has a delicious mixture of green-leafy and ripe-berry scents, harmonised with good-quality oak. The palate is fine and balanced with fine-grained tannins, real elegance and a lingering aftertaste. It's a stylish, beautifully put-together red. Try it with pink lamb fillets.

Voyager Estate Shiraz

Quality	▼ ▼ ▼ ▼ ▼
Value	★ ★ ★ ★ ★
Grapes	shiraz
Region	Margaret River, WA
Cellar	🍾 10+
Alc./Vol.	14.0%
RRP	$28.00

Only the second vintage of Voyager shiraz we've seen, and already they score two out of two on our card. Maker: Cliff Royle.

CURRENT RELEASE 2001   This will please those who enjoy pristine cool-grown shiraz as well as those who cherish some feral complexities. It has a deep purple–red colour and intense, rich, ripe aromas of black cherry and plum with spicy, meaty/gamy and animal hide overtones. The taste is lovely and smooth, with a fleshy texture and some density. Tannins are generous but supple. Impressive length and balance complete the picture. An excellent shiraz to drink with beef casserole.

PENGUIN BEST SHIRAZ

Voyager Estate Tom Price Cabernet Sauvignon

Quality	▼ ▼
Value	★ ★
Grapes	cabernet sauvignon
Region	Margaret River, WA
Cellar	🍾 1
Alc./Vol.	13.5%
RRP	$100.00

This would take our prize for the worst $100 wine we've ever tasted – if we had such an award. Mercifully, only 250 dozen were made.

CURRENT RELEASE 1995   Why this costs $100, and why it was deemed worthy of cellaring so long before release, we are unable to say. It has a green, edgy, metallic nose, smelling of cigar butt and assorted vegetal smells, but little evidence of ripe grapes. Its palate is likewise thin, green and washed out. It has little to do with the region's great reputation for cabernet. Our advice is to leave it on the shelf.

Warrabilla Reserve Durif

Durif suits the Rutherglen climate and the evidence is in big hearty red wines like this. Maker: Andrew Sutherland Smith.
CURRENT RELEASE 2001   This is a big thick wine in traditional Rutherglen durif style, made to be enjoyed by true aficionados. The colour is blackish and impenetrable, and it smells of lush dark berries, aniseed and earth. In the mouth it's as formidable as the nose suggests, with great intensity of weighty blackberry fruit dressed in a light veneer of French oak. Tannins are softer than we've come to expect from durif, yet still there. Good with brasied oxtail.

Quality	♟♟♟♟
Value	★★★★
Grapes	durif
Region	Rutherglen, Vic.
Cellar	➥ 2–10+
Alc./Vol.	14.5%
RRP	$22.00

Warrabilla Reserve Shiraz

At Warrabilla, Andrew Sutherland Smith says, 'Shiraz is our benchmark.' In common with many warmer Australian wine districts, shiraz is right at home in Rutherglen.
CURRENT RELEASE 2001   There's a Neanderthal regional charm to this young red. It opens with porty, cherry jam-like fruit that's simple and lacking finesse, but it has character. In the mouth it's warm, sweetly spicy and rich with dry, firm tannins behind. A red wine for the traditionalists, it will work well with a high quality steak and kidney pie.

Quality	♟♟♟♟
Value	★★★★
Grapes	shiraz
Region	Rutherglen, Vic.
Cellar	▯ 5
Alc./Vol.	14.5%
RRP	$19.00

Warrenmang Red Gold Reserve Shiraz

Made to celebrate Warrenmang's 25th anniversary, this is an unusual multi-vintage blend made up from the finest barrels of the 1997, '98 and 2000 vintages.
CURRENT RELEASE 1997, 1998 and 2000   This perfumed wine offers a sophisticated mix of berry fruit, peppermint, chocolate, cedary oak and spices on the nose. It's rich and starting to show some maturity in bouquet and flavour. The palate has smooth texture and it tastes fine and long with subtle complexity. Fine-grained, ripe tannins finish it off in lovely balance. Serve it with roast fillet of beef.

Quality	♟♟♟♟♟
Value	★★★
Grapes	shiraz
Region	Pyrenees, Vic.
Cellar	▯ 5+
Alc./Vol.	14.0%
RRP	$120.00

Water Wheel Shiraz

Quality 🍷🍷🍷🍷
Value ★★★★½
Grapes shiraz
Region Bendigo, Vic.
Cellar 2–8+
Alc./Vol. 14.5%
RRP $19.00

Water Wheel reds are no blushing violets. Syrupy ripeness, full body, plenty of alcohol, and big tannins make up the formula. It works well, especially for fans of the big red. Maker: Peter Cumming.

CURRENT RELEASE 2001 This has a ripe, sweet nose of blackberry and spice. Earthy notes add a savoury dimension and charry sweet oak is kept in the shadow of that ripe fruit. In the mouth it's full in body with warm spicy berry flavour of real concentration against a background of firm, grippy tannins. It delivers well on the time-honoured Water Wheel formula and sits well with steak and onions.

Wellington Pinot Noir

Quality 🍷🍷🍷🍷
Value ★★★★
Grapes pinot noir
Region various, Tas.
Cellar 5+
Alc./Vol. 13.6%
RRP $28.00

Wellington winemaker Andrew Hood makes about 25 different pinot noirs every vintage, for other people, mostly. His methods are remarkably simple, and often leave the more fussy pinot noir makers gobsmacked.

CURRENT RELEASE 2001 This is somewhat subdued for a Wellington pinot, and given the calibre of the vintage we suspect it will yield more and more character if allowed enough time. Subdued it may be on the nose, but the colour is deepish with youthful purple hues, and the palate is rich, full and smooth, with good flesh and density. It is already soft enough to drink well with barbecued quail.

Wendouree Cabernet Malbec

Quality 🍷🍷🍷🍷½
Value ★★★★
Grapes cabernet sauvignon; malbec
Region Clare Valley, SA
Cellar 2–15+
Alc./Vol. 13.4%
RRP $40.00 (cellar door)

The Bradys of Wendouree continue to make beautiful full-bodied reds that are never porty or over-oaked, in contrast to many of their brethren in the Clare. Just 250 cases were made.

CURRENT RELEASE 2000 Big, bold and ballsy, this traditional blend has a medium–deep red–purple hue and a raw, essency, blackcurrant, blackberry and blueberry aroma. It has excellent depth of nicely ripe fruit but needs time to build more complexity. The palate is tannic and concentrated as we'd expect. It needs time. Cellar! Then serve with hard cheeses.

Wendouree Cabernet Sauvignon

Every year, Wendouree's wines sell out within weeks of release, and bottles rarely find their way into retail shops. But as a matter of record, most years we review a few – we reckon they're among Australia's great wines. 200 cases produced. Makers: Tony and Lita Brady. CURRENT RELEASE 2000   If 2000 wasn't such as good year in Clare, it didn't worry Wendouree, whose yields are minuscule and vines are very old and deep-rooted, helping smooth out the vintage vagaries. This is a marvellous red: concentrated cassis and lightly crushed-leafy flavours, abundant powder-fine tannins; serious structure. It needs age, then drink it with aged cheeses.

Quality	🍷🍷🍷🍷🍷
Value	★★★★
Grapes	cabernet sauvignon
Region	Clare Valley, SA
Cellar	▬ 2–20+
Alc./Vol.	13.2%
RRP	$40.00 (cellar door)

West Cape Howe Cabernet Merlot

Established in 1997 to provide contract winemaking services to growers in south-west Western Australia. Wines are sourced from the company's own vineyard and various others through the Mount Barker and Denmark districts. Maker: Brenden Smith. CURRENT RELEASE 2002   A bright young wine with an appealing aroma of plummy fruit and cassis. There's also a hint of tobacco and a slightly stemmy edge. Oak is subtle and there's some succulent fruit on the palate, but some youthful bitterness on the finish intrudes. There's moderate length of flavour, but it falls off the palate a little into that astringent ending. Try it with a Beijing-style lamb stirfry.

Quality	🍷🍷🍷🍷
Value	★★★
Grapes	cabernet sauvignon 65%; merlot 35%
Region	Great Southern, WA
Cellar	🍷 3
Alc./Vol.	13.5%
RRP	$17.50

West Cape Howe Shiraz

The Great Southern region is proving to be yet another great place to grow shiraz; it seems to thrive in about 90 per cent of Australian vineyards. CURRENT RELEASE 2001   Plum and berry aromas of lovely penetrating intensity meet the nose; there's a lick of spice too, and a light-handed bit of sweet oak. In the mouth it's very classy with smoothly ripe, spicy flavour, medium body and good length. Not a rugged blockbuster even with 14.5 per cent alcohol, but this sums up just how well shiraz can do in cooler places, and in the right hands. Try it with lamb and kidney pie.

Quality	🍷🍷🍷🍷
Value	★★★★★
Grapes	shiraz; viognier
Region	Great Southern, WA
Cellar	🍷 4
Alc./Vol.	14.5%
RRP	$17.50

Westend 3 Bridges Durif

Quality	🍷🍷🍷
Value	★★★⟩
Grapes	durif
Region	Riverina, NSW
Cellar	🍾 3
Alc./Vol.	14.5%
RRP	$22.00

Durif has made a successful migration from Rutherglen in Victoria to the New South Wales Riverina. Its hearty red wines are striking a chord with the public; expect more to appear in the future. Bill Calabria's Westend version is one of the newest.

CURRENT RELEASE 2001   This is a straightforward, well-made red that should please a lot of people. The nose has raspberry, mint and blackberry aromas of good intensity with a chocolatey dressing of oak. The palate is ripe and tannins are balanced and dry. It will make easy, medium-bodied drinking in the short term. Serve it with chargrilled meats.

Western Range Accord Shiraz

Quality	🍷🍷🍷
Value	★★★⟩
Grapes	shiraz; viognier
Region	Perth Hills, WA
Cellar	🍾 4
Alc./Vol.	14.0%
RRP	$20.00

A consortium of wine-interested investors established the large Western Range vineyard in the Perth Hills to take advantage of the booming Western Australia wine industry. The first few wines have been very good. Maker: Mark Nairn.

CURRENT RELEASE 2001   This has a lot of ripe appeal. The nose has aromatic fruitcake smells with a measured overlay of spicy oak. In the mouth it's medium in body with intense berry flavours that dovetail into fine, grainy, dry tannins. A little viognier in the blend doesn't stand out much, but seems to add to the wine's fragrance. It will suit little medallions of fillet steak well.

Western Range Shiraz

Quality	🍷🍷🍷
Value	★★★
Grapes	shiraz
Region	Perth Hills, WA
Cellar	🍾 3
Alc./Vol.	14.0%
RRP	$16.00

The Western Range wines are based on vineyards in the Perth Hills. The region is nowhere near as fashionable as Western Australia's southern vineyards, but the robust styles produced are sure to please a wide market.

CURRENT RELEASE 2001   This has a deep colour and an appealing nose that's like a spiced plum chutney. There's a touch of oak adding another aspect, and the palate is medium–intense with dark fruit and oak flavour that leads through some firm tannins. A good match for a steak.

Wignalls Albany Pinot Noir

Wignalls have always made a speciality of pinot noir, making wines that have captured pinot's eccentric, erratic nature well.

CURRENT RELEASE 2001   Fragrant and full of pinot noir's foresty mysteries, Wignall's 2001 has a complex nose of gamy plum and strawberry with earth and a touch of decaying dry leaves. Cedary oak isn't intrusive, and it tastes savoury with spicy, earthy, red fruit flavours that are decadently rich and warm. Despite a whopping 15 per cent alcohol it's not too fumy or 'hot'. The dry finish has a lick of spicy oak and ripe tannins. Serve it with duck and braised root vegetables.

Quality	♟ ♟ ♟ ♟ ♟
Value	★ ★ ★ ┤
Grapes	pinot noir
Region	Great Southern, WA
Cellar	🍾 2
Alc./Vol.	15.0%
RRP	$30.00

Willow Bridge Estate Winemaker Reserve Shiraz

Willow Bridge is an ambitious large vineyard project in the Geographe region of Western Australia. Although it was only established six or so years ago, wine quality under winemaker Rob Bowen has already been impressive.

CURRENT RELEASE 2000   Smartly packed in one of those heavy burgundy bottles that usually signify wines with attitude, this doesn't disappoint. The colour is deep and the nose is complex, with herb and spice aromas dressing up a core of fleshy black cherry and black plum aromas. The palate is velvety-rich with real depth, length and sophisticated power. Oak plays a good citizen role. Lovely with steak and kidney pie.

Quality	♟ ♟ ♟ ♟ ♟
Value	★ ★ ★ ★ ┤
Grapes	shiraz
Region	Geographe, WA
Cellar	🍾 8
Alc./Vol.	14.5%
RRP	$30.00

Willow Creek Cabernet Sauvignon

Quality	♥♥♥♥
Value	★★★）
Grapes	cabernet sauvignon
Region	Mornington Peninsula, Vic.
Cellar	▮ 3
Alc./Vol.	13.5%
RRP	$25.00 (cellar door)

It has to be a pretty warm year on the Mornington Peninsula to get adequate ripeness in cabernet sauvignon. When it works (and that's not often, in our opinion), the best wines sometimes have a little hint of Bordeaux about them.
CURRENT RELEASE 2000   This has good depth of colour and the nose has an appealing, medium intensity bouquet of savoury, briary, blackcurrant fruit. Some cedary oak is woven in well. In the mouth it has medium intensity and weight with savoury but ripe flavours and a long, dry finish. A Bordeaux style red to serve with racks of lamb.

Quality	♥♥♥♥♥
Value	★★★★）
Grapes	cabernet sauvignon
Region	Mornington Peninsula, Vic.
Cellar	▮ 6+
Alc./Vol.	13.5%
RRP	$25.00 (cellar door)

CURRENT RELEASE 2001   This is a real step up in depth and character. It has a dark colour, intense dusty, leafy and blackcurrant cabernet nose, fine oak handling, and a taut, elegant, finely crafted palate of great style and length. Very fine tannins, too. Serve with cheddar.

Windowrie The Mill Cowra Cabernet Merlot

Quality	♥♥♥）
Value	★★★
Grapes	cabernet sauvignon; merlot
Region	Cowra, NSW
Cellar	➙ 1–5
Alc./Vol.	13.5%
RRP	$14.00

The Mill in question is an old stone flour mill built in the 1860s that serves as Windowrie's cellar-door area.
CURRENT RELEASE 2001   A potent young red with some extractive, almost tarry notes on the nose. There's also intense dark berries and vanillin oak behind. It all adds up to plenty of character in a medium-bodied package, although cabernet and merlot varietal traits aren't strongly stated. The palate has spicy black fruit flavours of good intensity, backed up by tinder-dry, half-bitter tannins. Roast a piece of porterhouse to go with this.

Wirra Wirra Church Block Cabernet Shiraz Merlot

Church Block was once a favourite of the suit-clad young cowboys who lunched every day at company expense, back before Paul Keating's posse rounded them up with the fringe benefits tax.
CURRENT RELEASE 2001   The label says 'keep a second bottle handy'. This is pretty good advice in our book, not just where Church Block is concerned, but with every highly rated wine in the *Guide*. This McLaren Vale red is middle of the road in every way: berry fruit, touches of earth and briar, some spicy oak, middling body and soft tannins. Drink it reasonably young with pot-roasted rabbit

Quality	🍷🍷🍷🍷
Value	★★★⯪
Grapes	cabernet sauvignon; shiraz; merlot
Region	McLaren Vale, SA
Cellar	🍾 3
Alc./Vol.	14.0%
RRP	$22.00

Wirra Wirra McLaren Vale Grenache Shiraz

Once the bread and butter of many Australian red wine producers, grenache-shiraz blends have a sort of 'back to the future' charm that's popular again right now.
CURRENT RELEASE 2001   Comfort food in a bottle. Grenache gives a raspberry note, and there are hints of spices and dried herbs with warmly jammy touches. The pongy farmyard smells that once characterised McLaren Vale grenache blends are missing, but it's not without interest. In the mouth it's ripe and mellow with berry flavours of juicy ripeness and good depth. It finishes dry with balanced tannins and a long warm finish. Great with braised osso buco.

Quality	🍷🍷🍷🍷
Value	★★★
Grapes	grenache; shiraz
Region	McLaren Vale, SA
Cellar	🍾 4
Alc./Vol.	14.5%
RRP	$30.00

Wirra Wirra McLaren Vale Shiraz

Shiraz loves McLaren Vale and McLaren Vale loves shiraz. It's at the foundation of the region's high standing in Australia, and internationally.
CURRENT RELEASE 2001   Mellow blackberry and black cherry jam smells tell the story of the big pillow of ripe fruit that makes this young shiraz so attractive. It's lightly influenced by oak which seasons rather than flavours it. The palate has generous proportions; it's full flavoured with good depth and smooth drinkability. Classic easy-sipping Aussie shiraz that would be good at a barbecue where the cook knows what he's doing (unfortunately the barbecue cook is nearly always a he!).

Quality	🍷🍷🍷🍷🍷
Value	★★★★
Grapes	shiraz
Region	McLaren Vale, SA
Cellar	🍾 5
Alc./Vol.	14.5%
RRP	$30.00

Wirra Wirra RSW Shiraz

Quality	🍷🍷🍷🍷
Value	★★★
Grapes	shiraz
Region	McLaren Vale, SA
Cellar	🍾 4
Alc./Vol.	14.5%
RRP	$48.00

RSW was Robert Strangways Wigley, who planted Wirra Wirra in 1894. Apparently Wigley's eccentric ways matched his middle name perfectly.
CURRENT RELEASE 2000   We found this a bit disappointing by RSW's usual high standards, especially after an excellent '99. The nose has earth and slightly raisiny blackberry aromas and there's a slight green thread through it. In the mouth it's warm and concentrated, but that little edge of greenness is there too. Tannins are sinewy and dry. Serve it with roast lamb and mint sauce.

Wirra Wirra Scrubby Rise

Quality	🍷🍷🍷🍷
Value	★★★⁺
Grapes	shiraz; cabernet sauvignon; petit verdot
Region	McLaren Vale, SA
Cellar	🍾 2
Alc./Vol.	13.5%
RRP	$16.00 ⑤

In the manner of such things, the Scrubby Rise vineyard is naturally flat and free of scrub. The wines slot in below the grander Wirra Wirras. Maker: Samantha Connew.
CURRENT RELEASE 2001   Wirra Wirra's lower-priced red shows a strongly traditional McLaren Vale accent in its slightly jammy, earthy personality. Plum and red berry aromas meet balanced oak and the stewed fruit flavours suggest a bygone age. Tannins are mild and unobtrusive. It all adds up to an honest red that would suit good quality grilled sausages well.

Wirra Wirra The Angelus

Quality	🍷🍷🍷🍷🍷
Value	★★★⁺
Grapes	cabernet sauvignon
Region	Coonawarra & McLaren Vale, SA
Cellar	🍾 8
Alc./Vol.	14.0%
RRP	$49.00 🍾

This premium cabernet from Wirra Wirra is a 60/40 Coonawarra–McLaren Vale blend. Cabernet blends of these two regions have a long and successful history.
CURRENT RELEASE 2000   As usual this Angelus improves a lot with air; we recommend decanting to get the best from it. It's an eminently satisfying style with an attractive nose of blackcurrant, crushed dry leaves, beef stock and cedar. In the mouth it has attractive medium body and good balance, with perhaps a tad less weight than usual. Overall it's a very tasty drop, well-made and complete with finely balanced ripe tannins backing it up. Just the thing for a rack of lamb.

Witchmount Estate Cabernet Sauvignon

In Victorian times Sunbury produced very fine wines, but the bubble burst and in the 1920s the vines disappeared. Now the region has been revitalised. Witchmount is one of the newest producers.
CURRENT RELEASE 2001   This raw youngster looks deep, dark and full of glass-staining promise. The nose is a concentrated mix of dark berries, earth, spices, bitter chocolate and subtle oak. In the mouth it has intense, unevolved cassis-like flavour, chocolatey richness and a savoury toasty touch. It's medium-bodied, succulent and well balanced, ahead of drying tannins on the finish. Still rather unruly, it should settle down with time in bottle. When it does, sip it with a rare porterhouse.

Quality	♥♥♥♥
Value	★★★⅟
Grapes	cabernet sauvignon
Region	Sunbury, Vic.
Cellar	2–6
Alc./Vol.	14.0%
RRP	$25.00

Witchmount Estate Lowen Park Cabernet Sauvignon

Witchmount's Lowen Park vineyard was only planted in 1998, but the quality points in the right direction. Maker: Matt Ramunno.
CURRENT RELEASE 2001   Deep purplish colour is a trademark of these young Witchmount reds; this one looks totally immature. The nose has real concentration with syrupy, blackberry aromas, a touch of licorice, dark chocolate and earthy spice. It tastes fruit-sweet and rather raw, with strong berry flavours dominating a subdued touch of oak. A wine with attractive texture and good balance that will work well with roast veal.

Quality	♥♥♥♥
Value	★★★★
Grapes	cabernet sauvignon; cabernet franc
Region	Sunbury, Vic.
Cellar	1–5
Alc./Vol.	14.0%
RRP	$22.00

Witchmount Estate Lowen Park Shiraz

The Lowen Park vineyard was planted by Witchmount less than five years ago. Fruit quality is already good. Maker: Matt Ramunno.
CURRENT RELEASE 2001   Purplish, dense, dark colour introduces this shiraz with some fanfare. The nose has spicy berry and dried-leaf aromas trimmed in sweet oak. The impression is of a heavily extracted wine that's a bit 'headachey' now. The palate is intense with ripe blackberry flavour that's pure and penetrating. Body and mouth-feel are good and it finishes with balanced dry tannins. All arms and legs at the moment, it should calm down in time. Serve it with braised beef and onions.

Quality	♥♥♥♥
Value	★★★⅟
Grapes	shiraz
Region	Sunbury, Vic.
Cellar	1–5
Alc./Vol.	14.0%
RRP	$22.00

Wolf Blass Black Label Cabernet Sauvignon Shiraz

Quality	🍷🍷🍷🍷¡
Value	★★
Grapes	cabernet sauvignon 53%; shiraz 47%
Region	McLaren Vale, Barossa Valley & Langhorne Creek, SA
Cellar	⬤ 1–10
Alc./Vol.	14.0%
RRP	$125.00 🍾

Not long ago the Black Label was an essay in overdone American oak, but it has taken a more moderate tack recently and looks somewhat better for it.
CURRENT RELEASE 1999   Some will love this wine, others will think it still a dinosaur. There's a lot of syrupy blackcurrant fruit on the nose and some meaty touches. That old raw oakiness is there too, but it's not as assertive. The palate is big-flavoured and ripe, still with good serves of dark fruit, toasted coconut and dark chocolate. Dry, grainy tannins back it up. It needs time to realise its potential. Try it with a rib-roast of beef.

Wolf Blass Brown Label Shiraz

Quality	🍷🍷🍷🍷
Value	★★★
Grapes	shiraz
Region	McLaren Vale & Barossa Valley, SA
Cellar	⬤ 2–8
Alc./Vol.	14.5%
RRP	$39.00

The Wolf Blass mob has a penchant for coloured labels: there's a red, white, green, black, gold, brown, grey, yellow, and a platinum label. What next: hot pink? raw umber? magenta or chartreuse?
CURRENT RELEASE 2001   Word has it the Blass winemakers have eased off the throttle with oak, but this still has an emphatic measure of coconutty vanillin wood, with syrupy blackberry fruit underneath. There's a suggestion of bourbon whiskey about it, it relies on charred barrels so much. The palate is obvious, full, ripe and oaky with a firm backbone of grainy tannins. Serve it with glazed beef ribs.

Wolf Blass Grey Label Cabernet Sauvignon

Quality	🍷🍷🍷🍷
Value	★★★
Grapes	cabernet sauvignon
Region	Langhorne Creek, SA
Cellar	⬤ 2–8
Alc./Vol.	13.5%
RRP	$42.00

The Wolf Blass labels have had a revamp and now look rather more tasteful than the baroque efforts that were such a trademark for so long.
CURRENT RELEASE 2001   An honest, well-made cabernet with plenty of character. The nose has blackcurrant and blackberry aromas with hints of cloves, mint and vanilla. There's less raw oak than in past wines, and it tastes ripe, warm and concentrated with good length and balanced tannins. Still immature, this will be good with a beef claypot dish when it's a bit older.

Wolf Blass Platinum Label Cabernet Sauvignon

In dollar terms Platinum Label used to slot in below the Black Label cabernet in the Wolf Blass red wine hierarchy. Now the situation has been reversed, with Platinum wearing a truly terrifying price tag.
Previous outstanding vintage: '98
CURRENT RELEASE 2000   Not quite as successful as the 1998 vintage, especially given the price hike. The nose has slightly vegetal aromas interwoven with dark berries and sweet, spicy oak. In the mouth it's medium-bodied with good length and structure, but the flavours are still slightly mulchy. Perhaps ripeness was an issue. Not a bad wine to enjoy with lamb racks with a minty crust.

Quality	♟♟♟♟
Value	✦ ⌐
Grapes	cabernet sauvignon
Region	Clare Valley, SA
Cellar	▮ 6
Alc./Vol.	13.0%
RRP	$150.00

Wolf Blass Platinum Label Shiraz

The 1998 edition of this special shiraz was the best Wolf Blass red we'd tasted in yonks. We're happy to say the 2000 vintage is every bit as good, but be warned: an already expensive wine has got a hell of a lot pricier.
Previous outstanding vintage: '98
CURRENT RELEASE 2000   The nose has spicy plum, sweet blackberry, mocha and vanillin oak aromas that blend together into a powerful yet refined bouquet. In the mouth it has good balance of ripe, spicy shiraz fruit and classy French oak, great depth of flavour and fine texture, ending in ripe smooth tannins. Serve it with venison.

Quality	♟♟♟♟♟
Value	✦✦
Grapes	shiraz
Region	Adelaide Hills, SA
Cellar	⊶ 1–10
Alc./Vol.	14.0%
RRP	$170.00

Wynns Cabernet Sauvignon

This Australian icon once had a white label, but to delineate it from its less prestigious shiraz sibling, it was made black in the 1960s. In recent vintages, the wine inside is probably better than ever.
CURRENT RELEASE 2000   This edition benefited from the inclusion of material normally reserved for John Riddoch, the super-premium version that wasn't made in 2000. The nose has essency, liqueurish blackcurrant aromas with cedary oak threaded through and the pleasant leafy edge of ripe young cabernet. In the mouth it's satisfyingly rich, with good length and concentration ahead of firm, dry tannins. Perfect with roast lamb, and even better with some bottle-age. Shop around for price.

Quality	♟♟♟♟♟
Value	✦✦✦✦✦
Grapes	cabernet sauvignon
Region	Coonawarra, SA
Cellar	⊶ 2–10+
Alc./Vol.	13.5%
RRP	$30.00 Ⓢ

Wynns Cabernet Shiraz Merlot

Quality	🍷🍷🍷🍷
Value	★★★★﹜
Grapes	cabernet sauvignon; shiraz; merlot
Region	Coonawarra, SA
Cellar	🍾 8+
Alc./Vol.	13.0%
RRP	$19.50 Ⓢ

In our view Wynns is one of the great red wine brands of Australia, but is in danger of being taken for granted as the myriad of new, groovy boutiques continue to hog the spotlight.

CURRENT RELEASE 2000   This is a genuinely elegant, but ripe, cabernet blend that shouts Coonawarra. It's a gentle wine of elegance and understatement: good colour; scented mulberry, raspberry fruit overlain by cedary, sandalwood aromas; the tannins smooth and fine-grained. A delicious drink. Try it with pink lamb.

Wynns Shiraz

Quality	🍷🍷🍷🍷﹜
Value	★★★★★
Grapes	shiraz
Region	Coonawarra, SA
Cellar	🍾 6
Alc./Vol.	14.0%
RRP	$18.00 Ⓢ

PENGUIN BEST BARGAIN RED

Is there another red wine in Australia that offers such pedigree, consistent quality and value as this one? Wynns Coonawarra Shiraz continues a great 50-year tradition in fine form. Maker: Sue Hodder.

CURRENT RELEASE 2001   Like the 2000 Wynns Cabernet, this 2001 Shiraz contains all the material that would normally be made into its super-premium big brother, Michael Shiraz. The result is a more concentrated drop – spicy, ripe and complete. Buy up big on these wines right now: Southcorp have big export plans for Wynns that could push the prices up on the home market.

Xanadu Lagan Estate Reserve Cabernet

Quality	🍷🍷🍷🍷
Value	★★﹜
Grapes	cabernet sauvignon 65%; cabernet franc 20%; merlot 15%
Region	Margaret River, WA
Cellar	🍾 6+
Alc./Vol.	14.0%
RRP	$70.00

The top-level reds in Margaret River are very expensive these days. They're not always worth it, but it's amazing how just one winery can start a chain reaction in pricing, as Leeuwin Estate did many years ago.

CURRENT RELEASE 1998   The bottle-age shows in the medium brick-red colour, and it opens up with an off-beat vermouth-like nose of ginger, angelica and mixed spice. The palate is dry and savoury, thanks to extended time in barrel, and displays secondary or developed, as opposed to primary or fruity, flavours. There is lot of tannin and oak here, giving a very savoury finish. It's too grippy and unbalanced, unless you serve it with a hearty meat dish. Try rump steak.

Xanadu Secession Merlot

Xanadu has made some thumping big, tannic merlots in the past, but this is the first we recall under the cheaper Secession label. A drink-now brand, this wine is soft and easy, which tallies with our impression that the winemaker has used some carbonic maceration.
CURRENT RELEASE 2002   It's just a pup, but that carbonic maceration has made it an easy wine to drink young. It smells like a French Beaujolais: raw, floral and grapey without appreciable oak. It's light and soft and easy on the gums. But it's also rather simple and a bit short. Would go with barbecued sausages.

Quality	🍷🍷🍷🍷
Value	★★★★
Grapes	merlot
Region	south-west WA
Cellar	🍾 4
Alc./Vol.	14.0%
RRP	$14.90

Xanadu Secession Rosé of Cabernet

Secession started off as a single blended dry white; now it's had pups. There's a whole family of Secessions.
CURRENT RELEASE 2002   The very pale, European colour of Xanadu rosés continues, and this is starting to develop a salmon pink/orange hue. It smells smoky and developed; that is, it's moved along from a simple fresh-grapey nose. It's sweetly perfumed and flavoured, with lemony and mineral flavours that seems to point to some white grapes in the mix. It's very dry and slightly tart to finish. Good balance and drinkability. It goes with tuna carpaccio.

Quality	🍷🍷🍷🍷
Value	★★★⭐
Grapes	cabernet sauvignon
Region	Margaret River, WA
Cellar	🍾 1
Alc./Vol.	13.5%
RRP	$15.00

Yalumba Coonawarra Merlot

Yalumba call this one of their 'Wines of Provenance', a way of describing what the French would call *terroir*, the sense of place and identity some wines have.
CURRENT RELEASE 2000   This treads a middle road between a traditional style of Australian dry red, and a modern varietal merlot. It has roasted sweet plum aromas, some foresty merlot undertones, an earthy touch and some cedary oak behind it. There's nice balance and smooth mouth-feel with a succulent fruity tang. It finishes soft and likeable. Try it with roast veal.

Quality	🍷🍷🍷🍷
Value	★★★⭐
Grapes	merlot
Region	Coonawarra, SA
Cellar	🍾 3
Alc./Vol.	13.0%
RRP	$25.00

Yalumba Coonawarra Shiraz

Quality	🍷🍷🍷🍷
Value	★★★½
Grapes	shiraz
Region	Coonawarra, SA
Cellar	5
Alc./Vol.	14.0%
RRP	$25.00

These Yalumba wines are very smartly presented with a label that makes them look like wines worth many dollars more. Ideal for impressing the impressionable.

CURRENT RELEASE 2000 This is a middle of the road Coonawarra shiraz that mates raspberry and blackberry pastille-like fruit with a good measure of vanillin oak. It smells and tastes clean and appetising with a medium-bodied palate, ripe almost cordially berry flavour, good length and balanced tannins. Great with lamb chops.

Yalumba Mawson's Cabernet Sauvignon Shiraz Merlot

Quality	🍷🍷🍷½
Value	★★★
Grapes	cabernet sauvignon; shiraz; merlot
Region	Limestone Coast, SA
Cellar	2
Alc./Vol.	13.0%
RRP	$22.00

Sir Douglas Mawson's Antarctic expeditions are the stuff of Australian legend, but not as many people know that his expeditions were partially fuelled by warming Yalumba wine.

CURRENT RELEASE 2000 This has a very dense youthful colour that suggests good intensity. With a bit of exposure to the air the nose confirms it, with appetising, briary, red berry and mulchy aromas and some dusty, spicy oak behind. In the mouth it's medium-bodied with a bit of austerity to it, and it ends with fine tannins. A good Irish stew sits well here.

Yalumba The Signature Cabernet Sauvignon and Shiraz

Quality	🍷🍷🍷🍷🍷
Value	★★★★
Grapes	cabernet sauvignon; shiraz
Region	Barossa Valley, SA
Cellar	8
Alc./Vol.	14.5%
RRP	$35.00

There's a long tradition behind this label, which kicked off in 1962 as a special binning of Galway Vintage Claret. Each vintage is labelled in honour of a particular employee, associate or friend of Yalumba.

CURRENT RELEASE 1998 From an excellent vintage, this is the best Signature for a long time. It's a concentrated ripe wine with lovely integration of mellow, spicy, blackberry-like fruit character and excellent use of oak. It's medium- to full-bodied, long and firm with grippy tannins, and while showing some mature traits, it should still live for many years. Try it with beef braised in red wine.

Yangarra Park Appellation Series Cabernet Sauvignon

Is this the future for Australian wine? Yangarra Park is owned by Kendall Jackson Wine Estates of California, USA. The wines are made with restraint, rather than in the over-the-top, super-concentrated style beloved of American commentators. Very commendable.
CURRENT RELEASE 2001   Not really very varietal, nor particularly regional, this is still a well put-together young cabernet. It has a deep and youthful colour, and a clean, appetising nose of black fruits with measured oak in support. Not especially complex, but it tastes admirably ripe and sweet with smooth, mellow flavour, ripe fine tannins, and excellent balance and structure for its type. Serve it with barbecued lamb steaks.

Quality	♥ ♥ ♥ ♥
Value	★ ★ ★
Grapes	cabernet sauvignon
Region	McLaren Vale, SA
Cellar	▮ 5
Alc./Vol.	13.0%
RRP	$28.00

Yangarra Park Appellation Series Shiraz

Yangarra Park is one of the largest single vineyards in the McLaren Vale region, with around 230 acres planted with both red and white grapes.
CURRENT RELEASE 2001   In common with the other Yangarra Appellation red, this doesn't stray too far down the bigger-is-better road. There's still plenty of everything in it though. The nose is ripe with attractive blackberry and plum-like fruit aromas of controlled power. There's a spicy touch to ripe sweet fruit, some earthy notes, well-integrated toasty mocha oak, smooth flavour and good length. A friendly, full-flavoured red that sits well alongside a rare porterhouse steak.

Quality	♥ ♥ ♥ ♥ ♥
Value	★ ★ ★ ╉
Grapes	shiraz
Region	McLaren Vale, SA
Cellar	▮ 6
Alc./Vol.	14.5%
RRP	$28.00

Yangarra Park Shiraz

This is the base label from the McLaren Vale outpost of USA wine producers Kendall Jackson. Maker: Peter Fraser.
CURRENT RELEASE 2001   This seems a bit washed-out compared to Yangarra Park's Appellation Shiraz. This is to be expected we suppose – it is a lot less expensive – but we'd have liked just a bit more concentration in it. It has raspberry and plum fruit with a modicum of toasty oak for seasoning. The palate is simple easy drinking without great distinction. Serve it with fried noodles with Chinese sausage, roast pork and vegetables.

Quality	♥ ♥ ♥ ♥
Value	★ ★ ★
Grapes	shiraz
Region	various
Cellar	▮ 2
Alc./Vol.	13.5%
RRP	$14.00

Yarra Ridge Cabernet Sauvignon

Quality	♟♟♟♟
Value	★★★⬩
Grapes	cabernet sauvignon
Region	Yarra Valley, Vic.
Cellar	▮ 2
Alc./Vol.	12.5%
RRP	$21.00 Ⓢ

The Beringer Blass map of Australia now includes two of the Yarra Valley's best known names: St Huberts and Yarra Ridge. St Huberts, true to its traditions, is more of an individual estate; Yarra Ridge acts as a clearing house for wines from all over the Yarra region.

CURRENT RELEASE 2000   Designed as a drink-now proposition, this has a savoury nose that hints at black fruit, clean earth, briar, mint and sweet oak. The palate is medium-bodied with fresh flavours that track the nose well, finishing in dry tannins. Drink it with veal schnitzel.

Yarra Ridge Pinot Noir

Quality	♟♟♟⬩
Value	★★★
Grapes	pinot noir
Region	Yarra Valley, Vic.
Cellar	▮ 2
Alc./Vol.	13.0%
RRP	$21.00

When the Yarra Ridge wines came on the scene around 20 years ago, aggressive marketing ensured they quickly carved out a solid slot in the marketplace. Now under Beringer Blass ownership, the estate continues to grow and the wines are found just about everywhere.

CURRENT RELEASE 2001   A simple, uncomplicated pinot that won't disappoint, for easy, early drinking. Cherry, spice and light caramel aromas meet the nose, and the palate is light and simply constructed, with a very gluggable fruity flavour and clean soft finish. Could be lightly chilled as a warm weather companion to cold ham and salad.

Yarra Valley Hills Pinot Noir

Quality	♟♟♟♟
Value	★★★
Grapes	pinot noir
Region	Yarra Valley, Vic.
Cellar	▮ 3
Alc./Vol.	14.0%
RRP	$20.00

This is the Yarra Valley arm of the expanding Garry Crittenden/Dromana Estate empire. The wine is made in a forthright style that should please those who think pinot is a bit wimpy.

CURRENT RELEASE 2001   Quite deep colour here, and the nose has an unusual dimension of ripeness to it. The smells are a bit 'dry reddish' rather than delicate or fine, but there's nothing wrong with that. In the mouth it has robust plummy flavour with some spice, and good depth and body. A touch of smoky oak and a framework of slightly firm tannins complete the picture. Serve it with fillet steak.

Yering Station Pinot Noir

Yering Station produces three levels of pinot noir: Barak's Bridge at the budget end, this standard label, and the luxurious Reserve wine. Maker: Tom Carson. CURRENT RELEASE 2001   This is a pale colour with a magenta edge to it. A fruity nose hints at strawberries; spicy oak is less pronounced than in the 2000 but it's there. The clean palate has red cherry flavours, light body, soft mouth-feel and a dry finish. Try it with Chinese BBQ pork.

Quality	♥♥♥♥
Value	★★★
Grapes	pinot noir
Region	Yarra Valley, Vic.
Cellar	▮ 2
Alc./Vol.	13.5%
RRP	$23.00

Yering Station Reserve Cabernet Sauvignon

Yering Station's main claims to fame, for its Reserve wines, are the often superb pinot noirs and chardonnays; this cabernet sauvignon doesn't attract quite the same attention but it's always a good style. CURRENT RELEASE 2000   This has a savoury nose that combines briary and earthy aromas with a charry touch of spicy oak and blackcurrant fruit of good intensity. The palate is medium-bodied with good length of tasty flavour, which folds seamlessly into finely poised tannins. A refined wine to enjoy with fillet steak.

Quality	♥♥♥♥
Value	★★★
Grapes	cabernet sauvignon
Region	Yarra Valley, Vic.
Cellar	▮ 5
Alc./Vol.	13.9%
RRP	$58.00

Yering Station Reserve Shiraz Viognier

The recent trend to blend a little viognier with top quality shiraz (à la francaise) has produced some superb wines in Australia. Now Yering Station has joined in with their Yarra Valley version. We're big fans of the style. CURRENT RELEASE 2001   A brilliantly coloured young red with a superb aroma of black plum, cherries, pepper, earth and spicy oak, and a mere hint of floral viognier influence. The palate is richly aromatic with spicy fruit of real depth and lovely intensity. It isn't heavy at all, but has good structure underpinning things in fine style. The finish is soft and long. Lovely drinking with Peking duck.

Quality	♥♥♥♥♥
Value	★★★⁴
Grapes	shiraz; viognier
Region	Yarra Valley, Vic.
Cellar	▮ 6
Alc./Vol.	13.9%
RRP	$58.00

Yering Station Shiraz

Quality	🍷🍷🍷🍷
Value	★★★
Grapes	shiraz; viognier
Region	Yarra Valley, Vic.
Cellar	2
Alc./Vol.	13.5%
RRP	$23.00

The first vineyard in Victoria was planted on this site in the Yarra Valley by William Ryrie in 1838. It became one of the most famous before the wine slump of the early 1900s killed it. Now it's back.

CURRENT RELEASE 2000 Typically cool-climate and new wave, this is miles away from the prevailing world concept of big Aussie shiraz. There's a hint of wildness to it with a light gamy touch to spicy black fruit and nicely fitted oak. The dry palate has medium-intensity spicy fruit and light to medium body, finishing savoury with moderate dry tannins. A good match for sautéed kidneys.

Zema Estate Family Selection Cabernet Sauvignon

Quality	🍷🍷🍷🍷½
Value	★★★
Grapes	cabernet sauvignon
Region	Coonawarra, SA
Cellar	7+
Alc./Vol.	13.5%
RRP	$47.00

Established in 1982, Zema Estate is a family concern with 61 hectares of vines in Coonawarra. The Zemas only make red and this wine is their flagship.

CURRENT RELEASE 2000 This is a much more oaky style than Zema has been known for in the past. The charred barrel scents mingle attractively with sweetly ripe, almost jammy berry aromas, and the whole lot translates onto a succulent palate that has loads of flavour and charm. The tannins are soft. It holds up well with food, and goes nicely with a confit of duck.

Zilzie Buloke Reserve Petit Verdot

Quality	🍷🍷🍷½
Value	★★★★
Grapes	petit verdot
Region	Murray Valley, Vic.
Cellar	1–4+
Alc./Vol.	13.5%
RRP	$10.00 (S)

Not a 'reserve' range, rather the name refers to the fact that part of the Forbes family ranch has been fenced off as a reserve for an endangered species of native casuarina tree, colloquially known as the buloke.

CURRENT RELEASE 2002 The colour is impressively deep and dark, but it is just a baby, of course. A very fruit-driven red, it's attractively scented with pepper and spices and is remarkably concentrated for a $10 red. It's surprisingly tannic too, which makes us wonder what market it's supposed to be aimed at. It needs more time; or else serve it with a hearty, rare steak.

Zilzie Buloke Reserve Sangiovese

Made from exotic grape varieties, the Zilzie cheapie reds are truly head-turning – and not just because of their colours. This one, for instance, really does taste like a sangiovese, more so than some other much more pricey efforts. Maker: Bob Shields.

CURRENT RELEASE 2002   Clean, fresh, ripe red-cherry, black-pepper and dried-herb aromas abound in this trimmer of a wine. There's a touch of bay leaf and the palate is lean and linear with real elegance and style, no obvious oak, but good length and balance, ending with firm, drying tannins. This is unnervingly Italianate! Use it to trick your friends, and enjoy it with osso buco.

Quality	▼ ▼ ▼ ▼
Value	★ ★ ★ ★ ★
Grapes	sangiovese
Region	Murray Valley, Vic.
Cellar	▮ 5
Alc./Vol.	13.5%
RRP	$10.00 ⑤

Zilzie Merlot

Zilzie is apparently an old Scottish word meaning first home. Whatever it means, we reckon it's a great name for a wine – distinctive and catchy.

CURRENT RELEASE 2001   The colour is excellent: a very good start. The nose has plum-pit, cassis, almost cabernet overtones with a hint of sweatiness. It's fruit-driven: oak takes a back-seat. The structure is lean and somewhat skeletal, with a big finish due to exuberant tannins. It needs food: try a steak sandwich.

Quality	▼ ▼ ▼ ▼
Value	★ ★ ★
Grapes	merlot
Region	Murray Valley, Vic.
Cellar	▮ 3
Alc./Vol.	13.0%
RRP	$17.00 ⑤

Zilzie Show Reserve Shiraz

The Zilzie wines have been turning heads since they debuted on the wine market a year or two back. They prove that inexpensive Riverland wines can be really excellent drinks.

CURRENT RELEASE 2001   This is an affordable shiraz of real flavour and quality. It has a dusty, chocolate and licorice-like character, with a smidgin of honeycomb. It's soft in the mouth and easy to drink, without great depth or concentration. It's good drinking already, and would suit grilled pork sausages.

Quality	▼ ▼ ▼ ▼
Value	★ ★ ★ ◗
Grapes	shiraz
Region	Murray Valley, Vic.
Cellar	▮ 4
Alc./Vol.	13.5%
RRP	$16.50 ⑤

White Wines

Alkoomi Riesling

Quality	♟ ♟ ♟ ♟
Value	★ ★ ★ ⁴
Grapes	riesling
Region	Great Southern, WA
Cellar	➥ 2–8+
Alc./Vol.	12.0%
RRP	$19.00 ⬙

Riesling is a star in Western Australia's Great Southern region and Alkoomi is consistently one of the flagship wines.
Previous outstanding vintages: '98, '99, '01
CURRENT RELEASE 2002   Typically, Great Southern rieslings start off life shy and reserved, but a few years' bottle-age starts building richness and complexity. Alkoomi 2002 is more up-front on the nose than usual, with intense, musky floral aromas, lime juice, pear and minerally elements. In the mouth it's truly austere, with dry minerally flavour and a firm backbone of lemony acidity giving a bit of astringency to the finish. Definitely a keeper. Thai seafood salad will suit it.

All Saints Chardonnay

Quality	♟ ♟ ♟
Value	★ ★ ★
Grapes	chardonnay
Region	Rutherglen, Vic.
Cellar	▐ 1
Alc./Vol.	14.0%
RRP	$16.50

Under the direction of Peter Brown, the All Saints white wines have taken a step up in quality. Whether Rutherglen really suits most white table-wine grapes is still a moot point.
CURRENT RELEASE 2002   There's a strong honey aroma to this chardonnay that has some appeal, and peachy fruit mixes in well. The palate has honeyed fruit and oak flavours of medium intensity, but there's hardness and some alcoholic warmth on the finish that makes it a bit coarse. Serve it with soft cheeses.

All Saints Riesling

Rutherglen and riesling aren't the stuff of legends, but All Saints don't do a bad job with it.
CURRENT RELEASE 2001   This is an old-fashioned, slightly broad wine, with dry lime cordial and light spice aromas. The palate follows suit, lacking a little 'cut' and refinement, but it has good varietal character, and it's clean and well-made. It's a shade short in the mouth, but well chilled it makes good inexpensive drinking. Try it with good fish and chips.

Quality	🍷🍷🍷
Value	★★★
Grapes	riesling
Region	Rutherglen, Vic.
Cellar	🍾 2
Alc./Vol.	12.5%
RRP	$15.00

Amberton Chardonnay

The Barossa is red wine country in many eyes, but there's a lot of chardonnay planted too. Now almost universal, this white grape was unknown there only 25 years ago.
CURRENT RELEASE 2002   A pale chardonnay that exhibits lots of juicy tropical fruit aromas along with a light herbal touch. A touch of oak stands slightly apart from things making it a bit disjointed, but the fruit-salady flavours are what it's all about really. The palate is simple, refreshing and pleasantly tangy. Serve with prawn cutlets.

Quality	🍷🍷🍷
Value	★★★
Grapes	chardonnay
Region	Barossa Valley, SA
Cellar	🍾 2
Alc./Vol.	13.5%
RRP	$16.50

Andrew Harris Mudgee Chardonnay

Andrew Harris is a man on a mission. He wants to tell the wine-drinking world just how good Mudgee chardonnay is. It's certainly a topic for discussion.
CURRENT RELEASE 2001   There isn't great refinement to this chardonnay, but then the price is pretty reasonable. The nose has some raw oak aromas and melon-like fruit, while the palate is quite full, round and juicy. It's a simple style, to enjoy well chilled with a pumpkin risotto. Whatever you do, drink it young; chardonnays like this usually fall apart quite quickly.

Quality	🍷🍷🍷
Value	★★★¾
Grapes	chardonnay
Region	Mudgee, NSW
Cellar	🍾 1
Alc./Vol.	13.0%
RRP	$16.00

Andrew Harris Orange Chardonnay

Quality	▼▼▼▼
Value	★★★
Grapes	chardonnay
Region	Orange, NSW
Cellar	🍷 3+
Alc./Vol.	12.8%
RRP	$35.00

This is the finest of the three new Harris chardonnays, as you might expect; Orange is a high-altitude, cool region that naturally produces delicate wines.
CURRENT RELEASE 2002 A challenging wine, this. It opens with a sweet confectionery, sweaty, oaky range of aromas and there is an overtone of sulfide. The palate is lighter-bodied, lean in profile, strongly citrusy in flavour and finishes firmly with some oak astringency. As it airs and warms in the glass it gets better and better and the slightly pongy nose cleans up nicely. Try it with a cheese soufflé.

Andrew Harris Three Regions Chardonnay

Quality	▼▼▼▼▼
Value	★★★★
Grapes	chardonnay
Region	Hilltops, Orange & Mudgee, NSW
Cellar	🍷 3+
Alc./Vol.	13.4%
RRP	$35.00

Andrew Harris has put together a trio of fine premium chardonnays from the 2002 vintage. This one's blended from three top New South Wales regions. Mudgee chardonnay by itself can lack the aromatics and structure of cooler climes. Maker: Frank Newman.
CURRENT RELEASE 2002 This is a complex and appealing wine, with a smoky, toasty, butterscotch, barrel-marked nose and rich toffee and citrus complexities in the mouth. There's a subtle hint of sulfide that doesn't mar it, but adds interest. A lovely deep, rich smooth chardonnay to serve with grilled crayfish.

Angoves Stonegate Verdelho

Quality	▼▼▼
Value	★★★
Grapes	verdelho
Region	Murray Valley, SA
Cellar	🍷 1
Alc./Vol.	13.0%
RRP	$8.00 $

Someone somewhere has said that verdelho is the 'new chardonnay'. Frankly, pronouncements that reduce wine to a fashion statement should be ignored. Drink what you like, when you like it.
CURRENT RELEASE 2002 A no-complications sort of white, juicy with pineappley fruit, and touched by a bit of herbaceous tang. In the mouth it's no challenge to the senses, but it's softly fruity, crisp and easy drinking. Try it with Singapore noodles.

Annie's Lane Chardonnay

Clare Valley chardonnay is often damned with faint praise, but it's not really all that bad. The great makers put more effort into riesling as their premier white wine, with the result that Clare chardonnay can be a bit of a bargain. Annie's Lane shows what we mean. CURRENT RELEASE 2002 Often discounted to low prices that don't quite reflect its quality, this has attractive melony fruit with a well-modulated touch of nutty oak in the mix. It's smooth in the mouth with succulent flavour, zesty acidity and a fragrant finish. Serve it with mild vegetable korma.

Quality	♟♟♟♟
Value	★★★★↓
Grapes	chardonnay
Region	Clare Valley, SA
Cellar	🍶 2
Alc./Vol.	13.0%
RRP	$17.00

Annie's Lane Copper Trail Riesling

The corporate shenanigans of latter years have changed the identities of a few historic vineyards and wineries. Annie's Lane, for example, was once known as Quelltaler. Whatever, riesling is always a star. CURRENT RELEASE 2002 This super riesling is made from the best fruit available at Annie's Lane. It's a classic in the making that only needs a bit of age to complete the picture. Right now it has much to offer: aromas of lime, spices, herbs and minerals, intense flavour and the underlying minerally firmness and power of the best. Keep for a few years, then try it with sugar-cured tuna.

Quality	♟♟♟♟♟
Value	★★★★
Grapes	riesling
Region	Clare Valley, SA
Cellar	➡ 1–10+
Alc./Vol.	12.5%
RRP	$37.00 🍷

Annie's Lane Riesling

Around a quarter of this 2002 riesling was bottled with a screw-cap. Why not all, we ask? Always among the best value varieties, the screw-top makes it even better. Maker: Carolin Dunn. CURRENT RELEASE 2002 Made in a time-honoured style rather than the forward type of riesling that comes under some Beringer Blass labels. The nose is austere and minerally with light floral touches and a hint of lime zest. In the mouth it's penetrating and dry with minerally flavour, tight structure and brisk acidity. A winner at the price, but needs time to evolve. Try it with grilled South Australian whiting.

Quality	♟♟♟♟
Value	★★★★
Grapes	riesling
Region	Clare Valley, SA
Cellar	➡ 1–6
Alc./Vol.	12.0%
RRP	$17.00 🍷

Ashwood Grove Sauvignon Blanc

Quality	♟ ♟ ♟ ﹖
Value	★ ★ ★ ★
Grapes	sauvignon blanc
Region	various, Vic.
Cellar	▮ 1
Alc./Vol.	13.0%
RRP	$12.75 ⑤

Ashwood Grove's base of operations has shifted from Swan Hill to the Yarra Valley, where an arrangement with Fergusson's Winery will allow them to develop wines for the toffs.

CURRENT RELEASE 2002   There's good varietal character in this straightforward young sauvignon. The nose has an appetising gooseberry tang with hints of asparagus, spiky green leaves and passionfruit. Green fruit and slightly vegetal flavours are clean and it finishes dry. Serve it with stir-fried asparagus drizzled with oyster sauce.

Ballabourneen Hunter Verdelho

Quality	♟ ♟ ♟
Value	★ ★ ﹖
Grapes	verdelho
Region	Hunter Valley, NSW
Cellar	▮ 1
Alc./Vol.	12.0%
RRP	$18.00

Yep, it's another new brand, folks. Step right up and give it a try. But seriously, we wonder how these new brands can ever compete against the big established name brands in a tight market.

CURRENT RELEASE 2002   It smells dusty/peppery and capsicum, in short like underripe grapes, and the palate is commensurately lean and angular. It's pretty plain and tartly acidic. The finish is dry and has a little firmness to it. Try serving it with tossed green salad and asparagus.

Bannockburn Chardonnay

Quality	♟ ♟ ♟ ♟ ♟
Value	★ ★ ★ ★
Grapes	chardonnay
Region	Geelong, Vic.
Cellar	▮ 4
Alc./Vol.	13.5%
RRP	$47.50

Bannockburn Chardonnay's complexity always makes it a wine to linger over as it opens up in the glass, and its consistency has few peers. Maker: Gary Farr.

CURRENT RELEASE 2001   This fine chardonnay has a brilliant, pale greenish-yellow colour, and subtle yet powerful characters that hint at figs, white peaches and almonds. Fine French oak is there too and it's folded in with scarcely a ripple. On further acquaintance matchsticky and earthy notes enter the equation, adding quite seductive French-accented elements. The palate is long and smooth-textured with a soft finish. Drink it cool, not chilled, with salmon.

PENGUIN BEST CHARDONNAY

Banrock Station The Reserve Chardonnay

Jacob's Creek has a Reserve, so why not Banrock? Sure, but we can't see these wines as being in the same league qualitywise. But then, they are a bit cheaper. CURRENT RELEASE 2002   The colour is light yellow and it has a whiff of extended ferment character, which just obscures the fresh fruit a little – not that this will worry most drinkers. The taste is light, lean, simple and lacks real depth. There are some basic melon and nectarine flavours, typical of chardonnay, but it doesn't really transcend the basic. It goes well with corn fritters.

Quality	♀ ♀ ♀ ¼
Value	★ ★ ★ ⌐
Grapes	chardonnay
Region	Murray Valley, SA
Cellar	▮ 1
Alc./Vol.	14.0%
RRP	$13.00 Ⓢ

Barak's Bridge Chardonnay

Yering Station's budget Yarra brand is named after William Barak, the local Aboriginal chief in the early days of the Lilydale district. Barak's Bridge was a large tree that was felled across the Yarra River at Yering. CURRENT RELEASE 2001   This dry style of chardonnay has some subtlety and complexity for a modest label. The nose and palate have creamy lees and slightly minerally qualities that add dimension to melon-like fruit. There's also an attractive, smooth yet slightly powdery texture which gives real palate interest. It finishes dry and clean. Good with pan-fried fish.

Quality	♀ ♀ ♀ ¼
Value	★ ★ ★ ⌐
Grapes	chardonnay
Region	Yarra Valley, Vic.
Cellar	▮ 1
Alc./Vol.	13.0%
RRP	$15.50

Barossa Valley Estate Spires Chardonnay Semillon

This label has heralded some very good-value reds and whites over the years. Barossa Valley Estate now has its own winery in the Barossa at Marananga (near Seppeltsfield). Maker: Stuart Bourne. CURRENT RELEASE 2001   This is ageing quite rapidly, and already has a deep yellow colour. The aromas are very much in the green herbal spectrum, reminiscent of parsley and basil. It's a bit green and underripe, but it's often discounted and is reasonable value for money. It could suit vegetarian lasagne.

Quality	♀ ♀ ¼
Value	★ ★ ★
Grapes	chardonnay; semillon
Region	Barossa Valley, SA
Cellar	▮ 1
Alc./Vol.	13.0%
RRP	$12.60 Ⓢ

Bethany Manse Semillon Riesling Chardonnay

Quality	🍷🍷🍷
Value	★★★﹜
Grapes	semillon; riesling; chardonnay
Region	Barossa Valley, SA
Cellar	🍾 1
Alc./Vol.	12.5%
RRP	$13.85 Ⓢ

The dictionary tells us a 'manse' is a dwelling occupied by a minister of religion, especially in Scotland. It also used to mean a measure of land considered sufficient to support one family. So there!

CURRENT RELEASE 2002   This is a soft, light, simple dry white which does reveal its riesling component in its subtle powder-puff-like fragrance. It is soft and smooth, gentle on the palate and easy to drink. It should be perfectly acceptable in its market niche. You could serve it to the vicar, and it suits a range of vegetable dishes.

Bethany Riesling

Quality	🍷🍷🍷🍷
Value	★★★★
Grapes	riesling
Region	Barossa Valley, SA
Cellar	🍾 5
Alc./Vol.	13.0%
RRP	$16.40

Bethany is named after the picturesque little Barossa town near the winery. It was one of the earliest settlements in the region, dating from the mid-nineteenth century.

CURRENT RELEASE 2002   This is a finer, more fragrant riesling than usual for Bethany, reflecting the cool summer. It has lovely lemon/lime juice and mineral aromas. There's a touch of sweetness in it but it's not enough to be noticed by most people. It's very easy to enjoy young, despite an apparent ability to age. Try it with pan-fried sardines.

Bindi Quartz Chardonnay

Quality	🍷🍷🍷🍷🍷
Value	★★★★
Grapes	chardonnay
Region	Macedon Ranges, Vic.
Cellar	🍾 5+
Alc./Vol.	14.4%
RRP	$45.00 (mailing list)

The tiny Bindi vineyard was first planted in 1988 by Bill Dhillon and son Michael (now the winemaker), with some over-the-shoulder help from Stuart Anderson. This vintage was reduced by 60 per cent by frost. *Previous outstanding vintages: '98, '00*
CURRENT RELEASE 2001   The Bindi style is very fine yet concentrated, with marvellous purity of fruit, unencumbered by excessive oak or malolactic character. Balance is the key, and this has it. Creamy, nutty, stone-fruit aromas are reflected on the palate, which is very fine and tightly focussed with great power and persistence. The texture is smooth and creamy too. It suits truffled egg pasta.

Bird In Hand 'Two In The Bush' Sauvignon Blanc Semillon

Well, at least the handle's different. Apparently the names both come from roads or mines in the Adelaide Hills. Both these grape varieties are very much at home in the Hills.

CURRENT RELEASE 2002   It's a good wine, showing a shy, lemongrass-type fragrance, with some greener capsicum and green-pea-like nuances. It's clean and fresh and the palate finishes nicely dry. It lacks a little oomph (note the low alcohol) but the corollary is that it has delicacy and great drinkability. Goes well with a light asparagus risotto.

Quality	♥ ♥ ♥ ♥
Value	★ ★ ★ ⸴
Grapes	sauvignon blanc; semillon
Region	Adelaide Hills, SA
Cellar	🍷 1
Alc./Vol.	10.8%
RRP	$20.00

Bloodwood Riesling

Very little riesling exists in the Orange region's vineyards, which seems a shame as it's one of the best varieties for the area, judging by results to date. Maker: Stephen Doyle.

CURRENT RELEASE 2002   Bread-doughy esters shroud the varietal fruit in the wine's youth, but it seems to have what it takes to turn into a lovely drink in time. It has a classically dry, lean – almost austere – palate. The finish is firm and clean with good length. Cellar short term while the wine comes out of its shell. Then drink with fish, such as flounder.

Quality	♥ ♥ ♥ ♥
Value	★ ★ ★ ★
Grapes	riesling
Region	Orange, NSW
Cellar	🍷 1–6+
Alc./Vol.	13.5%
RRP	$18.00 (cellar door)

Boggy Creek Vineyards Riesling

Boggy Creek Vineyards are at Myrhee, an isolated pocket of viticulture in the alpine foothills of north-eastern Victoria, beyond the King Valley. It's a lovely little backwater, miles away from the rat race.

CURRENT RELEASE 1999   An oddity this, a developed riesling from a little-known grower. The colour is still youthful, the bouquet is richly developed with oily lemon and lime fruit aromas, and the light toasty touch of some bottle-age. In the mouth it has rich citrus flavours, ripe and intense, good length and texture, and a long, savoury palate. It finishes dry and complete. Try with lemon chicken.

Quality	♥ ♥ ♥ ♥ ⸴
Value	★ ★ ★ ★ ★
Grapes	riesling
Region	King Valley, Vic.
Cellar	🍷 2
Alc./Vol.	12.0%
RRP	$15.00

Brangayne Isolde Reserve Chardonnay

Quality	🍷🍷🍷
Value	★★★↓
Grapes	chardonnay
Region	Orange, NSW
Cellar	🍾 3
Alc./Vol.	13.0%
RRP	$24.00

Lovers of Wagner will recognise the names from the opera *Tristan und Isolde*.
CURRENT RELEASE 2001   A very restrained chardonnay with a pale colour and a slightly sulfury herbal aroma. The flavours recall parsley and green apple. It's a clean, fresh, well-made wine, albeit a touch simple. Cool-climate subtlety is the order of the day. It should grow with time in bottle. The oak is nicely underplayed. It goes well with niçoise salad.

Brangayne Sauvignon Blanc

Quality	🍷🍷🍷🍷
Value	★★★↓
Grapes	sauvignon blanc
Region	Orange, NSW
Cellar	🍾 1
Alc./Vol.	12.0%
RRP	$20.00

The grapes are grown by the Hoskins family and wines are contract-made by Simon Gilbert at Mudgee.
CURRENT RELEASE 2002   This pale-coloured, fresh and vibrant wine has a fresh gooseberry-like aroma with green salad and vegetable notes – clean and not too pungent. It's light-bodied and delicate on the palate with some capsicum and melon flavour and a slight astringency to finish. It would suit fish fillets with roasted red capsicum purée.

Briar Ridge Early Harvest Semillon

Quality	🍷🍷🍷🍷🍷
Value	★★★★↓
Grapes	semillon
Region	Hunter Valley, NSW
Cellar	🍾 10
Alc./Vol.	11.0%
RRP	$19.00 Ⓢ

Briar Ridge's ownership is a confused picture. The brand and stock were bought by Beringer Blass a few years ago, the vineyards and winery are still owned by Sydney businessman John Davis. Neil McGuigan has overall control of winemaking.
CURRENT RELEASE 2002   A classically styled Hunter semillon that will reward patient cellaring, although it's a great accompaniment to white-fleshed fish in its youth. The colour is fairly pale and it has a restrained aroma of straw, hay and lemon, with a floral high note. In the mouth it is deliciously intense and refreshing, with plenty of bracing acidity and lowish alcohol. A top example of the steely style.

Briar Ridge Stockhausen Semillon

Interesting how the old heroes of the Hunter are valued, and invited into the wineries to make a special wine of their chosen style. This celebrates Karl Stockhausen, winemaker at Lindemans in the 1960s and '70s.

CURRENT RELEASE 2002   This is even more steely and restrained than the Early Harvest (see opposite) and promises to be longer lived. It has a pale lemon hue and a shy floral, powder-puff, immature semillon nose. It is very clean, lean, dry and tangy: a pristine youngster that begs to be put away in a dark cellar. It is soft enough to enjoy young with oysters, though.

Quality	♟ ♟ ♟ ♟ ♟
Value	★ ★ ★ ★
Grapes	semillon
Region	Hunter Valley, NSW
Cellar	➡ 2–10+
Alc./Vol.	10.5%
RRP	$21.50

Bridgewater Mill Sauvignon Blanc

The Petaluma concept for Bridgewater Mill was to blend grapes from three vineyards. This sets it apart from the top range, which are all single region wines. Makers: Brian Croser and Con Moshos.

CURRENT RELEASE 2002   The tropical-fruit aromas are so pungent this year that it smells like a southern Western Australia wine. Passionfruit is uppermost, then pawpaw, and the palate is lovely and soft, clean and dry to finish, with impeccable balance. It has palate extension and richness, and we suspect there's a touch of barrel in there somewhere. Take it to a vegetarian restaurant.

Quality	♟ ♟ ♟ ♟ ♟
Value	★ ★ ★ ★
Grapes	sauvignon blanc
Region	Adelaide Hills, Coonawarra & Clare Valley, SA
Cellar	▮ 2
Alc./Vol.	12.9%
RRP	$20.70 🍷

Broke Estate Lacrima Angelorum

'Tears of the angels', we assume, in which case their hankies must be in an awful state. This is sticky wine writ large.

CURRENT RELEASE 2000   The colour is a mature-looking deep gold/amber, and the complex bouquet is composed of dried apricot, honey, mixed peel and marmalade scents, all lifted by a twinge of volatility. It's sweet, soft, rich and broad on the palate, with a candied-pineapple taste, quite sweet but also fairly acidic. Drink it up soon, with a rich pavlova.

Quality	♟ ♟ ♟ ♟
Value	★ ★ ★
Grapes	not stated
Region	Hunter Valley, NSW
Cellar	▮ 1
Alc./Vol.	12.6%
RRP	$26.00 (375 ml)

Brokenwood Semillon

Quality	🍷🍷🍷🍷
Value	★★★★
Grapes	semillon
Region	Hunter Valley, NSW
Cellar	🍷 10
Alc./Vol.	11.0%
RRP	$20.00 Ⓢ

This made an early appearance in last year's guide but it's still current and we reckon it's worth a second look. Winemaker Iain Riggs recently won the Graham Gregory Award for service to the New South Wales wine industry.
CURRENT RELEASE 2002   The 2002s look like long-ageing wines, but a lot depends on how the wine is crafted. This is still pale-ish yellow and subdued, with refined grass/hay, mineral and lemon-juice fragrance. It's tautly structured and subtle in the mouth, with plenty of fruit but restrained, and needs more time. Serve it now with baked coral trout, or cellar.

Brookland Valley Sauvignon Blanc

Quality	🍷🍷🍷🍷
Value	★★★⯪
Grapes	sauvignon blanc
Region	Margaret River, WA
Cellar	🍷 2
Alc./Vol.	13.5%
RRP	$27.35

Brookland Valley's best sauvignon blanc grapes come from a block of vines on poor, sandy soil near the front gate. Founder Malcolm Jones said he planted them there for their looks, and it was just lucky they grew great fruit.
CURRENT RELEASE 2002   This has all the freshness, clarity of varietal character and concentration that we look for in sauvignon blanc. It smells of gooseberry and cashew nut, with great intensity in the mouth and a very long carry. Power-packed stuff! Try it with grilled chicken and tomato aioli.

Brookland Valley Verse One Semillon Sauvignon Blanc

Quality	🍷🍷🍷
Value	★★★★⯪
Grapes	semillon;
	sauvignon blanc
Region	Margaret River, WA
Cellar	🍷 2
Alc./Vol.	12.5%
RRP	$19.35 Ⓢ

These days Brookland Valley is half-owned by the vast BRL Hardy empire, which brings the winemaking under the aegis of Houghton's dynamo, Larry Cherubino. Founder Malcolm Jones still has a hand in things, too.
CURRENT RELEASE 2002   This continues the excellent value-for-money of the Verse One range. The aromas are of tangy capsicum, dusty nettles and herbs. Lemon/citrus flavours and fresh salad leaves on the palate. The finish is clean and fairly firm, and it has some all-important length. It would go with Balmain bugs.

Brown Brothers Patricia Noble Riesling

Brown Brothers are among the pioneers of botrytis-affected sweet white wines in Australia – their first commercial effort was in 1962. Patricia Brown is the family matriarch.

CURRENT RELEASE 1999   They've held it back for some bottle-age, as is the custom at Brown's, and the wine is a ripper. The colour is deep golden-amber and it smells of cumquat marmalade and honey, reflecting lots of botrytis and aged complexities. The riesling character is not obvious, while the palate has barley-sugar and grapefruit/lemon flavours. There's a lot of sugar here. Lively acidity keeps it fresh, but not harsh. A lovely drink with pavlova.

Quality	♀♀♀♀♀
Value	★★★★
Grapes	riesling
Region	King Valley, Vic.
Cellar	🍾 2
Alc./Vol.	10.0%
RRP	$48.00
	$27.00 (375 ml)

Brown Brothers Whitlands Sauvignon Blanc

Whitlands has proven a good investment for Browns, even though phylloxera was discovered there in the early days and must have given them some anxious moments.

CURRENT RELEASE 2002   This is the finest savvy we've ever seen from Browns. It has a pungent bouquet of greenish twiggy aromas, nettles and a sweaty overtone. In the mouth it's soft and fruity, with a pristine clean, dry finish. Slightly elevated acidity does not concern us. Try it with oysters and a subtle herbed vinaigrette.

Quality	♀♀♀♀♀
Value	★★★★⁺
Grapes	sauvignon blanc
Region	King Valley, Vic.
Cellar	🍾 2
Alc./Vol.	13.0%
RRP	$17.20

Bunnamagoo Estate Chardonnay

Quality	🍷🍷🍷🍷🍷
Value	★★★★
Grapes	chardonnay
Region	Bathurst, NSW
Cellar	🍾 1
Alc./Vol.	13.4%
RRP	$26.40

The property, just south of Bathurst, is owned by the Paspaley family of pearling fame, and the wine was made by Jon Reynolds of Orange.

CURRENT RELEASE 1999   This is a finer, less developed wine than the 2000, despite its extra age. The bouquet shows cream, butterscotch and hazelnut. It has more restraint and subtlety, despite also having some richness. A delightful wine indeed. It would suit prawn ravioli in burnt butter sauce.

Quality	🍷🍷🍷🍷
Value	★★★
Grapes	chardonnay
Region	Bathurst, NSW
Cellar	🍾 1
Alc./Vol.	13.4%
RRP	$24.20

CURRENT RELEASE 2000   The colour is full yellow and the wine is rich and forward in a style similar to the lower Hunter Valley – although Bathurst is higher and cooler. It has a resiny, cough-medicine-like bouquet and the profile is lean and taut, with hazelnut flavours and moderate length. It would suit KFC chicken.

Burge Family Olive Hill Dry Riesling

Quality	🍷🍷🍷🍷🍷
Value	★★★★⁴
Grapes	riesling
Region	Barossa Valley, SA
Cellar	🍾 6+
Alc./Vol.	12.5%
RRP	$15.80 (cellar door)

The Olive Hill vineyard is at Lyndoch, which is the higher and cooler end of the Barossa Valley floor. It helps explain how Rick Burge produces such fine riesling, normally the preserve of the Barossa Ranges/Eden Valley.

CURRENT RELEASE 2002   The 2002 summer was also very cool, and the result is a sublime riesling: refined, graceful and beautifully flavoured with lemon/lime, garden herb and fresh pear. It is soft, up-front and fruity, but also has a seamless purity and delicacy that will help it age. It suits grilled whiting.

Burge Family Winemakers Olive Hill Semillon

Rick Burge is probably not as well known as his cousin
Grant, and his output is much smaller, but the wines
are superb and deserve a wider audience. His winery
is at Lyndoch in the southern end of the Barossa.
CURRENT RELEASE 2002   The first sniff reveals the
presence of oak, which can be contentious in semillon.
But the oak is subtly handled and the wine is a blinder.
It has an inviting nutty aroma of toasted-cashew and
lightly toasty bread – not terribly varietal, but
delicious. It's rich, nutty and lemony in the mouth,
with white Bordeaux-like honey complexities. It's full-
bodied, of similar weight to chardonnay. A classy wine,
to serve with roast Barossa chook.

Quality	♆♆♆♆♆
Value	★★★★★
Grapes	semillon
Region	Barossa Valley, SA
Cellar	🍶 5
Alc./Vol.	12.8%
RRP	$19.80 (cellar door)

By Farr Chardonnay

Gary Farr's first wines from his new vineyard were
cheekily named Bannockburn By Farr, but the owners
of Bannockburn Vineyard, where he still makes the
wine, weren't amused. This is the fall-back position.
CURRENT RELEASE 2001   This really responded to
breathing, which probably means it responded to
both aeration and warming in the glass. It has a
complex array of scents: peach, nectarine, butter,
creamed nuts and a hint of marzipan. It's not as
big-boned as some Gary Farr chardonnays, but is
still powerful and rich. A very good chardonnay
that goes a treat with roast pheasant.

Quality	♆♆♆♆♆
Value	★★★⬧
Grapes	chardonnay
Region	Geelong, Vic.
Cellar	🍶 5
Alc./Vol.	13.5%
RRP	$53.00 🍾

By Farr Viognier

Gary Farr was awarded the Qantas/Australian Gourmet
Traveller Wine Magazine's winemaker of the year
award in 2002.
CURRENT RELEASE 2001   Yes, it is expensive, but it
is a remarkable wine and more like a good Condrieu
(the greatest French wine made from viognier) than
probably anything else in Australia. The colour is
medium yellow and the bouquet is very complex,
spicy and toasty from barrels. It's rich and full yet not
overblown. Impressive stuff! You could try it with
oven-roasted scampi.

Quality	♆♆♆♆♆
Value	★★★⬧
Grapes	viognier
Region	Geelong, Vic.
Cellar	🍶 2+
Alc./Vol.	13.5%
RRP	$53.00

Cape Mentelle Georgiana

Quality	♟♟♟♟
Value	★★★⁴
Grapes	sauvignon blanc 70%; semillon 15%; chenin blanc 15%
Region	Margaret River, WA
Cellar	🍾 1
Alc./Vol.	13.0%
RRP	$15.80

This is Cape Mentelle's 'entry level' dry white, named after Georgiana Molloy, a pioneer of Western Australia's south-west. The label features a tapestry made by Gemma Hohnen, daughter of Cape Mentelle's founder. CURRENT RELEASE 2002 This pale white has a pungent nose that's like a handful of crushed grasses, leaves and other things green. In this context 'green' doesn't mean lacking ripeness; in fact a succulent touch of tropical passionfruit aroma adds a touch of ripe lushness to it. The palate is tangy and clean-tasting with an intense thrill of fruit and a lively lick of acidity. Serve it with assorted crisp vegetables.

Cape Mentelle Semillon Sauvignon

Quality	♟♟♟♟
Value	★★★⁴
Grapes	semillon 54%; sauvignon blanc 46%
Region	Margaret River, WA
Cellar	🍾 1
Alc./Vol.	13.6%
RRP	$22.40

This is an almost universal blend in Margaret River with just about every winery having a go at it. Most of them are pretty good, with Cape Mentelle consistently one of the best. CURRENT RELEASE 2002 Lime, pawpaw and gooseberry aromas lead the way here, with much less herbaceousness than many in the region, a legacy of a little barrel-fermented wine in the blend. That bit of wood influence seems more marked than in previous vintages, and adds subtle complexity, depth and mouth-feel to the palate. It finishes clean with slight firmness. Good with eel, grilled Japanese style.

Capercaillie Hunter Gewürztraminer

Quality	♟♟♟♟♟
Value	★★★★★
Grapes	gewürztraminer
Region	Hunter Valley, NSW
Cellar	🍾 3
Alc./Vol.	12.5%
RRP	$17.00

It is surprising that the Hunter produces several rather good traminers, contrary to most people's expectations. Others are Little's and Audrey Wilkinson. CURRENT RELEASE 2002 The colour is pale and this is a restrained, dry, subtle wine as opposed to the big, fat, pungent style fashionable now in Alsace. The aromas are delicate but authentic gewürz: a lychee and jasmine-like fragrance. It's intense and lively in the mouth, with a rich, juicy middle, a clean dry finish and real finesse. It would go well with a spinach quiche.

Capercaillie Semillon

Alasdair and Trish Sutherland bought the former Dawson Estate in the Hunter Valley in 1995 and expanded the plantings, renaming it and establishing a name for fine reds and whites from the Hunter, Orange and other places.

CURRENT RELEASE 2001   This is what used to be termed a traditional Hunter chablis style. It is delicate, restrained, subtle and needs time to build complex flavours in the bottle with age. At present it's all about lemon/citron and grass/hay aromas, with minerally hints. It's steely, well made and finely balanced. Good now with sashimi fish, or cellar it.

Quality	♟♟♟♟
Value	★★★★
Grapes	semillon
Region	Hunter Valley, NSW
Cellar	▮ 10
Alc./Vol.	10.5%
RRP	$17.00

Carlyle Riesling

The Rutherglen region doesn't immediately spring to mind when you think of good riesling. The warm climate favours other grape varieties, but riesling? Rutherglen-based Carlyle winemaker Chris Pfeiffer's answer is to look to cooler parts of Victoria's north-east, like the King and Alpine Valleys, for riesling fruit. The strategy works well.

CURRENT RELEASE 2002   Varietal personality is very good in this riesling. There's fine concentration on the nose with lime-juice, sweet spice and light stone-fruit aromas that are very appealing. The palate is brightly flavoured and intense with lime and spicy flavours well balanced by zippy acidity.

Quality	♟♟♟♟
Value	★★★★┦
Grapes	riesling
Region	north-east Vic.
Cellar	▮ 4
Alc./Vol.	12.5%
RRP	$16.00

Cassegrain Fromenteau Limited Release Chardonnay

The Cassegrain winery at Port Macquarie is back under the control of John and Eva Cassegrain after a period in the wilderness, due to family feuds. Part of the Fromenteau vineyard is biodynamic. Maker: John Cassegrain.

CURRENT RELEASE 2001   The colour has developed some golden tinges and the development is starting to show in the buttered-toast bouquet. There are also tropical-fruit flavours galore, with some oak on palate adding to the hazelnut flavour. It has weight and warmth. Try it with chicken chasseur.

Quality	♟♟♟♟
Value	★★★┦
Grapes	chardonnay
Region	Hastings Valley & Northern Slopes, NSW
Cellar	▮ 2
Alc./Vol.	13.0%
RRP	$28.00

Cassegrain Northern Slopes Semillon

Quality	♟ ♟ ♟ ♟ ♟
Value	★ ★ ★ ★ ↓
Grapes	semillon
Region	Hastings Valley, NSW
Cellar	➡ 2–6+
Alc./Vol.	12.5%
RRP	$18.00

The warm, subtropical region of Port Macquarie on the New South Wales north coast hardly fits the conventional idea of a wine region, but Cassegrain does it well, especially with whites.

CURRENT RELEASE 2002   This bears an uncanny resemblance to the classical Hunter Valley Semillon. Not surprising really, the Hunter isn't all that far away. This Northern Slopes wine has lemon, mineral and straw aromas of a fresh purity that would do a Hunter winemaker proud, and the palate has clean-tasting dry fruit of good length and mouth-watering savour. We don't know much of the ageing potential of these wines, but our hunch is that it will live long and well. Try it with a seafood terrine.

Castle Rock Estate Chardonnay

Quality	♟ ♟ ♟ ♟
Value	★ ★ ★
Grapes	chardonnay
Region	Great Southern, WA
Cellar	▮ 1
Alc./Vol.	13.5%
RRP	$21.00

If you're bored with the sameness of many Australian chardonnays, try something like Castle Rock. It's in a leaner, tighter, more austere style that will polarise tasters. CURRENT RELEASE 1999   It would be safe to say that most aged Aussie chardonnays disappoint us big-time. A lot of '99s already look tired at four years old, but not this mature Western Australian. It has fascinating complexity on the nose – honeyed citrus, nuts, spice, hints of toast and minerals. The palate is dry and very firm with good intensity of long, steely flavours, and a savoury toasty, flinty finish. A confronting drier style. Try it with a rich crab dish.

Castle Rock Estate Riesling

Quality	♟ ♟ ♟ ♟ ♟
Value	★ ★ ★ ★
Grapes	riesling
Region	Great Southern, WA
Cellar	➡ 1–8
Alc./Vol.	12.5%
RRP	$18.50

This riesling, from the Porongurup range near Albany in southern Western Australia, is a most ageworthy wine. Very shy at first, they build lots of character with age. CURRENT RELEASE 2002   If you haven't experienced the satisfaction of cellaring white wines, this is a good place to start. As a youngster, there's a light floral note, and it's delicate and restrained with lemon/lime aromas and a minerally thread. It tastes dry and tightly structured. An austere accompaniment to grilled whiting now.

Celtic Farm Revenge Botrytis Semillon

Since a large number of Australians can claim some
Celtic ancestry, and since those same people often like
a bit of a drink, it's entirely appropriate that we have
a range of wines called Celtic Farm.

CURRENT RELEASE 2001   Right in the Riverina botrytis
mainstream, this sweetie smells of marmalade, honey,
apricot and spiced fruit that's lusciously appetising. It
tastes as delicious as the nose suggests with very sweet
peach and marmalade flavours, tightly balanced by
zesty acidity. It's not as powerful in the mouth as some
others, which isn't necessarily a bad thing. Try it with
ripe peaches.

Quality	♥♥♥♥
Value	★★★⅃
Grapes	semillon
Region	Riverina, NSW
Cellar	▮ 2
Alc./Vol.	13.5%
RRP	$26.00 (375 ml)

Chalkers Crossing Hilltops Semillon

French-born Celine Rousseau won the 2002 Qantas
Medal for the most promising young winemaker in the
country. This wine was 60 per cent fermented in French
oak; it barely shows.

CURRENT RELEASE 2002   It seems to be trying to out-
chablis chablis. It is a pale lemon-yellow in colour and is
developing slowly. The aromas are very subtle and have
yet to evolve: there are hints of mineral and pear, and
just a smidgin of smoky oak. It's very tight and restrained
in the mouth, with tautness and tang. It would go with
oysters and should reward even short-term cellaring.

Quality	♥♥♥♥
Value	★★★★
Grapes	semillon
Region	Hilltops, NSW
Cellar	▮ 5+
Alc./Vol.	13.5%
RRP	$18.00 ⅋

Chapel Hill Reserve Chardonnay

Chapel Hill make two chardonnays – an unplugged
version without oak, and this one which is made in
a take-no-prisoners oaky style.

CURRENT RELEASE 2001   This shines yellow with
some depth in the glass, and the nose is a powerful
statement that's reliant on lots of oak. Spices, vanilla
and new-sawn wood aromas tend to overtake melony
fruit, and the palate is big and richly endowed.
Everything is on a larger-than-life scale, making it
a chardonnay for those who think white wine is for
wimps. Serve it with roast chicken.

Quality	♥♥♥♥
Value	★★★⅃
Grapes	chardonnay
Region	McLaren Vale & Limestone Coast, SA; Great Southern, WA
Cellar	▮ 2
Alc./Vol.	13.5%
RRP	$24.00

Chapel Hill Unwooded Chardonnay

Quality	♟♟♟⁉
Value	★★★⁑
Grapes	chardonnay
Region	McLaren Vale 40%, Coonawarra 40% & Padthaway, SA 20%
Cellar	🍾 4
Alc./Vol.	13.0%
RRP	$15.00

Many wineries put out unoaked chardonnays. At Chapel Hill, Pam Dunsford believes in a cross-regional selection of fruit to enhance the flavour spectrum. It seems to work, as this is consistently one of the better wines.
CURRENT RELEASE 2002   As a rule, unwooded chardonnays are profoundly yawnworthy, but this is a better proposition. A fresh pale wine, with a honeyed nose of citrus and melon scents, that's light and pleasant. The palate is soft and likeable with smooth texture and a tangy end. Usually thought of as an early-drinking proposition, these wines can improve with age. Easy drinking with tempura.

Chateau Leamon Riesling

Quality	♟♟♟♟
Value	★★★⁑
Grapes	riesling
Region	Strathbogie Ranges, Vic.
Cellar	🍾 2
Alc./Vol.	14.6%
RRP	$17.00

Riesling isn't common in central Victoria, and not particularly suited to Chateau Leamon's Bendigo climate, so Ian Leamon sources his riesling from the cooler Strathbogie Ranges.
CURRENT RELEASE 2002   An unusual riesling and one that perhaps ought to have a warning label owing to its strong 14.6 per cent alcohol! It has real weight and character with a nose that's reminiscent of cosmetics, stone fruit, lime and herbs. In the mouth it's lush-textured with big stone-fruit and lime flavours, dovetailed into tingling acidity on the finish. A potent riesling to serve with ratatouille topped with poached eggs.

Chatto Riesling

Quality	♟♟♟♟♟
Value	★★★★★
Grapes	riesling
Region	Tamar Valley, Tas.
Cellar	🍾 7+
Alc./Vol.	12.5%
RRP	$19.50

Although winemaker Jim Chatto now works in the Hunter Valley, he is still dabbling in Tassie grapes. The results of his labours are much more than idle doodling.
CURRENT RELEASE 2000   At nearly three years, this is a sensational riesling! It has a bright mid-yellow colour and a fine, maturing buttered-toast bouquet. A gorgeous semi-mature riesling, it fills the mouth, yet retains finesse. The finish is classically dry, yet soft. It's ageing gracefully and should go on and on. Great with a cold salad of smoked chicken.

Chestnut Grove Verdelho

The verdelho grape has a long history in the West, being the basis of soft white wines for generations. Even newer operators like Chestnut Grove find space for it among their trendy chardonnay and sauvignon blanc vines. PS: the two gold medals on the bottle aren't gold medals at all.

CURRENT RELEASE 2002   A bright pale straw-coloured wine, this has light fruit-salad verdelho aromas of simple, direct personality. In the mouth it's soft and juicy, round and dry on the finish. An uncomplicated fruity dry white. Drink it with chilled prawns.

Quality	♟♟♟♗
Value	★★★
Grapes	verdelho
Region	Manjimup, WA
Cellar	▮ 1
Alc./Vol.	14.5%
RRP	$13.50

Chrismont Riesling

Arnie and Jo Pizzini's friendly cellar door is a hospitable spot to visit when touring the lovely King Valley high country of north-east Victoria.

CURRENT RELEASE 2002   There's a zippy tingle of gas in this young riesling and the nose is fresh with slightly estery aromas of lime and spiced apple. The palate has pure intensity of varietal flavour and good concentration. It hints slightly at sweetness, giving a feel of real depth and softness, ahead of a clean zesty tang at the end. Serve it with Vietnamese lemon-grass prawns.

Quality	♟♟♟♟♟
Value	★★★★★
Grapes	riesling
Region	King Valley, Vic.
Cellar	▮ 4
Alc./Vol.	13.2%
RRP	$14.00

Cockfighters Ghost Chardonnay

Poor old Cockfighter was a horse who drowned in the treacherous bogs of the Wollombi Brook one stormy night in the early days of the Hunter Valley. This vineyard lies next to the spot and Cockfighter's ghost is said to haunt these parts still. Spooky or what?

CURRENT RELEASE 2000   A more obvious Cockfighters Ghost than some previous wines. It has bright greenish-yellow colour and straightforward oaky aromas mingled with syrupy stone fruit and fig. The smoky wood leads the palate and fruit is subdued, giving a slightly hollow palate. Serve it with shark and chips.

Quality	♟♟♟♗
Value	★★★
Grapes	chardonnay
Region	Hunter Valley, NSW
Cellar	▮ 1
Alc./Vol.	14.0%
RRP	$18.50

Cockfighters Ghost Semillon

Quality	♥♥♥♥
Value	★★★ ⧸
Grapes	semillon
Region	Hunter Valley, NSW
Cellar	⊷ 1–7
Alc./Vol.	11.5%
RRP	$17.00 ⬤

Cockfighters Ghost semillon is made in classic style by Patrick Auld, a man with excellent Hunter Valley winemaking credentials.

CURRENT RELEASE 2002   The very pale colour of youth has a bright silvery sheen in this Hunter semillon. On the nose it has varietal/regional aroma of good intensity that's minerally with a hint of lemon and a light touch of Sunlight soap to it. It's understated and still too young, but not without hidden strength. In the mouth it has soft, dry, slightly neutral flavour characteristics and a little more flint than some others. Serve it with blue-swimmer crab.

Coldstream Hills Chardonnay

Quality	♥♥♥♥
Value	★★★
Grapes	chardonnay
Region	Yarra Valley, Vic.
Cellar	▮ 3
Alc./Vol.	13.5%
RRP	$26.50

The Coldstream Hills labels are graced with a new Yarra Valley vineyard photograph each year. The shutterbug is founder James Halliday, a man of many talents.

CURRENT RELEASE 2002   A richer Coldstream Hills Chardonnay, perhaps a reflection of a very small, highly concentrated Yarra Valley vintage. The nose is still slightly undeveloped but it has subtlety and finesse. There's melon fruit and a gentle seasoning of nutty oak. The palate has good depth and texture with a long dry finish. A classy drop to match with grilled scampi.

Cookoothama Botrytis Semillon

Quality	♥♥♥♥
Value	★★★
Grapes	semillon
Region	Riverina, NSW
Cellar	▮ 2
Alc./Vol.	11.5%
RRP	$23.00 (375 ml)

The Riverina region has made botrytised sweet white wine its own, even coining the term 'Riverina Gold' for it. Results have been spectacular.

CURRENT RELEASE 2001   Oak plays a big part on the nose of this golden wine, giving a toasted-wood note to the nose and dumbing down the sweet fruit aromas a little. The palate is better: intense marmaladey flavour of intense sweetness is at the core, and the oak is there too but in better harmony. Overall it's a good sweet wine, though not as complex or luscious as the best of them. Try it with crème brûlée.

Cookoothama Chardonnay

The two hands on the label commemorate the hard manual yakka put in by the generations who developed the agricultural lands along the Murrumbidgee River in New South Wales. CURRENT RELEASE 2001   A satisfying example of Riverina chardonnay, Cookoothama has a ripe peachy, buttery nose with a balanced oak input, and it tastes smooth and generous. The palate has good depth and ready drinkability, without great complications of flavour. It finishes with respectable length and a dry sign-off. Try it with pumpkin gnocchi.

Quality	♟♟♟♟
Value	★★★
Grapes	chardonnay
Region	Riverina, NSW
Cellar	▮ 1
Alc./Vol.	13.0%
RRP	$17.00

Coolangatta Estate Verdelho

This estate in the Shoalhaven region of New South Wales is part of a substantial tourist operation in a historic area full of interest. The wines, made by Tyrrells in the Hunter, are of good quality. CURRENT RELEASE 2002   Coolangatta's Verdelho sums up the variety well. It's a straightforward unoaked white wine with a sweet nose reminiscent of pineapple and other juicy tropical fruits. In the mouth it follows on as expected, smooth, fruit-sweet and easy, with the soft mid-palate counterbalanced well by bright acidity. Try it with sweet and sour chicken.

Quality	♟♟♟♟
Value	★★★
Grapes	verdelho
Region	Shoalhaven, NSW
Cellar	▮ 1
Alc./Vol.	12.0%
RRP	$18.00

Craiglee Chardonnay

Pat Carmody does things his own way with skill and intuition. With chardonnay he avoids the creamy malolactic ferment characters that are a big part of most cool-grown chardonnays, in favour of a more elegant, fruit-dominant style. CURRENT RELEASE 2001   For a relatively 'unworked' chardonnay, this always has plenty of personality. The 2001 has a honeyed nose with stone-fruit aromas and a touch of powdery-dry oak. In the mouth it has good intensity and persistence, but like some other Craiglee chardonnays it seems a little 'hot' with alcohol. There's plenty of flavour and a dry, slightly hard finish. Try it with crab cakes.

Quality	♟♟♟♟
Value	★★★
Grapes	chardonnay
Region	Sunbury, Vic.
Cellar	▮ 4
Alc./Vol.	14.0%
RRP	$30.00

Cranswick Autumn Gold Botrytis Semillon

Quality	♥♥♥♥
Value	★★★
Grapes	semillon
Region	Riverina, NSW
Cellar	▮ 2
Alc./Vol.	11.1%
RRP	$27.00 (375 ml)

Autumn Gold is very appropriately named. The deep, shining golden colour of Riverina botrytised semillon is brilliantly evocative of warm autumn days.
CURRENT RELEASE 1998   This wine has the deep colour of old gold and our bottle seemed quite developed. The nose has apricot, honey-nougat and nutty elements, as well as a veneer of spicy oak and some volatile lift. In the mouth it's penetrating, very sweet and lingering with some slightly aged flavours adding interest. A mature sweet white to enjoy with some cheese.

Crawford River Nektar

Quality	♥♥♥♥♥
Value	★★★⟩
Grapes	riesling
Region	Henty, Vic.
Cellar	▮ 2
Alc./Vol.	13.0%
RRP	$25.00 (375 ml)

Portland, on Victoria's south-west coast, has a growing number of vineyards nearby. Seppelt's vast Drumborg spread is the biggest, but Crawford River often tops the list for quality.
CURRENT RELEASE 2001   This is simply delicious, an intense botrytised sweet white with a juicy lime, sweet cumquat and spice nose of great purity. The palate has luscious sweetness and texture with penetrating citrus flavours and a long clean orange-perfumed finish. Serve it with fresh fruit.

Cullen Chardonnay

Quality	♥♥♥♥♥
Value	★★★⟩
Grapes	chardonnay
Region	Margaret River, WA
Cellar	➥ 1–6+
Alc./Vol.	14.0%
RRP	$53.00

Vanya Cullen doesn't trumpet her expertise with chardonnay, but she is one of our most accomplished practitioners. The proof is in wines like this. Her style is underplayed elegance, making wines that get better with every glass (and bottle).
CURRENT RELEASE 2001   A complex young chardonnay, still tight and unassuming, but a wine that will build wonderfully in bottle. In youth it's superbly understated, working together perfectly ripe citrus and melon-fruit, nutty, creamy winemaker input and the light spice of classy oak, with great aplomb. The finish is long and penetrating with a fragrant, slightly toasty aftertaste. Great with grilled scampi.

Cullen Sauvignon Blanc Semillon

Many Margaret River wineries make a white Bordeaux-inspired blend like this one, but few are as good. Maker: Vanya Cullen.

CURRENT RELEASE 2002   A deceptively pale wine, this has a pungent nose of real intensity. At the moment oak and lees influences are a little dominant, but ripe herbal fruit isn't far beneath. Good acidity gives it a little more 'cut' and elegance than usual, while the flavour is still deep and rich, very long, smoky and fine. It should develop well in bottle. An excellent companion to a smoked fish platter.

Quality	♥ ♥ ♥ ♥ ♥
Value	★ ★ ★ ★ ⌐
Grapes	sauvignon blanc 82%; semillon 18%
Region	Margaret River, WA
Cellar	🍷 5
Alc./Vol.	14.0%
RRP	$29.00

Dal Zotto Riesling

This did well in the Sydney International Wine Competition 2003, where wines are judged with food. Winemaker is the euphoniously named Otto Dalzotto.

CURRENT RELEASE 2002   This fresh young riesling has an inviting aroma of minerals and lemon juice, and a penetrating palate with intense fruit flavour that leaves the mouth with a rich, satisfying aftertaste. It's not entirely dry but is beautifully balanced and very long. It goes remarkably well with a mousse of Jerusalem artichokes.

Quality	♥ ♥ ♥ ♥ ♥
Value	★ ★ ★ ★ ⌐
Grapes	riesling
Region	King Valley, Vic.
Cellar	🍷 5+
Alc./Vol.	13.0%
RRP	$19.90

Dalfarras Sauvignon Blanc

Mrs Rosa Purbrick, the wife of winemaker Alister, is an artist and her maiden name was Dalfarra. She paints the pictures for the labels.

CURRENT RELEASE 2002   This is a light, clean, well-made dry white without too much pungency. Instead, it has aromas of straw, dried grass and dried herbs, clean and properly ripe. Fairly simple in flavour and structure, it would go well with grilled garfish.

Quality	♥ ♥ ♥ ♥
Value	★ ★ ★ ★
Grapes	sauvignon blanc
Region	not stated
Cellar	🍷 1
Alc./Vol.	12.5%
RRP	$14.00 Ⓢ

Dalfarras Verdelho

Quality	♔ ♔ ♔
Value	★ ★ ★
Grapes	verdelho
Region	not stated
Cellar	▮ 1
Alc./Vol.	13.5%
RRP	$16.50 ⑤

Dalfarras is a brand owned by Alister and Rosa Purbrick of Chateau Tahbilk. The labels are adorned by pictures of Rosa's handiwork with the paintbrush.

CURRENT RELEASE 2002   This has the passionfruity aroma typical of young verdelho, but also the simple and somewhat weak palate structure. It's very light and falls away at the finish, and the acidity is somewhat disjointed. It's a simple, easy-drinking white that many will enjoy. It goes with cold seafood and salads.

Dalrymple Fumé Blanc

Quality	♔ ♔ ♔ ♔
Value	★ ★ ★ ┩
Grapes	sauvignon blanc
Region	Pipers River, Tas.
Cellar	▮ 2+
Alc./Vol.	12.9%
RRP	$25.00

Winemaker Bert Sundstrup is constantly playing around with experimental wines, and this is one of them. It's matured in older barrels, and is one of the relatively few wines labelled fumé blanc still on the market.

CURRENT RELEASE 2002   Oak ageing has deepened the colour slightly, compared to unwooded sauvignon blanc of the same age. It has a complex bouquet showing quite a deal of attractive cedary oak, together with discernible gooseberry and tropical varietal fruit clues. The palate has quite impressive intensity and length. It's a wine that grows on you. Try it with barbecued garlic prawns.

Dalrymple Sauvignon Blanc

Quality	♔ ♔ ♔
Value	★ ★ ┩
Grapes	sauvignon blanc
Region	Pipers River, Tas.
Cellar	▮ 1
Alc./Vol.	12.9%
RRP	$34.00

This savvy, made by Dr Bertel Sundstrup, is usually the stand-out example of its variety in Tasmania but it doesn't scale the usual heights this year.

CURRENT RELEASE 2002   There is some forward development that shows in the colour and the wine smells of the steamed-asparagus and boiled-cabbage kinds of sauvignon blanc varietal character. The palate is tartly acidic and it lacks the fruit intensity to balance. It needs food: try it with poached mussels.

Dalwhinnie Moonambel Chardonnay

This vineyard is best known for its full-blooded reds, but the chardonnay has really been hitting its straps in recent years. Up to the 2001 vintage they were made by Don Lewis at Mitchelton.

CURRENT RELEASE 2001   A real beauty! The colour is light–medium yellow; the nose is all about honeysuckle, with an intriguing chablis-like chalky, flinty minerality. The palate is correspondingly fine and tautly structured, with great length and panache. This is serious chardonnay! Try it with grilled lobster.

Quality	♟ ♟ ♟ ♟ ♟
Value	★ ★ ★ ★
Grapes	chardonnay
Region	Pyrenees, Vic.
Cellar	▮ 5
Alc./Vol.	14.0%
RRP	$42.00

D'Arenberg The Broken Fishplate Adelaide Sauvignon Blanc

This wine's worth buying just to read the back label. It rabbits on in entertaining fashion about how the wine got its name, but also about why the label carries the designation of Adelaide.

CURRENT RELEASE 2002   Here's a dusty, minerally, non-vegetal style of sauvignon blanc. It may lack a little in fragrance, but the taste is pleasantly light and soft, with good balance and drinkability. The finish has a slight phenolic grip. It would suit caesar salad.

Quality	♟ ♟ ♟ ♟
Value	★ ★ ★
Grapes	sauvignon blanc
Region	Adelaide Hills & McLaren Vale, SA
Cellar	▮ 1
Alc./Vol.	13.0%
RRP	$19.90

D'Arenberg The Dry Dam Riesling

D'Arry Osborn reckons this is the best riesling D'Arenberg has made, and we wouldn't question that. The record cool of the 2002 season meant McLaren Vale made much finer whites than usual. The blend contains some grapes from Middleton, 40 kilometres further down the peninsula from the Vale.

CURRENT RELEASE 2002   It's a delicate, subtle wine that is looking slightly austere at this juncture. The colour is pale, the aromas earthy, flinty, minerally and subdued. It tastes earthy/minerally again, somewhat angular and austere yet it has intensity and needs more time. Serve with whiting à la meunière.

Quality	♟ ♟ ♟ ♟
Value	★ ★ ★ ★
Grapes	riesling
Region	Fleurieu Peninsula, SA
Cellar	▮ 5
Alc./Vol.	12.5%
RRP	$16.55

D'Arenberg The Hermit Crab Marsanne Viognier

Quality	♟ ♟ ♟ ♟
Value	★ ★ ★ ★
Grapes	marsanne; viognier
Region	McLaren Vale, SA
Cellar	🍷 2
Alc./Vol.	14.5%
RRP	$15.00

All the D'Arenberg Rhône-style whites from 2002 have very elevated alcohols. That maybe okay in ballsy McLaren Vale reds, but we'd question its wisdom in subtler dry whites.

CURRENT RELEASE 2002   Very Rhôney, this! It smells of apricot, honey and spice, which probably reflects the viognier more than the marsanne. The palate is soft, slightly sweet-tasting and has a definite oily viscosity. There's a scented, 'lady's handbag' aroma too. It has generous flavour, but finishes with some harshness from the alcohol. It would suit oily pasta with herbs and peas.

D'Arenberg The Lucky Lizard Chardonnay

Quality	♟ ♟ ♟ ♟ ♟
Value	★ ★ ★ ♦
Grapes	chardonnay
Region	Adelaide Hills, SA
Cellar	🍷 2
Alc./Vol.	14.5%
RRP	$25.00

The back label tells us that lizards sunning themselves on trellis posts sometimes get shaken into the mechanical harvesters, along with the grapes, but the caring new-age vigneron will stand by the crusher bin and fish out the lucky ones!

CURRENT RELEASE 2001   This is a rich and complex wine as you might expect from D'Arenberg. The colour is medium–full yellow; it smells of straw and silage over richer peach/nectarine fruit with well-integrated oak. The palate is full, rich and complex, while retaining some cool-grown finesse. It would go with sautéed Balmain bugs.

David Traeger Verdelho

Quality	♟ ♟ ♟ ♦
Value	★ ★ ★
Grapes	verdelho
Region	Goulburn Valley, Vic.
Cellar	🍷 2+
Alc./Vol.	14.0%
RRP	$20.00 Ⓢ 🥂

David Traeger has his winery and cellar-door sales in Nagambie. He recently sold the brand to Dromana Estate, but he continues to do what he did before, without getting involved in the affairs of Dromana.

CURRENT RELEASE 2002   Under its screw-cap, this wine is nice and fresh, with a shy dusty nose that opens to reveal floral and spicy aromas as well as hints of tropical fruits. It's lean and quite light considering its alcohol strength, again with tropical flavours on the finish. It's a decent wine that would go with buttery grilled asparagus.

De Iuliis Show Reserve Semillon

Michael De Iuliis is the young winemaker at this Broke Road winery. The first vines in the 20 hectare vineyard were planted in 1990, and grapes have been sold to Tyrrells for some years.

CURRENT RELEASE 1998   Full marks to a boutique winery for holding back a traditionally styled Hunter semillon for so long (it was released in May 2003). It has a medium–full yellow colour and a semi-mature bouquet of straw, lemon-soap and baked lemon pudding. It's soft and gentle in the mouth, maintaining remarkable finesse, and is surprisingly youthful for a five-year-old. It suits salmon and fennel frittata.

Quality	♥♥♥♥♥
Value	★★★★⅃
Grapes	semillon
Region	Hunter Valley, NSW
Cellar	▮ 4+
Alc./Vol.	11.0%
RRP	$20.00 (cellar door)

Deakin Estate Chardonnay

The brand is named after Alfred Deakin, Australia's second prime minister. He was a prime mover in starting the Murray Valley irrigation scheme, without which this wine might never have existed.

CURRENT RELEASE 2002   The colour is medium–light yellow and it does smell like a chardonnay, with traces of burnt toast, peachy fruit and a hint of smoky, toasty oak. In the mouth it is soft and flavoursome, but just lacks a little freshness and purity of fruit. There's a slightly beery, leesy note. All the same, it's a crowd-pleaser that would go well with chicken satays.

Quality	♥♥♥⅃
Value	★★★
Grapes	chardonnay
Region	Murray Valley, Vic.
Cellar	▮ 1
Alc./Vol.	14.0%
RRP	$10.00 Ⓢ

Deakin Estate Sauvignon Blanc

In 2002, even the hottest climatic regions turned in some pretty fine dry whites, thanks to an abnormally cool summer. Maker: Linda Jakubans.

CURRENT RELEASE 2002   There's a touch of the cat about this sauvignon, by way of high-toned, slightly sweaty aromatics that are not unusual in sauvignon blanc. The wine is very light in weight, perhaps lacking a bit of intensity, but at the price it's certainly acceptable. The palate is soft and clean with a nice dry finish. It would go with salads.

Quality	♥♥⅃
Value	★★★
Grapes	sauvignon blanc
Region	Murray Valley, Vic.
Cellar	▮ 1
Alc./Vol.	12.5%
RRP	$10.00 Ⓢ

DeBortoli Hunter Valley Chardonnay

Quality	🍷🍷🍷🍷
Value	★★★★⟩
Grapes	chardonnay
Region	Hunter Valley, NSW
Cellar	🍾 3
Alc./Vol.	13.5%
RRP	$20.00

Like the debut semillon under this label, this wine is remarkably undeveloped and subtle, considering its region and age. It underwent a small proportion of malolactic and French oak maturation.

CURRENT RELEASE 2000   The colour is medium–light yellow and it's fresh and youthful, smelling of melon and grapefruit with some hazelnut just beginning to develop. Oak takes a back seat. There are some citrus flavours in the mouth, too, and the acidity is crisp and lively and drives the wine nicely. It goes well with ravioli of ricotta and fresh herbs.

DeBortoli Hunter Valley Semillon

Quality	🍷🍷🍷🍷
Value	★★★⟩
Grapes	semillon
Region	Hunter Valley, NSW
Cellar	🍾 5+
Alc./Vol.	12.5%
RRP	$20.00 Ⓢ

Just over a year ago Griffith's DeBortoli family extended their empire by purchasing the former Lesnik Family's Wilderness Estate in the heart of Pokolbin, a plum site for tourist traffic. The wines they've released were presumably inherited from Lesnik, but finished off by the DeBortolis.

CURRENT RELEASE 2000   This is a pale lemon colour, which is little short of amazing for a three-year-old wine. It is similarly fresh and alive on the nose and palate: delicate fragrant herbal, grassy, lemony aromas are very appealing. It's minerally/chalky and somewhat French to taste, with pleasant subtlety and balance. It suits baked snapper.

Deen DeBortoli Vat 2 Sauvignon Blanc

Quality	🍷🍷🍷
Value	★★★★⟩
Grapes	sauvignon blanc
Region	Riverina, NSW
Cellar	🍾 1
Alc./Vol.	12.5%
RRP	$10.00 Ⓢ

This won a gold medal and trophy for the best sauvignon blanc at the 2002 Cowra Wine Show. The Show accepts unfinished wines (tank samples), so we're cynical about its awards for current-vintage whites. But we do happen to like this wine!

CURRENT RELEASE 2002   Most unusual to find such good value in Aussie sauvignon blanc! The colour is very light yellow and the nose is melony, peachy and not at all green. The taste is soft, fruity (but not sweet) and lemony, with some richness and warmth. A very quaffable young savvy at a bargain-basement price. Take it to a vegetarian restaurant.

Deen DeBortoli Vat 6 Verdelho

This range celebrates Deen DeBortoli, the patriarch of this family wine company. His sons and daughter are all actively involved in the business.
CURRENT RELEASE 2002   A sweaty, passionfruity nose is typical of the verdelho grape, and the wine is light and lively on the tongue, with exaggerated acidity. It lacks a bit of intensity and drive, but it's clean and well-made and would go well with seafoods. Try whitebait.

Quality	♟ ♟ ¦
Value	★ ★ ★
Grapes	verdelho
Region	Riverina, NSW
Cellar	⬧ 1
Alc./Vol.	13.5%
RRP	$13.80 Ⓢ

Delatite Pinot Gris

The grapes came from Delatite's own plantings of this vine, which is still relatively new to Australian vineyards but quite famous in northern Italy and Alsace.
CURRENT RELEASE 2002   The colour is very pale and youthful; the aroma recalls dried wildflowers and there's a trace of the 'dishcloth' character often found in Aussie pinot gris. In the mouth, it is lean and austere, with some astringency which is not helped by the warmth of high alcohol. It may benefit from a few months' cellaring to recover its balance. Then try it with pasta with clams or pippies.

Quality	♟ ♟ ♟
Value	★ ★ ★
Grapes	pinot gris
Region	Mansfield, Vic.
Cellar	⬧ 2
Alc./Vol.	14.0%
RRP	$20.60

Devil Bend Creek Chardonnay

This sous-marque of Moorooduc Estate has a suitably provocative title. Maker Rick McIntyre has recently built a new winery, barrel shed, home and restaurant, all from stabilised rammed earth. It's well worth checking out.
CURRENT RELEASE 2001   It's a fruit-driven wine on which oak has not been wasted. Hence the nectarine-like fruit is allowed to shine through. It has a smidge of sweetness on the palate, which has good weight and presence. It needs to be chilled. A straightforward but well-made, attractive ready-drinker. It goes with prawn and mango salad.

Quality	♟ ♟ ♟ ¦
Value	★ ★ ★
Grapes	chardonnay
Region	Mornington Peninsula, Vic.
Cellar	⬧ 1
Alc./Vol.	13.5%
RRP	$20.00

Devil's Lair Chardonnay

Quality	🍷🍷🍷🍷🍷
Value	★★★⦆
Grapes	chardonnay
Region	Margaret River, WA
Cellar	🍾 4
Alc./Vol.	13.5%
RRP	$42.20

Devil's Lair was established by Phil Sexton in 1985 and purchased by Southcorp in 1996. The winemaker is Stuart Pym.

CURRENT RELEASE 2001   This is a restrained chardonnay for this region, and is slow to get moving. It has a shy, nutty, nougat barrel-ferment nose, with a little butterscotch developing as it airs. It opens up into a concentrated, intense yet refined chardonnay palate with plenty of oak, but lovely balance and persistence. It is already complex and will continue in that direction. It drinks well with baked vegetables.

Devil's Lair Fifth Leg

Quality	🍷🍷🍷🍷
Value	★★★
Grapes	semillon; sauvignon blanc; chardonnay
Region	Margaret River, WA
Cellar	🍾 2
Alc./Vol.	13.0%
RRP	$17.40

This 'fruit salad' blend has a back label that makes an appeal to the young and groovy. But it's a whole lot better than some of the turgid bulldust we read on some back labels.

CURRENT RELEASE 2002   This is a very pleasant, easy-drinking dry white with just the subtlest whiff of oak. The colour is pale green–yellow and the aroma reminds of cut grass, with a nutty oak background. It's light-bodied and straightforward. The balance is good and the finish has some alcohol warmth. The oak seems to soften and slightly flatten the palate. It goes well with vegetarian yum cha.

D'Meure Chardonnay

Quality	🍷🍷🍷🍷🍷
Value	★★★★
Grapes	chardonnay
Region	Huon Valley, Tas.
Cellar	🍾 2
Alc./Vol.	13.9%
RRP	$25.00 (cellar door)

For a guy with one lonely hectare of vines, Dirk Meure certainly maintains a high level of quality among the three varieties he produces. Check out the pinot gris and pinot noir too.

CURRENT RELEASE 2001   The bouquet is mysterious: slightly cheesy, perhaps from a wild-yeast ferment? The wine is light-bodied, fruit-driven, subtle and beautifully balanced, with low-key oak and a little age development starting to creep in. It has a lovely spectrum of flavours, and a positive finish that lingers on, and continues that fine balance. Its intensity and fresh acid should ensure it continues to age gracefully. Try it with Tassie scallops.

D'Meure Pinot Gris

Dirk Meure bought Flowerpot, a tiny 1-hectare vineyard at Birch's Bay, in 2000, when he returned home after 30 years away from Tassie, his home state. Maker: Michael Vishacki.

CURRENT RELEASE 2001   More in the Alsace than the Italian style, for sure. It's remarkably pungent, spicy, and full of character. The acidity is high and lively on the palate but it also manages to be rich and full. It has a firm, dry finish so it would be best drunk with food. Dirk suggests Alsace onion tart, and we'd go along with that.

Quality	▯ ▯ ▯ ▯
Value	★ ★ ★ ⁺
Grapes	pinot gris
Region	Huon Valley, Tas.
Cellar	▮ 3
Alc./Vol.	13.9%
RRP	$25.00 (cellar door)

Domaine Epis Chardonnay

Aussie Rules great Alec Epis learnt the game at Boulder, near Kalgoorlie. Italian origins meant wine was in his blood, and an early coach, who gave players a swig on a bottle of port as a training aid, surely helped (?). Now Alec has his own patch in the lovely Macedon hills, north of Melbourne.

CURRENT RELEASE 2001   This follows a good 2000 vintage wine in fine form. It has all the cool-climate cues without any unripe characters. Nectarine, citrus and melon meet classy oak in fine partnership. The palate is succulent and long with fine texture, good intensity and clean acidity. Serve with cured salmon.

Quality	▯ ▯ ▯ ▯ ▯
Value	★ ★ ★ ⁺
Grapes	chardonnay
Region	Macedon Ranges, Vic.
Cellar	▮ 3
Alc./Vol.	13.5%
RRP	$35.00

Dowie Doole Chenin Blanc

Few wineries make an effort with chenin blanc in Australia, which means this consistent one from McLaren Vale is a bit of a rarity.

CURRENT RELEASE 2002   The colour is pale yellow and it has an attractive passionfruity aroma with a hint of sweatiness. The high alcohol adds weight and length to the palate and there's a hint of sweetness. It's not a wine of finesse, but it's a decent drink and fair value. Try it with cabbage rolls.

Quality	▯ ▯ ▯ ▯
Value	★ ★ ★ ⁺
Grapes	chenin blanc
Region	McLaren Vale, SA
Cellar	▮ 1
Alc./Vol.	13.5%
RRP	$14.00 🍷

Dromana Estate Chardonnay

Quality	♥♥♥♥♥
Value	★★★★→
Grapes	chardonnay
Region	Mornington Peninsula, Vic.
Cellar	♦ 3
Alc./Vol.	13.5%
RRP	$30.00

There's no doubt chardonnay is one of the handful of varieties that suit the Mornington Peninsula very well. This is the second-ranked of several chardonnays from the Dromana group.

CURRENT RELEASE 2001   Like all the best chardonnays, this is about a lot more than just simple fruit. It has creamy, nutty, sur lie characters, a hint of toast from oak, plus stone-fruit aromas, the whole lot nicely balanced so no single character dominates. The palate is dry, clean-tasting and smoothly textured, and the finish has good length. It has the appeal of Mornington's trademark subtlety. Try it with steamed prawns and beurre blanc.

Dromana Estate Reserve Chardonnay

Quality	♥♥♥♥♥
Value	★★★→
Grapes	chardonnay
Region	Mornington Peninsula, Vic.
Cellar	♦ 3+
Alc./Vol.	13.0%
RRP	$53.00

As with most true reserve wines, the output is limited in order to maintain the desired quality, by grape and barrel selection; 420 cases were produced. Makers: Garry and Rollo Crittenden.

CURRENT RELEASE 2001   Dromana's reserve wines continue to improve (you'd hope so, as the prices keep rising!). This has a light yellow hue and a lovely nose of toasted hazelnut, white peach and nectarine. The oak has been beautifully handled and the complexing factors have been subtly employed, resulting in a finely balanced, deep, layered wine. It has the structure to age for a few years, too. Serve with grilled crayfish.

Dunsborough Hills Semillon Sauvignon Blanc

Quality	♥♥♦
Value	★★★
Grapes	semillon; sauvignon blanc
Region	Margaret River, WA
Cellar	♦ 2
Alc./Vol.	12.5%
RRP	$15.70

This wine is sealed with a synthetic stopper in place of cork. We've been seeing fewer of these in the past year or so. Has the momentum gone out of the plastic fad?

CURRENT RELEASE 2002   The colour is almost water-clear, and it smells very subtle, too. Honeydew-melon, restrained capsicum and stalky aromas are hidden beneath some vestiges of bottling sulfur. The palate is light and lean and lacks a little intensity. It may build some more body after a few more months in the bottle. Try it with cucumber salad.

Dunsborough Hills Verdelho

Verdelho is a grape that's grown mostly in either the Hunter Valley of New South Wales or the various regions of Western Australia, especially Margaret River and the Swan Valley.

CURRENT RELEASE 2002   The colour is a pale lemon–yellow and it smells slightly floral, powder-puff scented. There's some spice on the palate and a trace of sweetness, finishing with mineral and green-apple flavours. It's well balanced and would suit a caesar salad.

Quality	￼ ￼ ￼ ￼
Value	★ ★ ★ ￼
Grapes	verdelho
Region	Margaret River, WA
Cellar	￼ 1
Alc./Vol.	13.5%
RRP	$15.70

Edwards Estate Sauvignon Blanc

Sauvignon blanc haters (and there are quite a few) should avoid wines like this, such liaisons always end in tears. Sauvignon lovers should get stuck in – it's a good example.

CURRENT RELEASE 2002   Very pale in colour, this sauvignon has a light touch of barrel ferment, but as with many such Margaret River blends, the oak lends a modicum of textural interest and depth, but little overt wood on nose and palate. This is really dominated by herb and citrus characters that are pleasantly tangy. It has a soft middle and a zesty acid finish. Try chicken and asparagus stirfry.

Quality	￼ ￼ ￼ ￼
Value	★ ★ ★
Grapes	sauvignon blanc
Region	Margaret River, WA
Cellar	￼ 2
Alc./Vol.	13.5%
RRP	$22.00

Edwards Estate Semillon Sauvignon Blanc

At Edwards Estate their mascot is a vintage yellow Tiger Moth named Matilda. She putters around at a leisurely pace over the Margaret River beaches from time to time.

CURRENT RELEASE 2002   A very pale white wine with uncompromisingly herbaceous, blackcurranty aromas of zippy intensity. A touch of barrel-ferment adds dimension but it's secondary to tart, confronting aromas and flavours with more sauvignon traits than semillon. It has good length and a bracing thread of sharp acidity woven through it. Think of serving it with sushi.

Quality	￼ ￼ ￼ ￼
Value	★ ★ ★
Grapes	semillon; sauvignon blanc
Region	Margaret River, WA
Cellar	￼ 2
Alc./Vol.	13.2%
RRP	$22.00

Eldridge Estate Chardonnay

Quality	🍷🍷🍷🍷
Value	★★★
Grapes	chardonnay
Region	Mornington Peninsula, Vic.
Cellar	🍾 2
Alc./Vol.	13.5%
RRP	$34.00

Chardonnay is the success story on the Mornington Peninsula, despite the noise local winemakers make about pinot noir. Yes, pinot can be excellent, but chards more often reach the heights.

CURRENT RELEASE 2001   This is a 'worked' style of chardonnay but it stops short of being overdone. Nose and palate have subtle peachy fruit, hints of earth, toffee and nuts – all very complex and in fine balance. Oak takes a secondary role, and the palate has smooth, creamy texture that's easy and satisfying. There's a little phenolic firmness to it, and it finishes very long and quite powerfully. Try it with salmon.

Element Chardonnay

Quality	🍷🍷🍷
Value	★★★★
Grapes	chardonnay
Region	various, WA
Cellar	🍾 1
Alc./Vol.	13.5%
RRP	$13.25 ⑤

Element is Sandalford's budget brand. The product's motto is 'born of earth, wind, fire and water, Element is the essence of nature'. Wow, heavy stuff.

CURRENT RELEASE 2002   This is just what you want in an inexpensive chardonnay. There's a light touch of oak but it doesn't dominate a core of figgy fruit. Aroma and flavour are clean and direct, and the soft palate has attractive depth with a soft finish. Good value with some quality fish and chips.

Elgee Park Family Reserve Chardonnay

Quality	🍷🍷🍷🍷
Value	★★★
Grapes	chardonnay
Region	Mornington Peninsula, Vic.
Cellar	🍾 2
Alc./Vol.	13.8%
RRP	$30.00

At Elgee Park, Baillieu Myer pioneered the present Mornington Peninsula wine industry in 1972. There had been some small-scale viticulture down there before, but nothing much had come of it; now there are vineyards everywhere.

CURRENT RELEASE 2001   This is a brightly coloured chardonnay that improves with air. The nose has earth, cashew and lactic touches to nectarine and fruit-compote aromas. Subtle oak adds to its complexity. In the mouth it's long and smooth with a slightly firm thread towards the end. It has plenty of character and a very long aftertaste. Serve it with pan-fried yellowtail.

Elgee Park Family Reserve Viognier

Elgee Park proprietor Baillieu Myer quotes a description of viognier as having '. . . the aroma of Marie Antoinette's boudoir and the texture of chicken soup in a glass'. We couldn't have said it better.

CURRENT RELEASE 2001   Pungent aromatics are what most viognier is all about, but this is a little less like old pot-pourri than some examples, capturing the florals, spices, hazelnut and musk of viognier well, but in a more reserved way. The musky palate has a lightly unctuous feel and the flavours reflect the fragrant perfume of the nose. It finishes light and dry. Try it with roast pork.

Quality	🍷🍷🍷🍷🍷
Value	★★★⸹
Grapes	viognier
Region	Mornington Peninsula, Vic.
Cellar	🍾 2
Alc./Vol.	13.4%
RRP	$35.00

PENGUIN BEST WHITE BLEND/ OTHER VARIETY

Elsewhere Chardonnay

The 2001 Tassie chardonnays often lacked fruit intensity, although they are generally very pleasant drinks. This was made by contract winemaker Andrew Hood in his customary fruit-driven style.

CURRENT RELEASE 2001   The colour is bright light yellow and the aroma reminds of passionfruit and mango, fruit leading the charge, and oak tucked into the background. It is fresh, clean and grapey to taste, with a finish that just falls away somewhat. A good easy-drinking chardonnay with cool-climate Tassie flavours. Try it with pumpkin ravioli and sage burnt butter.

Quality	🍷🍷🍷🍷
Value	★★★★
Grapes	chardonnay
Region	southern Tas.
Cellar	🍾 2
Alc./Vol.	13.0%
RRP	$20.00 (cellar door)

Empress Vineyard Chardonnay

Quality	🍷🍷🍷🍷
Value	★★★★½
Grapes	chardonnay
Region	Geelong, Vic.
Cellar	2
Alc./Vol.	13.2%
RRP	$22.00

Empress Vineyard is near Colac, a bit to the north of the lovely Otway Ranges. This region west of Geelong had a healthy wine industry in the late 1800s.

CURRENT RELEASE 2000 An interesting style of chardonnay with subtle complexity worked in well without obscuring fruit character. The nose has slightly syrupy white stone-fruit aromas, as well as chalky lees and nutty, tasty oak behind it. In the mouth it's smoothly textured with integrated fruit and oak flavours and a clean dry finish. Works well with baked snapper.

Ferngrove Chardonnay

Quality	🍷🍷🍷
Value	★★★
Grapes	chardonnay
Region	Great Southern, WA
Cellar	2
Alc./Vol.	13.0%
RRP	$18.00 ($)

Ferngrove Vineyard Estate, to give it its full name, is one of the newer stars in the Western Australian firmament, with ex-Houghton winemaker John Griffiths consulting and Ted Avery as general manager. Early releases have been exciting.

CURRENT RELEASE 2001 This is one of the lesser Ferngrove new releases, a fairly prosaic chardonnay, pale-ish of hue and simple in character. There is negligible oak apparent and there are simple green-melon and apple aromas, while the palate is light and a bit straightforward. Still, it's a very clean, well-made wine and won't cause any offence. Try it with fried fish fingers.

Ferngrove Cossack Riesling

Quality	🍷🍷🍷🍷½
Value	★★★★½
Grapes	riesling
Region	Great Southern, WA
Cellar	8
Alc./Vol.	11.8%
RRP	$21.00 ($)

Ferngrove's riesling vineyards are in the Frankland area of the Great Southern. They have over 400 hectares of vines and chief winemaker is John Griffiths.

CURRENT RELEASE 2002 This delicious riesling has already done well in the shows, and we add our seal of approval to the list. It is pale in colour and aromas of fresh flowers and dried flowers, plus hints of citrus, present themselves to the nose. The palate is taut and nervy, the finish dry and clean. It's light-bodied and we really like its delicacy. Goes well with salmon poached with leeks.

Ferngrove Sauvignon Blanc

Few new brands springing from new vineyards have launched with such immediate success as Ferngrove. Many of the wines have won gold or silver medals and the riesling harvested seven trophies from just two shows!

CURRENT RELEASE 2002   The first bottle was corked, but the second was a ripper. This is quite a commercial style, with a touch of sweetness, while the fragrant aromas remind of lemon juice and gooseberry. It's fruity and full in the mouth and the finish carries some alcohol warmth plus phenolic grip. It's not subtle, but very flavoursome. Try it with seafood cocktail.

Quality	¶¶¶¶
Value	★★★⁴
Grapes	sauvignon blanc
Region	Frankland River, WA
Cellar	▮ 1
Alc./Vol.	13.0%
RRP	$18.00

Ferngrove Semillon Sauvignon Blanc

Consultant winemaker John Griffiths, who also runs a university wine science course in Perth, has handed the reins over to former Leeuwin Estate winemaker Kim Horton for the 2003 vintage.

CURRENT RELEASE 2002   Typical herbal, capsicum and 'snapped twig' aromas of these varieties when grown in southern Western Australia are evident in this user-friendly dry white. It's clean, fresh and well-made, and a trace of sugar on the palate doesn't mar it. Easy drinking, with traditional caesar salad.

Quality	¶¶¶¶
Value	★★★⁴
Grapes	semillon; sauvignon blanc
Region	Frankland River, WA
Cellar	▮ 1
Alc./Vol.	12.5%
RRP	$15.00 ⑤

Fire Gully Semillon

Components of this wine were fermented in oak barrels and others in stainless steel tanks. The oak has been sensitively employed: you can barely detect it.

CURRENT RELEASE 2002   The snapped-twig aromas give this away as a Margaret River wine. It has a slightly developed colour and some herbal characters that range from dry hay to fresh garden herbs. There seems to be a smidgin of sweetness in the mouth, which doesn't interfere with the attractively tangy citrus, grapefruit, lemon/lime flavours that dance on the tongue. It's good with crab timbale.

Quality	¶¶¶¶
Value	★★★⁴
Grapes	semillon
Region	Margaret River, WA
Cellar	▮ 5
Alc./Vol.	13.0%
RRP	$26.35 ⧦

First Creek Botrytis Semillon

Quality	🍷🍷🍷🍷
Value	★★★★
Grapes	semillon
Region	Hunter Valley, NSW
Cellar	🍾 2
Alc./Vol.	9.7%
RRP	$19.80 (375 ml)

First Creek is another new brand, this time it's Hunter Valley contract winemakers Greg Silkman and Jim Chatto of Monarch Wines doing their own thing.
CURRENT RELEASE 2002   It's very sweet, for sure, but also an absolutely delicious sticky! The colour is mid-straw; the bouquet is rich in toasty, buttery, lemony and crème brûlée aromas, and it's clean as a whistle all round. The palate is rich, sweet, finely balanced and smooth, luscious in fact, with a stone-fruit flavour. Acidity is discreet but obviously adequate to preserve the lovely harmony of flavour. It would do a citrusy crème brûlée justice.

First Creek Three Degrees Verdelho

Quality	🍷🍷🍷
Value	★★★
Grapes	verdelho
Region	Hunter Valley, NSW
Cellar	🍾 1
Alc./Vol.	12.5%
RRP	$13.50 (cellar door)

Verdelho is one grape whose varietal character is hard to pin down. It changes like a chameleon according to the vineyard, region, season and maker.
CURRENT RELEASE 2001   This is yet another interpretation of verdelho: it smells almost as spicy as gewürztraminer, and there's some sweetness on the rich, fairly broad palate. It has spicy and pineapple flavours, and finishes with obvious acidity, which gives a touch of hardness. It needs food: try a vegetarian meal.

Flinders Bay Pericles Sauvignon Blanc Semillon

Quality	🍷🍷🍷🍷
Value	★★★★
Grapes	sauvignon blanc; semillon
Region	Margaret River, WA
Cellar	🍾 2
Alc./Vol.	13.0%
RRP	$18.25

The *Pericles* was a ship wrecked on the coast near Margaret River. The brand is one of several co-owned by former Sydney retailer Bill Ireland.
CURRENT RELEASE 2002   This is the style the Margaret River does so well. It's minerally, lemony and dusty herbal smelling, with an apparent kiss of oak. We like the fullness, richness and softness of the palate. A gentle and eminently drinkable dry white. It goes well with whitebait fritters.

Flinders Bay Verdelho

Matthew Flinders was a brilliant navigator, one of the early maritime explorers, who charted much of the coastline of southern Australia soon after European settlement, around 200 years ago.

CURRENT RELEASE 2002   The nose has a suggestion of powder puff about it, together with grass and hay. The colour is pale and it is a little on the bland side, although it is certainly easy to quaff because it's so undemanding. The acidity is somewhat steely, and it needs to be served with food, such as antipasto.

Quality	♟ ♟ ♟
Value	★ ★ ★
Grapes	verdelho
Region	Margaret River, WA
Cellar	▯ 1
Alc./Vol.	13.5%
RRP	$18.25

Fox Creek Semillon Sauvignon Blanc

A percentage of the semillon in this blend was barrel-fermented, which helps explain the cedary/toasty nutty aromas.

CURRENT RELEASE 2002   The colour is slightly developed light yellow, reflecting the use of some oak. The cedar, toast and nut aromas dominate any varietal character. It has softness and breadth on the palate, but lacks the cut and zip of these varieties. There are squashy-melon mouth-aromas and a hint of peach on the finish. It's a very pleasant soft dry white to have with fish balls.

Quality	♟ ♟ ♟ ♟
Value	★ ★ ★ ⋆
Grapes	semillon; sauvignon blanc
Region	McLaren Vale, SA
Cellar	▯ 1
Alc./Vol.	13.5%
RRP	$17.00 Ⓢ

Fox Creek Verdelho

Fox Creek has 60 hectares of vines at McLaren Vale and Willunga. Winemakers are Daniel Hills and Tony Walker. From the circuitous label-speak, we deduce that some of the grapes, but not all, came from McLaren Vale.

CURRENT RELEASE 2002   A fresh, spicy aroma introduces this excellent verdelho. There are mineral and earthy scents as well. In the mouth it is dry and soft, light-bodied and very attractive drinking. It has some texture and some McLaren Vale broadness. Not subtle, but generously flavoured and authentic. Serve it with calamari and chips.

Quality	♟ ♟ ♟ ♟
Value	★ ★ ★ ★
Grapes	verdelho
Region	South Australia
Cellar	▯ 1
Alc./Vol.	13.5%
RRP	$17.00 Ⓢ

Fox River Chardonnay

Quality	🍷🍷🍷🍷½
Value	★★★★★
Grapes	chardonnay
Region	Great Southern, WA
Cellar	3
Alc./Vol.	13.5%
RRP	$18.40 Ⓢ

This is the 'other' label of Goundrey Wines, of Mount Barker, WA. The company was sold by Jack Bendat during 2002. Maker: David Martin.

CURRENT RELEASE 2001 A remarkably good chardonnay considering its price and station. It has quite a deal of complexity from creamy/nutty and lightly herbal flavours, with stone-fruit nuances, and we suspect some barrel ferment. The palate has delicacy and finesse, with layers of flavour, and finishes with good balance. This is real value and would work with chicken satay.

Fox River Classic White

Quality	🍷🍷½
Value	★★★
Grapes	chenin blanc; semillon; verdelho
Region	Great Southern, WA
Cellar	1
Alc./Vol.	13.0%
RRP	$14.80 Ⓢ

Fox River, Fox Creek, Foxeys Hangout, Foxes Island (in New Zealand). It's all a tad confusing for simple folk like us. This is Goundrey's second label.

CURRENT RELEASE 2002 A nice, simple, well-made, easy-drinking soft white that would suit many informal occasions. It has a clean, candle-wax aroma with hints of lemon essence and without too much herbaceousness. It's light, soft and uncomplicated in the mouth, with a nicely balanced finish. Try it with asparagus risotto.

Frankland Estate Cooladerra Vineyard Riesling

Quality	🍷🍷🍷🍷
Value	★★★★
Grapes	riesling
Region	Great Southern, WA
Cellar	1–5+
Alc./Vol.	12.8%
RRP	$23.50

The soil here is rocky gravel on a steep ironstone knoll, the stoniest of the three vineyards. Owner is well-known Perth retailer, John Ahern.

CURRENT RELEASE 2002 It's uncanny that there's an echo of the Wachau in this wine, the Austrian region the Cullam/Smiths greatly admire. The aromas are very minerally, with hints of earth and wet rock. The theme continues in the mouth, where it's lean and austere, slightly forbidding in its steeliness, and it's hard to see great depth of fruit at this point. It's unready now but should reward cellaring. Then try it with sushi.

Frankland Estate Isolation Ridge Vineyard Riesling

Isolation Ridge is the name of the Cullam/Smith family's own property at Frankland. They now use the name on all their home-grown wines. Soil is gravel over loam over a clay base. Maker: Barrie Smith.
CURRENT RELEASE 2002   This is arguably the pick of the three Frankland rieslings this year, a deliciously steely style of riesling which should age long-term. It's pale-hued and smells of minerals, with subtle notes of lemon/citrus, green herbs and flowers. In the mouth it's a fuller style with real richness, concentration and length. Steely but not harsh, it will reward even short-term keeping. Serve with grilled flounder.

Quality	♥♥♥♥♥
Value	★★★★↑
Grapes	riesling
Region	Great Southern, WA
Cellar	🍶 6+
Alc./Vol.	13.0%
RRP	$23.50 🥂

Frankland Estate Poison Hill Vineyard Riesling

The Poison Hill vineyard is owned by Frankland's shearing contractor, and the soil is white clay. It was so-named because of the supposedly poisonous plants that grew there and were a threat to passing livestock.
CURRENT RELEASE 2002   The low alcohol reflects a delicate, subtle wine which has intriguing aromas of dried herbs: sage and thyme. There are also mineral and citrus notes. It's dry, clean and racy on the palate with appealing softness despite its austerity. It should cellar well, but drinks nicely now with crab and asparagus gratin.

Quality	♥♥♥♥♥
Value	★★★★
Grapes	riesling
Region	Great Southern, WA
Cellar	🍶 5+
Alc./Vol.	10.7%
RRP	$23.50 🥂

Galli Estate Chardonnay

The Galli family name is derived from 'gallo', which is Italian for rooster. Lorenzo Galli, founder of Galli Estate, came from Tuscany, where he worked in the wine game.
CURRENT RELEASE 2001   This is a forthright, pungent sort of chardonnay with plenty of winemaking input on the nose. Nutty, spicy oak and barrel ferment aromas are quite strong and there are creamy notes as well, with fig-like fruit hiding in the middle. The palate has good texture and grapefruity flavour, fine and smooth, although the fruit character is a little hidden by toasty oak. To be drunk with soft cheeses.

Quality	♥♥♥♥
Value	★★★★↑
Grapes	chardonnay
Region	Sunbury, Vic.
Cellar	🍶 2
Alc./Vol.	12.5%
RRP	$15.00

Galli Estate Semillon

Quality	🍷🍷🍷
Value	★★★
Grapes	semillon
Region	Sunbury, Vic.
Cellar	🍾 2
Alc./Vol.	13.5%
RRP	$15.00

Galli Estate is one of those rare new wineries that hit its stride straight away, producing some excellent wines right from the word go. The future holds much promise for this Melbourne-outskirts vineyard.

CURRENT RELEASE 2002   Delicacy to some wine drinkers is plainness and neutrality to others. This wine treads that fine line; it has citrus and lightly grapey aromas but do they lack intensity? The palate is simple and fuss-free with more happening than the nose suggests, smooth citrus flavours are pleasant enough, it finishes attractively dry, and it has presence. Overall it's a well-made semillon that just lacks a little oomph. Serve it with pan-fried garfish.

Gapsted Ballerina Canopy Chardonnay

Quality	🍷🍷🍷🍷
Value	★★★⯪
Grapes	chardonnay
Region	Tumbarumba, NSW & Alpine Valleys, Vic.
Cellar	🍾 2
Alc./Vol.	14.0%
RRP	$20.00

The Ballerina Canopy is a method of trellising that ensures vines can get plenty of sunshine in cooler climates. This translates to ripe, healthy fruit.

CURRENT RELEASE 2002   There's plenty of flavour in this satisfying young chardonnay. It begins with ripe stone-fruit, nougat, and butter-caramel aromas touched by some forceful spicy oak. The palate is creamy in texture with good body and lush flavours that linger long on the palate. Balance is good but the flavour is quite oaky. Serve it with seafood in a creamy sauce.

Garry Crittenden I Arneis

Quality	🍷🍷🍷🍷
Value	★★★⯪
Grapes	arneis
Region	King Valley & Mornington Peninsula, Vic.
Cellar	🍾 2
Alc./Vol.	14.0%
RRP	$25.00

Hunting for something really obscure? This may be just what the doctor ordered. Arneis is a relatively unknown Italian white grape grown in small patches north of Alba in Piedmont.

CURRENT RELEASE 2002   Subtlety and underplayed fruit character are the hallmarks of good Italian white wine, and this arneis doesn't disappoint. The nose has juicy pear, minerals and almond cordial, and it tastes soft and clean with a little whisper of sweetness to fill it out, and a touch of nutty firmness on the dry finish. A little fuller than previous vintages, this should work well with pan-fried scallops.

Gartelmann Benjamin Semillon

In 1996 Jorg and Jan Gartelmann bought this already
established vineyard in search of a healthy country
lifestyle. Wine quality is usually right in the regional
mainstream.

CURRENT RELEASE 2002   This is a very aromatic
Hunter semillon with a sherbetty lime and lemon nose
of good intensity and real presence. It's not quite as
reserved as many young Hunter sems in aroma, but
the palate is more traditional – dry, vinous and clean-
tasting with the sort of youthful reserve that augurs
well for a few years in the cellar. Serve it with fish in
a lemon butter sauce.

Quality	♛♛♛♛
Value	★★★✦
Grapes	semillon
Region	Hunter Valley, NSW
Cellar	▮ 5
Alc./Vol.	10.5%
RRP	$17.50

Gartelmann Botrytis Chenin Blanc

Botrytised chenin blanc is a rarity in Australia, but in
France some of the world's greatest sweet wines are
made from it, along the banks of the River Loire.
CURRENT RELEASE 2001   This has a high-toned,
honeyed nose with aromas of citrus peel and candied
fruits and, despite botrytis influence, it's fairly subtle.
In contrast to the nose, the palate is not as sweet as
most, with a very dry edge and penetrating citrus-peel
flavours. It finishes quite hot and rather coarse,
possibly due to high alcohol. An oddball sweet white
that might work with pâté and warm buttered toast.

Quality	♛♛♛♛
Value	★★★
Grapes	chenin blanc
Region	Hunter Valley, NSW
Cellar	▮ 1
Alc./Vol.	15.0%
RRP	$20.00 (375 ml)

Giaconda Aeolia

Made from the rare northern Rhône grape roussanne,
this is very much in the Giaconda mould, with plenty
of winemaker input rather than simple primary fruit.
Maker: Rick Kinzbrunner.
CURRENT RELEASE 2002   A tiny sniff of this wine tells
you that it's special. There's all the usual Giaconda
complexity, but it has a different enough varietal
personality to keep us fascinated. On the nose there are
hints of heather and flowering herbs as well as stone
fruit, nuts, wild honey, spice and smoky oak. The palate
is full and round in texture with sustained power and
great length. Lovely with a creamy lobster dish.

Quality	♛♛♛♛♛
Value	★★★
Grapes	roussanne
Region	Beechworth, Vic.
Cellar	▮ 3
Alc./Vol.	13.5%
RRP	$85.00

Giaconda Chardonnay

Quality	♟♟♟♟♟
Value	★★★
Grapes	chardonnay
Region	Beechworth, Vic.
Cellar	🍷 1–5+
Alc./Vol.	13.5%
RRP	$120.00

Giaconda might just be Australia's best chardonnay; its cult status makes it as rare as hen's teeth and very expensive, but if you can get hold of a bottle grab it, you deserve the best, occasionally.

CURRENT RELEASE 2001   The magic of Giaconda Chardonnay is the way it combines power with subtlety. The 2001 is typically complex with lots of winemaker-induced effort adding nutty, creamy, toasty touches to rich peach fruit at the core. Everything is interwoven so that nothing stands out, and texture and feel are as important as flavour. It's silky, long and complete. Serve cool with buttery salmon fillets.

Giaconda Nantua Les Deux

Quality	♟♟♟♟♟
Value	★★★♦
Grapes	chardonnay; roussanne
Region	Beechworth, Vic.
Cellar	🍷 1–4
Alc./Vol.	13.5%
RRP	$45.00

There's an air of mystery and romance about this wine with its allegorical name and Swan Lake label. It seems entirely appropriate to an artistic blend of chardonnay and roussanne. Maker: Rick Kinzbrunner.

CURRENT RELEASE 2002   This unusual blend has the Giaconda mark on it and an interesting fruit character almost defies description. But here goes! The nose has some eggy and matchsticky Frenchified smells, along with passionfruit and creamy notes, and notable spicy oak. The palate is richly endowed with spice and stone-fruit flavours and a creamy smooth, almost thick texture. It finishes dry. Serve it with soft cheeses.

Giant Steps Chardonnay

Quality	♟♟♟♟
Value	★★★★
Grapes	chardonnay
Region	Yarra Valley, SA
Cellar	🍷 2
Alc./Vol.	13.9%
RRP	$20.00

Giant Steps is the new Yarra Valley project of ex–West Australian brewer/winemaker Phil Sexton. The label features a fascinating allegorical picture of a child with a teddy bear about to climb a flight of stairs that lead to . . . enlightenment? Very artistic stuff.

CURRENT RELEASE 2001   First impressions are of lots of toasty oak and barrel effect here. On further acquaintance some attractive stone-fruit and mealy notes emerge. It tastes rich, oaky and perhaps a smidge volatile, with ripe fig-like fruit and alcohol sweetness at the heart of things. It has smooth texture and full flavour that's long and tasty. Try it with chargrilled salmon.

The Gorge Chardonnay

The Gorge is the second label of David Hook of Pothana vineyard at Belford, a northern sub-district of the Hunter. He's an early-adopter of screw-caps on chardonnay.
CURRENT RELEASE 2002   The wine is a lighter, simpler style of chardonnay, with negligible oak influence. It has a slightly sweaty, nectarine-like nose that's youthful and vibrant. It's light-bodied to taste, and while the aspirations are modest, so is the price. Clean and well-made. It goes with prosciutto and melon.

Quality	♥♥♥♥
Value	★★★★
Grapes	chardonnay
Region	Hunter Valley, NSW
Cellar	🍾 2
Alc./Vol.	12.5%
RRP	$16.00 🍷

The Gorge Mosto

This light, sweet white most resembles an Italian moscato. The word mosto means must – the unfermented juice of the grape. Maker: David Hook.
CURRENT RELEASE 2002   It's not muscat-based and therefore lacks the spicy grapey aromas of the muscat grape. But it's a delicious, refreshing light sweetie, with a mid-yellow colour and zingy fresh aromas of citrus – limes and lemons predominating. The palate is very vibrant and tangy, helped by the screw-cap no doubt, and the effervescence referred to on the back label is barely noticeable. Try it as an aperitif or with cake.

Quality	♥♥♥♥
Value	★★★★
Grapes	semillon
Region	Hunter Valley, NSW
Cellar	🍾 1
Alc./Vol.	9.5%
RRP	$20.00 🍷

The Gorge Verdelho

Not sure where this gorge is exactly, but David Hook's Pothana vineyard, where the wine was grown and made, is right beside the railway line where endless coal trains bring brown coal from the upper Hunter Valley mines to the docks at Newcastle.
CURRENT RELEASE 2002   This has a pale colour and an earthy, crushed-leaf and capsicum aroma that reminds more than distantly of sauvignon blanc. The taste is dry and high in acidity, creating an austere, slightly harsh finish. It needs food. Try it with Greek salad.

Quality	♥♥♥
Value	★★★
Grapes	verdelho
Region	Hunter Valley, NSW
Cellar	🍾 1
Alc./Vol.	12.5%
RRP	$16.00

Grant Burge Barossa Vines Chardonnay

Quality	▼▼▼⬗
Value	★★★★
Grapes	chardonnay
Region	Barossa Valley, SA
Cellar	🍶 1
Alc./Vol.	13.5%
RRP	$13.50 Ⓢ

Grant Burge's Barossa Vines range are just about the best-value Barossa wines around. Most of the competition at this price point is sourced from the big broadacre vineyards of the Murray Valley and Riverina. CURRENT RELEASE 2002 There's a generous amount of fruit character in this wine. It's slanted towards the pineappley, tropical-fruit style with little oak influence. It has good concentration for its type and the flavours are ripe and satisfying. Drink it well-chilled with Szechuan chicken.

Grant Burge Barossa Vines Semillon

Quality	▼▼▼▼
Value	★★★★★
Grapes	semillon
Region	Barossa Valley, SA
Cellar	🍶 1
Alc./Vol.	13.0%
RRP	$13.50 Ⓢ

This unassuming semillon is always cracking value, possibly because people overlook it in their rush to grab the chardonnays. CURRENT RELEASE 2002 This has a fresh, light, grapey nose with an appetising hint of citrus to it. In the mouth it's zesty-tasting with medium intensity and a clean, crisp finish. It has enough depth and interest to lift it above the ordinary, and it's always well-priced, so what are you waiting for? Serve it with shellfish pasta.

Grant Burge Summers Chardonnay

Quality	▼▼▼▼⬗
Value	★★★⭑
Grapes	chardonnay
Region	Barossa Valley, SA
Cellar	🍶 2
Alc./Vol.	13.5%
RRP	$20.00

Made from grapes grown on the Summers vineyard, and also eminently suitable for summer drinking. Or winter, spring and autumn as the case may be. CURRENT RELEASE 2002 A rich, ripe nose here, nicely balanced between melon-pineapple fruit, smoky barrel ferment and nutty lees character. In the mouth there's good depth of rich fruit and balanced oak flavours, and it's quite fine in texture and long in flavour. A satisfying chardonnay that offers plenty of character. Try it with a Thai chicken salad.

Grant Burge Thorn Eden Valley Riesling

In common with a number of other Grant Burge wines, this bears the name of one of the principal vineyards that provide grapes for the wine. In this case the Thorn Family Vineyard and Stephens Wyncroft Estate, both in the Eden Valley, are the sources.
CURRENT RELEASE 2002   This looks pale and very slightly spritzy. The nose has pristine varietal purity of the lime-zest type. It's more austere than most previous Thorn Rieslings with a steely thing that continues down the long tight palate with unusual intensity. It looks to have good ageing potential. It suits smoked trout pâté well.

Quality	♟ ♟ ♟ ♟ ♟
Value	★ ★ ★ ★ ★
Grapes	riesling
Region	Eden Valley, SA
Cellar	➥ 1–8
Alc./Vol.	12.5%
RRP	$17.00

Grant Burge Virtuoso

A problem for wine marketers is how to attract attention to your product on a crowded shelf. With a garish harlequin-coloured label and narrow clear-glass bottle, Virtuoso is guaranteed to be noticed.
CURRENT RELEASE 2002   There's a bit more lemony semillon character to this wine than usual. The sauvignon blanc component adds its particular herbaceous twist to things, but that semillon comes through on the long clean-tasting palate. It finishes crisp and long. Well-made and tasty, a good companion to vegetable tempura.

Quality	♟ ♟ ♟ ♟
Value	★ ★ ★ ★ ⟩
Grapes	sauvignon blanc; semillon
Region	Barossa Valley, SA
Cellar	▮ 2
Alc./Vol.	13.0%
RRP	$16.00

Grant Burge Zerk Semillon

Semillon makes entirely different wines in three of Australia's great regions: in Margaret River they tend to be herbaceous and zesty; Hunter River wines are delicate young, blossoming with age; and the Barossas are big and flavoursome.
CURRENT RELEASE 2002   A good chardonnay alternative with similar weight and construction, but quite different varietal cues. The nose is a full-throttle job, with lanolin, lemon and vanillin oak in real harmony. The palate has good body and length of lemon and nutty flavours, with a touch of firmness underneath. We'd prefer it young although it will undoubtedly live for some years. Try it with slow-roasted tuna steak.

Quality	♟ ♟ ♟ ♟
Value	★ ★ ★ ★
Grapes	semillon
Region	Barossa Valley, SA
Cellar	▮ 3
Alc./Vol.	13.0%
RRP	$17.00

The Green Vineyards Chardonnay

Quality	🍷🍷🍷🍷🍷
Value	★★★★
Grapes	chardonnay
Region	Yarra Valley, Vic.
Cellar	🍾 4
Alc./Vol.	13.5%
RRP	$36.00

A truly impressive wine made by perfectionist winemaker Sergio Carlei. Influenced by Giaconda's Rick Kinzbrunner in his early days, he employs minimalist techniques with super results.

CURRENT RELEASE 2001 Non-interventionist methods like Carlei's make wines of true complexity and interest, worlds away from the primary fruit/oak equation of so many Aussie chards. A great example with fine stone-fruit and citrus aromas beautifully integrated with creamy, nutty winery influences. In the mouth it has lovely smooth texture and depth with a seamless mix of flavours in perfect balance. It finishes tasty, long and clean. A wine worthy of lobster.

Grosset Polish Hill

Quality	🍷🍷🍷🍷🍷
Value	★★★★
Grapes	riesling
Region	Clare Valley, SA
Cellar	🍾 8+
Alc./Vol.	13.0%
RRP	$38.00 🍷

2002 seems to have been just about the perfect riesling vintage in the Clare Valley. Much anticipated, Jeff Grosset's 2002 rieslings don't disappoint – they are superb.

CURRENT RELEASE 2002 The more-ish qualities of this Polish Hill ensure that, once opened, a bottle disappears with untimely haste. The aromas are pure and essency. There are citrus-blossom, lime-juice, minerally notes and a yeasty touch, and the palate has real concentration, typical of the 2002 crop. It tastes spicy and minerally, but it's still reserved and tight in youth. Racy acidity underpins the palate with a zip. Great with smoked trout.

Grosset Watervale Riesling

Quality	🍷🍷🍷🍷🍷
Value	★★★★
Grapes	riesling
Region	Clare Valley, SA
Cellar	🍾 6+
Alc./Vol.	13.0%
RRP	$32.00 🍷

In some eyes this is the lesser of the two Grosset rieslings, but we don't think there's much between them. They're both excellent.

CURRENT RELEASE 2002 A gorgeously pure, appetising young riesling that is already a little more forward than its Polish Hill sibling. The nose is a riot of fruits – apple, white peach, passionfruit, lime – and a minerally thread adds firmness. In the mouth there's good flesh, tight structure, spicy flavour and a long finish. Its screw-cap should preserve and help it develop for many years, but it's also delicious right now. Try it with a crab dish.

Hamilton's Ewell Railway Chardonnay

Chardonnay from the Barossa Valley floor rarely shows much class, so we agree with this maker's approach, to make a fruit-driven style and sell it young and fresh. CURRENT RELEASE 2002   The colour is pale yellow and it has a dusty straw, melon aroma that's simple and straightforward, like the flavour. It's lean and narrow in profile, technically well-made and fresh, with a nice dry, well-balanced finish. Enjoy it with avocado salad.

Quality	♥ ♥ ♥ ♥
Value	★ ★ ★
Grapes	chardonnay
Region	Barossa Valley, SA
Cellar	🍷 1
Alc./Vol.	13.5%
RRP	$18.00

Hamilton's Ewell Stonegarden Riesling

Not to be confused with Orlando's famous riesling, Steingarten. Mark Hamilton, the owner, is a sixth-generation descendant of Richard Hamilton, a pioneer South Australian vigneron.
CURRENT RELEASE 2002   This is a very grassy, green-pea interpretation of riesling, and smells almost like a sauvignon blanc. No doubt it's a product of the very cool summer. However, the palate is lean and somewhat austere, with a very dry, hard acid finish. Its future is uncertain, but age may help soften it. It might work with a caesar salad.

Quality	♥ ♥ ♥ ♥
Value	★ ★ ★ ★
Grapes	riesling
Region	Eden Valley, SA
Cellar	➡ 1–5+
Alc./Vol.	13.0%
RRP	$18.00 🥂

Hardys Eileen Hardy Chardonnay

A matriarch of the family, Eileen Hardy made an important contribution to the then family-owned wine company, from 1938 to 1975. Group chief winemaker is Peter Dawson.
CURRENT RELEASE 2000   A very low-alcohol chardonnay, relatively speaking, reflecting its cool-climate origins in Tassie and Hoddles Creek – the highest part of the Yarra. Not surprisingly, the wine is restrained and fairly high-acid, lean and sinewy, and needing time to fill out. It has predominantly citrus and herbal flavours, with toasty oak and buttery malolactic combining to give a hazelnut overtone. It should be long-lived. It's already great to drink, with gratin of crab.

Quality	♥ ♥ ♥ ♥ ♥
Value	★ ★ ★ ★
Grapes	chardonnay
Region	Coal Valley, Tas., 65% & Yarra Valley, Vic., 35%
Cellar	🍷 6
Alc./Vol.	12.2%
RRP	$40.00

Heggies Chardonnay

Quality 🍷🍷🍷½
Value ★★★
Grapes chardonnay
Region Eden Valley, SA
Cellar 3
Alc./Vol. 14.5%
RRP $24.90

Louisa Rose is using wild yeasts and various other techniques once considered out of bounds, but we still find the Yalumba chardonnays a bit lacking in character, if seldom disappointing.

CURRENT RELEASE 2002 This is a soft, nicely balanced chardonnay with subtle oak and restrained personality. It is lean and narrow in profile without a lot of richness, and finishes with a suggestion of sweetness, which may be just the effect of high alcohol strength. It would go with a slice of runny ripe brie.

Heggies Riesling

Quality 🍷🍷🍷½
Value ★★★
Grapes riesling
Region Eden Valley, SA
Cellar 1–7+
Alc./Vol. 12.5%
RRP $20.00 (S)

Riesling is the grape for which Heggies was mainly planted in the early 1970s. There have been some rippers over the years; even the '79 – the first – can still open beautifully.

CURRENT RELEASE 2002 A very closed, shy wine that is possibly going through a phase (as some screw-capped rieslings do); it will surely recover within months. Light yellow in colour, it has vague hints of flowers, powder puff and a hint of ginger beer. Now, the acidity is prominent, making the palate harsher and more steely than we'd like. But remember, this is a style built to age, and 2002 was a very cool, but outstanding, vintage. Our rating may need to be revised upwards. Cellar, then serve with pan-fried whiting.

Heggies Viognier

Quality 🍷🍷🍷🍷½
Value ★★★★
Grapes viognier
Region Eden Valley, SA
Cellar 2+
Alc./Vol. 14.0%
RRP $20.00

The Yalumba mob are pioneers with viognier, producing no less than four examples – including a sticky. They were pivotal in organising the first viognier symposium in the Barossa in 2002.

CURRENT RELEASE 2002 There's no mistaking the grape's punchy bouquet of spices and honey, coupled with the richness and plump smoothness we expect to find in viognier's palate. There is weight and warmth from alcohol but it's not unbalanced. There's no obvious oak: it's all fruit, and plenty of it! A powerful wine that avoids fatness and does not entirely sacrifice subtlety. Try it with pasta and a creamy, seafood-based sauce.

Helm Classic Dry Riesling

Ken Helm is a great champion of the Canberra district, and most particularly its riesling. Not surprisingly his riesling is among the region's best.

CURRENT RELEASE 2002 This is a fine cool-climate riesling with a slightly Teutonic accent which gives it plenty of aromatic spice and lime zest, as well as Australian richness and intensity. The flavour is long and juicy with intense citrus flavours and a long fragrant aftertaste. Try it with Alsace onion tart.

Quality	🍷🍷🍷🍷﹙
Value	★★★★
Grapes	riesling
Region	Murrumbateman, NSW (Canberra region)
Cellar	🍷 5
Alc./Vol.	12.5%
RRP	$23.00

Henschke Green's Hill Lenswood Riesling

The Henschkes named their Adelaide Hills wines after former landowners or people whose names have been associated with the area. Hence Croft chardonnay, Abbott's Prayer merlot blend, Giles pinot noir, and this one.

CURRENT RELEASE 2002 A pale colour presages a reserved, undeveloped riesling which has a very spicy bouquet, with hints of flowers and powder-puff aromatics. It's quite full in the mouth, possibly reflecting alcohol, but also clean and refined, with softness and pleasing balance. It's deceptively smooth but we expect it to also age well. Food: try swordfish steaks.

Quality	🍷🍷🍷🍷﹙
Value	★★★﹢
Grapes	riesling
Region	Adelaide Hills, SA
Cellar	➡ 1–8+
Alc./Vol.	12.9%
RRP	$24.80 🔖 (cellar door)

Hewitson Riesling

Dean Hewitson was a winemaker at Petaluma for ten years before striking out on his own in 1996. He recently moved into a former milk factory in Adelaide which he reckoned would make a nice cool winery.

CURRENT RELEASE 2002 As you'd expect given his background at Petaluma and as a flying winemaker, Dean's riesling is spotlessly clean and refined. The colour is a pale lemon and the nose is shy, minerally, dried-herbs and floral, with a suggestion of grassiness. It's very understated riesling and needs time. It will drink well with grilled scampi.

Quality	🍷🍷🍷🍷﹙
Value	★★★★
Grapes	riesling
Region	Eden Valley, SA
Cellar	➡ 1–10+
Alc./Vol.	12.5%
RRP	$19.00 🔖

Higher Plane Chardonnay

Quality	♟ ♟ ♟ ♟
Value	★ ★ ★ ⅃
Grapes	chardonnay
Region	Margaret River, WA
Cellar	🍶 2+
Alc./Vol.	14.0%
RRP	$30.00

This wine was produced by Craig and Cathie Smith at Forest Grove. They barrel-fermented it in 100 per cent new French oak, and gave it a full malolactic.

CURRENT RELEASE 2001   A very oaky but very powerful chardonnay, which reflects the use of new barrels. It has a light/mid-yellow colour and buttery, toasty-oak and butterscotch aromas fill the glass. It's a full-on, intense style with lots of oak and complexities from malolactic and barrel work. A complex, very long-flavoured chardonnay that bodes well for this new producer. Don't over-chill it. It would suit buttery grilled marron.

Hill Smith Estate Sauvignon Blanc

Quality	♟ ♟ ♟ ♟
Value	★ ★ ★ ★
Grapes	sauvignon blanc
Region	Eden Valley, SA
Cellar	🍶 2
Alc./Vol.	12.0%
RRP	$19.60

Cool summers certainly result in a different spectrum of aromas in sauvignon blanc. The 2002s from the Adelaide Hills and Eden Valley are sharper and more tangy than usual. Maker: Louisa Rose.

CURRENT RELEASE 2002   The colour is pale and the aromas are dusty and herbaceous, like freshly cut green capsicum. The palate has very intense, jumpy, cucumber, green-apple and herbaceous flavours and is crisply crunchy and bracing. An extreme style that really wakes up the tastebuds. It would suit a salade composé.

Hollick Sauvignon Blanc Semillon

Quality	♟ ♟ ♟
Value	★ ★ ★
Grapes	sauvignon blanc; semillon
Region	Coonawarra, SA
Cellar	🍶 1
Alc./Vol.	12.5%
RRP	$17.50 ⑤

Lively acid is a hallmark of Ian and Wendy Hollick's dry whites. It helps them partner food, but some drinkers may find them a bit too tart on their own.

CURRENT RELEASE 2002   The colour is slightly developed yellow and the bouquet reminds of overripe honeydew melon. It has herbal/vegetal, squashy aromas, too. The taste is broad and figgy, with a hint of sweetness and a bracingly tart finish. Don't serve it too cold. It goes with antipasto.

Home Hill Kelly's Reserve Chardonnay

Planting of this tiny 4-hectare vineyard in the Huon Valley (half an hour south of Hobart) started in 1993. Ex-Rosevears and now Hunter Valley winemaker Jim Chatto consults.
CURRENT RELEASE 2001   This is a very fine, crisp, high-acid, almost chablis-esque, definitely cool-climate chardonnay. The oak is barely discernible and there are no obvious malolactic characters, but plenty of nectarine-like fruit. The palate is smooth, subtle and refined. It would drink well with poached scallops.

Quality	▼▼▼▼
Value	★★★↓
Grapes	chardonnay
Region	Huon Valley, Tas.
Cellar	▮ 3
Alc./Vol.	13.5%
RRP	$23.00

Hope Estate Chardonnay

Ten different batches, with varying treatments, were used to construct this wine; some had wild-yeast ferments, some were whole-bunch pressed. They all went into French oak and the result won a gold medal in the under-$20 classes at the 2002 Adelaide Wine Show.
CURRENT RELEASE 2001   The colour has developed into a medium golden yellow and the wine has a lot of smoky, toasty complexities that reflect oak as well as bottle-age. It is a rich, full-bodied chardonnay with a soft, gentle finish. Oak has been used to the limit, so don't over-chill it. You could try it with gnocchi.

Quality	▼▼▼▼
Value	★★★★
Grapes	chardonnay
Region	Hunter Valley, NSW
Cellar	▮ 2
Alc./Vol.	13.0%
RRP	$21.00 Ⓢ

Hope Estate Semillon

Ex-pharmacist Michael Hope took over the former Saxonvale winery and vineyards in the Broke Fordwich sub-region in 1996. He now has 55 hectares there.
CURRENT RELEASE 2002   A little more 'twiggy' and cedary than usual for Hunter semillon (more common in Margaret River), this is a light, delicate semillon with liberal mouth-watering acidity that jars a little at this stage of its life. There are straw and lemon-juice flavours as well, and the finish is all tangy jumpy lemon juice. It needs food: try freshly shucked oysters.

Quality	▼▼▼▼
Value	★★★★
Grapes	semillon
Region	Hunter Valley, NSW
Cellar	➥ 1–7+
Alc./Vol.	10.0%
RRP	$15.90

Hope Estate Verdelho

Quality	🍷🍷🍷⦙
Value	★★★⦙
Grapes	verdelho
Region	Hunter Valley, NSW
Cellar	🍾 3
Alc./Vol.	12.5%
RRP	$15.90

Owner Michael Hope's philosophy is to make 100 per cent estate-grown wines and keep the business 100 per cent family-owned. Vineyard manager is Neil Orton and winemaker is Josh Steele.

CURRENT RELEASE 2002   Five per cent of the wine was barrel-fermented to add spice and richness, but its effect is not obvious. The wine has the classic musk-stick varietal signature of Hunter verdelho, while the palate is full and subtly rich, up-front and easy to enjoy young. It has loads of fruit and flavour, a hint of sweetness that doesn't unbalance it, and slightly harsh acid on the afterpalate. It would be best with food, such as Singapore noodles.

Houghton Chenin Blanc

Quality	🍷🍷⦙
Value	★★★
Grapes	chenin blanc
Region	various, WA
Cellar	🍾 1
Alc./Vol.	12.5%
RRP	$14.00 Ⓢ

The Houghton company has quite a tradition of making chenin blanc in the Swan Valley. Indeed, chenin was the mainstay of the famous White Burgundy in its formative years.

CURRENT RELEASE 2002   There's really only one place in the world chenin makes interesting vino, and that's the Loire Valley. At least this simple, bland, basic soft white is fairly priced. It sure won't excite too many palates with its flavour! Our sample had a belt of sulfur at first, but by the time it reaches you that should have settled down. It has a faintly grassy, herbal fragrance and it tastes so sweet it's hard to find any fruit beneath. Serve it to the vicar with sponge cake.

Houghton Pemberton Sauvignon Blanc

Quality	🍷🍷🍷🍷🍷
Value	★★★★⦙
Grapes	sauvignon blanc
Region	Pemberton, WA
Cellar	🍾 2
Alc./Vol.	12.5%
RRP	$23.00 Ⓢ

Larry Cherubino seems to have upped the ante at Houghton since he took over as chief winemaker four years ago. At just 33, he has plenty of energy for what must be one of the longest and most arduous vintages in the country.

CURRENT RELEASE 2002   This is one of the finest wines we've seen out of Pemberton to date. It is simply delicious! The pungent tropical fruit aromas include some gooseberry and a hint of sweaty character that's typical of Western Australia, and it has tremendous cut and clarity in the mouth. Crunchy and vibrant, it goes well with sushi.

Houghton Semillon Sauvignon Blanc

This is part of Houghton's 'line series', which has a coloured diagonal line across the label. The grapes are sourced from all over Western Australia. Maker: Larry Cherubino.

CURRENT RELEASE 2002   A crisp, crunchy white that faithfully displays the signatures of both grape varieties, the semillon lemon-grassy and the sauvignon blanc sweaty and capsicum-like. It has some bite but stops short of tartness. The finish is clean, dry and well-balanced. It's an excellent salad wine.

Quality	♥♥♥
Value	★★★★
Grapes	semillon; sauvignon blanc
Region	various, WA
Cellar	2
Alc./Vol.	12.5%
RRP	$14.00 ⑤

Houghton White Burgundy

How can it be that in 2003 this wine is still labelled after a geographic region of France, and is therefore technically 'passing off'? Eventually the Australia–EU wine agreement will put the kybosh on European names. CURRENT RELEASE 2002   There have been some good wines under this label even as the price has come down. But the 2002 doesn't light our fire. A light, simple, bland wine – at least it's not too blatantly sweet. There are some edgy dry-grass and stalky aromas, plus a little bottling sulfur, and the palate is light and lean. Soft, balanced and easy to quaff, serve with fish and chips.

Quality	♥♥
Value	★★★
Grapes	chardonnay & others
Region	various, WA
Cellar	1
Alc./Vol.	13.5%
RRP	$14.00 ⑤

House of Certain Views Viognier

Why the bizarre name? Andrew Margan enjoyed a bottle of a famous Bordeaux red, Vieux Chateau Certan, while he was working in France as a flying winemaker. It's a fine example of mangled French. CURRENT RELEASE 2002   Our first viognier from Orange is a promising wine. It smells of musk stick and ripe banana, with hints of sweatiness and spices. It's quite big and full in the mouth, even slightly fat, with plenty of alcohol and this combines with acid to lend some astringency to the finish. It could suit chicken with apricots.

Quality	♥♥♥
Value	★★★
Grapes	viognier
Region	Orange, NSW
Cellar	2
Alc./Vol.	14.0%
RRP	$30.00

Howard Park Chardonnay

Quality	♟ ♟ ♟ ♟ ♟
Value	★ ★ ★ ★ ★
Grapes	chardonnay
Region	Great Southern, WA
Cellar	🍷 6+
Alc./Vol.	13.5%
RRP	$35.00 ⊗

This company has 60 hectares of vines in Margaret River, and more in Mount Barker, Porongurup and Frankland. With Michael Kerrigan as winemaker, it is going from strength to strength.

CURRENT RELEASE 2001   A terrific young chardonnay, built to age – as most Aussie chardonnays aren't. It has high acidity and taut, youthful structure, unevolved fruit and a light yellow colour. All this finesse and age-worthiness is enhanced by a screw-cap closure. The bouquet is hazelnut, nougat and toast with a suggestion of sulfide complexity but melon/grapefruit to the fore. The palate is fine and linear, and the acidity is fresh, so drink with food at this stage. Try it with prawns.

Howard Park Riesling

Quality	♟ ♟ ♟ ♟ ♟
Value	★ ★ ★ ★ ⸸
Grapes	riesling
Region	Great Southern, WA
Cellar	➝ 1–12+
Alc./Vol.	12.0%
RRP	$25.00 ⊗

This is the one riesling from Western Australia that consistently throws down the gauntlet to the Clare and Eden Valleys, especially in terms of cellaring potential. Maker: Michael Kerrigan.

CURRENT RELEASE 2002   As usual, this is a concentrated, high-acid wine that some drinkers may find intimidating in its youth. It has a powerfully spicy aroma of dried flowers, dried herbs, minerals and stone fruits. The palate is also rich and mouth-filling and the acid gives it some hardness. It will richly reward cellaring. You could drink it now with grilled marron and buttery sauce.

Hungerford Hill Chardonnay

Quality	♟ ♟ ♟ ♟
Value	★ ★ ★
Grapes	chardonnay
Region	Cowra & Tumbarumba, NSW
Cellar	🍷 1
Alc./Vol.	13.5%
RRP	$16.50

Hungerford Hill has two levels of chardonnay: this modestly priced version based on Cowra, and a much finer, more classic version from Tumbarumba. Philip John has done a great job in his first year as chief winemaker for this revamped brand with its new owner.

CURRENT RELEASE 2002   A fairly straightforward commercial chardonnay with a twist of sweetness. Oak impact is very light – it's all about fruit – and it's clean and well-made with some citrus and herbal fruit flavours. Drink it young, perhaps with cold grilled chicken and salad.

Hungerford Hill Tumbarumba Sauvignon Blanc

This brand is now being overseen by the very experienced former Southcorp winemaker, Philip John. Tumbarumba grows some of the raciest sauvignon blanc in the land.

CURRENT RELEASE 2002   This is seriously good sauvignon. It has lovely, bracing cool-climate 'cut' and tanginess, vivacious and refreshing to drink. The aromas are pure gooseberry: vibrant, intense and utterly delicious. It would suit a seafood soup.

Quality	♥♥♥♥♥
Value	★★★★⁴
Grapes	sauvignon blanc
Region	Tumbarumba, NSW
Cellar	▮ 2
Alc./Vol.	12.5%
RRP	$20.70

Hungerford Hill Verdelho

Verdelho from Gundagai? Now we've seen everything. This brand has become synonymous with New South Wales regional wine, and you often see unusual regions figuring on the labels.

CURRENT RELEASE 2002   It's not especially verdelho-like, but has more Hunter regional character perhaps than anything. It's straw-like – as opposed to the spicy kind of verdelho – and carries quite a lot of sweetness. It's medium-bodied, very fruity and should be a real crowd-pleaser. It could go with salads that involve fruit, such as mango.

Quality	♥♥♥
Value	★★★
Grapes	verdelho
Region	Hunter Valley & Gundagai, NSW
Cellar	▮ 1
Alc./Vol.	13.5%
RRP	$16.50

Huntington Estate Semillon Bin W1

Huntington has been turning out excellent semillon that often cocks a snoot at fancied Hunter brands. As we went to press, Mudgee vineyards were being washed away in floods, so we're not sure how the 2003 is cooking.

CURRENT RELEASE 2002   Another deliciously zingy semillon from 2002: there's an embarrassment of them! The aromas recall fresh lemon juice and they pole-vault out of the glass. It's crisp and tangy to drink, very fresh and vibrant with lemon/lime citrus and subtle green-herb flavours. The finish is crisp and dry and it would go beautifully with sushi.

Quality	♥♥♥♥♥
Value	★★★★⁴
Grapes	semillon
Region	Mudgee, NSW
Cellar	▮ 8
Alc./Vol.	11.8%
RRP	$13.50 (cellar door)

Ingoldby Chardonnay

Quality 🍷🍷🍷🍷
Value ★★★★½
Grapes chardonnay
Region McLaren Vale, SA
Cellar 2
Alc./Vol. 13.5%
RRP $15.00 (S)

The Ingoldby name has long associations with the McLaren Vale region, but these days it's a Beringer-Blass subsidiary. This chardonnay is a perennial bargain.

CURRENT RELEASE 2002 Sunshine in a bottle, just like the 2001! The nose has ripe syrupy fig and tropical-fruit aromas with some eggy chardonnay and buttery overtones. Sweet oak is folded in with a controlled hand. It tastes generous, with intense fruit and toasty oak in happy harmony. Try it well-chilled with Thai fish cakes and sweet chilli sauce.

Ingoldby Sauvignon Blanc

Quality 🍷🍷🍷½
Value ★★★
Grapes sauvignon blanc
Region McLaren Vale, SA
Cellar 1
Alc./Vol. 11.5%
RRP $14.00 (S)

McLaren Vale sauvignon blanc is a flavoury white wine that rarely has the sort of pungency and intensity of sauvignons from the nearby Adelaide Hills.

CURRENT RELEASE 2002 Fruit salad and light grassiness introduce a pleasant dry sauvignon from Ingoldby. It tastes fresh and zesty with citrus and herbaceous flavours that lead to a clean, dry finish. The best thing here would be a Vietnamese lemon and coriander-influenced prawn dish.

Jane Brook James Vineyard Verdelho

Quality 🍷🍷🍷
Value ★★★
Grapes verdelho
Region Swan Valley, WA
Cellar 1
Alc./Vol. 13.2%
RRP $18.00 (S)

Jane Brook is an Atkinson family affair. They have 12 hectares of vines in the Swan, 30 in Margaret River.

CURRENT RELEASE 2002 This opens with a typically sweaty Western Australia verdelho nose, which is pungent and striking, although it seems to mask a little sulfide. There is a dollop of sugar on palate, which is not overdone. It is a soft, light, easy-drinking, unabashedly commercial white wine. It would go with a prawn cocktail.

Jane Brook Plain Jane

Not a great name for engendering enthusiasm among the potential buyers, perhaps. But it has a ring of authenticity and candour about it.

CURRENT RELEASE 2002   This reminds us of walking into a sweetshop: it has a confectionery aroma which may be due to a kiss of sweet American oak, plus a passionfruit, tea-leafy and slightly sweaty fruit character. It has some freshness and life, and while a little light-on, it finishes with a dash of sweetness. It should appeal to smart alecs and handsome harrys. Serve with spring rolls.

Quality	▼▼▼╻
Value	★★★★
Grapes	chenin blanc; chardonnay
Region	Swan Valley, WA
Cellar	▮ 1
Alc./Vol.	12.5%
RRP	$12.00 Ⓢ

Jim Barry Lodge Hill Riesling

This is the Barry family's newer brand of riesling, the first being its Watervale riesling from the legendary Florita vineyard which supplied the early Leo Buring grapes. Lodge Hill is north of Clare and the terroir is quite different to Watervale.

CURRENT RELEASE 2002   The aromas are fresh-bready, straw-like and quite alluring. In the mouth it is classically dry, lean and taut, a somewhat angular youngster that seems a trifle austere now but will undoubtedly reward even short-term cellaring. A hint of bitterness at the finish is a slight concern, though. Cellar at least a year, then try it with any white-fleshed fish.

Quality	▼▼▼▼
Value	★★★╸
Grapes	riesling
Region	Clare Valley, SA
Cellar	⬤ 1–6+
Alc./Vol.	13.5%
RRP	$20.00 ⬯

Jones The Winemaker Chardonnay

Mandy Jones is the winemaker in question, and her uncle Les Jones was the founder. It's a very small outfit, selling most of its make through its Rutherglen cellar door.

CURRENT RELEASE 2001   This is a rip-snorter. It's very concentrated and full-on, and owes some of its power and persistence to alcohol. But it's packed full of flavour and has a heap of character. The colour is still palish, the bouquet reminding us of butter, hazelnut, nectarine and quince. Very ripe and complex, with sweet fruit flavour on palate and very full body. Not for the faint-hearted! Try with barbecued chicken and bacon kebabs.

Quality	▼▼▼▼╻
Value	★★★★
Grapes	chardonnay
Region	Tumbarumba, NSW
Cellar	▮ 3+
Alc./Vol.	14.5%
RRP	$25.00 (cellar door)

Kangarilla Road Chardonnay

Quality 🍷🍷🍷🍷
Value ★★★★
Grapes chardonnay
Region McLaren Vale, SA
Cellar 2
Alc./Vol. 14.0%
RRP $15.50

The Kangarilla Road runs from the hamlet of Kangarilla to McLaren Vale township. It passes through the heart of McLaren Vale vineyard country.

CURRENT RELEASE 2002 This is a fruit-dominated style that's made for easy, youthful enjoyment. It's pale in colour and the nose is juicy and appetising with pear and white-peach aromas, only lightly influenced by subtle oak. In the mouth it's smooth and fruit-sweet with good mouth-feel and long, succulently fruity flavours that remain fresh and easy to drink. Serve it with cold chicken.

Katnook Estate Chardonnay

Quality 🍷🍷🍷🍷
Value ★★★
Grapes chardonnay
Region Coonawarra, SA
Cellar 2
Alc./Vol. 14.5%
RRP $30.00

Katnook Estate was a pioneer with chardonnay in Coonawarra. The region remains solidly a place for red wine, but Katnook shows how well chardonnay can do there.

CURRENT RELEASE 2000 A little more age than most chardonnays on the market gives this wine a yellow–green colour of more depth than most. The nose shows some development as well, with rich, buttery, peachy fruit, and sensitive oak treatment in good balance. It tastes smooth with good texture and length, finishing toasty and lingering. Try it with baked snapper.

Katnook Estate Sauvignon Blanc

Quality 🍷🍷🍷🍷
Value ★★★
Grapes sauvignon blanc
Region Coonawarra, SA
Cellar 2
Alc./Vol. 13.5%
RRP $26.00

Katnook Sauvignon Blanc is one of Australia's pricier sauvignons, but it can hold its own in most company for zippy varietal personality.

CURRENT RELEASE 2002 Right in the Katnook mould, this has a pristine, ripe sauvignon blanc nose suggesting passionfruit, gooseberries and crushed nettles. The palate is snappy with pure varietal flavour, an attractive thread of austerity underneath, and a crisp finish. Try it with goat's cheese croutons.

Keith Tulloch Hunter Semillon

Keith Tulloch is descended from *that* famous Hunter wine family, and has worked for Rothbury Estate, Evans Family, Mount View Estate and others.

CURRENT RELEASE 2002   This trophy winner is a delicious youngster in the classic low-alcohol regional style, although we have seen some bottle variation. The good bottles are restrained and delicate, fresh and vibrant, with a subtle aroma in the lemon-juice to lemon-pith spectrum. Fresh herbs and doughy esters, too. In the mouth, it's fine, dry, lean and long. It's quite shy and unevolved and will richly reward patient cellaring. It goes well now with oysters.

Quality	♥♥♥♥♥
Value	★★★★↘
Grapes	semillon
Region	Hunter Valley, NSW
Cellar	♦ 10+
Alc./Vol.	11.8%
RRP	$26.00

Killerby Chardonnay

Killerby, originally established in the Geographe district, has incorporated a Margaret River vineyard into its operations in recent years, following a familiar pattern for Western Australian wineries.

CURRENT RELEASE 2001   There's some complexity here. The nose has oatmeal, cashew and almond touches to green melon and peach fruit. Spicy oak adds to a complex personality. In the mouth it has real impact with ripe-fruit and oaky flavours in the middle and a slightly hot finish. Try it with chicken sautéed in white wine.

Quality	♥♥♥♥
Value	★★★
Grapes	chardonnay
Region	Geographe & Margaret River, WA
Cellar	♦ 2
Alc./Vol.	14.5%
RRP	$30.00

Kingston Chardonnay

Bill Moularadellis and Kingston Estate look to have recovered well from the additives scandal of a few years back. We've liked their wines all along for their generosity and value.

CURRENT RELEASE 2002   There's a slight dumbness on the nose here. You can tell that it's not a weakie, but there's little aromatic definition to it. It has some syrupy tropical-fruit aromas and a hint of spicy oak. The palate is better with straightforward rich chardonnay flavours, moderately seasoned with oak. This is fair value. Try it with calamari stirfry.

Quality	♥♥♥◗
Value	★★★↘
Grapes	chardonnay
Region	Murray Valley, Vic.
Cellar	♦ 1
Alc./Vol.	13.5%
RRP	$14.00 ⑤

Kirrihill Estates Adelaide Hills Chardonnay

Quality	🍷🍷🍷🍷
Value	★★★★★
Grapes	chardonnay
Region	Adelaide Hills, SA
Cellar	🍾 3
Alc./Vol.	12.9%
RRP	$20.00

Kirrihill is one of the newer Clare Valley operations, but they have hit the market with a very good range of wines, very competently made by David Mavor and ex-Leasingham winemaker Richard Rowe.
CURRENT RELEASE 2001   A wine that fits the understated Adelaide Hills chardonnay style well. The nose has fig and melon aromas that are ripe and fragrant, yet almost delicate. There's a hint of barley sugar to it and a quietly complex lick of spicy oak. The palate is medium in body with smooth texture and juicy fruit flavour. Oak makes a subtle seasoning and fits like a glove. Try it with a blanquette of chicken.

Knappstein Riesling

Quality	🍷🍷🍷🍷🍷
Value	★★★★★
Grapes	riesling
Region	Clare Valley, SA
Cellar	🍾 10+
Alc./Vol.	13.0%
RRP	$21.00 🥂

The name Knappstein has been inextricably linked with riesling in Clare for decades. Long-time Knappstein winemaker Andrew Hardy maintains the faith with excellent wines.
CURRENT RELEASE 2002   The best Knappstein riesling for some time, courtesy of an excellent vintage. It smells attractive with ripe, exotic passionfruit aromas of lush succulence, mated to zesty lime-juice notes. It has a gorgeous pristine fruit quality continuing down the palate with intense, juicy varietal flavour that's tangy and dry. It's all backed up with persistent tingling acidity that should help it live for many years. Serve with a mixed shellfish platter.

Knight Granite Hills Riesling

Quality	🍷🍷🍷🍷🍷
Value	★★★★
Grapes	riesling
Region	Macedon Ranges, Vic.
Cellar	🍾 5
Alc./Vol.	13.0%
RRP	$20.00

The boulder-strewn hills around Baynton in the north Macedon Ranges are great riesling country. Maker: Llew Knight.
CURRENT RELEASE 2002   Granite Hills Riesling is always a very distinctive style. The 2002 has a musky, spicy nose of Alsace-like aromas with some sweet lime and minerals thrown in. In the mouth it's rich and slightly viscous with deep, long flavour, and a snappy dry finish marked by steely acidity. Serve it with a green vegetable stirfry.

Knots Carrick Bend Chardonnay

Ex-Balgownie winemaker Lindsay Ross has set up on his own in the Heathcote district. His Knots range of wines celebrates . . . knots. The Carrick Bend is a symmetrical knot, easily tied and untied.
CURRENT RELEASE 2002   An approachable young chardonnay with melon and peach-like aromas folded into spicy oak. In the mouth it has smooth texture and pleasantly ripe but fine flavour. It finishes with a softly honeyed nutty aftertaste that lasts well on the palate. A gentle oaked chardonnay that will taste great with pork fillets and peaches.

Quality	♥ ♥ ♥ ♥
Value	★ ★ ★ ⸸
Grapes	chardonnay
Region	central Victoria
Cellar	▮ 2
Alc./Vol.	14.0%
RRP	$20.00

Kooyong Chardonnay

This is a Mornington Peninsula name to watch, a no expense spared operation with real quality aspirations. So far its chardonnays have lived up to expectations.
CURRENT RELEASE 2001   Still very youthful, this Kooyong Chardonnay has an attractive smooth nose of fig, peach and citrus peel with subtly applied barrel influence. The impression is of freshness and life and the palate follows through accordingly with tangy flavour. It's light in the mouth, yet it has intensity, harmony and length with an attractive smoky aftertaste. Serve it with scallops roasted on the shell.

Quality	♥ ♥ ♥ ♥ ♥
Value	★ ★ ★
Grapes	chardonnay
Region	Mornington Peninsula, Vic.
Cellar	▮ 4
Alc./Vol.	13.0%
RRP	$39.00

The Lane Gathering Sauvignon Semillon

As of this year, Ravenswood Lane becomes simply The Lane. The wine's brand name is Gathering. Without explanation, it all looks kind of puzzling on the page.
CURRENT RELEASE 2002   The colour is very pale and the wine is backward in every way. It has a hint of acetone esteriness, but also some soft, non-pungent varietal fruit. In the mouth is where it really shines: it's light and delicate, the sort of wine you want more than one glass of, and it's dry but soft and finely balanced. We'd like to drink this with trout gravlax.

Quality	♥ ♥ ♥ ♥
Value	★ ★ ★
Grapes	sauvignon blanc; semillon
Region	Adelaide Hills, SA
Cellar	▮ 2
Alc./Vol.	13.5%
RRP	$25.00

Leasingham Bastion Riesling

Quality	♟♟♟♟
Value	★★★★★
Grapes	riesling
Region	Clare Valley, SA
Cellar	🍾 5
Alc./Vol.	13.0%
RRP	$14.50 ⑤ 🥂

One good turn deserves another. The Bastion red has been given a rousing reception by the media, the trade and you, the drinkers. Good enough reason for Leasingham to issue a whole family of Bastions. CURRENT RELEASE 2002   This is a serious riesling, and no second-rate cheapie. It's pale-coloured, citrusy-smelling with a high-toned spicy character, and is tart and jumpy to taste. It emphasises acid rather than fruit generosity but we suspect a few months in the bottle will soften it up. It finishes dry and mouth-watering. Best with food: try buttery scallops.

Leasingham Bin 7 Riesling

Quality	♟♟♟♟♟
Value	★★★★★
Grapes	riesling
Region	Clare Valley, SA
Cellar	🍾 10
Alc./Vol.	12.0%
RRP	$16.00 ⑤ 🥂

This winery has a distinguished history of riesling making. If you think Bin 7 is the goods (and we do), just watch out for the Classic, which is released with a couple of extra years' bottle-age. Maker: Kerri Thompson. CURRENT RELEASE 2002   The 2002 continues a remarkable succession of great value-for-money rieslings under this label, now with added value from a screw-cap. It's a fragrant, mineral and citrus-smelling youngster which has a delicate and very more-ish aroma and taste. The palate has lively acidity and this helps give it superb line and length – much like a Glenn McGrath delivery, really. It goes well with any grilled white-fleshed fish.

Leconfield Chardonnay

Quality	♟♟♟♟
Value	★★★★
Grapes	chardonnay
Region	Coonawarra, SA
Cellar	🍾 4
Alc./Vol.	13.0%
RRP	$19.00

Former Rouge Homme winemaker Paul Gordon is now working at Leconfield, and we are eager to see what effect he can exert, especially over the once-famous cabernet. CURRENT RELEASE 2002   This is a lively, yet slightly developed, wine which shows plenty of buttery/creamy malolactic character in its bouquet. Fine gooseberry and grapefruit flavours chime in on the lean palate, and it has a lively zinginess as well. It finishes with some alcohol warmth. It could benefit from a few more months in the bottle to harmonise fully. Try it with trout and bearnaise sauce.

Leconfield Old Vines Riesling

Of all the superb 2002 South Aussie rieslings, from the Clare and Eden Valleys, this Coonawarra wine pipped them all, emerging as the trophy winner at the 2002 Royal Adelaide Wine Show.

CURRENT RELEASE 2002   This is a classically restrained, shy, delicate riesling that promises to be long-lived. As a youngster, it's subtle and undeveloped, with aromas of dried flowers, lemon pudding and powder puff; while in the mouth it's steely, dry and a touch austere. The acidity is quite marked and it needs time. Will drink nicely with whiting quenelles.

Quality	🍷🍷🍷🍷🍷
Value	★★★★
Grapes	riesling
Region	Coonawarra, SA
Cellar	🍷 1–12+
Alc./Vol.	12.0%
RRP	$18.00 🖐

Lenswood Vineyards Sauvignon Blanc

Tim Knappstein has added the words 'Winemaker: Tim Knappstein' on the bottom of the front label, apparently thinking this will help the wine's street cred. We'd agree. He can't name the wine after himself, of course, as he sold the rights to his name, along with the winery, years ago.

CURRENT RELEASE 2002   A brilliant sauvignon blanc, its honeydew-melon, nectarine, pea-pod and herbal aromas remind us of New Zealand's finest. The palate is delicate and refined, with surprising softness, yet lots of acid giving cut and tang. An intense, seamless drink that would go well with flathead fillets and roasted red capsicum purée.

Quality	🍷🍷🍷🍷🍷
Value	★★★★★
Grapes	sauvignon blanc
Region	Adelaide Hills, SA
Cellar	🍷 2
Alc./Vol.	12.5%
RRP	$21.50

Lillydale Chardonnay

These chardonnays have won gold medals and trophies on occasion at the Southern Victorian Wine Show. They can be very good value for money.

CURRENT RELEASE 2001   This is a lighter, less arresting vintage of Lillydale Chardonnay, with a bright medium-yellow colour and a nutty, straw, hay-like aroma that just lacks a little in complexity. It has a light body and the flavours are a little straightforward. Oak plays a very minor role. Well-priced and very easy to drink. It would suit grilled chicken breast and salad.

Quality	🍷🍷🍷🍷
Value	★★★↓
Grapes	chardonnay
Region	Yarra Valley, Vic.
Cellar	🍷 2
Alc./Vol.	13.0%
RRP	$19.00 Ⓢ

Lindemans Bin 75 Riesling

Quality	♟ ♟ ♟ ♟
Value	★ ★ ★ ★ ★
Grapes	riesling
Region	Padthaway, SA
Cellar	🍶 5
Alc./Vol.	12.5%
RRP	$9.00 ⑤ 🥢

A new addition to the Lindemans Bin range, this is a remarkable wine that shows just how much high-quality riesling fruit was available from the excellent 2002 harvest. Maker: Wayne Falkenberg.

CURRENT RELEASE 2002 A highly attractive wine that totally transcends its lowly price point! Aromas of dried grass, herbs and lime juice greet the nose, and the taste is surprisingly intense and tightly structured, with an almost steely line to it. It doesn't rely on sugar. There's a flick of phenolic grip at the finish, but it's a great value wine. Try serving with a Thai chicken salad.

Lindemans Cawarra Chardonnay

Quality	♟ ♟ ♟
Value	★ ★ ★ ⸳
Grapes	chardonnay
Region	not stated
Cellar	🍶 1
Alc./Vol.	13.5%
RRP	$8.10 ⑤

Like its sister below, this wine is sealed with a plastic stopper. Mind you, don't call it a 'plastic cork' or the cork spin doctors will dump a tonne of press releases and pedantic letters on you!

CURRENT RELEASE 2002 This is a cut above the semillon chardonnay, for the same money. It at least tastes like the grape, with cashew-nut and peachy chardonnay fruit aromas, a vague suggestion of oak, and some sweetness on entry. It's a nice enough, cheap commercial style. It would suit stuffed cabbage rolls.

Lindemans Cawarra Semillon Chardonnay

Quality	♟ ♟ ♟
Value	★ ★ ★
Grapes	semillon; chardonnay
Region	not stated
Cellar	🍶 1
Alc./Vol.	13.5%
RRP	$8.10 ⑤

It's a tragedy the way the great Lindeman name has been allowed to decline at Southcorp, so that today it stands for little more than cheap, bland, supermarket fodder. We can't blame anyone in particular: it's the cumulative neglect of successive managements.

CURRENT RELEASE 2002 This is a shy, minerally, restrained white wine, which is just a bit too neutral and boring. The palate reflects semillon's lean angularity rather than chardonnay's pulpy richness. It needs more fruit and softness. You could serve it with steamed chicken and three veg.

Lindemans Reserve Padthaway Chardonnay

There was a time when this was a really good-value buy. In recent years the price has trod water and the quality has slid.

CURRENT RELEASE 2002   It's just a simple, herbal, rather boring, neutral dry white. The colour is light lemon and it smells of parsley. In the mouth, it has a thick, slightly coarse texture which is dull and leaden and out of whack with the very light, basic fruit. Strictly for party dips.

Quality	♀ ♀ ⑨
Value	★ ★ ★
Grapes	chardonnay
Region	Padthaway, SA
Cellar	🍶 1
Alc./Vol.	13.5%
RRP	$14.00 ⑤

Lindemans Reserve Verdelho

Having killed off most of the good things about Lindemans, the Southcorp marketers see no irony in advertising the fact that the once-proud company was founded in 1843 – in a discreet strip at the base of the label. How times have changed!

CURRENT RELEASE 2002   Sealed with a plastic stopper to protect it from taint, this wine has a fairly forward developed colour and personality. The aromas are of dry grass and straw and there's a hint of varietal spice. A very light palate lacks vibrancy, finishing with a leesy character. It's diffuse in structure and short at the finish. A basic dry white, to serve with salad.

Quality	♀ ♀ ⑨
Value	★ ★ ★
Grapes	verdelho
Region	not stated
Cellar	🍶 1
Alc./Vol.	13.0%
RRP	$13.00 ⑤

Little's Gewürztraminer

The Littles' white wines are often surprising, especially the gewürz, which only an optimist would expect to work consistently well in the Hunter.

CURRENT RELEASE 2002   The colour is light yellow and the bouquet is bath-powdery, fragrant and fresh, and very true to the grape. It's a fairly straightforward wine, clean and correct, although the finish doesn't sustain very well. It would suit onion quiche.

Quality	♀ ♀ ♀ ♀
Value	★ ★ ★ ★
Grapes	gewürztraminer
Region	Hunter Valley, NSW
Cellar	🍶 2
Alc./Vol.	12.5%
RRP	$16.00

Llangibby Estate Sauvignon Blanc

Quality	♟♟♟
Value	★★★
Grapes	sauvignon blanc
Region	Adelaide Hills, SA
Cellar	🍾 1
Alc./Vol.	12.5%
RRP	$20.00

This is another fairly new producer in the Adelaide Hills, growing grapes for other people and now starting to market a little of their own wine, which was made at Nepenthe.

CURRENT RELEASE 2002   This is a good wine, filled with attractively fragrant green-apple, passionfruit and straw aromas. It is soft and light on the tongue, with a touch of sweetness and finishes a little short. This is a minor quibble: it's fine wine, quaffable and more-ish. It goes well with cold salmon that's been poached with leeks and capers.

Madew Belle Riesling

Quality	♟♟♟♟
Value	★★★
Grapes	riesling
Region	Canberra region, NSW
Cellar	🍾 5
Alc./Vol.	11.0%
RRP	$25.00 🥂

Canberra district vineyards are doing good things with riesling, with few poor wines and a number of top-flight examples. This top wine is one of the latter. Maker: David Madew.

CURRENT RELEASE 2002   Canberra riesling is fine and aromatic, usually with good intensity but less minerally strength than South Australian wines. Madew Belle Riesling has lime, pear, floral and slatey notes to the nose, giving an aromatic introduction. In the mouth it has excellent sweet-sour balance, with the 'sweet' full flavours of ripe riesling, delicately supported by the 'sour' tingle of clean, dry acidity. Great companion to prawn stirfry with lemon grass.

Madew Chardonnay

Quality	♟♟♟♟
Value	★★★↘
Grapes	chardonnay
Region	Canberra region, NSW
Cellar	🍾 3
Alc./Vol.	13.3%
RRP	$25.00 🥂

The screw-cap onslaught continues. Riesling started the revolution and now it's spreading to chardonnays like Madew, various reds, just about everything. It's a move that consumers should welcome.

CURRENT RELEASE 2001   There's quite a bit of fruity charm on the nose of this quietly impressive Canberra district chardonnay. Citrus and white-peach aromas of attractive intensity head the bill, and nutty oak is admirably controlled. In the mouth it's agreeably persistent with fine texture and equilibrium. A subtle, delicate wine all round, and one that disappears all too readily. Try it with creamy fettuccine, cheese and chives.

Madew Riesling

This is the junior Madew Canberra riesling. Its sibling, Belle, has more intensity and character, but this wine is still very presentable. Maker: David Madew.
CURRENT RELEASE 2002   A bright young riesling with an attractive nose of spiced apple, lime and slate. The palate is a bit disjointed at the moment, with a fruit-sweet middle not quite integrating with high acidity, but it's early days. Time should help it all come together nicely. Try it with stewed capsicum, tomato and basil bruschetta.

Quality	♟♟♟♟
Value	★★★
Grapes	riesling
Region	Canberra region, NSW
Cellar	➤ 2–5
Alc./Vol.	11.6%
RRP	$22.00 ✍

Madfish Chardonnay

Howard Park has become a significant player in the Western Australia wine business in recent years. This multi-regional blend sits below the estate labels as a sort of introductory drop. It is always of good quality.
CURRENT RELEASE 2001   This bright youngster isn't just a 'second label', it can readily stand on its own. It smells of stone fruit that's slightly syrupy-sweet. Spicy oak plays a significant role, and maybe a little less would be better, but succulent flavour does come through. It's quite long-tasting and it finishes clean with a slightly toasty aftertaste. Serve with barbecued prawns.

Quality	♟♟♟♟
Value	★★★⯈
Grapes	chardonnay
Region	Margaret River & Great Southern, WA
Cellar	◗ 2
Alc./Vol.	14.0%
RRP	$22.00

Maglieri Chardonnay

Now owned by Beringer Blass, red wines remain Maglieri's forte. Their chardonnay is a middling McLaren Vale style that offers good value but no great refinement.
CURRENT RELEASE 2002   This is a no-fuss, straightforward affair of stone fruit, understated nutty vanillin oak, and a sweaty, warm-climate touch. It's smooth and easy in the mouth with melony flavour that finishes clean and dry, if a little short. It's a friendly chardonnay to enjoy chilled with the neighbours, if you're friendly with them. If you don't get on too well, turn up the music, and sip it with some chicken wings.

Quality	♟♟♟♟
Value	★★★⯈
Grapes	chardonnay
Region	McLaren Vale, SA
Cellar	◗ 2
Alc./Vol.	13.5%
RRP	$14.00 ⑤

Main Ridge Chardonnay

Quality	🍷🍷🍷🍷
Value	★★★⟩
Grapes	chardonnay
Region	Mornington Peninsula, Vic.
Cellar	🍾 4
Alc./Vol.	13.5%
RRP	$44.00 🍾

Proprietor/winemaker Nat White presides over the Mornington Peninsula's first commercial vineyard with grace and good humour. His chardonnays are deliberately made in a subtle and understated style that befits the man.

CURRENT RELEASE 2001   Very much in the restrained Main Ridge style, this wine opens with a slight earthy pong that disappears with air in the glass. Further acquaintance brings gentle aromas that combine white-peach fruit with touches of nuts, rock candy, pastry and butter. It's an elegant mouthful with very fine texture and lingering flavour of subtle richness. Fine, soft, complex, and lovely with delicate pan-fried fish.

Majella Riesling

Quality	🍷🍷🍷
Value	★★★
Grapes	riesling
Region	Coonawarra, SA
Cellar	➡ 1–4
Alc./Vol.	12.0%
RRP	$18.50

Majella's main claim to fame rests on red wines. Riesling is a less well-known part of the range. It's competently made, but it doesn't reach the heights of its red brothers.

CURRENT RELEASE 2002   The nose is a bit unyielding with dry mineral, lime and spice aromas that take a while to develop in the glass. It has an angular feel in the mouth, with firm lime fruit and a steely element. The finish has a touch of hardness that may mellow in time. Try it with little Vietnamese spring rolls wrapped in green herbs.

Margan Botrytis Semillon

Quality	🍷🍷🍷🍷
Value	★★★★
Grapes	semillon
Region	Hunter Valley, NSW
Cellar	🍾 3
Alc./Vol.	10.0%
RRP	$25.00 (375 ml)

This sweet Hunter semillon is made from 50 per cent botrytised grapes and 50 per cent non-botrytised cordon cut fruit, a combination of techniques designed to give complexity with lush sweetness.

CURRENT RELEASE 2002   A bright green–gold wine with a lush nose of apricot, tea-leaves, oak and a touch of volatility. The palate is mellow and very sweet, mouth-filling and lush. Tangy acidity keeps an exquisite balance of sweet and sour. Like some botrytised stickies with some volatility, it won't please the technocrats, but who cares? Drink it with some blue cheese and fruit.

Margan Semillon

Margan's semillon is a bit riper and more alcoholic than the time-honoured Hunter style, therefore it's more in the mainstream of modern white wine than most of its brethren.

CURRENT RELEASE 2002   There's real intensity on the nose here, lemon and lanolin aromas are quite punchy rather than delicate. It has a hint of fusty ferment smell as well, but this should disappear with time. The palate continues the concentrated theme – full slightly smoky flavour, good depth, and a tangy clean finish to provide balance. Roast some scallops on the shell to go with this.

Quality	🍷🍷🍷🍷
Value	★★★⁺
Grapes	semillon
Region	Hunter Valley, NSW
Cellar	➙ 1–5
Alc./Vol.	12.5%
RRP	$18.50

Marinda Park Sauvignon Blanc

Victoria's Mornington Peninsula doesn't spring to mind for its sauvignon blancs, but that hasn't stopped a lot of budding vignerons from planting the variety. The results are mixed to say the least.

CURRENT RELEASE 2002   An unusual sauvignon, 50 per cent fermented in old French oak and the balance in stainless steel. The result is a wine of some complexity, with grassy, crunchy, freshly cut capsicum aromas, and a dry-twig overtone. It's clean and vibrant, dry, subtle and well balanced. Try it with stir-fried green vegetables.

Quality	🍷🍷🍷🍷
Value	★★★⁺
Grapes	sauvignon blanc
Region	Mornington Peninsula, Vic.
Cellar	🍾 1
Alc./Vol.	13.0%
RRP	$19.00

Maxwell Verdelho

When he went looking for a new white grape to plant in his vineyard, Mark Maxwell chose verdelho. Probably a good decision since it suits the site well and its popularity is on the climb.

CURRENT RELEASE 2002   Very verdelho: juicy sweet on the nose with tropical-fruit aromas like banana and a hint of citrus. The palate is fruity and dry with direct uncomplicated flavour and a zippy acid finish. A friendly white to serve with a chicken and mango salad.

Quality	🍷🍷🍷
Value	★★★⁺
Grapes	verdelho
Region	McLaren Vale & Langhorne Creek, SA
Cellar	🍾 2
Alc./Vol.	14.0%
RRP	$16.95

McVitty Grove Pinot Gris

Quality	🍷🍷🍷¡
Value	★★★
Grapes	pinot gris
Region	Southern Highlands, NSW
Cellar	🍷 2
Alc./Vol.	11.9%
RRP	$22.50 ⧖

The Southern Highlands of New South Wales is a region that focuses on the towns of Bowral and Mittagong. There's a growing number of small vineyards there. This was made by Canberra winemaker David Madew.
CURRENT RELEASE 2002   The colour is light yellow and the wine has a slight spritz. It smells of dry tobacco and cedar, with a hint of smoked bacon. The taste is lean and dry, with some subtlety although the structure is somewhat broad. It pulls up a trifle short, and is not especially varietal. Try it with grilled garfish.

McWilliams Hanwood Chardonnay

Quality	🍷🍷🍷🍷
Value	★★★★★
Grapes	chardonnay
Region	Riverina & Hilltops, NSW, Coonawarra, SA & Yarra Valley, Vic.
Cellar	🍷 2
Alc./Vol.	13.5%
RRP	$11.50 Ⓢ

An amazingly good 2002 vintage in the Riverina, cooler and more temperate than usual, might just have given us the best Hanwood Chardonnay yet: it's as good as some wines selling for two or three times the price. Maker: Jim Brayne and team.
CURRENT RELEASE 2002   An eminently satisfying, poised young chardonnay, it opens with ripe, succulent fig and melon fruit, creamy buttery, malolactic touches and a hint of toasty oak, interesting and complex, and all in real harmony. In the mouth it's creamy and mellow with admirable depth and complexity, finishing long and dry. A well-integrated robe of oak completes the picture. Pan-fried fish would go nicely.

McWilliams Hanwood Verdelho

Quality	🍷🍷🍷¡
Value	★★★¡
Grapes	verdelho
Region	Riverina, NSW
Cellar	🍷 2
Alc./Vol.	13.5%
RRP	$11.50 Ⓢ

There must be a hell of a lot of verdelho planted around Australia, if the numbers that reach us are any indicator. McWilliams Hanwood differs from most by putting a little oak in the mix.
CURRENT RELEASE 2002   A brightly coloured verdelho with fruit on the nose subdued by some spicy oak. There are some tropicals in there as well, but it's quite chardonnay-like, without verdelho's usual riot of succulent fruit. The bit of wood works well in the mouth to give texture and weight, making it a more serious proposition than many others, although it tends to dominate the flavour. An interesting drink with poached chicken.

McWilliams Mount Pleasant Chardonnay

Chardonnay isn't what Mount Pleasant is traditionally about, but this wine can be surprisingly good. It's sharply priced, too. Maker: Phil Ryan.

CURRENT RELEASE 2002 This is a good middle-of-the-road chardonnay that offers a little bit extra. On the nose there are attractive melon notes, and there's a chalky suggestion of lees influence. Subdued oak leaves the fruit character to the fore and doesn't intrude too much on the smooth palate. It has gentle melony fruit and easy-drinking texture in the mouth, with a dry clean ending. Good with soft mild cheeses.

Quality	🍷🍷🍷🍷
Value	★★★★
Grapes	chardonnay
Region	Hunter Valley, NSW
Cellar	2
Alc./Vol.	13.5%
RRP	$16.00 (S)

McWilliams Mount Pleasant Early Release Elizabeth

No Australian white needs age so much as Hunter Valley semillon, and few so reward the patient collector. Mount Pleasant Elizabeth Semillon usually sells with around four years' bottle-age, but last year they test-marketed a screw-capped 2001 vintage through Vintage Cellars, as a youthful cellaring proposition.

CURRENT RELEASE 2001 This has the understated intensity that is the hallmark of good young Hunter semillon, but it seems just a fraction riper-tasting than usual, due probably to the 2001 vintage. It has citrus, light herbal and slightly herbaceous notes on the nose, and it tastes clean and subtle with a herbal hint. The finish is tinder-dry and it needs bottle-age to be at its best. A white wine to match up with grilled whiting.

Quality	🍷🍷🍷🍷½
Value	★★★★★
Grapes	semillon
Region	Hunter Valley, NSW
Cellar	3–10+
Alc./Vol.	10.5%
RRP	$15.55

McWilliams Mount Pleasant Elizabeth

Quality	🍷🍷🍷🍷🍷
Value	★★★★★
Grapes	semillon
Region	Hunter Valley, NSW
Cellar	🍾 8+
Alc./Vol.	11.0%
RRP	$18.50 Ⓢ

At Wine Australia 2002, McWilliams put on a 20-year retrospective tasting of Mount Pleasant Elizabeth. Not one wine was less than good, some were truly great. What other Australian white wine could boast such a record? An amazing bargain at the price.
Previous outstanding vintages: '82, '83, '86, '87, '89, '91, '93, '94, '95, '96, '98
CURRENT RELEASE 1999   This great Elizabeth is starting to turn from understated youthful, primary fruit character into something more interesting. The nose has aromas of lemon, honey and dry grass with a hint of toast. In the mouth it has impeccable balance with fine vinous flavour, a light aged touch and a tang to the finish. Try it alongside chilled king prawns.

McWilliams Mount Pleasant Lovedale Semillon

Quality	🍷🍷🍷🍷🍷
Value	★★★★
Grapes	semillon
Region	Hunter Valley, NSW
Cellar	🍾 10+
Alc./Vol.	11.0%
RRP	$42.00

Lovedale Semillons epitomise the best of the classic Hunter Valley style. Released with a few years' age, they develop beautifully, building superb, savoury complexity along the way. Maker: Phil Ryan.
Previous outstanding vintages: '74, '75, '79, '84, '86, '95, '96, '97
CURRENT RELEASE 1998   A superb semillon, and one that will only get better with more bottle-age. There's a deep, buttery, toasty overlay to still fresh lemon-curd aromas on the nose, with a honeyed thread creeping in. In the mouth, a fine, elegant feel, with dry flavours of savoury intensity turning slightly toasty before a long, clean finish. A classic in the making. Serve with roasted snapper.

McWilliams Mount Pleasant Maurice O'Shea Chardonnay

McWilliams top chardonnay is starting to look a little old-fashioned amongst the fine, elegant styles that come from cooler regions than the Hunter.

CURRENT RELEASE 2000 Oak and straightforward fruit character in chardonnay doesn't seem enough any more, in a world of complex winery techniques and cool-climate viticulture. The nose has big, toasty and slightly splintery oak input that dominates peach and honey fruit underneath. The stone-fruit flavours get more of a look-in on the powerfully built palate, but wood is still pronounced. Serve it with stir-fried chicken and almonds.

Quality	🍷🍷🍷🍷
Value	★★★
Grapes	chardonnay
Region	Hunter Valley, NSW
Cellar	🍾 3
Alc./Vol.	14.0%
RRP	$33.00

McWilliams Mount Pleasant Museum Elizabeth

Mount Pleasant keep back a bit of each vintage of Elizabeth for release as a more mature wine. This well-priced Museum Elizabeth is eight years old.

CURRENT RELEASE 1995 Not quite the wine the '94 was, but it does encapsulate the virtues of aged Hunter semillon. The nose is richly developed and full of savoury appeal. Primary lemony fruit has given way to the buttered toastiness of maturity, and the mellow palate continues this theme. Not as complex as usual, having more aged character and a bit less freshness, but still a lovely drop, worthy of special occasions. Try it with coconutty fried prawns.

Quality	🍷🍷🍷🍷½
Value	★★★★★
Grapes	semillon
Region	Hunter Valley, NSW
Cellar	🍾 2
Alc./Vol.	11.0%
RRP	$28.00

McWilliams Regional Collection Clare Valley Riesling

McWilliams used to be a bit of a sleeping giant, but, thanks to some dynamic management, they now have an excellent range of wines, from budget brands to Australian classics.

CURRENT RELEASE 2002 Not quite as refined as the best of Clare Valley riesling, this is still an attractive, affordable wine to drink relatively young. It has zesty lime, apple, and floral notes with light spiciness. It's slightly broader in the mouth than the best, but that makes it smooth and drinkable, and there's enough acidity to balance the spicy citrus flavours. Serve it with chicken and lemon grass.

Quality	🍷🍷🍷🍷
Value	★★★★½
Grapes	riesling
Region	Clare Valley, SA
Cellar	🍾 3
Alc./Vol.	13.0%
RRP	$17.50 (S)

McWilliams Regional Collection Eden Valley Riesling

Quality	🍷🍷🍷🍷🍷
Value	★★★★★
Grapes	riesling
Region	Eden Valley, SA
Cellar	🍶 5
Alc./Vol.	12.5%
RRP	$17.50 ⑤ 🥂

This Regional Collection brings together some of the most celebrated wine types from Australia's most celebrated regions and sells them at very reasonable prices. Good on 'em.

CURRENT RELEASE 2002   Great value in keeping with McWilliams' Regional Collection established form, this smells like a delicate pot-pourri of florals, pear and zesty citrus aromas. In the mouth it has real concentration, with rich pear-like fruit that's juicy and tangy, and typically 2002 South Australian riesling. It has good depth, but the flavour retains delicacy. A bargain to enjoy with Thai roast duck salad.

McWilliams Riverina Botrytis Semillon

Quality	🍷🍷🍷🍷🍷
Value	★★★★
Grapes	semillon
Region	Riverina, NSW
Cellar	🍶 5
Alc./Vol.	12.5%
RRP	$25.00 (375 ml)

This Riverina botrytis semillon doesn't attract the hype of De Bortoli Noble One, the regional flagship, but at its best it's finer, more elegant and, dare we say it, more like real French Sauternes, than any other Riverina sweetie we've seen.

CURRENT RELEASE 2000   This subtly complex wine travels the Riverina road in its light marmalade, apricot and honey/toffee aromas, but then it detours towards Europe with fine citrus, classy oak and earthy notes. The palate is sweet, silky and luscious with elegant, even subtle flavour. The finish is crisp with tangy acid and fragrant with quality oak. A first-class Australian sweet wine to sip on its own after dinner, or perhaps with a piece of mild blue cheese.

PENGUIN BEST SWEET WINE

Meadowbank Estate Sauvignon Blanc

Meadowbank offers an ongoing program of cultural activities which are worth a visit. You'll be well lubricated, of course, by Meadowbank's high-quality wines.
CURRENT RELEASE 2002   This is a pale, bright wine with a delicious surge of ripe sauvignon blanc aroma jumping out of the glass. It's like a thrilling mix of passionfruit, green fruits, green grass and sweat – sounds strange, but amazingly appetising! In the mouth it's soft and juicy with an entrancing sweet-sour see-saw that keeps it interesting. The aftertaste is mouth-wateringly long. Try it with crudités.

Quality	♥♥♥♥♥
Value	★★★★
Grapes	sauvignon blanc
Region	Coal River, Tas.
Cellar	🍶 2
Alc./Vol.	12.5%
RRP	$22.00

Meadowbank Riesling

Tasmania and riesling are a great combination. Add the sort of restaurant facilities available at Meadowbank, and it's an essential place to visit when in the 'Apple Isle'.
CURRENT RELEASE 2002   Meadowbank Riesling sits in that austere Tassie style that impresses us more with each edition of the *Guide*. It has a steely nose that's dry and quite austere. Mineral, lime and herbal notes are spring-like and pure. It tastes fine and long, light but intense, with a dry minerally finish. Try it with pan-fried trout with almonds.

Quality	♥♥♥♥♥
Value	★★★⁺
Grapes	riesling
Region	Derwent Valley, Tas.
Cellar	🍶 6
Alc./Vol.	12.0%
RRP	$24.00

Meerea Park Alexander Munro Semillon

Alexander Munro was present Meerea Park winemaker Rhys Eather's great-great-grandfather. He too was a winemaker – it must run in the blood.
CURRENT RELEASE 1998   A maturing Hunter semillon with a full green–yellow colour, and some of the concentration and savoury complexity that comes with age. At five years old it seems in a transitional phase, with buttered toast and minerally smells overtaking primary fruit on the nose, and the palate gives the impression of enhanced depth and richness. It's bone-dry and less giving than Mount Pleasant Elizabeth, for example, but with the right food, perhaps baked fish, it works well.

Quality	♥♥♥♥
Value	★★★★
Grapes	semillon
Region	Hunter Valley, NSW
Cellar	🍶 5
Alc./Vol.	11.0%
RRP	$25.00

Meerea Park Late Harvest Viognier

Quality	🍷🍷🍷🍷
Value	★★★
Grapes	viognier
Region	Hunter Valley, NSW
Cellar	🍾 2
Alc./Vol.	11.5%
RRP	$24.00 (375 ml)

Mmm! Late-harvested sweet viognier? This really is an unusual type of wine, but one of fascinating personality. CURRENT RELEASE 2002   Viognier is one of the most extravagantly aromatic grapes. This sweet white puts viognier to an unusual use, and gets away with it, although we doubt it will be to everyone's taste. There's the floral spice of the variety with hints of apricot and banana, and a touch of spicy oak. In the mouth it's silky-sweet and long-flavoured with apple and dried-apricot flavours that are long and soft. A weirdo wine to get people talking, it might just work with pâté.

Meerea Park Lindsay Hill Verdelho

Quality	🍷🍷🍷🍷
Value	★★★
Grapes	verdelho
Region	Hunter Valley, NSW
Cellar	🍾 3
Alc./Vol.	14.0%
RRP	$18.50

The Hunter Valley has a long history with verdelho, going back continuously to a time long before the current trend to plant it all over the place. Maker: Rhys Eather.
CURRENT RELEASE 2002   From the Upper Hunter, this verdelho has quite a bit of regional character in its make-up, and less of the typical varietal fruit salad. The nose has lemon, light tropical and stone-fruit aromas that are clean and agreeable. The palate is dry with good vinosity rather than simple fruit. It tastes clean and flinty dry on the finish, making it a good wine for prawn satays.

Meeting Place Chardonnay

Quality	🍷🍷🍷🍷
Value	★★★★★
Grapes	chardonnay
Region	Tumbarumba, NSW & Canberra, ACT
Cellar	🍾 2
Alc./Vol.	13.5%
RRP	$14.95 ⑤

The Meeting Place in question is Canberra, the site of BRL Hardy's new Kamberra wine centre. The centre produces wines sourced from the vineyard regions surrounding the national capital.
CURRENT RELEASE 2001   As you would expect from BRL Hardy, this is a very well-made commercial chardonnay. The colour is bright and youthful, and it smells of toasty oak and summer stone fruit, a creamy note adding a touch of quiet complexity. In the mouth it's clean and fresh with tangy peach-like fruit and fine integrated acidity. Tastes like wines of double the price from some boutique producers. Try it with pan-fried fish.

Meeting Place Riesling

Most of the Meeting Place wines are blends of
Canberra district fruit with grapes from other nearby
New South Wales vineyards, but this riesling is 100 per
cent Canberra. The region is evolving into a good
source of cool-climate rieslings.
CURRENT RELEASE 2002   Unlike an increasing
number of rieslings with screw-caps, this youngster
has a cork. It's a pale drop with a high-toned steely
nose that also brings aromas of limes, lemons and
some herbal notes. The palate is dry and austere with
a tangy acid finish. Try it with delicate white fish.

Quality	♥♥♥♥
Value	★★★
Grapes	riesling
Region	Canberra, ACT
Cellar	3
Alc./Vol.	12.0%
RRP	$14.95 ($)

Meeting Place Sauvignon Blanc

Much maligned, Canberra is really a great place to
visit, with first-class museums, galleries, places of
interest, and now a thriving wine industry on its
doorstep. And with BRL Hardy's Kamberra Wine
Centre in town, even more reasons to go.
CURRENT RELEASE 2002   This has substance and
drinkability, but it is rather neutral. The nose has citrus
and lightly grassy aromas with a hint of honey, and the
palate is clean and dry with acceptable intensity and
a crisp, high-acid finish. It just doesn't make the earth
move, for us at least. A straightforward companion
to some fritto misto of fish.

Quality	♥♥♥
Value	★★★
Grapes	sauvignon blanc
Region	Tumbarumba, NSW & Canberra, ACT
Cellar	1
Alc./Vol.	11.5%
RRP	$14.95

Merum Semillon

The small Merum vineyard is in the picturesque
Manjimup district of southern Western Australia. Wine
quality is excellent and winemaker/proprietor Mike
Melsom maintains an enviable standard of quality.
CURRENT RELEASE 2002   This semillon has some
of the herbaceous zest of sauvignon blanc. There are
touches of herbs, green peas and citrus to the tropical
fruit on the nose, and the palate is clean and dry,
medium-bodied with a dry finish. There's a little barrel
influence in the mix and the wood input gives mouth-
feel and persistence. A nicely balanced white to pal up
with Thai pad-see-iw noodles.

Quality	♥♥♥♥♥
Value	★★★★
Grapes	semillon 90%; chardonnay 10%
Region	Pemberton, WA
Cellar	2
Alc./Vol.	13.8%
RRP	$20.00

Mesh Eden Valley Riesling

Quality	▼▼▼▼▼
Value	★★★★
Grapes	riesling
Region	Eden Valley, SA
Cellar	🍾 10+
Alc./Vol.	13.0%
RRP	$27.00 🍷

Mesh is a collaborative effort between modern riesling guru Jeffrey Grosset and Robert Hill Smith, whose family company, Yalumba, has generations of experience making great riesling. A limited quantity was made in 2002, but it's worth seeking. Quality is exemplary.

CURRENT RELEASE 2002   This encapsulates the pristine, aromatic fruit of high-quality Eden Valley riesling. The nose is intense and surprisingly concentrated with classical floral, pear and citrus-accented aromas. It tastes intense, with great length and sustained flavour. A steely, firm structure should ensure good ageing potential. Serve it with vegetarian noodles, with tofu, sweet soy and fresh coriander.

Miramar Semillon

Quality	▼▼▼◗
Value	★★★★
Grapes	semillon
Region	Mudgee, NSW
Cellar	🍾 10+
Alc./Vol.	10.5%
RRP	$12.00 🍷
	(cellar door)

Ian McRae has been making good wine at Miramar for 25 years, and he is one of the better-kept secrets of the boutique wine scene.

CURRENT RELEASE 2002   The colour is very pale and it's a reserved wine all round. There are hints of passionfruit, chalk and slate to sniff, and the minerally characters continue on the palate, where it is delicate, tangy, fine and very dry. It has yet to really come out of its shell. It should age well. You could serve it with sushi.

Miranda High Country Chardonnay

Quality	▼▼▼▼◗
Value	★★★★★
Grapes	chardonnay
Region	King & Ovens Valleys, Vic.
Cellar	🍾 1
Alc./Vol.	14.0%
RRP	$13.50 Ⓢ

They're definitely doing something right at Miranda. This inexpensive chardonnay just gets better and better and the 2002 is absolutely amazing value.

CURRENT RELEASE 2002   Here's a wine that has been transformed in recent years into a much fresher, more delicate style. Along the way it's gained a touch of sheer class that has us reaching for superlatives, especially at the price. The colour is pale and it has fine grapefruit and lightly peachy fruit, smooth and well-harmonised with subtle oak into a lovely, lightly creamy wine of good length and freshness. A classy addition to yabbies and beurre blanc.

PENGUIN BEST BARGAIN WHITE

Mitchell Watervale Riesling

In 2002, perfect weather gave the Clare Valley
winemakers one of the best riesling vintages any of
them could remember, with many near-perfect wines
like this one. Maker: Andrew Mitchell.

**CURRENT RELEASE 2002   The perfect young
riesling appearance: bright, pale and distinctly
greenish. On the nose there's unusual richness
and succulence, with lime-like aromas, hints of
aromatic bakery spices and a touch of peach.
The full-bodied palate is sumptuously
constructed with spiced fruit flavour, and a
long lemony finish. A tour de force; drinks well
now, but long-ageing under its screw-cap
should build powerful complexity. Serve with
stir-fried chicken, lemon grass and chilli.**

Quality	🍷🍷🍷🍷🍷
Value	★★★★★
Grapes	riesling
Region	Clare Valley, SA
Cellar	🍶 10
Alc./Vol.	13.5%
RRP	$18.00 🗲

**PENGUIN WINE OF THE YEAR,
BEST WHITE WINE and BEST
RIESLING**

Mitchelton Blackwood Park Botrytis Riesling

Some of Mitchelton's vineyards enjoy perfect conditions
for the development of botrytis cinerea, the noble rot.
The grapes are usually harvested at least four weeks
after the main crop.

CURRENT RELEASE 2002   A tangy sweetie with
candied citrus peel, dried ginger, floral and lime aromas.
Varietal character remains distinct despite botrytis
influence, and it's not as lush nor as sweet as most
botrytis styles. The palate is juicy and spicy, with a dry
marmaladey finish. Try it with a rich chicken liver pâté.

Quality	🍷🍷🍷🍷
Value	★★★⁺
Grapes	riesling
Region	Goulburn Valley, Vic.
Cellar	🍶 3
Alc./Vol.	12.5%
RRP	$17.00 (375 ml)

Mitchelton Blackwood Park Riesling

Victoria's Goulburn Valley doesn't feature highly on the
national riesling map, but this has been a favourite of
ours over many years. It drinks well young, and it takes
age well: more so now it has a screw-cap.

CURRENT RELEASE 2002   A pale slightly green-tinged
colour looks just right, and the nose is light and
fragrant, reminiscent of blossom, lime and peach. The
palate follows with more softness and weight than
usual. Ripe citrus and passionfruit flavours are quite full
and there's a tang at the end. Serve with prosciutto.

Quality	🍷🍷🍷🍷🍷
Value	★★★★★
Grapes	riesling
Region	Goulburn Valley, Vic.
Cellar	🍶 5+
Alc./Vol.	13.5%
RRP	$17.00 Ⓢ 🗲

Molly Morgan Old Vine Semillon

Quality	🍷🍷🍷🍷🍷
Value	★★★★⁴
Grapes	semillon
Region	Hunter Valley, NSW
Cellar	🍷 6+
Alc./Vol.	10.0%
RRP	$20.00

Molly Morgan was a twice-transported convict who eventually became a large Hunter Valley landowner, known as 'Queen of the Hunter Valley'. This vineyard land was once hers.

CURRENT RELEASE 2001   If you want to taste Hunter Valley semillon with absolutely classic regional/varietal personality, try this. It has a complete, savoury nose reminiscent of citrus and minerals, and there's really surprising concentration at only 10 per cent alcohol. In the mouth the story's the same: penetrating flavour, good length, clean taste and a crisp finish. Like most good Hunter sems, it should build beautifully in bottle. Try it with pan-fried fish.

Monichino Botrytis Semillon

Quality	🍷🍷🍷🍷
Value	★★★★
Grapes	semillon
Region	Goulburn Valley, Vic.
Cellar	🍷 2
Alc./Vol.	9.6%
RRP	$16.00 (375 ml)

Monichino winery is well off the beaten track, at Katunga, near Shepparton in Victoria's central north. It's a warm place to grow grapes and susceptible to botrytis infection in the right circumstances.

CURRENT RELEASE 2001   This bright yellow–gold wine shows sweaty, light tangerine and peach aromas of real intensity. Is it sweet? And how! The very sweet flavour is stopped short of going over the top by long tangy acid, and it has good balance as a result. It has nice depth and persistence. A shade more finesse would give it a higher score. Try it with crème caramel.

Montalto Pennon Riesling

Quality	🍷🍷🍷🍷
Value	★★★⁴
Grapes	riesling
Region	Mornington Peninsula, Vic.
Cellar	🍷 3
Alc./Vol.	12.5%
RRP	$17.50

Riesling is an adaptable grape variety, so it's no surprise that it's producing good wine in various places around Australia, even regions with no riesling history to speak of, like the Mornington Peninsula.

CURRENT RELEASE 2002   Perhaps lacks the penetration and thrill of the best rieslings, but it's not a bad starting point for a new vineyard. It has a fresh varietal nose reminiscent of apple sauce, spice and lime, and there's a light minerally touch. The palate has dry spiced apple and lime flavours of good depth that end dry with lemony acidity. Try it with grilled garfish.

Moorilla Estate Chardonnay

Moorilla have their own design of bottles for some of
their wines. Embossed with the winery's logo, they are
certainly distinctive, but bloody hard to stack.
CURRENT RELEASE 2001   The nose has distinct
pineapple aromas with spicy oak in support. The
palate has juicy tropical-fruit flavour of reasonable
intensity but it feels a bit linear in the mouth, rather
than round and mouth-filling. A whisper of sulfur
and a finish that falls away a bit don't add to its charm.
Try it with cream cheese pastries.

Quality	♥♥♥♡
Value	★★★
Grapes	chardonnay
Region	Derwent Valley, Tas.
Cellar	▮ 2
Alc./Vol.	13.5%
RRP	$31.50

Moorilla Estate Reserve Chardonnay

Moorilla, on the outskirts of Hobart, is worth visiting,
and not just for its wines. It also has a fascinating
museum of antiquities.
CURRENT RELEASE 2001   This is a tasty, complex
chardonnay of real style. All the different influences of
ripe fruit, oak and winemaker input combine in fine
harmony. The nose has melon, nectarine, light vanilla
caramel and high-toned oak aromas. In the mouth it's
rich and smooth with citrus, white-peach and spicy
oak flavours, creamy texture and a long finish. Try it
with Tasmanian ocean trout.

Quality	♥♥♥♥♡
Value	★★★
Grapes	chardonnay
Region	Tamar Valley, Tas.
Cellar	▮ 3
Alc./Vol.	13.5%
RRP	$38.50

Moorooduc Estate Chardonnay

The subtext on the Moorooduc Estate Chardonnays
these days is 'wild yeast'. Maker Dr Richard McIntyre
believes that natural vineyard yeasts give more interest
to the finished wine than cultured strains.
CURRENT RELEASE 2001   A complex wine but
somehow a bit less 'wild' than The Moorooduc (see
below). The nose has subtle peach and cashew aromas
with light mealy and vanilla-cream touches, and some
of the earthiness that marks minimal-intervention
chardonnay. In the mouth it's smooth and even, with
some structure and a long, rather firm finish. Try it
with chicken salad, with mango and sesame.

Quality	♥♥♥♥♡
Value	★★★
Grapes	chardonnay
Region	Mornington Peninsula, Vic.
Cellar	▮ 3
Alc./Vol.	13.5%
RRP	$31.70

Moorooduc Estate The Moorooduc Chardonnay

Quality	🍷🍷🍷🍷🍷
Value	★★★
Grapes	chardonnay
Region	Mornington Peninsula, Vic.
Cellar	🍾 4
Alc./Vol.	13.5%
RRP	$60.00

Rick McIntyre is always striving for more quality and interest in his winemaking. As a result, his chardonnays are never boring.

CURRENT RELEASE 2001   This has a bright straw-yellow colour and a restrained, complex bouquet of fig, white peach, earth and some slightly feral 'Frenchy' qualities. There's also a hint of buttered toast and subtle nuttiness from oak. The palate is fine and long, and as much about easy texture and feel as flavour. A hint of yeast extract adds to the foreign feel of this wine, and there's beautifully integrated acidity on a long, slightly firm finish. Slow-roasted salmon cutlets work well here.

Moss Wood Ribbon Vale Semillon Sauvignon Blanc

Quality	🍷🍷🍷🍷
Value	★★★⁴
Grapes	semillon 54%; sauvignon blanc 46%
Region	Margaret River, WA
Cellar	🍾 1
Alc./Vol.	14.0%
RRP	$19.00

The Mugfords of Moss Wood purchased the Ribbon Vale vineyard in 2000 and have been working to improve it since. It's located in Caves Road, Willyabrup, some of the best wine country in the whole of Western Australia.

CURRENT RELEASE 2002   Straw-coloured and bright, this has juicy fruit-salad, green-salad and citrus aromas that are immediately attractive. Some herbal and chalky notes add more subtle interest. The palate is clean-tasting with good depth and a penetrating, clean finish. Serve it with asparagus and hollandaise.

Moss Wood Semillon

Quality	🍷🍷🍷🍷
Value	★★★
Grapes	semillon
Region	Margaret River, WA
Cellar	🍾 3
Alc./Vol.	14.5%
RRP	$32.00 🥂

Moss Wood boss Keith Mugford is a fan of screw-caps instead of corks to seal his bottles, so his latest semillon comes packed in both.

CURRENT RELEASE 2002   A powerful white wine, richly concentrated with aromas of citrus, herbs, minerals and nuts. The palate follows full-bodied and rich in flavour and texture. There's a slight warmth of alcohol too, 14.5 per cent, so be warned. (HH finds the alcohol makes the wine hot and clumsy.) As for the cork versus screw-cap issue, the screw-topped wine had a little more definition and freshness, the cork-sealed was slightly broader and more forward. Time will emphasise the superiority of the screw-cap. Serve with roast chicken.

Mount Horrocks Riesling

Mount Horrocks, relatively unknown not all that long ago, has stepped into the circle of top quality Clare-Watervale riesling producers with great aplomb. Proprietor/winemaker Stephanie Toole is a perfectionist, and it shows.

CURRENT RELEASE 2002 Another one of the growing band of screw-cap rieslings, this is a bright, pale wine with a minerally nose and sweet cinnamon, stewed-apple and lime aromas. The palate is tight and closed, but it has that feel of underlying sinewy strength and potential that marks the best. It finishes dry with lemony acidity and a minerally aftertaste. Serve it with little fried whitebait.

Quality	🍷🍷🍷🍷🍷
Value	★★★★
Grapes	riesling
Region	Clare Valley, SA
Cellar	2–8+
Alc./Vol.	13.0%
RRP	$27.80

Mount Horrocks Semillon

This semillon is always serious; low-yield, dry-grown fruit, barrel-fermented in French oak, lees stirred, and bottled under a screw-cap, it's a recipe for wine of character and impact. Maker: Stephanie Toole.

CURRENT RELEASE 2002 An object lesson in applying oak to semillon. The nose retains lightly tropical fruit and some citrus, with cashew and spice from solids and wood. It all dovetails together, and the palate benefits in richness and texture from the oak and yeast lees. There's a slight phenolic touch at the moment, but it will be better in a year or two. Try it with grilled swordfish steaks.

Quality	🍷🍷🍷🍷
Value	★★★
Grapes	semillon
Region	Clare Valley, SA
Cellar	4
Alc./Vol.	13.5%
RRP	$27.00

Mount Mary Chardonnay

The Mount Mary chardonnays walk their own path, often deviating significantly from mainstream Aussie style. There's no malolactic, for one thing. Maker: John Middleton.

CURRENT RELEASE 2001 This vintage is more developed than usual for Mount Mary, which can often be austere in youth and demanding years of cellaring. The colour is medium yellow and there's a lot of bready sur lie character in the bouquet. It's soft and smooth on the tongue, with lemon/citrus flavours, fine balance and a clean dry finish. It looks to be a relatively early-maturing vintage. We'd serve it with barbecued chicken.

Quality	🍷🍷🍷🍷
Value	★★★
Grapes	chardonnay
Region	Yarra Valley, Vic.
Cellar	4+
Alc./Vol.	13.8%
RRP	$43.00 (cellar door)

Mount Trio Chardonnay

Quality	♟♟♟♟
Value	★★★★⌐
Grapes	chardonnay
Region	Great Southern, WA
Cellar	▮ 3
Alc./Vol.	13.5%
RRP	$17.00

Chardonnay is Australia's favourite white wine, and it performs well just about anywhere it's planted. This comes from the Great Southern part of Western Australia. Maker: Gavin Berry.

CURRENT RELEASE 2001   Gavin Berry builds restrained complexity into chardonnay with great skill. From his own Porongurup vineyard, this has harmonious complexity: nothing overdone, everything in its place. There's stone fruit, citrus, a hint of butterscotch, and subtle barrel influence. The palate is medium in body with intense satisfying flavours that aren't big or overdone. A zesty tang of acidity and a long, toasty/savoury aftertaste complete the picture. Serve it with pan-fried fish.

Mount Trio Sauvignon Blanc

Quality	♟♟♟♟
Value	★★★★⌐
Grapes	sauvignon blanc
Region	Great Southern, WA
Cellar	▮ 2
Alc./Vol.	13.5%
RRP	$15.00

Western Australia's far south is a great place to visit, and surprisingly undiscovered by the hordes. Mount Trio wines come from the Porongorup region, a very atmospheric place.

CURRENT RELEASE 2002   Herbal and mineral aromas are the first thing you notice with this wine, but sweetly juicy fruit is there behind it, along with a sweaty touch. It tastes soft and mouth-filling for a sauvignon, with gooseberry flavours of good persistence and finish. Try it with stir-fried calamari.

Nepenthe Sauvignon Blanc

Quality	♟♟♟♟♟
Value	★★★★★
Grapes	sauvignon blanc
Region	Adelaide Hills, SA
Cellar	▮ 1
Alc./Vol.	13.0%
RRP	$18.00 🕳

Nepenthe has 25 hectares of vineyards at Lenswood and 40 hectares at Charleston in the Adelaide Hills, with untold varieties in them. It's come a long way fast, for a company less than a decade old.

CURRENT RELEASE 2002   Delicious gooseberry aromas and a hint of the famous (infamous?) cat's pee aroma here. The wine is clean, fresh and lively in the mouth: exactly what we want in a young savvy blanc. The palate has a pronounced tang and is dry and zesty on the finish. It would suit Chinese scallops with bean curd and broccoli.

Nepenthe Unwooded Chardonnay

Australian unoaked chardonnay often disappoints because it's made from lesser-quality fruit and left slightly sweet, assuming a less wine-aware clientele. Nepenthe's Peter Leske is more generous with quality than most.

CURRENT RELEASE 2002   The aromas of pungent tropical fruits in the passionfruit/pawpaw range suggest a little skin contact has been employed, but it's certainly a charmer to drink young. It's very grapey and simple, but also very fresh and lively, with a jolt of cleansing acidity to finish. A good bottle to take to a vegetarian restaurant.

Quality	♟♟♟♟
Value	★★★★
Grapes	chardonnay
Region	Adelaide Hills, SA
Cellar	▮ 2
Alc./Vol.	13.5%
RRP	$16.00 ⊗

Nugan Estate Frasca's Lane Vineyard Chardonnay

The Nugan name is well-known in Griffith, but the Nugan Estate is a fairly new venture, based on vineyards at Darlington Point near Griffith.

CURRENT RELEASE 2001   From King Valley fruit, this chardonnay is quite advanced and shows a medium–full yellow hue and plenty of 'legs' from glycerol. The bouquet is toasty, almost resinous, and reveals some bottle-age. There are roasted hazelnut characters, too. It is full-bodied with plenty of weight from oak and alcohol as well as fruit. It perhaps lacks a little richness of fruit, and would be best with food. Try roast chicken.

Quality	♟♟♟♟
Value	★★★
Grapes	chardonnay
Region	King Valley, Vic.
Cellar	▮ 1
Alc./Vol.	13.5%
RRP	$21.00 Ⓢ

Nugan Estate Frasca's Lane Vineyard Sauvignon Blanc

The back label explains that some French oak was used in the maturation of this wine, which explains the toasty nut character. Oak is fairly rare in delicate sauvignon blancs like this.

CURRENT RELEASE 2002   The colour is a nice, bright, light yellow and the wine smells of toasty oak, plus a hint of herbal varietal fruit in the background. The taste is light and lean, taut and nervy. The finish is dry and has a nice touch of sauvignon tang, but there's not a lot of varietal character. It's a pleasant, light-bodied, wooded dry white. Try it with cold chicken and salad.

Quality	♟♟♟♟
Value	★★★
Grapes	sauvignon blanc
Region	King Valley, Vic.
Cellar	▮ 1
Alc./Vol.	13.0%
RRP	$21.00 Ⓢ

O'Leary Walker Adelaide Hills Sauvignon Blanc

Quality	♟♟♟♟
Value	★★★
Grapes	sauvignon blanc
Region	Adelaide Hills, SA
Cellar	▮ 1
Alc./Vol.	12.5%
RRP	$21.00 ⧖

Messrs O'Leary and Walker have put together a great portfolio of South Australian wines, all of them representing top-quality regional classics at affordable prices. More power to them.
CURRENT RELEASE 2002   From the O'Leary family vineyard in the Adelaide Hills, this is in good Hills sauvignon vein, succulent, pure and vibrant. Nose and palate have tropical-fruit and crisp snow-pea characters of essency quality. Acid is tight and tangy and the palate is light yet reasonably intense. Good with steamed Chinese broccoli and oyster sauce.

O'Leary Walker Polish Hill River Riesling

Quality	♟♟♟♟♟
Value	★★★★⯪
Grapes	riesling
Region	Clare Valley, SA
Cellar	▮ 10+
Alc./Vol.	12.5%
RRP	$19.80 ⧖

Polish Hill River is a pretty sub-region of the Clare Valley. Its name is appearing more and more on labels as winemakers and consumers recognise the quality of riesling grown there.
CURRENT RELEASE 2002   Very much in the concentrated mould that typifies 2002 Polish Hill River rieslings. It has a bright, viscous green-tinged appearance, and a gorgeously intense nose of florals, passionfruit and pineapple, lime cordial and minerals. It tastes fresh and lively, with a concentrated palate of good depth, a steely spine and a dry finish. It should develop into a very rich wine. Great to sip with a Japanese bento box.

O'Leary Walker Watervale Riesling

Quality	♟♟♟♟♟
Value	★★★★★
Grapes	riesling
Region	Clare Valley, SA
Cellar	⬤► 2–10+
Alc./Vol.	12.5%
RRP	$21.00 ⧖

David O'Leary and Nick Walker can do no wrong with their own label. All the wines are high-quality, honest expressions of classic Australian wine types, and some of them, this riesling included, have that little extra that makes them very special.
CURRENT RELEASE 2002   This young riesling should be locked away for a while for its own good. At the moment it's tight and closed up with archetypal aromas of lime, apple and slate. In the mouth it has penetrating intensity and good depth of lingering flavour with a firm minerally backbone. Its solid construction should ensure long life. A great wine to enjoy with vegetable tempura.

Orlando Jacob's Creek Chardonnay

Jacob's Creek is one of the greatest success stories for Aussie wine. Sales now run to the tune of five million cases annually, four million of them going to export.

CURRENT RELEASE 2002 Like most of the Jacob's Creek range, this is an object lesson in how inexpensive need not mean uninspiring. This is cleverly made to incorporate fresh varietal melon and stone-fruit characters with a finely tuned touch of oak, into an easy-drinking and reasonably priced young white. The palate is soft and succulent with a clean, dry finish. Try it with Swiss-style cheese and crackers.

Quality	🍷🍷🍷½
Value	★★★★
Grapes	chardonnay
Region	not stated, SA
Cellar	🍾 1
Alc./Vol.	13.0%
RRP	$10.00 ($)

Orlando Jacob's Creek Riesling

This has often been the pick of the Jacob's Creek whites, perhaps as a result of riesling's unfashionable status in recent decades. It always has archetypal varietal characters and the price is often discounted.

CURRENT RELEASE 2002 Considering it usually sells for around $10, this is a ripper of a wine. The nose is sweetly aromatic, suggestive of bath powder, lime juice and a touch of spice. In the mouth it has good intensity with succulent lime-like flavour and a crisp finish. Buy it by the case. Try it with Asian flavours.

Quality	🍷🍷🍷🍷
Value	★★★★★
Grapes	riesling
Region	not stated, SA
Cellar	🍾 2
Alc./Vol.	12.0%
RRP	$10.00 ($)

Orlando Jacob's Creek Semillon Chardonnay

Australia is pretty much the only country in the world that blends semillon and chardonnay – it's a sort of unholy alliance between Bordeaux and Burgundy. But if it tastes good, why not?

CURRENT RELEASE 2002 The semillon fruit draws attention to itself, adding a green-herb, bracken, snapped-twig aroma; any contribution from the chardonnay is well in the background. The colour is palish and it's an all-round fresh, youthful drop. Light-bodied and simple, it needs to be drunk young, with a niçoise salad.

Quality	🍷🍷½
Value	★★★½
Grapes	semillon; chardonnay
Region	not stated
Cellar	🍾 1
Alc./Vol.	11.5%
RRP	$10.00 ($)

Orlando Jacob's Creek Semillon Sauvignon Blanc

Quality	♀ ♀ ♀
Value	★ ★ ★ ⧽
Grapes	semillon; sauvignon blanc
Region	not stated, SA
Cellar	▮ 1
Alc./Vol.	12.0%
RRP	$10.00 ⑤

This was once known as 'Chablis', a fact that really exemplifies how ridiculous the use of European wine names for Australian products could be. Real French Chablis is bone-dry chardonnay from the Burgundy region, dry-grown on chalk soil; Jacob's Creek is something else entirely. Thank heavens it's all changed.
CURRENT RELEASE 2002   No complications here. The nose has grapey, juicy aromas with a snappy edge that's like crushed nettles and grass. It tastes clean with medium-intensity herbaceous flavours, and a zing of tart acidity to give the palate a lift. Try it with a green vegetable salad.

Orlando St Helga Riesling

Quality	♀ ♀ ♀ ♀ ♀
Value	★ ★ ★ ★ ★
Grapes	riesling
Region	Eden Valley, SA
Cellar	⬤ 2–10
Alc./Vol.	12.5%
RRP	$18.00

A large part of Orlando's heritage revolves around superb riesling. For generations the company name has been a guarantee of quality and value. The tradition continues with St Helga.
CURRENT RELEASE 2002   There's a bit of steel in Orlando rieslings that sets them apart from the 'prettier' wines of a few other commercial producers. The 2002 St Helga also has some floral aromatics and lime-juice aromas that are fresh and inviting. In the mouth it's elegantly reserved in style with real spine and tangy acidity. The flavour is long and tangy. Try it with sushi.

Orlando Trilogy Semillon Sauvignon Blanc Viognier

Quality	♀ ♀ ♀ ⧽
Value	★ ★ ★ ⧽
Grapes	semillon; sauvignon blanc; viognier
Region	not stated
Cellar	▮ 1
Alc./Vol.	12.0%
RRP	$14.00 ⑤

The third part of the trilogy in this well-presented white is now viognier, where in previous vintages it was muscadelle. And yes, it does make it more interesting.
CURRENT RELEASE 2002   An attractively complex white wine, given its market niche. It smells herbaceous and it has green-pea and citrus aromas too. Touches of florals and spice from the viognier chime in nicely. In the mouth there are clean grassy flavours that are simple, and maybe not quite up to the promise of the nose, but overall a good-value, inexpensive white. Serve it with mee goreng.

Palandri Baldivis Estate Chardonnay

We love discovering really good wines that are also very cheap. It makes our day. This is one of them. Winemaker is Tony Carapetis.

CURRENT RELEASE 2002   The colour is a fresh, bright pale lemon and it just goes on and up from there. It smells of white peach, gooseberry and nougat – clean, fresh and undeveloped. It's light-bodied and fruity, with negligible oak influence, and there's a smidgin of sweetness that's below most people's threshold. It's a lovely drink now – eminently quaffable. Many vegetable dishes would suit.

Quality	♥♥♥♥
Value	★★★★↓
Grapes	chardonnay
Region	various, WA
Cellar	▮ 1
Alc./Vol.	13.5%
RRP	$12.00 ⑤

Peerick Sauvignon Blanc

The Peerick vineyard is on Wild Dog Track, Moonambel. The very cool 2002 summer enabled the sauvignon blanc to achieve ripe flavours as the sugar accumulation was more gradual than usual, say the proprietors Chris and Merryl Jessup.

CURRENT RELEASE 2002   An attractive wine with no trace of underripe green flavours, this has a pale lemon colour and a nose of snapped twigs and dry grass: clean, fresh, youthful and vibrant. The taste is light-bodied and bracingly crisp, dry and well-balanced. A delicious, mouth-watering example of the variety. It would suit stuffed zucchini flowers.

Quality	♥♥♥♥
Value	★★★↓
Grapes	sauvignon blanc
Region	Pyrenees, Vic.
Cellar	▮ 1
Alc./Vol.	12.5%
RRP	$20.00 ⑤

Penfolds Koonunga Hill Chardonnay

Koonunga Hill is the name of a Penfolds vineyard, established during Max Schubert's time at the northern end of the Barossa Valley. With the strange disregard for geography common among big Australian wine companies, the name is now simply a brand and the grapes have nothing whatever to do with Koonunga Hill.

CURRENT RELEASE 2002   It's a simple chardonnay, made to a price. There's little oak influence or other complexity and the palate reveals some residual sugar. It's light in weight, a trifle green and limey/herbal; an odd style that's not very varietal. It would suit KFC.

Quality	♥♥♥
Value	★★★
Grapes	chardonnay
Region	not stated
Cellar	▮ 1
Alc./Vol.	14.0%
RRP	$15.50 ⑤

Penfolds Reserve Bin 00A Chardonnay

Quality	🍷🍷🍷🍷🍷
Value	★★★★
Grapes	chardonnay
Region	Tumbarumba, NSW
	75% & Adelaide
	Hills, SA 25%
Cellar	🍾 3+
Alc./Vol.	13.5%
RRP	$60.00

The Penfolds team has declared its intention to stylistically distance the Reserve Bin chardonnay from Yattarna, mainly through fruit sourcing: this is, on the whole, high-altitude Tumbarumba while Yattarna is mostly Adelaide Hills.

CURRENT RELEASE 2000   This superb chardonnay really opens up with some air: don't serve it too cold! It starts with smoky, charred-oak and hints of green capsicum, developing peach and melon aromas with lovely complex smoke, honey, butter and citrus nuances. The palate is very intense, tightly focussed and has an incredibly long follow-through. A great chardonnay. Serve it with chicken galantine.

Penfolds Thomas Hyland Chardonnay

Quality	🍷🍷🍷🍷
Value	★★★
Grapes	chardonnay
Region	not stated
Cellar	🍾 2
Alc./Vol.	13.5%
RRP	$20.00 ⑤

The Thomas Hyland range was debuted by Southcorp just in time for Christmas 2002. It is one of the keys to the company's ambitious growth plans for Penfolds, which will see wine production under the Penfolds brand almost trebled to five million cases.

CURRENT RELEASE 2002   Barely a step up from the Koonunga Hill chardonnay, this somewhat bland chardonnay falls away on the finish. No question that it's clean and well-made, with a little more interest and less sweetness, but it's not in the same league as the Hyland reds. (It's okay at a discounted $14.99.) It would suit a prawn cocktail.

Penley Estate Chardonnay

Quality	🍷🍷🍷
Value	★★★
Grapes	chardonnay
Region	Coonawarra, SA
Cellar	🍾 1
Alc./Vol.	13.5%
RRP	$21.00

Past releases contained some McLaren Vale, but this is 100 per cent estate-grown Coonawarra fruit. Maker: Kym Tolley.

CURRENT RELEASE 2001   The squashy pineapple and pawpaw tropical aromas suggest the fruit got pretty ripe in 2001. There's a certain jamminess to the wine and the finish carries a whack of acid. It's not quite integrated and it's hard to see it improving from here. You could try it with ham steak and pineapple.

Petaluma Forreston Viognier

It isn't cheap, but then why should it be? Petaluma has proven the breadth of its skills by not only surpassing with traditional Australian varieties, but more recently venturing into, and mastering, grapes such as viognier.
CURRENT RELEASE 2001   The nose shows a talc-like perfume with a hint of spiciness, and rich stone-fruit flavours chime in on palate. The finish is very dry and clean, and the texture is a highlight: it's rich and sensual with some appealing viscosity. Don't chill it too much, and serve with flounder in a buttery sauce.

Quality	ᵞᵞᵞᵞᵞ
Value	★★★⁴
Grapes	viognier
Region	Adelaide Hills, SA
Cellar	🍾 2+
Alc./Vol.	13.8%
RRP	$33.00

Petaluma Hanlin Hill Riesling

The 2002 summer in Clare was the coolest on record, followed by an unusually long, dry, sunny and warm autumn, enabling the grapes to achieve full ripeness. Brian Croser reckons this could be as good as or better than the 1980, his favourite.
CURRENT RELEASE 2002   Time will tell, but as a youngster it is great and promises to cellar extremely well. If anything, it's more open than many of its peers, drinking beautifully from the word go. Pale lemon coloured, it smells intensely fragrant – of lemon essence, lime juice and dried wildflowers – which translates perfectly onto a palate of great fruit intensity, vivacity and persistence. It leaves mouth aromas that linger on. Great with lemon sole.

Quality	ᵞᵞᵞᵞᵞ
Value	★★★★★
Grapes	riesling
Region	Clare Valley, SA
Cellar	🍾 15+
Alc./Vol.	12.8%
RRP	$24.00

Petaluma Tiers Chardonnay

Tiers is the name of the original Petaluma vineyard, located next to the winery in the Piccadilly Valley. The soil contrasts with all the other Hills vineyard soils: much older and with a different structure and origin. And its wine is always different.
CURRENT RELEASE 2000   It has a bright, full yellow colour and a superb bouquet of citrus and pear with grapefruit leading the way, and a toasty background from subtle, integrated oak. The palate has great intensity, power and complexity. It really fills the mouth and the flavours linger long after the wine is gone. Outstanding chardonnay. Treat yourself to grilled lobster.

Quality	ᵞᵞᵞᵞᵞ
Value	★★★
Grapes	chardonnay
Region	Adelaide Hills, SA
Cellar	🍾 3+
Alc./Vol.	13.0%
RRP	$130.00

Peter Lehmann Reserve Riesling

Quality	🍷🍷🍷🍷🍷
Value	★★★★★
Grapes	riesling
Region	Eden Valley, SA
Cellar	🍾 4+
Alc./Vol.	13.0%
RRP	$24.85

This is the best reserve riesling since the stellar 1993, which won 27 trophies and 42 gold medals but alas was never released. The '97 has already won several accolades, including best riesling in the '98 and 2000 International Wine & Spirit Competitions in England. *Previous outstanding vintages: '82, '93*
CURRENT RELEASE 1997　A splendid wine, indeed. Semi-mature and starting to show deliciously toasty, lemon-pith and candle-wax aromas, it is still taut, linear and very much alive in the mouth. Dry, tangy and very long, it's enlivened by frisky acidity and would go beautifully with sole meunière.

Peter Lehmann Reserve Semillon

Quality	🍷🍷🍷🍷🍷
Value	★★★★
Grapes	semillon
Region	Barossa Valley, SA
Cellar	🍾 3
Alc./Vol.	13.0%
RRP	$24.85

This is the first release of a new-style, unwooded reserve semillon, and there are several more rippers waiting in the wings, especially the 2002. The plan is to hold it back for five years before sale. Semillon is managing director Doug Lehmann's favourite white variety.
CURRENT RELEASE 1998　Nutty, straw-like and lemon-essency aromas pour from the glass, and it's quite youthful for a five-year-old Barossa semillon. It's richly toasty and nutty to taste, lemony and fine for its years, with lovely balance and generosity of fruit, which lingers a long time on the aftertaste. It goes with roast stuffed Barossa chook.

Peter Lehmann Semillon

Quality	🍷🍷🍷🍷🍷
Value	★★★★★
Grapes	semillon
Region	Barossa Valley, SA
Cellar	🍾 5
Alc./Vol.	12.0%
RRP	$12.00 Ⓢ

Could there be a better value-for-money white wine in Australia right now? This very inexpensive dry white wins high praise and high scores wherever it is served to fair-minded tasters. The fact that retailers sell it for as little as $8.99 makes it an unbelievable bargain!
CURRENT RELEASE 2002　This fresh, vibrant, deliciously clean, fragrant young semillon smells of lemon and various citrus fruits, almost as perfumy as riesling, and tastes smoothly seamless, intensely fruity, crisp and tangy. Its intensity of fruit and fine balance, finishing pleasantly dry, make it a superb food wine or a refreshing drink on its own. Great with oysters.

Phaedrus Pinot Gris

Phaedrus's wines are quite inexpensive within the Mornington perspective, and that's the aim of their creators – to make if not the greatest Mornington wines, certainly some of the most affordable. It's a goal we applaud.

CURRENT RELEASE 2002   Some cynics have observed that pinot gris has a 'dishwater' character. Not all of them do, but this one does! It is something between cheesy and sweaty, quite unusual but distinctive and not disagreeable. The palate is soft and has a little broadness or thickness, some alcohol warmth and a slight grip to close. It could go with a mild brie-style cheese.

Quality	♀ ♀ ♀
Value	★ ★ ★
Grapes	pinot gris
Region	Mornington Peninsula, Vic.
Cellar	▮ 2
Alc./Vol.	13.0%
RRP	$18.00

Pierro Margaret River Chardonnay

Mike Peterkin and his team seem to have refined this wine a tad, which is probably no bad thing. Past vintages have been monsters, with lots of oak – albeit very good.

CURRENT RELEASE 2001   There are some smoky, subtle oak and slightly volatile characters – the last perhaps from wild ferments. It also has buttery malolactic and spicy French oak scents. There's a suggestion of sweetness on palate, from the generous alcohol and glycerol, and some thickness on the back palate. A complex wine that is still improving. Plenty of flavour and style here. Try it with crayfish.

Quality	♀ ♀ ♀ ♀ ♀
Value	★ ★ ★
Grapes	chardonnay
Region	Margaret River, WA
Cellar	▮ 5
Alc./Vol.	14.0%
RRP	$64.50

Pikes Reserve Riesling

In the best seasons, Neil Pike selects the best grapes from the original estate-grown vines for a Reserve bottling. It is a bit more austere and potentially long-living than the regular Pikes riesling.

CURRENT RELEASE 2002   The colour is pale yellow and it smells rather misleadingly of tropical fruits and lemon squash. It tastes much more austere than it smells: concentrated, very dry, reserved and flinty. There's a lovely mixture of citrus-fruit flavours – lemon, lime and grapefruit – and it promises a bright future with time. Then serve it with smoked trout mousse.

Quality	♀ ♀ ♀ ♀ ♀
Value	★ ★ ★ ★
Grapes	riesling
Region	Clare Valley, SA
Cellar	➴ 1–10+
Alc./Vol.	12.0%
RRP	$27.00 ⦾

Pikes Riesling

Quality	🍷🍷🍷🍷🍷
Value	★★★★★
Grapes	riesling
Region	Clare Valley, SA
Cellar	🍾 8+
Alc./Vol.	12.5%
RRP	$21.00 🔩

Where the screw-cap symbol appears at the end of the entry, it doesn't mean all of the wine is available with this kind of closure: some wineries do a proportion of their riesling this way, and you may have to specify screw-caps when you order.

CURRENT RELEASE 2002   This is a lovely, up-front style of riesling with a subtle trace of sweetness, but it's ostensibly dry to taste. Toasty bread aromas mingle with dried flowers and the palate is smooth and seamless, quite rich and easy to enjoy right now, although it will age well too. Serve with prawn, rocket and lychee salad.

Pipers Brook The Upper Slopes Riesling

Quality	🍷🍷🍷🍷🍷
Value	★★★⯪
Grapes	riesling
Region	Pipers River, Tas.
Cellar	🍾 5
Alc./Vol.	13.0%
RRP	$35.50

Andrew Pirie built Pipers Brook into Tasmania's leading wine company, but he lost control over the company when it went public. It was later taken over by Kreglinger, a Belgian group and, this February, Pirie was 'terminated' by the company's new owners.

CURRENT RELEASE 2000   Only 200 dozen of this single-site riesling, from the oldest riesling vines, was produced. It's a delicious medium-developed riesling which is starting to show glorious buttered-toast and baked lemon pudding flavours. It has years in front of it, though. The palate is already soft and gentle, with a seamless harmony. The only question is whether it's a bit low in acid to age long-term. Superb right now, with pan-fried flathead.

Plantagenet Hazard Hill Semillon Sauvignon Blanc

Quality	🍷🍷🍷
Value	★★★
Grapes	semillon; sauvignon blanc
Region	Great Southern, WA
Cellar	🍾 1
Alc./Vol.	14.0%
RRP	$12.00 ⑤

It's simply stunning just how many good blends of these two Bordeaux white grapes are coming out of Western Australia these days. Priced at entry level, Hazard Hill is another new brand that's over-delivering at the price.

CURRENT RELEASE 2002   Good, but not as good as the red under the same label. It's held back by very obvious sweetness, which, of course, will be enjoyed by many $10–$12 wine buyers. The sugar is accentuated by high alcohol. It's otherwise clean and well-made, with lemon-soap semillon aromas plus cashew-nut and lemon-pith scents. It could go with a green salad with chicken and mango.

Plantagenet Omrah Sauvignon Blanc

The Omrah label is a second-string label at Plantagenet, but some of the wines are surprisingly good. This is Exhibit A. Maker: Gavin Berry.
CURRENT RELEASE 2002   A very fine sauvignon blanc indeed. It smells intensely of gooseberry and tropical fruits, clean and pungent, with a crisp and crunchy palate structure, finishing with real varietal tang. There is a trace of sweetness but it doesn't interfere with the lovely balance and appealing style of the wine. It goes beautifully with grilled asparagus sprinkled with parmesan.

Quality	▼▼▼▼▼
Value	★★★★⁺
Grapes	sauvignon blanc
Region	Great Southern, WA
Cellar	▐ 1
Alc./Vol.	13.0%
RRP	$16.00 ⑤ ≋

Plunkett Blackwood Ridge Unwooded Chardonnay

Plunkett is a great name for a wine: we can just hear the dipper being dunked into the tank of fresh wine as the cellar-hand hauls up a sample for the laboratory. As in: 'Hey, Joe, go and plunkett the unwooded chardonnay, will ya?'
CURRENT RELEASE 2002   This is par-for-the-course unwooded chardonnay. It is a pretty basic sort of wine. It has a nice bright, light yellow hue and smells of slightly green, underripe fruit, which has a herbaceous character. The taste is light and lean, a trifle angular, with a little hardness on the finish. It won't offend. It would suit asparagus sandwiches.

Quality	▼▼▼▼
Value	★★★
Grapes	chardonnay
Region	Goulburn Valley, Vic.
Cellar	▐ 2
Alc./Vol.	13.5%
RRP	$16.00 (cellar door)

Plunkett Strathbogie Ranges Riesling

Sam Plunkett is the winemaker here. His family were Avenel sheep and cattle graziers when they took the decision to plant vines commercially in 1980. Their first experimental plantings were in the late '60s. They now have over 100 hectares of vines.
CURRENT RELEASE 2002   A spicy style of riesling, with a smidge of sweetness to help its early commercial acceptability. There are grapey and fruit-compote aromas too and the wine is a fuller, fruitier type of riesling. It's already drinking well, and suits crab cakes.

Quality	▼▼▼▼▼
Value	★★★★⁺
Grapes	riesling
Region	Strathbogie Ranges, Vic.
Cellar	▐ 6+
Alc./Vol.	12.5%
RRP	$16.00 (cellar door)

Pothana Belford Chardonnay

Quality	🍷🍷🍷🍷🍷
Value	★★★⌐
Grapes	chardonnay
Region	Hunter Valley, NSW
Cellar	🍾 3
Alc./Vol.	12.5%
RRP	$30.00

All David Hook's wines, from the inexpensive The Gorge range to the premium Pothana, bear the stamp of a highly competent, experienced winemaker. He's been at it for many years, working at Tyrrells, Lakes Folly, and numerous overseas postings as a 'flying winemaker'. He has 8 hectares on the Belford dome of limestone. *Previous outstanding vintages: '89, '91, '95, '00* CURRENT RELEASE 2001   Intensity with fineness is the catch-cry here. The colour is light yellow and it smells of butterscotch, peach and honey, the palate flavours similarly complex and layered. It's a lovely drink, finely nuanced and not oaky, overblown or alcoholic. It would suit steamed king prawns with beurre blanc.

Preece Chardonnay

Quality	🍷🍷🍷🍷
Value	★★★★
Grapes	chardonnay
Region	King & Goulburn Valleys, Vic.
Cellar	🍾 1
Alc./Vol.	14.0%
RRP	$16.00 Ⓢ

This is the kind of wine that's given Australia such a huge slice of the world export wine market in recent years: a soft, fruity chardonnay with attractive varietal character. Maker is veteran Don Lewis. CURRENT RELEASE 2002   Sunshine in a bottle! It's light and fresh, filled with clean peachy chardonnay fruit, oak very much in the background. There's no great depth or length, but it's a lovely easy-drinking, fruit-driven, soft white wine. Throw another prawn on the barbie!

Prentice Whitfield & Whitlands Pinot Gris

Quality	🍷🍷🍷🍷
Value	★★★
Grapes	pinot gris
Region	King Valley, Vic.
Cellar	🍾 2
Alc./Vol.	14.0%
RRP	$22.00 🥂

Founder Neil Prentice sold this brand to the Mornington Peninsula winery Tuck's Ridge. The winemaker there is Phillip Kittle. CURRENT RELEASE 2001   The colour is very light yellow and it smells of dry grass, straw and dried thyme. It's light and lean on the palate, clean and dry to finish. There is a trace of spice and it's clean and well-made. A pleasant and very drinkable dry white, to have with sautéed yabbies.

Preston Peak Verdelho

This winery is located at Ballandean, near Stanthorpe in the Granite Belt. Winemakers are Philippa Hambleton and Rod MacPherson.

CURRENT RELEASE 2002 The nose is all classic musk-stick verdelho fruit, estery and fresh. The wine has plenty of weight in the mouth, but finishes with some thickness which may be due to phenolics. It has generous spicy flavour throughout and some alcohol warmth and sweetness on the finish. It could go well with soy sauce lentils and tuna sashimi.

Quality 🍷🍷🍷
Value ★★★
Grapes verdelho
Region Granite Belt, Qld
Cellar 1
Alc./Vol. 13.7%
RRP $17.00 (cellar door)

Primo Estate La Biondina Colombard

The Grilli family are proud of their Italian heritage, and the name means something like 'The Blonde Bimbo', which we guess is the target market for the wine.

CURRENT RELEASE 2002 Some people get excited about this wine, but we can't quite figure out the reason for the fuss. The 2002 is a pretty basic white, smelling vegetal, sweaty and lemon-grassy with a hint of sauvignon blanc–like feline whiff, and the palate is simple and grapey with an obvious twist of sweetness. Try it with a tossed salad.

Quality 🍷🍷🍷
Value ★★★
Grapes colombard
Region Adelaide Hills, SA
Cellar 1
Alc./Vol. 12.0%
RRP $14.90

Provenance Pinot Gris

Not to be confused with Tasmanian winery Providence, this brand is produced by Scott Ireland, who works in the Geelong Region.

CURRENT RELEASE 2002 This has a very spicy, almost gewürztraminer-like nose – not so different to an Alsace version. It's intensely varietal, rich and ripe-smelling. In the mouth it's medium-weight, smooth yet intense, with a degree of richness and possibly a subtle influence of barrel ferment character. There's impressive concentration, power and length, and lots of alcohol without sacrificing balance. Try prawns in a buttery sauce.

Quality 🍷🍷🍷🍷🍷
Value ★★★★½
Grapes pinot gris
Region Geelong, Vic.
Cellar 2
Alc./Vol. 13.8%
RRP $25.00

Punt Road Chardonnay

Quality	♟♟♟︎
Value	★★★
Grapes	chardonnay
Region	Yarra Valley, Vic.
Cellar	🍷 2
Alc./Vol.	13.0%
RRP	$20.00 ⑤

The Punt Road reds offer great value for money, while the whites are good and fair value, but less exciting.
CURRENT RELEASE 2002   The aromas are of nuts, stone fruits, subtle oak and barrel-ferment characters. The taste is light-bodied and fairly lean, with moderate intensity and a clean, dry, well-balanced finish of modest length. It's a workmanlike chardonnay which would suit an asparagus risotto.

Punt Road Late Harvest Semillon

Quality	♟♟♟︎
Value	★★★⁺
Grapes	semillon
Region	Riverina, NSW
Cellar	🍷 2
Alc./Vol.	13.0%
RRP	$26.00 (500 ml)

Brands, brands, brands and more brands . . . Yarra Valley contract winemakers The Yarrahill have two labels – this one and Sticks. Winemakers are Kate Goodman and Rob Dolan. The grapes came from Yenda.
CURRENT RELEASE 2001   This is a pretty decent sweetie of the moderately luscious kind. No botrytis in the name, and it doesn't taste heavily botrytised either. Instead there are some greener capsicum and herbal notes among the honey and candied-fruit flavours. It's starting to show a lot of toasty, vanilla and crème brûlée development. The palate has moderate intensity and length. Try it with pavlova.

Punt Road Pinot Gris

Quality	♟♟♟︎
Value	★★★⁺
Grapes	pinot gris
Region	Yarra Valley, Vic.
Cellar	🍷 2
Alc./Vol.	13.5%
RRP	$18.00

Winemaker Kate Goodman has deliberately tried to do a bit more with this often-underwhelming grape variety, by barrel-fermenting a small proportion of it. What the back label describes as a 'hint of spicy French oak' is discernible, but nicely subtle.
CURRENT RELEASE 2002   Distinctly copper-coloured (what the northern Italians call 'ramato'), and that's not unusual for this grape. The aromas are sweetly floral and lightly spicy, with touches of cedar and twig. There is pleasing richness and weight on the palate, while the finish is long, dry and firm. It has real backbone, and should go well with food. We'd punt on stuffed zucchini flowers.

Punt Road Sauvignon Blanc

There were vines along Punt Road in the city of
Melbourne over a century ago. Hard to believe these
days, when you cruise along, stuck in the multi-lane
traffic.

CURRENT RELEASE 2002   The nose is all sweet
gooseberries, a touch of guava, and some squashy
asparagus-like aromas. The palate is lean and angular
with a little capsicum thrown in. There's a thread of
greenness in the wine. The finish is dry and a trifle
abrupt. It goes well with salads.

Quality	♥♥♥♥
Value	★★★⌐
Grapes	sauvignon blanc
Region	Yarra Valley, Vic.
Cellar	▮ 1
Alc./Vol.	11.5%
RRP	$19.00 ⓢ

Queen Adelaide Chardonnay

This sells in whopping quantities all over Australia.
It's down at the cheaper end of the market, but
don't treat it with disdain, it's actually pretty good.
CURRENT RELEASE 2002   Juicy, fruity white wine this,
just a simple drop, but it really tastes like chardonnay.
The nose has melon-like varietal aromas with no
perceptible oak, and the palate is smooth and
succulent with reasonable persistence. The finish is
reasonably dry and clean. Easy-drinking everyday
white wine. Sip it with Balinese fried chicken.

Quality	♥♥♥♥
Value	★★★★⌐
Grapes	chardonnay
Region	not stated
Cellar	▮ 1
Alc./Vol.	13.0%
RRP	$8.25 ⓢ

R.L. Buller & Son Beverford Chardonnay

Beverford is Buller's vineyard and winery at Lake Boga,
near Swan Hill on the Murray River. The winemaker
there is Richard Buller junior, brother of Andrew, who
runs the Rutherglen winery.
CURRENT RELEASE 2002   Basic river-grown
chardonnay is seldom that exciting, but you have to
consider the price. It ain't gonna break the bank. This
is picnic chardonnay, nothing more: the colour is pale-
ish and it smells minerally and slightly earthy, while
the palate is lean, simple and basic. It would go with
pan-fried yabbies.

Quality	♥♥♥
Value	★★★
Grapes	chardonnay
Region	Murray Valley, Vic.
Cellar	▮ 1
Alc./Vol.	13.5%
RRP	$13.00 ⓢ

R.L. Buller & Son Magee Semillon Chardonnay

Quality	♥ ♥ ♥
Value	★ ★ ★ ★
Grapes	semillon; chardonnay
Region	Murray Valley, Vic.
Cellar	▮ 1
Alc./Vol.	13.5%
RRP	$11.00 Ⓢ

Dry whites at this price are often innocuous and a bit bland, but the least we can expect is that they be fresh, subtle, balanced and provide good current drinking. This certainly does. Maker: Richard Buller.

CURRENT RELEASE 2002   This light-coloured, fresh white has a restrained aroma of cream and stone fruits, and doesn't have a lot of personality. It is, however, soft, clean, nicely balanced and smooth on the palate, without obvious residual sugar or coarseness. It's a friendly, gentle drink and we could easily enjoy quaffing it with a salad entrée.

R.L. Buller & Son Victoria Chardonnay

Quality	♥ ♥ ♥
Value	★ ★ ★
Grapes	chardonnay
Region	Murray Valley, Vic.
Cellar	▮ 1
Alc./Vol.	13.5%
RRP	$9.00 Ⓢ

The Victoria range is Buller's 'entry level' range: cheap and cheerful stuff for popping in the picnic Esky. It's made to a price, at the Beverford winery.

CURRENT RELEASE 2002   The colour is pale and there's a hint of sulfur hanging around, as it's a very young white. The result is that it lacks fruit aroma at present. The taste is very light and somewhat dilute, with mineral and earthy characters, while the palate seems low in acid and has a trace of sweetness for easy quaffing. Not a challenging drink, but at this price, few will mind. Fish and chips here.

Ralph Fowler Botrytis Semillon

Quality	♥ ♥ ♥ ♥
Value	★ ★ ★
Grapes	semillon 88%; sauvignon blanc 12%
Region	Limestone Coast, SA
Cellar	▮ 2
Alc./Vol.	12.5%
RRP	$25.70 (375 ml)

Ralph Fowler, who'd made his name at Tyrrells, Cassegrain and Leconfield/Richard Hamilton, left Coonawarra to set up his own venture in the emerging Mount Benson region several years ago.

CURRENT RELEASE 1999   The wine was all barrel-fermented in French oak, and it shows in the nutty, toasty edges to the complex honey, marmalade botrytis characters. The colour is golden and the wine also has lots of lemon/citrus on the palate. It's a tautly structured, finer style of sticky, not too oily or sugary, and has good length and style with a clean finish. It goes well with fruit salad.

Redbank Sunday Morning Pinot Gris

The first bottle we opened was badly cork-tainted. No wonder so many wineries are moving to screw-caps for this kind of light dry white. Such wines show taint more readily than some others, such as wooded whites and reds.

CURRENT RELEASE 2002   This is regularly one of the better pinot gris in Australia, a clean, soft, fruity, well-made wine with a floral kind of bouquet which, while attractive, isn't especially varietal. The palate has real delicacy and fine balance, finishing with citrusy acids and good persistence. It would suit pan-fried flathead.

Quality	♟♟♟♟
Value	★★★★
Grapes	pinot gris
Region	King Valley, Vic.
Cellar	▮ 2
Alc./Vol.	14.0%
RRP	$20.00

Renard Chardonnay

This new vineyard is not far from the Kooyong winery, where the wines are made. Both are in the lower-lying, warmer, Moorooduc Plains sub-region of the Mornington Peninsula.

CURRENT RELEASE 2001   This is a very forward, developed chardonnay: deep yellow to golden in colour and with a quite overblown bouquet. It has a smoky, almost medicinal character with hints of plasticine and caramel. The fruit underneath seems to have some herbaceous elements, which wouldn't tally with the highly successful 2001 vintage – but it is a very young vineyard. Try it with a creamy pasta dish.

Quality	♟♟♟♟
Value	★★♪
Grapes	chardonnay
Region	Mornington Peninsula, Vic.
Cellar	▮ 1
Alc./Vol.	13.0%
RRP	$29.80

Reynolds Moon Shadow Chardonnay

This was the only gold-medal wine and the clear champion at a tasting HH conducted in Orange a year ago. Only one reservation: we've seen several corked bottles of it.

CURRENT RELEASE 2000   When it's good it's very, very good. The colour is full buttercup yellow and it's very complex, with lots of barrel fermentation, butterscotch malolactic and mealy stirred-lees characters combining with fine peach/apricot and honeyed fruit. It's rich and satisfying, with bottle-aged characters contributing extra interest to what was already a complex wine. It would go well with a creamy French brie.

Quality	♟♟♟♟♟
Value	★★★★♪
Grapes	chardonnay
Region	Orange, NSW
Cellar	▮ 2
Alc./Vol.	13.0%
RRP	$25.00 Ⓢ

Richmond Grove Watervale Riesling

Quality	🍷🍷🍷🍷🍷
Value	★★★★★
Grapes	riesling
Region	Clare Valley, SA
Cellar	🍾 12+
Alc./Vol.	12.5%
RRP	$17.20 ⑤ 🍷

Time and time again, this wine is one of the best values on the market, and of course it's subject to some discounting, being a brand of the giant Orlando Wyndham Group. Makers: Bernie Hickin and John Vickery.

CURRENT RELEASE 2002   Fabulous lemon-zesty freshness here; a refined and yet pungent riesling with amazing vibrancy. Grass/hay, lemon, straw aromas; great intensity as well as finesse on palate. It's a superb drink now and will age gracefully for at least a decade. Serve it with grilled King George whiting.

Riddoch Chardonnay

Quality	🍷🍷🍷
Value	★★★
Grapes	chardonnay
Region	Coonawarra, SA
Cellar	🍾 1
Alc./Vol.	13.0%
RRP	$17.00 ⑤

Riddoch is the Katnook Estate second label, and the wines tend to be simpler and lighter than Katnook's. Maker: Wayne Stehbens.

CURRENT RELEASE 2001   It's a clean, well-made but straightforward chardonnay that lacks a bit in the interest department. The colour is light yellow, the aromas remind of peach skin with a spicy dimension, and the taste is light and a trifle short. The texture is oily and while it won't thrill, it doesn't offend either. It goes with chicken stirfry.

Rockbare Chardonnay

Quality	🍷🍷🍷
Value	★★★
Grapes	chardonnay
Region	McLaren Vale, SA
Cellar	🍾 2
Alc./Vol.	13.0%
RRP	$15.00

Rockbare is the new budget brand produced by former Southcorp winemaker Tim Burvill. He was one of several winemakers who found themselves out of a job when the axe was wielded following the Southcorp-Rosemount merger.

CURRENT RELEASE 2002   This seems to have been made to a price and for a certain market. It is really quite sweet, and it's not easy to taste the fruit underneath. The colour is pale and the aromas more mineral and slate than overt sunny peachiness. A basic, very commercial chardonnay that could stand a big chill. Try it with chicken and apricots.

Rosabrook Chardonnay

The Rosabrook reds have impressed us over the recent years, but this white won't turn too many heads. Rosabrook was almost sold to Palandri back in 2001, but the sale fell through and it's still privately owned.
CURRENT RELEASE 2002 Hardly a benchmark Margaret River chardonnay, but it won't embarrass either. The colour is pale lemon and it smells slightly herbaceous, simple and lightly oaked. The palate lacks a little intensity and length. It falls away on the finish and leaves you with a glimpse of toasty oak. Try it with Cantonese fish balls.

Quality 🍷🍷🍷
Value ★★½
Grapes chardonnay
Region Margaret River, WA
Cellar 3
Alc./Vol. 14.0%
RRP $21.50

Rosabrook Semillon Sauvignon Blanc

Blends of these two grapes are often thought to be a marriage made in heaven: the semillon provides backbone and palate intensity; the sauvignon blanc provides fragrance and fruitiness.
CURRENT RELEASE 2002 This is one of the lighter-bodied examples of the style, with aromas of cured meadow hay and a sweaty undertone, not unusual with sauvignon blanc. There are smoky notes, too, and the palate is just a trifle under-powered. It goes well with sushi.

Quality 🍷🍷🍷½
Value ★★★½
Grapes semillon; sauvignon blanc
Region Margaret River, WA
Cellar 1
Alc./Vol. 13.5%
RRP $18.20

Rosemount Estate Chardonnay

Will the Oatley family, Rosemount's founders, retain any ownership or control over Southcorp? At the time of writing, the company's future looks shaky indeed.
CURRENT RELEASE 2002 This is a decent if unexciting commercial chardonnay that doesn't disappoint, even if it doesn't raise the eyebrows like it once did. It is fruit-driven – peach and melon aromas with little oak influence – and has a slightly sweet entry followed by a light to medium-weight palate and a good balance between fruit, alcohol and sweetness. A plain but easygoing quaffer. It goes with prosciutto and melon.

Quality 🍷🍷🍷½
Value ★★★
Grapes chardonnay
Region not stated
Cellar 2
Alc./Vol. 13.0%
RRP $15.70 (S)

Rosemount Estate Giants Creek Chardonnay

Quality	🍷🍷🍷🍷🍷
Value	★★★★★
Grapes	chardonnay
Region	Hunter Valley, NSW
Cellar	🍾 3+
Alc./Vol.	13.0%
RRP	$20.00

This is a single-vineyard wine from an Upper Hunter vineyard which consistently produces chardonnay of quite different character to Roxburgh, Rosemount's other great chardonnay vineyard. Maker: Andrew Koerner.
CURRENT RELEASE 2001   This is simply the best Giants Creek we can recall. It is a stunner. Creamy nougat, butter, toasty aromas mingle with hints of fig, peach and nectarine, and the oak handling has been exemplary (only some of the barrels were new). It's tautly structured and lively in the mouth, clean and refined with layers of flavour. A classy chardonnay to serve with fish and beurre blanc.

Rosemount Estate Hill of Gold Chardonnay

Quality	🍷🍷🍷🍷🍷
Value	★★★★★
Grapes	chardonnay
Region	Mudgee, NSW
Cellar	🍾 3
Alc./Vol.	14.0%
RRP	$20.00 Ⓢ

This wine's name reflects the history of Mudgee, which was once a prosperous gold-mining district. Rosemount bought an established vineyard called Hill of Gold, which has been planted for over 30 years, and added it to their expanding Mudgee holdings.
CURRENT RELEASE 2002   This is a delicious young, fruit-driven chardonnay, reflecting the excellent 2002 Mudgee vintage. It has bright citrusy fruit and is light-bodied but intense and beautifully balanced. The freshness of primary fruit really captivated us. There's a subtle touch of oak on the mid-palate that's in no way assertive. Lovely drinking right now, with salmon and asparagus quiche.

Rosemount Estate Sauvignon Blanc

Quality	🍷🍷🍷🍷
Value	★★★★
Grapes	sauvignon blanc
Region	not stated
Cellar	🍾 1
Alc./Vol.	13.0%
RRP	$15.70 Ⓢ

Rosemount was a model wine business, its stunning growth capably managed while family-owned. Now, as part of Southcorp, things have gone off the rails.
CURRENT RELEASE 2002   The aromas are clean and inviting, with a lemony, grassy tang. In the mouth, it's lean and angular, lacking a little mid-palate. It's ripe-tasting, clean and dry to finish with modest persistence. A very decent and well-priced wine. It needs to go with fresh oysters.

Rosemount Estate Semillon Chardonnay

We do wonder how companies like Rosemount can get away with appending the word 'estate' onto their name. It suggests all the grapes were grown on their own vineyards, which patently isn't the reality.

CURRENT RELEASE 2002 The split-label range has always been good value for money, and this is no exception. It has a shy but pleasant nose of straw/bracken semillon-like fruit and a soft but fairly broad palate. There are straw/hay flavours and it's a little floppy in structure. A straightforward quaffing dry white. Try it with fish cakes.

Quality	🍷🍷🍷
Value	★★★½
Grapes	semillon; chardonnay
Region	not stated
Cellar	🍾 1
Alc./Vol.	13.0%
RRP	$11.70 ($)

Rosemount Estate Semillon Sauvignon Blanc

The Rosemount split-label indicates blends of two grapes, and a price level below the diamond-label series. They are reliable quality wines, if rarely exciting.

CURRENT RELEASE 2002 This is a straightforward, easy-drinking dry white that won't offend, and the price is right. It has a straw-like, slightly mineral aroma, and a soft, fruity palate that finishes clean and dry with a little phenolic grip. It's for immediate drinking and goes well with steamed dim sum.

Quality	🍷🍷🍷
Value	★★★½
Grapes	semillon; sauvignon blanc
Region	not stated
Cellar	🍾 1
Alc./Vol.	13.0%
RRP	$11.70 ($)

Rosemount Estate Show Reserve Semillon

It's an indication of just how neglected the marketing of Lindemans wines has been over the years that Southcorp is now producing just two semillons and they're both Rosemount. Once upon a time Lindemans was second to none in Hunter semillon, with up to three bottlings a year, plus mature 'classic' releases.

CURRENT RELEASE 2002 It's a lovely, varietally correct semillon with restrained lemon aromas and a hint of riesling-like aromatics, not unusual in the 2002s. The palate is dry and refined, with light alcohol delicacy and a lovely clean, soft acid finish. Finesse aplenty! Try it with a shellfish platter.

Quality	🍷🍷🍷🍷½
Value	★★★★
Grapes	semillon
Region	Hunter Valley, NSW
Cellar	🍾 6
Alc./Vol.	12.5%
RRP	$23.40 ($)

Rosily Vineyard Sauvignon Blanc

Quality	🍷🍷🍷🍷🍷
Value	★★★★★
Grapes	sauvignon blanc
Region	Margaret River, WA
Cellar	🍾 2+
Alc./Vol.	13.0%
RRP	$16.00

The Rosily team hit the ground running with their first crop of whites, released about three years ago. Dan Pannell of Picardy consulted in their early days. CURRENT RELEASE 2002   This is a delicious sauvignon blanc. It has a lifted aroma of gooseberry and minerals with a sweaty overtone that's quite common in Western Australian whites, and there's a subtle hint of oak. It tastes frisky and clean and very refreshing. Bracing acidity, concentrated flavour and a very long aftertaste mark this as a high-quality wine. It would suit a tossed salad of grilled scallops, rocket, mango and vinaigrette.

Rosily Vineyard Semillon

Quality	🍷🍷🍷🍷
Value	★★★⯨
Grapes	semillon
Region	Margaret River, WA
Cellar	🍾 2
Alc./Vol.	13.9%
RRP	$20.00

This vineyard is named after a member of the early French expeditions to the west coast of Australia. Comte François de Rosily was on two voyages to Western Australia and served as France's chief hydrographer. CURRENT RELEASE 2001   Barrel fermentation and maturation make oak a feature of the wine, as in previous releases. The blurb describes it as 'subtle'. It contributes to the toasty-bread, roasted-nut aromas, but we found this vintage somewhat harsh and hot on the finish. It is big on flavour but a tad heavy-handed. The alcohol is high at 13.9 per cent. It might go with barbecued marinated chicken.

Rosily Vineyard Semillon Sauvignon Blanc

Quality	🍷🍷🍷🍷
Value	★★★★
Grapes	semillon 60%; sauvignon blanc 40%
Region	Margaret River, WA
Cellar	🍾 3
Alc./Vol.	13.5%
RRP	$18.00

Two families, Mike and Barb Scott and Ken and Dot Allan, planted this vineyard at Willyabrup in 1994. More recently, they've built their own winery and employed Mike Lemmes as winemaker. CURRENT RELEASE 2002   This is a very seductive wine thanks in part to cleverly used French oak for a percentage of the blend. It smells of lemon and herbs and 'snapped-twig' regional character, plus a little smoky, toasty oak. This adds extra dimension and length to the palate. A wine of substance which could keep for a few years, and would go well with chargrilled king prawns.

Ross Hill Chardonnay

Ross Hill vineyard is on Griffin Road, Orange, just next door to the district's pioneer, Bloodwood Estate.
CURRENT RELEASE 2001   This is a good wine, although one could fault it for being forward in development and a little hot on the finish, even though the alcohol strength is apparently not high. It has a medium–full yellow hue and smells of butter, peach and toasted nuts, with some appealing complexity. It's less rewarding on the palate, fairly light in weight, and plain with an oily texture and some heat in the finish. It would go well with milk-fed veal.

Quality	♥♥♥♥
Value	★★★⅃
Grapes	chardonnay
Region	Orange, NSW
Cellar	▍ 2
Alc./Vol.	13.3%
RRP	$18.00 (cellar door)

Rothbury Estate Brokenback Semillon

Brokenback is a famous old vineyard on the Broke Road in the outer limits of the Pokolbin sub-region. These days it's divided among three owners, the others being Kulkunbulla and Tyrrells.
CURRENT RELEASE 2002   The colour is bright lemon yellow and there are fresh green-apple aromas together with nettle and dried-herb nuances. It's bright and jumpy in the mouth with fresh acid coupled with clean, dry, intense semillon flavour and excellent length. A classic Hunter style, and well worth cellaring. You could serve it now with snapper quenelles.

Quality	♥♥♥♥♥
Value	★★★★⅃
Grapes	semillon
Region	Hunter Valley, NSW
Cellar	▍ 10
Alc./Vol.	10.5%
RRP	$24.00 ⑤

Rothbury Estate Hunter Verdelho

Australia is the only place on earth that regularly makes a big commercial success of dry white wines made from this Madeira grape. It's a niche item that's growing rapidly.
CURRENT RELEASE 2002   This has a big flowery aroma that helps it stand out in a line-up of verdelhos. Touches of passionfruit, cashew nut and citrus give it a boost. There is some spice, too, and the wine has quite a dollop of sweetness, making it very juicy in the mouth. The aftertaste is a trifle mawkish, but it's a good drink and well-priced. Serve with prawn and mango salad.

Quality	♥♥♥
Value	★★★⅃
Grapes	verdelho
Region	Hunter Valley, NSW
Cellar	▍ 1
Alc./Vol.	11.5%
RRP	$13.85 ⑤

Rothbury Estate Neil McGuigan Series Chardonnay

Quality	▼▼▼⁅
Value	★★★⁆
Grapes	chardonnay
Region	Mudgee, NSW
Cellar	➥ 1–4
Alc./Vol.	13.5%
RRP	$18.00 Ⓢ

This wine reflects Neil McGuigan's personal taste for a finer, leaner style of chardonnay with a long, soft finish. CURRENT RELEASE 2002   The colour is pale and it smells young and undeveloped, with nougat and nutty aromas, hints of minerals and citrus, and it's yet to unfold its full potential. The palate is determinedly lean and narrow in profile: indeed, a chablis style from Mudgee! You could enjoy it now with scallops and salad, or cellar and let it develop more richness and complexity.

Rothbury Estate Neil McGuigan Series Semillon

Quality	▼▼▼▼⁅
Value	★★★★⁆
Grapes	semillon
Region	Hunter Valley, NSW
Cellar	▮ 5
Alc./Vol.	10.5%
RRP	$18.00 Ⓢ

If anyone should know all about how to make a good Hunter semillon, it's Neil McGuigan. He's been doing it for 24 years. CURRENT RELEASE 2002   This is a very fine semillon, as you might expect. The colour is pale and it's fresh, youthful and restrained. The aromas are of straw, hand cream and lemon-soap – typical of the style. The taste is light-bodied, delicate and balanced. It finishes dry but soft. We think it's going to be a medium-term wine, and it drinks well young, with oysters.

Ryan Free Run Chardonnay

Quality	▼▼▼
Value	★★★
Grapes	chardonnay
Region	Hunter Valley, NSW
Cellar	▮ 1
Alc./Vol.	12.9%
RRP	$18.00 Ⓢ

Free-run is winemaker's jargon for the liquid that flows by gravity alone from the red fermenter when you pull the plug. The rest, which comes out under duress, is pressings. With white wine the distinction is very blurred and we're willing to wager this wine's got no more right to the name than any other. CURRENT RELEASE 2001   It's a simple, fruit-driven wine which doesn't show any evidence of oak, but smells and tastes of green herbs, especially parsley. Light, simple, basic dry white wine. It would suit a Greek salad.

Rymill Sauvignon Blanc

Rymill is owned by Peter Rymill's Old Penola Pastoral
Company and has a very substantial 170 hectares of
vines. Rymill is a descendant of John Riddoch, the
'father' of Coonawarra.
CURRENT RELEASE 2002   This is a simple style
of sauvignon, with a palish colour and an aroma of
fresh-cut grass, capsicum and perhaps lantana. It's a
bit straightforward in the mouth, but perfectly good
wine and well-priced too. It goes with cold seafood
and capsicum salad.

Quality	🍷🍷🍷
Value	★★★
Grapes	sauvignon blanc
Region	Coonawarra, SA
Cellar	🍾 1
Alc./Vol.	13.0%
RRP	$16.00 Ⓢ

Saddler's Creek Classic Hunter Semillon

The smart packaging of Saddler's Creek wines is no
surprise when you know the winery was started by a
group of people from Classic Packaging, a company
that supplies oak barrels and packaging materials to
the wine industry.
CURRENT RELEASE 2002   Typical Hunter semillon
aromas of Sunlight soap and lanolin come through
in the bouquet, and there's still a vestige of bottling
sulfur which will soon disappear. There's a lively
tanginess to the palate and a hint of sweetness,
resulting in a nice sherbetty mouth-feel. It's squeaky-
clean and well-balanced, easy to enjoy young and
not as austere as some. It would go well with sushi.

Quality	🍷🍷🍷🍷
Value	★★★★
Grapes	semillon
Region	Hunter Valley, NSW
Cellar	🍾 5
Alc./Vol.	12.0%
RRP	$19.00 ⬤

Saddler's Creek Reserve Chardonnay

Big, oaky chardonnays are alive and well in the Hunter.
They're what the area does naturally (well, at least the
big part) and, although fashion has changed, there still
seem to be plenty of takers.
CURRENT RELEASE 2000   Released at three years old,
this is full-frontal chardonnay! It's a bright, full yellow in
colour, and smells of new French barrels, together with a
particular rubbery, medicinal character that's typical of
a certain kind of Hunter chardonnay. The taste is big,
thick, heavy and oaky; there's a phenolic grip to close
and the oak gives a certain astringency. A big, fat, heavy-
handed chardonnay, which would suit chicken satay.

Quality	🍷🍷🍷
Value	★★★
Grapes	chardonnay
Region	Hunter Valley, NSW
Cellar	🍾 1
Alc./Vol.	14.0%
RRP	$35.00 (cellar door)

Saddler's Creek Verdelho

Quality	♀ ♀ ♀
Value	★ ★ ⁺
Grapes	verdelho
Region	Hunter Valley, NSW
Cellar	▮ 1
Alc./Vol.	13.0%
RRP	$19.00

Saddler's Creek is run by the affable John Johnston for a syndicate of owners. They buy in grapes from other regions, such as shiraz from McLaren Vale, as well as making Hunter wines – a common mix of activities in the region today.

CURRENT RELEASE 2002 Verdelho is often a rather plain, even bland, varietal, and the purists wonder what makes it so popular. This has a fairly neutral personality, while the palate has some weight from alcohol and a little residual sweetness. There is a slight phenolic grip to close. It's a basic dry white and would go with cold chicken and salad.

Saltram Sauvignon Blanc

Quality	♀ ♀ ♀
Value	★ ★ ★ ⁺
Grapes	sauvignon blanc
Region	not stated
Cellar	▮ 1
Alc./Vol.	12.0%
RRP	$10.00 Ⓢ

Saltram's simple varietal wines like this one can be very good value, obviously benefiting from the economies of scale available to owners Beringer Blass.

CURRENT RELEASE 2002 This has a grapey, slightly herbal nose that's clean enough, but a bit broad and clumsy. The palate is simple in flavour and structure, lightly herbaceous and tropical-fruity, with a slightly short finish. Not bad at the price, and will suit spicy Thai takeaway.

Saltram Semillon

Quality	♀ ♀ ♀ ♀
Value	★ ★ ★ ★
Grapes	semillon
Region	not stated
Cellar	▮ 2
Alc./Vol.	12.0%
RRP	$10.00 Ⓢ

Saltram Semillon occupies one of the lower rungs on the white-wine ladder, but it remains a pleasant drink, proof that you don't need to be a millionaire to enjoy a daily glass.

CURRENT RELEASE 2002 A straw-coloured young wine with an attractive and very typical semillon aroma. It's a bit lemony, a bit soapy, and pleasant in a mouth-watering, clean way. Snappy fresh flavour, smooth texture and a pleasant dry lemony-fragrant finish complete the picture. Drink it with fish and chips.

Sandalford Margaret River Chardonnay

Margaret River chardonnay is one of Australia's great whites. Sometimes it can be very powerful but Sandalford's version is usually more restrained. Maker: Paul Boulden.

CURRENT RELEASE 2000   A pale yellow–green colour looks the goods, and a complex nose has notable but well-integrated nutty barrel influence to cashew and stone-fruit aromas. The palate is very long and succulent in flavour. It has a smooth texture and restrained flavour yet it's quite rich and mouth-filling. Try it with grilled marron.

Quality	▾▾▾▾▾
Value	★★★↗
Grapes	chardonnay
Region	Margaret River, WA
Cellar	🍶 2
Alc./Vol.	13.5%
RRP	$29.00

Sandalford Margaret River Semillon

Semillon performs well at Margaret River, although early examples were perhaps a little too much like sauvignon blanc. Nowadays mature vines, better viticulture and thoughtful winemaking add up to some very good wines.

CURRENT RELEASE 2002   Following a trend, Sandalford's 2002 has some barrel influence to add complexity. The wood leads the way, dominating attractive, vinous, lemony fruit character with nutty, spicy, oaky touches. The palate is clean and dry to taste, and the oak better integrated than on the nose. Tangy acid gives it zesty appeal, and should help it improve with bottle-age. Try it with fried chicken.

Quality	▾▾▾▾
Value	★★★↗
Grapes	semillon
Region	Margaret River, WA
Cellar	🍶 3
Alc./Vol.	12.0%
RRP	$21.00 🐚

Sandalford Margaret River Verdelho

Another winery having a bit of an each-way bet; 50 per cent of this wine was bottled under cork, the rest with a screw-cap. Which was better? Read on.

CURRENT RELEASE 2002   This is a graphic illustration of the advantages of screw-caps on young white wines. Tasted together, blind, the cork-sealed wine is duller on the nose and flatter in the mouth. The screw-top version has a feel of purity with gentle tropical fruit-salad characters, and touches of citrus and herbs. It's medium-bodied and dry finishing with some ageing potential.

Quality	▾▾▾▾
Value	★★★↗
Grapes	verdelho
Region	Margaret River, WA
Cellar	🍶 4
Alc./Vol.	13.5%
RRP	$19.50 🐚

Schild Estate Riesling

Quality	🍷🍷🍷🍷
Value	★★★✦
Grapes	riesling
Region	Barossa Valley, SA
Cellar	🍾 5+
Alc./Vol.	12.5%
RRP	$17.00 🥂

Ed Schild took over this family property at the age of 15, in 1956. Today it is the largest single-owner private property in the Barossa. Over the years, nearly all the grapes have been sold to big makers, and the Schild Estate label is a relatively new name.

CURRENT RELEASE 2002   A near-ethereal floral scent meets the nose, and green-apple and citrus touches are very subdued. The palate is tight and dry, a little more open than the nose suggests, with lime and apple flavours of good length and a crisp sign-off. Good with shellfish.

Schild Estate Unwooded Semillon

Quality	🍷🍷🍷🍷
Value	★★★
Grapes	semillon
Region	Barossa Valley, SA
Cellar	🍾 2
Alc./Vol.	12.5%
RRP	$18.00

Semillon is widely planted in the Barossa Valley where it was once oddly known as madeira. The style of Barossa semillon varies from overwhelming oaky types to fresh, simple wines like this one.

CURRENT RELEASE 2002   This is a simple, unfussy dry white, with a light lemony nose that leads pleasantly to a straightforward palate that's soft, fruity and clean-finishing. It doesn't have great personality, but there's nothing wrong with it, and you could do far worse for more dollars. Nice with fried whitebait.

Schinus Sauvignon Blanc

Quality	🍷🍷🍷🍷
Value	★★★
Grapes	sauvignon blanc
Region	not stated
Cellar	🍾 1
Alc./Vol.	13.0%
RRP	$15.00

Garry Crittenden of Dromana Estate on the Mornington Peninsula uses the Schinus wines as an entrée into the budget end of the market. Made largely from non-regional fruit, they are very good value.

CURRENT RELEASE 2002   This has likeable sauvignon personality and it won't break the bank. On the nose the herbaceous traits of this grape variety are kept well in check with subdued crushed-leaf aromas hiding behind fruity tropical 'two fruits' smells. The palate has soft fruitiness that balances well with crisp acidity and a fresh, dry finish. Try it with a goat's cheese and tomato salad.

Scotchmans Hill Sauvignon Blanc

In 20 years of astute work the Browne family has built this operation on Victoria's picturesque Bellarine Peninsula into a household name, particularly in the smart restaurants of Melbourne and Sydney.
CURRENT RELEASE 2002   Strong varietal aromas in the green-bean and gooseberry range power the nose of this young sauvignon. This uncomprising varietal character continues on the palate, which is snappy and fresh with good acidity. It has real presence and depth, and it finishes crisp with good length of flavour. Serve it with grilled asparagus and prosciutto.

Quality	♟♟♟♟
Value	★★★
Grapes	sauvignon blanc
Region	Geelong, Vic.
Cellar	▮ 1
Alc./Vol.	13.0%
RRP	$22.50

Seppelt Jaluka Chardonnay

The Rosemount-led Southcorp schemozzle of recent times meant that after the merger a lot of wines in their portfolio weren't brought to the attention of the *Guide*'s hardworking authors. These relaunched Seppelt wines are an example, but we finally got hold of some.
CURRENT RELEASE 2002   This is a very refined chardonnay of lovely restrained complexity. It combines fruit-sweet aromas and secondary characters in fine harmony. There are touches of nectarine, fig, butterscotch and subtle toasty oak, and it has real succulence. The palate is silky in texture and long on the finish. Try it with salmon.

Quality	♟♟♟♟♟
Value	★★★★┤
Grapes	chardonnay
Region	various, Vic.
Cellar	⬤ 1–3
Alc./Vol.	13.5%
RRP	$29.00

Shadowfax Pinot Gris

Pinot gris has gone in all over the cooler vineyard regions of Australia, with mixed results; the good ones lean more towards the Alsace style than the Italian.
CURRENT RELEASE 2002   This smells like a combination of those dried fruits, honeys and nuts that populate the shelves of a health-food shop. All this makes it an exotic thing indeed, and the palate is appropriately rich in flavour and mellow mid-palate with full body and a soft finish. Just the thing if you're looking for a change. Try it with grilled chicken and Italian mustard fruits.

Quality	♟♟♟♟
Value	★★★
Grapes	pinot gris
Region	Adelaide Hills, SA; Geelong, Vic.
Cellar	▮ 2
Alc./Vol.	13.5%
RRP	$24.00

Shadowfax Sauvignon Blanc

Quality	♟ ♟ ♟ ♟
Value	★ ★ ★ ⸑
Grapes	sauvignon blanc
Region	Adelaide Hills, SA
Cellar	▮ 1
Alc./Vol.	12.5%
RRP	$19.00

This Werribee vineyard complex doesn't just confine itself to Victorian region wines. You might find McLaren Vale Shiraz or in this case Adelaide Hills Sauvignon Blanc graced by the smart Shadowfax label. Quality is good.
CURRENT RELEASE 2002   This is in good form, a wine with an intense grape, tropical and gooseberry aroma. In the mouth it has zippy clean flavours that follow the elements on the nose. Tart acidity underpins it with freshness and it finishes clean and fresh. A little more depth mid-palate would give it a higher score. Serve it with yabbies and beurre blanc.

Shane Warne Collection Chardonnay

Quality	♟ ♟ ♟ ♟
Value	★ ★ ★ ★ ★
Grapes	chardonnay
Region	Murray Valley, Vic.
Cellar	▮ 1
Alc./Vol.	13.5%
RRP	$15.00

Warnie is never far from the news, and some of the media pressure faced by high-profile sportsmen like him must make life very difficult. A calming glass of wine is what's needed, and now Shane Warne has his own drop to do the trick.
CURRENT RELEASE 2002   This is great value. Nose and palate have stone-fruit character of clean intensity, along with some nutty, buttery-rich touches and a dab of vanillin oak. There's good depth and persistence, and it finishes crisp and fresh. Try it with prawns.

Shaw and Smith M3 Vineyard Chardonnay

Quality	♟ ♟ ♟ ♟ ⸑
Value	★ ★ ★ ⸑
Grapes	chardonnay
Region	Adelaide Hills, SA
Cellar	▮ 3
Alc./Vol.	13.5%
RRP	$34.00

The wine quality is consistently excellent in the Adelaide Hills, a region that boasts a who's who of Australian wine names: Henschke, Petaluma, Knappstein, Shaw and Smith . . .
CURRENT RELEASE 2001   There's some of what wine buffs call 'artefact' to this wine. That is, simple chardonnay fruit is influenced by winemaker and winery influence, providing refined character and complexity. It looks relatively pale, and the nose and palate have subtle nutty and creamy nuances. Delicately fragrant white peach is at the core. The effect of savoury subtlety and refinement gets more interesting the more you drink. Try it with grilled prawns.

Shaw and Smith Sauvignon Blanc

This is the benchmark for Adelaide Hills sauvignon
blanc. Now it's made in a new showplace winery that's
worth a weekend visit. Maker: Martin Shaw.
**CURRENT RELEASE 2002   In the best years, and
2002 is exactly that, this is a truly exciting
wine. It smells pure and lively with gooseberry,
lime and a lush hint of fruit salad on the nose.
These deliciously zesty qualities track down the
palate with real depth of juicy flavour that's
long, tangy and super-appetising. Shaw and
Smith launch this wine accompanied by all
sorts of yum cha goodies, which isn't a bad
idea at all.**

Quality	🍷🍷🍷🍷🍷
Value	★★★★★
Grapes	sauvignon blanc
Region	Adelaide Hills, SA
Cellar	🍶 1
Alc./Vol.	13.0%
RRP	$22.00

**PENGUIN BEST
SAUVIGNON BLANC**

Shottesbrooke Chardonnay

Shottesbrooke Chardonnay is stylistically a bit out of
the McLaren Vale mainstream, being less broad and
rich than most. Maker: Nick Holmes.
CURRENT RELEASE 2001   The nose is surprisingly
delicate in this young McLaren Vale chardonnay, quite
at odds with many from the district. There are fragrant
stone-fruit and citrus aromas with a light dressing of
oak. The palate is smooth, and not big but intensely
flavoured, with a feeling of real finesse. A clean crisp
finish provides a low-key ending. Good with tofu and
Chinese greens with oyster sauce.

Quality	🍷🍷🍷🍷
Value	★★★★
Grapes	chardonnay
Region	McLaren Vale, SA
Cellar	🍶 2
Alc./Vol.	13.0%
RRP	$15.50

Sirromet Queensland Chardonnay

There's a typically Queensland feel of entrepreneurial
get-up-and-go about the Sirromet operation. Aimed
as much at the tourist trade as the confirmed wine
drinker, but quality so far has been good.
CURRENT RELEASE 2001   Please excuse us if we see
some tropical fruit in this wine, but it does come from
Queensland after all. It's a sunny yellow colour, and
the nose has touches of pineapple and soft peachy
fruit. Nutty oak is in balance and it tastes smooth,
if a tad short. Try it with Queensland tiger prawns
and spanner crabs.

Quality	🍷🍷🍷🍷
Value	★★★
Grapes	chardonnay
Region	South Burnett 62% &
	Granite Belt 38%,
	Qld
Cellar	🍶 1
Alc./Vol.	13.5%
RRP	$16.00

Skillogalee Gewürztraminer

Quality	🍷🍷🍷🍷
Value	★★★★
Grapes	gewürztraminer
Region	Clare Valley, SA
Cellar	🍾 2
Alc./Vol.	14.0%
RRP	$18.50 🥂

There was a time when Aussie winemakers got all excited by gewürztraminer, but today it's a curiosity made by only a handful. Those few who persist, like Skillogalee, generally make a good fist of it.

CURRENT RELEASE 2002   Gewürztraminer has amazing aromatic power and good examples can be almost over the top. Skillogalee is a case in point. A deceptively pale wine with an exotic, complex nose reminiscent of rosewater, almond Turkish delight, and perhaps Asian spices like coriander. The palate is dry with deep richness of flavour and a lingering spicy aftertaste. It's characterful enough to stand up to a pongy washed-rind cheese.

Skillogalee Riesling

Quality	🍷🍷🍷🍷🍷
Value	★★★★★
Grapes	riesling
Region	Clare Valley, SA
Cellar	➥ 1–5
Alc./Vol.	13.0%
RRP	$19.50 🥂

After years in the wilderness, we sense that riesling's fortunes are turning. Clare Valley wines have never had a better vintage.

Previous outstanding vintages: '97, '99

CURRENT RELEASE 2002   A tingle of gas clings to the glass after pouring. The colour is pale, bright and green-tinged – all fine indicators of breeding. The nose is slightly closed-up, but has good intensity, with aromas of lime, flowers, spices and wet slate. In the mouth, a clean minerally flavour needs bottle-time to develop complexity. This vintage's added richness shows in its depth of flavour and viscous texture, while tangy acidity keeps things brisk and lively. Good with Thai stirfry.

Smithbrook Sauvignon Blanc

Quality	🍷🍷🍷🍷
Value	★★★★⯪
Grapes	sauvignon blanc 86%; semillon 14%
Region	Pemberton, WA
Cellar	🍾 2
Alc./Vol.	13.0%
RRP	$17.50

Smithbrook's sauvignon blanc uses a proportion of material fermented in old oak to add depth and texture, but not much in the way of flavour. It's an excellent style. Maker: Michael Symons.

CURRENT RELEASE 2002   Pale, almost water-like in appearance, this has a thrilling, pure varietal aroma of exquisite juicy charm. Tropical-fruit, lime and herbal touches add dimension while the very light barrel influence helps it avoid the over-the-top excesses of many sauvignons. The palate is smooth and dry. Try it with yellow tomato bruschetta.

Sorrenberg Chardonnay

Beechworth has quietly worked itself into the wine world's consciousness as a place renowned for quality. The best vineyards are Giaconda, Castagna and Sorrenberg.

CURRENT RELEASE 2001   A chardonnay that evolves and grows more fascinating the longer you leave it in the glass. Honeyed melon, citrus and subtle nutty, creamy lees complexity add bouquet, flavour and textural interest. There's also a Frenchified earthy touch. Oak is very subtle and there are hints of toffee to the long, silky stone-fruit flavours. It shows a slightly hot finish, but that won't worry most fans. A good wine to sip with grilled tuna.

Quality	🍷🍷🍷🍷🍷
Value	★★★★
Grapes	chardonnay
Region	Beechworth, Vic.
Cellar	🍷 4
Alc./Vol.	13.9%
RRP	$35.00

St Hallett Blackwell Barossa Semillon

Oak-influenced semillon is a wine type that's often promoted by Barossa wine people as one of their own. It's offered as a chardonnay alternative to a sometimes sceptical wine-drinking public.

CURRENT RELEASE 2001   A brilliant green–yellow colour flashes in the glass, and the nose has a lemony tang that matches the look. Oak is in there adding some nuttiness and interest. The wood is well-integrated on the palate which is round, dry and clean-tasting. A successful example of the style. Try it with pan-fried white-fleshed fish.

Quality	🍷🍷🍷🍷
Value	★★★⊰
Grapes	semillon
Region	Barossa Valley, SA
Cellar	🍷 2
Alc./Vol.	13.0%
RRP	$19.50

St Hallett Semillon Sauvignon Blanc

Semillon and sauvignon blanc enjoy a special harmony. The blend is a standard for hundreds of Australian wineries.

CURRENT RELEASE 2002   St Hallett's sem sauv is a cut above a lot of them. The nose has a winey thing to it, rather than just grapey fruit aroma. The aromas are zesty, suggesting lemon, grass and herbs. A clean, crisp palate follows, with some softness in the middle, and a tasty and satisfying sign-off. Good to sip with vegetable antipasto.

Quality	🍷🍷🍷🍷
Value	★★★⊰
Grapes	semillon; sauvignon blanc
Region	Barossa Valley & Adelaide Hills, SA
Cellar	🍷 2
Alc./Vol.	12.5%
RRP	$16.50 Ⓢ

Starvedog Lane Chardonnay

Quality	🍷🍷🍷🍷🍷
Value	★★★
Grapes	chardonnay
Region	Adelaide Hills, SA
Cellar	🍷 1
Alc./Vol.	13.5%
RRP	$28.50

Starvedog Lane is based in the Hahndorf area of the Adelaide Hills. There's no mistaking the German origins of this district. Lederhosen and oom-pah-pah bands don't seem out of place at all.

CURRENT RELEASE 2000   Lemon-yellow in colour, this shows appetising and quite forceful grapefruity cool-climate chardonnay aromas. The nose is dressed up in smoky oak with light caramel and mineral touches. In the mouth it has deep, rich flavour that flows into a firm bone-dry finish and a lightly toasty aftertaste. A tasty companion to crab pancakes.

Starvedog Lane Sauvignon Blanc

Quality	🍷🍷🍷🍷🍷
Value	★★★
Grapes	sauvignon blanc
Region	Adelaide Hills, SA
Cellar	🍷 2
Alc./Vol.	13.0%
RRP	$21.50

The Adelaide Hills region is a lovely place to visit for good food and wine. Sauvignon is right at home there.

CURRENT RELEASE 2002   Pale and bright, this young sauvignon has a nose of citrus, green-fruit and crushed-leaf aromas of tart austerity. The palate has a lot more give than the nose would suggest, with succulent tropical and blackcurrant fruit of good length and intensity, but that austerity returns on the finish. Fine Adelaide Hills sauvignon blanc no doubt, but truly one for the fans. Try it with Thai minced chicken salad.

Stella Bella Pink Muscat

Quality	🍷🍷🍷🍷
Value	★★★
Grapes	red frontignac
Region	Margaret River, WA
Cellar	🍷 1
Alc./Vol.	7.0%
RRP	$17.00 (375 ml)

Pink muscat? This pretty little wine would look good on a Valentine's Day table in the shimmering, heady haze of hormones and new romance that typifies such occasions. It's low in alcohol, which might help control any foolishness.

CURRENT RELEASE *non-vintage*   A delicately pale, rose-pink colour and a light grapey nose suggests a carefree little drink, and that's what this is. It's sweet and fresh, tasting like a handful of crushed ripe grapes. A tingle of acidity keeps it succulent and clean. A lovely, fruity variation on the low-alcohol moscato style. Drink it with fresh fruit.

Sticks Chardonnay

Sticks Chardonnay is always a middle-of-the-road Yarra Valley chardonnay that offers plenty of ripe flavour at a good price. There should be more of 'em.
CURRENT RELEASE 2002 A pale young chardonnay with a nose of stone fruit, honey and a whisper of nutty oak. In the mouth it has ripe, juicy flavour and a smooth feel that runs through to an even-textured dry finish. A well-made ripe wine to enjoy with a chicken club sandwich.

Quality	♥♥♥♥
Value	★★★★
Grapes	chardonnay
Region	Yarra Valley, Vic.
Cellar	🍶 2
Alc./Vol.	13.0%
RRP	$15.00

Sticks Sauvignon Blanc

Sauvignon blancs aren't among the Yarra Valley's classics, but in recent years we've seen a big increase in their numbers. Sticks is a reasonably priced example. Maker: Rob 'Sticks' Dolan.
CURRENT RELEASE 2002 Certainly no chance of mistaking the grape variety here, it has a typically varietal herbaceous aroma with a hint of fresh shelled peas to it. The palate is clean-tasting with straightforward citrus and green-bean flavours, a soft middle and a dry finish. Serve it with some mussels.

Quality	♥♥♥♥
Value	★★★⟩
Grapes	sauvignon blanc
Region	Yarra Valley, Vic.
Cellar	🍶 1
Alc./Vol.	12.0%
RRP	$15.00

Stonehaven Stepping Stone Chardonnay

The Stepping Stone name appeared last year with a very good Coonawarra cabernet that well and truly over-delivered at its price. Now there's a chardonnay to keep it company. Maker: Tom Newton.
CURRENT RELEASE 2002 There's complexity here that lifts it above the $10–$15 pack. The nose has nutty notes that suggest some lees influence, and a creamy touch adds interest to aromas of melon and peach. In the mouth it has smooth texture with soft peachy flavour and a dry finish. Try it with scallop brochettes.

Quality	♥♥♥♥
Value	★★★★⟩
Grapes	chardonnay
Region	Padthaway, SA
Cellar	🍶 1
Alc./Vol.	13.5%
RRP	$13.80 Ⓢ

Stonehaven Viognier

Quality	♟♟♟♟
Value	★★★★⅃
Grapes	viognier
Region	Padthaway, SA
Cellar	▯ 1
Alc./Vol.	13.5%
RRP	$18.00 Ⓢ

Viognier has certainly captured the imagination of a lot of Australian winemakers, with good examples springing out of vineyards all over the country. Whether Australian wine drinkers will embrace it long term is a moot point.

CURRENT RELEASE 2002   More affordable than many viogniers, this has light apricot, floral and powdered ginger aromas that are quite exotic. Although it's not mentioned on the label, there looks to be a touch of mellow oak in the mix, giving depth and texture rather than aroma and flavour. The palate is smooth and easy to like, with fragrant flavour and typically soft acidity. Try it with scallops.

Stonier Chardonnay

Quality	♟♟♟♟⅃
Value	★★★★★
Grapes	chardonnay
Region	Mornington Peninsula, Vic.
Cellar	▯ 2
Alc./Vol.	13.5%
RRP	$21.00

Stonier's 'second' chardonnay doesn't reach the heights of the excellent Reserve wine, but we think it's a great buy, offering good cool-climate Victorian quality at a lower price tag than many also-rans. Maker: Tod Dexter.

CURRENT RELEASE 2001   A super-fine, stylish white wine. The nose has mild-mannered grapefruit and white-peach aromas with a lovely vanilla caramel overlay that's subtly tempting. The palate is silky-smooth with complex flavour, medium body and a long-lasting aftertaste. A class act, even better when you realise it sells for less than a lot of overrated chardonnays from the same area. Try it with sugar-cured salmon.

Quality	♟♟♟♟⅃
Value	★★★★⅃
Grapes	chardonnay
Region	Mornington Peninsula, Vic.
Cellar	▯ 3
Alc./Vol.	14.0%
RRP	$24.00

CURRENT RELEASE 2002   Another attractive edition of this consistent chardonnay. Perhaps a bit richer than the 2001, it has peach, citrus, and cream-toffee aromas that are very appealing. It's really an object lesson in how to build complexity into chardonnay without sacrificing finesse. The palate has clean grapefruit and stone-fruit flavour with smooth texture, zippy acidity, and a long finish.

Stonier Reserve Chardonnay

Is this the best chardonnay from the Mornington Peninsula? Although there are a lot of pretenders to the title these days, each vintage of Stonier Reserve comes up with the goods. Maker: Tod Dexter.

CURRENT RELEASE 2001 Harmony is the key to this lovely chardonnay; no one element in its make-up stands out. Ying and yang balance perfectly. The nose blends nectarine-like fruit, oatmeal, nutty touches, earth and smoky oak in a way that keeps you coming back to the glass. In the mouth it's concentrated, yet it has true finesse with fragrant long flavour, smooth depth, fresh lemony acidity and a lingering slightly toasty aftertaste. Dig deep and serve with lobster.

Quality	🍷🍷🍷🍷🍷
Value	★★★★
Grapes	chardonnay
Region	Mornington Peninsula, Vic.
Cellar	🍾 4
Alc./Vol.	13.5%
RRP	$41.50

Straws Lane Gewürztraminer

There isn't much gewürztraminer in the Macedon Ranges region, although the Alsace varieties might do well there.

CURRENT RELEASE 2002 Like most gewürztraminers, when you raise a glass of this to the nose its overt aromatics are a shock to the system. Straws Lane has lychee, floral-talc and lime aromas that are intense, but there is also a slight dullness that suggests a hint of oxidation somewhere. The palate is plainer than the nose suggests, with lightly spicy dry flavours and quite a firm finish. Lacks a little freshness. Try it with Thai ginger chicken.

Quality	🍷🍷🍷
Value	★★½
Grapes	gewürztraminer
Region	Macedon Ranges, Vic.
Cellar	🍾 2
Alc./Vol.	11.0%
RRP	$25.00

Suckfizzle Augusta Sauvignon Blanc Semillon

Quality	♗♗♗♗
Value	✱✱
Grapes	sauvignon blanc; semillon
Region	Margaret River, WA
Cellar	🍷 2
Alc./Vol.	13.0%
RRP	$42.00

The name comes from the Great Lord Suckfizzle, a creation of fourteenth-century monk, medico, writer and wine buff Rabelais. The label features a huge winged foot crushing some grapes, a Monty Pythonesque image in keeping with the general feel of things.

CURRENT RELEASE 2001   Made along the lines of the dry whites of Bordeaux, this blend has a lot of smoky, nutty oak on the nose. The wood dominates herbaceous green-tinged fruit character and the palate dances to the same tune. It finishes rather harsh and mean with austere acidity. Try it with fried sardines.

Tahbilk Chardonnay

Quality	♗♗♗
Value	✱✱✱
Grapes	chardonnay
Region	Goulburn Valley, Vic.
Cellar	🍷
Alc./Vol.	13.5%
RRP	$16.00 ⑤

It's a worry that this is still on sale, as it's already showing aged development that's not benefiting the wine, so it's past its best.

CURRENT RELEASE 2000   The colour is full yellow and it smells like a simple, parsley-scented wine with bottle-aged character. It's fairly lean and drying out, with some grip at the finish, making the palate seem slightly hollow. Drink up soon, perhaps with roast stuffed chicken.

Tahbilk Marsanne

Quality	♗♗♗
Value	✱✱✱
Grapes	marsanne
Region	Goulburn Valley, Vic.
Cellar	🍷 3
Alc./Vol.	13.0%
RRP	$14.00 ⑤

Tahbilk, once Chateau Tahbilk and now minus the French castle nomenclature, continues to promote the cause of marsanne. At one stage the Goulburn Valley had the world's biggest plantings.

CURRENT RELEASE 2001   The colour is still nice and light and youthful, and it has a strange aroma of mineral, sulfur and lemon juice, airing to display parsley-like herbal notes. The palate is harsh and acidic, lean and bordering on hollow, and it lacks fruit depth. Perhaps a bit more time will help it along. Or serve with food, such as crab cakes.

Talga Chardonnay

This comes from the established Hunter family winery, Little's. Although made from Canberra grapes, by Suzanne Little, it's vinified in the Hunter for Littles' 'other' operation, the Talagandra Wine Co.
CURRENT RELEASE 2001   A very smart chardonnay, reflecting the fine quality of cool-grown Canberra grapes. It has a mid-yellow colour and smells of complex lemony fruit and nutty integrated oak and developed characters, full of interest and charm. It's fruit-driven and on the lean side; dry-finishing, soft and smooth, with excellent persistence. Try it with Cantonese lemon chicken.

Quality	♟ ♟ ♟ ♟
Value	★ ★ ★ ★
Grapes	chardonnay
Region	Canberra region, NSW
Cellar	▮ 2
Alc./Vol.	13.5%
RRP	$24.00

Taltarni Fiddleback White

Taltarni's winemakers blend this to a price and a style; hence there is a 'fruit salad' of grape varieties and several regions.
CURRENT RELEASE 2002   This is a light yellow coloured, slightly nondescript wine, with hints of musk sticks, stone fruits and earthiness. It's light, soft, simple and grapey on the tongue, and the finish carries a trace of phenolic coarseness and tart acidity. Best with food: try crumbed lamb's brains.

Quality	♟ ♟ ♟
Value	★ ★ ★
Grapes	chardonnay; sauvignon blanc; chenin blanc; riesling
Region	Pyrenees 57% & Murray Valley 38%, Vic.; mystery 5%
Cellar	▮ 1
Alc./Vol.	13.0%
RRP	$12.40 ⑤

Taltarni Sauvignon Blanc

We remember earlier days when Taltarni called this wine a fumé blanc. That name has all but disappeared now, and its passing isn't lamented – it was very confusing.
CURRENT RELEASE 2002   This is a simple, estery youngster with a trace of sweetness. Its varietal character is only moderate and it lacks a bit of the sauvignon 'cut' that we like. The palate is broad and the finish is a touch hot, from elevated alcohol and a hint of volatility. It could go with a cold vegetable terrine.

Quality	♟ ♟ ♟
Value	★ ★ ★
Grapes	sauvignon blanc
Region	Pyrenees, Vic.
Cellar	▮ 1
Alc./Vol.	13.5%
RRP	$19.50

Tamar Ridge Riesling

Quality	❦❦❦❦❦
Value	★★★★
Grapes	riesling
Region	Tamar Valley, Tas.
Cellar	🍾 10+
Alc./Vol.	13.5%
RRP	$21.00

Joe Chromy's Tamar Ridge has quickly become a leading Tasmanian brand. Chromy made his money in export beef cattle and entered the wine industry by buying Rochecombe and Heemskerk in the 1990s, which he then sold on.

CURRENT RELEASE 2002   Almost Alsatian in style, this racy, minerally wine displays Tassie riesling at its best. The nose is very spicy, faintly herbal, and undeniably cool-grown. There's almost a suggestion of traminer. It has plenty of flavour in the mouth, with richness and depth. The acidity is fairly elevated leading to a touch of hardness, which time will resolve. Try it with grilled Tassie scallops and salad.

Tamburlaine Orange Sauvignon Blanc

Quality	❦❦❦❦
Value	★★★★
Grapes	sauvignon blanc
Region	Orange, NSW
Cellar	🍾 2
Alc./Vol.	13.0%
RRP	$24.00 🥂

Tamburlaine has recently started making wines from Orange grapes, from its own vineyard planted at Borenore in 1996. A percentage of all the white wines is under Stelvin screw-caps. Maker: Mark Davidson.

CURRENT RELEASE 2002   This is a clean, tangy, cool-climate sauvignon blanc which smells of confectionery, pepperminty, estery young varietal fruit. It's soft and smooth in the mouth, not too pungent, and has a clean dry finish with a little sauvignon tanginess. Very well-balanced. It goes with niçoise salad.

TarraWarra Estate Chardonnay

Quality	❦❦❦❦❦
Value	★★★⸺
Grapes	chardonnay
Region	Yarra Valley, Vic.
Cellar	🍾 2
Alc./Vol.	14.3%
RRP	$46.00

The TarraWarra label has been getting smaller and smaller over the years. It's almost invisible! The wine makes up for it in size. Maker: Clare Halloran.

CURRENT RELEASE 2001   2001 was a very hot summer, and this is a big, rich, gutsy wine as you might expect. It's not a wine of subtlety or finesse, having caramel, butter, cedar and mealy, toasty characters. The texture is ultra-rich and viscous, with fruit-sweetness and oak well married in. It has just enough acid to keep the whole thing enlivened. The lingering clean, dry finish avoids heaviness. It would suit a rich crayfish dish.

Tarrington Chardonnay

This has been getting some fashionable support among the Melbourne cognoscenti. Our bottle certainly didn't justify a detour.
CURRENT RELEASE 2001   The colour is pale and it smells sulfury and bland, breathing to reveal marzipan. The palate is lean, tight and ungiving, with a firm, slightly hard finish. It certainly has some intensity and perhaps cellaring will bring it out of its shell, but without a track record you'd need to be an optimist. If you're into the most austere kinds of French Chablis, you might go for this. Try oysters.

Quality	♟♟♟
Value	★★┤
Grapes	chardonnay
Region	Tarrington, western Vic.
Cellar	➥ 1–3
Alc./Vol.	13.5%
RRP	$30.00 (cellar door)

Tatachilla Adelaide Hills Chardonnay

The grapes for this wine were grown at Lenswood and Hahndorf. The Adelaide Hills is undoubtedly one of the top three or four chardonnay regions in Australia these days.
CURRENT RELEASE 2001   Great value here, as this is a delicious, harmonious and quite refined style of chardonnay that seduces rather than overpowers. It has a smoky, nutty, hazelnut bouquet that is quite complex, while the structure is soft, light to medium-bodied, restrained and well-balanced. There are some Burgundy-like qualities that impress the more it warms in the glass. It would suit a goat's cheese soufflé.

Quality	♟♟♟♟♟
Value	★★★★
Grapes	chardonnay
Region	Adelaide Hills, SA
Cellar	▮ 3
Alc./Vol.	13.5%
RRP	$20.00 Ⓢ

Tatachilla Adelaide Hills Sauvignon Blanc

We tried this under both screw-cap and cork, in the same blind tasting, and scored and described the two bottles almost identically. When cork's good, it's very good; trouble is you never know when it's going to be crook.
CURRENT RELEASE 2002   This has a herbal, honeydew-melon aroma, with hints of grass and lime leaves. Some pear as well. The palate has a touch of succulence, and lots of fruit flavours and aromas. It's well-balanced without great power or intensity of palate, but a very good drink with caesar salad.

Quality	♟♟♟♟
Value	★★★┤
Grapes	sauvignon blanc
Region	Adelaide Hills, SA
Cellar	▮ 1
Alc./Vol.	13.0%
RRP	$20.00 Ⓢ ⧤

Thomas Semillon

Quality	🍷🍷🍷🍷🍷
Value	★★★★⧸
Grapes	semillon
Region	Hunter Valley, NSW
Cellar	🍾 8+
Alc./Vol.	10.0%
RRP	$20.00 (cellar door)

Andrew Thomas streeted the 2002 Hunter Valley Wine Show, winning the trophies for both 2001 and 2002 vintage Semillons – a superhuman effort for such a micro-boutique-sized operation. He's a former Tyrrells winemaker, which helps explain it.
CURRENT RELEASE 2002 'Thommo' is a Hunter traditionalist and that means low-alcohol, unwooded semillon which can be steely in youth and ages brilliantly. His 2002 is exemplary of this: a pale yellow coloured, classically straw/hay and lemon scented wine that needs time to unfold its full glory. In the mouth it's lean, tangy and intensely minerally. It will cellar for years, but drinks well now with flathead cooked à la meunière.

Thorn–Clarke Sandpiper Riesling

Quality	🍷🍷🍷🍷
Value	★★★★
Grapes	riesling
Region	Eden Valley, SA
Cellar	🍾 4+
Alc./Vol.	12.0%
RRP	$16.00 🥂

Thorn-Clarke is a highly promising new producer in the Barossa and Eden Valleys, headed up by former Perth mining geologist David Clarke. They have a thoughtfully constructed three-tier range of wines, with Jim Irvine as consultant winemaker.
CURRENT RELEASE 2002 This is a fine but very soft young riesling which seems to have a fairly low acid level, but that's all okay for early drinking. There are subdued but pleasantly mineral aromas and a touch of bottling sulfur that will soon dissipate. It's smoothly fruity and nicely balanced in the mouth, and drinks well young. Good with pan-fried whiting.

Three Ponds Chardonnay

Quality	🍷🍷🍷⧸
Value	★★★
Grapes	chardonnay
Region	Hunter Valley, NSW
Cellar	🍾 1
Alc./Vol.	13.5%
RRP	$18.00 (cellar door)

Mount Eyre is a 24-hectare vineyard at Broke, established in 1996. It already has three brands on the market: Mount Eyre, Three Ponds and Neptune. No wonder the poor old wine market is congested!
CURRENT RELEASE 2000 This is a typical Hunter chardonnay: it has a nicely restrained medium yellow colour and a resiny, cough-medicine character that is a Hunter chardonnay hallmark. It is a full, broad style in the mouth and carries a fair quota of residual sugar. It certainly has stacks of flavour, but fine and subtle it is not! Horses for courses. It would suit chicken chasseur.

Tim Adams Riesling

Tim Adams has been running his own winery in the Clare Valley for more than 15 years. He's the brother of Simon Adams, former Yalumba and now Cellarmasters chief winemaker in the Barossa.

CURRENT RELEASE 2002   Tim Adams makes rieslings to last, and they can seem a trifle austere in youth. This already has a nice floral nose, reminding of bunches of dried wildflowers. It's delicate, refined, dry and minerally in the mouth, finishing just a touch hard. It has good fruit depth and taut structure, and should blossom with time. Try it with whole baked snapper.

Quality	????
Value	★★★★
Grapes	riesling
Region	Clare Valley, SA
Cellar	➛ 1–15
Alc./Vol.	12.5%
RRP	$16.00

Tin Cows Chardonnay

TarraWarra Estate's owner Marc Besen is an inveterate collector of art, and the grounds of the property are strewn with sculptures. Grazing cows made of corrugated iron are among them.

CURRENT RELEASE 2001   This is a lighter, simpler wine than its big brother under the TarraWarra Estate label. It nevertheless has some butterscotch and honey complexities, although the freshness of the primary fruit isn't as evident as we might have expected. It's a light to medium-bodied wine which finishes clean and dry, even if it's a trifle short. It goes well with san choy bow.

Quality	???
Value	★★★
Grapes	chardonnay
Region	Yarra Valley, Vic.
Cellar	▮ 2
Alc./Vol.	13.1%
RRP	$25.50

Torbreck The Bothie

This is a new adventure for Torbreck, which shows they're willing and able to try new things. It's quite an unusual style, though, and not the usual light, easy-quaffing Barossa fronti. Only 400 cases made. CURRENT RELEASE 2002   The colour is pale and it has a pungent aroma of muscat grapes: rose petals, frangipani, rather ripe and broad, not light and zingy like a low-alcohol fronti. The taste is very sweet and a trifle clumsy. It fails to sing like the best Beaumes-de-Venise, but if you enjoy that style, you'll probably like this. Chill it well, and it could go with a citrus fruit flan for dessert.

Quality	???
Value	★★★
Grapes	white frontignac
Region	Barossa Valley, SA
Cellar	▮ 2
Alc./Vol.	14.5%
RRP	$27.00

Tower Estate Clare Valley Riesling

Quality 🍷🍷🍷🍷½
Value ★★★★
Grapes riesling
Region Clare Valley, SA
Cellar → 1–10+
Alc./Vol. 13.5%
RRP $24.00 (cellar door)

The grapes were sourced from Brian Barry's Jud's Hill vineyard. The 2002 Clare vintage produced rieslings capable of cellaring for a very long time.

CURRENT RELEASE 2002 The colour is pale and the aromas and flavours are quite undeveloped; it will be a slow-maturing, long-living wine. There are some glimpses of passionfruit, mango and gooseberry, and the palate is searingly intense and sharply acidic at this stage. It begs to be tucked away for a few years, and then drunk with gravlax of trout.

Trentham Estate Chardonnay

Quality 🍷🍷🍷½
Value ★★★½
Grapes chardonnay
Region Murray Valley, Vic.
Cellar 🍾 2
Alc./Vol. 13.5%
RRP $16.00 (\$)

The Murphy brothers, Tony and Patrick, are based on the Murray River at Gol Gol where they make some great value wines. They also have a restaurant with river views.

CURRENT RELEASE 2002 The bouquet has some caramel from oak and early development, which is not unusual in hot-area whites. The palate carries rich peachy, buttery flavour and some sweetness. It could build a bit more character with a few more months in bottle. Drink it with roast chicken.

Trentham Estate Viognier

Quality 🍷🍷🍷🍷
Value ★★★★★
Grapes viognier
Region Murray Valley, NSW
Cellar 🍾 1
Alc./Vol. 13.0%
RRP $19.00 (\$)

The Murphy brothers, Tony and Patrick, produce wines well above their station from their substantial vineyards at Trentham Cliffs, near Mildura.

CURRENT RELEASE 2002 This has a stack of flavour and a fairly warm, alcohol finish. It has a nose of dry straw and Eastern spices. In the mouth, it's smoothly fruity yet dry and clean at the finish. Despite its big flavour it has some subtlety and good balance. Serve it with crumbed lamb's brains.

Trentham Murphy's Lore Semillon Chardonnay

Like the play on words here! The Murphy brothers run the place, of course. The winery is thus named because it's located at Trentham Cliffs.
CURRENT RELEASE 2002   The aromas are of slightly sharp-edged green, herbaceous semillon grapes. There's some sweetness on the palate and it's a simple, grapey, quaffing white wine that will appeal to the uninitiated but won't offend more seasoned drinkers. It goes well with Cantonese fish balls.

Quality	¶ ¶ ¶
Value	★★★⁴
Grapes	semillon; chardonnay
Region	Murray Valley, NSW
Cellar	▯ 1
Alc./Vol.	11.5%
RRP	$10.00 Ⓢ

Tucks Ridge Chardonnay

Tucks Ridge was started by a group of wine people in 1988 and today is owned by Peter Hollick. Only one third of the wine undergoes a malolactic.
CURRENT RELEASE 2001   This is an attractive chardonnay that doesn't labour the barrel and other non-grape-derived flavours as many peninsula chardonnays do. The colour is still light yellow and there are well-harmonised mineral, oak and melon aromas, coupled with nutty, mealy, butterscotch touches. It's very soft and drinks well now, with caesar salad.

Quality	¶ ¶ ¶ ¶
Value	★★★
Grapes	chardonnay
Region	Mornington
	Peninsula, Vic.
Cellar	▯ 2
Alc./Vol.	13.5%
RRP	$25.00

2–Bud Spur Chardonnay

A two-bud spur is what's left on the vine after pruning; many of them, in fact. From these, the following year's growth – shoots, fruit, leaves and tendrils – will magically emerge. Contract winemaker is Michael Vishacki at Panorama.
CURRENT RELEASE 2001   This won a controversial gold medal at the 2003 Tasmanian Regional Wine Show: contentious because it had a trace of sulfide, which the judges saw as adding extra interest. It also has intense grapefruit, passionfruit and pineapple flavours, together with oak and other buttery complexities. A rich, multi-layered wine to fascinate all but arch-technocrats! Serve with creamy fish pie.

Quality	¶ ¶ ¶ ¶ ¶
Value	★★★★⁴
Grapes	chardonnay
Region	southern Tas.
Cellar	▯ 2
Alc./Vol.	13.6%
RRP	$18.00

Two Rivers Stone's Throw Semillon

Quality	♟ ♟ ♟
Value	★ ★ ★
Grapes	semillon
Region	Upper Hunter Valley, NSW
Cellar	♦ 3
Alc./Vol.	11.7%
RRP	$14.60 ⑤

Two Rivers is part of the Inglewood group, based in the Upper Hunter where there are indeed two rivers, the Hunter and the Goulburn (no relation to its namesake in Victoria).

CURRENT RELEASE 2002   A fairly plain, commercial style of Hunter semillon which lacks a bit of character, and finishes with a little sweetness. There are some grass/hay and straw aromas, and the palate could use more depth and intensity. It's a perfectly decent wine at the price. Take it to a vegetarian restaurant.

Tyrrells Lost Block Semillon

Quality	♟ ♟ ♟ ♟ ♟
Value	★ ★ ★ ★ ★
Grapes	semillon
Region	Hunter Valley, NSW
Cellar	♦ 6
Alc./Vol.	11.0%
RRP	$17.00 ⑤

The story goes that they forgot about this block of vines one harvest, and inadvertently let the grapes get riper than usual, producing a wine with an interesting character. So, how come they went back to picking early? The alcohols are low in traditional style, like all Tyrrell semillons.

CURRENT RELEASE 2002   Chalky, minerally early-picked semillon aromas are the order of the day. Dry grass/hay and lemon juice with slight floral highlights, too. It's classically dry, minerally and almost austere in the mouth: dry, taut, tangy and deliciously mouth-watering. It goes with quick-barbecued calamari.

Tyrrells Stevens Reserve Semillon

Quality	♟ ♟ ♟ ♟ ♟
Value	★ ★ ★ ★ ★
Grapes	semillon
Region	Hunter Valley, NSW
Cellar	♦ 6
Alc./Vol.	10.5%
RRP	$23.00 ⑤

An individual vineyard semillon from George and Neil Stevens' highly regarded vineyard at Pokolbin. Winemaker is Andrew Spinaze.
Previous outstanding vintage: '96
CURRENT RELEASE 1998   This is still a very young Hunter semillon of the traditional style – in an austere mode. It's still in its developmental phase and needs more time. The aromas are dusty, lemony and straw/hay-like. The palate is very tart and lean, with lemon-citrus flavours and a hint of Sunlight soap. It's very tangy and needs to be drunk with a cold seafood platter, or cellared further. It will become richer and more buttered-toasty with more time.

PENGUIN BEST SEMILLON

Vintage Plane Semillon Sauvignon Blanc

No, it's not a new label from Tim Knappstein, as far as we know. Although Tim is the noted vintage aeroplane aficionado in the Hills. Remember: eight hours between bottle and throttle, though.
CURRENT RELEASE 2002   This is a subtle, minerally style of sauvignon blanc. It's lean, tangy and dry to finish, just right for washing down summer seafoods and salads. Dry-straw aromas combine with a taut, slightly angular profile, and it has a dry, minerally, almost steely finish. It would go well with fish in salsa verde.

Quality	♥♥♥♥
Value	★★★
Grapes	semillon; sauvignon blanc
Region	Adelaide Hills, SA
Cellar	1
Alc./Vol.	11.6%
RRP	$24.00

Voyager Estate Chardonnay

Voyager Estate is one of the many Western Australian wineries whose wines keep on improving. Stuart Pym moved to Devil's Lair a couple of years back and handed over the winemaking to his able deputy, Cliff Royle.
CURRENT RELEASE 2001   This is a more restrained chardonnay than usual, which may just be the year. Whatever, it's a fine wine that will grow with time in the bottle. It's light yellow and has a subtle almond, crushed-nuts aroma which is a little undeveloped at this stage. It reveals some good qualities in the mouth and we expect it to repay short-term keeping. Then serve with pan-sautéed yabbies.

Quality	♥♥♥♥♥
Value	★★★♦
Grapes	chardonnay
Region	Margaret River, WA
Cellar	1–3+
Alc./Vol.	13.5%
RRP	$33.00

Voyager Estate Sauvignon Blanc Semillon

Voyager Estate started life as Freycinet in the '70s. It changed its name when purchased by mining magnate Michael Wright, whose mining company is also named Voyager. Maker: Cliff Royle.
CURRENT RELEASE 2002   Some nutty barrel-ferment characters add interest to this classic Margaret River blend, making it more complex than some. There are herbal and citrus flavours as well, and the palate is fairly full and smooth with a touch of tannin grip, possibly from oak, which helps dry the finish. It goes well with chargrilled vegetables.

Quality	♥♥♥♥
Value	★★★♦
Grapes	sauvignon blanc; semillon
Region	Margaret River, WA
Cellar	2
Alc./Vol.	13.3%
RRP	$20.50

Wandin Valley Estate Reserve Semillon

Quality	♀♀♀♀♀
Value	★★★★
Grapes	semillon
Region	Hunter Valley, SA
Cellar	← 2–8
Alc./Vol.	11.0%
RRP	$18.00

At Wandin Valley Estate there's a village-green-inspired cricket ground, although the Hunter Valley climate isn't exactly as Wodehouse would have it. Semillon is a particular strength at this winery.

CURRENT RELEASE 2002   Perhaps more intense on the nose than many young semillons, this has attractive mineral and citrus aromas that are very appetising. In the mouth it's clean and dry, with the usual subtlety of young Hunters that you just know will mature handsomely. Try it with trout meunière.

Water Wheel Chardonnay

Quality	♀♀♀♀
Value	★★★¾
Grapes	chardonnay
Region	Bendigo, Vic.
Cellar	▮ 2
Alc./Vol.	14.5%
RRP	$20.00 ➳

A real water wheel near the winery used to power an old flour mill back when times were simple. Now modern technology has given this bottle a reliable screw-cap. Maker: Peter Cumming.

CURRENT RELEASE 2002   Water Wheel is never a delicate chardonnay, but it's always well-made, generously constructed and keenly priced. The 2002 has peach and citrus fruit on the nose, along with a herbal touch and underplayed nutty oak. In the mouth it's big and ripe, with a warm 14.5 per cent alcohol giving an impression of sweetness and some heat to the finish. Try it with Balinese fried chicken.

Wellington Iced Riesling

Quality	♀♀♀♀♀
Value	★★★★
Grapes	riesling
Region	various, Tas.
Cellar	▮ 2
Alc./Vol.	9.5%
RRP	$24.85 (375 ml)

This reliably brilliant, non-botrytised sweetie is made from juice that's been freeze-concentrated before fermentation. It's a kind of high-tech ice-wine, shortcutting the German technique of leaving grapes on the vines until the first freeze of winter, harvesting and pressing while the grapes are partly frozen.

CURRENT RELEASE 2002   This is not a very sweet or rich wine, but a thrillingly racy, medium–sweet white with pungent citrus and flowery varietal fruit, with honey and herbaceous overtones. It's spotlessly clean, fresh and well-made; a delicious dessert wine to serve with fruit salad.

Wellington Tasmanian Chardonnay

Andrew Hood prides himself on making chardonnay without malolactic fermentation, so much so that he declares it on his back label. The high natural acid should enable the wines to age well.

CURRENT RELEASE 2000 We've tried several bottles. One was very aged and apparently suffering from cork failure; the best bottle seemed to be ageing very well for a three-year-old. It has a developing bouquet of nougat, smoke and stone fruits; the palate is restrained, taut and retaining its focus. An understated, subtle style which would drink well with barbecued king prawns.

Quality	🍷🍷🍷🍷
Value	★★★★
Grapes	chardonnay
Region	various, Tas.
Cellar	🍾 2
Alc./Vol.	13.0%
RRP	$24.85

Wellington Tasmanian Riesling

At his winery at Cambridge, near Hobart, Andrew Hood is a contract winemaker for well over 20 small vineyards dotted around Tasmania. Wellington is his own brand.

CURRENT RELEASE 2001 This is starting to show some development, and with it some touches of silage and honey, which are typical of Tassie white wines generally. There are also lemon-butter, toast and grass/hay aromas. The taste is very soft, fruity and gentle. It's a balanced, easygoing wine which is drinking well now, and is ageing faster than usual for Wellington. It goes with dressed rocket salad with scallops.

Quality	🍷🍷🍷🍷
Value	★★★★
Grapes	riesling
Region	various, Tas.
Cellar	🍾 3
Alc./Vol.	12.7%
RRP	$19.90

West Cape Howe Chardonnay

West Cape Howe winemaker Brenden Smith worked at Goundreys at Mount Barker for four years in the 1990s, giving him plenty of experience with Great Southern chardonnay.

CURRENT RELEASE 2002 Fine, ripe grapefruit and fig aromas lead the way here, under a veneer of spicy, nutty oak. It smells and tastes very fresh and new, with succulent fruit and barley-sugar notes following down the smooth juicy palate. The flavours are quietly fragrant with toasty oak, and citrus-like acidity and a slight phenolic grip give structure. A chardonnay of understated elegance to accompany steamed marron with dill mayonnaise.

Quality	🍷🍷🍷🍷
Value	★★★½
Grapes	chardonnay
Region	Great Southern, WA
Cellar	🍾 3
Alc./Vol.	13.5%
RRP	$23.00

West Cape Howe Mount Barker Riesling

Quality	🍷🍷🍷🍷
Value	★★★⁴
Grapes	riesling
Region	Great Southern, WA
Cellar	➦ 1–5
Alc./Vol.	11.5%
RRP	$19.00 🥂

Western Australia's Great Southern has quietly assumed a position as one of Australia's great places for riesling. The style is quite austere and ageworthy.

CURRENT RELEASE 2002   This is rather neutral in youth, pale and tightly closed up with lime and minerally aromas of some austerity. The palate has fine texture and is slightly dumb at the moment; like most southern Western Australian rieslings, it really needs time to open up. The finish is clean and slate-dry. Keep it for a couple of years, then try it with grilled delicate fish.

West Cape Howe Semillon Sauvignon Blanc

Quality	🍷🍷🍷🍷
Value	★★★⁴
Grapes	semillon; sauvignon blanc
Region	Great Southern, WA
Cellar	🍾 1
Alc./Vol.	13.0%
RRP	$17.50

West Cape Howe's logo is two golden seahorses, commemorating the first Europeans to explore this corner of the world in 1627. They were Dutchmen aboard the 'Gulden Zeepaard' (Golden Seahorse).

CURRENT RELEASE 2002   Refreshing wines like this are just what the Fremantle doctor ordered – in Western Australia they sit wonderfully well with the climate and lifestyle. This has deliciously succulent aromas of passionfruit and a bright grassy note. The palate is ripe with tropical-fruit flavour and a tang of gooseberry. Serve it with the freshest of shellfish, preferably by the Indian Ocean.

Will Taylor Adelaide Hills Sauvignon Blanc

Quality	🍷🍷🍷🍷
Value	★★★
Grapes	sauvignon blanc
Region	Adelaide Hills, SA
Cellar	🍾 1
Alc./Vol.	13.5%
RRP	$20.45 🥂

Adelaide lawyer Will Taylor has built a successful merchant business in recent years, based on bottling high-quality examples of tried and tested Australian regional classics.

CURRENT RELEASE 2002   There's some blackcurrant on the nose, along with mineral and lightly herbaceous aromas. In the mouth it's dry with lively acidity, but it's rather plain and a bit lacking in the pristine juicy fruit that's such a part of the best 2002 Adelaide Hills sauvignons. There's nothing wrong with it, it just doesn't press our buttons the way wines like Shaw and Smith and Tim Knappstein's Lenswood do. Try it with black pepper and lemon-grass squid.

Willow Creek Tulum Chardonnay

This is a big wine for a Mornington Peninsula chardonnay, and as if to confirm the point it's in a big heavy version of the normal chardonnay bottle. Maker: Phil Kerney.

CURRENT RELEASE 2001   A bright, green-tinged, yellow colour introduces a larger-than-life type of chardonnay. It has a complex nose of peach, syrupy figs, barley sugar, and smoky nutty oak. The palate is richly worked with creamy texture and long flavour ahead of a dry finish. Serve it with lobster.

Quality	▼▼▼▼▼
Value	★★★᛫
Grapes	chardonnay
Region	Mornington Peninsula, Vic.
Cellar	▮ 1
Alc./Vol.	13.5%
RRP	$32.50

The Wilson Vineyard Riesling

The Wilson vineyard is in the Polish Hill River sub-region, where the soils are slatey and the wines tend to be flintier and more austere than other parts of the Clare Valley.

CURRENT RELEASE 2002   The colour is pale and the aromas are minerally, earthy and of grass/hay, rather than flowers or overt citrus. It is very delicate, subtle and dry in the mouth, a restrained style that epitomises the Polish terroir. Linear acidity and a minerally finish complete the picture. It needs cellaring, then serve with a shellfish platter.

Quality	▼▼▼▼
Value	★★★★
Grapes	riesling
Region	Clare Valley, SA
Cellar	➡ 1–8+
Alc./Vol.	13.0%
RRP	$20.00

Windowrie Cowra Chardonnay

Windowrie is a significant name in the Cowra region. Much of their grape production goes to other makers, but they have two labels, The Mill, and Cowra, for their own wine.

CURRENT RELEASE 2002   This is a simple fruity chardonnay, very much in the juicy, ripe Cowra style. Oak is imperceptible, the nose dominated by peach and fig aromas that are clean and ripe. In the mouth it's rather plain, but it won't cause offence, and the price tag is very reasonable. There's a slight hardness to the finish which doesn't intrude when it's well-chilled and served with something like cold chicken.

Quality	▼▼▼
Value	★★★᛫
Grapes	chardonnay
Region	Cowra, NSW
Cellar	▮ 1
Alc./Vol.	13.5%
RRP	$10.00

Wirra Wirra Adelaide Hills Chardonnay

Quality 🍷🍷🍷🍷
Value ★★★½
Grapes chardonnay
Region Adelaide Hills, Vic.
Cellar 3
Alc./Vol. 13.5%
RRP $26.00

Wirra Wirra have been moving away from McLaren Vale in search of high-quality chardonnay material. The 2001 vintage is the first wine they've made entirely from Adelaide Hills fruit and it augurs well for the future.

CURRENT RELEASE 2001 A bright greenish colour and the nose is refined and stylish, thankfully with oak blended in seamlessly. There's citrus and melon, and some pleasant nutty touches add dimension. The palate is fine and clean, not powerful but nicely intense. The finish is clean and dry with a fragrant whisper of toasty oak in the background. Try it with crisp-fried whole flounder.

Wirra Wirra Hand Picked Riesling

Quality 🍷🍷🍷🍷
Value ★★★
Grapes riesling
Region McLaren Vale, SA
Cellar 4+
Alc./Vol. 12.5%
RRP $17.00

Hand-picking is giving way to machine-harvesting in many vineyards. So much so that Wirra Wirra advertise the fact that they still do things the old-fashioned way. Many feel that fruit quality is better.

CURRENT RELEASE 2002 A pale young riesling with a light whiff of sulfur on opening the screw-cap. It evolves into a straightforward nose of mixed citrus aromas that aren't as up-front or as lush as they are in some South Australian 2002 rieslings. The palate is clean and dry with pleasant lime flavours. A good wine, but it lacks a little excitement. Try it with pad thai noodles.

Wolf Blass Chardonnay

Quality 🍷🍷🍷½
Value ★★★★½
Grapes chardonnay
Region not stated
Cellar 2
Alc./Vol. 13.0%
RRP $12.00 (S)

This is the wooded version of the yellow-labelled chardonnay bearing the Wolfgang Blass name. The Blass winemakers have changed the style of this wine in recent years, throttling back on the oak a bit and letting the fruit shine through. A good move.

CURRENT RELEASE 2002 A smart buy at the price. It smells ripely of pear, peach and cashew with a balanced touch of nutty oak. The palate has light to medium weight and intensity, with smooth mouth-feel and a clean crisp finish. Try it with crisp fried chicken.

Wolf Blass Gold Label Riesling

Wolf Blass Gold Label has been an impressive riesling for some years. It's made in a precocious style that wins many friends. With the 2002 vintage, Gold Label has joined the screw-cap brigade – a big plus.
CURRENT RELEASE 2002   This has a lovely fresh nose of light floral scents and some classical lime, green-apple and pear notes. The palate has mouth-watering dry riesling flavour, a penetrating citrus tang, good persistence and a fine, long dry finish. Serve it with pan-fried garfish fillets.

Quality	♟♟♟♟⸮
Value	★★★★
Grapes	riesling
Region	Clare & Eden Valleys, SA
Cellar	▮ 6
Alc./Vol.	11.5%
RRP	$21.00 ⑤ 🥂

Wolf Blass Unwooded Chardonnay

Herr Wolf Blass used to say 'no wood, no good'. He was speaking about red wines of course, but in our view the same could go for chardonnay. Many of the unoaked breed are pretty ordinary in our opinion: the Blass version is a passable example.
CURRENT RELEASE 2002   This Wolf Blass 2002 Unwooded is an easy-drinking drop. The fruity nose is grapey and dry with a nice touch of melon. In the mouth it's soft and easy-drinking, if a little plain, and it finishes soft and clean. Try it with a simple seafood pasta.

Quality	♟♟♟
Value	★★★
Grapes	chardonnay
Region	not stated
Cellar	▮ 1
Alc./Vol.	12.5%
RRP	$12.00 ⑤

Woodstock Semillon Sauvignon Blanc

This only has a 'dash' of sauvignon blanc in it, but they've chosen to mention it on the front label anyway. The super-cool 2002 summer led to many stand-out whites from hot areas, such as this. They're finer and more varietally intense than usual.
CURRENT RELEASE 2002   The colour is pale lemon and it has marvellous freshness and fragrance. It smells invitingly of fresh lemon juice, with a creamy nutty overtone. The taste is light, refreshingly crisp and dry, with mouth-watering fruit and superb balance. Herbs, citrus and creaminess are combined on the palate. There's abundant acid but it's not tart. It would go well while young with oysters.

Quality	♟♟♟♟♟
Value	★★★★★
Grapes	semillon; sauvignon blanc
Region	McLaren Vale, SA
Cellar	▮ 6+
Alc./Vol.	13.0%
RRP	$14.00 🥂 (cellar door)

Wyndham Estate Bin 777 Semillon

Quality	♥♥♥♥
Value	★★★★
Grapes	semillon
Region	Hunter Valley, NSW
Cellar	🍾 3
Alc./Vol.	12.0%
RRP	$15.00 ⊠

Wyndham Estate's white wines are usually a better bet than the reds. Bin 777 is one of the better examples.
CURRENT RELEASE 2002   This is a pale young white which is a little more giving than most young Hunter semillons. The nose has citrus aromas with a light herbal touch, and the palate has smooth texture, clean flavour and relatively soft acidity, making it an earlier-drinking style. Good value and often discounted, it goes well with fried prawns.

Wynns Chardonnay

Quality	♥♥♥♥
Value	★★★★⁺
Grapes	chardonnay
Region	Coonawarra, SA
Cellar	🍾 2
Alc./Vol.	13.5%
RRP	$16.75 Ⓢ

The Wynns Coonawarra label has long been associated with red wine, but don't ignore the great-value whites. Once upon a time this chardonnay suffered from a surfeit of raw oak, but skilled barrel fermentation and new winery techniques have made recent wines quite classy.
CURRENT RELEASE 2002   The nose has citrus blossom, white peach, apricot jam and subtle nutty, smoky oak. The flavours are ripe and satisfying with a hint of oak towards the end. It's easy-textured and a little light on the finish, but great value. A pleasant commercial style to drink with grilled chicken.

Wynns Riesling

Quality	♥♥♥♥
Value	★★★★★
Grapes	riesling
Region	Coonawarra, SA
Cellar	━ 1–6+
Alc./Vol.	13.0%
RRP	$16.75 Ⓢ ⊠

This is a remarkable wine with a long history and a great record for quality over many years. It's usually discounted and it also improves with bottle-age. What more could you ask?
CURRENT RELEASE 2002   This pale wine is still dumb in youth but it should develop well. The nose has lemon and green-apple aromas of good varietal definition. In the mouth it's shy and reserved with a flinty touch to the dry palate. Not as floral-fragrant as some past Wynns Rieslings, but it's early days. A great cellar builder on discount. Try it with chilled soba noodles on a warm day.

Xanadu Secession Chardonnay

This is Xanadu's unwooded chardonnay. It comes in a clear-glass claret bottle, which is a departure from the norm. Maker: Jurg Muggli.

CURRENT RELEASE 2002   This is a very good example of unwooded chardonnay, a poorly catered category in Australia. It has a fresh melon, nectarine aroma with a nettley lift, and again a fresh, lively, uncomplicated taste which finishes clean and tangy, thanks to good acidity. It's not complex, but that's not the point. A very attractive easy-drinking chardonnay, which would suit stir-fried vegetables.

Quality	🍷🍷🍷🍷
Value	★★★★
Grapes	chardonnay
Region	various, WA
Cellar	🍾 2
Alc./Vol.	13.5%
RRP	$14.90 Ⓢ

Xanadu Secession Semillon Sauvignon Blanc

Secession was inspired by the Viennese Secession, a movement in painting, and harks back to the slightly zany, but inspired, early days of the Lagan family's Chateau Xanadu. Maker: Jurg Muggli.

CURRENT RELEASE 2002   Pristine fruit, clean and wholesome but just a trifle same-ish. The gooseberry-like aromas are tangy and fresh, and it has reasonable depth of flavour in the mouth, finishing dry and balanced with respectable persistence. A good wine in which the semillon dominates. It would go well with caesar salad.

Quality	🍷🍷🍷🍷
Value	★★★★
Grapes	semillon; sauvignon blanc
Region	Margaret River, WA
Cellar	🍾 1
Alc./Vol.	13.0%
RRP	$14.90 Ⓢ

Xanadu Semillon Sauvignon Blanc

'For he on honey dew hath fed, and drunk the milk of paradise', etc, etc . . . The legend of Xanadu was what inspired Conor Lagan's parents to set up this winery. Now it's a big public company, there seems to be less poetry about.

CURRENT RELEASE 2002   Dusty herbaceous regional fruit and a kiss of oak are the aromas that greet the nose. It's almost peppery in its dusty fruit, and the palate is high-acid tangy, slightly pinched in the fruit department and the oak becomes more apparent as you sip. The finish is clean and very dry. It goes with fish in a capsicum purée.

Quality	🍷🍷🍷🍷
Value	★★★⬩
Grapes	semillon; sauvignon blanc
Region	Margaret River, WA
Cellar	🍾 2
Alc./Vol.	13.0%
RRP	$18.00

Xanadu Show Reserve Semillon

Quality	♥♥♥♥
Value	★★★
Grapes	semillon
Region	Margaret River, WA
Cellar	🍷 4
Alc./Vol.	13.5%
RRP	$35.00 (cellar door)

Xanadu released a special white and red to mark the occasion of its 25th anniversary in 2003. *Tempus fugit!* It seems like just yesterday Xanadu was a new boutique – now it's a fairly big public company. Only 500 cases of each were produced. Maker: Jurg Muggli.

CURRENT RELEASE 2000   The wine has been aged in French oak puncheons, and it shows. It is smart oak, though, giving a lovely cedary, toasty fragrance, but the problem is, oak dominates so totally! The taste is clean, dry, very long and powerful, with again predominant oak flavours, although it has good structure and a nice clean finish. Of its style, a very good wine. Try smoked chicken salad.

Yangarra Park Chardonnay

Quality	♥♥♥♥
Value	★★★★
Grapes	chardonnay
Region	various, south-eastern Australia
Cellar	🍷 1
Alc./Vol.	13.5%
RRP	$15.00

This American-owned concern is based on an ex-Normans vineyard at McLaren Vale, also sourcing grapes from other regions. It may be the power of suggestion, but we think this chardonnay speaks with an almost Californian accent.

CURRENT RELEASE 2001   There's some fruit salad and peach on the nose here, and it tastes ripe and round with juicy fruit character. Oak is well in hand, and the palate has smooth drinkability and depth. It's not overly complex, which is fine in a wine that's obviously intended as a no-fuss drop to guzzle young. Serve it with spring rolls.

Yarra Edge Single Vineyard Chardonnay

Quality	♥♥♥♥
Value	★★★
Grapes	chardonnay
Region	Yarra Valley, Vic.
Cellar	🍷 2
Alc./Vol.	13.0%
RRP	$30.00

This Yarra Valley vineyard is now associated with Yering Station. Heavily 'worked' chardonnay has been a speciality for some years.

CURRENT RELEASE 2000   A lot of winemaking influence has shaped this Yarra Valley chardonnay. It opens with smoky, earthy and leesy influences, hints of cashew and almond, and a heart of honeyed nectarine-like fruit. In the mouth it's more about texture and richness than overt flavour, with a smooth layered feel to it. Subtle fruit is matched to smoky oak which gives it a long toasty aftertaste. Try it with salmon.

Yarra Valley Hills Chardonnay

Since its purchase by Dromana Estate, the Yarra Valley Hills wines are made by Garry Crittenden and Judy Gifford Watson. Early results are promising.
CURRENT RELEASE 2001 An attractive, complete type of chardonnay which is good value. The colour is bright yellow–green and the nose has full, rich fig, peach and nutty spicy oak aromas. The palate has a full flavour to match the nose and it's smooth-textured with a clean finish. A drink-now chardonnay which will accompany richer fish dishes well.

Quality	🍷🍷🍷🍷
Value	★★★★½
Grapes	chardonnay
Region	Yarra Valley, Vic.
Cellar	1
Alc./Vol.	13.5%
RRP	$19.00

Yering Station Chardonnay

Many Yarra Valley vineyards established in the heady days of nineteenth-century winemaking are back in business. Yering Station is one of the most impressive.
CURRENT RELEASE 2001 Oak plays a big part in Yering Station's standard chardonnay. Too much so? Certainly the smoky, nutty, spicy oak dominates at the moment. Some ripe stone fruit is there mid-palate but it struggles to find its way through the wood. A well-made chardonnay and that oak treatment shows a skilled hand, but we think less would have been better. Serve it with smoked cod.

Quality	🍷🍷🍷½
Value	★★★
Grapes	chardonnay
Region	Yarra Valley, Vic.
Cellar	2
Alc./Vol.	13.0%
RRP	$20.00

Yering Station Reserve Chardonnay

Yering Station's Reserves follow the trend to bottle *really* special wines in big, toe-breakingly heavy bottles. It certainly makes you take notice, and in this case the wine warrants the attention. Maker: Tom Carson.
CURRENT RELEASE 2001 As always, a subtle creation with plenty going on. The nose has subtle fruit skilfully woven into nutty, creamy aromas, a hint of Frenchy burnt match and a dusty veneer of classy oak. In the mouth it has finesse and elegance, with that understated power that marks the best. It finishes long and savoury with a tasty seasoning of toasty oak. Blow the budget with a grilled lobster.

Quality	🍷🍷🍷🍷🍷
Value	★★★½
Grapes	chardonnay
Region	Yarra Valley, Vic.
Cellar	3
Alc./Vol.	13.5%
RRP	$58.00

Zarephath Porongurup Riesling

Quality	▼▼▼▼
Value	★★★★
Grapes	riesling
Region	Great Southern, WA
Cellar	🍾 8+
Alc./Vol.	12.5%
RRP	$18.00 ⬓

The biblical name signifies wines made from the vineyard run by a Benedictine community in the Porongurup Ranges near Albany, Western Australia. Maker: Robert Diletti at Castle Rock Estate.
CURRENT RELEASE 2002   Pale lemon coloured and refined, this youngster is very restrained in its youth and should reward cellaring. It has a shy, bready aroma from fermentation esters and this will soon give way to more citrusy varietal aromas. It's light-bodied and delicate; a subtle wine which already displays a delicious array of flavours and a little mid-palate richness. It would be a good match for sushi.

Zilzie Buloke Reserve Sauvignon Blanc

Quality	▼▼▼⁀
Value	★★★★
Grapes	sauvignon blanc
Region	Murray Valley, NSW
Cellar	🍾 1
Alc./Vol.	11.5%
RRP	$10.00 Ⓢ

Winemaker at Zilzie is Bob Shields, who's been around the Riverland wine industry for yonks. He was the winemaker who originally put Alambie/Salisbury Estate on the map.
CURRENT RELEASE 2002   Ripe, non-pungent, warm-climate sauvignon blanc flavours, here – nothing green or vegetal. It's a light wine with straw/hay and melon aromas that are clean and fresh, but fairly straightforward, and the palate is soft, dry and well-balanced. Try it with avocado and salad.

Zilzie Show Reserve Chardonnay

Quality	▼▼▼▼⁀
Value	★★★★★
Grapes	chardonnay
Region	Murray Valley, Vic.
Cellar	🍾 2
Alc./Vol.	13.0%
RRP	$16.50

The Forbes family has farmed at Zilzie Estate in north-western Victoria since 1911. Their wine involvement is quite recent; they now have a fully fledged winery and Bob Shields is chief winemaker.
CURRENT RELEASE 2002   It's hard to believe this was made from Riverland fruit, so refined, subtle and classy it is. It has beguiling aromas of passionfruit and citrus with subtle use of oak, and the finish is delicious despite slightly harsh acidity. Overall, it's quite soft and should be good with food. We'd suggest cold smoked chicken and salad.

Zilzie Viognier

Surprising things can happen when modern viticulture and winemaking methods are intelligently applied to hot, dry-land viticulture. The Forbes family of Zilzie have turned many heads this past two years, since their dramatic appearance on the wine market.
CURRENT RELEASE 2002   This tastes like the viognier grape should taste. It's distinctly varietal and would put quite a lot of more expensive efforts in the shade. It smells rich and spicy, with traces of honey and apricots. There's no evidence of oak, but it has good texture and some warmth from alcohol, plus a lot of style and good balance. It would go well with roast chicken in a rich sauce.

Quality	♥♥♥♥
Value	★★★★⸴
Grapes	viognier
Region	Murray Valley, Vic.
Cellar	▮ 1
Alc./Vol.	13.0%
RRP	$14.00 ⓢ

Sparkling Wines

All Saints Carlyle Sparkling Shiraz

Quality	🍷🍷🍷🍷
Value	★★★♦
Grapes	shiraz
Region	Rutherglen, Vic.
Cellar	🍾 2
Alc./Vol.	14.0%
RRP	$25.00

North-east Victoria can produce a good sparkling red; perhaps the slightly jammy thing that's a regional characteristic fits well with this mellow wine style. CURRENT RELEASE 2000   On the nose there's a smooth stewed-berries aroma along with a slight earthiness, some vitamin B tablet yeastiness from bottle-fermentation and toasty touches from oak. In the mouth it's rich with attractive fruitcakey flavours. Sweetness is well-controlled and smoky oak and firm tannins support it well. It finishes dry and slightly firm. Try it with pork ribs and plum sauce.

Andrew Garrett Sparkling Shiraz

Quality	🍷🍷🍷🍷
Value	★★★
Grapes	shiraz
Region	not stated
Cellar	🍾 2
Alc./Vol.	14.0%
RRP	$21.85

This has been around for a while, perhaps reflecting how hard it is to flog some sparkling reds. On the back label it says that it was 'bottle-fermented in time for the best celebrations of the millennium'. CURRENT RELEASE 1998   There are a lot of South Australian red wine smells here and there's also a slight mushroomy touch that suggests some lees ageing. The nose has dark-berry, earth and sweet-oak aromas, and the palate is robustly flavoured. Sweetness is middling and it finishes with dry but balanced tannins. Serve it with a prune-stuffed loin of pork.

Andrew Garrett Vintage Chardonnay Pinot Noir

Andrew Garrett, the man, now has nothing to do with Andrew Garrett, the wine company. The company is now part of the Beringer Blass group, and Garrett has a new entity called Andrew Garrett Vineyard Estates. Confused?

CURRENT RELEASE 1999   A pretty good sparkler for the price. The bead is fine and the nose is subtle with apple, citrus and a hint of praline to it. In the mouth it has fine dry flavour, not bolstered by sweetness like some of its competitors, and a smooth, creamy feel, counterpointed by a zesty crispness at the end. Serve it as an aperitif.

Quality	🍷🍷🍷🍷
Value	★★★★
Grapes	chardonnay; pinot noir
Region	not stated
Cellar	🍷 2
Alc./Vol.	11.5%
RRP	$19.50

Bay of Fires Pinot Noir Chardonnay

BRL Hardy's Bay of Fires winery, which is the renamed Rochecombe, is operated by young winemaker Fran Austin. This bubbly would have been put together by BRL Hardy's former white winemaker Glenn James and sparkling winemaker Ed Carr.

CURRENT RELEASE 1997   There is a complex, slightly rubbery aged character about it, but this wine is full of personality, reflecting its considerable time (four years) on yeast lees. The palate has richness and body, with a superb array of flavours and finishes with excellent balance. It would do justice to cheese puffs.

Quality	🍷🍷🍷🍷🍷
Value	★★★★
Grapes	pinot noir; chardonnay
Region	Tasmania 82% & Yarra Valley, Vic. 18%
Cellar	🍷 2
Alc./Vol.	12.0%
RRP	$27.00

Bindi Cuvée Two Chardonnay Pinot Noir

Bindi describes its wines as 'multi-vintage', and this is an authentic way of describing the blending process – a combination of vintages from 1993 to '96 is disgorged after six years on the sediment.

CURRENT RELEASE *non-vintage*   An extreme style, emphasising aged complexity at the expense, some might say, of freshness and primary fruit. A deep yellow colour, it has some sherry-like aldehyde characteristics, but also great complexity of dried fruit, dried-wildflower and roasted-hazelnut aromas. It's a big wine with masses of flavour and personality. The finish is clean and lingers on. It's dry without harshness or phenolic grip. A delicious drink with smoked chicken and salad.

Quality	🍷🍷🍷🍷🍷
Value	★★★⯪
Grapes	chardonnay; pinot noir
Region	Macedon Ranges, Vic.
Cellar	🍷 1
Alc./Vol.	12.0%
RRP	$35.00 (cellar door)

Brown Brothers King Valley Pinot Chardonnay NV

Quality	🍷🍷🍷🍷
Value	★★★★
Grapes	pinot noir; chardonnay
Region	King Valley, Vic.
Cellar	2
Alc./Vol.	12.0%
RRP	$17.80 (S)

PENGUIN BEST BARGAIN BUBBLY

The higher altitudes of the King Valley seem well suited to sparkling base-wines, and Browns have started to bag some major show trophies with their vintage cuvées.

CURRENT RELEASE *non-vintage* A good-value everyday bubbly with a hint of greenness to its fruit, but also some attractive champagne-like character. It has a lively mousse and hints of candy and meringue, plus some greener herbal aspects. In the mouth it's smooth, and dry with very good drinkability. Delish with almond bread.

Chandon Rosé Vintage Brut

Quality	🍷🍷🍷🍷🍷
Value	★★★★
Grapes	pinot noir 53%; chardonnay 45%; pinot meunier 2%
Region	various cool vineyards across southern Australia
Cellar	2
Alc./Vol.	12.5%
RRP	$33.00 (S)

PENGUIN BEST SPARKLING WINE

In some key export markets Australian Chandon sparkling wines are known as Green Point, to avoid confusion with the other Moet et Chandon subsidiaries. Rumour has it that Moet think the Aussie Chandon the best outside France.

CURRENT RELEASE 1998 This '98 edition of the onion-skin pink Chandon is up there with the best of the breed. The complex nose is a rich melange of red fruits, vanilla bean and smoky pinot noir. It has great depth and full, smoky, yeasty flavour, and the palate is seriously structured, dry and firm. This is a wine for serious food, try with grilled salmon cutlets.

Chandon Vintage Brut

Quality	🍷🍷🍷🍷
Value	★★★
Grapes	chardonnay 49%; pinot noir 46%; pinot meunier 5%
Region	various cool vineyards across southern Australia
Cellar	2
Alc./Vol.	12.7%
RRP	$33.00 (S)

Last year Chandon sparkling wines enjoyed a 30 per cent sales increase, and why not? Quality is excellent.

CURRENT RELEASE 1998 A well-made, classy sparkle, although possibly not quite up to the standard of some past vintages. A complex bouquet with biscuit and vanilla-cream aromas is woven into fine fruit, and the palate is creamy-smooth and long-tasting. A little broader and less elegant in the mouth than usual, but it's still a sparkling wine of a high standard that won't disappoint too much. We suggest it as a festive aperitif.

Cofield Sparkling Shiraz

Max Cofield is Rutherglen's sparkling red man, producing some good red bubblies for an increasing number of fans.
CURRENT RELEASE 2000   This has medium depth of colour and a lasting, fine bead. The nose has red and blackberry aromas that are sweetly appealing, rich, and complex with hints of earth and leather. In the mouth it's hearty in flavour and a little drier than some of its brethren. Ripe, fine-grained tannins add dimension to the palate and it finishes long and savoury. A good sparkling burg to enjoy with glazed and baked ham.

Quality	🍷🍷🍷🍷
Value	★★★
Grapes	shiraz
Region	Rutherglen, Vic.
Cellar	3
Alc./Vol.	14.6%
RRP	$29.00

Croser

Croser is blended in the Champagne manner from various vineyards of different aspect that bring certain characteristics to the blend. In good vintages it excels in finesse.
CURRENT RELEASE 2000   Typically reserved and undeveloped, this pale sparkler is very classy. It has a very fine, persistent mousse and beautifully pure, refined aromas. The nose has light citrus and macaroon touches, and it's low in bottle-ferment, yeast-derived influence, only adding the lightest trace of vanilla and biscuit. The palate is superfine and delicate with spring-like freshness that lasts long in the mouth. A fine aperitif.

Quality	🍷🍷🍷🍷
Value	★★★
Grapes	pinot noir; chardonnay
Region	Adelaide Hills, SA
Cellar	4
Alc./Vol.	12.5%
RRP	$36.00

Dalrymple Blanc de Blancs

Bertel and Anne Sundstrup established their 10-hectare vineyard in 1987. Anne's sister Jill Mitchell runs cellar-door sales. Their father Bill Mitchell established a famous early Tamar Valley vineyard, Tamarway, in the early '70s. They still make a wine from it.
CURRENT RELEASE 1998   Definite chardonnay character here: it's a fine, soft, peachy style of fizz, without a great deal of secondary complexities, but it is terrifically youthful, fresh and vibrant, with marvellous acidity. It's just the thing for raw oysters.

Quality	🍷🍷🍷
Value	★★★
Grapes	chardonnay
Region	Pipers River, Tas.
Cellar	3+
Alc./Vol.	11.8%
RRP	$30.00

Deakin Estate Brut

Quality	🍷🍷
Value	★★★↓
Grapes	mainly chardonnay
Region	Murray Valley, Vic.
Cellar	🍾 1
Alc./Vol.	13.0%
RRP	$10.00 ⑤

The Riverland may not be the ideal place to grow grapes for bubbly, but Deakin Estate doesn't overreach itself. They release the wine young and capitalise on its fresh fruit, and don't try to get yeast lees or age-derived complexity into the wine.

CURRENT RELEASE *non-vintage*   It's pale yellow in colour and is fairly plain and neutral to smell, while the palate is clean, fresh and again fairly simple, but at least it's light, refreshing and undemanding. It finishes fairly dry, considering its price point and aspirations. It's a well-made bubbly to serve with pretzels and chips.

Eaglehawk Sparkling Chardonnay

Quality	🍷🍷
Value	★★★
Grapes	chardonnay
Region	not stated
Cellar	🍾 1
Alc./Vol.	10.5%
RRP	$10.00 ⑤

Eaglehawk wines are at the bottom end of the Wolf Blass pyramid. We prefer the Eaglehawk still table wine to this sparkling, but it's a passable drink on a tight budget.

CURRENT RELEASE *non-vintage*   The nose is fruity and grapey in a way that almost suggests some muscaty input. In the mouth it has soft stone-fruit flavour with a hint of residual sugar and a crisp finish. A simple sparkling wine of no great fault, but no great distinction either. Take it to the in-laws' place.

Elderton Ashmead Family Reserve Sparkling Shiraz NV

Quality	🍷🍷🍷
Value	★★★
Grapes	shiraz
Region	Barossa Valley, SA
Cellar	🍾 3
Alc./Vol.	13.5%
RRP	$48.00

Sparkling burgundy is an Aussie icon, so it's entirely appropriate to celebrate special events with it. This red fizz was produced to commemorate Elderton's twenty-first vintage.

CURRENT RELEASE *non-vintage*   This has a good fine bubble and a mature red colour. The nose shows maturity in slightly leathery aromas and mellow smells of spicy dark fruitcake. A touch of oak is there, but it doesn't take over. In the mouth it's smooth with notable sweetness and a slightly hard finish. Serve it with profiteroles and chocolate sauce (we're serious).

Fox Creek Vixen

When the parties of visiting foreign wine media and buyers tour Australian wine regions they are invariably plied with sparkling red as the wine to relax with after a day's yakka. They go away thinking Australians are a very odd breed indeed.

CURRENT RELEASE *non-vintage*   This is a young, bold, straightforward sparkling red with an impressive purple–red colour and a high-impact fruit-and-oak aroma. Spiced plums, dark chocolate and oak are uppermost, with some earthy regional notes. It certainly has rich fruit but it needs more age and mellowness. Try it with Cantonese honey-glazed pork.

Quality	♟ ♟ ♟ ♟
Value	★ ★ ★
Grapes	shiraz; cabernet franc
Region	McLaren Vale, SA
Cellar	▯ 5+
Alc./Vol.	14.0%
RRP	$23.00

Grant Burge Pinot Noir Chardonnay

This wine has changed style to a pale pink, almost a light rosé style. Because pinot noir is a red grape, it's not unusual for it to leave a faint pink tinge, even in sparkling wines that aren't intended as rosé styles.

CURRENT RELEASE *non-vintage*   The smoky, pinoty aromas go hand-in-hand with the pale pink colour and the wine tastes quite youthful, with a trace of sweetness from the expedition liqueur. As usual, it is a high-quality, well-balanced bubbly and excellent value for money. Try salmon gravlax.

Quality	♟ ♟ ♟ ♟
Value	★ ★ ★ ★
Grapes	pinot noir; chardonnay
Region	not stated
Cellar	▯ 2
Alc./Vol.	12.0%
RRP	$20.00

Hanging Rock Macedon

The eighth Hanging Rock cuvée is based on vintages spanning eleven years, 1987–97. A true multi-vintage, the aged complexity of the older components introduces extra character to the blend.

CURRENT RELEASE *non-vintage Cuvée 8*   This is a brilliant wine, although its extreme aged character polarises technocrat tasters. The colour is deep yellow–gold, and it smells of roasted hazelnuts (a bit like an old chardonnay), breads both toasted and freshly baked, as well as smoky, biscuity inflexions. The palate is extremely dry, quite rich, and very complex. It's at the big and mature end of the spectrum. Try it with pan-fried fish entrée, or even quail canapés.

Quality	♟ ♟ ♟ ♟ ♟
Value	★ ★ ★ ⬩
Grapes	pinot noir; chardonnay
Region	Macedon Ranges, Vic.
Cellar	▯ 1
Alc./Vol.	12.5%
RRP	$41.50

Hardys Arras Chardonnay Pinot Noir

Quality	🍷🍷🍷🍷
Value	★ ★ ★
Grapes	chardonnay; pinot noir
Region	mainly Tasmania
Cellar	⬥ 1–3
Alc./Vol.	12.5%
RRP	$53.00

A bronze-medal winner at the 2002 Royal Adelaide Wine Show, while the Sir James '98 Vintage scored gold. We saw the wines the same way. Perhaps the Arras should have been kept longer on lees – but then, five years is quite a while!

CURRENT RELEASE 1997   The colour is medium yellow with a brassy tinge, and the aromas are of subtle pastry and earthy scents, just a trifle subdued. Likewise the palate: it's delicate, subtle, restrained, with refinement and balance, it just isn't singing at this stage. (Two bottles sampled.) You could try it with choux pastries filled with mushroom.

Hardys Omni

Quality	🍷🍷🍷
Value	★ ★ ★ ⟩
Grapes	not stated
Region	not stated
Cellar	🍾 1
Alc./Vol.	12.0%
RRP	$12.00 Ⓢ

This has wowed us from time to time, not with its dazzling quality mind you, but its keen value for money. It's a lovely mouthful of fizz for a tenner (on special).

CURRENT RELEASE *non-vintage*   The colour was medium–light yellow with brassy reflections, suggesting our sample had been in its bottle for some time. This impression was confirmed by the nose, which was somewhat developed and had lost its freshness. The palate had simple, light flavour without much depth or interest, ending with a lick of sweetness. It had pleasant balance and good drinkability. Hopefully, your bottle will be fresher! Serve it with vol au vents at a party.

Hardys Sir James Pinot Noir Chardonnay

Quality	🍷🍷🍷🍷🍷
Value	★ ★ ★ ★ ★
Grapes	pinot noir; chardonnay
Region	Yarra Valley, Vic. & Tasmania
Cellar	🍾 2
Alc./Vol.	12.5%
RRP	$25.00 Ⓢ

This wine often trumps the far more expensive Arras in shows and other blind tastings. It's because Sir James Vintage is accessible, up-front, open and obvious, while Arras is an exercise in delicacy and is built to last.

CURRENT RELEASE 1998   This seems a more subtle, restrained, chardonnay-driven style than previous vintages. It has a complex eggy, lemon/citrus and grass/hay aroma, which is very chardonnay-like, and the taste is fine and taut, clean and subtle. The liqueur sweetness is well-integrated. We loved the focus, intensity and direct fruit character of this wine. It would suit oysters with a lemony Thai dressing.

Hardys Sir James Sparkling Shiraz

If sparkling wine is the epitome of the blender's art, this is a good example of that art. It's a mixture of several regions and, we suppose, several vintages. Makers: Ed Carr and team.

CURRENT RELEASE *non-vintage*   The colour is dark blood-red and it has a vigorous mousse. The aromas remind of sweet, ripe blood plum and black cherry and there is a touch of oak giving a mocha aspect. The high-impact palate has quite a belt of tannin as well as gas and acid, and it goes remarkably well with the right sort of food, such as smoked salmon with leek salad.

Quality	♀♀♀♀
Value	★★★♦
Grapes	shiraz
Region	McLaren Vale 48%, Clare Valley 45%, Padthaway 4% & other 3%, SA
Cellar	🍶 4
Alc./Vol.	14.0%
RRP	$27.00

Houghton Pemberton Chardonnay Pinot Noir

This is one of the new Houghton regional range. We reviewed it last year but it's still current and we think it's worth another look. Maker: Larry Cherubino.

CURRENT RELEASE 1998   There's an intriguing bacony character that may be a whisper of sulfide: whatever, it adds extra complexity to the bouquet, which also has meringue and smoky, meaty pinot noir characters. The palate is light in weight and has real delicacy and style. The finish is clean and balanced with a smidge of sweetness from the expedition liqueur. It would be delicious with gravlax of trout.

Quality	♀♀♀♀♀
Value	★★★★
Grapes	chardonnay; pinot noir
Region	Pemberton, WA
Cellar	🍶 1
Alc./Vol.	13.0%
RRP	$27.00

Jansz Australia Premium Cuvée

You might expect this to be a Tasmanian wine, given the provenance of the brand, which is now owned by Yalumba. But it's a schizophrenic mixture of regions, including some Tasmania.

CURRENT RELEASE *non-vintage*   This is a very pleasant sparkler, with some smoky and bready development to sniff, reflecting some time on yeast lees, plus green-apple fruit. The palate is soft and open-knit, nicely balanced, and shows some sweetness from the expedition liqueur. The aftertaste is fairly dry, not all that complex, but it makes a good aperitif, with smoked oysters.

Quality	♀♀♀♀
Value	★★★♦
Grapes	chardonnay; pinot noir
Region	various, including Tas., SA & Vic.
Cellar	🍶 2
Alc./Vol.	12.0%
RRP	$23.00 ⑤

Jansz Tasmania Vintage

Quality	🍷🍷🍷🍷½
Value	★★★½
Grapes	pinot noir; chardonnay
Region	Pipers River, Tas.
Cellar	2
Alc./Vol.	12.5%
RRP	$37.50

We reviewed this last year but it is still current, so here we go again. The wine may be technically a year older but it's still fresh and maturing superbly.

CURRENT RELEASE 1997 A typically complex, developed Tasmanian bubbly, which emphasises complexities rather than primary fruit. There are creamy/buttery dairy characters from malolactic fermentation, plus roasted hazelnuts and in the mouth it has fine balance, with evident sweetness from the expedition liqueur which is harmonised by flavour and acidity. The aftertaste is clean, refreshing and very long.

Knappstein Chainsaw Sparkling Shiraz

Quality	🍷🍷🍷🍷
Value	★★★½
Grapes	shiraz
Region	Clare Valley, SA
Cellar	1–5
Alc./Vol.	14.0%
RRP	$26.00

These vines have been delicately 'pruned' with a chainsaw, twice. When shiraz was out of fashion they were chopped off and grafted over to chardonnay, then out came the saw again when shiraz made a comeback.

CURRENT RELEASE 2000 A raw youngster that needs a bit more schooling. Plum, meat, licorice and earthy characters are big, and there's a whisper of oak, but the complexity and interest that age brings to sparkling reds is only starting to build. The palate is smooth with balanced sweetness and a dry finish, but it needs bottle-age to be at its best. Try it with glazed pork chops.

Lake Barrington Alexandra

Quality	🍷🍷🍷🍷
Value	★★★½
Grapes	pinot noir; chardonnay
Region	northern Tas.
Cellar	3
Alc./Vol.	12.5%
RRP	$35.00

This tiny north-west Tasmanian vineyard is somewhat isolated from the state's other vineyards. Its public face is Maree Taylor, a Launceston dietician, whose father Barry Flude manages the vineyard. Alexandra is Maree's young daughter.

CURRENT RELEASE 1998 With contract winemaker Steve Lubiana's help, Lake Barrington has made a succession of excellent bubblies, and this is one of the best. Minerally, slatey aromas arise from the glass together with meaty, lees-aged pinot noir characters. The palate has delicacy as well as softness, and a pleasingly fine texture, finishing with balanced acidity. Try it with sushi.

Majella Sparkling Shiraz

More and more wineries are making a sparkling red. Standards are generally very high but we often wonder (1) when you drink 'em, (2) what you drink 'em with, and (3) who you drink 'em with. Irate fans answer: (1) anytime, (2) anything, and (3) with anyone. CURRENT RELEASE 2001   A lush aroma that reminds us of juicy blackberries, spice and new leather is a good introduction. The palate is smooth and slightly sweet, yet clean and crisp. It has good length and a fine finish with soft tannins. A fresh style of sparkling shiraz to sip, with anything and anyone at anytime.

Quality	♟ ♟ ♟ ♟
Value	★ ★ ★
Grapes	shiraz
Region	Coonawarra, SA
Cellar	▮ 2
Alc./Vol.	13.5%
RRP	$38.00

McWilliams Hanwood Pinot Noir Chardonnay Brut

The great value that comes under McWilliams' Hanwood label extends to sparkling wine as well as table wine. This reasonably priced fizz has style well above its station.
CURRENT RELEASE *non-vintage*   There's a level of residual sugar in this sparkling wine that doesn't quite measure up to its 'Brut' tag; it's really too sweet for that. That doesn't mean it's an unattractive bubbly though, in fact the nose and palate are very appealing with lively stone-fruit and appley aromas, a whisper of smoky complexity and a soft smooth flavour. It signs off dry with commendable length. A great party wine.

Quality	♟ ♟ ♟ ♟
Value	★ ★ ★ ★ ↓
Grapes	pinot noir; chardonnay
Region	Riverina, NSW
Cellar	▮ 1
Alc./Vol.	12.0%
RRP	$11.50 ⑤

McWilliams Hanwood Sparkling Shiraz

All the big companies do a sparkling red these days, and a competitive new market niche has been created by good, budget-priced examples like Hanwood.
CURRENT RELEASE *non-vintage*   This is a lighter, gentler type of sparkling red than the hearty styles that have so many fans. The bubble is persistent and the nose has cherry and vanilla aromas of fresh, easy appeal. In the mouth there's controlled sweetness, and the smooth texture and soft tannins make it very likeable. It would suit bacon-wrapped prunes off the barbecue.

Quality	♟ ♟ ♟ ♟
Value	★ ★ ★ ★ ↓
Grapes	shiraz
Region	Riverina, NSW
Cellar	▮ 1
Alc./Vol.	12.5%
RRP	$11.50 ⑤

Meeting Place Chardonnay Pinot Noir Pinot Meunier

Quality	🍷🍷🍷🍷
Value	★★★★⅃
Grapes	pinot noir 47%; chardonnay 37%; pinot meunier 16%
Region	Tumbarumba, NSW
Cellar	🍷 2
Alc./Vol.	12.0%
RRP	$14.95 Ⓢ

This bubbly from BRL Hardy comes from Tumbarumba, another of the new cool-climate New South Wales vineyards. It benefits from the legendary Ed Carr touch that's evident right across the company's sparkling wine portfolio.

CURRENT RELEASE 2000   Here's a sparkling wine with quality well beyond its price tag. It smells rich and nutty with a heart of citrus and stewed pear-like fruit aromas, trimmed in slightly bready notes. The palate is full and nutty with surprising length and a snappy thread of mouth-watering acidity to keep it fresh. Serve it with little seafood pastries.

Morris Sparkling Shiraz Durif

Quality	🍷🍷🍷🍷
Value	★★★★
Grapes	shiraz; durif
Region	Rutherglen, Vic.
Cellar	🍷 5
Alc./Vol.	14.0%
RRP	$19.00

The legendary Rutherglen durif doesn't just make big tarry reds, it's also a good base for sparkling burgundy. Morris leads the way with this worthwhile shiraz-durif blend.

CURRENT RELEASE *non-vintage*   A more rustic sparkling red than most of the non-Rutherglen breed. The colour shows some age, and the nose combines syrupy-sweet berry aromas with a hint of licorice and a touch of the barnyard. It adds up to complexity, and the palate follows through with full, round flavour based on fruit sweetness and depth. The sweetness mid-palate is tempered by balanced dry tannins, and the finish is long and tasty. Enjoy it with cheddar.

Mount William Macedon

Quality	🍷🍷🍷🍷⅃
Value	★★★★
Grapes	chardonnay
Region	Macedon Ranges, Vic.
Cellar	🍷 2
Alc./Vol.	12.0%
RRP	$30.00

Like many Macedon Ranges vignerons, Murray Cousins of Mount William makes upmarket bottle-fermented sparkling wine. As French counterparts in Champagne have found, it can be hard to ripen grapes for table wines in such cool climes, but for fizzies it's just right.

CURRENT RELEASE 1999   A lively appearance with a foamy, creaming mousse. The nose is fresh and subtle with apple, citrus and lightly nutty bottle-ferment aromas. In the mouth it's fine and delicate in flavour and tingly with high acidity. Some might be sensitive to that acidity, but the rest should enjoy this crisp wine as a zappy aperitif.

Orlando Jacob's Creek Chardonnay Pinot Noir Brut Cuvée

Amazingly this wine won a gold medal at the Cairns
Wine Show. We are dumbfounded!
CURRENT RELEASE *non-vintage*   Orlando's Trilogy
sparkler is a better buy than this label, judging by our
sample. The Jacob's Creek moniker will guarantee its
success, whatever we think. The nose is rather neutral
with light appley fruit of only moderate intensity. The
palate has fresh apple and citrus flavours that are crisp,
light and simple. A good wine to serve at a party.

Quality	♟ ♟ ♟
Value	★ ★ ★
Grapes	chardonnay; pinot noir
Region	not stated
Cellar	▮ 1
Alc./Vol.	12.0%
RRP	$12.00 Ⓢ

Orlando Trilogy

Consistently one of the best of the inexpensive
bubblies, Trilogy looks the goods too, with smart
packaging giving it a classy feel.
CURRENT RELEASE *non-vintage*   This hits the spot
with smooth tropical and citrus fruit plus some lightly
toasty hints. In the mouth it's creamy and soft with a
little trace of sweetness to aid easy drinkability. Try it
with canapés.

Quality	♟ ♟ ♟ ♟
Value	★ ★ ★ ★
Grapes	pinot noir; chardonnay; pinot meunier
Region	not stated
Cellar	▮ 1
Alc./Vol.	12.0%
RRP	$14.90 Ⓢ

Pirie Pinot Noir Chardonnay

What will become of the Pirie sparkling now that its
namesake has left the company? It's a bit like Andrew
Garrett without the man.
CURRENT RELEASE 1997   The '97s in Tassie seem
to be a fairly high-acid, austere crop of bubblies. This
has a full yellow colour, showing some maturity, and
a certain herbaceous or silage-like character that is
typical of Tassie wines in cool years. There's a trace
of greenness in the wine and this shows in the finish,
which is a touch hard. The finish doesn't carry as
well as we'd have liked. It would go with crab and
avocado timbale.

Quality	♟ ♟ ♟ ♟
Value	★ ★ ★
Grapes	pinot noir; chardonnay
Region	Pipers River, Tas.
Cellar	▮ 2
Alc./Vol.	12.0%
RRP	$53.80

Radenti Chardonnay Pinot Noir

Quality	♟♟♟♟♟
Value	★★★★⟩
Grapes	chardonnay; pinot noir
Region	East Coast, Tas.
Cellar	🍾 2
Alc./Vol.	12.0%
RRP	$34.00 (cellar door)

Freycinet is banned from using its own name on its sparkling wine, thanks to legal action by the Spanish fizz company Freixenet. The ban applies to *all* Freycinet's wines on the export market! Maker: Claudio Radenti.

CURRENT RELEASE 1997   This is an extreme style, an immensely complex bubbly which is heavily influenced by malolactic fermentation, bottle-age, lees-contact and a little oak as well. It's very creamy and buttery, with toasty aged complexities. In the mouth it's very rich, full-bodied and multi-layered, showing a little biscuity character from barrels, and some Tassie 'silage' vegetal hints. A rewarding drink: the finish goes on and on. Chicken satays would do.

Red Hill Estate Blanc de Blancs

Quality	♟♟♟♟
Value	★★★★
Grapes	chardonnay
Region	Mornington Peninsula, Vic.
Cellar	🍾 3
Alc./Vol.	13.0%
RRP	$25.00

Red Hill have decided to continue making separate blanc and noir styles, as they did in 1998, instead of the pinot noir–chardonnay blends of the past. They certainly are contrasting wines, and well illustrate the difference between the grape varieties.

CURRENT RLEASE 2000   This also has youth on its side, which emphasises the fresh, fruit-driven, zippy-acid style. It's very tangy and lean and the flavours and acidity on the palate are piercing. The discreet aromas are of melon rind and green apple. It's the perfect wine for freshly shucked oysters.

Red Hill Estate Blanc de Noirs

Quality	♟♟♟♟⟩
Value	★★★★
Grapes	pinot noir
Region	Mornington Peninsula, Vic.
Cellar	🍾 2
Alc./Vol.	13.0%
RRP	$30.00

The estate vineyard is one of the highest and coolest in the Mornington Peninsula, and is well-suited to producing fine sparkling wines. Winemaker is Michael Kyberd.

CURRENT RELEASE 1999   The red grapes give a much richer, fuller style of wine in contrast to the blanc de blancs. It has a smoky, bready pinot bouquet and tastes softer, richer and fruitier, and a slight impression of sweetness is apparent – from the combined effects of the pinot fruit and the expedition liqueur. A delicious wine of excellent balance, it would suit smoked salmon.

Rosemount Sparkling Chardonnay

This is a basic sparkling wine at a similarly unambitious, often discounted, price. With all the diamonds on Rosemount labels, no wonder it's a favourite with baseball-mad Americans.

CURRENT RELEASE *non-vintage*   The colour is light yellow and it has a very straightforward, neutral aroma that is reflected in the mouth flavour, which is similarly mono-dimensional. There's a trace of iced-pastry aroma. Yeast autolysis plays little part in the wine. It's soft and fairly liqueur-sweet to taste, and would do for elevenses with almond bread.

Quality	♥ ♥ ♥
Value	★ ★ ★
Grapes	chardonnay
Region	not stated
Cellar	▮ 1
Alc./Vol.	12.5%
RRP	$16.00 Ⓢ

Seaview Brut Vintage

Synonymous a generation ago with hearty, satisfying McLaren Vale cabernets, this once great Seaview name is now a Southcorp budget 'brand', best known for cheap sparkling wines like this one.

CURRENT RELEASE 2001   Inexpensive and popular, you could do a lot worse for a lot more dollars. The nose is pleasant with sweet fruit, nougat and a touch of biscuit. It tastes smooth and satisfying with slightly more weight than we expect from such wines. The finish is a tad hard, but it's good value. Use it as an all-rounder for parties or a sip in the garden on a hot day.

Quality	♥ ♥ ♥ ♥
Value	★ ★ ★ ★ ★
Grapes	not stated
Region	not stated
Cellar	▮ 1
Alc./Vol.	11.5%
RRP	$9.60 Ⓢ

Seaview Chardonnay Blanc de Blanc

Blanc de Blanc sparkling wines are usually finer, more delicate and lighter in texture than wines with pinot noir in the blend. In Seaview's case it's still quite a full style.

CURRENT RELEASE 1999   This has been in the market for a while now which hasn't done it any harm. The relative depth of yellowish colour here indicates a richer wine than many B de B types, and the nose confirms it with complex macaroon-like aromas. The palate is lighter than expected, pulling up a bit short with a rather firm touch of aldehyde at the end. Serve it with cheese goujeres.

Quality	♥ ♥ ♥ ♥
Value	★ ★ ★
Grapes	chardonnay
Region	not stated
Cellar	▮ 1
Alc./Vol.	12.5%
RRP	$21.00 Ⓢ

Seaview Pinot Noir Chardonnay Brut

Quality	▼▼▼▼
Value	★★★
Grapes	pinot noir; chardonnay
Region	not stated
Cellar	1
Alc./Vol.	12.5%
RRP	$21.00 Ⓢ

Through no fault of consumers or fans of its wine, the once great Seaview name has been sacrificed to brand rationalisation by successive Southcorp owners over the years. First came the debacle of it being renamed Edwards and Chaffey; now the brand is reserved exclusively for sparkling wines.
CURRENT RELEASE 1998 This has an explosive foaming bubble, and it has a very attractive personality. There are subtle stewed-apple and citrus-fruit characters folded into attractive biscuity and lightly toasty touches. It tastes creamy and long with easy complexity and a dry finish. Serve it with seafood pancakes.

Seaview Sparkling Shiraz

Quality	▼▼▼▼
Value	★★★
Grapes	shiraz
Region	not stated
Cellar	2
Alc./Vol.	12.5%
RRP	$9.60 Ⓢ

Sparkling red's fortunes have changed radically since it had a near-death experience a couple of decades ago. Now everybody seems to be making one and they cover all price points, from the staggeringly expensive to cheapies like Seaview.
CURRENT RELEASE non-vintage This no-fuss sparkling red has a sweetly fruited nose of red berries and a hint of licorice. In the mouth it's pleasantly smooth with some berry sweetness and chocolatey notes mid-palate, ahead of a soft, easy finish. A crowd-pleaser to enjoy with pâté and crusty bread.

Seppelt Fleur de Lys Pinot Noir Chardonnay

Quality	▼▼▼▼
Value	★★★★★
Grapes	pinot noir; chardonnay
Region	various, Vic. & NSW
Cellar	1
Alc./Vol.	12.5%
RRP	$12.60 Ⓢ

The Seppelt name used to be hidden away on the Fleur de Lys bottle, but now it's writ large on the label and capsule. A good thing, since few Australian wineries have anything like the sparkling-wine heritage of Seppelt.
CURRENT RELEASE non-vintage At the price, this is very good value. There's some nectarine-like fruit on the nose and evidence of bottle-ferment in a rich, nutty, biscuity overlay. The palate is smooth and creamy with good depth and a clean biscuity finish. A wine that seems to have stepped up a notch in the last year. Try it with little pre-dinner nibbles.

Seppelt Fleur de Lys Vintage Pinot Noir Chardonnay

The senior Fleur de Lys has always been a favourite of ours in the value for money stakes. It used to be released with the amazing bonus of long age in Seppelt's cellars. The last vintage we saw was 1995, but the time machine has been accelerated to 1999 in this latest edition.

CURRENT RELEASE 1999   A pale sparkling wine with a fine bead that has a delicate bouquet of citrus, apples and pastry. There's some depth of character and a nice lick of bready flavour in the mouth, giving a dimension of smooth complexity. The flavour is long and firm-finishing. Try it with goujons of fish.

Quality	♥♥♥♥
Value	★★★★
Grapes	pinot noir; chardonnay
Region	not stated
Cellar	🍶 2
Alc./Vol.	12.5%
RRP	$18.00 ⑤

Seppelt Great Western Brut Reserve

Just how brut is brut? It's a term usually reserved for the very driest of sparkling wines, but lower-priced 'bruts' like Great Western Brut Reserve usually flirt with a little sweetness.

CURRENT RELEASE *non-vintage*   This is a pretty neutral sort of gargle with some citrus and a whisper of aldehyde on the nose. A simple palate has some soft sweetness in the middle to fill it out a bit. It finishes clean and fresh. Drink it at the car races.

Quality	♥♥◗
Value	★★★
Grapes	not stated
Region	not stated
Cellar	🍶
Alc./Vol.	11.5%
RRP	$8.25 ⑤

Seppelt Great Western Imperial Reserve

One of the authors has a bottle of this bought for a wedding in 1946. It wasn't opened for some reason and survives to this day, never to be opened for fear of what might be inside. We only mention it to illustrate how long Great Western Imperial Reserve has been a part of Australian wine culture.

CURRENT RELEASE *non-vintage*   This is an easy-to-like, unfussed sparkler with an appealing aroma that's a bit like tinned pears. It tastes smooth and likeable with soft flavours and an unintimidating finish. Something to stock up with, for a cork-poppin' sort of party.

Quality	♥♥♥
Value	★★★★
Grapes	not stated
Region	not stated
Cellar	🍶
Alc./Vol.	11.5%
RRP	$8.25 ⑤

Seppelt Original Sparkling Shiraz

Quality	♥♥♥♥♥
Value	★★★★★
Grapes	shiraz
Region	Barossa Valley, SA & Great Western, Vic.
Cellar	🍾 4
Alc./Vol.	14.0%
RRP	$19.00 Ⓢ

No other example of sparkling red has the same iconic status as Seppelt, and few can match it for quality and value. It really is the genuine article.

CURRENT RELEASE 1998   The packaging may have changed but the product remains a great-value example of a very Aussie wine. The nose is very complex with raspberry, spice, earth and subtle bottle-ferment complexities, all tied together into a lovely 'winey' thing. In the mouth it's mellow and velvety, with a dab of sweetness, kept perfectly in balance with the subtle aged flavours and ripe, fine tannins. Perfect with a baked Christmas ham.

Seppelt Salinger

Quality	♥♥♥♥♥
Value	★★★★
Grapes	pinot noir; chardonnay
Region	not stated
Cellar	🍾 3
Alc./Vol.	12.5%
RRP	$28.00 Ⓢ

Salinger was conceived as a flagship sparkling wine, giving Seppelt a product to go head-to-head with swanky wines at the pricey end of the market. Despite its quality, it's become a discount brand, and now it's released much younger than before.

CURRENT RELEASE 2000   Southcorp have pushed the pedal to the metal with Salinger, accelerating from the 1995 vintage to the 2000 in the space of a year. This hasn't compromised it excessively – the 2000 still has real finesse. Citrus and apple characters are smoothly integrated with lightly bready touches into a subtle, long wine, and it has an appetising, gentle tang. A fine aperitif.

Seppelt Show Sparkling Shiraz

Quality	♥♥♥♥♥
Value	★★★⁍
Grapes	shiraz
Region	Great Western, Vic.
Cellar	🍾 4
Alc./Vol.	13.0%
RRP	$65.00

Many claim that this is Australia's best sparkling red and we wouldn't argue. It's the granddaddy of them all, consistently of excellent quality, with form on the board over many decades, and it ages improbably well.

CURRENT RELEASE 1991   An aged dark brick-red colour testifies to its 12 years, and the nose has tons of bottle-aged complexity. There are suggestions of leather, berry jam, earth, warm spices and old oak that conjure up thoughts of a bygone age. In the mouth it's velvet-smooth, with great length of complex, subtly rich flavour. Nothing is obvious, but it fascinates you long after simpler wines have palled. Serve it with roast turkey.

Starvedog Lane Chardonnay Pinot Noir Pinot Meunier

The first German settlers in South Australia established themselves at Starvedog Lane. They spread out to found Hahndorf and other settlements in the Adelaide Hills and elsewhere. Wine was often a part of their culture.
CURRENT RELEASE 1999   This has a pale colour and a fine, creamy foam. On the nose there's light fruit with a savoury touch that hints at parsley or celery. There are also some minerally notes and only a little biscuity bottle-ferment character. It tastes dry with pleasant mouth-filling texture, yet quite delicate cool-climate fruit flavours. The finish is very long, fragrant and clean. Serve it with cucumber sandwiches.

Quality	🍷🍷🍷🍷🍷
Value	★★★⟩
Grapes	chardonnay; pinot noir; pinot meunier
Region	Adelaide Hills, SA
Cellar	🍾 2
Alc./Vol.	12.0%
RRP	$28.50

Stoniers Cuvée

A chardonnay–pinot sparkling wine is a logical extension of the Stonier range, and it gives the winery team something to sip at the end of the vintage. Maker: Tod Dexter.
CURRENT RELEASE 1999   A good first effort, this bubbly has a real touch of classical charm. The nose combines eggy chardonnay aromas with patisserie, vanilla and biscuity touches. It tastes smooth and dry, with very fine texture, persistent flavour and a tart, tangy finish. Excellent as an aperitif, perhaps with some oysters.

Quality	🍷🍷🍷🍷🍷
Value	★★★⟩
Grapes	chardonnay; pinot noir
Region	Mornington Peninsula, Vic.
Cellar	🍾 2
Alc./Vol.	13.5%
RRP	$45.00

Taltarni Brut NV

This has become a single-vintage wine, much as Yellowglen's standard wines have. Market research must dictate that bubbly drinkers like a year on their labels, for what it's worth.
CURRENT RELEASE 2000   The blend of Pyrenees and Clover Hill is proving a winning formula for Taltarni. It has a smoky, earthy, straw-like pinot-dominant bouquet that is quite complex and intriguing. It has a deal of richness in the mouth and we like its generosity of flavour, even if it lacks a little finesse. It tastes fairly full-bodied, as though the alcohol is on the higher side. Serve it with devils on horseback.

Quality	🍷🍷🍷
Value	★★★★
Grapes	chardonnay; pinot noir
Region	Pyrenees, Vic. & Pipers River, Tas.
Cellar	🍾 1
Alc./Vol.	13.0%
RRP	$20.00 Ⓢ

Tamar Ridge Josef Chromy Selection Blanc de Noirs

Quality	🍷🍷🍷🍷🍷
Value	★★★★
Grapes	pinot noir
Region	Pipers River, Tas.
Cellar	🍾 3
Alc./Vol.	12.0%
RRP	$38.00

Joe Chromy owns the Kayena vineyard on the Tamar River, and he has quickly established Tamar Ridge as an outstanding producer. Stop Press: Chromy has just sold Tamar Ridge to the Gunn's timber people.
CURRENT RELEASE 1996   A superbly complex, character-filled bubbly. At nearly seven years it still has a light yellow hue, and the bouquet is filled with smoky, marshmallow, biscuity, grilled-nut and honeysuckle complexities. The acid level is high but the palate is creamy-textured and fine. The balance is impeccable and the wine shows no sign of tiring. Try it with grilled scampi.

Tamar Ridge TRV

Quality	🍷🍷🍷🍷
Value	★★★⸺
Grapes	pinot noir; chardonnay
Region	Tamar Valley, Tas.
Cellar	🍾 3
Alc./Vol.	12.0%
RRP	$25.00

This is the 'regular' Tamar Ridge bubbly, disgorged a little earlier than the blanc de noirs. The acid certainly betrays its cool-climate origins. Maker: Michael Fogarty.
CURRENT RELEASE 1997   A tangy Taswegian, with high acid typical of cool climates, and chardonnay-led aromas of iced pastries, cream and eggs, with a hint of milk powder – probably from the malolactic fermentation. There are candy flavours, too, which translate onto the palate along with honeysuckle. It shows some mellowing from maturity, but the finish is quite steely. It has good persistence, and would drink well with raw oysters.

Touchwood Coal River Cuvée

Quality	🍷🍷🍷🍷🍷
Value	★★★★
Grapes	pinot noir; chardonnay
Region	Coal Valley, Tas.
Cellar	🍾 3+
Alc./Vol.	12.5%
RRP	$28.00 (mail order)

This won the trophy for the best sparkler at the 2003 Tasmanian Regional Wine Show. The vineyard was planted 10 years ago by Peter and Tina Sexton, and the wines are made at Moorilla Estate by Michael Glover.
CURRENT RELEASE 1998   This fine, reserved sparkler is just starting to hit its straps, having built complexity and richness with age. The nose has mineral and yeast complexity, while the palate delivers excellent depth and persistence, with lovely softness and harmony. It's a fine balance between vibrant fruit and complexity due to lees-ageing and time in bottle. Serve with mushroom-filled puff pastries.

Trentham Estate Brut

The Murphy families run this operation at Red Cliffs. Patrick Murphy looks after the vineyards and Anthony Murphy makes the wines.

CURRENT RELEASE 2002   As you'd expect from a 2002 bubbly, this is a fruit style with no appreciable yeast influence nor developed character. Its colour is pale and it has a grapey, young, floral aroma, with perhaps even a suggestion of riesling. There's a hint of sweetness. It's delicate, fruity and young to taste, with crisp citrusy acidity and the zing and cut to go well with oysters.

Quality	♟ ♟ ♟
Value	★ ★ ★
Grapes	chardonnay; pinot noir
Region	Murray Valley, NSW
Cellar	▮ 1
Alc./Vol.	11.5%
RRP	$19.00 Ⓢ

Wolf Blass Chardonnay Pinot Noir

Wolf Blass came to Australia in the 1960s to make simple sparkling wine in the Barossa Valley. These days his name is borne by some altogether more flash drops like this keenly priced example.

CURRENT RELEASE *non-vintage*   A cleverly put together sparkling wine that offers great value, especially as it's sure to be discounted further at the big stores. It smells quite rich and serious with dry, candied-fruit aromas dressed up in richer yeasty notes. The palate is round and quite deeply flavoured, with bready touches adding character and interest. It finishes clean and dry. Try it with chicken sandwiches.

Quality	♟ ♟ ♟ ♟
Value	★ ★ ★ ★ ⁑
Grapes	chardonnay; pinot noir
Region	not stated
Cellar	▮ 1
Alc./Vol.	10.5%
RRP	$13.00 Ⓢ

Wolf Blass Vintage Pinot Noir Chardonnay

The Wolf Blass name isn't synonymous with sparkling wine, but we've been impressed with some of the flavoursome fizz that appears with the Blass name on it.

CURRENT RELEASE 1999   Pale, green-tinged straw in colour, this has citrus and green-apple aromas and a bit of toasty, nutty bottle-ferment complexity underneath. The palate has an easy feel with good depth, and flavour that's long, dry and satisfying. A flavoursome sparkler to enjoy with prosciutto.

Quality	♟ ♟ ♟ ♟
Value	★ ★ ★ ⁑
Grapes	pinot noir; chardonnay
Region	not stated
Cellar	▮ 2
Alc./Vol.	11.5%
RRP	$22.50

Wyndham Estate S222 Sparkling Chardonnay

Quality	🍷🍷🍷🥂
Value	★★★⯛
Grapes	chardonnay
Region	not stated
Cellar	🍷 1
Alc./Vol.	12.0%
RRP	$14.50 Ⓢ

Chardonnay makes excellent sparkling-wine base, and these days it finds its way into nearly all quality Aussie fizz, all the way up from the budget brands to the prestige cuvées.

CURRENT RELEASE *non-vintage*   A sharply priced sparkler that won't disappoint. The nose is clean and uncomplicated with pleasant citrus, peach and marshmallow aromas. The palate follows the straightforward, likeable theme without great complication. It's smooth and creamy with a little touch of sweetness in the middle. Balanced acid keeps it refreshing. A good wine to get a party going.

Yarrabank Cuvée

Quality	🍷🍷🍷🍷🥂
Value	★★★⯛
Grapes	chardonnay; pinot noir
Region	Yarra Valley & Mornington Peninsula, Vic.
Cellar	🍷 4
Alc./Vol.	12.5%
RRP	$35.00

The second Franco-Australian sparkling-wine enterprise to open in Victoria's Yarra Valley, Yarrabank doesn't make as much noise as its competing neighbour Chandon, but its wines are excellent.

CURRENT RELEASE 1999   Tasted not long after release, this is a wine that will benefit from a little age 'on the cork'. It's pale and foamy with a delicate smoky, slightly minerally aroma that's clean and inviting. The palate is rich and intense with lovely texture and vanilla-cream flavour that's very long and fine. Despite crisp acidity, the finish is soft and lingering. A first-class aperitif to serve with the freshest oysters.

Yellowglen Cuvée Victoria

Quality	🍷🍷🍷🍷🥂
Value	★★★
Grapes	pinot noir; chardonnay
Region	Adelaide Hills, SA
Cellar	🍷 2
Alc./Vol.	12.0%
RRP	$35.00

Yellowglen's top drop is bottled in an elegant, glitterylabelled, skittle-shaped bottle. Grapes for this and the rest of the Yellowglen range are sourced all over the place these days, rather than from the original Ballarat base.

CURRENT RELEASE 1999   Pale and very fizzy, Yellowglen's prestige cuvée is a delicate aperitif-style wine with a subtle nose of minerals, lightly honeyed fruit and nuts. In the mouth it has pleasantly crisp stonefruit and nutty flavours of good persistence and texture. It's subtle and quite refined, and to our mind the best Cuvée Victoria so far. A delicate aperitif to match sushi.

Yellowglen Vintage Crémant

'Crémant' means creaming. The term is reserved by the winemakers of Champagne for wines that are somewhat less explosively bubbly than the norm. At Yellowglen we think it means slightly sweet, as the effervescence in this crémant looks to be about the same as the standard sparklers.

CURRENT RELEASE 2000 Pale yellow–green in colour, this has a fairly persistent fine bubble, and a plain but clean nose of soft stone-fruit aromas. In the mouth it has smooth flavour and a round mouth-feel with a trace of sweetness providing a bit of interest mid-palate. The finish is crisp. Try it with cream cheese and fruit.

Quality 🍷🍷🍷½
Value ★★★
Grapes chardonnay; pinot noir
Region not stated
Cellar 1 bottle
Alc./Vol. 11.5%
RRP $17.85 (S)

Yellowglen Vintage Pinot Noir Chardonnay

These days Yellowglen is all things to all people, making everything from bargain-basement fizz to flash cuvées in suitably curvaceous bottles.

CURRENT RELEASE 2000 The colour here is a deeper straw than the Vintage Cremant, probably due to more pinot noir in the blend. It smells fresh and light with a pleasant creamy apple and citrus aroma. The palate is smooth with a lightly creamy feel to it, and a zesty touch of acidity to end with. A fresh party sparkler at a reasonable price.

Quality 🍷🍷🍷🍷
Value ★★★½
Grapes pinot noir; chardonnay
Region not stated
Cellar 1 bottle
Alc./Vol. 11.0%
RRP $17.85 (S)

Yellowglen Y

The big letter Y on the bottle has become a bit more stylised and there's more of a story on the back, but the package remains fashionably minimalist. This wine fits around the middle of the Yellowglen range.

CURRENT RELEASE *non-vintage* Bright-coloured and fine in bead, this looks the goods. The nose is simpler than we expected, with light citrus and apple aromas, and a little yeast lees influence. It tastes straightforward, clean and zippy, but perhaps too uncomplicated when some of the competition offer a good measure of complexity in this price point. Not bad though. Serve it before dinner.

Quality 🍷🍷🍷½
Value ★★½
Grapes chardonnay; pinot noir
Region not stated
Cellar 1 bottle
Alc./Vol. 11.5%
RRP $23.85 (S)

Fortified Wines

All Saints Museum Release Rare Muscat

Quality	🍷🍷🍷🍷🍷
Value	★★★
Grapes	red frontignac
Region	Rutherglen, Vic.
Cellar	🍾
Alc./Vol.	18.0%
RRP	$395.00 (500 ml)

These fantastic Rare fortifieds from All Saints have been repackaged in natty half-litre decanters, a bit like the 'pichet' you get in a French café. Here are superb, majestic wines worth doffing your hat for.

CURRENT RELEASE *non-vintage* The solera this is drawn from is over 70 years old, and it shows. This is exquisitely intense and profoundly aromatic and flavoursome. Toffee, raisin, vanilla caramel and dried muscatel characters combine in gorgeous harmony on nose and palate, and the aftertaste lasts forever. It's extremely expensive but wines like this are very rare. A superb example to serve with nougat and good coffee.

All Saints Museum Release Rare Tokay

Quality	🍷🍷🍷🍷🍷
Value	★★★
Grapes	muscadelle
Region	Rutherglen, Vic.
Cellar	🍾
Alc./Vol.	18.0%
RRP	$395.00 (500 ml)

When aficionados talk of the pinnacle of Rutherglen fortified wines, they always mention Chambers and Morris, but don't often include All Saints. We reckon these Museum Releases are among the crème de la crème.

CURRENT RELEASE *non-vintage* From a 40-year-old solera that's been quietly resting in the All Saints cellars, this is exquisite tokay. It has a khaki edge to nut-brown colour, and the nose is striking with malt, syrupy tea, burnt sugar and roasted nuts. In the mouth it's lush, very sweet and amazingly persistent in flavour, with a lovely nutty-sweet aftertaste. Great with nuts, dried fruit, and maybe coffee.

All Saints The Keep Muscat

The Keep is a new All Saints range of fortifieds that fits in at the more basic end of things, rather than amongst the ancient blends that are causing such excitement in the USA.

CURRENT RELEASE *non-vintage* This is a young muscat with fleshy muscatels, a hint of raisin and some lifted florals on the nose. The palate is very sweet with a syrupy dollop of essency, raisiny muscat in the middle and a lingering, sweet, Turkish-delight sort of finish. Definitely a fortified for the sweet tooth, but very attractive nevertheless. Serve it with vanilla ice-cream.

Quality	🍷🍷🍷🍷
Value	★★★½
Grapes	red frontignac
Region	Rutherglen, Vic.
Cellar	🍾
Alc./Vol.	18.0%
RRP	$26.00 (500 ml)

All Saints The Keep Tawny Port

All Saints winery is actually a castle and 'the keep' is a well-known Rutherglen landmark. Fortified wines sleep soundly beneath the battlements.

CURRENT RELEASE *non-vintage* The colour is a reddish mahogany. It smells of molasses, raisins and subtle spirit – more fruity and forward than most South Australian wines of similar type. There's a hint of dark chocolate as well, and the palate is warm, round and liqueurish. It finishes long with a nice nutty sweetness that turns dry at the end. Good with coffee and cake.

Quality	🍷🍷🍷🍷
Value	★★★★½
Grapes	grenache; shiraz; mourvèdre
Region	Rutherglen, Vic.
Cellar	🍾
Alc./Vol.	18.0%
RRP	$15.00

All Saints The Keep Tokay

The All Saints winery was built to the design of an old Scottish castle, the keep being the main tower, or stronghold, of a castle.

CURRENT RELEASE *non-vintage* This is a pleasant introduction to All Saints Rutherglen Tokay at a competitive price. It smells of honey, light malt and butterscotch with some clean fresh spirit behind it. In the mouth it's grapey-sweet with a lush feel that's really quite addictive. The aged depth that characterises the most ancient wines is absent here, instead it's forward and fresh with delicious length of toffee flavour that lingers long afterwards. Try it with coffee and dessert nougat.

Quality	🍷🍷🍷🍷
Value	★★★★½
Grapes	muscadelle
Region	Rutherglen, Vic.
Cellar	🍾
Alc./Vol.	18.0%
RRP	$26.00 (500 ml)

Baileys Founder Liqueur Muscat

Quality	♥♥♥♥
Value	★★★½
Grapes	red frontignac
Region	Glenrowan, Vic.
Cellar	▮
Alc./Vol.	18.0%
RRP	$20.20 ⑤

The rich red soils of Baileys Glenrowan vineyards are well-suited to both fortified and gutsy dry red grape production. The company is owned by Beringer Blass these days.

CURRENT RELEASE *non-vintage*   This is a charming young muscat, full of lovely raisiny, muscaty fruit and some aged complexity giving gunsmoke and toasty-nut characters. The colour is a nice deep walnut/russet red, with a tawny edge. The entry is rich and sweet, liqueury and unctuous, with some fiery spirit astringency. It's a pleasant drink although it won't raise the roof. It goes well with Meredith Blue cheese.

Baileys Founder Liqueur Tokay

Quality	♥♥♥½
Value	★★★
Grapes	muscadelle
Region	Glenrowan, Vic.
Cellar	▮
Alc./Vol.	18.0%
RRP	$20.20 ⑤

Why Founder, you might ask? Well, you might just founder if you have too much of it.

CURRENT RELEASE *non-vintage*   The colour is mid-russet to tawny, with youthful reddish glints. It smells more like tawny port than tokay: nutty and simple with an unusual red grapey aspect, plus some genuine toffee-apple, typical tokay flavour in the mouth. The palate is slightly fiery and hot, a little disjointed, with liberal sweetness coming to the rescue. A nice drink, with after-dinner caramels and espresso.

Baileys Founder Tawny Port

Quality	♥♥♥½
Value	★★★½
Grapes	not stated
Region	Glenrowan, Vic.
Cellar	▮
Alc./Vol.	18.0%
RRP	$20.20 ⑤

Baileys was established by Varley Bailey in 1870, in the Warby Ranges near Glenrowan, as the label reminds us.

CURRENT RELEASE *non-vintage*   This port is attractively reddish-russet coloured and the bouquet's dominant feature is a vinegar fly taint, which far from being a turn-off actually seems to add to the character and complexity of the wine. There is a hint of rancio although it's not a very old port. The palate is deeper, richer and more layered than many ports of its level, which is the style of north-east Victorian tawnies. It's nicely clean and reasonably dry to finish. It goes well with aged cheddar.

Benjamin Tawny Port

Ben Chaffey – the Benjamin, whose name is recorded for posterity on this port – had much to do with the establishment of irrigation along the Murray River, where Mildara, the company that produces this port, was founded.
CURRENT RELEASE *non-vintage* The colour is medium–light amber tawny and it smells light and simple, with some nutty port aromas but not a lot of complexity or aged character. It's light-bodied and pretty sweet in the mouth, without much of a finish. But it is a very decent drink and fair value at the price. It goes with dried fruits and nuts.

Quality	♟ ♟ ♟
Value	★ ★ ★
Grapes	not stated
Region	not stated
Cellar	🍾
Alc./Vol.	17.5%
RRP	$16.90 Ⓢ

Brown Brothers Liqueur Muscat

Why use 'liqueur' to describe these famous, natural, Australian wines? Liqueurs are, of course, not wines at all, but usually spirits-based drinks with added flavours.
CURRENT RELEASE *non-vintage* A more concentrated, obviously older wine than the Reserve, it has a medium–full tawny brown colour with an amber rim. The bouquet is rich, ripe and raisiny, with toffee and dried-muscatel character of real age and rancio. In the mouth the rich, profound and lusciously sweet flavours reverberate around the palate, intense and lingering, with a clean drying aftertaste. You'll want another sip! Great with brandied figs and mascarpone.

Quality	♟ ♟ ♟ ♟ ♟
Value	★ ★ ★ ★
Grapes	red frontignac
Region	north-east Vic.
Cellar	🍾
Alc./Vol.	18.0%
RRP	$28.60 (375 ml)

Brown Brothers Reserve Muscat

Browns call this cheaper wine their Reserve Muscat, while the better wine is just Liqueur Muscat. This one comes in a 750 ml bottle with a stopper; the other comes in a half-bottle with a full-length cork. Mysterious!
CURRENT RELEASE *non-vintage* Cork stoppers can suffer from cork taint; this year, the trace of dusty earthiness in the bouquet, coupled with a rather short finish, pointed to subliminal cork taint. We opened a second bottle, and the wine was much better. Still excellent value, with lots of sweet, youthful muscat fruit on both nose and palate, and rich raisiny palate flavours. Lovely with Meredith Blue cheese.

Quality	♟ ♟ ♟ ♟
Value	★ ★ ★ ★ ⅃
Grapes	red frontignac
Region	north-east Vic.
Cellar	🍾
Alc./Vol.	18.0%
RRP	$18.80

Brown Brothers Reserve Port

Quality 🍷🍷🍷
Value ★★★½
Grapes not stated
Region north-east Vic.
Cellar 🍾
Alc./Vol. 18.0%
RRP $14.80 ($)

We're not sure who this is reserved for, but it's the bottom of the Browns range in price terms.
CURRENT RELEASE *non-vintage* This is quite a respectable port at its price, with a deepish hue of burnished mahogany and a lot of youthful red reflections. It's very grapey and young, with vanilla, brandy spirit, chocolate and mint in the bouquet. It's very sweet to taste, and a little lollyish, finishing with some bitterness and heat from fiery spirit. Try it with dried fruits.

Brown Brothers Very Old Tokay

Quality 🍷🍷🍷🍷½
Value ★★★
Grapes muscadelle
Region north-east Vic.
Cellar 🍾
Alc./Vol. 18.0%
RRP $26.80 (375 ml)

This is a consistently pleasing wine which won our Best Fortified award five years ago, when it was $28 a full bottle. The price has risen and it's recently been repackaged in half-bottles, so it's not quite the amazing value it once was. But it's still good!
CURRENT RELEASE *non-vintage* The colour is burnished mahogany with a yellow rim, indicating genuine age. It has a lovely aroma of malt extract, with hints of cold tea-leaf and fish oil – all very tokay-like and very appealing. The taste is smooth and mellow, finely balanced and intensely flavoured, with plenty of liqueury sweetness. It concludes with drying acid and spirit that leaves your mouth clean and wanting more! It's great with stilton cheese.

Campbells Rutherglen Muscat

Quality 🍷🍷🍷🍷
Value ★★★½
Grapes red frontignac
Region Rutherglen, Vic.
Cellar 🍾
Alc./Vol. 17.5%
RRP $19.00 (375 ml)

This is the base level of liqueur muscat under Rutherglen's excellent four-rank classification. Winemaker Colin Campbell promoted the idea. And the classy conservative packaging is a plus.
CURRENT RELEASE *non-vintage* Youthful colour – a pinkish-red tawny – and a fresh raisiny, grapey aroma give a preview of the type of wine we have here. No great age, but it doesn't lack character. The nose also has a hint of Turkish delight to it, and it tastes sweet and raisiny with reasonable depth and smooth texture. Clean spirit adds its bit and it finishes sweet and clean. Try it with muscatels, nuts and cheese.

Chambers Dry Flor Sherry

There was a time when most Rutherglen wineries produced a broad range of sherries but these days only a couple keep the tradition alive. Bill Chambers is one of them.
CURRENT RELEASE *non-vintage*   This is a rather old-fashioned Australian dry flor style, unlike the lower-alcohol Spanish type. The nose has developed essency flor characters that give nutty, savoury notes, richer than the classic fino type. The palate is yeasty, nutty and slightly toasty with excellent depth and length, finishing long and dry. Serve it with canapés.

Quality	▮▮▮▮▮
Value	★★★★★
Grapes	palomino
Region	Rutherglen, Vic.
Cellar	▮
Alc./Vol.	18.0%
RRP	$15.00

Chambers Grand Rutherglen Muscat

Of all the famous 'muscateers' of Rutherglen, Bill Chambers is justifiably one of the real legends. In recent years these wines have attracted attention from overseas, so their rarity will no doubt increase.
CURRENT RELEASE *non-vintage*   This has an attractive deep tawny-brown colour and a lovely intense liqueurish nose. There are notes of malt, toffee, raisins and florals. The flavour is sweet and luscious with good depth of aged material in the blend. It's still fresh and intensely luscious with penetrating sweetness and a long raisiny finish. Try it with a steamed pudding.

Quality	▮▮▮▮▮
Value	★★★★⯪
Grapes	red frontignac
Region	Rutherglen, Vic.
Cellar	▮
Alc./Vol.	19.0%
RRP	$56.00 (375 ml)

Chambers Old Vine Muscadelle

The muscadelle grape is also known in Rutherglen as tokay. As we embrace more PC names for our wines there's danger of some confusion, but whatever it's called it's one of only a couple of wine types that are exclusively Australian. Be patriotic and get stuck into it.
CURRENT RELEASE *non-vintage*   Amber-coloured, this has a lush nose that's like homemade coconut toffee, malt and butterscotch with some aged hints. The palate is deliciously sweet with very deep flavour that's intense and long. It finishes with a lingering treacly aftertaste. Lovely with good vanilla ice-cream.

Quality	▮▮▮▮▮
Value	★★★★⯪
Grapes	muscadelle
Region	Rutherglen, Vic.
Cellar	▮
Alc./Vol.	18.0%
RRP	$46.00 (375 ml)

Chambers Oloroso

Quality	▼▼▼▼▼
Value	★★★★★
Grapes	palomino; muscadelle
Region	Rutherglen, Vic.
Cellar	▮
Alc./Vol.	18.0%
RRP	$23.00

Sweet oloroso sherry is just as much at home with a soup based on good stock, as it is with a lavish afternoon tea, or as an after-dinner tipple. Chambers is a fine example.
CURRENT RELEASE *non-vintage*   Initial impressions here are of a sweet dessert style with lovely raisiny notes, a hint of toffee and a fairly sweet palate. It's very deep in flavour, but the clean, long and dry finish brings another dimension, as does the toasted nutty, aged rancio character. The palate is long and rich and delicious. Serve it with nuts and dried fruit.

Chambers Rutherglen Tokay

Quality	▼▼▼▼
Value	★★★★⅃
Grapes	muscadelle
Region	Rutherglen, Vic.
Cellar	▮
Alc./Vol.	18.5%
RRP	$23.00

The subtitle on this wine, and the correct varietal name, is Muscadelle, but to most of us it's still Tokay and that's how we'll know it for some time yet.
CURRENT RELEASE *non-vintage*   This has a pale golden amber colour and an archetypal sweet varietal nose, reminiscent of cold tea, honey and caramel with a nice lick of clean spirit. The palate is pure and sweet, straightforward in flavour with a lush texture and a long sweet aftertaste. Serve it chilled with chocolate cake.

Clocktower Port

Quality	▼▼▼⌁
Value	★★★
Grapes	not stated
Region	not stated
Cellar	▮
Alc./Vol.	17.5%
RRP	$8.75

Eagle-eyed wine buffs will note that the back label of this port states the producer as Mildara Wines, yet the building pictured on the front is the Yalumba winery at Angaston in the Barossa. Some years ago Mildara bought all of Yalumba's fortified-wine stocks and continues to make, blend, and sell them under their old identities.
CURRENT RELEASE *non-vintage*   This mahogany-coloured sweet fortified is a fairly straightforward wine with a mahogany colour and a nose of raisiny dried fruit and lifted spirit. The palate is sweet and clean-tasting with agreeable flavour, though no great complexity or aged character. Try it with caramel fudge.

DeBortoli Black Noble

This is an unusual style of fortified wine, made from botrytis-affected semillon and pedro grapes. It fits the nowadays little-used descriptor of an old sweet white, rather than port or sweet sherry.

CURRENT RELEASE *non-vintage*   This is a lovely sweet wine that displays considerable aged character and colour. It's dark amber, almost black in colour, and smells old and rancioed, with hints of burnt sugar and honey, which probably come from the botrytis – not unlike very old German beerenauslese. It's very sweet, fairly high in acid, and a little leaner than, say, muscat or tokay. Delicious with dried fruit and nuts.

Quality	♟♟♟♟♟
Value	★★★♦
Grapes	semillon; pedro ximinez
Region	Riverina, NSW
Cellar	▮
Alc./Vol.	18.0%
RRP	$33.80 (375 ml)

DeBortoli Old Boys Tawny Port

It's funny how clubby and male-orientated port is; almost as if women don't drink it at all. When they give it names like Club and Directors Special and Old Boys, it's a self-fulfilling prophecy.

CURRENT RELEASE *non-vintage*   This is a serious style of tawny, a high-quality wine that shows real aged character. The bouquet reminds of old leather armchairs and roasted nuts, with dried-fruit highlights. It is rich and complex and finishes relatively dry – as all the best tawnies do. It would be good sipped with an after-dinner espresso.

Quality	♟♟♟♟♟
Value	★★★★
Grapes	not stated
Region	Riverina, NSW
Cellar	▮
Alc./Vol.	18.5%
RRP	$35.75

DeBortoli Show Liqueur Muscat

We had to double-check the price of this muscat, as it seemed too good to be true. At a time when the older Rutherglen muscats are soaring, this one is holding a very drinkable price.

CURRENT RELEASE *non-vintage*   It's a very good muscat, although the bouquet is drying out a little and there's not a lot of muscat fruit showing. It is very complex, though, and the palate is intense and rich, with medium lusciousness, and plenty of rancio and acid helping to dry it off and give it a clean finish that leaves you wanting more. It's good with caramels and coffee.

Quality	♟♟♟♟
Value	★★★★♦
Grapes	red frontignac
Region	not stated
Cellar	▮
Alc./Vol.	18.5%
RRP	$17.50

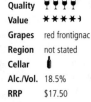

PENGUIN BEST BARGAIN FORTIFIED

Director's Special Tawny Port

Quality	♀♀♀
Value	★★★
Grapes	not stated
Region	not stated
Cellar	▮
Alc./Vol.	17.5%
RRP	$12.60 ⑤

There was a time when Director's Special was a highly regarded, premium-priced port that would have added lustre to the managing director's office bar. But its price and status have slipped somewhat over the years.
CURRENT RELEASE *non-vintage*   This is a young, straightforward port with a sweetish grapey aroma, displaying fruity young material but not a lot of age. There may be a touch of muscat in it too. It's sweet and slightly fiery on the tongue, with a noticeable belt of acid at the finish. Then it falls away to a slightly disjointed finish. A decent young port made to a price. Try it with dried figs and dates.

Director's Special 10 Year Old Premium Port

Quality	♀♀♀♀
Value	★★★
Grapes	not stated
Region	not stated
Cellar	▮
Alc./Vol.	17.5%
RRP	$20.50 ⑤

This was a long-standing Yalumba port, until Mildara bought it along with Clocktower and Galway Pipe some years ago.
CURRENT RELEASE *non-vintage*   The colour is a nice deepish tawny–russet, and it smells of old leather armchairs, smoke, vanilla, spices and seasoned timber. It's a port of character and depth, with a bigger, richer, fatter structure than its younger brother. It's soft and gentle to taste, but falls away a little at the finish, which concludes with a lick of tannin. It goes with mild blue cheeses.

Grant Burge Age Unknown Liqueur Muscat

Quality	♀♀♀♀
Value	★★★
Grapes	red frontignac
Region	Barossa Valley, SA
Cellar	▮
Alc./Vol.	19.0%
RRP	$40.00

Rutherglen winemakers' liqueur muscats are superb and have become international currency in recent years, but other regions have a style of their own.
CURRENT RELEASE *non-vintage*   Not as aromatic nor as lush as the Rutherglen version, this Barossa wine has a nose of raisiny muscatel fruit that's sweet and attractive. The palate is middling in lusciousness with relatively high acid. The 'age unknown' on the label gives the impression of great age and yes, there is some nutty, toasty rancio in the background and on the long finish, but the dominant impression is of youth. Serve it with ice-cream.

Grant Burge Aged Tawny

Just how aged is aged? This tawny seems quite youthful to us. It has a very swanky bottle for a $13 wine.
CURRENT RELEASE *non-vintage*   The tawny colour suggests age, but the nose has youthful fruity aromas and grapey spirit. It smells straightforward and clean. The palate is pleasant with clean raisiny flavour, attractive intensity and good length. It's not bad at the price. Try it with coffee and conversation.

Quality	▼▼▼◗
Value	★★★
Grapes	grenache; shiraz; mataro
Region	Barossa Valley, SA
Cellar	▮
Alc./Vol.	19.0%
RRP	$13.25

McGuigan Personal Reserve Tawny Port

Brian McGuigan has the extraordinary achievement of creating and bringing to fruition two big and highly successful wine companies in his lifetime, first Wyndham Estate and now Brian McGuigan Wines.
CURRENT RELEASE *non-vintage*   This is a gutsy style of tawny port, which has echoes of sherry and also muscat – which is not all that unusual in Aussie tawnies. It has a toffee, rancio and slightly volatile bouquet displaying considerable age. In the mouth it's rich and chocolatey with masses of flavour from fruit and wood-aged complexities. It would go with rich chocolate cake.

Quality	▼▼▼▼◗
Value	★★★★
Grapes	not stated
Region	not stated
Cellar	▮
Alc./Vol.	18.5%
RRP	$26.00 (500 ml)

McWilliams Amontillado Medium Dry Sherry

A substantial, heavy-based, clear-glass bottle graces this sherry, giving it a look of real substance. The wine inside is an unusual mixture of flor sherry characters and sweetness.
CURRENT RELEASE *non-vintage*   The colour is an unusual golden amber. The nose is like a true wood-aged amontillado with pungent flor yeast and aged rancio characters giving savoury interest. In the mouth a note of mid-palate sweetness is grafted onto aged flor flavours and a tinder-dry backbone. Somehow the whole thing doesn't quite come together in our opinion, but it does work reasonably well as an unusual aperitif, lightly chilled.

Quality	▼▼▼◗
Value	★★★◗
Grapes	not stated
Region	Riverina, NSW
Cellar	▮
Alc./Vol.	18.0%
RRP	$18.00

McWilliams Family Reserve Old Tawny Port

Quality	🍷🍷🍷🍷
Value	★★★★⟩
Grapes	not stated
Region	Riverina, NSW
Cellar	🍶
Alc./Vol.	18.0%
RRP	$13.25

We're not sure how many of the McWilliams family drink the Family Reserve port. Not many we suspect, but they could do a lot worse.

CURRENT RELEASE *non-vintage*   This really is a bargain, when you consider its quality relative to more trendy dessert wines. It has a mature tawny colour, and a nose of raisins and assorted dried fruits, aged spirit and a nuttiness that betrays a hint of older material in the blend. The palate is sweet with some depth and good persistence. A good wine to enjoy with some dried fruit and coffee.

McWilliams Show Reserve Liqueur Muscat

Quality	🍷🍷🍷🍷🍷
Value	★★★⟩
Grapes	muscat gordo blanco
Region	Riverina, NSW
Cellar	🍶
Alc./Vol.	18.5%
RRP	$69.50

Conventional wisdom says that the best muscats come from Rutherglen, and that they are made from the red frontignac grape. This outstanding old muscat proves there are exceptions to every rule: it's made from muscat gordo blanco, and comes from the New South Wales Riverina.

CURRENT RELEASE *non-vintage*   A truly delicious old fortified of enormous character and aged complexity. It has a dark, olive-tinged colour indicating great age, and the impression is reinforced by the beautifully concentrated nutty, raisiny nose and palate. The flavour is lusciously sweet and profound with a powerful lingering aftertaste. Try it with coffee and florentines.

Morris Liqueur Tokay

Quality	🍷🍷🍷🍷⟩
Value	★★★★★
Grapes	muscadelle
Region	Rutherglen, Vic.
Cellar	🍶
Alc./Vol.	17.5%
RRP	$16.90 (500 ml)

The 'Canister' tokay – it's packed in a tin-lidded cardboard canister – is a perennial favourite of ours. Quality is unchanging from year to year, a tribute to the Morris family's skill at blending.

CURRENT RELEASE *non-vintage*   This delicious honeyed fortified has an amber colour that shines promisingly in the glass. The style is spot-on, a great illustration of what makes Rutherglen tokay so charming. The tea-leaf, caramel and malty aromas lead to a luscious, sweet palate of rich malty flavour and good length. A clean tang keeps it lively. Just the thing to enjoy with top-notch vanilla ice-cream and wafers.

Morris Old Premium Liqueur Muscat

David Morris is in control of an amazing library of fortified material – some very old and some as fresh as last year's vintage. They are kept in cask at Morris's Rutherglen winery and drawn on for blending wonderful wines like this.

CURRENT RELEASE *non-vintage*   Simply superb, this old blend has a deep colour with an olive edge and a deliciously concentrated bouquet and palate. Raisiny muscatel, honey, nutty rancio, old-leather and toffee characters are gorgeously complex and profound; it has extraordinary length of flavour and wonderful lusciousness. Sip it reverentially with some nuts.

Quality	♟ ♟ ♟ ♟ ♟
Value	★ ★ ★ ★ ★
Grapes	red frontignac
Region	Rutherglen, Vic.
Cellar	▮
Alc./Vol.	17.5%
RRP	$45.70 (500 ml)

Morris Old Premium Liqueur Tokay

In many ways the Morris Old Premium fortified wines are a tribute to the work of generations of Morris family winemakers. All have been responsible for building up maturing stocks of wonderful wines.

CURRENT RELEASE *non-vintage*   Great age is indicated by the brown–green colour here, and it's confirmed in bouquet and flavour. The nose has cold-tea, malt-toffee, vanilla, toasted-almond and old-furniture aromas of great complexity. In the mouth it's lusciously sweet and amazingly long-flavoured with lovely richness and depth. The aftertaste seemingly lasts forever. Simply great with coffee and chocolates.

Quality	♟ ♟ ♟ ♟ ♟
Value	★ ★ ★ ★ ★
Grapes	muscadelle
Region	Rutherglen, Vic.
Cellar	▮
Alc./Vol.	18.0%
RRP	$45.70 (500 ml)

Noon Winery V.P.

Thanks to the Australia–EU wine agreement, you will see the word 'port' on Aussie wine labels less and less; 'VP' gets the message across. Drew Noon made it from his lowest-yielding old grenache vines.

CURRENT RELEASE 2001   Bigger, richer, more lushly fruited and opulent than most VPs, with a smooth, sweet afterpalate that makes it a delight to drink even at this tender age. The colour is youthful deep purple–red, and it has a superb aroma of blackberry fruit and nuts with a floral spirit/fruit lift. The taste is rich and fruity. It's a big wine, sweet and liqueury, but with remarkably gentle tannins. Try it with blue cheese.

Quality	♟ ♟ ♟ ♟ ♟
Value	★ ★ ★ ★ ★
Grapes	grenache; shiraz
Region	McLaren Vale, SA
Cellar	▮ 20
Alc./Vol.	19.7%
RRP	$18.00 (500 ml) (cellar door)

Penfolds Grandfather Port

Quality	♟♟♟♟♟
Value	★★★
Grapes	shiraz; mataro
Region	Barossa Valley, SA
Cellar	◦
Alc./Vol.	18.5%
RRP	$89.50

This old tawny blend maintains enviable consistency. First released in the 1960s, from memory with a 1945 vintage-dated wine, these days it's blended from a very old solera, and limited bottlings ensure the nucleus of very old wine isn't depleted.

CURRENT RELEASE *non-vintage*   This is a lovely old thing. It's a pity more people don't enjoy the delights of wines like this, but then there'd be less for us. Grandfather has very complex malt, raisin, nutty and vanillin notes on the bouquet, and there's a harmonious lick of aromatic spirit. The palate is smooth, mellow and long-finishing with a dry end. Sip it with some dried fruit and nuts.

Peter Lehmann Cellar Reserve Old Tawny

Quality	♟♟♟♟♟
Value	★★★★
Grapes	not stated
Region	Barossa Valley, SA
Cellar	◦
Alc./Vol.	19.1%
RRP	$20.00 (500 ml) (cellar door)

This is only available at the winery, presumably because they don't have enough old port stocks to share it around the retail trade – another good reason to pay them a visit.

CURRENT RELEASE *non-vintage*   A good port, appropriately priced. It has a lightish tawny colour and the bouquet reminds of molasses and dried fruits, with a peppery undercurrent. The palate has good richness and body; it's warm and resonant, with a little tannin grip and a clean, almost austere, dry aftertaste. That's one hallmark of a serious tawny. It goes well with freshly shelled walnuts.

Queen Adelaide Tawny

Quality	♟♟♟♟
Value	★★★★♪
Grapes	not stated
Region	not stated
Cellar	◦
Alc./Vol.	18.5%
RRP	$7.00

Inexpensive port has always had a poor reputation in Australia with connotations of four-penny dark, paper-bag-encased bombo, and alcoholism just around the corner. In reality today's crop are pretty good drinks, and absolutely nothing to be ashamed of. Queen Adelaide is a good example.

CURRENT RELEASE *non-vintage*   A fairly simple young tawny style with a light raisiny, grapey nose with hints of vanilla and citrus peel. The palate is light to medium-bodied for the style, but it has pleasant nutty-sweet flavour and a dry finish. Take it to warm you up on a midnight fishing expedition.

R.L. Buller & Son Rare Liqueur Muscat

'Rare' is the highest grade for the fortified muscats and tokays of Rutherglen, so this is Bullers' top bottling. R.L. was Reginald, grandfather of present winemakers Andrew and Richard, and the son was the late Dick Buller, their dad.

CURRENT RELEASE *non-vintage* A deep burnished wood colour, with complex aged character aplenty in the bouquet, along with some of the superphosphate character in the tokay. It could use a smidge more muscat fruit character. The taste is very intense, rich, layered and lively, with some acidity poking through the wall of lush, sweet flavour. It suits gorgonzola cheese.

Quality	🍷🍷🍷🍷½
Value	★★★½
Grapes	red frontignac
Region	Rutherglen, Vic.
Cellar	🍾
Alc./Vol.	18.0%
RRP	$65.00 (375 ml)

R.L. Buller & Son Rare Liqueur Tokay

It's a quaintly olde worlde way to identify the producer on a wine label: 'R.L. Buller & Son', but somehow it seems appropriate for this very traditional family winery in Rutherglen, one of Australia's oldest and most venerated wine regions.

CURRENT RELEASE *non-vintage* A very old, wonderfully complex, luscious, treacly style of tokay. It's deepish tawny–amber and smells of toffee apples, with undertones of malt and caramel, with a curious whiff of superphosphate, which it shares with the muscat above. Marvellous viscosity and decadent richness, finishing cleanly despite all that sweetness. It's great with after-dinner espresso coffee and chocolates.

Quality	🍷🍷🍷🍷½
Value	★★★½
Grapes	muscadelle
Region	Rutherglen, Vic.
Cellar	🍾
Alc./Vol.	18.0%
RRP	$65.00 (375 ml)

Sandalford Sandalera

A unique dessert wine with mysterious origins. Its aged character makes it a bit like sweet Madeira. The makers have finally realised its value and the price has skyrocketed.

CURRENT RELEASE *non-vintage* Our latest tasting of this special wine suggested that it might need a little freshening, it seemed just a little faded. The nose has loads of rancio and volatile complexities, along with nutty and vanillin aromas. In the mouth it's sweet and long with a toasty aftertaste that sticks around for ages. Acidity is very high. Try it with petits fours and coffee.

Quality	🍷🍷🍷🍷½
Value	★★★
Grapes	who knows? Probably verdelho and others
Region	Swan Valley, WA
Cellar	🍾
Alc./Vol.	18.0%
RRP	$118.00 (500 ml)

Seppelt Barossa Valley Rare Tawny DP90

Quality	♟♟♟♟♟
Value	★★★★⌐
Grapes	mostly shiraz & grenache
Region	Barossa Valley, SA
Cellar	▮
Alc./Vol.	21.0%
RRP	$65.00 (500 ml)

Is this Australia's best old tawny port style? So few people sip great ports these days, but they're missing out big-time. Smartly repackaged in line with a general revamp of Seppelt fortifieds, the quality remains superb and it's actually come down in price. Blended by James Godfrey.

CURRENT RELEASE *non-vintage*   Subtlety is the thing. Fragrant and aromatic with a lovely aged, spirity edge, and super complexity. There are hints of grilled nuts, dried fruit, peel, vanilla, leather and toffee, it has amazing length and finesse, and finishes remarkably dry and lingering. Try it with walnuts, dried fruits, maybe a little cheddar.

Seppelt Grand Rutherglen Tokay DP57

Quality	♟♟♟♟⌐
Value	★★★★★
Grapes	muscadelle
Region	Rutherglen, Vic.
Cellar	▮
Alc./Vol.	17.0%
RRP	$27.00

These excellent fortifieds used to be in half-bottles, an ideal size to consume fresh and in prime condition, rather than being left half-full in some cupboard. Inexplicably, the new Southcorp has reversed this, and is again packing them in large 750 ml bottles.

CURRENT RELEASE *non-vintage*   This lovely, intense, amber-coloured wine isn't as luscious as some; instead it has a penetrating, aged, sweet varietal personality that's incredibly more-ish. Cold-tea, toffee, honey, lemon and toasted nut characters are complex and lingering, and the finish is clean, long, deliciously sweet but not cloying. Try it with soft blue cheese.

Seppelt Para Liqueur Port

Quality	♟♟♟♟⌐
Value	★★★★★
Grapes	grenache; shiraz; mataro
Region	Barossa Valley, SA
Cellar	▮
Alc./Vol.	19.0%
RRP	$20.00

Once there was only one vintage-dated Para Liqueur Port. Collecting it became an absurd mania for many people who should have known better. These days there are two wines: the one with the vintage year, and this cheaper numbered edition.

CURRENT RELEASE *non-vintage. Bottling 121*   Over the years this once luscious style has evolved into a drier more elegant style and we like it. The colour is an aged tawny, and the nose has raisin, almond nougat, nuts and honeyed elements. There's lovely aged flavour mid-palate, rich and complex, and the finish is dry and clean. Serve it with crostoli and coffee.

Seppelt Rutherglen Muscat DP33

A revamp of the Seppelt fortified wines has regraded the Rutherglen muscats and tokays along the lines of classification devised by the Rutherglen winemakers. From the bottom to the top, they are Rutherglen, Classic, Grand, and Rare.

CURRENT RELEASE *non-vintage*   Incredibly well-priced for 750 ml of muscat, this has a pale amber–tawny colour and a fragrant grapey, raisiny nose with a hint of Turkish delight. There's no evidence of great age in the blend, but it has finesse and its fresh personality is lush, sweet and long. A lighter style, but intense and very easy to sip. Serve it with some cheese and biscuits.

Quality	♟♟♟♟♟
Value	★★★★★
Grapes	red frontignac
Region	Rutherglen, Vic.
Cellar	▮
Alc./Vol.	17.0%
RRP	$17.00

Seppelt Rutherglen Rare Muscat GR113

This is based on a single vintage wine from 1983 that's been snoozing at Seppeltsfield ever since, with a little bit bottled off every so often to show us just how good it is.

CURRENT RELEASE *non-vintage*   This is a super-intense liqueur muscat of exquisite concentration and luscious depth. The bouquet has profound raisin, toffee, malt and almond scents, and it lasts and lasts on the palate. Muscats like this are among the world's most exquisite wines. A steal at the price. Try it with the best dark chocolates and coffee.

Quality	♟♟♟♟♟
Value	★★★★★
Grapes	red frontignac
Region	Rutherglen, Vic.
Cellar	▮
Alc./Vol.	17.5%
RRP	$65.00 (500 ml)

Seppelt Rutherglen Rare Tokay DP59

DP stands for 'duty paid', a throwback to those days when a customs officer was stationed at Seppeltsfield. He watched where the spirit went and made sure the government got its cop.

CURRENT RELEASE *non-vintage*   This has that remarkable khaki-edged colour that indicates great age, and a bouquet of incredible concentration. Maybe it's overdue for a little freshening with youthful material, but it's still quite remarkable. It smells of dark toffee, nuts and vanilla and tastes fresher than the nose indicates with super-sweet, profound, complex flavour of great persistence. Simply gorgeous with Meredith blue cheese.

Quality	♟♟♟♟♟
Value	★★★★★
Grapes	muscadelle
Region	Rutherglen, Vic.
Cellar	▮
Alc./Vol.	17.5%
RRP	$65.00 (500 ml)

Seppelt Rutherglen Tokay DP37

Quality	🍷🍷🍷🍷🍷
Value	★★★★★
Grapes	muscadelle
Region	Rutherglen, Vic.
Cellar	🍾
Alc./Vol.	17.0%
RRP	$17.00

This is the base-grade Tokay in the new Seppelt fortified range. Liqueur tokay is one of only a couple of wine types that can claim to be unique to Australia, so be patriotic and sup up!

CURRENT RELEASE *non-vintage*   A delicious young tokay, without the complexities of great age perhaps, but special in its own way. It's a copper-coloured wine with a bouquet of homemade toffee and cold sweet tea. The palate is sweet and luscious but not heavy, and it has a long sweet finish. Another Seppelt bargain fortified. Try it chilled with a chocolate dessert.

Seppelt Show Amontillado DP116

Quality	🍷🍷🍷🍷🍷
Value	★★★★★
Grapes	palomino
Region	Barossa Valley, SA
Cellar	🍾
Alc./Vol.	22.0%
RRP	$20.00

This must be a record: wine company repackages wine in 750 ml bottles instead of 375 ml, price stays the same (actually, it's fallen slightly!). These great sherries are now extraordinary bargains!

CURRENT RELEASE *non-vintage*   A pearl in the Seppelt fortified collection, this is a glittering old-gold colour with a complex bouquet of nuts, citrus peel, and vanilla toffee. The palate has slightly sweetish citrus-like flavours counterpointed by a hint of savoury yeastiness, a nutty touch and a very dry tang. Balance is superb, and it seems a shade drier than it used to. It works beautifully with a traditional onion soup.

Seppelt Show Fino DP117

Quality	🍷🍷🍷🍷🍷
Value	★★★★★
Grapes	palomino
Region	Barossa Valley, SA
Cellar	🍾
Alc./Vol.	15.5%
RRP	$20.00

With fino sherry, freshness is an absolute must. With this in mind, it's odd that Southcorp have removed the bottling date from the back label of DP117, and repackaged it from 375 ml bottles into ones twice the size. Maybe the new bosses aren't sherry drinkers.

CURRENT RELEASE *non-vintage*   An excellent aperitif! This pale wine has a nutty, yeasty, appley personality as bracing as a sea breeze, and it tastes clean and alive with a bone dry, piercing, appetising finish. Drink it as fresh as possible and don't leave opened bottles in the cupboard, they go stale quickly. Chill it with some anchovy-stuffed olives.

Seppelt Show Oloroso DP38

We've noticed a mini-renaissance in sherry drinking recently – what used to be a granny's drink is becoming just slightly groovy. Mind you, this is a sweet sherry of real style (not exactly Granny's tipple). Now in 750 ml bottles, it's blended by fortified wine master James Godfrey.

CURRENT RELEASE *non-vintage* **An inviting amber colour, this is super-complex with a fascinating interplay between wood, controlled oxidation, wine, spirit and age. The bouquet has vanilla, dried fruits, spice and nuts, and the palate treads a lovely delicate line between sweetness and tangy acidity. The finish lasts forever. Try it with cake and coffee.**

Quality	🍷🍷🍷🍷🍷
Value	★★★★★
Grapes	palomino; grenache
Region	Barossa Valley, SA
Cellar	🍾
Alc./Vol.	20.0%
RRP	$20.00

PENGUIN BEST FORTIFIED WINE

Stanton and Killeen Vintage Port

Few wineries keep the vintage port tradition alive these days, but thankfully there are VP aficionados like Chris Killeen to maintain the faith.

Previous outstanding vintages: '82, '83, '85, '86, '88, '90, '91, '92, '93, '95

CURRENT RELEASE 1997   There's an extra dimension over the '98 in this wine. It has a wonderfully integrated, powerful bouquet with less raw fruit. Deep plum-pudding, spice and spirit aromas lead to a full-bodied palate of profound, complex flavour that has a very dry, firm background, and a long sweetly aromatic aftertaste. A lovely wine with a great future ahead of it. Try it with cheddar when it's grown up.

Quality	🍷🍷🍷🍷🍷
Value	★★★★★
Grapes	shiraz; touriga nacional; durif; tinta cao; tinta barroca; cabernet sauvignon
Region	Rutherglen, Vic.
Cellar	➤ 4–15+
Alc./Vol.	19.0%
RRP	$27.00 🍾

CURRENT RELEASE 1998   There's real power on the nose here, a super-intense berry, black-cherry and spice bouquet that's very appealing. Clean spirit adds to a complex mix, and the palate is similarly ripe and potent. It's sweet, but not jammy like some Aussie VPs, with a fragrant long and very firm palate. Keep it for years, then serve it with blue cheese and walnuts.

Quality	🍷🍷🍷🍷🍷
Value	★★★★↓
Grapes	shiraz; touriga nacional; durif; tinta barroca; tinto cao
Region	Rutherglen, Vic.
Cellar	🍾 3–15
Alc./Vol.	18.5%
RRP	$27.00 🍾

Wynns Samuel Port

Quality	♥ ♥ ♥ ♥ ♥
Value	★ ★ ★ ★
Grapes	cabernet sauvignon; touriga
Region	not stated
Cellar	▮
Alc./Vol.	18.5%
RRP	$12.50 Ⓢ

Styled after a port served at Samuel Wynn's Colonial Wine saloon in Melbourne 80 years ago, this individual style combines cabernet with the Portuguese touriga. When it was introduced to the market it was described as a 'new' style, drier and more elegant than the syrupy Aussie standard.

CURRENT RELEASE *non-vintage*   The colour is paler than most port types, and the nose has dried-fruit and lightly toasty, nutty rancio aromas. In the mouth it's sweet, but not overwhelmingly so, with relatively light body, and a long, pleasantly nutty aftertaste. A surprisingly elegant and well-priced fortified to try with soft, creamy blue cheese.

Wine Terms

The following are commonly used winemaking terms.

Acid   There are many acids that occur naturally in grapes and it's in the winemaker's interest to retain the favourable ones because these promote freshness and longevity.

Agrafe   A metal clip used to secure champagne corks during secondary bottle fermentation.

Alcohol   Ethyl alcohol (C_2H_5OH) is a by-product of fermentation of sugars. It's the stuff that makes people happy and it adds warmth and texture to wine.

Alcohol by Volume (A/V)   The measurement of the amount of alcohol in a wine. It's expressed as a percentage, e.g. 13.0% A/V means there is 13.0% pure alcohol as a percentage of the total volume.

Aldehyde   An unwanted and unpleasant organic compound formed between acid and alcohol by oxidation. It's removed by sulfur dioxide.

Allier   A type of oak harvested in the French forest of the same name.

Aperitif   A wine that stimulates the appetite.

Aromatic   A family of grape varieties that have a high terpene content. Riesling and gewürztraminer are examples, and terpenes produce their floral qualities.

Autolysis   A Vegemite or freshly baked bread taste and smell imparted by spent yeast cells in sparkling wines.

Back Blend   To add unfermented grape juice to wine or to add young wine to old wine in fortifieds.

Barrel Fermentation   The process of fermenting a red or white wine in a small barrel, thereby adding a creamy texture and toasty or nutty characters, and better integrating the wood and fruit flavours.

Barrique   A 225-litre barrel.

Baumé   The measure of sugar in grape juice used to estimate potential alcohol content. It's usually expressed as a degree, e.g. 12 degrees Baumé juice will produce approximately 12.0% A/V if it's fermented to dryness. The alternative brix scale is approximately double Baumé and must be divided by 1.8 to estimate potential alcohol.

Bentonite   A fine clay (drillers mud) used as a clarifying (fining) agent.

Blend   A combination of two or more grape varieties and/or vintages. *See also* Cuvée.

Botrytis Cinerea   A mould that thrives on grapevines in humid conditions and sucks out the water of the grapes thereby concentrating the flavour. Good in white wine but not so good in red. (There is also a loss in quantity.)

Breathing   Uncorking a wine and allowing it to stand for a couple of hours before serving. This introduces oxygen and dissipates bottle odours. Decanting aids breathing.

Brix   *see* Baumé.

Brut   The second lowest level of sweetness in sparkling wine; it does not mean there is no added sugar.

Bush Vine   Although pruned the vine is self-supporting in a low-to-the-ground bush. (Still common in the Barossa Valley.)

Carbonic Maceration   Fermentation in whole (uncrushed) bunches. This is a popular technique in Beaujolais. It produces bright colour and soften tannins.

Charmat Process   A process for making sparkling wine where the wine is fermented in a tank rather than in a bottle.

Clone (Clonal)   A recognisable subspecies of vine within a varietal family, e.g. there are numerous clones of pinot noir and these all have subtle character differences.

Cold Fermentation   (Also Controlled Temperature Fermentation) Usually applied to white wines where the ferment is kept at a low temperature (10–12 degrees Centigrade).

Cordon   The arms of the trained grapevine that bear the fruit.

Cordon Cut   A technique of cutting the fruit-bearing arms and allowing the berries to dehydrate to concentrate the flavour.

Crush   Crushing the berries to liberate the free-run juice (*q.v.*). Also used as an expression of a wine company's output: 'This winery has a 1000-tonne crush'.

Cuvée   A Champagne term meaning a selected blend or batch.

Disgorge   The process of removing the yeast lees from a sparkling wine. It involves freezing the neck of the bottle and firing out a plug of ice and yeast. The bottle is then topped up and recorked.

Dosage   Sweetened wine added to a sparkling wine after disgorgement.

Downy Mildew   A disease that attacks vine leaves and fruit. It's associated with humidity and lack of air circulation.

Drip Irrigation   An accurate way of watering a vineyard. Each vine has its own dripper and a controlled amount of water is applied.

Dryland Vineyard   A vineyard that has no irrigation.

Esters   Volatile compounds that can occur during fermentation or maturation. They impart a distinctive chemical taste.

Fermentation   The process by which yeast converts sugar to alcohol with a by-product of carbon dioxide.

Fining   The process of removing solids from wine to make it clear. There are several methods used.

Fortify   The addition of spirit to increase the amount of alcohol in a wine.

Free-run Juice   The first juice to come out of the press or drainer (as opposed to pressings).

Generic   Wines labelled after their district of origin rather than their grape variety, e.g. Burgundy, Chablis, Champagne etc. These terms can no longer legally be used on Australian labels. *Cf.* Varietal.

Graft   Changing the nature/variety of a vine by grafting a different variety onto a root stock.

Imperial   A 6-litre bottle (contains eight 750-ml bottles).

Jeroboam   A 4.5-litre champagne bottle.

Laccase   A milky condition on the surface of red wine caused by noble rot. The wine is usually pasteurised.

Lactic Acid   One of the acids found in grape juice; as the name suggests, it's milky and soft.

Lactobacillus   A micro-organism that ferments carbohydrates (glucose) or malic acid to produce lactic acid.

Lees   The sediment left after fermentation. It consists mainly of dead yeast cells.

Malic Acid   One of the acids found in grape juice. It has a hard/sharp taste like a Granny Smith apple.

Malolactic Fermentation   A secondary process that converts malic acid into lactic acid. It's encouraged in red wines when they are in barrel. If it occurs after bottling, the wine will be fizzy and cloudy.

Mercaptan   Ethyl mercaptan is a sulfur compound with a smell like garlic, burnt rubber or asparagus water.

Méthode Champenoise   The French method for producing effervescence in the bottle; a secondary fermentation process where the carbon dioxide produced is dissolved into the wine.

Methoxypyrazines   Substances that give sauvignon blanc and cabernet sauvignon that added herbaceousness when the grapes aren't fully ripe.

Mousse   The froth or head on sparkling wines.

Must   *see* Free-run juice.

Noble Rot   *see* Botrytis cinerea.

Non-vintage   A wine that is a blend of two or more years.

Oak   The least porous wood, genus *Quercus*, and used for wine storage containers.

Oenology   The science of winemaking.

Organic Viticulture   Growing grapes without the use of pesticides, fungicides or chemical fertilisers. Certain chemicals, e.g. copper sulfate, are permitted.

Organic Wines   Wines made from organically grown fruit without the addition of chemicals.

Oxidation   Browning and dullness of aroma and flavour caused by excessive exposure to air.

pH   The measure of the strength of acidity. The higher the pH the higher the alkalinity and the lower the acidity. Wines with high pH values should not be cellared.

Phenolics   A group of chemical compounds which includes the tannins and colour pigments of grapes. A white wine described as 'phenolic' has an excess of tannin, making it taste coarse.

Phylloxera   A louse that attacks the roots of a vine, eventually killing the plant.

Pigeage   To foot-press the grapes.

Pressings   The juice extracted by applying pressure to the skins after the free-run juice has been drained.

Pricked   A wine that is spoilt and smells of vinegar, due to excessive volatile acidity. *Cf.* Volatile.

Puncheon   A 500-litre barrel.

Racking   Draining off wine from the lees or other sediment to clarify it.

Saignée   French for bleeding: the winemaker has run off part of the juice of a red fermentation to concentrate what's left.

Skin Contact   Allowing the free-run juice to remain in contact with the skins; in the case of white wines, usually for a very short time.

Solero System   Usually a stack of barrels used for blending maturing wines. The oldest material is at the bottom and is topped up with younger material from the top barrels.

Solids   Minute particles suspended in a wine.

Sulfur Dioxide (SO_2)   (Code 220) A chemical added since Roman times to wine as a preservative and a bactericide.

Sur Lie   Wine that has been kept on lees and not racked or filtered before bottling.

Taché   A French term that means 'stained', usually by the addition of a small amount of red wine to sparkling wine to turn it pink.

Tannin   A complex substance derived from skins, pips and stalks of grapes as well as the oak casks. It has a preservative function and imparts dryness and grip to the finish.

Terroir   Arcane French expression that describes the complete growing environment of the vine, including climate, aspect, soil, etc., and the direct effect this has on the character of its wine.

Varietal   An industry-coined term used to refer to a wine by its grape variety, e.g. 'a shiraz'. *Cf.* Generic.

Véraison   The moment when the grapes change colour and gain sugar.

Vertical Tasting   A tasting of consecutive vintages of one wine.

Vigneron   A grapegrower or vineyard worker.

Vinegar   Acetic acid produced from fruit.

Vinify   The process of turning grapes into wine.

Vintage   The year of harvest, and the produce of a particular yeast.

Volatile   Excessive volatile acids in a wine.

Yeast   The micro-organism that converts sugar into alcohol.

Tasting Terms

The following terms refer to the sensory evaluation of wine.

Aftertaste   The taste (sensation) after the wine has been swallowed. It's usually called the finish.

Astringent (Astringency)   Applies to the finish of a wine. Astringency is caused by tannins that produce a mouth-puckering sensation and coat the teeth with dryness.

Balance   'The state of . . .'; the harmony between components of a wine.

Bilgy   An unfortunate aroma like the bilge of a ship. Usually caused by mouldy old oak.

Bitterness   A sensation detected at the back of the tongue. It's not correct in wine but is desirable in beer.

Bouquet   The aroma of a finished or mature wine.

Broad   A wine that lacks fruit definition; usually qualified as soft or coarse.

Cassis   A blackcurrant flavour common in cabernet sauvignon. It refers to a liqueur produced in France.

Chalky   An extremely dry sensation on the finish.

Cheesy   A dairy character sometimes found in wine, particularly sherries.

Cigar Box   A smell of tobacco and wood found in cabernet sauvignon.

Cloudiness   A fault in wine that is caued by suspended solids that make it look dull.

Cloying   Excessive sweetness that clogs the palate.

Corked   Spoiled wine that has reacted with a tainted cork, and smells like wet cardboard. (The taint is caused by trichloroanisole.)

Creamy   The feeling of cream in the mouth, a texture.

Crisp   Clean acid on the finish of a white wine.

Depth   The amount of fruit on the palate.

Dry   A wine that does not register sugar in the mouth.

Dull   Pertaining to colour; the wine is not bright or shining.

Dumb   Lacking nose or flavour on the palate.

Dusty   Applies to a very dry tannic finish; a sensation.

Earthy   Not as bad as it sounds, this is a loamy/mineral character that can add interest to the palate.

Finesse   The state of a wine. It refers to balance and style.

Finish   *see* Aftertaste.

Firm   Wine with strong, unyielding tannins.

Flabby   Wine with insufficient acid to balance ripe fruit flavours.

Fleshy   Wines of substance with plenty of fruit.

Flinty   A character on the finish that is akin to sucking dry creek pebbles.

Garlic   *see* Mercaptan (in Wine Terms).

Grassy   A cut-grass odour, usually found in semillon and sauvignon blancs.

Grip   The effect on the mouth of tannin on the finish; a puckering sensation.

Hard   More tannin or acid than fruit flavour.

Herbaceous   Herbal smells or flavour in wine.

Hollow   A wine with a lack of flavour in the middle palate.

Hot   Wines high in alcohol that give a feeling of warmth and a slippery texture.

Implicit Sweetness   A just detectable sweetness from the presence of glycerin (rather than residual sugar).

Inky   Tannate of iron present in a wine which imparts a metallic taste.

Integrated (Well)   The component parts of a wine fit together without gaps or disorders.

Jammy   Ripe fruit that takes on the character of stewed jam.

Leathery   A smell like old leather, not necessarily bad if it's in balance.

Length (Long)   The measure of the registration of flavour in the mouth. (The longer the better.)

Lifted   The wine is given a lift by the presence of either volatile acid or wood tannins, e.g. vanillin oak lift.

Limpid   A colour term usually applied to star-bright white wine.

Madeirised   Wine that has aged to the point where it tastes like a madeira.

Mouldy   Smells like bathroom mould; dank.

Mouth-feel   The sensation the wine causes in the mouth; a textural term.

Musty   Stale, flat, out-of-condition wine.

Pepper   A component in either the nose or the palate that smells or tastes like cracked pepper.

Pungent   Wine with a strong nose.

Rancio   A nutty character found in aged fortifieds that is imparted by time on wood.

Residual Sugar   The presence of unfermented grape sugar on the palate; common in sweet wines.

Rough   Unpleasant, aggressive wines.

Round   A full-bodied wine with plenty of mouth-feel (*q.v.*).

Sappy   A herbaceous character that resembles sap.

Short   A wine lacking in taste and structure. *See also* Length.

Spicy   A wine with a high aromatic content; spicy character can also be imparted by wood.

Stalky   Exposure to stalks, e.g. during fermentation. Leaves a bitter character in the wine.

Tart   A lively wine with a lot of fresh acid.

Toasty   A smell of cooked bread.

Vanillin   The smell and taste of vanilla beans; usually imparted by oak ageing.

Varietal   Refers to the distinguishing qualities of the grape variety used in the wine.

Directory of Wineries

Abbey Vale
Wildwood Rd
Yallingup WA 6282
(08) 9755 2277
fax (08) 9755 2286
www.abbeyvale.com.au

Abercorn
Cassilis Rd
Mudgee NSW 2850
(02) 6373 3106
www.abercornwine.com.au

Affleck Vineyard
RMB 244
Millynn Rd
(off Gundaroo Rd)
Bungendore NSW 2651
(02) 6236 9276

Ainsworth Estate
Ducks Lane
Seville Vic. 3139
(03) 5964 4711
fax (03) 5964 4311
www.ainsworth-estate.com.au

Alambie Wines
(see Cranswick Estate)

Albert River Wines
1–117 Mundoolun
Connection Road
Tamborine Qld 4270
(07) 5543 6622
fax (07) 5543 6627
www.albertriverwines.com.au

Alkoomi
Wingeballup Rd
Frankland WA 6396
(08) 9855 2229
fax (08) 9855 2284
www.alkoomiwines.com.au

All Saints Estate
All Saints Rd
Wahgunyah Vic. 3687
(02) 6033 1922
fax (02) 6033 3515
www.allsaintswine.com.au

Allandale
Lovedale Rd
Pokolbin NSW 2320
(02) 4990 4526
fax (02) 4990 1714
www.allandalewinery.com.au

Allanmere
(see First Creek)
www.allanmere.com.au

Allinda
119 Lorimer's Lane
Dixon's Creek Vic. 3775
(03) 5965 2450
fax (03) 5965 2467

Amberley Estate
Wildwood & Thornton Rds
Yallingup WA 6282
(08) 9755 2288
fax (08) 9755 2171

Anderson Winery
Lot 13 Chiltern Rd
Rutherglen Vic. 3685
(03) 6032 8111

Andraos Bros. Wines
150 Vineyard Rd
Sunbury Vic. 3429
(03) 9740 9703
fax (03) 9740 9795
www.andraosbros.com.au

**Andrew Garrett
Vineyard Estates**
134A The Parade
Norwood SA 5067
(08) 8364 0555
fax (08) 8364 5799
www.andrewgarrett.com.au

Andrew Harris
Sydney Rd
Mudgee NSW 2850
(02) 6373 1213
fax (02) 6373 1296

Angove's
Bookmark Ave
Renmark SA 5341
(08) 8595 1311
fax (08) 8595 1583
www.angoves.com.au

Annie's Lane
(see Beringer Blass)

Antcliffe's Chase
RMB 4510
Caveat
via Seymour Vic. 3660
(03) 5790 4333

Apsley Gorge
'The Gulch'
Bicheno Tas. 7215
(03) 6375 1221
fax (03) 6375 1589

**Armstrong
Vineyards**
(not open to public)
(08) 8277 6073
fax (08) 8277 6035

Arrowfield
Denman Rd
Jerry's Plains NSW 2330
(02) 6576 4041
fax (02) 6576 4144
www.arrowfieldwines.com.au

Arthurs Creek Estate
(not open to public)
(03) 9714 8202

Ashton Hills
Tregarthen Rd
Ashton SA 5137
(08) 8390 1243
fax (08) 8390 1243

Ashwood Grove
(not open to public)
(03) 5030 5291

Auldstone
Booth's Rd
Taminick via Glenrowan
Vic. 3675
(03) 5766 2237
www.auldstone.com.au

Austins Barrabool
50 Lemins Rd
Waurn Ponds Vic. 3216
(03) 5241 8114
fax (03) 5241 8122

Avalon
RMB 9556
Whitfield Rd
Wangaratta Vic. 3677
(03) 5729 3629

Baileys
Taminick Gap Rd
Glenrowan Vic. 3675
(03) 5766 2392
fax (03) 5766 2596
www.beringerblass.com.au

Baldivis Estate
(see Palandri)

Balgownie
Hermitage Rd
Maiden Gully Vic. 3551
(03) 5449 6222
fax (03) 5449 6506
www.balgownie.com

Ballingal Estate
(see Riverina Estate)

Balnaves
Penola-Naracoorte Rd
Coonawarra SA 5263
(08) 8737 2946
fax (08) 8737 2945
www.balnaves.com.au

Bannockburn
(not open to public)
Midland Hwy
Bannockburn Vic. 3331
(03) 5281 1363
fax (03) 5281 1349

Banrock Station
(see Hardys)

Barak's Bridge
(see Yering Station)

Barambah Ridge
79 Goschnicks Rd
Redgate via Murgon
Qld 4605
(07) 4168 4766
fax (07) 4168 4770

Barossa Settlers
Trial Hill Rd
Lyndoch SA 5351
(08) 8524 4017

Barossa Valley Estate
Seppeltsfield Rd
Marananga SA 5355
(08) 8562 3599
fax (08) 8562 4255
www.brlhardy.com.au

Barratt
(not open to public)
PO Box 204
Summertown SA 5141
(08) 8390 1788
fax (08) 8390 1788

Barrington Estate
700 Yarraman Rd
Wybong NSW 2333
(02) 6547 8118
fax (02) 6547 8039
www.barringtonestate.com.au

Barwang
(see McWilliams)

Basedow
161–165 Murray St
Tanunda SA 5352
(08) 8563 3666
fax (08) 8563 3597
www.basedow.com.au

Bass Phillip
Tosch's Rd
Leongatha South
Vic. 3953
(03) 5664 3341

Batista
PO Box 88
Manjimup WA 6258
tel/fax (08) 9772 3530

Bay of Fires
(see Hardys)

Belgenny
Level 8, 261 George St
Sydney NSW 2000
(02) 9247 5577
fax (02) 9247 7273
www.belgenny.com.au

Beresford
49 Fraser Ave
Happy Valley SA 5159
(08) 8322 3611
fax (08) 8322 3610
www.beresfordwines.com.au

Beringer Blass
77 Southbank Blvd
Southbank Vic. 3000
(03) 9633 2000
fax (03) 8626 3451
www.beringerblass.com.au

Berrys Bridge
Forsters Road
Carapooee
St Arnaud Vic. 3478
(03) 5496 3220
fax (03) 5496 3322

Best's Great Western
Western Hwy
Great Western Vic. 3377
(03) 5356 2250
fax (03) 5356 2430

Bethany
Bethany Rd
Bethany
via Tanunda SA 5352
(08) 8563 2086
fax (08) 8563 2086
www.bethany.com.au

Bianchet
187 Victoria Rd
Lilydale Vic. 3140
(03) 9739 1779
fax (03) 9739 1277
www.bianchet.com

Bidgeebong
(no cellar door)
PO Box 5393
Wagga Wagga NSW 2650
(02) 6931 9955
www.bidgeebong.com

Bindi
(not open to public)
145 Melton Rd
Gisborne Vic. 3437
(03) 5428 2564
fax (03) 5428 2564

Bird in Hand
Pfeiffer & Bird In Hand Rds
Woodside SA 5244
(08) 8389 9488
fax (08) 8389 9511
www.OlivesOilWine.com

Birdwood Estate
PO Box 194
Birdwood SA 5234
(08) 8263 0986

Blackjack Vineyard
Calder Hwy
Harcourt Vic. 3452
(03) 5474 2528
fax (03) 5475 2102

Blass
(see Wolf Blass)

Bleasdale
Wellington Rd
Langhorne Creek SA 5255
(08) 8537 3001
www.bleasdale.com.au

Blewitt Springs
Recreational Rd
McLaren Vale SA 5171
(08) 8323 8689
www.hillsview.com.au

Bloodwood Estate
4 Griffin Rd
via Orange NSW 2800
(02) 6362 5631
www.bloodwood.com.au

Blue Pyrenees Estate
Vinoca Rd
Avoca Vic. 3467
(03) 5465 3202
fax (03) 5465 3529
www.bluepyrenees.com.au

Blues Point
(see Southcorp Wines)

Bookpurnong Hill
Bookpurnong Road
Bookpurnong Hill
Loxton SA 5333
(08) 8584 1333
fax (08) 8584 1388
www.salenaestate.com.au

Boston Bay
Lincoln Hwy
Port Lincoln SA 5605
(08) 8684 3600
www.bostonbaywines.com.au

Botobolar
Botobolar Lane
PO Box 212
Mudgee NSW 2850
(02) 6373 3840
fax (02) 6373 3789
www.botobolar.com

Bowen Estate
Penola-Naracoorte Rd
Coonawarra SA 5263
(08) 8737 2229
fax (08) 8737 2173

Boyntons of Bright
Ovens Valley Hwy
Porepunkah Vic. 3740
(03) 5756 2356

Brands Laira
Naracoorte Hwy
Coonawarra SA 5263
(08) 8736 3260
fax (08) 8736 3208
www.mcwilliams.com.au

Brangayne
49 Pinnacle Rd
Orange NSW 2800
(02) 6365 3229

Bremerton
Strathalbyn Rd
Langhorne Creek SA 5255
(08) 8537 3093
fax (08) 8537 3109
www.bremerton.com.au

Briagolong Estate
118 Boisdale St
Maffra Vic. 3860
(03) 5147 2322
fax (03) 5147 2400

Brian Barry
(not open to public)
(08) 8363 6211

Briar Ridge
Mount View
Mt View NSW 2321
(02) 4990 3670
fax (02) 4998 7802
www.briarridge.com.au

Bridgewater Mill
Mount Barker Rd
Bridgewater SA 5155
(08) 8339 3422
fax (08) 8339 5253

Brindabella Hills
Woodgrove Cl.
via Hall ACT 2618
(02) 6230 2583

Broke Estate
Wollombi Rd
Broke NSW 2330
tel/fax (02) 6579 1065

Brokenwood
McDonalds Rd
Pokolbin NSW 2321
(02) 4998 7559
fax (02) 4998 7893
www.brokenwood.com.au

Brook Eden
Adams Rd
Lebrina Tas. 7254
(03) 6395 6244

Brookland Valley
Caves Rd
Willyabrup WA 6284
(08) 9755 6250
fax (08) 9755 6214
www.brlhardy.com.au

Brown Brothers
Meadow Crk Rd
(off the Snow Rd)
Milawa Vic. 3678
(03) 5720 5500
fax (03) 5720 5511
www.brown-brothers.com.au

**Browns of
Padthaway**
PMB 196
Naracoorte SA 5271
(08) 8765 6063
fax (08) 8765 6083
www.browns-of-padthaway.com

Buller & Sons, R.L.
Calliope
Three Chain Rd
Rutherglen Vic. 3685
(02) 6032 9660
www.rlbullerandson.com.au

Buller (R.L.) & Son
Murray Valley Hwy
Beverford Vic. 3590
(03) 5037 6305
fax (03) 5037 6803
fax (03) 6032 8005
www.rlbullerandson.com.au

**Burge Family
Winemakers**
Barossa Hwy
Lyndoch SA 5351
(08) 8524 4644
fax (08) 8524 4444
www.burgefamily.com.au

Burnbrae
Hargraves Rd
Erudgere
Mudgee NSW 2850
(02) 6373 3504
fax (02) 6373 3601

By Farr
(no cellar door sales)
101 Kelly Lane
Bannockburn Vic. 3331
Tel/fax (03) 5281 1979

Calais Estate
Palmers Lane
Pokolbin NSW 2321
(02) 4998 7654
fax (02) 4998 7813

Callatoota Estate
Wybong Rd
Wybong NSW 2333
(02) 6547 8149

Cambewarra Estate
520 Illaroo Rd
Cambewarra NSW 2541
(02) 4446 0170
fax (02) 4446 0170

Campbells
Murray Valley Hwy
Rutherglen Vic. 3685
(02) 6032 9458
fax (02) 6032 9870
www.campbellswines.com.au

Canobolas-Smith
Cargo Rd
Orange NSW 2800
(02) 6365 6113
fax (02) 6365 6113

Canonbah Bridge
Merryanbone Station
Warren NSW 2824
(02) 6833 9966
www.canonbah.com.au

Cape Clairault
via Caves Rd
or Bussell Hwy
CMB Carbunup River
WA 6280
(08) 9755 6225
fax (08) 9755 6229

Cape Mentelle
Wallcliffe Rd
Margaret River WA 6285
(08) 9757 3266
fax (08) 9757 3233

Capelvale
Lot 5
Capel North West Rd
Capel WA 6271
(08) 9727 2439
fax (08) 9727 2164
www.capelvale.com

Capercaillie
Londons Rd
Lovedale NSW 2325
(02) 4990 2904
fax (02) 4991 1886
www.capercailliewine.com.au

Casa Freschi
30 Jackson Av
Strathalbyn SA 5255
Tel/fax (08) 8536 4569
www.casafreschi.com.au

Cascabel
Rogers Rd
Willunga SA 5172
(08) 8557 4434
fax (08) 8557 4435

Casella Carramar Estate
Wakley Rd
Yenda NSW 2681
(02) 6968 1346

Cassegrain
Fern Bank Crk Rd
Port Macquarie NSW 2444
(02) 6583 7777
fax (02) 6584 0353

Castle Rock Estate
Porongurup Rd
Porongurup WA 6324
(08) 9853 1035
fax (08) 9853 1010
www.castlerockestate.com.au

Chain of Ponds
Main Adelaide Rd
Gumeracha SA 5233
(08) 8389 1415
fax (08) 8389 1877
www.chainofpondswines.com.au

Chalkers Crossing
387 Grenfell Rd
Young NSW 2594
(02) 6382 6900
fax (02) 6382 5068
www.chalkerscrossing.com.au

Chambers Rosewood
Corowa-Rutherglen Rd
Rutherglen Vic. 3685
(02) 6032 8641
fax (02) 6032 8101

Chandon
Maroondah Hwy
Coldstream Vic. 3770
(03) 9739 1110
fax (03) 9739 1095
www.chandon.com.au

Chapel Hill
Chapel Hill Rd
McLaren Vale SA 5171
(08) 8323 8429
fax (08) 8323 9245
www.chapelhillwine.com.au

Charles Cimicky
Gomersal Rd
Lyndoch SA 5351
(08) 8524 4025
fax (08) 8524 4772

Charles Melton
Krondorf Rd
Tanunda SA 5352
(08) 8563 3606
fax (08) 8563 3422
www.charlesmeltonwines.com.au

**Charles Sturt
University**
Boorooma St
North Wagga Wagga
NSW 2678
(02) 6933 2435
fax (02) 6933 2107
www.csu.edu.au/winery

Chateau Leamon
Calder Hwy
Bendigo Vic. 3550
(03) 5447 7995
www.chateauleamon.com.au

Chatsfield
O'Neill Rd
Mount Barker WA 6324
(08) 9851 1704
fax (08) 9841 6811
www.chatsfield.com.au

Chatto
(see First Creek)

Chestnut Grove
PO Box 335
Manjimup WA 6258
(08) 9772 4345
fax (08) 9772 4543
www.chestnutgrove.com.au

Chrismont
Upper King Valley Rd
Cheshunt Vic. 3678
(03) 5729 8220
fax (03) 5729 8253

Clarendon Hills
(not open to public)
(08) 8364 1484

Classic McLaren
PO Box 245
McLaren Vale SA 5171
tel/fax (08) 8323 9551

Cleveland
Shannons Rd
Lancefield Vic. 3435
(03) 5429 1449
fax (03) 5429 2017
www.cleveland.winerydirect.
com.au

Clonakilla
Crisps Lane
Murrumbateman
NSW 2582
(02) 6227 5877
www.clonakilla.com.au

Cloudy Bay
(see Cape Mentelle)

Clover Hill
(see Taltarni Vineyards)

Cobaw Ridge
Perc Boyer's Lane
East Pastoria
via Kyneton Vic. 3444
(03) 5423 5227

Cockfighter's Ghost
(see Poole's Rock)

Cofield
Distillery Rd
Wahgunyah Vic. 3687
(03) 6033 3798

Coldstream Hills
31 Maddens Lane
Coldstream Vic. 3770
(03) 5964 9410
fax (03) 5964 9389
www.southcorp.com.au

Connor Park
59 Connor Road
Leichardt Vic. 3516
(03) 5437 5234
fax (03) 5437 5204
www.bendigowine.com.au

Constable Hershon
1 Gillards Rd
Pokolbin NSW 2320
(02) 4998 7887
fax (02) 4998 7887

Coolangatta Estate
Coolangatta Resort
via Berry NSW 2535
(02) 4448 7131
fax (02) 4448 7997
www.coolangattaestate.com.au

Coombend
Swansea Tas. 7190
(03) 6257 8256
fax (03) 6257 8484

**Cope Williams
Winery**
Glenfern Rd
Romsey Vic. 3434
(03) 5429 5428
fax (03) 5429 2655
www.cope-williams.com.au

Coriole
Chaffeys Rd
McLaren Vale SA 5171
(08) 8323 8305
fax (08) 8323 9136

Cowra Estate
Boorowa Rd
Cowra NSW 2794
(02) 6342 3650

Crabtree Watervale Cellars
North Tce
Watervale SA 5452
(08) 8843 0069
fax (08) 8843 0144

Craig Avon
Craig Avon Lane
Merricks North Vic. 3926
(03) 5989 7465

Craigie Knowe
Cranbrook Tas. 7190
(03) 6223 5620

Craiglee
Sunbury Rd
Sunbury Vic. 3429
(03) 9744 4489
fax (03) 9744 4489

Craigmoor
Craigmoor Rd
Mudgee NSW 2850
(02) 6372 2208

Craigow
Richmond Rd
Cambridge Tas. 7170
(03) 6248 5482

Craneford
Main St
Springton SA 5235
(08) 8568 2220
fax (08) 8568 2538
www.cranefordwines.com

Cranswick Estate
Walla Ave
Griffith NSW 2680
(02) 6962 4133
fax (02) 6962 2888
www.cranswick.com.au

Crawford River
Condah Vic. 3303
(03) 5578 2267

Crofters
(see Houghton)

Cullens
Caves Rd
Willyabrup
via Cowaramup WA 6284
(08) 9755 5277
fax (08) 9755 5550
www.cullenwines.com.au

Currency Creek
Winery Rd
Currency Creek SA 5214
(08) 8555 4069

Dalfarras
(see Tahbilk)

Dalrymple
Pipers Brook Rd
Pipers Brook Tas. 7254
(03) 6382 7222

Dalwhinnie
Taltarni Rd
Moonambel Vic. 3478
(03) 5467 2388

Dal Zotto
Edi Road
Cheshunt Vic. 3678
(03) 5729 8321
fax (03) 5729 8490

D'Arenberg
Osborn Rd
McLaren Vale SA 5171
(08) 8323 8206
www.darenberg.com.au

Darling Estate
(by appointment only)
Whitfield Rd
Cheshunt Vic. 3678
(03) 5729 8396
fax (03) 5729 8396

Darling Park
Lot 1 Browne Lane
Red Hill 3937
(03) 5989 2732
fax (03) 5989 2254

David Traeger
399 High St
Nagambie Vic. 3608
(03) 5794 2514

David Wynn
(see Mountadam)

Deakin Estate
(see Katnook Estate)

De Bortoli
De Bortoli Rd
Bibul NSW 2680
(02) 6964 9444
fax (02) 6964 9400
or
Pinnacle Lane
Dixons Creek Vic. 3775
(03) 5965 2423
Fax (03) 5965 2464
www.debortoli.com.au

De Iuliis
Lot 21 Broke Rd
Pokolbin NSW 2320
(02) 4993 8000
fax (02) 4998 7168

Delamere
4238 Bridport Rd
Pipers Brook Tas. 7254
(03) 6382 7190

Delatite
Stoney's Rd
Mansfield Vic. 3722
(03) 5775 2922
fax (03) 5775 2911

Demondrille
RMB 97 Prunevale Rd
Prunevale
via Harden NSW 2587
(02) 6384 4272
fax (02) 6384 4292

Dennis's of McLaren Vale
Kangarilla Rd
McLaren Vale SA 5171
(08) 8323 8665
fax (08) 8323 9121
www.daringacellars.com.au

Derwent Estate
Lyell Hwy
Granton Tas 7030
tel/fax (03) 6263 5802

Devil's Lair
(not open to public)
PO Box 212
Margaret River WA 6285
(08) 9757 7573
fax (08) 9757 7533
www.southcorp.com.au

Diamond Valley Vineyards
Kinglake Rd
St Andrews Vic. 3761
(03) 9710 1484
fax (03) 9710 1369
www.diamondvalley.com.au

Dominion Wines
Upton Rd, via Avenel
Strathbogie Ranges
Vic. 3664
(03) 5796 2718
fax (03) 5796 2719

Doonkuna Estate
Barton Hwy
Murrumbateman
NSW 2582
(02) 6227 5811
fax (02) 6227 5085

Dowie Doole
182 Main Rd
McLaren Vale SA 5171
(08) 8323 7314
fax (08) 8323 7305

Drayton's Bellevue
Oakey Creek Rd
Pokolbin NSW 2320
(02) 4998 7513
fax (02) 4998 7743
www.draytonswines.com.au

Dromana Estate
Bittern-Dromana Rd
Dromana Vic. 3936
(03) 5987 3800
office (03) 5987 3177
fax (03) 5981 0714
www.dromanaestate.com.au

Dunsborough Hills
(see Old Station)

Eden Ridge
(see Mountadam)

Elan Vineyard
17 Turners Rd
Bittern Vic. 3918
(03) 5983 1858

Elderton
3 Tanunda Rd
Nuriootpa SA 5355
(08) 8862 1058 or
1800 88 8500
fax (08) 8862 2844
www.eldertonwines.com.au

Eldridge Estate
120 Arthurs Seat Road
Red Hill Vic. 3937
(03) 5989 2644
fax (03) 5989 2089
www.eldridge-estate.com.au

Elgee Park
(no cellar door)
Junction Rd
Merricks Nth
PO Box 211
Red Hill South Vic. 3926
(03) 5989 7338
fax (03) 5989 7553
www.elgeeparkwines.com.au

Eppalock Ridge
Metcalfe Pool Rd
Redesdale Vic. 3444
(03) 5425 3135

Evans & Tate
Lionel's Vineyard
Payne Rd
Jindong WA 6280
(08) 9755 8855
fax (08) 9755 4362
www.evansandtate.com.au

Evans Family
Palmers Lane
Pokolbin NSW 2320
(02) 4998 7333

Eyton on Yarra
Cnr Maroondah Hwy &
Hill Rd
Coldstream Vic. 3770
(03) 5962 2119
fax (03) 5962 5319
www.eyton.com.au

Fergusson's
Wills Rd
Yarra Glen Vic. 3775
(03) 5965 2237
www.fergussonwinery.com.au

Fermoy Estate
Metricup Rd
Willyabrup WA 6284
(08) 9755 6285
fax (08) 9755 6251
www.fermoy.com.au

Fern Hill Estate
Ingoldby Rd
McLaren Flat SA 5171
(08) 8383 0167
fax (08) 8383 0107
www.fernhillestate.com.au

Ferngrove
Ferngrove Rd
Frankland WA 6396
(08) 9855 2378
fax (08) 9855 2368
www.ferngrove.com.au

Fettler's Rest
(see Jindalee)

Fiddler's Creek
(see Blue Pyrenees Estate)

Fire Gully
(see Pierro)

First Creek
Monarch Wines
McDonalds Rd
Pokolbin NSW 2320
(02) 4998 7293
fax (02) 4998 7294
www.firstcreekwines.com.au

Fleur De Lys
(see Seppelt)

Flinders Bay
(see Old Station)

Fontys Pool
(see Cape Mentelle)

Fox Creek
Malpas Rd
Willunga SA 5172
(08) 8556 2403
fax (08) 8556 2104
www.foxcreekwines.com.au

Fox River
(see Goundrey)

Frankland Estate
Frankland Rd
Frankland WA 6396
(08) 9855 1555
fax (08) 9855 1549

Freycinet Vineyard
Tasman Hwy
Bicheno Tas. 7215
(03) 6257 8574
fax (03) 6257 8454

Gabriel's Paddocks
Deasy's Rd
Pokolbin NSW 2321
(02) 4998 7650
fax (02) 4998 7603
www.gabrielspaddocks.com.au

Galafrey
Quangellup Rd
Mount Barker WA 6324
(08) 9851 2022
fax (08) 9851 2324

Galah Wines
Box 231
Ashton SA 5137
(08) 8390 1243

The Gap
(see Mount Langi Ghiran)

Gapsted Wines
Great Alpine Road
Gapsted Vic. 3737
(03) 5751 1992
fax (03) 5751 1368
www.gapstedwines.com

Garden Gully
Western Hwy
Great Western Vic. 3377
(03) 5356 2400

Garry Crittenden
(see Dromana Estate)

Gartelmann
Lovedale Rd
Lovedale NSW 2321
(02) 4930 7113
fax (02) 4930 7114
www.gartelmann.com.au

Gembrook Hill
(by appointment only)
Launching Place Road
Gemrook Vic. 3783
(03) 5968 1622
fax (03) 5968 1699

Gemtree
Kangarilla Rd
McLaren Vale SA 5171
(08) 8323 8199
fax (08) 8323 7889

Geoff Merrill
291 Pimpala Rd
Woodcroft SA 5162
(08) 8381 6877
fax (08) 8322 2244

Geoff Weaver
(not open to public)
2 Gilpin Lane
Mitcham SA 5062
(08) 8272 2105
fax (08) 8271 0177
www.geoffweaver.com.au

Giaconda
(not open to public)
(03) 5727 0246
www.giaconda.com.au

Gilbert's
Albany Hwy
Kendenup WA 6323
(08) 9851 4028
(08) 9851 4021

Glenara
126 Range Rd Nth
Upper Hermitage SA 5131
(08) 8380 5277
fax (08) 8380 5056
www.glenara.com.au

Glenguin
Lot 8 Milbrodale Rd
Broke NSW 2330
(02) 6579 1011
fax (02) 6579 1009

Golden Grove Estate
Sundown Rd
Ballandean Qld 4382
(07) 4684 1291
www.goldengrove.com.au

Goona Warra
Sunbury Rd
Sunbury Vic. 3429
(03) 9744 7211
fax (03) 9744 7648

The Gorge
(see Pothana Vineyard)

Goundrey
Muir Hwy
Mount Barker WA 6324
(08) 9851 1777
fax (08) 9848 1018
www.goundreywines.com.au

Gramp's
(see Orlando)

Grand Cru Estate
Ross Dewell's Rd
Springton SA 5235
(08) 8568 2378

Grant Burge
Jacobs Creek
Barossa Valley Hwy
Tanunda SA 5352
(08) 8563 3700
Fax (08) 8563 2807
www.grantburgewines.com.au

Green Point
(see Chandon)

The Green Vineyards
1 Albers Rd
Upper Beaconsfield
Vic. 3808
(03) 5944 4599

Greenock Creek
Radford Rd
Seppeltsfield SA 5360
(08) 8562 8103
fax (08) 8562 8259

Grosset
King St
Auburn SA 5451
(08) 8849 2175
fax (08) 8849 2292
www.grosset.com.au

Grove Estate
Murringo Rd
Young NSW 2594
(02) 6382 6999
fax (02) 6382 4527

Gulf Station
(see De Bortoli)

Hainault
255 Walnut Road
Bickley WA 6076
(08) 9293 8339
fax (08) 9293 8339

Half Mile Creek
(see Beringer Blass)

Hamilton
Willunga Vineyards
Main South Rd
Willunga SA 5172
(08) 8556 2288
fax (08) 8556 2868
www.hamiltonwinegroup.com.au

Hamilton's Ewell
Barossa Valley Way
Nuriootpa SA 5355
(08) 8562 4600
fax (08) 8562 4611
www.hamiltonewell.com.au

Hanging Rock
Jim Rd
Newham Vic. 3442
(03) 5427 0542
fax (03) 5427 0310
www.hangingrock.com.au

Hanson Wines
'Oolorong'
49 Cleveland Ave
Lower Plenty Vic. 3093
(03) 9439 7425

Happ's
Commonage Rd
Dunsborough WA 6281
(08) 9755 3300
fax (08) 9755 3846
www.happs.com.au

Harcourt Valley
Calder Hwy
Harcourt Vic. 3453
(03) 5474 2223

Hardys
Reynella Rd
Reynella SA 5161
(08) 8392 2222
fax (08) 8392 2202
www.brlhardy.com.au

Harewood Estate
Scotsdale Rd
Denmark WA 6333
(08) 9840 9078
fax (08) 9840 9053

Haselgrove Wines
Sand Rd
McLaren Vale SA 5171
(08) 8323 8706
fax (08) 8323 8049
www.haselgrove.com.au

Hay Shed Hill
Harmans Mill Rd
Willyabrup WA 6285
(08) 9755 6234
fax (08) 9755 6305

Heathcote Winery
183 High St
Heathcote Vic. 3523
(03) 5433 2595
fax (03) 5433 3081
www.heathcotewinery.com.au

Heathfield Ridge
Cnr Caves Rd and
Riddoch Hwy
Naracoorte SA 5271
(08) 8762 4133
fax (08) 8762 0141
www.hthfieldwine.com.au

Heggies
(see Yalumba)

Helm's
Yass River Rd
Murrumbateman
NSW 2582
(02) 6227 5536 (A.H.)
(02) 6227 5953

Henschke
Moculta Rd
Keyneton SA 5353
(08) 8564 8223
fax (08) 8564 8294
www.henschke.com.au

Heritage Wines
Seppeltsfield Rd
Marananga
via Tununda SA 5352
(08) 8562 2880

Hewitson
16 McGowan Ave
Unley SA 5061
(08) 8271 5755
fax (08) 8271 5570
www.hewitson.com.au

Hickinbotham
Nepean Hwy
Dromana Vic. 3936
(03) 5981 0355
fax (03) 5981 0355
www.hickinbothamwinemakers.
com.au

Highbank
Penola-Naracoorte Rd
Coonawarra SA 5263
(08) 8737 2020
www.highbank.com.au

Highwood
(see Beresford)

Hill Smith Estate
(see Yalumba)

Hillstowe Wines
104 Main Rd
Hahndorf SA 5245
(08) 8388 1400
fax (08) 8388 1411
www.hillstowe.com.au

Hollick
Racecourse Rd
Coonawarra SA 5263
(08) 8737 2318
fax (08) 8737 2952
www.hollick.com

Holm Oak
11 West Bay Rd
Rowella, Tas. 7270
(03) 6394 7577
fax (03) 6394 7350

Home Hill
38 Nairn St
Ranelagh Tas. 7109
(03) 6264 1200
fax (03) 6264 1059
www.homehillwines.com.au

Homes
(see Massoni Home)

Honeytree
16 Gillards Rd
Pokolbin NSW 2321
tel/fax (02) 4998 7693

Hope Estate
Cobcroft Rd
Broke NSW 2330
(02) 6579 1161
fax (02) 6579 1373

Horseshoe Vineyard
Horseshoe Rd
Horses Valley
Denman NSW 2328
(02) 6547 3528

Houghton
Dale Rd
Middle Swan WA 6056
(08) 9274 5100
fax (08) 9250 3872
www.brlhardy.com.au

House of Certain Views
(see Margan)

Howard Park
Scotsdale Rd
Denmark WA 6333
(08) 9848 2345
fax (08) 9848 2064
www.howardparkwines.com.au

Hugh Hamilton Wines
PO Box 615
McLaren Vale SA 5171
(08) 8323 8689
fax (08) 8323 9488
www.hamiltonwines.com.au

Hugo
Elliott Rd
McLaren Flat SA 5171
(08) 8383 0098
fax (08) 8383 0446

Hungerford Hill
(see Cassegrain)

Huntington Estate
Cassilis Rd
Mudgee NSW 2850
(02) 6373 3825
fax (02) 6373 3730

Inglewood
18 Craig Street
Artarmon NSW 2064
(02) 9436 3022
fax (02) 9439 7930

Ingoldby
Kangarilla Rd
McLaren Vale SA 5171
(08) 8383 0005
www.beringerblass.com.au

Innisfail
(not open to public)
(03) 5276 1258

Ivanhoe
Marrowbone Rd
Pokolbin NSW 2320
(02) 4998 7325
www.ivanhoewines.com.au

James Irvine
Roeslers Rd
Eden Valley SA 5235
PO Box 308
Angaston SA 5353
(08) 8564 1046
fax (08) 8564 1046

Jamiesons Run
(see Beringer Blass)

Jane Brook
Toodyay Rd
Middle Swan WA 6056
(08) 9274 1432
fax (08) 9274 1211
www.janebrook.com.au

Jansz
(see Yalumba)

Jasper Hill
Drummonds Lane
Heathcote Vic. 3523
(03) 5433 2528
fax (03) 5433 3143

Jeanneret
Jeanneret Rd
Sevenhill SA 5453
(08) 8843 4308
fax (08) 8843 4251
www.ascl.com/j-wines

Jeir Creek Wines
Gooda Creek Rd
Murrumbateman
NSW 2582
(02) 6227 5999

Jenke Vineyards
Jenke Rd
Rowland Flat SA 5352
(08) 8524 4154
fax (08) 8524 4154
www.jenkevineyards.com

Jim Barry
Main North Rd
Clare SA 5453
(08) 8842 2261
fax (08) 8842 3752

Jindalee
(not open to public)
13 Shepherd Court
North Geelong Vic. 3251
(03) 5277 2836
fax 5277 2840
www.jindaleewines.com.au

Jingalla
Bolganup Dam Rd
Porongurup WA 6324
(08) 9853 1023
fax (08) 9853 1023

John Gehrig
Oxley Vic. 3678
(03) 5727 3395

Joseph
(see Primo Estate)

Juniper Estate
Harmans Rd Sth
Cowaramup WA 6284
(08) 9451 7277
fax (08) 9458 6015
www.juniperestate.com.au

**Kangarilla Road
Winery**
Kangarilla Rd
McLaren Flat SA 5171
(08) 8383 0533
fax (08) 8383 0044

Kara Kara
Sunraysia Hwy
St Arnaud Vic. 3478
(03) 5496 3294
fax (03) 5496 3294
www.pyrenees.org.au/
karakara.htm

Karina Vineyards
RMB 4055
Harrisons Rd
Dromana Vic. 3936
(03) 5981 0137

Karl Seppelt
(see Grand Cru Estate)

Karrivale
Woodlands Rd
Porongurup WA 6324
(08) 9853 1009
fax (08) 9853 1129

Karriview
RMB 913
Roberts Rd
Denmark WA 6333
(08) 9840 9381

Katnook Estate
Riddoch Hwy
Coonawarra SA 5263
(08) 8737 2394
fax (08) 8737 2397
www.katnookestate.com.au

Kays Amery
Kays Rd
McLaren Vale SA 5171
(08) 8323 8211
fax (08) 8323 9199

Keith Tulloch
Hermitage Road Winery
Hermitage Rd
Pokolbin NSW 2320
(02) 4990 7867
fax (02) 4990 7171
www.keithtullochwine.com.au

Kies Estate
Barossa Valley Way
Lyndoch SA 5351
(08) 8524 4110

Kilikanoon
PO Box 205
Auburn SA 5451
tel/fax (08) 8843 4377
www.kilikanoon.com.au

Killawarra
(see Southcorp Wines)

Killerby
Minnimup Rd
Gelorup WA 6230
(08) 9795 7222
fax (08) 9795 7835
www.killerby.com.au

Kingston Estate
Sturt Hwy
Kingston-on-Murray
SA 5331
(08) 8583 0244
fax (08) 8583 0304

Knappstein Wines
2 Pioneer Ave
Clare SA 5453
(08) 8842 2600
fax (08) 8842 3831
www.knappsteinwines.com.au

Knights
Burke and Wills Track
Baynton
via Kyneton Vic. 3444
(03) 5423 7264
mobile 015 843 676
fax (03) 5423 7288

Kooyong
110 Hunts Rd
Tuerong Vic. 3933
(03) 5989 7355
fax (03) 5989 7677
www.kooyong.com

Koppamurra
(no cellar door)
PO Box 110
Blackwood SA 5051
(08) 8271 4127
fax (08) 8271 0726
www.koppamurrawines.com.au

Kulkunbulla
PO Box 6265
Silverwater DC NSW 1811
(02) 9848 2103
fax (02) 9898 0200

Kyeema
(not open to public)
PO Box 282
Belconnen ACT 2616
(02) 6254 7557

Laanecoorie
(cellar door by
arrangement)
RMB 1330
Dunolly Vic. 3472
(03) 5468 7260

Lacache
(see Cape Mentelle)

Lake Breeze
Step Rd
Langhorne Creek SA 5255
(08) 8537 3017
fax (08) 8537 3267

Lake's Folly
Broke Rd
Pokolbin NSW 2320
(02) 4998 7507
fax (02) 4998 7322
www.lakesfolly.com.au

Lamont's
Bisdee Rd
Millendon WA 6056
(08) 9296 4485
fax (08) 9296 1663
www.lamonts.com.au

Lancefield Winery
Woodend Rd
Lancefield Vic. 3435
(03) 5433 5292

The Lane
Ravenswood Lane
Hahndorf SA 5245
(08) 8388 1250
fax (08) 8388 7233
www.ravenswoodlane.com.au

Langmeil
Cnr Langmeil & Para Rds
Tanunda SA 5352
(08) 8563 2595
fax (08) 8563 3622
www.langmeilwinery.com.au

Lark Hill
RMB 281
Gundaroo Rd
Bungendore NSW 2621
(02) 6238 1393

Laurel Bank
(by appointment only)
130 Black Snake Lane
Granton Tas. 7030
(03) 6263 5977
fax (03) 6263 3117

Leasingham
7 Dominic St
Clare SA 5453
(08) 8842 2555
fax (08) 8842 3293
www.brlhardy.com.au

Leconfield
Riddoch Hwy
Coonawarra SA 5263
(08) 8737 2326
fax (08) 8737 2285
www.leconfield.com.au

Leeuwin Estate
Stevens Rd
Margaret River WA 6285
(08) 9757 0000
fax (08) 9757 0001
www.leeuwinestate.com.au

Leland Estate
PO Lenswood SA 5240
(08) 8389 6928

Lengs & Cooter
24 Lindsay Tce
Belair SA 5052
(08) 8278 3998
(08) 8278 3998
fax (08) 8278 3998

Lenswood Vineyards
3 Cyril John Crt
Athelstone SA 5076
(08) 8365 3766
fax (08) 8365 3766
www.knappsteinlenswood.
com.au

Lenton Brae
Caves Rd
Willyabrup WA 6280
(08) 9755 6255
fax (08) 9755 6268

Leo Buring
(see Southcorp Wines)

Lillydale Vineyards
Davross Crt
Seville Vic. 3139
(03) 5964 2016
www.mcwilliams.com.au

Lillypilly Estate
Farm 16
Lilly Pilly Rd
Leeton NSW 2705
(02) 6953 4069
fax (02) 6953 4980
www.lillypilly.com

Lindemans
McDonalds Rd
Pokolbin NSW 2320
(02) 4998 7501
fax (02) 4998 7682
www.southcorp.com.au

Littles Winery
Lot 3 Palmers Lane
Pokolbin NSW 2320
(02) 4998 7626
fax (02) 4998 7867
www.littleswinery.com

Logan
(not open to public)
(02) 9958 6844
www.loganwines.com.au

Long Gully
Long Gully Rd
Healesville Vic. 3777
(03) 5962 3663
fax (03) 59807 2213

Longleat
Old Weir Rd
Murchison Vic. 3610
(03) 5826 2294
fax (03) 5826 2510
www.longleatwines.com

Lovegrove
Heidelberg Kinglake Road
Cottlesbridge Vic. 3099
(03) 9718 1569
fax (03) 9718 1028

Lowe Family
Ashbourne Vineyard
Tinja Lane
Mudgee NSW 2850
(02) 4998 7121
fax (02) 4998 7393
www.lowewine.com.au

Madew
Westering Vineyard
Federal Hwy
Lake George NSW 2581
(02) 4848 0026
fax (02) 4848 0026

Madfish
(see Howard Park)

Maglieri
RSD 295 Douglas Gully Rd
McLaren Flat SA 5171
(08) 8383 2211
fax (08) 8383 0735
www.beringerblass.com.au

Main Ridge
Lot 48 Williams Rd
Red Hill Vic. 3937
(03) 5989 2686

Majella
Lynn Rd
Coonawarra SA 5263
(08) 8736 3055
fax (08) 8736 3057
www.majellawines.com.au

Malcolm Creek
(open weekends and
public holidays)
Bonython Rd
Kersbrook SA 5231
tel/fax (08) 8389 3235

Marienberg
2 Chalk Hill Rd
McClaren Vale SA 5171
(08) 8323 9666
fax (08) 8323 9600
www.marienberg.com.au

Margan Family
1238 Milbrodale Rd
Broke NSW 2330
tel/fax (02) 6579 1317
www.margan.com.au

Maritime Estate
Tuck's Rd
Red Hill Vic. 3937
(03) 5989 2735

Martindale Hall
(see Andrew Garrett
Vineyard Estates)

Massoni Home
(by appointment only)
Mornington-Flinders Rd
Red Hill Vic. 3937
(03) 5981 8008
fax (03) 5981 2014
www.massoniwines.com

Maxwell
Cnr Olivers & Chalkhill Rds
McLaren Vale SA 5171
(08) 8323 8200
www.maxwellwines.com.au

McAlister
(not open to public)
RMB 6810
Longford Vic. 3851
(03) 5149 7229

McGuigan
Cnr Broke & McDonalds Rds
Pokolbin NSW 2320
(02) 4998 7700
fax (02) 4998 7401

**McLarens on the
Lake**
(see Andrew Garrett
Vineyard Estates)

McWilliams
Hanwood NSW 2680
(02) 6963 0001
fax (02) 6963 0002
www.mcwilliams.com.au

Meadowbank
Glenora Tas. 7140
(03) 6286 1234
fax (03) 6286 1133

Meerea Park
Lot 3 Palmers Lane
Pokolbin NSW 2320
(02) 4998 7006
fax (02) 4998 7005
www.meereapark.com.au

Merricks Estate
Cnr Thompsons La. &
Frankston-Flinders Rd
Merricks Vic. 3916
(03) 5989 8416
fax (03) 9629 4035

Miceli
60 Main Creek Rd
Arthur's Seat Vic. 3936
(03) 5989 2755

Middleton Estate
Flagstaff Hill Rd
Middleton SA 5213
(08) 8555 4136
fax (08) 8555 4108

Milburn Park
(see Cranswick Estate)

The Mill
(see Windowrie Estate)

Mintaro Cellars
Leasingham Rd
Mintaro SA 5415
(08) 8843 9046

Miramar
Henry Lawson Dr
Mudgee NSW 2850
(02) 6373 3874

Miranda Wines
57 Jordaryan Ave
Griffith NSW 2680
(02) 6962 4033
fax (02) 6962 6944
www.mirandawines.com.au

Mirrool Creek
(see Miranda Wines)

Mitchell
Hughes Park Rd
Sevenhill via Clare SA 5453
(08) 8843 4258

Mitchelton Wines
Mitcheltstown
Nagambie 3608
(03) 5794 2710
fax (03) 5794 2615
www.mitchelton.com.au

Molly Morgan
Talga Rd
Allandale NSW 2321
(02) 4930 7695
fax (02) 9235 1876
www.mollymorgan.bizland.com

Monichino
1820 Berry's Rd
Katunga Vic. 3640
(03) 5864 6452
fax (03) 5864 6538

Montara
Chalambar Rd
Ararat Vic. 3377
(03) 5352 3868
fax (03) 5352 4968

**Montrose/Poets
Corner**
Henry Lawson Dr
Mudgee NSW 2850
(02) 6373 3853
www.poetscornerwines.com.au

Moondah Brook
(see Houghton)

Moondarah
(see Prentice)

Moorilla Estate
655 Main Rd
Berridale Tas. 7011
(03) 6249 2949

Moorooduc Estate
Derril Rd
Moorooduc Vic. 3933
(03) 5978 8585

**Mornington
Vineyards Estate**
(see Dromana Estate)

Morris
off Murray Valley Hwy
Mia Mia Vineyards
Rutherglen Vic. 3685
(02) 6026 7303
fax (02) 6026 7445

Moss Brothers
Caves Rd
Willyabrup WA 6280
(08) 9755 6270
fax (08) 9755 6298
www.mossbrothers.com.au

Moss Wood
Metricup Rd
Willyabrup WA 6280
(08) 9755 6266
fax (08) 9755 6303
www.mosswood.com.au

Mount Avoca
Moates Lane
Avoca Vic. 3467
(03) 5465 3282
www.mountavoca.com

Mount Horrocks
Curling St
Auburn SA 5451
(08) 8849 2243
fax (08) 8849 2265
www.mounthorrocks.com

Mount Hurtle
(see Geoff Merrill)

Mount Ida
(see Beringer Blass)

Mount Langi Ghiran
Warrak Rd
Buangor Vic. 3375
(03) 5354 3207
fax (03) 5354 3277
www.langi.com.au

Mount Mary
(not open to public)
(03) 9739 1761
fax (03) 9739 0137

Mount Pleasant
Marrowbone Rd
Pokolbin NSW 2321
(02) 4998 7505
fax (02) 4998 7761
www.mcwilliams.com.au

Mount Prior Vineyard
Cnr River Rd & Popes La.
Rutherglen Vic. 3685
(02) 6026 5591
fax (02) 6026 5590

Mount William Winery
Mount William Rd
Tantaraboo Vic. 3764
(03) 5429 1595
fax (03) 5429 1998

Mountadam
High Eden Ridge
Eden Valley SA 5235
(08) 8564 1101
www.mountadam.com

Mulyan
North Logan Rd
Cowra NSW 2794
(02) 6342 1336
fax (02) 6341 1015
www.mulyan.com.au

Murrindindi
(not open to public)
(03) 5797 8217

Neagle's Rock
Main North Rd
Clare SA 5453
(08) 8843 4020

Nepenthe Vineyards
(not open to public)
(08) 8389 8218
www.nepenthe.com.au

Nicholson River
Liddells Rd
Nicholson Vic. 3882
(03) 5156 8241

Ninth Island
(see Pipers Brook)

Noon Winery
(cellar door seasonal)
Rifle Range Rd
McLaren Vale SA 5171
tel/fax (08) 8323 8290

Normans
(see Xanadu)

Notley Gorge
(see Rosevears Estate)

Nugan Estate
Darlington Point Rd
Wilbriggie NSW 2680
(02) 6968 5311
fax (02) 6962 5399

Oakridge Estate
864 Maroondah Hwy
Coldstream Vic. 3770
(03) 5964 3379
fax (03) 5964 2061
www.oakridgeestate.com.au

Oakvale Winery
Broke Rd
Pokolbin NSW 2320
(02) 4998 7520
www.oakvalewines.com.au

Old Kent River
Turpin Rd
Rocky Gully WA 6397
(08) 9855 1589
fax (08) 9855 1589

Old Station
PO Box 40
Watervale SA 5452
(02) 9144 1925

O'Leary Walker
Main Rd
Leasingham SA 5452
(08) 8271 1221
fax 08 8357 1457
www.olearywalkerwines.com

Orlando
Barossa Valley Way
Rowland Flat SA 5352
(08) 8521 3111
fax (08) 8521 3102
www.jacobscreek.com.au

Osborn's
Ellerina Rd
Merricks North Vic. 3926
(03) 5989 7417
fax (03) 5989 7510

Padthaway Estate
Riddoch Hwy
Padthaway SA 5271
(08) 8765 5039
fax (08) 8765 5097

Palandri
Bussell Hwy
Margaret River WA 6285
(08) 9755 5711
fax (08) 9755 5722
www.palandri.com.au

Palmer Wines
Caves Rd
Willyabrup WA 6280
(08) 9797 1881
fax (08) 9797 0534

Pankhurst Wines
Woodgrove Rd
Hall ACT 2618
(02) 6230 2592

Panorama
1848 Cygnet Coast Rd
Cradoc Tas. 7109
Tel/fax (03) 6266 3409

Paracombe
Paracombe Rd
Paracombe SA 5132
(08) 8380 5058
fax (08) 8380 5488

Paradise Enough
(weekends & holidays only)
Stewarts Rd
Kongwak Vic. 3951
(03) 5657 4241
www.paradiseenough.com.au

Paringa Estate
44 Paringa Rd
Red Hill South Vic. 3937
(03) 5989 2669

Parker Coonawarra Estate
Riddoch Hwy
Coonawarra SA 5263
(08) 8737 3525
fax (08) 8737 3527
www.parkercoonawarraestate.
com.au

Passing Clouds
Powlett Rd
via Inglewood
Kingower Vic. 3517
(03) 5438 8257

Pattersons
St Werburghs Rd
Mount Barker WA 6324
(08) 9851 2063
fax (08) 9851 2063

Paul Conti
529 Wanneroo Rd
Woodvale WA 6026
(08) 9409 9160
fax (08) 9309 1634

Paul Osicka
Graytown Vic. 3608
(03) 5794 9235
fax (03) 5794 9288

Paulett's
Polish Hill River Rd
Sevenhill SA 5453
(08) 8843 4328
fax (08) 8843 4202

Peel Estate
Fletcher Rd
Baldivis WA 6210
(08) 9524 1221

Pendarves Estate
Lot 12 Old North Rd
Belford NSW 2335
(02) 6574 7222
www.winedoctor.md/wine.htm

Penfolds
(see Southcorp Wines)

Penley Estate
McLean's Rd
Coonawarra 5263
(08) 8736 3211
fax (08) 8736 3124
www.penley.com.au

Penny's Hill
Main Rd
McLaren Vale SA 5171
(08) 8556 4460
fax (08) 8556 4462
www.pennyshill.com.au

Pepper Tree Wines
Halls Rd
Pokolbin NSW 2320
(02) 4998 7539
fax (02) 4998 7746
www.peppertreewines.com.au

Pepperjack
(see Beringer Blass)

Peppers Creek
Cnr Ekerts & Broke Rds
Pokolbin NSW 2321
(02) 4998 7532

Petaluma
(not open to public)
(08) 8339 4122
fax (08) 8339 5253
www.petalumalimited.com.au

Peter Lehmann
Para Rd
Tanunda SA 5352
(08) 8563 2500
fax (08) 8563 3402
www.peterlehmannwines.
com.au

Petersons
PO Box 182
Mount View Rd
Mount View NSW 2325
(02) 4990 1704

Pewsey Vale
(see Yalumba)

Pfeiffer
Distillery Rd
Wahgunyah Vic. 3687
(02) 6033 2805

Phillip Island Wines
Lot 1 Berrys Beach Rd
Phillip Island Vic. 3922
(03) 5956 8465
www.phillipislandwines.com.au

Pibbin Farm
Greenhill Rd
Balhannah SA 5242
(08) 8388 4794

Picardy
(not open to public)
(08) 9776 0036
fax (08) 9776 0036
www.picardy.com.au

Picarus
C/- Winetrust Estates
(no cellar door sales)
(02) 9816 4088

Piccadilly Fields
(not open to public)
(08) 8390 1997

Pierro
Caves Rd
Willyabrup WA 6280
(08) 9755 6220
fax (08) 9755 6308

Pikes
Polish Hill River Rd
Seven Hill SA 5453
(08) 8843 4370
fax (08) 8843 4353
www.pikeswines.com.au

Pipers Brook
3959 Bridport Hwy
Pipers Brook Tas. 7254
(03) 6332 4444
fax (03) 6334 9112
www.pbv.com.au

Pirie
(see Pipers Brook)

Pirramimma
Johnston Rd
McLaren Vale SA 5171
(08) 8323 8205
fax (08) 8323 9224

Pizzini
King Valley Road
Wangaratta Vic. 3768
(03) 5729 8278
fax (03) 5729 8495

Plantagenet
Albany Hwy
Mount Barker WA 6324
(08) 9851 2150
fax (08) 9851 1839

Plunkett's
Cnr Lambing Gully Rd &
Hume Fwy
Avenel Vic. 3664
(03) 5796 2150
fax (03) 5796 2147
www.plunkett.com.au

Poole's Rock
(not open to public)
Lot 41 Wollombi Road
Broke NSW 2330
(02) 6579 1251
fax (02) 6579 1277

Port Phillip Estate
261 Red Hill Rd
Red Hill Vic. 3937
(03) 5989 2708
fax (03) 5989 2891
www.portphillip.net

Portree Vineyard
RMB 700
Lancefield Vic. 3435
(03) 5429 1422
fax (03) 5429 2205
www.portreevineyard.com.au

Pothana Vineyard
Pothana Lane
Belford NSW 2335
(02) 6574 7164
fax (02) 6574 7209

Preece
(see Mitchelton Wines)

Prentice
(no cellar door sales)
PO Box 4
Red Hill South, Vic. 3937
(03) 5989 9063
fax (03) 5989 9068

Preston Peak
Wallangarra Rd
Wyberba
Wallangarra Qld 4383
tel/fax (07) 4630 9499

Primo Estate
Cnr Old Port Wakefield &
Angle Vale Rds
Virginia SA 5120
(08) 8380 9442
fax (08) 8380 9696
www.primoestate.com.au

Prince Albert
Lemins Rd
Waurn Ponds Vic. 3221
(03) 5243 5091
fax (03) 5241 8091

Provenance
(cellar door sales by
appointment)
PO Box 74
Bannockburn Vic. 3331
(03) 5265 6055
fax (03) 5265 6077
www.provenancewines.com.au

Providence
236 Lalla Rd
Lalla Tas. 7267
(03) 6395 1290
fax (03) 6395 2088
www.providence-
vineyards.com.au

Punt Road
St Huberts Rd
Coldstream Vic. 3770
(03) 9739 0666
fax (03) 9739 0633
www.puntroadwines.com.au

Punters Corner
Cnr Riddoch Hwy &
Racecourse Rd
Coonawarra SA 5263
(08) 8737 2007

Queen Adelaide
(see Seppelt)

Quelltaler Estate /
Annie's Lane
Main North Rd
Watervale SA 5452
(08) 8843 0003
fax (08) 8843 0096
www.beringerblass.com.au

Radenti
(see Freycinet Vineyard)

Ralph Fowler
Lot 101 Limestone Coast Rd
Mount Benson SA 5275
(08) 8768 5000
fax (08) 8768 5008
www.ralphfowlerwines.com.au

Red Edge
(not open to public)
(03) 9337 5695

Red Hill Estate
53 Red Hill-Shoreham Rd
Red Hill South Vic. 3937
(03) 5989 2838
www.redhillestate.com.au

Redbank
Sunraysia Hwy
Redbank Vic. 3478
(03) 5467 7255

Redgate
Boodjidup Rd
Margaret River WA 6285
(08) 9757 6488
fax (08) 9757 6308
www.redgatewines.com.au

Redman
Riddoch Hwy
Coonawarra SA 5263
(08) 8736 3331
fax (08) 8736 3013

Renmano
Renmark Ave
Renmark SA 5341
(08) 8586 6771
fax (08) 8586 5939
www.brlhardy.com.au

Reynell
(see Hardys)

Reynolds
Quandong Winery
Cargo Rd
Cudal NSW 2864
(02) 6364 2330
fax (02) 6364 2388
www.reynoldswine.com.au

Ribbon Vale Estate
(see Moss Wood)

Richmond Grove
(see Orlando)

Riddoch
(see Katnook Estate)

Rimfire
C/- PO Maclagan Qld 4352
(07) 4692 1129
www.rimfirewinery.com.au

Riverina Estate
700 Kidman Way
Griffith NSW 2680
(02) 6962 4122
fax (02) 6962 4628
www.riverinaestate.com.au

Robinvale Wines
Sealake Rd
Robinvale Vic. 3549
(03) 5026 3955
fax (03) 5026 1123
www.organicwines.com

Rochford
Romsey Park
via Woodend Rd
Rochford Vic. 3442
(03) 5429 1428
www.rochfordwines.com.au

Rockford
Krondorf Rd
Tanunda SA 5352
(08) 8563 2720
info@rockfordwines.com.au

Romsey Vineyards
(see Cope Williams)

Rosabrook Estate
Rosa Brook Rd
Margaret River WA 6285
(08) 9757 2286
fax (08) 9757 3634

Rosemount
Rosemount Rd
Denman NSW 2328
(02) 6547 2467
fax (02) 6547 2742
www.southcorp.com.au

Rosevears Estate
1A Waldhorn Drive
Rosevears Tas. 7277
(03) 6330 1800
fax (03) 6330 1810

Rosily Vineyard
Yelverton Rd
Willyabrup WA
tel/fax (08) 9755 6336

Rothbury Estate
Broke Rd
Pokolbin NSW 2321
(02) 4998 7555
fax (02) 4998 7553
www.beringerblass.com.au

Rothvale
Deasy's Rd
Pokolbin NSW 2321
(02) 4998 7290

Rufus Stone
(see Tyrrell's)

Rumball
(no cellar door)
(08) 8332 2761
fax (08) 8364 0188

Ryan Family Wines
Broke Estate
Wollombi Rd
Broke NSW 2330
(02) 6579 1065
fax (02) 6579 1065
www.ryanwines.com.au

Ryecroft
Ingoldby Rd
McLaren Flat SA 5171
(08) 8383 0001
www.southcorp.com.au

Rymill
The Riddoch Run
Vineyards (off Main Rd)
Coonawarra SA 5263
(08) 8736 5001
fax (08) 8736 5040
www.rymill.com.au

**Saddlers Creek
Winery**
Marrowbone Rd
Pokolbin NSW 2321
(02) 4991 1770
fax (02) 4991 1778
www.saddlerscreekwines.com.au

Salisbury
(see Cranswick Estate)

Salitage
Vasse Hwy
Pemberton WA 6260
(08) 9776 1599
fax (08) 9776 1504
www.salitage.com.au

Saltram
Angaston Rd
Angaston SA 5353
(08) 8564 3355
www.beringerblass.com.au

Sandalford
West Swan Rd
Caversham WA 6055
(08) 9274 5922
fax (08) 9274 2154
www.sandalford.com

Sandhurst Ridge
156 Forest Drive
Marong Vic. 3515
(03) 5435 2534
fax (03) 5435 2548
www.bendigowine.org.au

Sandstone Vineyard
(cellar door by
appointment)
Caves & Johnson Rds
Willyabrup WA 6280
(08) 9755 6271
fax (08) 9755 6292

Scarborough Wines
Gillards Rd
Pokolbin NSW 2321
(02) 4998 7563

Scarpantoni
Kangarilla Rd
McLaren Flat SA 5171
(08) 8383 0186
fax (08) 8383 0490
www.scarpantoni-wines.com.au

Schinus
(see Dromana Estate)

Scotchman's Hill
Scotchmans Rd
Drysdale Vic. 3222
(03) 5251 3176
fax (03) 5253 1743
www.scotchmanshill.com.au

Seaview
Chaffeys Rd
McLaren Vale SA 5171
(08) 8323 8250
www.southcorp.com.au

Seppelt
Seppeltsfield
via Tanunda SA 5352
(08) 8562 8028
fax (08) 8562 8333
www.southcorp.com.au

Sevenhill
College Rd
Sevenhill
via Clare SA 5453
(08) 8843 4222
fax (08) 8843 4382
www.sevenhillcellars.com.au

Seville Estate
Linwood Rd
Seville Vic. 3139
(03) 5964 2622
fax (03) 5964 2633

Shadowfax
K Road
Werribee Vic. 3030
(03) 9731 4420
fax (03) 9731 4421
www.shadowfax.com.au

Shantell
Melba Hwy
Dixons Creek Vic. 3775
(03) 5965 2264
fax (03) 9819 5311
www.shantellvineyard.com.au

Sharefarmers
(see Petaluma)

Shaw & Smith
(weekends only)
Lot 4 Jones Rd
Balhannah SA 5242
(08) 8398 0500
fax (08) 8398 0600
www.shawandsmith.com.au

Shottesbrooke
1 Bagshaws Rd
McLaren Flat SA 5171
(08) 8383 0002
fax (08) 8383 0222
www.shottesbrooke.com.au

Simon Hackett
(not open to public)
(08) 8331 7348

Skillogalee
Skillogalee Rd
via Sevenhill SA 5453
(08) 8843 4311
fax (08) 8843 4343
skilly@capri.net.au

Smithbrook
(not open to public)
(08) 9772 3557
fax (08) 9772 3579
www.smithbrook.com.au

Sorrenberg
Alma Rd
Beechworth Vic. 3747
(03) 5728 2278

Southcorp Wines
Tanunda Rd
Nuriootpa SA 5355
(08) 8568 9389
fax (08) 8568 9489
www.southcorp.com.au

Springwood Park
(see Andrew Garrett
Vineyard Estates)

St Hallett
St Halletts Rd
Tanunda SA 5352
(08) 8563 7000
fax (08) 8563 7001
www.sthallett.com.au

St Huberts
Maroondah Hwy
Coldstream Vic. 3770
(03) 9739 1118
fax (03) 9739 1015
www.beringerblass.com.au

St Leonards
St Leonard Rd
Wahgunyah Vic. 3687
(02) 6033 1004
fax (02) 6033 3636
www.allsaintswine.com.au

St Mary's Vineyard
V and A Lane
via Coonawarra SA 5263
(08) 8736 6070
fax (08) 8736 6045

St Matthias
(see Moorilla Estate)

Stanley Brothers
Barossa Valley Way
Tanunda SA 5352
(08) 8563 3375
fax (08) 8563 3758
www.stanleybros.mtx.net

Stanton & Killeen
Murray Valley Hwy
Rutherglen Vic. 3685
(02) 6032 9457

Stein's Wines
Pipeclay Rd
Mudgee NSW 2850
(02) 6373 3991
fax (02) 6373 3709

Stephen John Wines
Government Rd
Watervale SA 5452
(08) 8843 0105
fax (08) 8843 0105

**Stoney Vineyard/
Domaine A**
Teatree Rd
Campania Tas. 7026
(03) 6260 4174
fax (03) 6260 4390

Stonier's Winery
362 Frankston-Flinders Rd
Merricks Vic. 3916
(03) 5989 8300
fax (03) 5989 8709
www.stoniers.com.au

Stumpy Gully
1247 Stumpy Gully Rd
Moorooduc Vic. 3933
(03) 5978 8429
fax (03) 5978 8419

Summerfield
Main Rd
Moonambel Vic. 3478
(03) 5467 2264
fax (03) 5467 2380

Tahbilk
Tahbilk Vic. 3607
via Nagambie
(03) 5794 2555
fax (03) 5794 2360
www.tahbilk.com.au

Talijancich
26 Hyem Rd
Herne Hill WA 6056
(08) 9296 4289
fax (08) 9296 1762

Tallarook
(not open to public)
(03) 9818 3455
www.tallarook.com

Taltarni Vineyards
off Moonambel-Stawell Rd
Moonambel Vic. 3478
(03) 5467 2218
fax (03) 5467 2306
www.taltarni.com.au

Talunga
Lot 101 Adelaide-
Mannum Rd
Gumeracha SA 5233
(08) 8389 1222
fax (08) 8389 1233

Tamar Ridge
Auburn Road
Kayena Tas. 7270
(03) 6394 7002
fax (03) 6394 7003

Tamburlaine Wines
McDonalds Rd
Pokolbin NSW 2321
(02) 4998 7570
fax (02) 4998 7763
www.mywinery.com

Tanglewood Downs
Bulldog Creek Rd
Merricks North
(03) 5974 3325

Tapestry
Merrivale Wines
Olivers Rd
McLaren Vale SA 5171
(08) 8323 9196
fax (08) 8323 9746
www.merrivale.com.au

TarraWarra
Healesville Rd
Yarra Glen Vic. 3775
(03) 5962 3311
fax (03) 5962 3311
www.tarrawarra.com.au

Tatachilla Winery
151 Main Rd
McLaren Vale SA 5171
(08) 8323 8656
fax (08) 8323 9096
www.tatachillawinery.com.au

Taylors
Mintaro Rd
Auburn SA 5451
(08) 8849 2008
www.taylorswines.com.au

Temple Bruer
Angas River Delta
via Strathalbyn SA 5255
(08) 8537 0203
fax (08) 8537 0131
www.templebruer.net.au

Tempus Two
(see McGuigan)

T'Gallant
Lot 2 Mornington-
Flinders Rd
Main Ridge Vic. 3937
(03) 5989 6565
fax (03) 5989 6577

Thalgara Estate
De Beyers Rd
Pokolbin NSW 2321
(02) 4998 7717

Thomas Wines
PO Box 606
Cessnock NSW 2325
tel/fax (02) 4991 6801

Thorn-Clarke
PO Box 402
Angaston SA 5353
(08) 8564 3373
fax (08) 8564 3255
www.thornclarkewines.com.au

Tim Adams
Wendouree Rd
Clare SA 5453
(08) 8842 2429
fax (08) 8842 2429
www.timadamswines.com.au

Tim Gramp
PO Box 810
Unley SA 5061
(08) 8379 3658
fax (08) 8338 2160

Tin Cows
(see TarraWarra)

Tintilla
Hermitage Rd
Pokolbin NSW 2335
(02) 6574 7093
fax (02) 6574 7094

Tisdall
Cornelia Creek Rd
Echuca Vic. 3564
(03) 5482 1911
fax (03) 5482 2516

Tollana
(see Southcorp Wines)

Tom
(see Andrew Garrett
Vineyard Estates)

Torbreck
Roennfeldt Rd
Marananga SA 5360
(08) 8562 4155
fax (08) 8562 4195

Torresan Estate
Manning Rd
Flagstaff Hill SA 5159
(08) 8270 2500

Tower Estate
Broke & Halls Rds
Pokolbin NSW 2321
(02) 4998 7989
www.towerestatewines.com.au

Trentham Estate
Sturt Hwy
Trentham Cliffs
via Gol Gol NSW 2738
(03) 5024 8888
fax (03) 5024 8800
www.trenthamestate.com.au

Tuck's Ridge
37 Red Hill-Shoreham Rd
Red Hill South Vic. 3937
(03) 5989 8660
fax (03) 5989 8579

Tulloch
(see Inglewood)

Turkey Flat
James Rd
Tanunda SA 5352
(08) 8563 2851
fax (08) 8563 3610
www.turkeyflatvineyards.com.au

Turramurra Estate
295 Wallaces Rd
Dromana Vic. 3936
(03) 5987 1146
fax (03) 5987 1286
www.turramurra.citysearch.
com.au

Two Hands
Seppeltsfield Rd & Sturt
Hwy
Greenock SA 5360
(08) 8562 8282
fax (08) 8562 8200
www.twohandswines.com

Two Rivers
(see Inglewood)

Tyrrell's
Broke Rd
Pokolbin NSW 2321
(02) 4993 7000
fax (02) 4998 7723
www.winefutures.com.au

Vasse Felix
Cnr Caves & Harmans Rds
Cowaramup WA 6284
(08) 9755 5242
fax (08) 9755 5425
www.vassefelix.com.au

Veritas
94 Langmeil Rd
Tanunda SA 5352
(08) 8563 2330

Virgin Hills
(not open to public)
(03) 5422 3032
www.virginhills.com.au

Voyager Estate
Stevens Rd
Margaret River WA 6285
(08) 9757 6358
fax (08) 9757 6405
www.voyagerestate.com.au

Wandin Valley Estate
Wilderness Rd
Rothbury NSW 2321
(02) 4930 7317
fax (02) 4930 7814
www.wandinvalley.com.au

Wantirna Estate
(not open to public)
(03) 9801 2367

Warburn Estate
(see Riverina Estate)

Wards Gateway Cellars
Barossa Valley Hwy
Lyndoch SA 5351
(08) 8524 4138

Warrabilla
Murray Valley Hwy
Rutherglen Vic. 3687
tel/fax (02) 6035 7242
www.warrabillawines.com.au

Warramate
27 Maddens Lane
Gruyere Vic. 3770
(03) 5964 9219

Warrenmang
Mountain Ck Rd
Moonambel Vic. 3478
(03) 5467 2233
fax (03) 5467 2309
www.bazzani.com.au/
warrenmang

Waterwheel Vineyards
Lyndhurst St
Bridgewater-on-Loddon
Bridgewater Vic. 3516
(03) 5437 3060
fax (03) 5437 3082

Wedgetail
(not open to public)
(03) 9714 8661

Wellington
(Hood Wines)
489 Richmond Rd
Cambridge Tas. 7170
(03) 6248 5844
fax (03) 6248 5855

Wendouree
Wendouree Rd
Clare SA 5453
(08) 8842 2896

Westend
1283 Brayne Rd
Griffith NSW 2680
(02) 6964 1506
fax (02) 6962 1673

Westfield
Memorial Ave
Baskerville WA 6056
(08) 9296 4356

Wetherall
Naracoorte Rd
Coonawarra SA 5263
(08) 8737 2104
fax (08) 8737 2105

Wignalls
Chester Pass Rd
Albany WA 6330
(08) 9841 2848
www.wignallswines.com.au

Wild Duck Creek
Springflat Rd
Heathcote Vic. 3523
(03) 5433 3133

Wildwood
St Johns Lane
via Wildwood Vic. 3428
(03) 9307 1118
www.wildwoodvineyards.com.au

Will Taylor
1 Simpson Pde
Goodwood SA 5034
(08) 8271 6122

Willespie
Harmans Mill Rd
Willyabrup WA 6280
(08) 9755 6248
fax (08) 9755 6210

Willow Creek
166 Balnarring Rd
Merricks North Vic. 3926
(03) 5989 7448
fax (03) 5989 7584
www.willow-creek.com

**The Willows
Vineyard**
Light Pass Rd
Barossa Valley SA 5355
(08) 8562 1080

The Wilson Vineyard
Polish Hill River
via Clare SA 5453
(08) 8843 4310
www.wilsonvineyard.com.au

Winchelsea Estate
C/- Nicks Wine Merchants
(03) 9639 0696

Windowrie Estate
Windowrie Rd
Canowindra NSW 2804
(02) 6344 3264
fax (02) 6344 3227
www.windowrie.com

Wingfields
(see Waterwheel Vineyards)

Winstead
Winstead Rd
Bagdad Tas. 7030
(03) 6268 6417

Wirilda Creek
Lot 32 McMurtrie Rd
McLaren Vale SA 5171
(08) 8323 9688

Wirra Wirra
McMurtrie Rd
McLaren Vale SA 5171
(08) 8323 8414
fax (08) 8323 8596
www.wirra.com.au

Wolf Blass
Sturt Hwy
Nuriootpa SA 5355
(08) 8562 1955
fax (08) 8562 2156
www.beringerblass.com.au

Wood Park
Kneebone Gap Rd
Bobinawarrah Vic. 3678
(03) 5727 3367
fax (03) 5727 3682

Woodstock
Douglas Gully Rd
McLaren Flat SA 5171
(08) 8383 0156
fax (08) 8383 0437
www.woodstockwine.com.au

Woody Nook
Metricup Rd
Metricup WA 6280
(08) 9755 7547
fax (08) 9755 7547

Wyanga Park
Baades Rd
Lakes Entrance Vic. 3909
(03) 5155 1508
fax (03) 5155 1443

Wyndham Estate
Dalwood Rd
Dalwood NSW 2321
(02) 4938 3444
fax (02) 4938 3422
www.wyndhamestate.com.au

Wynns
Memorial Dr.
Coonawarra SA 5263
(08) 8736 3266
fax (08) 8736 3202
www.southcorp.com.au

Xanadu
Boodjidup Rd
Margaret River WA 6285
(08) 9757 2581
fax (08) 9757 3389
www.xanaduwines.com.au

Yaldara
Gomersal Rd
Lyndoch SA 5351
(08) 8524 4200
fax (08) 8524 467
www.simeon.com.au

Yalumba
Eden Valley Rd
Angaston SA 5353
(08) 8561 3200
fax (08) 8561 3392
www.yalumba.com

Yarra Burn
Settlement Rd
Yarra Junction Vic. 3797
(03) 5967 1428
fax (03) 5967 1146
www.brlhardy.com.au

Yarra Glen
(see Andrew Garrett
Vineyard Estates)

Yarra Ridge
Glenview Rd
Yarra Glen Vic. 3775
(03) 9730 1022
fax (03) 9730 1131
www.beringerblass.com.au

Yarra Valley Hills
(see Dromana Estate)

Yarra Yering
Briarty Rd
Gruyere Vic. 3770
(03) 5964 9267

Yarraman Road
(see Barrington Estate)

Yellowglen
White's Rd
Smythesdale Vic. 3351
(03) 5342 8617
www.beringerblass.com.au

Yeringberg
(not open to public)
(03) 9739 1453
fax (03) 9739 0048

Yering Station
Melba Hwy
Yering Vic. 3775
(03) 9730 1107
fax (03) 9739 0135
www.yering.com

Zarephath
Moorialup Rd
East Porongurup WA 6324
tel/fax (08) 9853 1152
www.zarephathwines.com

Zema Estate
Penola-Naracoorte Rd
Coonawarra SA 5263
(08) 8736 3219
fax (08) 8736 3280
www.zema.com.au

Zilzie
Lot 66 Kulkyne Way
Karadoc Vic. 3496
(03) 5025 8100
fax (03) 5025 8116
www.zilziewines.com

PRINCIPAL WINE REGIONS

WESTERN AUSTRALIA
1 Swan Valley
2 Perth Hills
3 South-west Coastal
4 Margaret River
5 Pemberton/Manjimup
6 Great Southern

SOUTH AUSTRALIA
7 Riverland
8 Clare Valley
9 Barossa Valley
10 Eden Valley
11 Adelaide Hills
12 McLaren Vale
13 Langhorne Creek
14 Coonawarra

TASMANIA
15 Tamar Valley
16 Derwent Valley
17 Coal River
18 East Coast
19 Piper's River

VICTORIA
20 Henty/Drumborg
21 Murray Valley
22 Sunraysia
23 Gippsland
24 Mornington Peninsula

25 Yarra Valley
26 Sunbury
27 Geelong/Bellarine
   Peninsula
28 Grampians/Great Western
29 Macedon Ranges
30 Heathcote
31 Bendigo
32 Pyrenees
33 Rutherglen
34 King Valley
35 Beechworth
36 Goulburn Valley

NEW SOUTH WALES
37 Murray Valley
38 Tumbarumba
39 Riverina
40 Canberra District
41 Hilltops/Young
42 Cowra
43 Shoalhaven
44 Southern Highlands
45 Orange
46 Mudgee
47 Hunter Valley
48 Hastings Valley

QUEENSLAND
49 Granite Belt
50 South Burnett

437

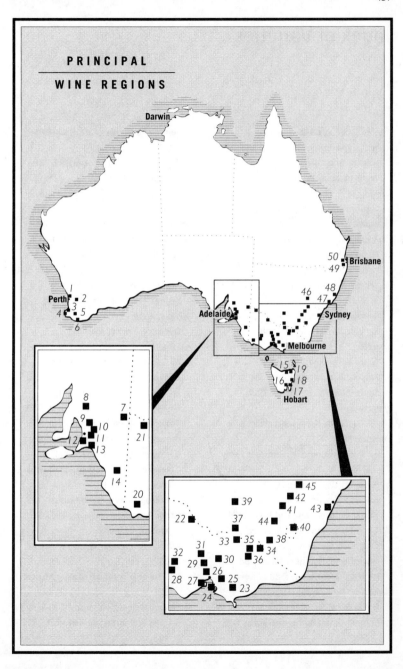

PRINCIPAL
WINE REGIONS

Darwin

Brisbane
50
49
48
46
47
Perth 1
2
3
5 Adelaide
4
6 Sydney
Melbourne
0
15 19
16 18
17
Hobart

8
9 7
10
12 11 21
13
14
20

45
39 42
41 43
22 37 44 40
33 35 38
34
31 30 36
32 29
28 27 26 25
24 23

Index of Varieties

White wines

White wines (sweet)